Ius Gentium: Comparative Perspectives on Law and Justice

Volume 80

Series Editors

Mortimer Sellers, University of Baltimore, Baltimore, MD, USA
James Maxeiner, University of Baltimore, Baltimore, MD, USA

Editorial Board

Myroslava Antonovych, Kyiv-Mohyla Academy, Kyiv, Ukraine
Nadia de Araújo, Pontifical Catholic University of Rio de Janeiro,
Rio de Janeiro, Brazil
Jasna Bakšic-Muftic, University of Sarajevo, Sarajevo, Bosnia and Herzegovina
David L. Carey Miller, University of Aberdeen, Aberdeen, UK
Loussia P. Musse Félix, University of Brasilia, Federal District, Brazil
Emanuel Gross, University of Haifa, Haifa, Israel
James E. Hickey Jr., Hofstra University, South Hempstead, NY, USA
Jan Klabbers, University of Helsinki, Helsinki, Finland
Cláudia Lima Marques, Federal University of Rio Grande do Sul,
Porto Alegre, Brazil
Aniceto Masferrer, University of Valencia, Valencia, Valencia, Spain
Eric Millard, West Paris University, Nanterre Cedex, France
Gabriël A. Moens, Curtin University, Perth, WA, Australia
Raul C. Pangalangan, University of the Philippines, Quezon City, Philippines
Ricardo Leite Pinto, Lusíada University of Lisbon, Lisboa, Portugal
Mizanur Rahman, University of Dhaka, Dhaka, Bangladesh
Keita Sato, Chuo University, Tokyo, Japan
Poonam Saxena, University of Delhi, New Delhi, India
Gerry Simpson, London School of Economics, London, UK
Eduard Somers, University of Ghent, Gent, Belgium
Xinqiang Sun, Shandong University, Shandong, China
Tadeusz Tomaszewski, Warsaw University, Warsaw, Poland
Jaap de Zwaan, Erasmus University Rotterdam, Rotterdam, Zuid-Holland,
The Netherlands

More information about this series at http://www.springer.com/series/7888

Janos Jany

Legal Traditions in Asia

History, Concepts and Laws

 Springer

Janos Jany
Pázmány Péter Catholic University
Budapest, Hungary

ISSN 1534-6781   ISSN 2214-9902   (electronic)
Ius Gentium: Comparative Perspectives on Law and Justice
ISBN 978-3-030-43730-5   ISBN 978-3-030-43728-2   (eBook)
https://doi.org/10.1007/978-3-030-43728-2

© Springer Nature Switzerland AG 2020
This work is subject to copyright. All rights are reserved by the Publisher, whether the whole or part
of the material is concerned, specifically the rights of translation, reprinting, reuse of illustrations,
recitation, broadcasting, reproduction on microfilms or in any other physical way, and transmission
or information storage and retrieval, electronic adaptation, computer software, or by similar or dissimilar
methodology now known or hereafter developed.
The use of general descriptive names, registered names, trademarks, service marks, etc. in this
publication does not imply, even in the absence of a specific statement, that such names are exempt from
the relevant protective laws and regulations and therefore free for general use.
The publisher, the authors and the editors are safe to assume that the advice and information in this
book are believed to be true and accurate at the date of publication. Neither the publisher nor the
authors or the editors give a warranty, expressed or implied, with respect to the material contained
herein or for any errors or omissions that may have been made. The publisher remains neutral with regard
to jurisdictional claims in published maps and institutional affiliations.

This Springer imprint is published by the registered company Springer Nature Switzerland AG
The registered company address is: Gewerbestrasse 11, 6330 Cham, Switzerland

Contents

Chapter 1
Introduction

One of the most important inspirations to writing this book was H. Patrick Glenn's magnum opus, *The Legal Traditions of the World*, certainly one of the most important books in the past decades. Glenn's work focuses in addition to the Continental and the Common law traditions on the Jewish, Islamic, Hindu and Confucian legal traditions but dedicates less attention to other contemporary Asian legal traditions (which is fully understandable given its global perspective), though there are quite a number of them (such as Japanese or Buddhist law), and disregards past legal traditions such as that of the Ancient Near East. Hence, the present work embarks on supplementing these hiatuses within the framework of a book focusing exclusively on Asia.

Contemporary Asian societies are studied either by economics or by political science but less by legal studies or sociology. The picture thus gained is a bit one-sided as there are more at play than just different numbers of economic growth. In fact, the causes of growth (in numbers, in area, and in influence) are not only due to economics and prosperity but also determined by social factors, one important one among them is tradition in general and legal tradition in particular. To name only a few evident examples just consider the traditional structures that have kept China among the major powers for millennia, or those that have elevated Japan to be a leading economic power of the world, or have ensured tremendous cultural influence to India. These social structures are rooted in the legal traditions, while law itself is also the result of social understanding, hence an inseparable thread is formed between the social system and the legal tradition (*ubi societas, ibi ius*), which exists to this day, despite several attempts at radically changing it (for instance, Mao Zedong, Pol Pot). All these destructive tendencies have not only failed, but have expressly strengthened the traditional legal structures they strove to eliminate. Actually, Confucianism which the earlier communist leadership tried to liquidate by all means is again on the rise in the post-Mao era witnessing and partly causing the global emergence of China. The economic miracles of the Asian Tigers can also be traced back to the proper wielding of the advantages of a modern legal system with the traditional approach to law and society, and the mix of the two was able to achieve results of global significance very rapidly.

© Springer Nature Switzerland AG 2020
J. Jany, *Legal Traditions in Asia*, Ius Gentium: Comparative Perspectives
on Law and Justice 80, https://doi.org/10.1007/978-3-030-43728-2_1

The traditional legal approach, however, is not the key to success in every case because it is not generally an operational model for every social problem. The ever-deeper crisis of the Islamic world, visible to all by now, just shows that rigid insistence on tradition, the lack of adaptive capacity, and rejecting the challenges of modernity lead to explosion resulting in armed violence. Thus, the traditional legal approach is not a miracle tool for the solution of every social problem (as representatives of political Islam think), nor is it a conservative, atavistic world, full of superstitions unable to change and hindering development as it is thought by the apostles of modernisation and by some Western social scientists.

The key is to have a balanced view on traditional legal systems not distorted by ideological, political or economic preferences. The present book is, therefore, not a plea for traditional law, neither is it an argument against it; it explores them as they are and what they have become as a result of their specific historical development. To do so one has to abandon the Eurocentric worldview that has been prevalent for a long time in social sciences. Asian legal systems should not be compared to any western legal tradition. Instead, we have to approach them on the basis of their own concepts, history, and mental structure. This method, recalling the Weberian understanding of '*verstehende Soziologie*' is capable of protecting us against the attitude advocating the cultural superiority of the West devoted to the belief of the Western civilising mission in the rest of the world. In our globalised world, there is no longer any room for a Euro-centric worldview, and we should get acquainted with the legal understanding of other societies as they are and not as westerners would like them to be. By the same token, however, the post-colonial interpretation, reflecting the bad conscience of the late colonising powers is also misleading because of its ideology-driven approach. To avoid ideological agendas and see things as they are is a precondition to achieve meaningful scholarly results. Therefore, despite all fashionable deconstructions, I think that though maximum objectivity is out of reach in social sciences yet striving towards it with maximum efforts is the basic condition of all scholarly work. This is what I attempt in the following chapters.

Obviously the question may arise whether there is any sense in writing about Asian legal history. Should we answer affirmatively, the next question would be whether a single author would be able to do so, considering the enormous dimension of the legal material, the large number of languages and cultures such a study would touch upon? The answer to the first question is affirmative. No one would be surprised at coming across a book about European history or the history of European law, even if the very concept of Europe has a variety of meanings and changes according to time and place (Europe was something different in the Greek poleis, in Rome, in the Middle Ages and the Renaissance, in the age of the nation-states and nowadays). Yet we take it for granted and teach European legal history in the belief that such a thing does exist, whereas it is evident that the medieval Spanish law, formed in the struggle against the Moors, has very little in common with the laws of the Germanic tribes in Scandinavia. In brief: Europe is almost as diverse historically, culturally and legally as Asia, but we accept it as a natural condition, while the complexity of Asia makes us rather uncertain to write about Asian legal history. I think it is worth taking the first steps, the success of which would encourage others to walk on the same line. This new approach is emerging on the horizon, though not in legal studies, but in philosophy. The Companion Encyclopaedia of Asian Philosophy comprising everything from the concepts of Medieval Muslim mystics to the Daoist teaching is a good example for this trend. The present book also embarks on something similar in the field of the traditional understanding of law. It is quite unique and new in this effort as no similar work, comprising of the entire spectrum of Asian law that has been written thus far.

To answer the second question, it is, of course, impossible for any researcher to have an equally deep knowledge on the history, culture and legal world of all of Asia, as it is also impossible for a single person to master the several hundred languages involved. As I am qualified both in law and in oriental studies, my experience focuses primarily on the legal tradition of the Middle East (Persian, Jewish and Islamic law), which I have researched intensively during the past decades. From this, it is quite a big step to explore the legal world of the Far East which, at a first sight, would rather encourage one to produce an edited volume with various contributors. That, however, would be just as problematic as a single-author approach because it is practically impossible to assemble a group of authors having qualifications in both law and philology who would be capable of writing about Chinese, Japanese, Mongolian or Burmese law with equal authenticity and professional competency. In addition to the personnel issues, the conceptual problem, a natural consequence of any omnibus volume is a difficulty of at least on the same level, as every author has his or her own style, points of consideration, argumentation and worldview which cannot be standardised even if the strictest editorial principles are observed. As a result, the most important feature of a single-author work would be lost, that is, the uniform outlook, the logically constructed arguments, the problem-sensitivity and the attempts at solutions stretching over the entire work, in other words, elements that make a scholarly work truly what it is. The result would be, instead, the editing of smaller units existing side by side as autonomous chapters, and this is what I wanted to avoid. Thus, there was nothing left but the long process of learning and research for years the result of which is the present book. I did not embark on the impossible task of learning the languages of all the societies involved in the book. Despite this I have based my arguments on primary legal sources which made the use of translations (mostly English, but also German, French and Spanish) inevitable. The result is, therefore, not optimal but optimised to the situation, an outcome which could be acceptable despite its faults and shortcomings.

There is no such thing as an Asian legal system and legal understanding: various legal systems and understandings exist parallel to each other, and their most visible common characteristic is that each of them have developed on the continent called Asia. Clearly, there is hardly any common point between Jewish law, deeply rooted in the traditions of the Ancient Near-East, and Japanese law based on Shintō and strongly exposed to Chinese influence, just to grasp the two opposite ends of the spectrum. To this one can add the customs of the nomadic Mongols or those of the peasant culture of Laos. Despite this truism, there are some elements that are shared by all Asian legal traditions which I will discuss at some length in the conclusions section. These elements are partly the results of adaptations and partly due to a similar way of thinking. One can identify some dominant (legal) cultures which develop their own legal, political and social understandings upon which the normative structure is built. As a next step, these concepts emerge elsewhere too, with local variants, as a result of legal export or adaptation, depending on perspective. Chinese law is a classic example which has fundamentally influenced the Korean, Vietnamese and Japanese legal thinking (to varying extents in these countries). In these societies, the local traditions subsequently coloured or modified the received legal wisdom but could neither squeeze it out nor subdue it. The same happened in India too, where Hindu (legal) culture expanded over the neighbouring Southeast Asia, resulting in the comprehensive influence of Hindu law over the legal systems of these societies despite the fact that they were Buddhist (with the exception of the Khmers), and had their own (mostly tribal) legal tradition.

As these examples show, the present work focuses not on contemporary legal trends but on the traditional legal systems which have been rather poorly studied in the recent past. This might be due to the widespread belief that traditional legal systems conserve backwardness and are a hindrance to modernisation. They are conceived as the world of irrationality adherent to superstitions, being just remnants of the past, and their burdensome presence just hinders the process of modernisation and the realisation of values considered as universal (while they are strongly West-specific).

A significant part of the twentieth century was spent on politics based on the above logic which forced modernisation along a mostly Western pattern against traditional structures (the socialist-communist path was also a Western ideology in the Asian countries!). Since the academic view did not differ fundamentally, the two trends mutually strengthened each other and dominated for decades. As a result, numerous Eastern states adopted Western constitutions (sometimes as word by word translations), and produced civil, criminal, and procedural laws along French, Swiss and German patterns (and texts), to implement a western type of legal system. Dealing with such laws did not mean any difficulty for a western lawyer, for they represented a familiar world: well-known laws and legal values were met in a slightly different form. One does not have to know the language, history, religion, and the legal tradition of the receiving country since neither of them determines the laws, nor are they interesting, according to the dominant attitude. In other words, the study of Japanese and Indian (or any other western-based) constitution was not essentially different from the study of European public law. No surprise, that while a significant number of books and papers dealing with such topics have been published, scholarly works dealing with the traditional understanding of law were on the margins. Actually, the basic idea was that modernisation would sweep off or eliminate the archaic social elements, superstitions, religiosity and traditional legal customs. This expectation was fundamentally false, and the consequences have turned out to be quite dramatic in some societies (mostly in Muslim countries). Contrary to the expectations, after the failures and controversial results of modernisation, the traditional structures have surfaced with such vigour that entire societies have been shaken by it to this day. This phenomenon, called re-traditionalisation first appeared in the 1970s during the formation of re-Islamisation, and its first victory, the Islamic revolution in Iran took Western public opinion and political leadership as a complete surprise. Social scientists were also unable to predict it, as they failed by the emergence of global Jihadism and the Arab Spring as well. The increasingly militant Islamic movements, organisations and terrorist groups all act in the name of Islamic law, and though they are incessantly struggling against each other, what links them together is that they consider Western cultural (legal) influence as their enemy, while their most important aim is to introduce traditional Islamic law, about which they think (falsely) it would solve all their problems immediately.

It would be misleading however, to think that the new policy to return to the inherited traditions is happening only in the Islamic world. In China, Confucianism has been experiencing its flowering once again, and this is openly supported by the Chinese state governed by a so-called Communist regime (see the Confucius Institutes all over the world). Moreover, recent works are also being published, which not only consider the Confucian interpretation of societal structure as something to be followed by the Chinese society but they also recommend this understanding for the solution of some global problems, and discuss it through its relationship to democracy, capitalism, law and gender equality (see, for example: Bell–Chaibong 2003). We can witness a similar progress in India today: at the latest elections the engine of the Indian independence movement, the National Congress Party which was in power for decades, was defeated by a party which declared a return to Hindu tradition as its political programme. Cambodia, having got rid of the terrible Communist heritage of Pol Pot has not only restored the freedom of religion but has made Buddhism state religion, regarding it as their own cultural tradition. As these examples show, re-traditionalisation is not only a political programme and a slogan in campaigns, but a real strategy supported by an ever growing majority of people in an increasingly large space of Asia. This fact in itself justifies paying particular attention to the traditional legal systems.

Parallel to the ever growing significance of the local (legal) tradition, Western way of legal thinking is on the retreat also in countries which have nothing to do with anti-colonialism or supporting global Jihadism. Saudi Arabia has never experimented with westernising modernisation although it is dependent on Western (American) military aid and is tied to global capitalism with hundreds of wires. Despite this, Islamic (Wahhābi-Hanbali) law remains the law of the country, a leadership that does not even consider the policy of a Western legal modernisation. Turkey, once a leading country in westernisation and a model for those countries that wanted to go along the same way, for the past decade has been run by a government which is becoming more and more Islamic and less and less West-oriented. India, which after gaining independence established its new, secular legal system on the Anglo-American model, is now witnessing a slow erosion of its western legal values and a re-emergence of the traditional Hindu law, promoted by Hindu nationalists. Contemporary China is also turning its back towards the demands to follow the Western legal pattern in some areas (human rights).

Needless to say, re-traditionalisation and the loosening of western influence is a long process connected to the success of the independence movements, to sovereignty regained, and to the controversial effects of westernisation. In addition to these, we can add the most recently growing global insignificance of the former colonising powers and particularly that of the European countries, and the rapid global economic and demographic decline of Europe. The vacuum just emerging has been increasingly filled by Asian countries. Thus, looking at these developments from a historical perspective, colonisation and Western legal influence connected to it would merely be a historical intermezzo, a period of "dark age" after which the Asian countries would once again return to their own traditions, and take back their global positions they had prior to colonisation (As a reminder: in the eighteenth century it was China that produced one third of the global production, and the largest city on Earth was not London or New York, but Ayutthaya, the capital of Siam). We should bear in mind: from a global perspective, the European legal understanding (together with its unique historical experience and a great deal of other cultural patterns and trajectories) is an exception, and not the rule. Thus, the present writing does not present received Western law, partly because its history has been written by others, and partly because the research of the genuine traditions is becoming an urgent task beneficial for both social sciences and legal practice.

1.1 Structure

The discussion of such a variety of traditional legal systems cannot be accomplished without organising principles. Therefore, I have placed the regional approach as the centre of the study, which is, although, more than a simple geographic point of view: it considers historical, religious and cultural relations as well.

For this purpose I have arranged the various traditions into legal circles, a term which is not identical to neither legal tradition nor legal system; though, I use both in these pages. For the purpose of this book, a legal system is understood as a totality of laws in a particular state (e.g. Chinese law (=Chinese legal system), etc.). By contrast, a legal tradition is also composed of laws but they are not a product of political law making and their boundaries are less clear cut as that of a legal system. Islamic legal tradition for example, is not a legal system of any state yet it is a legal tradition which influences heavily the legal systems of various Muslim countries and constitutes as a legal tradition with fundamental principles, legal theology and laws. The concept of legal circles was first formulated by M. B. Hooker, who called them legal world and applied this structure restrictively to South-East Asia only (*A Concise Legal History of South-East Asia*: Clarendon Press: Oxford, 1978: 6.). There is however, good reason to expand the idea to all of Asia in order to find a proper framework for the study of genuine legal traditions. Hooker specified the Chinese, the Indian and the Islamic legal world which fits perfectly not only to South-East Asia but to the entire continent. I changed legal world to legal circles because these entities resemble in fact a circle with a dominant legal system in the centre and more satellite legal systems around it (more on this in the following pages). For the purpose of this book however, I had to go a step further and this is why I have added the Ancient Near Eastern legal circle. For the sake of completeness, I added also studies about customary laws which do not constitute a legal circle with definitive boundaries since they are to be found all over Asia.

The concept of legal circle is more useful as an analytic tool rather than civilisation, though, evidently, Chinese (Confucian), Indian (Hindu) and Islamic traditions are at the same time civilisations. Civilisation is however, a term lacking a clear definition. Civilisation theorists such as Spengler, Toynbee and Elias, to mention only outstanding authorities, disagree not only on the exact meaning and the number of civilisations, but also on the markers on which the classification is based (is it religion as Huntington believed, or social-political structure, or language, or all these combined?). I did not want to place the study of Asian legal traditions on such shaky grounds. To this problem one may add that civilisation and legal tradition is by far not the same thing, the latter having a semi-autonomy due to its own peculiarity, historical circumstances and adoptions. To illustrate: while no one doubts the existence of Indian (Hindu) and Chinese (Confucian) civilisation, the idea of Buddhist (Southeast Asian) civilisation emerges only sporadically, if ever. The autonomy of a Buddhist (Southeast Asian) civilisation could be a subject to debate for civilisation theorists but not for scholars approaching the problem from the perspective of legal tradition: the autonomy of the Buddhist legal tradition is beyond doubt and should be treated separately from both India and China (this is why there is a separate chapter dedicated to it).

It is also clear that Asian legal traditions vary in their importance, considering some important factors in quantity and quality (the number of people following it, its territory of influence, the regional importance of the state's power, cultural domination, literacy, social structure and its importance, niveau of sciences in general and jurisprudence in particular). I call important legal traditions with dominating presence and regional influence: *dominant legal traditions* and *satellite legal traditions* those which are linked to them not as their equal. It is not necessarily jurisprudence and its fine scientific elaboration that make a legal tradition dominant. Chinese legal culture has not become dominant because of its refinement, as it concentrates only on penal law and administration. Yet Chinese law had its backing in the influence of the Chinese culture in general and its military forces in particular. The same applies to Islamic law, which has conquered a significant part of Asia by arms and a smaller part by commerce. The Indian dominance, however, was not due to the armed forces, but rather to the spread of Buddhism, which mediated also a series of Indian cultural elements, jurisprudence among them, that were not particularly Buddhist.

A legal circle is, therefore, not a monolith structure but a composite one, with a dominant legal tradition in its centre and a number of satellite traditions attached to it. Once again, examples help to clarify: in the Chinese legal circle the dominant legal tradition is Chinese law, followed by the Japanese, Korean, and Vietnamese legal traditions. In the Indian legal tradition Hindu law dominates, followed by an autonomous but intellectually subordinate legal tradition, that of the Buddhist societies which are further divided to local variants, such as the Thai-Lao or the Mon-Burmese legal traditions. It was however, a dilemma deciding how to classify the Japanese legal tradition, which though it had been under significant Chinese influence has several genuine legal institutions and a unique way of thinking. In the end, I put Japanese law into the Chinese legal circle but dedicated a separate chapter to it symbolising its autonomy.

As every categorisation, this one is also the result of somewhat arbitrary and subjective choices. This is particularly true about the Islamic legal circle. Islamic law is linked by numerous threads to the customs of pre-Islamic Arabia, which, in its turn is inseparable from the legal traditions of the Ancient Near East. Had I made this obvious fact the basis of arrangement, I would have had to discuss the entire legal tradition of the Near East under the heading of the Islamic legal circle, a nonsense, as some Near Eastern legal traditions emerged millennia before Islam. To complicate: Islamic law could be found not only in the Near and the Middle East, but also in faraway regions such as Malaysia or Indonesia. To insist on the Islamic legal circle would have resulted in classifying everything from Babylon to Indonesia under this umbrella term. To avoid this, I introduced the historical legal tradition of the Ancient Near East as the fourth legal circle, including cuneiform law, Jewish law, Persian law and the legal culture of Eastern Christianity. The legal tradition of Pre-Islamic Arabia was classified under the Islamic legal circle as its immediate antecedent, but its linkage to other Near Eastern traditions should not escape our attention.

Systemic difficulties have not yet disappeared entirely though. All these legal circles share a common feature, that is, all are written cultures. This means that important legal texts are put into writing and both jurisprudence and legal practices rest on literacy, at least to some extent (obviously, rural adjudication is rather oral than literary). A study focusing on Asia could not ignore societies based on oral cultural tradition firstly, for the sake of completeness, secondly, because millions of people live according to oral, tribal, customary laws (about 100 million only in India). Therefore, a fifth legal circle has been created, consisting of tribal customary laws. It differs from the other four circles in the way that it is independent of time, place, people, and religion. There is no dominant legal circle and the satellite legal circle is also missing. The only thing that brings these heterogeneous groups together is orality and the lack of a state. Of course, in theory these customary laws could find their place also among the satellite legal traditions in a particular legal circle. For example, Pashtunwali, the customs of the Pashtun tribes could be discussed in the Islamic legal circle as well as, they are Muslims and their customs are not independent from Islam. The various tribal laws in India could be dealt with in the Hindu legal circle, etc. But I chose a different path to show that there are a variety of similarities between the various customary laws of Asia. Therefore, I put all these together as the fifth legal circle which enabled me not only to demonstrate the general characteristics of customary laws but also to elaborate a new, Asia-specific classification of customary laws which would not have been possible had I placed the various customary laws under the heading of a dominant legal circle.

After arranging the legal material I had to structure the book in a way that makes comparisons meaningful and enables me to formulate general conclusions at the end. Therefore, every chapter is based on the same structure, consisting of three parts: the first part is about legal history, the second about the basic postulates of legal thinking (philosophy of law) followed by the third part about the major legal institutions. As legal history and legal philosophy does not exist independently from history and philosophy in general, whenever it was meaningful, I emphasised broader interrelationships too. I have indicated the leading role of the dominant legal cultures by longer and more detailed chapters whereas the description of the satellite legal traditions is shorter and less articulated. This is also due to the fact that satellite legal traditions follow mostly the norms of the dominant legal cultures and these have already been presented in subchapters dedicated to the most important fields of law (private law, criminal law, procedural law) in the dominant legal cultures. This structure was also dictated by the necessity to avoid any repetition, a basic requirement in such a long work.

Wherever possible, I have placed jurisprudence into the web of other disciplines in order to show both the complex structure of scholarship and the importance of jurisprudence within it. This has two reasons. One is to have a glimpse on the cultural settings in a broad perspective, the other is to learn the relative importance of jurisprudence vis-á-vis other disciplines. This is important because the best indicators to assess the importance of law in a particular society are jurisprudence's position within a web of science and the importance of legal training in a complex system of education. To illustrate using two examples: in the Chinese legal circle the role of law is not significant, it is merely an order of the state (emperor) and this is the reason why it is only about criminal law and administration. No wonder there is no jurisprudence as a discipline in its own right, it is only one element among the many in the corpus of classical texts, the knowledge of which is considered the most important element of erudition. Hence, law in itself is not taught, only to clerks as one element out of the many in their training. In contrast, in both the Jewish and Islamic religions, law is the most important system where the authorities are the leaders and the most influential sages of their respective community. Again, no surprise that the educational system is also organised around legal training, meanwhile other subjects such as theology, philosophy, and medicine are either missing or play a marginal role only.

Thus, I did not write merely on the history of law, since the spectrum of the book is far broader than just a positivist narrative of legal history, and also touches upon subjects such as scholarly life, legal schools and their great scholars, as well as some arts related to law (mostly literature). Besides legal history and jurisprudence, I devoted some pages also to legal practice and everyday life, which demanded the combination of sociological and dogmatic approach even though these two do not always peacefully coexist. The methodological approach was to start with legal dogmatics based on sources (statutes, judgments, works on jurisprudence) enlarged with socio-economic data wherever I was able to find some. These chapters do not contain an all-round and exhaustive discussion of the topic, my aim was rather to highlight the most important and significant characteristics, as too much detail would hinder the complex understanding. Limiting the length was very important, therefore, these chapters are rather encyclopaedic summaries and not analytical elaborations of some minor legal problems. Each chapter comes to an end with a sub-chapter devoted to the role of traditional law in the modern age. Islamic law is the only exception to it because the problem is so complex (Islamism, traditionalism, fundamentalism) and meandering, that I have dedicated a full chapter to it. Chapters on the modern age do not embark on the discussion of the modern legal system (a topic for another long book) but concentrate only on the role the traditional legal cultures play nowadays in these societies.

1.2 History

In writing this book I have strongly relied on the results of previously learned knowledge. Studying oriental legal systems is not a novelty, yet it is not as much of a classical discipline as Roman law or European and American legal history. Its reason is that Eastern societies were less known before the eighteenth century when the study of Roman law was already a discipline dating back to long centuries.

Colonisation was a great driving force to learning about Eastern societies as European countries had to govern huge countries, the culture of which were alien to them. The study of languages first came about to be followed by other disciplines related to texts such as religious studies, philosophy, historiography and literature (because linguists deciphered Eastern languages, ancient or modern, which enabled text-oriented disciplines to develop). Among them was Law, but never a favourite as was literature and religion. Driven also by practical considerations and not only by scientific interest the study of law emerged when legal professionals began to flourish among colonial administrators. Colonial administration was not an easy business after all, it was in search for local legal traditions to adjudicate the cases they had to solve, giving an extra impetus to legal research, at least in some areas such as India. Where such needs were absent, as in the case of the Ancient Near East, legal history began to flourish only after deciphering the cuneiform writing and experiencing some luck of archaeology, which had unearthed legal documents lost for millennia (the Code of Hammurabi being the greatest discovery ever since). It is small wonder that Jewish law was much better known at the time (due to knowledge of the Old Testament) when we did not know anything as now about Mesopotamian law or next to nothing about traditional laws of Southeast Asia or Japan.

Apart from historic legal traditions which remained rather the domain of scholars of a particular field, (Mesopotamian law is studied mostly by Assyrologists and not by lawyers), living legal traditions were dealt with primarily by colonial administrators in whose interest it was to get acquainted with the local customs. The first steps were, thus, largely not taken by scholars motivated by academic interest but by colonial administrators, judges, and even adventurers, that is, persons who got in touch with Eastern cultures on the spot. These people were not interested in the philosophical background of a norm nor were they interested in the linguistic problems caused by a legal text, but i n the practical utility of a law during the procedure they had to master. For the sake of more clarity and application, the legal matter was re-organized and at times 'codified' upon private initiative, but these texts have provoked resistance among the local population and this is why such projects (e.g. Sparks Code) had to be abandoned immediately.

In the beginning, legal scholars were largely absent and when their first representatives emerged, like Sir Henry Maine in India, they were students of Roman law who had viewed local legal traditions through the lenses of Roman law and their own legal tradition, both considered supreme. Yet it was an important period because the first translations of the great texts of the Asian legal traditions (Manu, Narada, the Burmese Dhammathat collections, Hammurabi) were produced during this period. Obviously, these translations cannot be used without caution today, though they were a significant step ahead in their own age. Legal scholars remained absent or underrepresented in the coming decades as well, leaving the field mostly to oriental studies, with a consequence that it had been studied mostly by philologists. More substantial scholarly interest was beginning to unfold in the first part of the twentieth century, at a time when the knowledge accumulated and the number of texts learned had been significantly expanding. This was also the time when colonial rule was slackening and subsequently disappearing, hence the considerations of colonial administration were pushed into the background and academic projects took their place.

Truly outstanding works were produced when orientalists of legal qualifications or interest (such as Joseph Schacht in the field of Islamic law, Robert Lingat in Indian and Southeast Asian law, J. D. M. Derrett in Indian and Jewish law, Werner Menski in Indian law) had begun their pioneering works, or when philologists and lawyers joined hand and combined the achievements and methods of philology and jurisprudence (like Driver and Miles in the field of Babylonian law). Nevertheless, current jurisprudence still does not consider the area as its own, whilst traditional oriental studies continue to focus on their own agenda, mainly philology and literature. Sadly, since there is an academic field where interdisciplinary approach and team work may produce meaningful and significant results, it is the research of Asian legal traditions, yet hardly any progress can be noticed. Though, centres researching Asian law have been opened at some legal faculties at American universities, they only prove that the necessity of opening jurisprudence in this direction has been recognised in some places (Harvard). But, despite lip service to the importance of interdisciplinary research there is hardly any breakthrough.

Despite adverse conditions there have always been scholars who, driven by academic interest, were able to accomplish significant results. In the study of Ancient Near Eastern law such a person was Jean Vincent Scheil, the first editor of the Code of Hammurabi, who published the text for the first time by his *edition princeps*. The most comprehensive historical, legal and linguistic commentary of the text was produced by Driver and Miles in the 1950s, which still continues to be an important work of reference for everyone working on Babylonian law. Since then archaeology contributed enormously to our understanding of Mesopotamian law as thousands of legal documents has been unearthed and published. These cuneiform tablets are documents produced during procedures of individual cases, found either in private archives or in temples or state archives (city, palace), but some "statutes" have been unearthed too, such as the Law of Ur-Nammu, Lipit-Ishtar or the Law of Eshnunna. Therefore, Codex Hammurabi is no longer the only reference and source for our understanding of Mesopotamian law. The increasingly diversified state of the arts was brilliantly summarised by Korosec in his long writing in a volume dedicated to

Oriental laws in the 1960s, which was followed in the coming decades by text editions
and translations of legal sources into German (Haase) and English (Roth, Hoffner).
Over the course of the last decades, it was perhaps the late Raymund Westbrook who
had the greatest impact on the study of Ancient Near Eastern legal history, partly
because of his insight and provocative questions and partly because of his last edited
volume, an encyclopaedic summary of what we now know about Near Eastern law.

Research on Jewish law has been unbroken for two millennia by the continuous
efforts of Jewish Rabbis who consider it as their most important task and social mission. Contrary to Mesopotamian law, there was thus no need to wait for archaeological excavations and for the deciphering of unknown languages and writing systems.
Additionally, Christianity kept the tradition of the Old Testament alive, hence Jewish
law was (superficially) known in Europe for centuries, and great scholars such as
Grotius made references to it in their moral or legal argumentations. Yet Talmudic
legal tradition and the somewhat naïve admiration of Christianity significantly differ
from the critical methods of modern scholarship which has begun with the work of
Julius Wellhausen, the founder of biblical scholarship in the late nineteenth century.
His work was followed by academics of the coming generations among whom Martin Noth and Gerhard von Rad deserve particular attention. After the Second World
War, some legal scholars also joined in, David Daube, an authority also in Roman
law and legal history being the most influential among them. In the generation after
Daube, a growing number of legal scholars devoted their scholarly work to Jewish law and its relationship to other Mediterranean legal traditions (cuneiform law,
Roman law, Islamic law). Luckily, an increasing number of universities and academic
research centres were created for the study of Jewish law, academic homes to dozens
of eminent specialists working in this field among whom the legal historian Calum
Carmichael (a disciple of Daube) and the legal philosopher Bernard S. Jackson may
be the best known scholars also for a wider audience. Menachem Elon, a former
deputy chairman of the Supreme Court of Israel is also among the most important
contributors whose four volumes, magnum opus, is a must read for everyone in this
field. In sum, the research on Jewish legal tradition continues in three parallel ways,
following either the Rabbinic method, Biblical studies, or legal history proper.

Since Muslim scholars have too been placing Islamic law into the focus of their
activities for centuries, the history of research on Islamic law resembles the situation of Jewish law in this regard. Yet, at the same time this approach is based, not
surprisingly, on the religious postulates of Islam. Therefore, it does not meet the
methodological requirements of critical modern science. The knowledge of Islamic
law in Europe had not been as widespread as that of the Jewish law of the Old Testament; in addition, it was burdened by a series of prejudices. Modern scientific activity
on Islamic law and its various understandings began in the late nineteenth and early
twentieth centuries by eminent scholars such as the German Theodor Nöldeke, the
Hungarian Ignaz Goldziher, the Dutch Snouck Hurgronje and Gotthelf Bergsträsser
of Breslau. Their scholarly tradition was continued by Joseph Schacht, a disciple of
Bergsträsser and Hurgronje, who set new direction for research of Islamic law in his
ground breaking classical, *The Origins of Muhammedan Jurisprudence,* published
in 1950. This work still remains a point of reference for everyone working in this

field, whether it is following the thesis of Schacht or criticizing it. It is a work no one can avoid, one just has to take a position, be it a positive, or a negative stand. This Goldziher-Schacht "school" dominated academic opinion for a long time, but recently an increasing number of scholars have started to doubt the merit of Schacht's approach. As a result, scholars of Islamic law have split up into camps, comprising of the followers of Schacht and their opponents. Unfortunately, the debate is not only academic, but has also political and ideological over tunes because critics of Schacht accuse him of approaching Islam with prejudices and being an advocate of colonialism and orientalism, not a word of praise by far in the academic world today. One of his masters, Hurgronje, has worked, it is true, for the Dutch colonial administration, but neither Goldziher nor Schacht himself have ever worked outside academia. Classical Islamic law was studied also by N. J. Coulson (who agreed with Schacht on the most important points) and by J. N. D. Anderson who was also engaged in studying contemporary socio-legal problems throughout the Islamic world. In the past decades interest in Islamic law has increased enormously due to various factors, international politics being an important one among them. The number of scholars has multiplied, and research centres of Islamic law have been created in Western universities. These centres and the study of Islamic law in general still remain primarily within the framework of oriental/Islamic/Middle Eastern studies and only few legal faculties join the trends (Harvard). Scholars working in these academic centres contribute enormously to our understanding of Islamic law and make the research of Islamic law a truly vivid and interesting discipline.

Contrary to the flourishing research on Jewish and Islamic law, scholarly activity on Persian (Zoroastrian) law and the legal tradition of Eastern Christianity hardly exists at all today. The situation was not as tragic a century ago when Georg Hoffmann first published the Syrian Acts of Martyrs (1880) and with this the research of the legal tradition of Eastern Christianity began in Germany, a homeland to historical, oriental and Biblical studies. Research attained maturity as a result of the admirable oeuvre of Eduard Sachau in the first two decades of the twentieth century. Sachau edited and translated with commentary a great deal of Syriac legal sources not only of the Christian legal tradition (Jesubocht, Simeon, Mar Abha) but also Roman legal texts in the Syrian language (Syrian-Roman law book, leges Constantini Theodosii Leonis). His text editions are extremely reliable, useful even to this day. Meanwhile his contemporary, the German Oskar Braun continued the work of Hoffmann with the publication and analysis of the Syrian Acts of Martyrs, a treasury of Syrian Christianity and Persian criminal law. Research was shifted from Germany to Leuven (Belgium) in the two decades after the Second World War where Arthur Vööbus' two significant works about the history of the school of Nisibis and their statutes were published, to be followed by the translation of perhaps the most important work of the Church of the East, the two volumes *Fiqh al-Nasraniya* (Jurisprudence of Christianity) of Ibn al-Taiyib by Wilhelm Hoenerbach and Otto Spies. Their work was continued by Walter Selb in Vienna, who had written extensively on the history of the legal tradition of Eastern Christianity, but after his death not a single scholar cares about his academic legacy. The history of the study of Persian law is even less heartening, as it has never been in the interest either of Iranian studies oriented towards linguistics or of legal history. Here once again the first steps were taken in Germany by a contemporary of Sachau, Christian Bartholomae, one of the most influential scholars in Iranian studies, who has published on the legal sources of the Sasanid period, but his work was not continued for decades by anyone. This has been changed in the 1970s when Mansour Shaki in Prague and Anahit Perikhanian in Leningrad started to work intensively on the history of Persian law. Maria Macuch from Berlin (Freie Universität) joined in from the 1980s with her edition, translation and commentary to the most important law book of Persian legal history, establishing herself as a well-known authority in this field.

The study of Hindu law has attracted perhaps the most outstanding scholarly minds, among whom we can find both linguists and legal scholars. Colonization of India meant a British-style indirect rule for centuries, which left the legal tradition of local population intact. As a result of this policy, British administrators were in need to learn more about local customs in order to adjudicate legal cases brought before their tribunal. The first step was taken by Sir William Jones, a genius of languages and a polymath, a miracle child of eighteenth-century England, who translated the *Manavadharmashastra* into English for the first time in 1794. In addition to his knowledge of Greek, Latin, Persian, Arabic and Hebrew, Jones obtained also legal training, which enabled him to work as a judge for a short period of time. As he sympathized with the American colonial population he tried to solve the political conflict through negotiations, but failed. Later he was transferred to Calcutta as a judge where he got acquainted with Indian civilisation and dedicated the rest of his life to research this culture; hence Manu's translation was just one part of his oeuvre. After Jones, another giant of early scholarly research was Max Müller who founded and edited the series *Sacred Books of the East* containing the edition and translation of a great deal of important texts of eastern civilisations, including some works on Hindu law. Julius Jolly, a German scholar also translated several Hindu legal sources (Narada, Vishnu Brihaspati) and published a pioneering monograph about the history of Hindu law (*Recht und Sitte*). The next century witnessed the work of scholars who were talented enough to step in the footsteps of their eminent predecessors. This series of researchers is opened by the Indian P. V. Kane, who explored the history of the dharmaśāstras in his five volumes magnum opus in the late 1960s (*History of the Dharmaśāstra*). The French Robert Lingat, qualified in both oriental studies and law, was his contemporary who dedicated his life to Hindu and Southeast Asian laws. In his now classic work, he reconsidered the entire history of Hindu law and thus laid down the foundations of modern scholarship. His work, though strongly relying on Kane and Max Müller, is unique in its content, argumentation, and in the consistent system in which it presents this huge and complex material. His work continues to be a primary reference for everyone working in this field. Its significance is indicated also by the fact that one of his junior contemporaries, J. Duncan M. Derrett, who established himself as an equal authority, had translated it personally from French to English (*The Classical Law of India*). Unfortunately, Lingat did not live to see it, as he died one year before its publication (1973). In addition to Hindu law, Lingat was also an authority in the history of Siamese (Thai) law, where he established his fame with his three-volume opus on the history of Thai law published in the Thai language

(1939–1940). J. D. M. Derrett was a researcher of no lesser format, who dedicated a series of monographs to Indian law, both historic and modern (*Religion, Law, and the State in India*). His broad classical and oriental learning (he knew also Latin, Greek, and Aramaic) allowed him to write in addition to Hindu law also about Jewish law as contained in the *Mishnah* and the legal relevance of the New Testament (*Studies in the New Testament*). After his retirement the research of Hindu law still continues to flourish with leading authorities such as Ludo Rocher and Werner Menski, and the younger generation too is establishing itself with significant publications.

Since Buddhism was considered to be a religion not focusing on this worldly affairs and thus not interested in issues regulated by law (politics, economy, society) the study of Buddhist law was neglected for long. According to this line of thinking, Buddhist law is nothing more than rules regulating the life of monks (*vinaya*). This is why research of Buddhist law has emerged only recently and it is currently struggling for a broader acceptance as a genuine discipline. The driving forces behind this are two contemporary academics, Rebeca French engaged in Tibetan legal anthropology, and Andrew Huxley studying Buddhist texts in Pali language. In contrast, the study of Buddhist societies goes back to more than a century, driven by practical considerations. As the British set foot in Burma after the Anglo-Burmese war, they faced practical problems similar to those in India. Since legal works containing mostly genuine Burmese legal material survived in quite a large number, British officials turned to these texts hoping that they could be used as simple legal manuals. This effort had led to the translation of some important texts but to the failure of the Sparks Code as well. Outstanding among the text were the two most important Burmese collections of law, the *Manugye dhammathat* (Richardson: 1847), and the *Wagaru Dhammathat* (by John Jardine, the Judicial Commissioner of British Burma, 1892). The next decades were determined by the scholarly influence of Emil Forchhammer who did not see more in the Burmese (and any other Southeast Asian) law, but a local variant of the Indian legal tradition, lacking any particular originality. This rather widespread opinion was later refuted by Robert Lingat, who has shown that the literary form in fact followed the Indian pattern, but the contents of the texts did not reflect Indian law but contain genuine Burmese legal tradition. Continental Southeast Asian legal tradition was researched by the British and the French, the archipelago, a Dutch colony at that time was explored by the Dutch, headed by Cornelius van Vellenhoven in the early twentieth century. Vellenhoven was a legal scholar who sympathised with the local legal traditions and dedicated his entire oeuvre to their study, establishing the *adat*-law school. What is more, he even defended the local customs against Dutch policy aiming at 'codification' and the transplantation of the Dutch law. His work was continued by Ter Har, also a member of the *adat*-law school. After the Second World War, M. B. Hooker established himself as the leading authority in Southeast Asian law who dedicated his entire career to the study of Southeast-Asian laws, producing publications of source materials and monographs.

The study of Chinese law once again had a different past, simply because China was not colonised and the formal authority of the ruling dynasty remained intact. Consequently, neither the bureaucrats of the British nor of any other colonising power had to take over the difficult task of local governance and the administration of justice. To this we can add that law was not an important field of study in China, and sinologists followed this traditional Chinese attitude. Therefore, modern scholarship also focused on the Confucian classics, literature, historical chronicles, Daoist, Buddhist and other philosophical texts. Scrutiny was never focused on law which was discussed, whenever necessary, within the framework of philosophy and history. This approach is clearly seen in the works of leading sinologists such as Henry Maspero and Étienne Balázs. During the Mao era, traditional law disappeared almost completely from the horizon in the works of Chinese scholars but Western academia was also not interested in it. During that period, writings produced on Chinese law in the West were rather about the horror of labour camps, lawlessness, and terror administered through law. A typical example of this approach is the work of Laszlo Ladany (*Law and Legality in China*). During the last decades however scholarly interest in Chinese legal history is growing rapidly producing an increase in publications about both traditional and modern Chinese law. New research centres were also created in Western universities promoting further study in this field. As a result, there are good chances for Chinese legal history as a discipline in obtaining some autonomy within sinology and put an end to its being merely a neglected area of Chinese philology. Scholars who did a lot to achieve this end are Geoffrey MacCormack, originally a Professor of Roman law at Edinburgh, and Randall Peerenboom, an eminent scholar of traditional and modern Chinese law and a scientific advisor to several international organisations.

As it can be seen from the above legal research relating to Asian legal traditions is unbalanced: while some areas look back to a history of hundred years others are just beginning to take off. Comparative studies, however, are missing: any research expanding over legal circles or individual legal traditions aiming at exploring common features and trends of development are non-existent.

1.3 Transliteration

Transliteration of names and judicial terms was also a source of headache. Here two conflicting trends should have been balanced. One is a clear editorial demand to follow the same rules in one book, that is, transliteration of foreign names and terms should follow the same rules and principles throughout the work. The other demand is not to distort already accepted practices of some disciplines where rules of transliteration are already established for long. To overrule such usages in the sake of uniformity within one book might cause more trouble than merit. In short, it is impossible to elaborate a coherent system of transliteration if one has to do with dozens of Asian languages from Sumerian to Japanese and relying simultaneously on divergent practices of oriental philology. Here again there was no chance to reach the optimum only a workable system framed by compromises. Therefore, I have left out symbols that make reading difficult and would cause lots of technical problems as dots under some consonants (t; s; d) in the transliteration of Semitic languages, but have made use of ^{c} to indicate ayn in the same languages. As it is customary in scientific transliteration, long vowels are indicated by ā; ē; ī; ō; ū. The transliteration of Chinese words and phrases follows the official system of China, the Pinyin standard. Exceptions were made only with names and terms which are already Englicised.

Reference

Bell–Chaibong (2003) Confucianism for the modern world. Cambridge University Press, Cambridge

Part I
The Ancient Near Eastern Legal Circle

Chapter 2
Cuneiform Law

2.1 Mesopotamian Law in the Third Millennium

2.1.1 City States

Archaeological evidence of human existence from the sixth millennium BCE has been unearthed in Mesopotamia, but little is known about those communities. The fifth millennium Ubaid-culture shows signs of cultural continuity but decisive changes can be observed with the emergence of Uruk culture (4000–2900 BCE). The use of wheel, the growing production of metal, and the invention of cuneiform script towards the end of this period were changes of epic significance. Technical development had been followed by the growth of population and social differentiation not experienced previously.

Historiography is still indebted to offer an explanation of the emergence of states acceptable to all. According to the most popular hypothesis, states developed out of the necessity of organising community labour (irrigation canals, the construction of palaces and temples) around the leader controlling these works. According to another less known hypothesis, advocated by Forest: cities came into existence out of competition among clans wishing to ensure their power by erection of buildings. This rivalry had led then to the emergence of different cities, home to competing clans. Despite theoretic uncertainty, the flourishing of early city states (2900–2340 BCE) such as Ur, Eridu, Uruk, Sippar, Shuruppak, Girsu, Lagash, and Umma, to mention only the most important centres of South Mesopotamia, is a remarkable development in the early history of mankind. These city states organised labour, established political order and a hierarchic social structure which guaranteed their success. Demographic growth was one important consequence. According to modern estimates, rates of urbanization reached the remarkable ratio of 80%, resulting in the rapid expansion of these cities. The territory of Shuruppak reached 100 ha, its population a figure between 15 and 30 thousand. The population of Lagash, one of the greatest Sumerian cities had a population between 36,000 and 100,000 people

© Springer Nature Switzerland AG 2020
J. Jany, *Legal Traditions in Asia*, Ius Gentium: Comparative Perspectives on Law and Justice 80, https://doi.org/10.1007/978-3-030-43728-2_2

in its heyday.[1] As these cities were located in a relatively narrow strip of territory, expansion of arable land (necessary to feed an increasing number of population) was possible only to the detriment of other cities resulting in continuous warfare, something not experienced previously. The relatively good documented war between Umma and Lagash is just one typical example. To win these wars, some cities created alliances, the most important being that of Ur, Uruk and Umma. Other cities reacted to this threat with the same policy, therefore, solution remained out of reach and endemic political chaos prevailed. The ongoing crisis of the city states was resolved by the Akkadians in the end, newcomers who established their own rule over the Sumerian cities and founded the first empire in Mesopotamian history.[2]

In the political structure of these cities, the ruler was primarily the representative and protector of the city towards the gods who decided on fate. In order to understand this role of the king, it is of importance that there had been a close contact between the city and its godhead, and the ruler played a mediating role between the secular and the divine spheres. As these spheres were not separated from each other, no competition evolved between the political and the religious authorities (contrary to Egypt and Persia). The ruler as high priest took an active part in cultic deeds, erected temples and substituted them in their daily operations. The king as the head of the political community, however, exercised both legislative and judicial functions and took over military leadership, too. In addition to these, large territories of land were concentrated under his control. There were two terms to refer to the ruler by, but we no longer understand the difference inherent in this distinction. Both *lugal* (big man), and *en* (with *ensi* as its variant) indicate the ruler. Modern scholarship thinks that the former is used when reflecting on his secular functions, while the latter is used to indicate his religious functions. Original usage was, however, not so clear cut and, therefore, the dual meaning of *en* (king, high priest) continues to be a source of many scientific problems to this day. The king's family had also an important role in politics: the ruler's wife maintained diplomatic contacts to wives of other rulers, was a priestess, and possessed large landed property. The king's children were also significant landowners, and sons not inheriting the throne were endowed with high-ranking political and priestly offices. In brief: the king and his family controlled the state and religious life connected to it. Popular assembly (*unkin*) was perhaps an important political institution too, at least in the early phase of development, to which the epic of Gilgamesh provides some evidence. When kingly power was enlarged, in the later stage of development, these assemblies lost their significance and subsequently disappeared.[3]

Social structure was diversified, though the exact legal status of each class still awaits clarification. Society was headed by the *lugulabi*, aristocrats consisting of leading officials and the group of *ugula* following them. Middle class consisted of *shub-lugals*, owners of small plots of land which was mostly cultivated by the *iginudu* ("who did not lift their eyes"). The number of slaves was not significant as was their

---

[1] Kuhrt (1995: 32), Korošec (1964: 59).

[2] Kuhrt (1995: 22–31).

[3] Wilcke (2003: 146), Korošec (1964: 60–61), Kuhrt (1995: 33–35).

economic role. Social inequality was a major threat to political stability and some rulers wanted to reduce tensions. Such a king was UruKaGina (Uruinimgina) of Lagash, whose "reform tablet" had reached us. It is not considered as law by modern scholarship, and this is the reason why UruKagina does not enter the book of records with producing the first law book in history. Still, it is a valuable source of information, because the texts not only declare the reforms of the king but also enumerate the old laws he wanted to change. We learn from this text the power of the *lugulabi* and the *ugula*, and also some of their misdeeds and abuse of power. According to the words of the king himself, the aim of his reforms was to protect widows and orphans, symbols of disenfranchised people in the Near-East. Accordingly, he abolished some duties of payment (prayer bread, fee of obsequies, etc.) and protected the ownership of the poor (house, garden, donkey) by ruling that, contrary to previous practice, the powerful should not take them away without compensation. Protection against debt slavery is also an important point in the text, as debt slavery was becoming increasingly frequent in that historical period when people were often forced to sell their children and themselves into slavery. There are some passages in the text, however, which are difficult to understand. One such passage is the ruling according to which a woman could previously have two husbands but this was no longer the case. The interpretation of this paragraph is problematic. Some scholars see the abolition of polyandry in it (Edzard, Korošec), while others interpret it as the abolition of *ius primae noctis*. The most recent explanation understands the text as a hint to the remarriage of widows (Wilcke). Despite these uncertainties, it is clear that the Sumerian marriage was monogamous, and polygamy was just as atypical as polyandry, concubinate, however, may have been a tolerated institution.[4] UruKAgina's reforms did not take for a long time (if anything at all was implemented), because after seven years in power he was overthrown by his chief enemy, Lugalzagesi, ruler of Umma.

2.1.2 Akkadians

The political unity of South Mesopotamia was the achievement of the nomadic Akkadians living originally further north, under the leadership of their legendary king, Sharrukīn I (2340–2284). The Akkadian Empire reduced the former city states to less important administrative and economic centres and created a territorial state with a capital, Agade, a city newly founded. These were enormous changes in the political system which solved the endemic rivalries of the former city states. Regaining strength, the new empire set out towards highly successful conquests under successive generations of talented kings. By the twenty-second century, however, the empire was weakened and some regions began to break away. Internal erosion was doubled by the Guti invasion which contributed to the disintegration of the Akkadian Empire, though perhaps to a lesser extent than earlier historiography believed. The centre of resistance was the city of Uruk headed by its legendary king, Utu-hegal

---

[4]Korošec (1964: 63), Kuhrt (2005: 39–40), Neumann (2003: 68–69), Wilcke (2003: 160).

who defeated the Guti troops. It was not he, but his rivals in Ur who established a
new and successful dynasty and this is how the Third Dynasty of Ur came to power.
With this, the political centre was shifted to the city of Ur which continued the policy
of the Akkadian Empire and tolerated no return to the previous political landscape
dominated by the city states. The hegemony of the dynasty and that of the city lasted
for a century (2112–2104), ending in internal chaos. The invading armies of Elam
attacking from the east put an end not only to the power of Ur, but also to the last
Sumerian state. The fall of the Third Dynasty of Ur indicates both the end of the
third millennium and the last flourishing period of the Sumerian culture (referred to
as Sumerian renaissance). Akkadian rule was more than a mere change of dynasties
or ruling elites, it brought about a complete turn in political structure and style. The
fragmented political landscape of the city states with their endemic wars was unable
to find a way out of a long crisis, therefore, a new way of thinking with a state on
a larger territorial base was introduced. The Akkadian Empire was not only larger
than the former city states, but rested on different principles. This new political entity
was not just a conglomerate of cities but a state with definite (and constantly growing) territory, populace, and political structure, headed by the king with his newly
created administration and army. One result was the growing power of the ruler who
became more and more a despot of unlimited power while his mediating role toward
the gods was pushed to the background. This new state advocated centralisation and
étatism resulting in constant warfare and conquest of faraway territories out of reach
for the former cities. Military success again strengthened the political centre which
has found its symbolic expression in the divination of the ruler and newly created,
exaggerated titles (*shar kibrātim arba'im*: ruler of the universe (lit.: four cardinals)).
All these changes were introduced by Sharrukīn I during his long reign lasting for
56 years. Sharrukin was wise enough to know that his newly created state will meet
opposition from the cities and their ruling elites, therefore he had their walls pulled
down in order to prevent further armed resistance. Yet, at the same time he granted
new positions to the leading members of the former elites who were empowered
to rule the cities continuously, not as independent sovereigns, but as subordinate
officials of the king. In so doing, he bribed the former defeated rulers, secured his
supreme position and guaranteed an effective administration. These governors were
still designated *ensi*, but this term no longer reflected their previous political position.
To secure and check the loyalty of these governors he stationed military garrisons
in some cities. Agade, the newly created capital which still awaits excavation, was
the political centre of the realm without the rivalry of the local previous elites, thus
a perfect location to rule over former enemies. Seen from this angle, the Akkadian
Empire was a state in which one victorious city extended its dominance over other
city states, but it is misleading. The idea of unity was on the rise, which found its
expression also in unifying the calendars, weights and measures by which Akkadian
kings promoted trade among cities and with more distant places (Indus valley). It
is small wonder that Sharrukīn's glory lasted for centuries and the Akkadian king
became the hero of many legends.[5]

---

[5]Korošec (1964: 64), Kuhrt (1995: 48–55).

In this newly created militaristic regime, law was hardly important as a tool of governance. Unsurprisingly, n o oyal edicts or laws are known from this period. Legal life could be reconstructed only with the help of documents produced during everyday life. Most of these tablets were produced to document sale and purchase, loans and their securities. Sumerian language continued to play a central role in the contracts particularly because the legal formulas developed previously were still in use. Legal formulas and clauses, already in practice for centuries were very important in drafting contracts because legal effects were linked to the precise observation of them. This ensured the application of the Sumerian formulas in documents written in Akkadian language. The contracts were written on clay tablets, or chiselled into stone in particularly important cases (*kudurru*). The best example for the latter is the so-called Manishtūshu-obelisk, recording the land purchase of the Akkadian ruler Manishtūshu (2274–2260).[6]

Akkadian political structure remained intact with modifications during the reign of the Ur III Dynasty. The ideal image of the ruler was no longer that of a brave warrior, the archetpye of the militaristic Akkadians, but that of an educated king who masters languages (five), is skilled in music and poetry, is qualified in the science of divination, and who personally takes part in the most important religious cults. Sumerian renaissance was not accomplished to the detriment of the Akkadians, who still remained an important part of the new state of Ur, the rulers of which called themselves kings of Sumer and Akkad. Important offices in the central administration and the still existent office of the *ensi* were in the hands of the royal family and their allies and the local elite. The office of the *ensi* could be inherited within his family. In the military administration along the border the *sagin* was an important figure. Those areas were under the direct control of the *sukkalmah*, who acted as viceroy and governed the entire administration. The importance of the *sukkalmah* is indicated also by the fact that it entered the Elamite language. Civilian and military administration was perhaps separated in some (central) regions, but there is no clear evidence for that. The system of taxation was well organized, which required a centralised bureaucracy. State administration, the armed forces and the temples were supplied from taxes mostly paid in kind.[7]

The idea of law and social justice, once raised by UruKAgina, returned to the agenda and its realisation counted as one of the duties of kings. Again, no wonder that in this period a law book was created, presumably by the second ruler of Ur, Shulgi. It was attributed for long to the founder of the dynasty, Ur-Nammu, therefore, the code is known as the law of Ur-Nammu, despite the fact that an ever growing number of scholars doubt the accuracy of this designation. Irrefutable evidences are missing, though the arguments of those who think that it was Shulgi's law, are convincing. Accordingly, Ur-Nammu reigned only for a couple of years. of which he spent almost exclusively at war, meanwhile Shulgi dedicated his almost half a century rule to the consolidation of power and legislation fits rather to this policy.

---

[6]Neumann (2003: 70–72), Korošec (1964: 64–67).
[7]Lafont and Westbrook (2003: 188), Kuhrt (1995: 55–55, 61), Korošec (1964: 68).

The code is extant only in fragments, the text of which was published for the first time in 1954 by Samuel Noah Kramer, an eminent scholar of Sumerian studies.[8]

The structure of the code consists of three elements, a prologue, the legal rules proper and an epilogue cursing of those who did not observe the law. This structure had an effect for long centuries as every law book after Ur-Nammu's code followed this pattern. The full text of the code is not yet known, but it is expanding by every new discovery of fragments: the original edition consisted only of five passages, while in the latest edition already thirty-three articles could be read.[9] This is not the entire text which is supposed to have around fifty articles, the rest being only in unintelligible fragments. Important feature of the texts is its conditional wording, sentences beginning with the Sumerian word *tukumbi* ('if') introducing the provisions.[10] In the prologue the ruler boasts with his military deeds and his new policy: he regulated river trade, made maritime trade possible again (in the Persian Gulf), and protected the widows, the orphans and the poor against the powerful.[11]

The laws in the text do not give a comprehensive regulation of a topic, they contain only norms pertaining to a few issues. The law focuses on penal regulations related to homicide, assault and various sexual crimes. A person committing homicide deserves death sentence (1. §), yet the code is not based on lex talionis: assaults are punished by pecuniary compensation, the sum of which depends on the severity of the injury caused and the status of the persons (freeman, slave) involved (18–22. §). An interesting feature of the law is that it does not punish slaves fleeing from their owners but rewards those who catch and bring them back (17. §). Those accusing others falsely of sorcery were administered by water ordeal (13. §), a rule taken over by the Code of Hammurabi (2. §). Witnesses who turned out to be perjurers were obliged to pay pecuniary compensation (28. §). Theft was punished by pecuniary compensation, the sum of which was several times the value of that of the stolen object and sale into slavery was not exceptional either.[12] Land ownership is dealt with only briefly and through the lenses of criminal law: wrongdoers who illegally cultivate someone else's land, or flood someone else's land with water, should pay compensation the sum of which is exactly stipulated by law (30–31. §). To sum up, the law is rather about crimes and punishments, but here *lex taionis* is missing, death penalty is just an exception and not the rule which is, by contrast, compensation. All this, is in sharp contrast to the rules of the *Code of Hammurabi* composed two centuries later.

It is not the law book, but the judicial documents called *ditilla* which disclose some aspects of contemporary legal life and allow for an insight into everyday life. According to these texts, the Sumerian family was monogamous and patriarchal, where the woman had a subordinate role: a marriage contract was concluded by her guardian in her stead, and there was no need for her consent. To pronounce divorce

---

[8]Kuhrt (1995: 64), Roth (1995: 1), Kramer (1954).

[9]Roth (1995: 15–21).

[10]Neumann (2003: 74).

[11]See the prologue of the law: Roth (1995: 15–17).

[12]Neumann (2003: 75–76).

was also the husband's unilateral decision and his right was hardly limited. If the husband pronounced divorce without proper justification, he had to pay divorce money to his wife. In property issues however, women had their say and could decide upon their ownership. Only male children had the ability to inherit, as the heir (*ibila*) inherited not only the material goods of the deceased person but also his social position and standing, and had to guarantee the continuity of the name and the family. In this capacity, the heir had also ritual obligations and had to present sacrifices on the behalf of the deceased. In this archaic way o f hinking, inheriting the property was only of secondary importance. This is reflected also by the fact that if a brother of a man died without an heir, he could inherit, but was not considered as an heir. Local differences, however, were responsible for some variations. In the city of Nippur only the eldest son was regarded as an heir, whereas in Lagash all the sons were considered as such. But it was generally observed in all cities that a widow could not inherit, her husband could care for her by *inter vivos* gifts if he so pleased.[13] Scribes, whose literacy and practice in writing legal documents was essential, were important actors in legal life. Scribes were professionals authorised to draw up documents after long and tiresome studies in the *e-dubba* (house of writing), whose sufferings during studies were documented by lamentations and literary works.

2.2 Babylon

Modern historiography divides Babylonian history into Old, Middle and New Babylonian periods. The beginning of the Old Babylonian period was marked by the settlement of the Amurrus, a nomadic tribe of Semitic origin in Mesopotamia. In the beginning, Babylon was nothing more than a city subordinated to the Assyrians during the reign of Shamshi-Adad I (1813–1781), but after the death of this powerful Assyrian ruler Hammurabi (1792–1750), a member of the Amurru elite extended his authority by alliances and wars, the last waged against his former ally, Zimrilim, the ruler of Mari. With clever politics he created an empire which was equal in size to the formal state of Ur. After his death Babylonia continuously lost its influence but remained intact for another one and half centuries, however the successful military campaign (1595) of the Hittite ruler, Murshilish I destroyed it creating a power vacuum in Mesopotamia. Now Kassites, a nomadic tribe of unknown origin took their chance and settled in Mesopotamia and later took over political control as well.[14]

The Kassite rule had expanded to several centuries (1595–1155) and ensured political stability, peace, economic and cultural prosperity. The Kassite Babylon—which corresponds to the Middle Babylonian period—produced prominent rulers like Agum, Kurigalzu and Burraburiash, who once again elevated Babylon to the

---

[13] Korošec (1964: 71–72), Lafont and Westbrook (2003: 206–204).

[14] The origin of the Kassites is unknown: according to majority view they came from the Iranian mountains (Zagros); they have even been linked to Indo-European peoples based on some divine names, but it is inconclusive (Kuhrt 1995: 333).

major powers. The twelfth century however witnessed chaos and disintegration; and Kassite Babylon was destroyed by Elam, a traditional enemy of Mesopotamian states, now at the peak of its power. Elamites under the leadership of their famous king, Shutruk-Nahhunte, had taken away the Code of Hammurabi as booty to Susa, the capital of Elam. This is the reason why excavations in Babylon had never unearthed the Codex, despite serious efforts of archaeologists working in Susa. As the campaign of Shutruk-Nahhunte was unknown in that time, the presence of the Code in Susa caused some headache for modern scholarship. As Elamites were unable to manage their newly conquered territories, Babylon again witnessed a power vacuum resulting in a long transitory period during which the power of Assyra was again on the rise. To counter Assyrian hegemony, Babylon formed alliance with Elam and the allies waged numerous wars against the Assyrians, none of them successful. Resistance was finally destroyed by Ashshur-bān-apli, perhaps the cruellest ruler of Assyrian history by several campaigns against Elam during the middle of the seventh century. Elam was destroyed completely, but Babylon, a city of cultural, political and economic importance was spared. The importance of Babylon is proven by the fact that it was governed by a viceroy, usually one of the sons of the Assyrian king, because some Assyrian kings tried to consolidate disputes of succession to the throne by appointing one of his sons as his successor and another as the viceroy of Babylon (such as Ashshur-ah-iddina). Things changed with the settlement of the nomadic Chaldeans who had taken over Babylon and made every effort to resist Assyrian hegemony. To achieve this goal, they formed alliance with the Medes, nomadic newcomers on the Iranian plateau. The allied forces launched successful attacks against the Assyrians, and Babylonians did not only win their freedom back under the rule of Nabū-apla-usur I, but also annihilated Assyria. With this, Babylon entered its New-Babylonian phase of history when it became once again a major power together with the Medes, their former allies. The most prominent ruler of this period was Nabū-kudurri-usur II, a successful conqueror who occupied Jerusalem (597), and deported the Jews to Babylon as captives. New Babylonian history came to a sudden end when as a result of the disorders of Nabū-na'id's policy, the Babylonians were unable to resist the Persian army led by Cyrus II, who had created an unprecedented empire in its size that of the Achaemenians.

Social justice, highlighted by both UruKAgina and Ur-Nammu in the previous centuries continued to be an important principle in the Old Babylonian period, now referred to as *kittu* and *mēsharu*. *Kittu* and *mēsharu* were thought of as being connected to cosmic order to which even gods are bound and should be followed during legislation and the administration of justice. Thus, law did not originate from the divine as in the case of Jewish and Islamic law, but rested on a universal principle independent from the will of the divine. It is however, equally important that gods were its guardians, particularly Shamash, the Sun god. Hence, law was primarily secular in its content and orientation, linked to the divine sphere with abstract principles. This ensured the power of the rulers to enact laws provided they keep justice in view. Hammurabi refers also to these two concepts in his prologue, saying that "*to provide just ways for the people of the land (in order to attain) appropriate behavior,*

I established truth and justice as the declaration of the land, I enhanced the well-being of the people".[15] Though law was not divine in its origin yet it was the chief god, Marduk, who commanded the king to provide justice (prologue v. 14–24) and he himself had won the ability of righteousness from Shamash so that he may be able to create proper laws.[16] *Kittu* and *mēsharu* balanced and completed each other in the legal system because *mēsharu* to be understood as a Babylonian understanding of *equitas* moderated the formal rigour of the traditional law (*kittu*) when it would have resulted in unjust outcomes.[17]

The first two centuries of the Old Babylonian period witnessed very important law collections to emerge. It was during this period that the *Laws of Lipit-Ishtar*, the *Laws of Esnunna*, and the *Laws of Hammurabi* were created. The *Laws of Lipit-Ishtar* is the law collection of Lipit-Ishtar (1934–1924), a king of Isin, ruling before Babylon dominated Mesopotamian politics. Sumerian language was still in use, at least in official communication, witnessed by several contemporary legal documents and by this law collection too, which was composed in Sumerian. The text found in the city of Nippur, followed the triple structure for which Ur-Nammu established the precedent: it consists of a prologue and an epilogue, the legal norms being placed between them. The text of the law that has come down to us is fragmentary; originally it may have contained forty paragraphs.[18] The law deals primarily with issues of family law, inheritance, and ownership, but penal law is missing from it (that is, from the text we know). It is not a comprehensive code but raises atypical and exceptional problems like the inheritance of a son born of a prostitute (27. §).

The *Laws of Eshnunna*[19] (nineteenth–eighteenth centuries) has the name of its city and not that of the ruler, promulgating it simply because we do not know him, though he might be king Dadusha, an assumption still waiting verification.[20] This law book is the second largest text after the Laws of Hammurabi to which it is connected with several ties. The law book came into being during the transition period from the end of Ur III to the rise of Babylon, which is also reflected in the contents of the law. The *Laws of Eshnunna* is thus an important link between the Sumerian laws and the Babylonian legal system being an amalgam of old (Sumerian) laws and new legal understanding, therefore the text deserves particular attention. Novelties brought about by the law could be summarised as follows. (1) This is the first law written in Akkadian and not Sumerian any more, in a city located further north; (2) This is the only Mesopotamian law book that contains procedural laws as well, defining the competency of the judiciary on the basis of the crimes committed (48. §). It is the king who presides over cases punished by death, about other crimes,

[15]Code *Hammurabi*: prologue v. 14–24 in Roth (1995: 80–81).
[16]Albertz (1997: 115–117).
[17]Westbrook (2003b: 364).
[18]Neumann (2003: 83).
[19]The text was first edited by Albrecht Goetze in 1948. Reuven Yaron dedicated a separate monograph to the law in which he also published his own translation (Yaron 1969). The most recent textual edition can be found in Roth's collection of laws (Roth 1995).
[20]Korošec (1964: 86).

punished by 20–60 sheqels are in the power of local courts to decide. (3) The *Laws of Eshunna* fixes prices and tariffs of wages, maximises the price of some listed products (oil, bitumen, barley) and even fixes the lowest wage of workers (boatman, harvester), though the violation of these rules is not sanctioned. In so doing it is a direct predecessor to the *Laws of Hammurabi* which also contain large paragraphs on these issues.

In addition to these, rather technical changes, a fundamental new way of thinking is also discernible. Sumerian laws were always formulated in conditional form applied to everyone ("if a man"). By contrast, the *Laws of Eshnunna* continued the conditional form but the laws were no longer intended for anyone but only for social classes defined in the very law text. In doing so, the law was adjusted to the social structure of the early Old Babylonian period, differing enormously from that of the late Sumerian period. Now the law texts distinguish between the *awēlum* and the *mushkēnum*, both free in their status. Therefore, the new wording at the beginning of each conditional sentence is: "if an *awēlum*" or "if a *mushkēnum*", a novelty not in style but in principle. The definition of these categories has been an evergreen point of debate in Assyriology far away from being settled even today. Some scholars think that *awēlum* and *mushkēnum* are two different social strata, *awēlum* being free citizens, meanwhile *mushkēnum* were persons depending on the royal palace, some kind of a royal employee.[21] By contrast, modern scholarship tends to believe that *awēlum* has rather a meaning of "someone", a free man, or "gentleman", figuring as a general subject in the sentence to which *mushkēnum* are exceptions about which particular laws are formulated.[22] According to a third view, it hints to *mushkēnum*s in the law collections being the result of a kind of legal archaism since this category features only rarely in the legal documents of this historical period.[23] The interpretation of these terms have a particular significance in our understanding of the laws because they often provide rules only for *awēlum*s but not for *mushkēnum*s ("if an *awēlum*"), and it is far from clear whether these laws were applied also to *mushkēnum*s or not. In short: it is clear that there were differences in judicial status but it is impossible for us to see what these differences were in social status and wealth. Perhaps *mushkēnum*s were not always inferior to *awēlum*s but the lack of strict consistency in the laws (both in Eshnunna and Hammurabi) prevents us to say something definite. Some laws pertain only to *wardum*s, a third social category in the text, but its interpretation causes no problem as it means slaves.

The *Laws of Eshnunna* consist of about sixty paragraphs, which seem to follow some editing principles according to which the text is arranged by legal subject matter, though the structure is not as clear as in the *Laws of Hammurabi*. The first part contains rules of prices and wages (1–14. §), the second larger part is about family law, inheritance and contracts (15–41. §), while the third part enlists wrongdoings and crimes together with their sanctions. The law punishes only adultery and sexual

---

[21]Diakonov (1971).

[22]Driver and Miles (1952: 409), Yaron (1969: 84–88), Postgate (1992: 239–240), Kuhrt (1995: 114), Westbrook (2003a: 377).

[23]Petschow (1965: 150).

offences with death penalty (26, 28. §), and the *lex taliones* is again completely missing, anyone committing assault has to pay pecuniary compensation (42–47. §).

Clearly the most famous law of Mesopotamian legal history is that of *Hammurabi* chiselled by scribes into a 2.25 m tall black diorite slab. This extraordinary work was explored by a French archaeological expedition led by de Morgan in Susa in 1901–1902, from where it was transported to Paris and it is still housed in the Louvre. The text was first translated by Vincent Scheil. It was he who had arranged the law into paragraphs as the text, similarly to all other Near-Eastern laws, it does not contain any division or separating mark. To this he took the word "*shumma*" ('if') because according to his assumption (proved to be right), a new unit of thought began with every sentence starting with the word 'if'. As a result, he had identified 282 paragraphs, and this division is accepted still to this day. The Elamites however, who brought away the law as their booty had removed a certain part of the text for unknown reasons, and this is why some 35 paragraphs are missing from the text as we now know it. During the course of the twentieth century, the law was translated into modern languages, and attracted brilliant scholars who have written commentaries to it. Outstanding among them are the work of Koschaker, a legal historian with a qualification also in Assyriology,[24] and the edition, translation and commentary (both philological and legal) of Driver and Miles.[25]

We do not know when the Laws were written, despite the fact that all the names of Hammurabi's reigning years are known. Babylonian custom has it that the years were not recorded by numbers but by names which reflect the most important events of a particular year. It is striking therefore, that no year was named after the Law, that is, it was not regarded by the Babylonian king as an accomplishment important enough to attach the year of its creation to it (and the year was named after another event regarded as more important). Though the name of his second year reflects to *mēsharu*, it certainly is no hint to the Laws, but to a *mēsharu*-edict, issued by Hammurabi. To promulgate, *mēsharu*-edicts was a political custom going back to a long Mesopotamian tradition, according to which a new ruler after ascending to power, abolished previous debts of the inhabitants of his realm and so restored their freedom thus meting out 'justice' to all.[26] As kings usually promulgated *mēsharu*-edicts at the beginning of their reign, Hammurabi's second year name refers to this custom and not to his laws. In short, Hammurabi himself has not regarded his laws as an important achievement worthy of even a year's name, it was later generations, Babylonians and their neighbours, who with the passage of time thought of it as a peculiar intellectual product, even as a symbol of Babylon itself (this is the reason why the Elamites took it away as a booty), a sign of Babylonian cultural dominance.

Contrary to previous scholarly assumption the work cannot be considered as a code because it does not give a comprehensive regulation of a particular era or

---

[24] Koschaker (1917).

[25] Driver and Miles (1952, 1955).

[26] Kuhrt (1995: 110); Hardly any *mēsharum*-edict survived from this period, the only exception is that of the Babylonian king *Ammi-Saduqa* (seventeenth century). For a detailed analysis of the text see Finkelstein (1961).

field, but focuses on different matters in a casuistic form.[27] According to Driver and Miles, even the ruler himself did not regard his work a 'code', and his objectives are precisely set in the prologue.[28] Eilers however, has challenged even the normativity of the law saying that the text was just a legislator's ideal which was never realised.[29] Landsberger and Kraus took up the same position with the hypothesis that the law book was merely the product of 'scholarly' activities characteristic of Mesopotamian scribes, similarly to the omen-lists and to medical works.[30] According to Finkelstein's view, projecting back modern concepts such as legislation to Ancient Near-East is anachronistic from the outset, therefore these laws should be regarded as royal admonitions and 'testaments' in which the ruler proved to public opinion and to the gods that he had done his mission as a good shepherd and righteous ruler.[31] Those who deny the normativity of the laws add a further argument to their point, according to which there is hardly a judicial document or sentence containing reference to the laws (meanwhile documents are abundant), even Hammurabi's reforms did not seem to be realised, for they are not reflected in the documents either. Against these arguments, Korošec sees them as an exaggeration and has pointed out that there was no reference to other laws either, whilst no one questions their normativity. The fact that centuries after its writing the Laws were copied shows a continuous interest in the text despite that it was not used in daily practice in the New Babylonian era.[32] Recently Westbrook stressed the scholarly nature of the work again and its royal ideology. Dedicating a paper to this issue, he stresses that the only normative legal text in this period was the *mēsharum*-edict meanwhile, *Hammurabi's Laws* did not possess such feature.[33] By contrast, however, according to Postgate's balanced view the normativity of *Hammurabi's Laws* cannot be disputed, as it was future-oriented and prescriptive. It took contemporary juridical practice as its basis and composed abstract rules on its legacy while also reforming some previous laws.[34]

The law follows the centuries-old tripartite structure of prologue, epilogue and the legal norms placed between them. The composition of the Laws follows clear principles or at least tendencies, more consistent than the *Laws of Eshnunna*. The structure of the Laws can be summarised as follows: procedural rules pertaining to witnesses and false accusers (1–5. §), wrongdoings and harms committed against private, temple and palace properties, and crimes usually deserving death penalty (6–25. §); particular rules pertaining to various military officers (26–41. §); laws of contracts and damages (42–127. §); family law including sexual offences together with some rules of inheritance (127–195. §); bodily injuries and their punishments

---

[27] Korošec (1964: 99).
[28] Driver and Miles (1952: 45).
[29] Eilers (1932: 8–9).
[30] Kraus (1960).
[31] Finkelstein (1961: 103).
[32] Korošec (1964: 99).
[33] Westbrook (1989).
[34] Postgate (1992: 289–290).

(197–215. §); particular rules about wages, professions (physician, builder, shepherd, mariner, etc.) and their liabilities (216–277. §); laws related to slaves (278–282. §).

In family law, the patriarchal and monogamous family model known from the Sumerian period prevailed, but allowed for broad exceptions in favour of the husband. He could take a second wife if his first wife fell ill, was a priestess or 'neglected her household', whatever that means (141, 145, 148. §). To marry, parties had to sign a contract, if there was no contract, the marriage was regarded as invalid (128. §). Usually it was not the parties themselves who signed the contract but their guardians, the consent of the woman as a condition is not mentioned in the law. A man was obliged to hand over a sum called *terhātum* the nature of which is highly disputed among historians of Babylonian law. According to Koschaker, it was the purchasing price, consequently, he called Babylonian marriage *Kaufehe* and regarded *terhātum* as the *arrha sponsalicia* of Roman law.[35] This opinion, however, was challenged by many who understand *terhātum* not as a purchasing price but as a gift. Accordingly, this is proven by the fact that the Laws refer to marriages without *terhātum* (139.) and some contemporary documents miss *terhātum* altogether.[36] The last moment of a wedding ceremony was the introduction of the bride to the husband's house. Until that moment, either party could change his/her mind and withdraw from the contract without any sanctions. If parties changed their minds afterwards, the bridegroom lost the *terhātum* or the girl's guardian had to pay back the sum twofold (159–160. §). The wife was equipped with a dowry (*sheriktum*) which remained in her own and her family's ownership. She could take her dowry if she remained childless and her husband divorced her (138. §) or when she divorced her husband because he disparaged her (142. §). After the wife's death, her dowry was inherited by her sons.

Sumerian law, as we have seen, left the widow in desperate circumstances as she could not inherit from her husband. To overcome this problem a husband could stipulate *inter vivos* a gift (*nudunnū*) for her wife to guarantee a living for her after his death. Thus, a widow was dependent on the mercy of her husband as *nudunnū* was by far not her right. It was therefore, a fundamental change brought about by Hammurabi, whose laws ensured a son's share for her from the heritage of her deceased husband. In addition, a widow was entitled to remain in the house where she had lived with her deceased husband, whose heir could not force her out. Should they do so, they were fined parallel with the widow's rights restored (172. §). It was therefore, not a mere propaganda and empty phrase that Hammurabi provided "just ways for the widow" in order that "the mighty not wrong the weak" (epilogue: xlvii: 59) but also his policy which has found its way into the Laws.

Divorce was the husband's privilege but then he had to repay the dowry and the *terhātum*, or instead of the latter pay divorce money (138–139. §). A wife could initiate divorce only if she could prove to the authorities of her city quarter that her husband disparaged her. If she was in fact without fault and her husband's wrong could be proven the authorities permitted the divorce simultaneously with the return of her dowry (142. §). The procedure took place at the *bābtum* (gate) because in

---

[35] Koschaker (1917: 130–137).
[36] Korošec (1964: 107).

the Ancient Near-East, courts were usually located at the city gate or in the temple (there was no Babylonian word for court).[37] Contemporary legal documents prove that divorce by the wife was in practice even when the husband's wrong could not be proven. In this case however, the wife had to give up her claim to her dowry and it was she who had to pay the divorce money.[38] The Laws regulate illicit sexual behaviour in the framework of marriage law and not among the rules of crimes. Prominent among them was the violation of the incest taboo by the father with his daughter or daughter in law and the mother with his son (154–157. §). In the latest case, both were put to death, while the father should be cast into water only when he slept with his daughter in law but not with his daughter (in this case he was banished from the city). Rape of a virgin woman was awarded with death penalty (130. §). In the case of adultery, both parties could be killed (throwing them into the river) but if the husband spared the life of his wife, her lover could not be killed either (129. §). If a wife had her husband killed for the sake of another man, she had to be impaled (153. §), a clear example of an archaic way of legal thinking, the mode of execution reflecting the motive of the crime committed.[39]

Laws of penal law are discussed in two distinct units. Crimes against property are discussed at the beginning of the law, whereas rules pertaining to crimes against persons could be read at the end of the text. Those committing crimes against property are called thieves, irrespective of whether they had 'stolen' an object or a human being (minor child). Laws relating to theft are contradictory: according to one law the thief must be killed (6. §), while according to another law, the thief had to restore the stolen good 30-fold or tenfold (depending on the owner: if it was the palace, then 30-fold, if a commoner, tenfold), and should be killed only if he was unable to do so (8. §). According to Koschaker, there is no contradiction but a historical development: the old law proposed the death sentence for a thief while the new legal understanding highlighted pecuniary penalty in its stead.[40] As a complete novelty to Sumerian laws, Hammurabi's laws are based on *lex talionis* pertaining to assaults and injuries. It is perhaps by no way an accident that the laws following *lex talionis* are grouped together in an individual unit of the Laws (196–215. §), separated from other criminal legal rulings. This might be due to the fact that the king himself was of Amurru origin and these laws may reflect the customary laws of this nomadic tribe, so different from that of the Sumerians, that would make the Laws a composite of old (partly) Sumerian laws,[41] Amurru customary law and some newly introduced reforms of the king.[42] Perhaps the maximisation of debt slavery in three years should be recorded among these reforms (117. §).

---

[37]For more on judicial organisation see Postgate (1992: 276–282).

[38]Neumann (2003: 93).

[39]For more on this custom see Franke (2000).

[40]Koschaker (1917: 74).

[41]Petschow has shown in relation to land rent that the provisions of the CH were rooted in Babylonian legal practice (1984: 212).

[42]Edzard (2004: 125).

The *Laws of Hammurabi* had a fundamental influence in Mesopotamia during the successive centuries, although it was less and less applicable in everyday legal life. At any rate, not a single law has come down to us from the Middle Babylonian period, though it would be hazardous to infer *ex silentio*. The most important documents of this period are the *kudurru*s. The *kudurru* (border, border stone) is a stone slab marking the ownership of a certain plot of land. Presumably, the *kudurru* was placed at the border of the plot and a copy of it was kept in the temple archives, though recent assumption has it that they were actually kept in the temples and not out at the border of plots. Divine figures and symbols are to be seen at the upper end of the *kudurru*s recalling the divine safeguard of the legal deeds. As far as their content is concerned, they mostly contain grants of landed property by the rulers including also the settlements built on them. Among the grantees high ranking officials, priests and temples are found most frequently.[43]

The New Babylonian period produced no Laws, but rather a large number of commercial and marriage contracts. There is also a legal text presumably from the city of Sippar which came into being around 700 BCE, now in the British Museum in London. The text consists of 15 paragraphs some of which only in fragments. The laws are about some issues of agriculture and irrigation, marriage, sale and inheritance. We do not know what this tablet is: some believe it is a fragment of a law book, while others think it is only a text for practice from a scribe's school.[44]

2.3 Assyria

Similarly to Babylonian history, Assyrian history also has three periods: the Old Assyrian (2000–1800), the Middle Assyrian (1400–1050) and the New Assyrian (934–610) periods. The name of Assyria is derived from the name of the city of *Ashshur* which was a flourishing city already around 2000 BCE. The settlement was already surrounded by walls, had shrines and proper water supply which presumes advanced material culture. The city owes its riches to its important strategical location in the trade route between Asia Minor and South Babylonia. The city of growing riches fell prey to Shamshi-Adad I who after taking over the city, created an extensive empire by conquests to which even Hammurabi was subordinated in the first years of his reign. After the death of Shamshi-Adad I, his empire declined, and the leading role was taken over by Babylon. This Assyrian city-state shows a particular arrangement of public law. The ruler heading the state was not called as king, but rather as a deputy of the god *Ashshur*. It was only Shamshi-Adad I who, following a southern example, started to call himself *sharru*, that is, king, reflecting his growing authority. The city was governed by the *alum*, the city council. The *alum* had the right to issue

---

[43] Korošec (1964: 143–144), Kuhrt (1999: 337).

[44] San Nicolo considered the text as a law book, Driver and Miles defined it as a text produced by students in a school. Currently the majority follow this view: Korošec (1964: 188–189), Neumann (2003: 101–102).

decrees (*awat ālim*: the order of the *ālum*) and adjudicate legal matters (*din ālim*). This governing body controlled diplomatic activities and could assert its policy also through messengers sent abroad. The *limmum*, an office won by lot, was a curious Assyrian institution. Though the *limmum* did not have a defined competency, still he must have possessed serious social and political influence due to this social prestige. This is also indicated by the fact that royal authority was incompatible with the office of the *limmum*. Each year was named after the person bearing the office of the *limmum*, as each person was only in office for a year. Presumably, the city-state was governed by the richest merchants who were members of the *alum*, and the *limmum* was also one of them. The ruler, by contrast, had a prominent role in cultic activities, was responsible for public construction works and controlled the administration of justice.[45]

The caravans of the Assyrian merchants reached distant regions of Asia Minor, where they established city quarters (*kārum*: wharf, referring to water transport) and commercial depots (*wabartum*: guest). The *wabartum*s, smaller units in more desolate regions were subordinated to the administrative authority of the *kārum*. Commercial activity was carried on by bigger families (*bītum*) and clans through their extensive networks. Younger family members were responsible for trade in more distant regions, which explains some particularities of Assyrian law which taken as a whole did not differ from Babylonian laws. One such feature was that the Assyrian merchants, when marrying local women of Asia Minor did not pay *terhātum*, but this was compensated when they paid divorce money, multiple in sum, usually in silver. After having paid the divorce money, they returned to Assyria and married an Assyrian woman because according to Assyrian law a legitimate heir could issue only from a marriage with an Assyrian woman. Another particular Old Assyrian legal device was the commercial usage of a document proving debts. The basis on which the idea developed was a tablet containing the sum and entitlement of a debt together with the name of the debtor and his creditor. Later on, only the sum of the debt was written on it but the name of the party was substituted by *tamkaru*, meaning merchant. Thus anyone in the possession of such a document was entitled to claim the debt from the debtor, that is, the tablet could be used as a means of payment by the actual possessor of the document. Transfer of the document about the debt was at the same time the transfer of the claim the tablet proved and this could be used as a particular kind of payment 1300 years before the invention of monetary economy (which was attributed by Herodotus to Croesus the King of Lydia).[46]

The long travels of the Assyrian merchants and their staying away for years determined the family structure as well, particularly regarding the rights of women. As the heads of the families were away for long, some of their roles, particularly the management of home affairs, were taken over by their wives during the absence of their husbands. As a result, women were of equal standing with men in many respects in the Old Assyrian period (but only then!): they were entitled to be parties in contracts (sale, purchase, loans) and in juridical procedure (they could launch

---

[45]Kuhrt (1995: 88–89).
[46]Kuhrt (1995: 92–94), Korošec (1964: 148–149).

lawsuits), their share was equal to other male family members in the bequest, could dispose of their property (could issue testaments) and had their say in family relations (could initiate divorce).[47]

Due to the scarcity of sources hardly anything is known about Assyrian history between the eighteenth and sixteenth centuries. Assyria became a major power during the reign of Ashshur-uballit (1365–1330) when it was a rival to Babylon, Egypt and the Hittites. The power of Assyria was further enhanced by Tukulti Ninurta I (1244–1208) with successful campaigns towards the south. Tukulti-apil-ēsharra I (1114–1076) continued expansion towards the north since his conquest of the south was stopped by the Babylonians. After his death, the Middle Assyrian Kingdom began to disintegrate the entire history of which is unknown to us. Foremost among the reasons is the settlement of the Arameans, a nomadic persons whose continuous attacks resulted in the loss of the occupied territories.

In the Middle Assyrian period, the former political structure was eroded and it disappeared since Assyria was no longer a city state of merchants but a centralised territorial state headed by an autocrat and his army. Though the office of the *limmum* wasn't abolished, it lost its political and social significance during the coming centuries. By contrast, the king became an autocrat whose will was implemented by an army and an increasingly well-organised administration, loyal only to the monarch. The king disposed of the enormous material and human resources accumulated during the conquests which were used for huge programmes of construction. His cultic function remained important, by which he tried to win the support of the gods and particularly that of Ashshur for himself and for his country. Imperial bureaucracy was also on the rise. In the royal centre the grand vizier (*sakallu rabiu*) played an important role having military, administrative and judicial functions, and was considered as the second most important person after the king. The royal palace was managed (construction, maintenance, personnel) by another high-ranking officer (*rab ekalli*), while the eunuchs controlled the harem. The provinces were administered by governors (*bēl pāhāti*); their most important task was to provide supply, and guarantee the safety of transport the maintenance of communications. The governors were controlled by central officers (*qēpu*) created intentionally for this purpose.[48]

Legal sources that have reached us from the Middle Assyrian period are palace decrees and the so-called Middle Assyrian Law. Palace decrees are about the daily routine of the royal court and particularly that of the harem. These texts regulate how to settle conflicts among women and also the punishment of courtiers guilty in misbehaviour. Unfortunately, however, some texts are too fragmentary to decipher.[49] The Middle Assyrian Laws (MAL) being the most important legal source of the period, allow an insight into everyday legal life.[50] MAL consists of several tablets which are marked by the letters of the Latin alphabet (A, B, C, etc.). Thus, MAL A identifies the first tablet of the Middle Assyrian Laws. MAL is not law but a private

---

[47] Veenhof (2003: 448).

[48] Lafont (2003: 522–523).

[49] Text editions Roth (1995: 195–209), Kuhrt (1995: 364).

[50] Text edition Roth (1995: 153–194).

collection, though it is not clear whether it was part of a royal library or was written by a scribe for his own use.[51] Some scholars believe that the tablet containing marriage law was actually law, the aim of which was to reform this field of law. Therefore, Driver and Miles regarded this part of the texts as novella. According to Koschaker, however, the first tablet of MAL was the work of a legal scholar who had compiled the legal material from various sources.[52] We do not know when MAL came into being: according to some views it was written between 1450 and 1250, whereas others date it to the end of the eleventh century. It is also probable that the tablets were not written at the same time but came into being in different periods. Koschaker thinks of two phases in its development; according to him the first two tablets came into exisistence later and the rest contain earlier legal material.[53] MAL A, containing marriage law and the legal position of women, is in the best condition of all the tablets, it is also the longest with 59 paragraphs. Other tablets which are about contracts and ownership are rather fragmentary. Middle Assyrian Laws continue the old Mesopotamian tradition of casuistic approach, each new law beginning with the word *shumma* (if) like in the Laws of *Eshnunna* and *Hammurabi*.

Taken as a whole, Assyrian marriage law was not different from Babylonian marriage law. In Assyria, too, a marriage came into being with the payment of the *terhātum* and a marriage contract signed by the parties, on the girl's side by her guardian. A husband was entitled to punish his wife and her lover in case of adultery. A husband could either kill both on the spot or cut her wife's nose. If he choose the latter the court sentenced her lover to castration. The husband could forgive his wife but in that case he could not take revenge on the lover (15. §). Contrary to Babylonian law, however, middle Assyrian law ensured the husband matrimonial rights to "correct" his wife with brutal physical violence such as beating, mutilating her ears, tearing off her hair and striking (59. §). A marriage came into being also by the cohabitation of the parties: if a widow lived in the house of a man for two years the cohabitation resulted in a legally valid marriage and subsequently the woman could not leave (34. §).

Married women could enter the public only if they were veiled while unmarried girls and the prostitutes were prohibited to wear a veil. Should a prostitute violate this prohibition, she was punished by fifty strikes of blows with rods and the same punishment was due to a man who did not take a prostitute who was veiled to a law court (40. §). The importance of veiling is indicated also by the provision, according to which if a man had put a veil on his concubine in front of witnesses, she was considered as his lawful wife (41. §). The marital status of a woman had an effect also on penal sanctions: if a married woman was raped the punishment was death, but if a virgin girl was raped her father could demand to hand over the culprit's wife to be raped and the girl entered the house of the rapist. If he had no wife he had to pay threefold of the value of the maiden and marry her, but should her father decline this he could give his daughter in marriage to whomever he pleased (55. §).

---

[51] Roth (1995: 153–154).
[52] Korošec (1964: 155–156).
[53] Korošec (1964: 153).

A particular type of marriage in the Assyrian marriage law was when the wife remained in her father's house after the wedding and her husband visited her regularly. This *natolocal* type of marriage is unique in the Ancient Near East and not widespread elsewhere, too, but as legal anthropology has shown it is known by some peoples (for instance among the Nagyar in Africa).[54] Koschaker believed this particular type of marriage (Besuchsehe) was without the husband's authority (*manus*) but recently this hypothesis has been challenged. Those who doubt Koschaker's thesis, point out to laws according to which such a wife was financially responsible for her husband's debts, her husband could divorce her at any time, and after the death of her husband she could remarry only if neither her father-in-law nor her sons were alive. All this shows that the wife was a member of her husband's and not of her former family; hence, it is difficult to assume the lack of the husband's authority.[55] At any rate, several provisions of MAL deal with the rules of such marriages, particularly with propriety rights and inheritance (25–27, 32–33, 36, 38. §).

During her marriage a woman had limited rights to property: if she gave any object of value to a slave, her husband could cut off her ear and could claim that object back (4. §). If she gave it to someone else, the recipient was responsible for theft (6. §). At the same time the wife was responsible for her husband's debts (32. §). The husband could sell his wife and daughter to pay his debts. Daughters were usually sold not because of a debt but in order to preserve their lives: in case of famine people sold their girls to others so that those families should look after them and thus they may survive.[56] All in all, the situation of women was far more adverse than in the neighbouring Babylon and it significantly deteriorated in comparison to the earlier Old Assyrian period.

Assyria became a hegemon power during the New Assyrian period which consists of two sub-periods: during the first period between 934 and 745, attempts were made to renew traditions left over from the Middle Assyrian period regarding legitimacy as well as territorial claims. The second period between 745 and 610, was the time of hitherto never experienced territorial expansion which Assyrians tried to consolidate by unprecedented terror. The foundations of the great power status of Assyria were laid down by Ashshur-dān II (934–912), particularly by his successful wars against the Arameans. His foreign policy was continued by Tukulti-ninurta II, making it possible for Ashshur-nāsir-apli II to continue further expansion. Though, during the reign of Shulmānu-ashsharīdu III and Shamshi-Adad V, some difficulties arose in the form of internal revolts and struggles for the throne, but Tukulti-apil-ēsharra III (744–727) again restored great power status. During the reign of Sīn-ahhē-eriba (704–681), Ashshur-ah-iddina (680–669), and particularly of Ashshur-bān-apli (668–631), the hegemony of Assyria and its terror reached its peak. In the decades after the death of Ashshur-bān-apli, Assyria was weakened and the Babylonian-Medean coalition annihilated it in 610 BCE. Based on the Middle Assyrian legacy, imperial administration was further developed. The realm was divided into provinces. Each province

---

[54]Rouland (1994: 194).

[55]Korošec (1964: 154–155).

[56]Lafont (2003: 533, 539).

had a capital and it was usually named after it (of Niniveh, Kalhu, etc.). Governors heading the provinces were responsible for ensuring internal peace, collection of taxes and safety of roads and merchants. Governors had to supply the deported and to recruit manpower for the army and for construction works. The cities in the provinces were important allies of the ruler who granted them privileges in return. These privileges were realised in contracts, which were chiselled in stone and erected in the cities. Residents of the cities could directly turn to the king with their complaints, and it was the religious duty of the king to adjudicate the cases brought to him correctly, keeping in view the accords, customs and local tradition, despite the fact that the Assyrian ruler stood above the law. The king was bound to his subjects, to the members of his army and to the personnel of his palace by oaths of loyalty, which was also required of subjugated local rulers. Those who swear an oath of loyalty promised to be ready to die for the king, to prevent all revolt and conspiracy, to obey the king, to take their part in military enterprises and to avoid the king's enemies. People not observing their oath were considered godless evil who violated the divine order, the restoration of which was the right and duty of the Assyrian king by merciless punishments[57] (an Assyrian *bellum iustum*-ideology with similarities to the same Roman ideology at the time of the *fetiales*).

Neither laws nor any private collections have been found from the New Assyrian period, therefore legal life can be reconstructed only on the basis of extant judiciary documents and contracts. These contracts contain sanctions for parties violating the agreement such as bringing sacrifices to the temple, piercing their tongue, giving their children to some gods as burning sacrifice and committing suicide.[58] Obviously, these texts have no hint to social reality, that is, we cannot say what was actually realised from all these horrifying sanctions for violating a private contract. Be that as it may, it is nevertheless evident that parallel to the militarisation of Assyria, the importance and refinement of law disappeared together with the fruitful commercial activities of the merchants and the respect for their women and their rights. By contrast, a hegemonic, centralised power emerged with a king being above the law, which terrorised subjugated people *en masse* to such an extent that this attitude entered the contracts of private persons. Periods of Assyrian law reflect, therefore, not only different historical periods but also different legal concepts and understandings.

2.4 The Hittite Empire

The Hittites or, as they called themselves, the *nesita*, were Indo-European persons arriving in Asia Minor in the early second millennium. They established first what we now call the Old Hittite Empire, which was succeeded by the New Hittite Empire with a short, transitory period between the two phases.

---

[57] The survey is based on Kuhrt (1995: 478–500, 506, 514–517).
[58] Korošec (1964: 162).

The Old Empire began to emerge from the gloom of the earlier period at the time of Hattushili I (1650–1620). His successor Murshili I (1620–1590), was already waging wars to the south and east from the capital city of Hattusha in the heart of Anatolia. During a successful raid he occupied and ransacked the city of Babylon, acquiring huge booty and putting an end to the Old Babylonian kingdom (see the chapter on Babylon). After the successful reign of Murshili, however, internal disintegration weakened the realm which was presumably due to the inappropriate distribution of the huge war booty. In this seventy year long internal chaos, those having the upper hand for a short period were crowned as kings to be dethroned by succeeding competitors almost immediately. No wonder nothing is known about these rulers besides their names. It was Telipinu (1525–1500) who put an end to the assassinations of kings with a new law regulating the succession of kings. He established primogeniture as the underlying principle of succession to the throne and a criminal procedure against kings who ascended to the throne by violent means. This law stabilised the Hittite kingdom in the long run, as it was respected by the next generations with only one exception, for which a long apology was written. Despite the long term effect of the law after the death of Telipinu, the Old Kingdom disintegrated. Following a transitory period, the history of the New Kingdom, headed by a new dynasty began. Only after defeating the Gasga, a nomadic people from the north threatening even the capital entered the Hittite kingdom to contemporary world politics during the reign of Shuppiluliuma I (1370–1330). This king significantly enlarged the territory of his realm with successful wars to the south and east and annexed Syrian territories too. At the peak of his power, the Egyptian pharaoh acknowledged him as his equal and wanted to have friendly relations with him. After the fall of the Amarna reforms in Egypt, the widow of the young king Tutanhamon asked for one of Shuppiluliuma's sons to become her husband. The Egyptian aristocracy however wanted to hinder the ascent of a foreign king on the Egyptian throne and had the prince assassinated during his travel to Egypt. The succeeding war was waged by the Hittite king, Muwattali (1295–1282) against Ramses II, the conquering pharaoh. The battle near Qādesh was a struggle of giants from which Ramses II hardly escaped alive and Hittites stopped the ascendancy of the Egyptian army to Syria, thus defending the territorial and political status quo. Status quo was also put into writing and this is how the Egyptian-Hittite peace treaty (concluded by Ramses II with Hattushili III (1275–1245), the successor of Muwattali) came into being in 1269 BCE. This peace treaty is an outstanding document in the history of diplomacy and this is the reason why its copy decorates the wall of the UN headquarters in New York. The treaty ensured decades of peace in the Levant. After the death of Hattushili III, the empire of the Hittites disintegrated within a few decades and disappeared from history around 1200 BCE, the causes of which is still awaiting explanation.

The king heading the Hittite kingdom was the paramount political authority in a web of hierarchies operated by complex institutional and personal relations. The title of the king was *labarna* who was addressed as "My Sun", referring to the royal symbol of the winged Sun.[59] The ruler was also the representative of the Storm God,

---

[59] Haase (2003a: 128–129).

the possessor of the land. Religion played an important part in Hittite political life not only in royal ideology but also in everyday practice. The king was therefore a high priest at the same time, one who was regarded as a god after his death. Contrary to Ancient Near Eastern practice, a queen played significant role in both the royal court and in international politics: she had diplomatic correspondence of her own and is a subject of international treaties on equal rank to the kings.[60]

Two important tasks of the Hittite kings were to head the army and to act as high priest. A Hittite king personally led the military operations as it was usual in the Ancient Near East. Equally significant, was their cultic functions which was more important among the Hittites than among other Near Eastern cultures. A Hittite king was the high priest of all the gods of Hatti *ex officio*, and though he was not a god during his lifetime, he enjoyed particular divine respect after his death. A cult was developed for the deceased ruler who was burnt and placed in a stone grave. Kings were in contact with the gods through prayers and ritual. Both were important as the king represented his folk among the gods who decided on fate. This is why kings composed prayers by which they tried to avert harm hitting their country. Particularly the prayers of Murshili II against pestilence are heart-rending in which he prays to gods to stop this epidemic with enormous devastation on the population (the pestilence was brought in the country, most probably, by Hittite soldiers during the wars of Shuppiluliuma). Religious festivals were also in the centre of royal ideology and everyday practice, therefore Hittite kings travelled long weeks to the venues of various festivities in their empire. Spring festival lasting for 32 days and the 21 days autumn festival were the two most important among them. Cultic purity was one of the cornerstones of Hittite religious, thinking the non-observance of which manifested in punishments (such as pestilence). This explains the innumerable stipulations for the ruler's ritual purity which had to be observed with rigour. For instance, when a king returned with an army from a lost war, both the king and the queen had to be handed over to the gods of the enemies to avoid more harm from them. For this purpose, a man and a woman dressed in royal garments were handed over to the enemy. In so doing, the king and his wife liable for the defeat were "punished" with the help of their proxies and at the same time the safety of the realm was guaranteed.[61] The ruler was also the supreme judge of the kingdom and there was no remedy against his final judgment. If anyone disregarded the judgment of the king, his entire house was destructed, while disregarding the judgment of other officials was awarded by capital punishment.[62] The cruel punishments served not only the centralisation of power but guaranteed that righteousness (*handandatar*) prevailed. It was not the king's justice but that of the gods, the ruler merely asserted it.[63]

Hittite rulers appointed officials whose competencies and responsibility were defined in detail in documents called *ishiul* (contract). Later on, this document served

---

[60] Haase (2003b: 626–628).

[61] Kuhrt (1995: 275).

[62] Hittite lawbook 173a.

[63] Güterbock (1954: 232) (page numbers follow the 1997 edition).

as a template to contracts signed with client kings (see below). Officials had to personally swear loyalty to the king. The capital city was governed by the *hazannu*, who had to provide internal security. For this purpose, the city gate was sealed each night and was reopened next morning. Defence was the most important task of officials acting in other cities. Garrisons were stationed along the borders under military commanders. High ranking officials belonging to either the 'powerful' or the 'king's sons' who were often linked to the ruler by dynastic marriages. This elite also benefited from huge land donation by the king, who wanted to reward them and pay off their loyalty. These lands were not identic with the territories of vassal kings, or defeated rulers who were left in office as kings, but were subjugated to the Hittite king. As these rulers were also called kings, now it is understandable why the Hittite king, their master, was called great king. The territorial competencies of a vassal ruler were determined by the Hittite king at his own discretion and put into writing in *ishiul*s, signed by both parties. Curiously, then, the Hittite kingdom was managed on contractual basis, signed by the ruler and his vassal kings and officials. These contracts were kept in the royal archive and therefore could be checked at any time if necessary. Vassal kings had to swear the oath of loyalty too. As such loyalty was not a matter of course, it was continuously controlled for which dynastic marriages were perfect tools. While having a wife from the Hittite royal family was regarded as a great honour, these marriages were effective controls on the ambitions of the subjected rulers since their wives remained in close contact with the Hittite king himself. Another means of control was that subjected kings had to visit the king annually, hand over the taxes imposed on them and to give him their gifts. Loyalty of vassal kings was of paramount importance, since it was they who provided internal and external peace and defence, produced an army of appropriate size and participated in wars, and reported on important issues based on information of spies.[64]

What we know about Hittite law rests upon two documents. One is the edict of Telipinu, according to which the throne was inherited by the first rank son of the king. In the absence of such a son, the throne was inherited by the second rank son of the king. If there was no male issue at all, the husband of the female child first in rank would become king.[65] Should anyone ascend to the throne violently or bypassing these rules, the *panku* (presumably a council consisting of the leading members of the aristocracy and the army) was his court to judge him with the right to pronounce even capital punishment. The *panku* thus had the right to remedy illegal ascendancy but had no power to interfere into the election of kings.[66]

The most important source of Hittite law is a collection of laws first written down already during the Old Kingdom, which has come down to us in some copies containing some variants.[67] At some points the text refers to old rules replaced by new laws which suggest legal reforms, the essence and tendency of which was to

---

[64] Kuhrt (1995: 266–271).

[65] Telipinush's edict, 28; Haase (2003b: 625).

[66] Güterbock (1954: 230) (the page numbering follows the 1997 edition).

[67] Full text in English is in Roth (1995: 217–241); in German in Haase (1963). The most recent critical edition and commentary is Hoffner (1997).

replace earlier severe punishments with milder penalties. In so doing, the law replaced corporal punishments with fines or reduced the amount of fines. Unfortunately the text does not tell us the name of the ruler in whose reign the Laws came into being, but according to scholarly consensus it was Telipinu. This law collection is not a law Code and no serious scholar thought otherwise prior to the time when the legislative nature of the *Code of Hammurabi* was not yet challenged.[68] Presumably, difficult cases of judicial practice together with their rules were put together in the collection for guiding scribes and officials. The text contains some 200 paragraphs but this structure, too, is the result of modern scholarship (Hrozny). It was written in conditional form; the sentences opening with the word *takku* (if) introduce a new unit of thought.[69] The text was found in the Hittite capital from under the ruins of the building of the supreme court.[70] Since it is not a code, the Laws do not give a comprehensive regulation of a given field, but have some rules on homicide, assault, marriage, land tenure, theft, wages, prices, damages and sexual offences. The laws pertaining to these are grouped more or less consistently together, that is, the editor followed some editorial principles which makes the structure of the Hittite Laws similar to other Ancient Near Eastern laws.

Taken as a whole, Hittite marriage law resembles Babylonian and Assyrian family law. Family structure was patriarchal which is important because according to Goetze this specificity of Hittite law makes this immigrated Indo-European people different from the original settlers of Asia Minor, among whom traces of matriarchate can be discovered.[71] The marriage was concluded between the son-in-law and the girl's guardian; before the wedding both parties could withdraw from the contract but in that case the guardian had to repay the bride price twofold or the groom forfeited the bride price he paid previously (29–30. §). Levirate was known as when the widow was married to the male brother or another relative of the deceased (193. §). Elopement of girls seems to be a rather common usage in which Hittite kings did not wish to interfere leaving it to the private parties to resolve, sometimes a lethal business. A modern reader hears the resigned tone in the laws:

> If anyone runs off with a woman, and a group of supporters goes after them, if 3 men or 2 men are killed, there shall be no compensation: "you have become a wolf". (37. §)[72]

In case of adultery, the husband was entitled to kill his wife and her lover on the spot or bring them to the royal court. Even at court he had the right to decide whether he wished the death penalty for the both his wife and her lover or not. If not, clemency was the rule for both persons, that is, resembling Near Eastern custom, he could not save his wife while destroying her lover (198. §). A man was master not only of his wife but also of his children: he had the right to sell his children to slavery, or to hand over a son for a person he killed to the relatives of the plaintiffs (44. A §).

---

[68] Koschaker defined it as a collection of judgments (Entscheidungssammlung): Haase (2003a: 133).

[69] Korošec (1964: 180).

[70] Haase (2003b: 620).

[71] Goetze (1974: 111–112).

[72] Hoffner (1997: 44).

In the field of criminal law, *lex talionis* is missing, compensation is the underlying principle. When inflicting injuries (to the head or blinding someone) one had to pay compensation, the sum of which was reduced to the half (from 40 to 20 shekels) by the law reform (7–9. §). Intentional killing was distinguished from homicide during quarrel when one had to bury the victim, care for his house and give 4 persons to the victim's family as compensation (men or women). The number of persons was reduced to 2 if death was the result of an accident or the victims were slaves (1–3. §). Hittite merchants were particularly protected by law, as their killing resulted in an enormous amount of compensation, 4000 shekels of silver, never again featuring in the whole text (5. §). Corporal punishments and bodily mutilation are almost completely missing from the laws, occurring rarely (95. §) and only in respect of burglarizing slaves, whose nose and ears were disfigured. The lack of *lex talionis* distinguishes Hittite law from the *Code of Hammurabi*, and the lack of bodily mutilation distinguishes it from Assyrian law.

The law collection devoted particular attention to illicit sexual behaviour, particularly incest and rape, in a separate part of the text (187–200. §). In the case of rape, women were not regarded as victims per se, because if the crime was committed in the mountains, that is, where women could not defend themselves, it was the man who was punished by death. By contrast, if the crime was committed in a house it was the woman's crime and she should be punished by death, and not the man. Thus, Hittite law represented the third variant to the same problem next to the Laws of Hammurabi and the Old Testament. The Laws of Hammurabi punished the man in every case, meanwhile the Old Testament only did if the act had taken place out in the field; should it happen in the city, both parties were considered guilty. The Hittite Laws have long rules on necrophilia and bestiality, not featuring in other Near Eastern law texts. In the whole, bestiality is a capital offence but the king could spare the life of the guilty who remained nevertheless in the status of ritual impurity (199. §).

Cultic and ritual considerations are the motives of some crimes, peculiar to the Hittite laws. Such an act is sorcery with a snake (170. §), or sowing someone else's land, the latter being an offence against the gods; earlier it was punished by unprecedented brutality but after the reform it was sufficient to bring a sacrifice (166–167. §).[73] Violating boundaries was not an act against neighbours but against gods, particularly against the Sun God and the Storm God. Anyone violating boundaries had to present sacrifices and swear to the gods that with the act no quarrel was intended (168–169. §). Since the ritual purity of kings was of paramount importance for the wellbeing of the ruler and his folk, acts against his ritual purity was sanctioned with unprecedented cruelty, otherwise missing from the Hittite legal understanding. Persons guilty of such acts were put to death by beheading or hanging together with their families. For example, royal shoemakers could use only ox-hide from the royal kitchen and coach-makers could use only goat skin also from there; should they act otherwise they were executed together with their family. A similar destiny was due to the water carrier if he did not pour the water through a filter so that to keep it

---

[73] Haase (2003b: 647–648).

free of hair.[74] Despite these rules, Hittite law remained a secular law as all other Mesopotamian legal systems never evolving into a religious law. The peculiar ritual rules in the law only show the importance of rituals and purity in Hittite religion, royal ideology, and everyday practice.

There are some rules in the laws that cause some headache to scholars. One such is the rule according to which a slave rising against his master would "go into the clay jar" (173b. §). Originally, perhaps, it was not for death penalty but we should interpret it literally, that is, slaves were put into large vessels in which they had the chance to think about their deeds while sitting in the jar for a long time. Later, however, the meaning was transformed to mean death penalty and revolting slaves were cooked in a cauldron or buried alive.[75] The wording, according to which after the husband asked for the death penalty on his adulterous wife and her lover "they shall roll the wheel" is completely unintelligible even for experts in Hittite philology (198. §). According to some speculations, it refers to the way of execution while according to rival theories the wheel was a royal symbol and therefore this passage does not refer to the way of punishment but to the presence of the king.

Despite these uncertainties, we have a fairly good understanding of Hittite law which resembles the Mesopotamian laws with local particularities. It is the law of an agricultural society reflecting the problems of such a community. No wonder rules pertaining to agriculture dominate the laws, such as the problem of hiring animals, damages done to animals and fields, theft of animals and etc. What distinguishes Hittite law from Mesopotamian laws is its focus on rituals and purity and a lenient attitude toward crimes and punishments. Family relations and conflicts remained in the hand of the pater familias who regulated all these issues at his own discretion, sometimes with violence and Hittite kings did their best not to be involved. For kings, what was at stake was that all their decisions be followed (death for those who rejected the king's judgment) and their ritual purity saved at all costs, including severe punishments. In all other fields, the law was rather lenient and more humanistic than the Laws of Hammurabi and the Assyrian laws. This is also due to the fact that Hittite society was less centralised and the power of the state did not extend to some social relations, leaving them to society to resolve. By contrast, Assyria was a centralised state with a centralised bureaucracy which inferred deeper into the life of society, creating a legal system on this model.

---

[74]Haase (2003b: 651).
[75]Hoffner (1997: 219–220).

References

Sources

Codex Eshnunna: In: Roth MT (1995) Law collections from Mesopotamia and Asia Minor. Scholars Press, Atlanta, Georgia; Haase R (1963) Die Keilschriftlichen Rechtssammlungen in deutscher Übersetzung. Harrassowitz, Wiesbaden

Laws of Hammurapi: In: Roth MT (1995) Law collections from Mesopotamia and Asia Minor. Scholars Press, Atlanta, Georgia; Haase R (1963) Die Keilschriftlichen Rechtssammlungen in deutscher Übersetzung. Harrassowitz, Wiesbaden

Laws of Lipit-Ishtar: In: Roth MT (1995) Law collections from Mesopotamia and Asia Minor. Scholars Press, Atlanta, Georgia; Haase R (1963) Die Keilschriftlichen Rechtssammlungen in deutscher Übersetzung. Harrassowitz, Wiesbaden

Laws of Ur-Nammu: In: Roth MT (1995) Law collections from Mesopotamia and Asia Minor. Scholars Press, Atlanta, Georgia; Haase R (1963) Die Keilschriftlichen Rechtssammlungen in deutscher Übersetzung. Harrassowitz, Wiesbaden

Laws of the Hittites: In: Roth MT (1995) Law collections from Mesopotamia and Asia Minor. Scholars Press, Atlanta, Georgia; Hoffner H (1997) The Laws of the Hittites. A critical edition. E. J. Brill, Leiden, Köln, New York; Haase R (1963) Die Keilschriftlichen Rechtssammlungen in deutscher Übersetzung. Harrassowitz, Wiesbaden

Middle Assyrian Laws: In: Roth MT (1995) Law collections from Mesopotamia and Asia Minor. Scholars Press, Atlanta, Georgia; Haase R (1963) Die Keilschriftlichen Rechtssammlungen in deutscher Übersetzung. Harrassowitz, Wiesbaden

Literature

Albertz R (1997) Die Theologisierung des Rechts im Alten Israel. Religion und Gesellschaft. Studien zu ihrer Wechselbeziehung in der Kulturen der Antiken Vorderen Orient. Ugarit Verlag, Münster

Diakonov I (1971) On the structure of old Babylonian society. In: Klengel H (hrsg) Beiträge zur socialen Struktur des alten Vorderasiens. Berlin

Driver G, Miles J (1952, 1955) The Babylonian laws, vol I–II. Clarendon Press, Oxford

Edzard DO (2004) Geschichte Mesopotamiens. Von den Sumerern bis zu Alexander der Großen. C. H. Beck, München

Eilers W (1932) Die Gesetzstele Chammurabis. Der Alte Orient 31:3–4

Finkelstein J (1961) Ammisaduqa's edict and the Babylonian "law-codes". J Cuneif Stud 15:91–104

Franke S (2000) "Magische Praktiken" im Codex Hammurapi. Z Altorient Biblische Rechtsgesch 6:1–16

Goetze A (1974) Kulturgeschichte kleinasiens. C. H. Beck, München

Güterbock G (1954) Authority and law in the Hittite kingdom. J Am Orient Soc 17:16–24. Reprinted: Hoffner H (ed) Perspectives on Hittite civilization: selected writings of Hans Gustav Güterbock. The Oriental Institute of the University of Chicago, Chicago, Illinois

Haase R (1963) Die Keilschriftlichen Rechtssammlungen in deutscher Übersetzung. Harrassowitz, Wiesbaden

Haase R (2003a) Recht im Hethiter-Reich. In: Manthe U (hrsg) Die Rechtskulturen der Antike. Vom Alten Orient bis zum Römischen Reich. C. H. Beck, München

Haase R (2003b) The Hittite kingdom. In: Westbrook R (ed) A history of ancient Near Eastern law. Handbuch der Orientalistik, vols 1–2. Brill, Leiden

Hoffner H (1997) The Laws of the Hittites. A critical edition. E. J. Brill, Leiden, Köln, New York

Korošec V (1964) Keilschriftrecht. In: Orientalisches Recht. Handbuch der Orientalistik, Erste Abteilung, Ergänzungsband III. Brill, Leiden, pp 49–219

Koschaker P (1917) Rechtsvergleichende Studien zur Gesetzgebung Hammurapis. Veit and Comp, Leipzig

Kramer SN (1954) Ur-Nammu law Code. Orientalia 23:40–51. Roma

Kraus F (1960) Ein zentrales problem des altmesopotamischen Rechtes: was ist der Codex Hammurabi? CRRA 9:283–296. Geneva

Kuhrt A (1995) The ancient near east C 3000-330 BC, vol I–II. Routledge, New York, London

Kuhrt A (2005) Az Ókori Közel-Kelet (ford. Mohay Gergely). Stud Orient 4. Pázmány Péter Katolikus Egyetem Bölcsészettudományi Kar, Piliscsaba

Lafont S (2003) Middle Assyrian period. In: Westbrook R (ed) A history of ancient Near Eastern law. Handbuch der Orientalistik, vols 1–2. Brill, Leiden

Lafont B, Westbrook R (2003) Neo-Sumerian period (Ur III). In: Westbrook R (ed) A history of ancient Near Eastern law. Handbuch der Orientalistik, vols 1–2. Brill, Leiden

Neumann H (2003) Recht im antiken Mesopotamien. In: Manthe U (hrsg) Die Rechtskulturen der Antike. Vom Alten Orient bis zum Römischen Reich. C. H. Beck, München

Petschow H (1965) Zur Systematik und Gesetztechnik im Codex Hammurapi. Z Assyrol 1965:146–172

Petschow H (1984) Die §§ 45 und 46 des Codex Hammurapi. Ein Betrag zum altbabylonischen Bodenpachtrecht und zum Problem: Was ist der Codex Hammurapi? Z Assyrol 74:181–212

Postgate N (1992) Early Mesopotamia. Society and economy at the dawn of history. Routledge, London, New York

Rouland N (1994) Legal anthropology. Stanford University Press, Stanford, California

Roth MT (1995) Law collections from mesopotamia and asia minor. Scholars Press, Atlanta, Georgia

Veenhof K (2003) Old Assyrian period. In: Westbrook R (ed) A history of ancient Near Eastern law. Handbuch der Orientalistik, vols 1–2. Brill, Leiden

Westbrook R (1989) Cuneiform law codes and the origins of legislation. Z Assyrol 79:201–222

Westbrook R (2003a) A history of ancient Near Eastern law. Handbuch der Orientalistik, vols 1–2. Brill, Leiden

Westbrook R (2003b) Old Babylonian period. In: A history of ancient Near Eastern law. Handbuch der Orientalistik, vols 1–2. Brill, Leiden

Wilcke C (2003) Early Dynastic and Sargonic period. In: Westbrook R (ed) A history of ancient Near Eastern law. Handbuch der Orientalistik, vols 1–2. Brill, Leiden

Yaron R (1969) The Laws of Eshnunna. Magnes Press, The Hebrew University of Jerusalem, Jerusalem

Chapter 3
Jewish Law

3.1 Political and Legal Institutions in the Pre-Talmudic Period

The history of Jewish law and society in the early nomadic period is less known. The Bible calls this period the age of judges, though these judges were rather tribal and clan leaders controlling only limited territories. The core of the first Jewish kingdom began to develop under the reign of Saul, who was initially hardly more than a military leader in the stateless political landscape of Palestine. The victory over the Philistines may have played a significant role in the election of Saul as king but his authority continued to be limited to the southern territories. Resistance against Saul ultimately promoted the leader of the rebels, the later King David to power. David occupied Jerusalem and made it his capital; subsequently he waged wars against the Philistines and other neighbouring cities and peoples. As a result of his victories, he extended the borders of his new state beyond the territories inherited from Saul, but his rule still did not extend over entire Palestine. Yet the occupation and integration of the hitherto independent city-states was a significant step ahead in creating a new kingdom. Solomon, his successor did not continue his father's policy of conquest but rather supported trade and culture. His famous temple well indicates his commitment to this policy. After his death, however, the kingdom was split: Israel was born under the leadership of Jeroboam in the north, and Judah under the kingship of Rehoboam in the south. With the accession to power of Omri, a successful military leader, Israel experienced success and international recognition. Omri made Samaria his capital which remained the centre of Israel for the next one and a half centuries, up to the Assyrian conquest (722 BCE). Omri subjugated the Moabites and created a broad international alliance, primarily against the increasingly expanding Assyrians. Stagnation followed the assassination of the last ruler of the Omri dynasty. After a brief flourishing period under the rule of Jeroboam II, the independent Israeli state was annihilated by the Assyrians (in the 720s). Parallel to the fall of Israel, Judah could still preserve its autonomy where a religious and legal reform was introduced under the rule of king Josiah. In the next century, Judah was

© Springer Nature Switzerland AG 2020
J. Jany, *Legal Traditions in Asia*, Ius Gentium: Comparative Perspectives on Law and Justice 80, https://doi.org/10.1007/978-3-030-43728-2_3

unable to resist, however, the Babylonian forces and Jerusalem also fell (597 BCE) in this great game of super power politics of the Ancient Near East. With this, the last Jewish state vanished. Babylonians, following an age old Near Eastern political custom, carried Jewish captives to Babylon in order to prevent revolts. This is how the Babylonian exile started, notably for merchants, craftsmen and the intelligentsia. The sudden victory of the Persians over Babylonian forces put an end to the exile and the decree of the Persian king, Cyrus II (539 BCE) made the return for the Jews possible. Soon works on the Second Temple began but no independent Jewish state was created: Palestine was integrated into the Persian Empire and became part of a larger satrapy. Persian rule came to an end with Alexander the Great's campaigns but subsequent Hellenism resulted in serious internal and religious tension which manifested in the revolt of the Maccabees who attempted to create an autonomous state under the authority of a religious leader. However, the state of the Hasmoneans was being increasingly threatened by the expansion of Rome and was made a client state under the rule of Antipater. Herod the Great proved to be a faithful ally of Rome but after his death the Romans introduced direct rule. The revolt against the Romans provoked by religious, economic and social tensions broke out in 66 CE which ended in the siege of Jerusalem and its final occupation (Titus). Jerusalem and the Temple were destroyed, yet resistance to the Romans continued. After the defeat of the revolt led by Simon (bar Kokhba') in 135 CE, a significant part of the population left the Roman Empire and was seeking refuge in Babylonia dominated by the Parthians and subsequently by the Sasanian Persians. Babylonia Jews enjoyed autonomy during the reign of the Parthians which was later, after Sasanians had taken over power, limited but never reduced completely. This is the reason why Babylonia for centuries remained the centre of Jewish intellectual life. In the beginning, Islamic conquest was hardly more for Jews than a change of the elite who demanded obedience and taxes from them. Thus, Babylonian Jewish community continued to exist and the academies could still preserve their intellectual influence over Jewish communities for another three centuries or a bit more. Afterwards however, the central role of Babylon ended and the history of Jews was associated with the history of those European, North African and Middle Eastern states where they settled down.

The basic unit of social structure was the extended family (*bēt'ab:* the father's house), which consisted of the members of two or more generations and of the servants belonging to the house, if there were any of them. Subjects of land ownership were also the families as the basic units of agricultural activity. Members of the extended families married from outside, though there are references to marriages between half brothers and sisters. The extended families were controlled by the heads of the family who disposed of property, administered justice concerning family members and determined external relations by marriages. Clans were made up by families who usually settled in a village or a smaller town. The leaders of the clans were the elders, that is, heads of the families, who in keeping with customs of the Ancient Near East, were seated in the gate of the village or town while providing justice. Several clans constituted tribes, though these were rather territorial units opposed to a large group based on descent. The geographical origin of the names of tribes (Gilead, Ephraim) also indicates the territorial roots of these units. At the same time the belief in descent from a common ancestor was alive which was manifest in marriage customs and perhaps in joint activities too. The leaders of the tribes were called by various designations, one of which was judge (*shōfet*), referring to their leading role in the administration of justice. These judges were also military commanders waging wars against the Philistines and other rival groups, usually with their private armies. At the dawn of history women could also be judges, proved by the prophetess *Deborah*.[1] As ritual was not yet centralized, the gathering place of the tribes functioned also as the centre of cultic activity.

Things had been changed with the ongoing centralisation by a hitherto never seen political figure, the king. Since the first Jewish state evolved from this tribal society, it was by no means a complete break with the past. Power remained in the hands of the king and his family, the members of which enjoyed privileges and important offices. Since the Jewish state was born during the wars with the Philistines, it is no wonder that the most important office by far was that of the military commander. The system of public administration became more refined under the kingship of David, a ruler of an increasingly centralised state with headquarters in Jerusalem. David's governance relied on the services of the Levites and on foreign mercenaries. As a result, tribal cohesion for the support of rule lost from its weight. To oversee public administration was the task of the 'chancellor', while the secretary controlled diplomatic correspondence and the supervisor of forced labour headed public works. Like in other Near Eastern kingdoms (e.g. Mari), court prophets (like Natan) provided the much needed ideological support for royal power. This administrative structure was not changed significantly at the time of Solomon but as a result of building programmes, its supervisor had acquired an eminent place in the hierarchy.[2]

During the Persian period, Judah was a small province being only a part of the satrapy called 'beyond the river' (*ebir nāri*). It was Persian policy that satrapies were governed by members of the Persian aristocracy and the royal family, but smaller units were left to the local elite to govern. This is what happened in Judah too, where Jews enjoying religious and some legal autonomy were governed by the local leaders whose most important task toward the king was to collect taxes and hand them over in due time. A military contingent of the king was stationed there, the leader of which resided in Jerusalem. The Second Temple was built during the Persian period, which contributed significantly to the preservation of Jewish identity without any political significance: the high priest was an important figure in ritual but not in politics. In short, religious and legal autonomy had its limits controlled by the Persian elite.[3]

Judicial organisation was non-existent in the period of the judges, as these tribal leaders administered justice in person, without formalities. Their judgments were based on local and tribal customs known to all and not on promulgated laws. Violation of basic tribal norms could provoke public outrage and armed clashes (when the residents of Gibea, a Benjaminite city, abusing the guest's rights raped the guest's concubine, Israeli tribes took up arms against the Benjaminites to punish them:

---

[1] Miller-Hayes (2003: 89–91).

[2] Miller-Hayes (2003: 136; 176–177; 197).

[3] Fried (2004: 233).

Judges 19–20). Judicial organisation began becoming more differentiated when the administration of the kingdom reached maturity. Head of the administration of justice was the ruler himself (see Solomon's judgement), but there was a royal court system as well. In addition to royal judges, law courts consisting of local leaders ('elders') were also active in small towns and villages which continued to provide justice in the city gates. The king was both a first instance and a court of appeal, though the institutional mechanism of appeal was missing. The king was a forum of legal remedy as the applicants could turn directly to him with their complaints, but he could also intervene into the procedure of cases any time if he deemed it necessary for any reason.[4] Priestly courts also existed but presumably their competency was limited to the Temple as their jurisdiction was narrow and had far less authority than in the coming centuries when the kingdom no longer existed.[5]

Judicial organisation had changed significantly throughout the course of centuries because the function of the royal judiciary had to be taken over by other institutions. As a result, it was the *Sanhedrīn* that had become the most important judicial forum in the Second Temple period and the subsequent centuries. There is some confusion about the role of the *Sanhedrīn* in legal life. According to rabbinic sources, the *Sanhedrīn* was an organ consisting of leading legal scholars, headed by the *nāśī*, which administered justice and issued ordinances in the framework of its legislative functions. By contrast, Greek sources have it as a political decision-making body headed by the king or the high priest. To overcome such contradictions some scholars suggested that there were two *Sanhedrīn*s, one political and one legal institution.[6] Others believe that there is no need to postulate two institutions, as the contradiction in the sources is due to the fact that they reflect different historical periods: the *Sanhedrīn* of the Greek sources was a completely different institution from that of the rabbinic sources.[7] What complicates matter is that the term *Sanhedrīn* was in use to also denote local courts of 23 members, otherwise called *bēt dīn* (house of judgment), resulting in some confusion. To make things clear, the central judiciary in Jerusalem was called Great *Sanhedrīn*, which was, however, not an appellate court of the local courts but decided on issues regarded as very important. The Great *Sanhedrīn* had jurisdiction over the high priest,[8] the ruler of a tribe or a given territory,[9] and a false prophet.[10] Capital punishments of local courts for a rebellious son, a false witness or one who leads a town to apostasy should be confirmed by the *Sanhedrīn* in Jerusalem before implementation.[11] The Great *Sanhedrīn* as a legislative institution

---

[4]Westbrook (1988: 134).

[5]Westbrook (1996: 3; 8–9).

[6]The various opinions are surveyed by Mantel (1965: 60–64).

[7]Segal (1996: 129), Mantel (1965: 55–58).

[8]M Sanh. II.1.

[9]Sanh. 16a.

[10]M Sanh. I.5.

[11]Tos Sanh. 11.6.

issued ordinances called *takkanah* which were to follow by everyone in the fields of ritual purity, agriculture and civil law.[12]

During the period of the *tannaim* (10–220) and the *amoraim* (220–500), it was the *nāśī* who gained prominence. The history of the term goes back to the beginning of Jewish history when tribal chiefs and local leaders were designated by it. Prior to the establishment of the monarchy, the term lost significance but returned again when Jewish leaders emerged who did not want to call themselves kings, as they were no rulers by law. *Simon Bar Kokba'*, for example, was one among them who called himself *nāśī* on his coin.[13] Rabbinic tradition has, however, a different interpretation and calls *nāśī* the head of the *Sanhedrīn*. We do not know when this usage was introduced: some think it was Hillel the Elder (first century) who was the first Pharisee *nāśī*, while others believe that R. Yūda (second century) was the first such person. Contrary to the uncertainties concerning the beginning of the Pharisee understanding of the term, we definitely know the end of its history: it was the *Codex Theodosianus* in 425 which abolished the office once and for all (XVI: 8: 22). The political function of the *nāśī* began around 70 CE as earlier political system did not make it either possible or necessary. The Romans acknowledged the *nāśī* as a political leader of the Jews though he did not govern a particular territory but a dispersed Jewish community instead. Imperial Roman law protected him and his office. The *nāśī* as a person belonged to the *spectabiles*, whose public verbal abuse was punishable, while his office was called *honoraria praefectura* by the *Codex Theodosianus* (Cod. Theod. XVI. 8. 11–15). As the representatives of the Jewish community, *nāśī*s also negotiated with Roman authorities but despite this, they were never considered as kings neither by Roman nor by Jewish law.[14]

The objective of the administration of the *nāśī* was to lead and control Jewish communities in the Roman Empire. Lacking political power this could be done only through legal means rested on social prestige. *Nāśī*s were, therefore, legal scholars or properly speaking, only highly qualified legal scholars could be appointed to this office. The most important task of the *nāśī* was to preside over the great *Sanhedrīn* (*bēt dīn ha-gadōl*), as a sign of his prestige and undisputed scholarly reputation. *Nāśī*s developed some techniques to achieve their goal. One such a mean was legal advice to the dispersed communities which ensured the uniform interpretation of Jewish law and its application. *Nāśī*s thus answered all the questions put forth to them by the Jewish communities living in the Roman Empire, whatever they were about. To control faraway communities, *nāśī*s sent their emissaries themselves highly qualified legal scholars, with a watching eye. As a fine could only be imposed by a properly qualified legal scholar, the emissaries of the *nāśī* presided over local law courts and passed judgments. In addition, they were entitled to remove any of the religious or lay officials from their office, provided they did not observe the principles and rules of the law. To ordain legal scholars was a privilege of the *nāśī*, a very important function in preserving the continuity of Jewish legal tradition and

---

[12]Cohn (1974a: 562), Mantel (1965: 84).

[13]Nasi in Encyclopaedia Judaica, vol 12, 834–836. (G. J. Blidstein).

[14]Mantel (1965: 239).

scholarship. Previously, disciples were ordained by the very scholar who was their teacher, but in the Late Antiquity *nāśīs* centralised this right to themselves (the right of ordination was transferred to the academies when the office of the *nāśī* was abolished in the fifth century). *Nāśīs* had a judiciary of their own also filled with legal scholars of reputation. This law court was, however, not a court of appeal but issued ordinances (*takkana*) to be followed by other courts as well. As religious leaders, *nāśīs* were empowered to pronounce excommunication (*herem*). Excommunication could be of shorter period (one week, thirty days) or of indeterminate duration.[15] After the abolition of the office of the *nāśī*, Jews were left without a political leader. Though the *Codex Theodosianus* regarded them as Roman citizens (II. 1.10.), their legal autonomy was further decreased: the decisions of the law courts qualified only as arbitration.[16]

Jews living in Babylon had their own leader called *rēsh galūta'*, an office similar to that of the *nāśī*. Babylonian *rēsh galūta'*s claimed direct descent from David by the male line (*nāśīs* by the female line) and were called *rabbana'* (our Lord) or *mār*. Babylonian *rēsh galūta'*s headed the Jewish communities living in the Parthian and the Persian (Sasanian) empires, appointed market inspectors and judges to adjudicate private legal disputes.[17] The power of the *rēsh galūta'* was challenged by the Babylonian academies, independent bodies of learning and teaching where outstanding legal scholars were not always ready to accept the *rēsh galūta'*s jurisdiction, resulting in long struggles the detail of which is not our concern here.

3.2 Jewish Law in the Pre-Talmūdic Period

Legal history of the period of the judges and the early kingdom is lesser known, but it is beyond doubt that tracing back the laws of Moses to these periods is a historical anachronism. No wonder judgements do not refer to the laws of *Moses* since they did not exist at that time.

This early period of Jewish law contains rules important for a peasant society, regulating family matters, inheritance and conflicts produced by agricultural activities (the goring ox, land ownership and cultivation, hired workers, etc.). This is the reason why early Jewish law has so much in common with cuneiform laws. Jewish kings had legislative power of their own, as did every king in the Ancient Near East. The Jewish legal system was, therefore, secular in its early phase, based on tribal customary laws and promulgated royal laws while religious law was either non-existent or insignificant.

In this regard, the so called reforms of king *Josiah* was of importance, about which the Old Testament informs us (II Kings 22–23.30; II Chron. 34–36). Accordingly, in

---

[15]Mantel (1965: 221–234).

[16]Rabello (1996: 153–154).

[17]Mantel (1965: 240–243); Tos Sanh 5a.

his 18th regnal year (622 BCE) a "book of law' was found during works in the Temple. When learning about it, the king asked the prophetess Huldah who confirmed the significance of the law book without hesitation. Next, the king summoned the people, informed them about the law book and took an oath of submitting himself to its rules. Needless to say, the story is curious enough to provoke scholarly disputes, since we do not know what was 'found' and why it was to be confirmed by a prophetess of less reputation. The majority of scholars tend to believe that it was the *Deuteronomy* or at least a part of it that had been found, but we cannot rule out the possibility that it was the work of High Priest Hilkīa, the finder, who produced it to promote Yahwist theology, now on the rise.[18]

Yahwist theology was in fact helpful to preserve Jewish identity and law after the fall of Israel and Judah. According to this understanding, law was not secular in its origin, neither as customary law nor royal law, but it is God who shapes its content in order to make his requirements clear. In this re-formulation, law is a moral and religious guidance for every Jew to be followed regardless of time and space, that is, it is binding when there is no longer a Jewish state. It was, therefore, a gradual reinterpretation of the role, function and origin of the law, transforming Jewish law from a secular law to a religious law in the long run. This change was coupled with a legal reform intended to protect the poor in social and economic life by prohibitions and restrictions (interest, debt slavery) in order to win backing to the new legal understanding. Details of the story are important: the king no longer promulgates law, he just reads it out once it is found, that is, the king is not the lawmaker, only its servant. The law originates from God, this is why it was found by the high priest and confirmed by a prophetess, and the king swears an oath to follow it without questioning its content. The king is, therefore, subordinate to the law and God, and has lost his capacity to legislate. This was a long process called die *Theologisierung des Rechts*, which transformed the theoretical foundations of law but left its content intact apart from some minor modifications. This is what was extremely needed after the fall of the last Jewish kingdom, since only divine law was able to preserve Jewish identity. With the fall of the kingdom, no king was able to legislate and adjudicate, but luckily Jewish law was transformed from a secular state-based law to a religious law based on *Personalitätsprinzip*, which is operational without state power as well. Moses was no king, but a prophet, chosen by God to his revelation, therefore a perfect candidate to mediate his law which is eternal regardless of ever changing political situation, since a law based on revelation and divine will had stronger legitimacy than royal legislation and customary law. Parallel to this, cultic activities were centralised to Jerusalem, religious syncretism was punished by death and the central judiciary was reinforced (Deut. 17. 8–13).[19]

This new legal thinking is not peculiar only to the Deuteronomy since Exodus (20, 22–23, 19) has a similar logic. The source material for laws in Exodus was believed local custom for long but recent scholarship has challenged this view. Accordingly, the composer was familiar with cuneiform legal material as well, and this is the reason

---

[18] Westbrook (1996: 3), Miller and Hayes (1986: 394), Smith (1971: 40–51).
[19] Albertz (1997: 120–127).

why so many laws i n Exodus have their parallel in Mesopotamian laws both in form and content. During the time of Assyrian occupation, it was possible to have access to cuneiform laws and this is exactly what the author did. While drawing the laws on Mesopotamian models (and, of course, local customary laws, too) he changed the lawgiver from the king to God and this is how YHWH replaced Hammurabi as supreme legislator. In so doing, the author turned his Mesopotamian model against the Mesopotamian conquerors and this is how loyalty to law became the focus and symbol of national solidarity and identity replacing obedience to the king with obedience to God. Codex Hammurabi was, therefore, not only a model for individual pieces of casuistic law, but also for the larger framework which was cleverly adapted to the situation of Jews, now under Assyrian hegemony. Deuteronomy, composed just some decades later followed the same line and logic.[20]

Foreign domination continued to have impact on Jewish law. Persian rule resulted in regaining some autonomy and Jews were allowed to return to Palestine. One among them was Ezra, a wise man well versed in Moses's law, who taught the law after returning to Jerusalem (7 Ez. 6; 10.). Later rabbinic tradition granted an exalted position to Ezra, seeing in his person the re-newer of the law who could have been given the *Tōra*, had Moses not preceded him.[21] Based on this tradition, Wellhausen believed a century ago that the *Pentateuch* (the Five Books of Moses) originated in Babylon and got to Judah by *Ezra.* This view is not accepted by everyone, therefore it is an open question whether or not Ezra's law is identical with the *Pentateuch*[22] or, alternatively, these are two separate legal corpuses and Ezra's law disappeared from history together with him.[23] Despite these disputes, the majority of scholars think that the final reduction of the *Pentateuch* was accomplished by the end of the Persian period (early fourth century BCE) at the latest.[24]

The last reduction of the laws of Moses put no end to disputes, legal and religious. During the Second Temple period, we can witness rival intellectual groups to emerge with different understandings of law, among others. Samaritans separated and continued to rely on their own law and legal interpretation which was still alive during the Islamic conquest. This was also the time when the Pharisees and the Sadduceans elaborated their own doctrines, which were hardly compatible to each other. At the end of this period, both John the Baptist and Jesus were confronted with legal problems, though these were not essential to their teachings. The Qumran community, separating itself from the majority, developed its own legal understanding while highlighting ritual purity and their role in salvation. While everyone accepted the *Pentateuch*, its content was interpreted differently. The Qumran community had legal norms of its own (the Damascus Document, the Temple Scroll, the Community Rule, War Scroll), the bases of which were also the laws of Moses. John the Baptist was condemned to death because he warned the ruler that he was not exempt to respect

---

[20]Wright (2009: 350).

[21]R. Yōse in Tos Sanh. 4.7.

[22]Blenkinsopp (2001: 56–62) with critical remarks.

[23]Smith (1971: 125).

[24]Grabbe (2001: 100), Piattelli and Jackson (1996: 25).

the law (Mark 6. 14–29). Pharisees on the other hand were keen to follow the law and this is the reason why they put forth legal questions to Jesus (*Shabbāt*, washing hands before eating, giving due wages to the workers, etc.).

We should understand the emergence of the *Sanhedrīn* against this background as it was not only a judicial body but also a forum of constant debates between the Pharisees and the Sadducees. There were few issues on which the two groups came to a consensus since they differed both in underlying principles and detail. The Pharisees (*perūshīm*; from the word to separate) believed in the resurrection of the body and divine providence, denied by the Sadducees. The Pharisees attributed outstanding significance to the issues of ritual purity and thus followed rules of purity prescribed for priests, even though they were laymen. In addition, they stressed the importance of teaching; in particular, the teaching of law[25] and were filled with pride because of their mastery in law.[26] The Pharisees also had some customs of their own called oral law, denied by the Sadducees who did not believe that God had revealed anything else beside the written law. Pharisees were previously believed to be a politically influential group but this view has been modified in the previous decades. It was Jacob Neusner who called them a "pure food club" based on the fact that their basic concern was ritual purity during eating. Sanders agrees, but would rather call them "purity club" as it was ritual purity in general which was at the heart of their teaching, not only dietary laws, which were rather part of their ritualistic understanding. Despite this, to see a withdrawn and isolated group in the Pharisees would be another extreme, therefore, the truth may lie in between, that is, they were neither a powerful, nor an isolated group of no significance.[27]

By contrast, Sadducees (*Cedūqīm*) were aristocrats, rich merchants and priests, that is, an influential group of leading persons whose name may derive from the high priest *Cādoq*. This unpopular group stressed its distance from the common people and maintained good relations with the Roman political elite. They denied everything the Pharisees believed in: the resurrection of the body, the immortality of the soul, the existence of angels and the validity of the oral law of the Pharisees. Sadducees dominated the *Sanhedrīn* for a long time and it was a joyful event for the Pharisees when they took it over from them. Sadducees stressed the importance of the temple cult and were not satisfied with the mere teaching of the law and ritual purity. Their close relation to the Temple explains not only their success but also their demise: after the destruction of the Temple they disappeared from history.[28] The legal interpretation of the Sadducees was believed for long as literalist and narrow but recent scholarship modified this view. They interpreted the law, it is true rather differently from the Pharisees, and rejected the oral law of their opponents but this does not make them literalists. Sadducees had their own customs and laws

---

[25] Piattelli-Jackson (1996: 44).

[26] Flavius (1980: 474).

[27] Neusner (1971: 305), Sanders (1990: 242–245).

[28] Encyclopaedia Judaica 14, 620–622 (Menachem Mansoor).

despite the fact that they denied it in order to show that they had no extra-Biblical traditions.[29]

After the demise of the Sadduceans, the destruction of the Temple and the annihilation of the Qumranians by the Romans the Pharisee interpretation of the law survived without rivals. The leading Pharisee legal scholars of this period were called 'pairs' (*zugōt*) in the rabbinic literature who played central role in handing down legal tradition. According to Pharisee understanding, oral law reached the pairs through Moses, Joshua, the elders, the prophets and next they mediated the legal tradition to the Pharisees and Rabbis. Thus, it is the continuity of tradition that invested the pairs with outstanding significance. Until the emergence of the last pairs in the chain of tradition, Hillel and Shamm'ay, oral law was undivided, but from this time on Pharisee legal tradition was fragmented between schools (*bēt*, literally: house), that is, followers of Hillel and Shamm'ay. Rabbinic legal tradition was developed as a result of the scientific debates between these two schools with rival understandings. Although we know very little about the disputes of the founding fathers the number of points of disagreements during the next generations reached the figure of 350. It is important to note that both understandings were valid and accepted and neither of them was superior to the other. This immanent legal pluralism continues for centuries and remains one of the basic principles of Jewish law with no attempt to declare one interpretation as the only official version. As they themselves put it, both schools were the "voice of the living God", though Rabbis understood also the disadvantages of such a system.[30] It is impossible to say in general terms what the difference between these schools were, as disagreements manifested rather in details of technical importance. Despite this, Jewish tradition has it that it was Hillel's school that was more lenient and the school of Shamm'ay was rather strict, though such a generalisation is clearly an oversimplification. Some see social differences between the schools: accordingly, followers of Shamm'ay would be representatives of the upper and richer middle class, while followers of Hillel belonged rather to lower social strata. This and similar generalisations however, explain little about the teachings of the schools and have no analytical value.[31] With these legal debates we enter the period of the *tannaim*, when the early schools of Hillel and Shamm'ay— which were only informal entities based on the personal relationship between masters and their disciples – begun to develop into more complex academic organisations called academies. This is the first step in a long way, as these academies reached maturity only in the subsequent centuries. Nevertheless, this first step in transforming schools to academies was important for the history of Jewish law. During the period of the *tannaim*, the *Sanhedrīn* continued to exist, now as a rabbinic institution with no disputes with the Sadduceans any longer.[32]

With the backing of institutions such as the *Sanhedrīn* and the academies, Jewish law continued to flourish during the period of the *tannaim*, marked by eminent legal

---

[29]Sanders (1990: 103–107).

[30]Tos Sanh 7:1.; T Sanh 88b.

[31]Enc. Judaica, vol 4B, 737–740 (Shmuel Safrai).

[32]Stemberger (1996: 8–11), Goodblatt (1975: 267–272).

scholars as Rabban Gamalī'el and Yōhanān ben Zakk'ay, who later followed R. ᶜAqība (put to death by the Romans for participating in the revolt of Bar Kokba') and Rabbi Yūda Ha-Hāśī, the redactor of the *Mishna*. Rabbi Yūda Ha-Nāśī (also known as Rabbenu HaQadosh) was regarded as the most outstanding scholar of the *tannaim* and this is the reason why he was referred to as *the* rabbi, whose name was further enhanced by his redaction of the Mishnah. Though not his personal work, but that of a group of legal scholars headed by R. Yūda, the importance of the *Mishna* makes R. Yūda known for long centuries to come.[33] The aim of the compilation is subject to debate. Some scholars understand the Mishnah as some kind of a code reflecting contemporary legal practice while others see it as a compilation for educational purpose, still others believe it as an academic work.[34] Be that as it may, the compilation is a valuable source of Jewish law arranged in a topical structure. The work has six orders (*sedarīm*), divided into tractates, though the structure as we now know it is not the original arrangement, as it was constantly re-organised in order to keep with the needs of later generations.[35] Individual orders deal with comprehensive areas of law, while tractates discuss issues of detail within them. The orders are the following: (1) *Zerāīm* (seeds): rules related to agriculture; (2) *Mōᶜēd* (holidays): rules related to religious festivities; (3) *Nashīm* (women): rules related to family law; (4) *Nezikīn* (damages): rules of private law and procedure; (5) *Qodashīm* (sacred things): Temple rules; (6) *Tohorōt* (purities): rules of purification.[36] Soon comments and additions were made to the various tractates and this is how the Tosefta', a subsidiary work to the *Mishna* came into being. The new legal material was arranged according to the structure of the *Mishna*, that is, Tosefta' follows the structure of the Mishnah, though the relationship of the two texts is problematic, giving rise to different scholarly theories.[37]

The endeavour to put the rabbinic understanding of Jewish law into writing reached its zenith with the compilation of the *Talmūd*. The *Talmūd* (teaching) is a storehouse of questions, answers and doctrines that emerged during the study of the *Mishna*, hence it is at the same time a commentary to the *Mishna*. As there were two academic centres, Palestine and Babylon, two *Talmūd*s were produced, each region having its own text. It is important to note that these are two, independent works and not variants of the same text. The *Palestinian Talmūd* (PT) was compiled during the fourth or fifth century, most probably in Tiberias. The repetitions and self-contradictions in the text have led some researchers to see only a loosely compiled collection in it without any editorial principles. Though the majority rejects this view as it is still beyond doubt that if there were organising principles, they are not as clear as in the Babylonian *Talmūd*.[38]

---

[33]Stemberger (1996: 138).

[34]Stemberger (1996: 133–139).

[35]Stemberger (1996: 121).

[36]For a complete English translation see Neusner (1988).

[37]Stemberger (1996: 150–158), Neusner (2002) has the English version of the text.

[38]Stemberger (1996: 164–173).

The *Babylonian Talmūd* (BT) is a longer and better structured work which is more than a commentary on the *Mishna* but rather a kind of encyclopaedia of Jewish wisdom: besides legal arguments it also contains legendary biographies of rabbis, anecdotes and legends, observations in mathematics, biology and astronomy. Due to this complexity, it significantly precedes the PT by its popularity and importance. Similarly to the *Tosefta*' its structure follows the *Mishna* but there are tractates in the *Mishna* which have no parallels in the *Talmūd*. We do not know when exactly BT was put to writing but it certainly does not have only one editor, perhaps it was the work of generations as a result of continuous editing and interpolation. Despite this, it is fair to say that the core of the text was already in existence around the second part of the Persian Sasanian period, that is, by the end of the period of the *saboraīm* (fifth–sixth centuries).[39]

3.3   Jewish Law in the Post-Talmūdic Period

Post-Talmūdic history of Jewish law has four periods: that of the *saboraīm* (fifth–sixth centuries); the *ge'ōnīm* (seventh to eleventh centuries), the *rishonīm* (eleventh–fifteenth centuries) and the *aharonīm* (from the fifteenth century to the present age).

It was the period of the *saboraīm* when the final redaction of the *Talmūd* was completed. In addition, academies reached maturity also in the period of the *saboraīm*. While previously, schools were less formalised and its operation was left to the personal relationship of the master and his disciples now more institutionalised academies called *yeshīva* dominated Jewish jurisprudence. The academies of the *saboraīm* and the *ge'ōnīm* functioned both as schools of legal training and courts. Since professors of the academies were eminent legal scholars, disputants turned to them out of their free will in order to settle their disputes and this is how academies evolved into courts too, a peculiar feature of Jewish law not shared by other legal schools in the Near East (Islamic madrasa) or elsewhere. In addition to the academies, other courts were also in operation, judges were appointed by the *nāśī* in Palestine and the *rēsh galūta*' in Babylon.[40]

Babylonian academies in Sura and Pumbedita were headed by the *gā'ōn* (hence the name of the period), who controlled the judiciary, appointed officials, and disposed of the only effective means of law enforcement, excommunication of private individuals. *Gā'ōn*s were not only administrative but also intellectual leaders, who in addition to works in jurisprudence had written works in various fields (such as theology) as well. Due to their widely known and appreciated theoretical works, the most famous *gā'ōn*s were Saᶜadya and Rav Hai.[41] Babylonian academies as intellectual centres influenced not only Mesopotamia and its neighbourhood, but also faraway regions such as North-Africa or even Europe, as Jewish communities turned to them for

---

[39]Lifshitz (1996: 175–180), Stemberger (1996: 191–197).

[40]Lifshitz (1996: 170–178).

[41]Libson (1996: 197–203; 229–234).

help or legal advice concerning their daily legal life and disputes. The pre-eminence of the Babylonian academies remained for centuries when local scholarly centres emerged all around Europe in the period of the *rishonīm* and thus there was no need to turn to the Babylonian academies any longer. Students of these academies obtained professional training in jurisprudence, legal practice and argumentation. They were seated in rows, the most eminent students sitting in the first row, close to the professor. If one member was missing from the rabbinic court for whatever reasons, the most eminent disciple from the first row was called to join the court in order to have a proper composition of the court for the proceeding. Students were expected not only to learn huge amount of texts by heart but also to participate in legal disputes among themselves and with their professors. Scholarly discussions were organised also for legal scholars outside the academies, devoted to a particular legal problem or tractate of a text. There was a fixed period in the year called the days of the *kalla*, during which only academic disputes were organised. These scholarly debates and exchange of ideas contributed also to the final redaction of the *Talmūd*.[42]

The period of the *ge'ōnīm* witnessed a gradual change in Jewish economic history, with far reaching consequences in social structure and law. Jewish society was composed of agricultural communities for long centuries, but Jews began to give up living from agriculture and turned towards trade and industry instead. Legal scholars were in the lead in this respect as a great number of them took part in long distance trade, though some of them remained agriculturalist. As a result of this societal change, laws on agriculture lost their significance and what was needed in its stead was law merchant. The isolation of Jewish communities allowed by agriculture was no longer possible since trade brought along a more intensive interaction with other communities residing in Mesopotamia among whom Muslims had the upper hand. Jews came into more intensive contact with their Muslim fellows and this is the reason why some laws of Islamic law entered Jewish law. Islamic law penetrated into Jewish substantial law in the form of commercial contracts between private persons, in which parties applied Islamic law for their business if one of the parties was a Muslim, or in a form of custom (*minhag*). Jewish legal scholars were aware of this tendency and did not welcome it unanimously, but ultimately they allowed for the acceptance of Islamic law in issues related to commercial activities. The increasing popularity of the Muslim courts among the Jews made the Geonim to introduce some innovations in the law to make it more flexible and thus to make it unnecessary to turn to the Muslim courts.[43]

Far reaching changes could also be observed in jurisprudence. One of them was a shift in language from Aramaic to Arabic. As a result, breaking from centuries old tradition, Arabic gained acceptance also in law. Another change was the emergence of a new literary genre of jurisprudence, the *responsum*-literature with a brilliant carrier in the centuries to come. A *responsum* is an answer to a legal problem asked by a private individual in writing. Questions embrace every field of law, but sometimes

---

[42]Goodblatt (1975: 155–170; 283).

[43]Libson (1996: 200; 224–225); for more on Islamic law and geonic custom see Libson (2003: 92–103).

they may touch upon the interpretation of some parts of the Bible and the *Talmūd*, or the explanation of an expression difficult to understand. Questions were sent from distant places such as North Africa, Egypt and Hispania, showing the leading position of the Babylonian academies in contemporary Jewish society. Questions were usually collected and sent to the academies by merchants travelling there; the answers arrived in the same way to the addressees. To avoid abuses, the texts usually repeated the question in order to make it clear precisely to what the answer was given (Muslim legal scholars applied the same technique in their *fatwās*). These answers weighed in heavily first because they reflected the legal interpretation of the academy as a corporate body of Jewish jurisprudence, second because they were compulsory and could not be neglected during adjudication. To promote their rulings, *responsa* were collected and edited in compilations out of which more than twenty are extant.[44]

The outstanding work in jurisprudence in the period is the collection *Halakhōt Gedolōt* ("Great laws"), which followed the structure of the *Talmūd*. The work gives an outline of the Talmudic legal material, therefore, it is shorter and easier to overview and implement in practice. No wonder it was highly popular, proven by a great deal of references to it also in theoretical works. We do not know who produced it and this is the reason why several *gā'ōn*s are suggested as its authors, but clear proof is lacking. Presumably, it was written in the ninth century in order to summarise oral law systematically and defend it against the critiques of the Karaite movement gaining strength in this period which rejected oral law.[45]

Valuable source material came to light from the Cairo *Geniza*. The thousands of legal and economic documents discovered there make it possible to learn the daily life of Jewish communities in detail. *Geniza* means a room or an isolated part of a synagogue where manuscripts out of use and daily routine were stored. Though some of the documents were destroyed, nevertheless the dry climate in Egypt guaranteed the survival of the Cairo *Geniza* and its documents. The best known expert of the Cairo *Geniza* is S. D. Goitein who published the results of his decades of research in several volumes. Based on his results it became clear that the synagogue was the intellectual, educational and legal centre of the Jews.[46] Legal scholars were considered as religious and spiritual leaders of the community who controlled religious life, adjudicated legal disputes, wrote *responsa* and theoretical works in jurisprudence. Lacking any political and administrative power, it was only their social prestige that made their decisions effective. Jewish courts were denied the right to implement penal sanctions, therefore excommunication and at times flogging were the only tools of law enforcement in their hands. Ancient customs going back to biblical times continued to exist in that period, consequently the days of proceedings remained Monday and Thursday. The economic documents testify to extensive long-distance trade while marriage contracts offer an insight into the everyday implementation of family law.[47]

---

[44]Libson (1996: 207–208), Bazak and Passamaneck (1978: xxi–xxiv), Elon (1994: 1468–1473).

[45]Encyclopaedia Judaica vol. 7, 1168–1170.; Elon (1994: 1155).

[46]Goitein (1988: 417).

[47]Goitein (1999: 206–208; 311–344).

The settlement of Jewish communities outside the Levant (North Africa, Iberian Peninsula, Europe) resulted in two important consequences. One such a result was the emergence of the Ashkenazi and Sephardic communities. While Ashkenazi Jews live in West, East and Northern Europe, Sephardic Jews live in North Africa and Hispania, and later, when they were expelled from Spain, in the Ottoman Empire and Greece. The second important consequence was the decline of the Babylonian academies, since these faraway communities established their own structure and leadership and were unwilling to be subordinated to Babylonian academies any longer. As a result, new scientific centres emerged, medieval Muslim Spain being the most influential among them, producing commentaries, *responsa*, and legal compilations. It is Maimonides (1135–1204), the physician, philosopher and legal scholar who was the most outstanding authority in Spain in the medieval period or generally in Jewish intellectual history. He wrote the first complete commentary to the *Mishnah*. The aim of Maimonides was to define rules at points where the *Mishnah* did not have any or contains merely contradictory views. It is this approach that made it soon a popular work. He has written also a good number of *responsa* which were also influential due to its author's scientific authority. Being the leading intellectual of his time, he was approached from both the eastern and the western communities with questions embracing all aspects of Jewish (legal) life. Since Maimonides answered all the questions with care and proper investigation, his influence could be felt in almost every field of law. His most famous work is, however, the *Mishne Tōra*, meant to be a work of 'codification'. *Mishne Tōra* was a novelty both in its form and content. Maimonides was unwilling to follow the centuries old Jewish scientific custom of redaction which grouped together contradictory scholarly opinions relating to the same issue without a clear statement of the final outcome, best exemplified by the *Talmūd*. By contrast, he neglected scholarly disputes and focused rather on the legal norms themselves. In order to do so, he even abandoned the structure of the *Talmūd* and organised his legal material around legal problems, arriving at a clear order of the laws comprising of 14 units (*sefer*). Some of the *sefer*s resemble the orders of the *Mishnah* (Taharah, Nashim, Zeraim, Nezikim), still others are new. The aim of Maimonides with this work was to teach law to a wide audience and to struggle against the Karaites rejecting oral law. Therefore, he discussed the rules of Jewish law in a form understandable to all and had oral law fitted into the entire system of law. Though some of his colleagues criticised this work because of its novelty in form and content, yet it became one of the most outstanding works in Jewish jurisprudence. In the following centuries, commentaries were written to it showing its unbroken popularity, Yemeni Jews accept this work as the codification of law to this day. Maimonides was, however, not only a legal scholar but also a physician and a philosopher producing outstanding results in these disciplines as well. He had written scholarly works on medicine too, and as a famous doctor he became the Muslim ruler's physician despite him being a Jew.[48] As a philosopher, he became the interpreter of Aristotle and tried to harmonise reason with revelation. His *Guide*

---

[48] Shochetman (1996: 276–279).

for the Perplexed[49] is as important a work in Jewish philosophy as his *Mishne Tōra* in Jewish law, with the same fate: followed by many and harshly criticised by some, it became the best known Jewish philosophical work ever. Its influence reaches out beyond the boundaries of the Jewish community as it influenced both Muslim and Christian thinkers, above all Thomas Aquinas and Duns Scotus. Maimonides' talent and scholarly activities could be compared best to his Muslim contemporary, Ibn Rushd, who was also a legal scholar, a physician and a philosopher of the Aristotelian tradition, producing his own legal 'code' of the Mālikite school of law. Not only contemporaries but also residing in the same city, the two polymaths of Cordoba had enormous impact on both their own tradition and Christian Europe. No wonder their statues stand close to each other in their home town.

Substantive Jewish law was also been modified by Jews living in Muslim Spain. While according to the Bible, polygamy was allowed and a man could divorce his wife without proper justification, now polygamy became restricted. In fact, the ban on polygamy was introduced by the *takkana* of the Ashkenazi scholar, R. Gershom (herem de Rabbenu Gershom) which was never adopted among the Sephardis as a source of law yet local customs were in favour of monogamy anyway. In addition, legal scholars tried to improve the position of women, enlarging their property rights during marriage and in the law of inheritance. It was again Maimonides who stood for the legal protection of women: according to his legal interpretation no married woman was to be forced to live marital life, should it be otherwise, it would qualify as sexual offence. The influence of Maimonides is shown by the fact that in a similar case a modern court of Israel based its judgment on his view.[50]

Ashkenazi Jews developed their own scientific tradition which was by far not inferior to that of the Sephardic Jews. One among their outstanding authorities was Rashi (Rabbi Solomon ben Isaac), a legal scholar living in France (d. 1105) whose commentary to the *Talmūd* is the most famous work written in this genre. Its importance is shown by the fact that the basic text and the commentary are put together in the *Talmūd* editions as if they constituted a single work and would be inseparable. Rashi's work inspired others and this is how a new literary genre came into being, the authors of which were called Tosaftists (not to be confused with the Tosefta'). Tosafist took the *Talmūd* and Rashi's commentary as their basis and compared them to other texts in order to dissolve existing contradictions. Every school had its own collection of texts in the major centres of France and Germany and they also reached Spain. Concerning substantive law, there was a revolution in the field of marriage law where *herem de Rabbenu Gershom* was introduced in the tenth century which made monogamy not only a local custom (as in Spain), but prohibited polygamy expressis verbis and forbade to divorce a wife against her will.[51]

When Joseph Qaro published his *Shulhān Arūk* ('Prepared Table') in Venice (1565), this work made its author immediately a famous scholar. It was similar to Maimonides' *Mishneh Tōrah* in its purpose, as Joseph Qaro also wanted to produce a

---

[49]Maimonides (1974).

[50]Shochetman (1996: 294).

[51]Grossman (1996: 303–304; 317–320).

comprehensive compilation of Jewish law, which he did. *Shulhān Arūk* was, of course, more modern, with a clear style understandable to all. During the course of writing, Joseph Qaro had taken earlier works into account and also studied independent legal doctrines that were not represented in them. In addition to Maimonides, he relied on other medieval authors too, and in the case of controversies he formulated his rule on the basis of majority opinion. If majority opinion was not to be identified for whatever reasons, he accepted the doctrines of earlier authorities. Though criticised in some of its detail, the authority of the entire work was never challenged. From that moment on, the *Mishne Tōra* of Maimonides was replaced by the *Shulhān Arūk* and nowadays it is still the most popular collection of law.[52] It is still one of the basic texts for legal education and serves as a guide for everyday life. *Shulhān Arūk* is also a dividing line between earlier scholars and the moderns: earlier legal scholars were declared as having greater authority than contemporaries and the subsequent generations. As a consequence, scholars belonging to the 'moderns' (*aharonīm*) could discuss the works of their predecessors (*rishonīm*) but could not modify them because of their missing authority. This is not a new phenomenon, a similar view also emerged in the post-*Talmūd*ic period when later generations were considered as less competent scholars than their predecessors.[53] It is worth noting in brief that the same point of view can be observed in Islamic law too, where the authority of classical scholars could not be challenged and later generations (*muta'akhirūn*, the Arabic equivalent of *aharonīm*) could not compete with them.

Excommunication remained the most effective means of law enforcement as Jewish courts still were lacking penal competencies. It was, therefore, widely used even against famous members of the community such as Baruch Spinoza (1656, Amsterdam).[54] Enlightenment and the subsequent intellectual and social movements however, made the Jewish communities and their traditional legal system face an increasingly difficult situation to which no response could be given by such simple methods. The new, hitherto unprecedented legal problems caused by modernity, divided Jewish communities regarding their attitude toward traditional law. Orthodox Jews remain faithful to the *Tōrah* and the traditions, while reformists stress the importance of adapting the law to current social conditions. Between these two extremes, conservatives try to follow a middle path in balancing tradition and change, stressing the importance of traditional Jewish law and also the need of its flexible interpretation.

3.4 Sources of Jewish Law

Halakha (literally: walking; or the way of walking) is the proper term for law or the body of traditional Jewish law comprising of rules relating to mundane (marriage,

---

[52]Passamaneck (1996: 339).

[53]Fram (1996: 365).

[54]Novak (1996: 383).

property, inheritance, contracts, etc.) and religious (rite, cult, purity, festivals, etc.) issues. It is usually contrasted to *aggada*, a term denoting a complexity of non-legal texts such as moral teaching, exegesis, legendary biographies, wisdom literature. It would be a mistake, however, to sharply separate these two fields because there is an interchange between the two. As wisdom could also be observed in the law, legal arguments could also find their backing in *aggadic* literature (*aggada*, however, could only support a legal argument or view but it could not be used against a *halakhic* argument). *Halakah* is comprised of biblical commandments (613) and rabbinic law or following the rabbinic categories, of written and oral law. Written law (*Tōra shebeketab*) refers to the biblical commandments given to Moses by God during the revelation at Sinai, while oral law (*Tōra shebeᶜal-pe*) refers to the Pharisee and rabbinic law. According to rabbinic understanding, Moses obtained oral law also by revelation which was passed on to the rabbinic sages through Josiah, the elders, the prophets and the 'pairs'. This body of laws was in fact the custom of the Pharisees, rejected by their opponents, the Sadduceans in Antiquity and the Karaites in the Middle Ages.

Needless to say, the epistemological value of written and oral law differ, as oral law only supplements written law but never modifies it. It has therefore, contrary to their names, nothing to do with their form (oral or written), since oral law was also put to writing, as we have seen in the previous chapter (*Mishnah, Tosefta' Talmūd, Mishne Tōra, Shulhān Arūk*). Oral law made it possible to apply biblical rules to ever changing social realities and create new norms based on biblical legal tradition. The result was (beyond systemic limits) a flexible legal system and the central position of legal scholars who became the scholars par excellence with the passage of time, a monopolistic position after the destruction of the Second Temple which lend jurisprudence central role in Jewish intellectual life.

Besides the written law-oral law dichotomy, rabbinic jurisprudence developed other categories as well. One such a category is called tradition (*dibrei kabbala*), reflecting on non-legal biblical texts. Biblical texts could also be source of law even when they contain no legal material (e.g. the books of the Prophets, etc.) when legal scholars have established legal rules on their ethical meaning or wisdom. These are called *dibrei kabbala* as they are not explicit biblical laws, yet they are based on biblical texts. Another classification distinguishes between Biblical (*de-oraita*) and rabbinic (*de-rabbanan*) law. All what features in the Bible was naturally Biblical and, as such, written law, while others were rabbinic. It is not easy to decide sometimes on where a particular rule would belong. For instance, rules of *dibrei kabbala* are based on biblical texts but were formulated by legal scholars and thus one can easily find arguments for both positions. No wonder the classification of rules has caused long debates in the Middle Ages. It was more than the self-entertainment of academic jurisprudence, since legal consequences were at stake. This is because according to rabbinic hermeneutic principles, Biblical law had to be interpreted strictly while rabbinic law more leniently, and it was evidently very important for the litigants which principle applied to their case.[55]

---

[55]Elon (1994: 203–214).

Jewish legal sources are interpreted by various hermeneutic principles and techniques called *midrāsh* (interpretation). The most common techniques of interpretation are contextual interpretation, *a fortiori* arguments, analogy, and the distinction between general and particular rules. These and other inferences are sometimes linked to great scholars and this is how, for example, 'Hillel's seven rules' came into being but it proves only what a famous scholar he was and not historical facts. Needless to say, to engage in *midrash* requires serious training and proper scientific qualifications. To know texts by heart is an obvious precondition to which practice in logic and reasoning are added. Mastery in rhetoric and argumentation was one among the most important qualifications for a legal scholar. As the Talmud has it, a candidate for the Sanhedrin must be able to prove that an unclean animal is actually clean.[56] Inferences and rules arrived at with the help of *midrāsh* are not to be confused with norms supported by *asmakta*. The basic difference between the two is that with the help of interpretation one produces a law by way of inference from a given text. By contrast, in case of *asmakta* the law already exists, usually as rabbinic law, but in order to enhance its legitimacy and authority, the law is connected to a biblical text supporting its content, evidently, the law does not derive from the given biblical text as it exists independently from it. Thus, biblical text is not the source of the law, but only its backing and this is the reason why it is called *asmakta*, support.[57]

Individual doctrines of legal scholars existed parallel to each other, which were subjects of continuous scholarly debates either in the sessions of the *Sanhedrīn* or during the *kalla*-days, discussions organised by the academies. Each scholar of proper qualification could develop his own doctrine and there was a tolerated legal pluralism guaranteeing the epistemological equivalence of them. This came to a halt, however, when there was a voting concerning a particular rule in order to establish the *halakha* for a given case. Majority opinion is sufficient, that is, there is no need to come to the consensus of all legal scholars (contrary to Islamic law) and scholars of the minority opinion should follow the law established by their colleagues by majority vote. Majority vote is not intended to restrict legal pluralism but to establish order and clarity in some hotly debated issues where priority was given to settle the issue once and for all to the detriment of constant debates. Jewish scholars take this seriously: if a scholar continues to cling to his own doctrine and does not accept majority opinion after voting was completed, he will be called a 'revolting elder' (*zāqēn mamre*), which could lead to his excommunication regardless his fame and scholarly reputation (this was the fate of the scholar R. Eliezer ben Hyrcanus).[58]

Majority opinion of legal scholars is therefore, a legal source for a particular *halakha* not subject of other legal sources. It is not a necessary precondition to vote for the law in every case, since some legal scholars have the right to determine what the law is by their individual actions. As we have seen in the previous chapter, the *nāśī* and his court had the power to enact orders during the period the *tannaim* and *amoraim*. Orders are of two kinds: *gezera* is a prohibition, *takkana* is prescribing positive

---

[56]Porton (2005: 250–268).

[57]Ehrman (1974: 171–172).

[58]Gilat (1968: 479–493).

action. After the decline of the academies, the right to issue orders was transformed to leading scholars of the Jewish communities of the diaspora. Jewish scholars made use of it, in fact sometimes resulting in gradual changes in legal understanding and attitude. For example, monogamy, clearly a ground breaking novelty in family law was introduced in medieval Europe by such a method (see R Gershom's herem).[59]

It is clear now that legal scholars have the capacity to enact and modify the law, although in theory they have no legislative power, of course, since the Lawgiver is only God. The various methods of interpretation, majority, vote and orders supplement existing law solely on the basis of academic jurisprudence. Society at large is not completely denied the right however to modify law and this is the reason why custom (*minhāg*) was taken into account not only during adjudication but also in scientific discussion. Custom had an important role in determining *halakha* when there was a debate among scholars concerning the law relating to a particular issue. If custom was clearly in favour of one view, then it was established as legal norm while competing doctrines were neglected in order to keep the law in accordance with legal practice and the custom of society at large. Similarly, custom could fill the gap in the legal system if there were issues for which no laws were established. In such cases, custom was taken into account and adjudication followed *minhāg*. Customs were important from the very beginning of Jewish legal history proven by, among others, the wedding ceremony going back to thousands of years (weddings were held customarily on Wednesdays because the day of court proceedings was Thursday and possible disputes could be remedied immediately). The laws of foreign legal cultures were also adopted by *minhāg* (the law merchant of Islamic law in the Middle Ages) as it was the parties who put them into their own agreements and made them binding for themselves.[60]

3.5 Substantive Law

3.5.1 Family Law and Law of Inheritance

In the early biblical period, laws on marriage were different from the later, more sophisticated rules which were sometimes at variance with the nomadic usages of the Hebrew tribes. In that period polygamy was permitted, moreover, according to a biblical narrative it was not against the law to marry two sisters (Jakob), though later on it became prohibited by the laws of Moses (Lev. 18:18).

In the Biblical period, marriage was rather an alliance between families and it was therefore not left to the parties to decide alone. Such negotiations were the responsibility of the family fathers, though adult males were also entitled to act on their own. No guardian was needed neither for widowed and nor divorced women. In

---

[59]Enactments are analysed in detail in Elon (1994: 477–880).
[60]Elon (1994: 896–899).

the majority of the cases, however, it was the guardian of the girl who decided about her marriage. Men were, as a rule, free to choose their mate but in some particular cases they had no option. One such a situation was rape, when the rapist was forced to marry his victim provided she was a girl not yet engaged. The other case when marriage was obligatory is levirate, that is, a man was obliged to marry the widow of his childless brother. Should he refuse to do so, he was humiliated at court in public (the widow removed her sandals and spat into his face). Monetary issues weighed heavily in the agreements and it is the reason why *mohar* had to be paid to the girls' father at engagement. *Mohar* was paid either in money or in any valuable goods as it was usual in the Near-East. Sporadic references hint at the custom to serve for the bride, otherwise unknown in the Ancient Near East. Accordingly, a groom did not pay for his wife but had to work for the father of the bride for a period agreed upon by the parties (Jacob served Laban for 7 years). Later on, this custom fell out of use and disappeared from Jewish legal history. The engagement was completed when the *mohar* was handed over and the girl qualified as married, despite the fact that the legal effects of the marriage had not yet set in for the parties (in the case of rape for example, it qualified as a crime against a married woman). Upon handing over the *mohar*, the son-in-law could demand his wife for which wedding ceremonies were celebrated, followed by consummation which actually completed the marriage. Contrary to the *mohar*, the dowry given to the wife was a financial supply for her should her husband pass away, because widowed women had no other means to guarantee their living. It is thus understandable why her husband had limited rights and control over her dowry. Divorce was the man's privilege as he could separate from his wife by a unilateral declaration.[61]

In the Second Temple period, polygamy and divorce became debated issues not only among legal scholars but also in the society at large (both the New Testament and the Qumran texts condemn both). In this period, the idea of the *ketuba* emerged as a pecuniary allocation promised to the wife for the unilateral divorce by the husband (its name originates from the verb meaning 'to write' as this agreement had to be committed to writing). *Ketuba* was subject to serious disputes in jurisprudence because some scholars believed it was a Biblical rule while others thought it was rabbinic.[62] In the period of the *tannaim* and the *amoraim*, a number of *takkana*s were produced to regulate details of marriage law. As a result, a new body of law emerged, that became the basis for the post-Biblical system of marriage law. Accordingly, engagement was the first step which could be concluded either by the partiers themselves or by their representatives. Engagement was usually an oral promise in which conditions were also defined. Either party could retract from the engagement but pecuniary compensation had to be paid, the sum of which was determined by the parties or local customs. Wedding consisted of two subsequent acts: the first one was the *qiddushin*, during which the bridegroom provides some valuable goods (money; nowadays it is a ring) to his bride in front of witnesses together with a marriage

---

[61] Westbrook (1996: 10–13), Falk (2001: 145–153).
[62] Piattelli-Jackson (1996: 47–48).

document and her *ketuba*. *Qiddushin* is followed by *nissu'in*, when the girl is led to her husband's house.[63]

Jewish marriage law elaborated a complicated system of hindrances to marriage. Distinction was made between two categories: one is the prohibited and invalid and the other the prohibited but valid marriages. Marriages that violated the prohibition of incest (on the male line), a marriage with two sisters, with an already married woman and with a non-Jew belonged to the first category. Prohibited but not invalid marriages are those which disregard some particular rules (like the waiting period of three months for a divorced woman; a high priest could not marry a divorced woman, a woman divorced for the second time or widowed could not be married by her first husband, etc.). A marriage concluded in the name of a minor boy by his guardian (boys qualified as adults after their thirteenth birthday) was also invalid, but a marriage concluded in the name of a minor girl (up to her twelfth birthday) did not qualify as *ipso iure* invalid, despite the fact that it was opposed at the time of the *Talmūd*. If the *qiddushin* was concluded in the name of a minor girl, she qualified as a married woman from this time but when she became twelve years old she could make a statement about her intent regarding her marriage. If she did not reject it or was silent about it her consent was regarded as given. Polygamy remained on the agenda for centuries and Talmūdic sages made some efforts to hammer out conditions for polygamy that were increasingly difficult to meet. Polygamy was finally prohibited for the Ashkenazi Jews by the *herem de-Rabbenū Gershom* referred to above.[64]

It was the husband's duty to provide housing, food, and garments for his wife, to maintain wedlock, to ensure her nursing when she was ill, and to pay ransom for her when she was taken into captivity. Legal scholars made every effort to define these duties as precisely as possible but in some cases they had to rely ultimately on local customs. It was, however, an underlying principle that with a marriage, women's social status could not be deteriorated, they could only obtain a higher social esteem. Consequently, if the wife's social status was higher before marriage than that of her husband's, she was entitled to a maintenance, keeping with her social prestige irrespective of her husband's social and financial condition. Similarly, the wife's duties were defined by this principle: a woman of a higher social status was obliged to such works only which were in keeping with her rank, but she was not obliged to do other works that were expected from a woman of lower status. Wives were also protected against their husband's arbitrary decisions about divorce, therefore, the unilateral declaration of the husbands was not effective any longer and Jewish law tried to limit divorce to the consensus of the parties (except some cases when courts obliged husbands to declare divorce and their wives to accept it such as illness, a suspected adultery, or refusal of wedlock). When divorce was inevitable a document called *get* was produced in order to regulate everything. These documents are highly formalistic in both form and content (formalism is indicated by the fact that the *get*s

---

[63] Satlow (2001: 76–77; 162–182).
[64] Schereschewsky (1974: 353–377).

are written in many cases in Aramaic language even today, though there is no such a linguistic requirement).[65]

Law of inheritance was just another legal way to consolidate patriarchal, clan based family structure. Biblical law favoured male descendants to inherit. A first born son received his own share being at his disposal as the story of Esau proves, but this right could be forfeited by undignified behaviour. Inherited land could be divided among the heirs by drawing lots or could be kept intact, thus making the heirs joint owners. To die without an heir was a situation one wanted to avoid at every cost and this is the reason why levirate marriage emerged, as the aim of such a marriage was precisely to create heirs to a deceased brother. If there was no male offspring, girls inherited the bequest. If there were no descendants, the inheritance was returned to the agnatic relatives.[66]

In the post-Biblical period, rules of inheritance were refined and supplemented. Biblical rules have nothing to say about the father's right to inherit his son, therefore, *Mishnah* makes this possible, creating a system of inheritance based on the agnatic family structure. The first *parentela* consisted of the direct descendants, that is, children of the deceased person, followed by their descendants and so on. The second parentela consists of the deceased's father and his descendants, while the father's father and his relatives belong to the third *parentela*. A nearer *parentela* not only enjoyed priority over other *parentela*s but also excluded them. Jewish law follows *ius representationis*, as an heir already dead was replaced by his descendants up to his proportion in the bequest ("inheritance in the grave"). First born son's share was the double of the portion of his brothers. A husband was an heir to his wife preceding all other heirs, while his wife was not his heir, an asymmetric situation which legal scholars wanted to balance. This is the reason why they restricted a husband's rights towards his wife's heirs and improved the rights of the widows. A rule was set already at the *tannaic* period that sons of a deceased woman would inherit after the death of their father, the *ketubba* and dowry of their mother and their share after their father. According to the *takkana* issued for the Ashkenazi Jews, the dowry of a wife who died childless within a year had to be returned to her heirs or to the person who gave the dowry to her. According to a medieval *takkana* from Toledo, the bequest of a deceased wife had to be distributed among her husband and children equally. The objective of these orders was to hinder the transfer of wealth from the female line to the husband's line. Parallel to this, development rights of widows were also extended. Though, she still could not inherit from her husband, yet some rights were guaranteed to her: she could demand her *ketubba*, dowry and property brought into the marriage and also her maintenance, rights that rested on her husband's heirs as obligations. Except in some particular situations, girls were still denied the right to inherit (they could inherit merely if there were no boys), but their situation was improved by legal scholars as it was the heirs' obligation to provide maintenance and a proper dowry for them corresponding to their social status.[67]

---

[65] Schereschewsky (1974: 377–420).

[66] Westbrook (1996: 15).

[67] Schereschewsky (1974: 445–452).

3.5.2 Criminal Law

Penal law was—similarly to family law—subject of important changes during the
centuries in the history of Jewish law. Biblical law followed *lex talionis* for crimes
against persons. Accordingly, homicide was punished by death and bodily injuries
by the same injury (an eye for an eye, a tooth for a tooth, a hand for a hand, a foot
for a foot: Exodus 21.23).

Lex talionis was subject to debates for long centuries in the post-Biblical period
resulting in its final elimination. The main argument against *lex talionis* was that
it is impossible to find exactly the same wrong for the perpetrator as a punishment
that he caused for the victim. A classic example was the case of a half blind man: if
such a man was completely blinded by an aggressive action it is impossible to find
a proper punishment: if the perpetrator would be blinded for one eye his situation
would be far better than that of the man completely blinded by him; by contrast,
if he would be blinded completely, his penalty would transgress his wrongdoing
which is against the principle of *lex talionis*. As a result of such considerations, *lex
talionis* fell out of practice and was replaced by pecuniary punishment. In biblical
law, the method of execution of capital punishments was stoning with the penalty
of burning featuring only twice. At the time of the *Mishna*, beheading and choking
were introduced and legal scholars began to specify exact punishments for every
crime. The aim of this reform was to find a more humane method and choking was
considered as the most humane mode of execution, causing minimum mutilation.
Stoning remained the penalty for sexual crimes, blasphemy, idolatry, the violation of
the *shabbāt*, and also for revolting sons and witches.[68] Burning was the penalty of
the adulterous daughter of a high priest and a man who had parallel sexual relations
with a woman and her daughter (which was against Leviticus 21:9.[69] Death by the
sword was the penalty of murderers and inhabitants of an apostate city.[70] Chocking
was introduced for persons assaulting their parents (Exodus 21:15) or stealing their
Jewish neighbours (Exodus 21:16), legal scholars not accepting majority decision
(revolting elder), a false prophet, a person telling prophecies in the name of an idol,
a man committing adultery with a priest's daughter and persons falsely accusing
such a girl with adultery. Much of these remained on paper, however, partly because
Jews were denied the right to implement death penalty by their overlords (Romans,
Persians), partly because to pronounce death sentence was the prerogative of the
Sanhedrīn and after its demise no court remained with the same power. Despite this,
whenever Jews had the opportunity to implement penal sanctions (like in Hispania
under the reign of the Umayyad caliphs) they wanted to do so but could not bring
Sanhedrīn back to life. In order to avoid violating the law in prescribing penalties

---

[68] M Sanh 7: 4–8: 5.

[69] M Sanh 9: 1.

[70] M Sanh 9: 1. In the case of execution by the sword it was always the edge and not its tip that had
to be used. Tos Sanh 14: 6.

that were in the power of the *Sanhedrīn*, Jewish courts applied sanctions missing from earlier law as death by hunger.[71]

Biblical law lays emphasis on sexual crimes: incest, adultery, homosexuality and bestiality were all criminal acts deserving the death penalty (Leviticus 18:22; 20:13) by stoning. A girl who did not prove to be a virgin at the consummation of her marriage was also punished by stoning, but if her husband accused her falsely he had to be flogged (Deut. 22:13–21). Adulterers, both the woman and her lover were punished by death (Deut. 22:22). Presumably it was the husband's right to punish his wife and her partner (similarly to other Near-Eastern legal systems), but later he was denied this right and death penalty could be pronounced only within the framework of a proper procedure at court. Penalty for rape varied according to circumstances: if it was committed "in the field", that is, not in an inhabited location where it was impossible for the girl to ask for help and defend herself, only the man was punished by death. By contrast, if it was committed in a town, that is, where the girl could ask easily for help, both parties were sentenced for stoning on the assumption that it was not against her wish, therefore, she is not an innocent victim (Deut. 22:23–27). Rape of a girl not yet engaged did not result in capital punishment but the man was obliged to pay compensation to the girl's father and to marry her with the restriction that he could never divorce her (Deut. 22:28–29). Talmūdic law extended the compensation to the physical and mental sufferings the girl had to endure and guaranteed her the right to refuse such a marriage.[72]

Asylum was a particular legal institution of Jewish law already in existence in biblical times (Deut. 19:1–13). There were towns guaranteeing asylum for those who fled there. The number of these towns was originally three to which other three cities were added (such as Shehem and Hebron), later to be completed with additional 42 cities. Asylum was a legal device against blood feud, deeply rooted in a tribal society. If someone committed manslaughter, he could escape from the relatives of the deceased by fleeing into one of the asylum towns where relatives were unable to kill him. If he escaped to one of the first six cities, asylum was a right obtained automatically but should he moved to other cities asylum was to be asked for from the local authorities. The fugitive had to report local authorities about his case which guaranteed him protection for the period of the procedure at court investigating what was reported. If the fugitive was able to prove that he committed involuntary manslaughter, he was taken back to the city where he could live without being disturbed. By contrast, should the court find him guilty in murder, he was sentenced to death. As these rules clearly show blood feud was an integral part of the legal system in biblical times, but later it was pushed into the background. In the post-Biblical period blood feud was out of practice and legal scholars discussed what new functions the persons have who were entitled originally to blood feud. Some scholars believed they were private accusers, others thought they were persons entitled to start a suit at court, meanwhile, according to a third interpretation, they had the right to execute the sentence of the court (this corresponds to the understanding of

---

[71]M Sanh 11: 1; Cohn (1974a: 525–529).
[72]Cohn (1974a: 485–487).

Muslim legal scholars). Everybody agreed however, that a blood feud inside asylum cities was murder.[73]

3.5.3 Laws of Procedure

The competency of the courts depended on the number of its members, which in its turn reflected its social and legal prestige. We cannot speak about a judicial hierarchy in the modern sense of the world, though in theory a larger court could overrule the judgment of a lesser court. This right, however, is not a systemic consequence of the judicial hierarchy but follows from the principle according to which a sentence of a court could be altered only by a court which is bigger in size and wisdom. The competencies and the number of the court members were defined according to the importance of the cases: the more important a case was, the more members the courts had. As a result, the most important cases were adjudicated by the Great *Sanhedrīn* of 71 members in Jerusalem.

Lesser courts consisting of only three members adjudicated property issues, compensation, sexual abuse and false denial of a girl's virginity, and the procedure related to the removal of shoes (breaking off the levirate).[74] Divorce and petty wrongs punished by fees and flogging belonged also to the competency of the three member courts.[75] By contrast, procedures related to crimes with capital punishment were conducted by courts of twenty-three members.[76]

The great *Sanhedrīn* of seventy-one members could in theory discuss all cases but there were particular issues regarding which had exclusive competency. It was this court that adjudicated proceedings against particular persons such as a false prophet, the high priest, a tribe and its chief, a 'revolting elder',[77] a revolting son, a false witness, a person encouraging people to worship an idol and persuading an entire city to become idolatrous. A death penalty of a lesser court had to be approved also by the great *Sanhedrīn* before the execution took place.[78]

Procedural law had a long history by the time it achieved its sophisticated form in the *Mishna*, the *Tosefta* and the *Talmūd*. Procedural law, particularly criminal procedure, was one of the hotly debated issues between the Pharisees and the Sadducees, legal sources that had reached us, reflect the Pharisee attitude. In disputes of private law, a law suit began with the claim of the plaintiff.[79] The jurisdiction of the court was defined by the defendant's place of residence. Parties were summoned for the hearing by the court. Courts discussed the cases in the order of the receipt of

---

[73]Cohn (1974a: 531–532).

[74]M Sanh 1: 1–1: 3.

[75]T Sanh 2a; Git. 5b.

[76]M Sanh 1: 4; T Sanh 2a.

[77]A legal scholar not accepting a halakha established by majority rule.

[78]M Sanh 1: 5–1: 6; T Sanh 2a; Tos. Sanh 11: 7.

[79]Tos Sanh 6: 3.

the claims, but particular rules were established in favour of some persons (widow, orphan, scholars). Cases in which women also participated had to be grant priority so that they may not have to wait for long.[80]

The hearing began early in the morning and continued without break up to the time of meal and had to be completed by sunset.[81] Later on, the hearing was also permitted to last late at night if it could not be finished during the day.[82] It was prohibited to hold a hearing on *Shabbāt* and on holidays.[83] Evidence had to be provided by the parties. If, however, either of the parties stated that there is evidence, but was unable to present it because it is not at his disposal, the court called the third party possessing the evidence to present it, threatening all who held back evidence by *herem*.[84] What is more, litigants also had the right to call upon those present in the synagogue that they should come forth if they had evidence supporting their statements and to be witnesses.[85]

After hearing of the parties and the witnesses the court discussed the case in which disciples of legal scholars could also participate and join in the discussion.[86] It was an important principle that decisions were to be made by consensus wherever possible, if consensus was impossible the court decided by majority vote.[87] A sentence had to be made on the day of the hearing and any delay was seen as a violation of the biblical command of fair judgment (Leviticus 19:15). Decisions were made public orally and were committed to writing only if the parties so requested.[88]

Criminal procedure followed the rules of private procedure with important differences in detail. Criminal procedures also had to be conducted in daytime and to be closed at sunset, and a sentence for the acquittal of the accused had to be made public on the same day. By contrast, a sentence against the accused should be postponed to the next day, thus enabling judges to discuss the case during the whole night and arrive at a final sentence after this long debate and a new voting.[89] This rule is one among the many which proves that Pharisee and rabbinic legal understanding was in favour of the accused and did everything possible to interpret the law to their benefit. We should come across more such rulings in what follows. Needless to say, no hearing was permissible at *Shabbāt* and on holidays and also on the previous days otherwise the pronouncement of the sentence condemning the accused would take place on a *Shabbāt* or a holiday.[90] It was a peculiar law of criminal procedure that on one day only one case was permissible to discuss, a rule which was interpreted

---

[80]Falk (1972: 102–103), Cohn (1974b: 575–576).

[81]M Sanh 4: 1.

[82]T Sanh 34b.

[83]M Sanh 4: 1.

[84]Falk (1972: 103–104), Cohn (1974b: 577–578).

[85]Falk (1972: 122).

[86]M Sanh 4: 1.

[87]M Sanh 4: 1.

[88]Cohn (1974b: 577–579).

[89]M Sanh 5: 5.

[90]M Sanh 4: 1.

very strictly. Accordingly, if accused persons of the same criminal act were punished differently (if, for instance, the man was to be condemned to choking and the woman to burning in the case of adultery), the procedure had to be conducted in two separate days showing that criminal procedure focused on the accused and not on the crime. This also explains the rule that more sentences could be made on the same day only if the accused were sentenced to the same punishment.[91]

A criminal procedure started with the claim of the accuser but there were some cases in which the court initiated the procedure ex officio. Procedures relating to homicide started with the claim of the person entitled originally to blood feud as he was the one who was given the right to execute the sentence of the court.[92] After hearing the parties, it was continued with the hearing of the witnesses. At the beginning, the court warned the witnesses about the consequences of perjury to be followed by their testimony.[93] After hearing the witnesses, the court checked what was heard and it was taken extremely seriously: the slightest difference among the testimonies could result in their rejection. The accused could be present during the hearing of the witnesses and the checking of their statements. What is more, anyone but particularly disciples of legal scholars were entitled, even encouraged, to speak in the interest of the accused.[94] In addition, later the possibility to speak in the interest of the accused was extended after the period when the sentence was already passed. Therefore, it was announced by a messenger who called upon everyone knowing anything which could lead to the acquittal of the accused to come forward and make a testimony. This right was pushed to the extreme when it was guaranteed to the accused already condemned and led to the place of execution: if his new statement was relevant he was turned back and the court discussed the case again.[95] By contrast, he was not permitted to say anything against his case, should had he done so, he was silenced immediately.[96] This was a new, rabbinic understanding as self-confession leading to death penalty is known from the Bible (2 Sam 1:16). To reject such statements was a ground-breaking new understanding of criminal procedure with the important consequence that Jewish law rejected torture altogether. These rules prove again the efforts of Jewish legal scholars to favour the accused during the procedure.

The discussion of the court began after hearing the statements of the witnesses and the accused. It had to first decide whether the testimonies were acceptable or not. If they were unacceptable for any reason (e.g. they contradicted each other), a sentence of acquittal followed. If the testimonies were accepted, the court began to consider the case. First, arguments in favour of the accused were pronounced followed by consideration arguing against the acquittal of the accused. There we can find another rule favouring the accused: if one judge made an argument in favour of acquittal,

---

[91] Tos Sanh 7: 2; T Sanh 46a.

[92] T Sanh 33b.

[93] M Sanh 4: 5.

[94] M Sanh 5: 4.

[95] Cohn (1974a: 582–584).

[96] Tos Sanh 9: 4.

he could not change his mind during the entire procedure, while those judges who were first against it could later change their mind in the favour of acquittal.[97] In order to avoid the influence of respected scholars and judges over other members of the court, at first the younger members formulated their own view.[98] Voting followed the discussion: if consensus or majority vote was in favour of acquittal it was to be pronounced on the same day otherwise the sentence was postponed to the next day.[99] Next morning the scribes of the court counted again the votes. Majority decision was interpreted differently (again to help the accused): a one-vote majority was needed for a sentence for acquittal but a two-vote majority was requested for sentences declaring the accused person guilty.[100]

In sentences condemning the accused to death, the way of execution was to be defined precisely but courts were not obliged to justify their sentences. An accused condemned to death was regarded as a dead person immediately, as anyone could kill him without committing murder,[101] a rule referred to by *Maimonides*, too.[102] Sentences came to force upon making them public and were implemented without delay. In order to relieve the sufferings of the condemned and to stupefy him, wine sprinkled with the seed of pine incense was given to him. Customarily, this was offered by the women of Jerusalem but should they fail to do so the community had to arrange for it.[103] Persons condemned to death had to confess their sins before execution so that they may obtain spiritual salvation after death.[104]

In the Biblical period, public execution by the state was unknown, sentences were therefore implemented with the participation of the witnesses and the entire population.[105] Stoning was a way of execution in which all the inhabitants of the community threw stones on the condemned until he/she died. Stoning had to be started by the witnesses and if that resulted in death no one else had to throw stones any longer.[106] The person to be stoned was taken to a place marked for this purpose which was twice as tall as he/she was.[107] He was divested of his garments but women were not to be stoned naked.[108] Stoning was re-interpreted by Talmūdic legal scholars, who put an end to throwing stones to the convicted persons until death. As the result of the new interpretation, convicted persons were pushed down from a certain spot

---

[97]M Sanh 5: 5.

[98]Tos Sanh 7: 2.

[99]M Sanh 5: 5.

[100]M Sanh 4: 1. This rule was established by analogy: since death penalty could be inflicted on the basis of two testimonies so at least a two votes majority is needed to pronounce guilt: Tos Sanh 3:7.

[101]T Sanh 17a; 71b; Cohn (1974b: 583).

[102]Rosner (1981: 115).

[103]T Sanh 43a. Cf the testimony of the New Testament too.

[104]M Sanh 6: 2.

[105]Daube (1986: 408).

[106]M Sanh 6: 4; T Sanh 45b.

[107]M Sanh 6: 4.

[108]Tos Sanh 9: 6. Not everyone agreed to this, to the dispute see T Sanh 45a.

high enough to lead to death for sure.[109] Strangulation had to be done by the witnesses by winding a shawl around the neck of the condemned and to pull the two ends in opposite directions.[110] Legal scholars considered strangulation as the least painful way of execution,[111] while no one could be executed by an arrow or spear.[112]

3.6 Jewish Law in the Modern Age

As this chapter demonstrated, Jewish law existed independently of any state for thousands of years relying not on the force but on the prestige of law. A new situation emerged when Palestine became a British Mandate after the First World War, though British did not want to infer to the legal life of the local population deeply. As a result, local laws and customs remained in force supplemented by common law and equity.

The British accepted the rabbinic courts and set up a kind of rabbinic supreme court—unknown to the traditional *halakha*—as a new institution in 1921. That new court issued a series of *takkana*s, primarily in the field of procedural and family law in order to enhance the rights of women, a trend also continued in modern Israel. It is important to note that the legal system of Israel does not rest on the traditional Jewish law, but belongs to the common law family, creating room for political, religious and legal debates about the role of Jewish law in Israeli legal system. Yet at the same time, the legitimacy of secular legislation had to be proved also for advocates of Jewish law. Interestingly, the legitimacy of secular legislation in Israel is proven by making use of an argument of Shamuel, an *amoraic* scholar living on the turn of the third century when the Sasanians came to power in Iran and changed the liberal religious policy of the Arsacid Parthians. In this period, Jewish autonomy was restricted and Jewish communities had to follow some of the laws of the Sasanian empire, among others, in paying tax. To reach a compromise and ensure Jewish autonomy to continue, Shamuel acknowledged the legitimacy of the legal system of Sasanian Iran accepting their tax as lawful. This was expressed by a very short sentence of him, subject to legal debates for the coming centuries. His *dina demalkhuta dina* (the law of the kingdom is law) figures among the most frequently cited arguments to guarantee the legitimacy of secular laws from the perspective of Jewish law. Compromise is still on the agenda to solve the competition of these two parallel legal systems. As a result, the state of Israel acknowledges rabbinic courts and their decisions in personal status, marriage and inheritance but extends its own legislation to other fields of law.[113]

---

[109]Cohn (1974a: 526–529).

[110]M Sanh 7: 3.

[111]Tos Sanh 12: 5.

[112]Tos Sanh 14: 6.

[113]For the role of Jewish law in modern Israel see Sinclair (1996) and Elon (1994 vol. IV).

References

Sources

Bazak J, Passamaneck S (1978) Jewish Law and Jewish life. Selected Rabbinical Responsa. Union of American Hebrew Congregations, New York

Flavius J (1980) A zsidók története (ford. Révay József). Európa Könyvkiadó, Budapest

Ganzfried S (1961) Code of Jewish Law. Kitzur Shulhan Arukh. Hebrew Publishing Company, New York

Hebrew–English Edition of the Babylonian Talmud. The Soncino Press, London, 1997

Maimonides (1974) The guide of the perplexed. The University of Chicago Press, Chicago

Neusner J (trs.) (1988) The Mishnah. Yale University Press, London

Neusner J (trs) (2002) The Tosefta. Peabody, St. Louis

Rosner F (1981) Maimonides' Commentary on the Mishnah. Tractate Sanhedrin. Sepher-Hermon Press, NewYork

Literature

Albertz R (1997) Die Theologisierung des Rechts im Alten Israel. Religion und Gesellschaft. Studien zu ihrer Wechselbeziehung in den Kulturen der Antiken Vorderen Orients. Ugarit-Verlag, Münster, pp 115–131

Blenkinsopp J (2001) Was the Pentateuch the civic and religious constitution of the Jewish Ethnos in the Persian Period? In: Watts W (ed) Persia and Torah. The theory of imperial authorization of the Pentateuch. Society of Biblical Literature No. 17. Atlanta, pp 41–62

Cohen A (1991) An introduction to Jewish Law. Feldheim Publishers, Jerusalem

Cohn H (1974a) Criminal law. In: Elon M (ed) The principles of Jewish Law. Keter Publishing House, Jerusalem, pp 469 553

Cohn H (1974b) Practice and procedure. In: Elon M (ed) The principles of Jewish Law. Keter Publishing House, Jerusalem, pp 574–584

Daube D (1961) Texts and interpretation in Roman and Jewish Law. A Special London University Lecture (School of oriental and African Studies, 1961 Nov. 21.). In: Carmichael C (ed) Nyomtatva megjelent: collected works of David Daube, vol 1. University of California Press. Berkeley, pp 173–204

Daube D (1986) Witness in the Bible and Talmud. In: Carmichael C (ed) Collected works of David Daube, volume one. University of California Press. Berkeley, pp 401–424

Ehrman Z (1974) Asmakhta. In: Elon M (ed) The principle of Jewish Law. Keter Publishing House, Jerusalem

Elon M (1974) The principle of Jewish Law. Keter Publishing House, Jerusalem

Elon M (1994) Jewish Law. History, sources, principles, vol I–IV. The Jewish Publication Society, Philadelphia

Falk Z (1972) Introduction to Jewish Law of the second commonwealth. Leiden, Brill

Falk Z (2001) Hebrew laws in Biblical times: an introduction. Brigham Young University Press, Provo, Utah

Fram E (1996) Jewish Law from the Shulhan Arukh to the enlightenment. In: Hecht et al (eds) An introduction to the history and sources of Jewish Law. Clarendon Press, Oxford, pp 19–56

Fried L (2004) The priest and the great king. Temple–Palace relations in the Persian Empire. Biblical and Judaic studies, vol 10. Eisenbrauns, Winana Lake

Gilat YD (1968) Rabbi Eliezer ben Hyrcanus. A scholar outcast. Bar-Ilan University Press, Tel Aviv

Glenn P (2000) Legal traditions of the world. Sustainable diversity in Law. Oxford University Press, Oxford

Goitein SD (1988) A mediterranean society, vol V. University of California Press, Berkeley

Goitein SD (1999) A mediterranean society, vol. V. University of California Press: Berkeley, Los Angeles, London

Goodblatt D (1975) Rabbinic instructions in Sasanian Babylonia. Leiden, Brill

Grabbe L (2001) The law of Moses in the Ezra Tradition. In: Watts W (ed) Persia and Torah. The theory of imperial authorization of the Pentateuch. Society of Biblical literature no. 17. Atlanta, pp 91–113

Grossman A (1996) Ashkenazim to 1300. In: Hecht et al (eds) An introduction to the history and sources of Jewish Law. Clarendon Press, Oxford, pp 299–323

Jany J (2012) Judging in the Islamic, Jewish and Zoroastrian legal traditions. A comparison of theory and practice. Cultural diversity and law series. Ashgate, GB

Karasszon I (2004) Ezsdrás személye és műve. In: Az Ószövetség varázsa. Új Mandátum kiadó, Budapest, pp 70–100

Kirschenbaum A (1991) The role of punishment in Jewish criminal law: a chapter in Rabbinic penological thought. Jewish Law Ann 9:123–143

Knoppers G (2001) An Achaemenid imperial authorization of Torah in Yehud? In: Watts W (ed) Persia and Torah. The theory of imperial authorization of the Pentateuch. Society of Biblical literature no. 17. Atlanta, pp 41–62

Libson G (1996) The age of the geonim. In: Hecht et al. (eds) An introduction to the history and sources of Jewish Law. Clarendon Press, Oxford, pp 197–244

Libson G (2003) Jewish and Islamic Law. A comparative study of custom during the Geonic Period. Harvard series in Islamic Law, vol. 1. Harvard University Press, Cambridge, Massachusetts

Lifshitz B (1996) The age of the Talmud. In: Hecht et al (eds) An introduction to the history and sources of Jewish Law. Clarendon Press, Oxford, pp 169–196

Mantel H (1965) Studies in the history of the Sanhedrin. Harvard University Press, Cambridge

Novak D (1996) Modern Responsa: 1800 to the present. In: Hecht et al (eds) An introduction to the history and sources of Jewish Law. Clarendon Press, Oxford, pp 19–56

Miller J, Hayes J (2003) Az ókori Izrael és Júda története (ford. Erdős Ágnes). Studia Orientalia 3. Pázmány Péter Katolikus Egyetem Bölcsészettudományi Kar, Piliscsaba

Passamaneck S (1996) Toward sunrise in the East 1300–1565. In: Hecht et al (eds) An introduction to the history and sources of Jewish Law. Clarendon Press, Oxford, pp 19–56

Piattelli D, Jackson B (1996) Jewish Law during the second temple period. In: Hecht et al (eds) An introduction to the history and sources of Jewish Law. Clarendon Press, Oxford, pp 19–56

Porton G (2005) Hermeneutics: a critical approach. In: Neusner J, Avery-Peck J (eds) Encyclopaedia of Midrash. Biblical interpretation in formative Judaism, vol 1. Brill, Leiden, pp 250–268

Rabello M (1996) Jewish and Roman Jurisdiction. In: Hecht et al (eds) An introduction to the history and sources of Jewish Law. Clarendon Press, Oxford, pp 141–167

Sanders EP (1990) Jewsih Law from Jesus to the Mishnah. Five studies. SCM Press, London

Satlow M (2001) Jewish Marriage in Antiquity. Princeton University Press: Princeton

Schereschewsky B (1974) Family law and inheritance. In: Elon M (ed) The principle of Jewish Law. Keter Publishing House, Jerusalem

Segal P (1996) Jewish Law during the Tannaitic Period. In: Hecht et al (eds) An introduction to the history and sources of Jewish Law. Clarendon Press, Oxford, pp 397–421

Shilo Sh (1974) Dina demalkhuta dina. In: Elon M (1974) The principles of Jewish Law. Keter Publishing House, Jerusalem

Shochetman E (1996) Jewish Law and Spain and the Halakhic activity. In: Hecht et al (eds) An introduction to the history and sources of Jewish Law. Clarendon Press, Oxford, pp 271–299

Sinclair D (1996) Jewish Law in the State of Israel. In: Hecht et al (eds) An introduction to the history and sources of Jewish Law. Clarendon Press, Oxford, pp 397–421

Smith M (1971) Palestinian Parties and politics that shaped the old testament. Columbia University Press, New York

Stemberger G (1996) Introduction to the Talmud and Midrash, 2nd edn. T&T Clark, Edinburgh
Westbrook R (1988) Studies in Biblical and Cuneiform Law. Cahiers de la revue Biblique 26. Gabalda, Paris
Westbrook R (1996) Biblical Law. In: Hecht et al (eds) An introduction to the history and sources of Jewish Law. Clarendon Press, Oxford, pp 1–18
Wright DP (2009) Inventing God's Law. How the covenant code of the bible used and revised the laws of Hammurabi. Oxford University Press, Oxford

Chapter 4
Persian Law

4.1 State and Society in Ancient Persia

The first Indo-European people migrating to the Near East were the Hittites in the second millennium BCE, followed by the Iranians (Medes and Persians) in the next millennia. The Medes and the Persians are mentioned for the first time in Assyrian sources, in the annals of the Assyrian king Shulmānu-asharīdu III (836; 844 BCE), which leads us to believe that they arrived in what is now Iran in the ninth century BCE. The western part of Iran was the eastern periphery of Mesopotamian civilization, with no stable state organisation or any other power which could detent the newcomer, nomadic people. In the absence of any organised resistance, they settled down along the borderline, the Medes in the north, the Persians in the south, near to Elam. The territory of the Medes belonged however to the Assyrian sphere of interest, hence they waged several wars against their powerful neighbour. The constant warfare against the most powerful Mesopotamian state made the Medes join forces and this is how a kingdom emerged from a tribal alliance. The founder and first ruler of the Medes was Khshathrīta (Phraortes by Herodotus), who stood firm against the Assyrians. After his death the Assyrians in alliance with the Scythians defeated the Medes and controlled them for some decades. Uvakhshathra, the most outstanding king of the Medes, however first expelled the Scythians and then made an alliance with the Babylonians against the Assyrians which they defeated in long years of warfare. As a result, Media emerged as a leading power in Mesopotamia, no less powerful than Babylon in its most successful decades of history. It was a surprise therefore, that such a great power was so rapidly conquered by Kurush II (Cyrus), king of the Persians, who defeated Astyages, the last king of the Medes in battle.

Persian tribes settled in the vicinity of the ancient kingdom of Elam, played no role whatsoever in the history of the ancient Near East for centuries. It was Cyrus, the grandson of Astyages on the female line, who united Persian tribes and started a military campaign of unprecedented success against his overlord and the neighbouring kingdoms. After defeating Astyages he conquered Lydia and Babylon.

© Springer Nature Switzerland AG 2020
J. Jany, *Legal Traditions in Asia*, Ius Gentium: Comparative Perspectives on Law and Justice 80, https://doi.org/10.1007/978-3-030-43728-2_4

His conquests were continued by his son Kabūjiya (Cambyses II), who occupied Egypt but died during his way back home. In the political chaos after his death, Dārayavahu (Darius I), also a member of the ruling Achaemenid dynasty, gained power and continued the militaristic foreign policy of his predecessors and waged wars against the Scythians and the Greek cities. The real oeuvre of Darius was not his military victories but the consolidation of the Achaemenid state: he introduced new money (Daric), established public administration, an effective system of taxation and introduced a very rigid etiquette at the Persian court. The first signs of decline were already felt when his son Xerxes lost the Greek wars, followed by slow disintegration under his successors. In the second part of Achaemenid history, effective government control vanished and the Persian king lost real power to the provincial governors who became local authorities sometimes waging wars against each other. Revolts and famines contributed to more chaos and this how the empire fell victim to Alexander at the end of its history.

The Persian state was headed by the king who had absolute power. In this sense, the state of the Achaemenians was the direct heir to the political understanding of the Mesopotamian kingdoms. Contemporary sources (Herodotus, The Book of Esther) testify that the will of the king had the force of law not limited by Persian tradition. The king was the lawgiver for the empire yet not a single law or its fragment has come down to us from that period. In addition to legislation, adjudication was also the ruler's prerogative as the king was the supreme judge of the empire, though Persian policy granted legal autonomy to the various ethnic groups to resolve their own disputes. The most important concern of the Persian king was no doubt the public administration of such a huge empire. It was Darius I who divided the state into provinces (satrapies) for administrative and taxation purposes. The size of the provinces varied and was sometimes identical with the territory of formerly independent states (such as Egypt). The number of provinces is subject to dispute as Herodotus (Book III: 89–97) contradicts the inscription of Darius himself. Several theories have been put forth to overcome contradictions, none of them enjoying scholarly consensus.[1]

A province was headed by a satrap (*khshachapāvan*), a term going back to the kingdom of the Medes, but Darius granted new meaning to it when he integrated former local authorities into his own centralised administrative system. A satrap was responsible for civilian administration only because the military was not under his control. The separation of civilian and military administration was an effective means of control in the hands of the Persian kings to prevent the concentration of power in the provincial governors and the disintegration of the realm. Despite this, satraps were very important figures in the administrative and political machinery of the Persian kingdom, being responsible for internal security, the collection of taxes and managing local economy (satraps were entitled to mint silver coins). A satrap disposed of only a small number of personal bodyguards which was large enough to protect him but small enough for other purposes. After some decades however, satraps extended their control over the military administration as well, partly because the kings lost the game

---

[1] Wiesehöfer (1996: 60), Dandamaev and Lukonin (1989: 98–99).

against their governors and partly because the increasingly frequent revolts had to be suppressed by the satraps rapidly and effectively which was impossible without a proper military organisation. When satraps began to use their forces also against each other or the central government, the catastrophic consequences soon undermined the stability of the empire and made it vulnerable to attacks as the rapid military successes of Alexander clearly show.[2] Provinces consisted of smaller administrative units, the administrative head of which were frequently called also satrap. These local leaders were under the control of the satrap governing the province and were recruited from both the Persian and the local elite. Territories enjoying a relative autonomy were also part of this centralised system as autonomy was, of course, not freedom. One among these was Yūda which constituted part of the fifth province according to Herodotus (*ebir nāri*: 'beyond the river'). According to a previous scholarly consensus, autonomies granted by the Persian central government resulted in a relative freedom of the people, provided they paid their taxes in due time and remained loyal to their overlords. Recent findings challenge this view and point to the fact that Yūda was governed by a provincial leader appointed by the Persians right from the beginning up to the time of Alexander, while the local organs of authority did hardly function, and the local officials served the Persian great power interests.[3] Susa, an ancient city of Elam was chosen for administrative capital while Persepolis was built to be the ceremonial centre of the realm where rulers were crowned, reception of envoys took place and oaths of loyalty were sworn during the festivities of the New Light (Nawa Raucha) festival.

The head of the central administration was the *hazārapati* (commander of thousands), who was originally the commander of the elite military unit called the 'ten thousand immortals', that is: the bodyguard of the king and a special force created by Darius. *Hazārapati* were the second persons after the king in rank, as more and more important issues were delegated to them to resolve. As a result, *hazārapati* evolved into a central figure of the court, which not only controlled the elite military unit but also the chancellery. In addition, it was again the *hazarapati* who managed diplomatic negotiations and accompanied the envoys to the ruler. The financial well-being of the realm was trusted to the chief treasurer, the *ganzbabara* and the book-keeper, the *hāmārakara* while the *frasaka* was responsible for legal issues. Royal decisions and resolutions were published by messengers (*azdākara*). This system of central administration had its counterpart at provincial level guaranteeing the appropriate machinery of each unit. Communication between the units of central and local administration was ensured by the imperial post organised along Assyrian pattern. Official documents were not written in Old Persian, as one may assume, but in Aramaic, a widely used language of this period. Aramaic texts sent by the royal post were translated to local languages and made public in the local vernacular in order to make them understandable for everyone. As a consequence, a new formalistic language, the so-called imperial Aramaic came into being. As its writing system was less complicated than that of the cuneiform script, the latter begun to disappear. As

---

[2]Dandamaev and Lukonin (1989: 100–103).
[3]Fried (2004: 233).

this example shows, Persian kings resolved the problem of communication, not an easy task by far in such a multi-ethnic society. Besides communication, control was another difficult task to accomplish as both the central bureaucracy and the provincial governors were to control. For this reason, Persian kings sent "secretaries" to the chancellery of the satraps whose task was, among others, to inform the king from every decision or correspondence at local levels. Secret agents called the 'king's ears' (*gaushaka*) were sent in every part of the realm to collect information about civilian and military commanders. Officials called *tīftāye* and *pati-ākhsha* belonged also to the intelligence service but lack of sources prevents us to know more about them.[4] Besides public administration the judiciary was also established. The royal judge (*dāta-bara*) was the official to adjudicate in the royal court, while the local elite ran the local courts. The Persian system of administration had a long lasting impact on the Near East, it was taken over by succeeding dynasties too. Basic terms such as *data* (law), *dātabara, ganzabara* and *hāmārakara* entered contemporary languages such as Akkadian, Armenian and Hebrew.[5]

After the disintegration of the Achaemenid Empire, the Seleucids became masters of Iran and the largest part of the former Persian realm. Seleucids were descendants of Seleucos, a military commander of Alexander who defeated his rivals after the death of Alexander. Their rule did not last for long, as they were unable to resist a nomadic Iranian tribe coming from the east, the Parni, later to be known as the Parthians, and lost Iran and Mesopotamia to them. Effective Parthian control was established by Mithridates I, who laid down the foundations of a new hegemon in the Near East (second century BCE), conquering the heartland of the former Achaemenid Empire. It was Mithridates the Great who made the Parthian Empire a superpower and consolidated the realm. In so doing, he established a friendly relationship with the Chinese emperor and signed a treaty with him. He followed the same policy towards the Romans too, but they opted for conflicts instead, and this is how a rivalry began, which resulted in constant warfare for centuries. Though Roman forces were routed at Carrhae in Syria, later Romans gained the upper hand and defeated the Parthians in several military campaigns. However, Romans were unable to defeat them completely and the Parthian Empire remained intact with no loss of territory.[6] It was, therefore, a complete surprise again that a Persian petty king called Ardakhshēr was able to accomplish in a couple of years what the Romans were unable to do in two centuries. But this is exactly what happened and the Parthian ruling dynasty, the Arsacids, lost power to the Sasanians, descendants of Ardakhshēr, at the beginning of the third century AD. Ardakhshēr's son and successor, Shābuhr I, inherited a strong empire from his father and continued the aggressive foreign policy of the Parthians against the Romans, now in decline. This is how two great victories were won against the arch enemy without long lasting effects. During the long reign of Shābuhr II in the fourth century, Sasanian power was on his zenith. The next century witnessed lost military campaigns against the Hephtalites or White Huns invading from the

---

[4]Dandamaev and Lukonin (1989: 111–113).
[5]Frye (1963: 100).
[6]Schippmann 1980: 33–73.

east, followed by internal chaos. Against this background, it is understandable why Khosrau I is regarded as one of the most talented Persian kings who defeated the Hephtalities, reorganised the empire and made it stronger than ever. In so doing, he was also a great patron of Iranian culture, granting to it a long period to flourish. His grandson, Khosrau II, waged a long war against the Byzantine Empire which weakened the empire both militarily and economically. After his murder, the ruling dynasty was unable to reorganise the empire again and lost against the invading Arab-Muslim army which ended the history of Ancient Iran (651).

The administration of the kingdom was built on the inherited pattern of the Achaemenians, with some changes. The empire consisted of two kinds of territories: one was in the direct control of the king and the other in the hands of vassal kings, the number of which varied. Provinces under the king's control (corresponding to the *praefecturae* of Tacitus) were headed by satraps (*stratēgoi* according to Greek texts) with the help of some dignitaries. Territories in the hands of the vassal kings enjoyed autonomy, provided they paid the tax levied and were loyal to the Parthian ruler. Authority was inherited within the royal families acknowledged by the Parthian king. The designation King of kings, an epithet of Iranian monarchs has thus perfect sense: the great king was king of his subordinate vassal kings. If vassal kings and other noble men were no longer loyal to the great king, the ruling dynasty lost his power: the Parthians to the Sasanians, the Sasanians to the Muslims.[7] We do not know the number of vassal kingdoms precisely; according to a Persian source, the number of the vassal kings in the last decades of the Parthian rule reached the number of 240, a somewhat exaggerated number.[8]

With the coming to power of the Sasanians, two tendencies began to unfold. One is the rising political power of the Zoroastrian church, the other is the constant ongoing tendency toward centralisation. Zoroastrian church as a centralised entity with hierarchical structure was non existent before the third century, which does not mean, of course, that Iranian were not Zoroastrians previously. But Zoroastrianism was adapted to the historical reality in which Sasanians needed ideological support, which they obtained from the Zoroastrian clergy in exchange of growing political power. As a result, Sasanian state building and Zoroastrian church building went hand in hand. Zoroastrianism became the state religion and the royal title: Mazda-worshiper (*mazdā-yasna*), was introduced as a constant epithet of the kings. At the same time, Zoroastrian clergy was organised into a hierarchic structure modelled on the public administration of the state. As the king was the head of the state with the title of king of kings, so too was the chief *mōbed* the head of the church with the same logic in his title (*mōbedān mōbed*). He was not only a powerful chief of the clergy, but at the same time the advisor to the king ex officio and the second most important political figure in the realm. According to this new concept, state and religion were twins born from the same womb never to be separated.[9] Here religions means state Zoroastrianism, an understanding which resulted in narrowing the autonomy of

---

[7] Wiesehöfer (1996: 145).

[8] Kār Nāmag-i Ardakhshēr, in Nyberg (1964: 1).

[9] Ibn Isfandiyār (1320: 17).

religious minorities and sometimes also their prosecution (Manicheans, Christians, Jews), a complete break with the liberal religious policy of the Parthians. As a result, *Ērān-shahr* as a new ideology emerged as the Sasanians identified their state with the country of the Aryans, that is, *Ērān-shahr,* linked to Zoroastrianism as a state religion.[10] This combined national and religious ideology was projected back to the Achaemenians on which Sasanians based their fabricated genealogy. This tendency was hallmarked by the creation of a unified national culture, the emphasis on dynastic continuity, the demonization of Alexander the Great, the codification of religious texts of orthodox Zoroastrianism, and the creation of a powerful Zoroastrian church.[11]

Sasanians inherited the political structure of the Parthian kingdom which they started to modify right from the beginning. Though vassal kings were allowed to remain in power, provided they were loyal to their new master, their competency was nevertheless reduced. It was expressed symbolically by extinguishing their royal fire combined with a general prohibition for everyone to have a fire of his own, except the Persian king.[12] In order to understand this religious symbolism, we should bear in mind the central role and importance of the fire cult in Zoroastrianism in general and the Parthian custom to light the royal fire for every vassal king when ascending to throne in particular, which was extinguished only at the vassal king's death, to be lit again for his own purpose by his descendant. The message was clear: the king is no longer the king of his vassals but an omnicompetent authority without rivals. Despite this, vassal kings were important for the central administration and this is the reason why they were allowed to remain in place at least in provinces along the border. Studying the royal inscription of Shābuhr I (Res Gestae Divi Saporis or the inscription at Kaᶜba-yi Zardosht: ShKZ), it is evident that local rulers (MLK'- *shāh*) were important in places such as Merv, Adiabene and Kirman; that is, provinces along the borders but not in the central territory of the empire; perhaps the leader of the Sakas (Scyths) was designated as king for the same reason too.[13] Parthian noble families retained their wealth and power for the next centuries to come and remained therefore key players in Sasanian politics and the military. It is not by accident that the same royal inscription of Shābuhr I mentions some of them (Warāz, Kārin and Sūrēn families) as particularly important pillars of the realm (the head of the Sūrēn family was the chief commander of the Parthian army routing the Romans in the battle of Carrhae).[14] Territories not belonging to the vassal kings were called *shahr* ('country, province'), headed by the *shahrab*, that is, the satrap. Such territories were originally in the hands of either the defeated Parthian royal family or in the Sasanian royal family. A s i nhe Achaemenid Empire satraps were responsible for the civilian administration, the military having its own structure. Provinces were further divided into smaller units called *ōstān*, headed by the *ōstāndār*.[15]

---

[10]Gnoli (1989: 157–162).

[11]Gnoli (1989: 175–178).

[12]Ibn Isfandiyār (1942: 25).

[13]ŠKZ 28–29: Back (1978: 348–349).

[14]ŠKZ 29.

[15]Wiesehöfer (1996: 186), Daryaee (2009: 126).

Early Sasanian public administration was based on both the Achaemenid and the Parthian model, which resulted in a sophisticated structure. Central administration was headed by the *bidakhsh,* whose office is usually titled as viceroy or grand wizier (ShKZ: 29). Clear Achaemenid heritage in both function and designation are the offices of the *hazāruft,* the commander of the royal bodyguard (the *hazārapati* of the Achaemenians), the *ganzvar* (Old Persian *ganzabara*), the chief treasurer, and the *āmārgar* (Old Persian *hāmārakara*) an official responsible for auditing the accounts. Public administration was separated from the management of the royal court in which the *sālār-ī darīgān* played the central role. A *darbed* supervised the gatekeepers, while the control of the servants was the task of the *paristagbed.* Royal hunts were organised by the *nakhchirbad.* Kings were advised by councillors (*andarzbed*) and queens had their own advisers too (ShKZ: 33). As the title *mogān-andarzbed* suggests, priests were also among the advisors. The function of the *argbed* is disputed, some scholars think he was the commander of a fortress (the name indicates such an understanding) while others believe he was the chief official controlling taxation.[16] In addition to these offices, there was a food master (*grastebed*) and a cup-bearer (*mayyār*) also at the royal court.[17] Sources refer to an office called *framādār* (commander), but we do not know his competencies. The highly powerful commander of king Yazdagerd II, Mihr-Narseh titles himself *wuzurg-framādār* (great commander) on his bridge-inscription but this, too, does not bring us any closer to the exact competencies of this office.[18]

Day to day machinery of this complicated system was ensured by the scribes (*dibīr*), who enjoyed great esteem. According to the royal inscription of Shābuhr I, the head of the scribes (*dibīrbed*) was such an important figure, that a sacrifice had to be made in his favour.[19] Scribes were exempt from paying taxes, had fast horses and wore garments appropriate to their office. On some particular occasions, *dibīrbed*s took part in important decisions such as electing a new king (Shābuhr II appointed his brother as his successor in the presence of the high priest and the head of the scribes). Scribes were trained in a school called *dibīristān,* from where the most talented fund their way directly into the central administration.[20] However, a rigid social system prevented talented people from entering the noble circle of scribes; therefore, the caste-like social structure of the Sasanian society hindered social mobility in this respect too. Scribes were organised into 'chancelleries' (*dīwān*), that is, units on which the whole administrative system was based. Though plagued by massive corruption, the system itself was effective and this is the reason why it served as a model for the administration of the caliphate in the long centuries after the fall of the Sasanians. Important facts and decisions were kept in registers subdivided by topics, thus court sentences (*dād dibīray*), lands for taxation (*shahr āmār dibīray*),

---

[16]Wiesehöfer (1996: 186–189).

[17]ŠKZ: 30.

[18]Back (1978: 498).

[19]ŠKZ: 34.

[20]Tafazzoli (2000: 23–27).

the treasury (*ganz āmār dibīray*), fires (*ātash āmār dibīray*) and the pious foundations (*ruwānagān dibīray*) had their separate registers.[21]

Zoroastrian church further refined its structure, which enabled some of its dignitaries to take part directly in managing state affairs in the second half of the Sasanian period, notably in adjudication. Priests known as *mōbed, rad* and *ērbed* were at the same time leading figures of the judiciary, notably in criminal cases, some of which were delegated into their exclusive competency. Religious minorities (primarily the Christians and the Jews) enjoyed relative autonomy, headed by the bishops and the *rēsh galūta'*, the leader of the Babylonian Jews, who were also charged with the collection o f taxes levied on these communities by the king. Should they fail to do so, Persian kings retaliated with brutal violence, sometimes ending up in mass persecutions even when law was against the king (the first mass persecution of Christians took place when Christians refused to pay the tax arbitrarily raised to its double of what was agreed upon previously, because *Shābuhr* wanted to finance his campaign against Rome out of this extra income).[22] Apart from such particular cases coloured by power struggles, the influence of the Zoroastrian clergy and foreign policy considerations, religious minorities could follow their own law resulting in the flourishing of their jurisprudence (Christian law collections, the Babylonian Talmud).

Military administration remained separated from the civilian up to the sixth century. The army was headed by the *arteshtārān sālār* ('leader of the soldiers') while the *spāhbed* worked in subordination to him. The cavalry, very important for the Persian army, was under the command of the *aspbed,* while the defence of fortresses was the task of the *dizbed,* all enlisted in the inscription of Shābuhr as important military officers.[23] The reforms of Khosrau I changed this structure as he divided the empire into four territories and united civilian and military administration. The four territories (*pāygōsh*) were: *apākhtan* (north), *khorāsān* (east), *nēmrōz* (south), and *khwarwarān* (west) governed by powerful commanders who were directly responsible to the king. Khosrau created four *spāhbed*s (previously there was only one in the centre) and placed them at the head of each *pāygōsh.* Their work was assisted by the *pāygōshbān*s and by the *marzbān*s (frontier guards) who had to defend the borders and govern the areas under their control.[24] Tax administration remained exempt from this new structure and the old system based on 37 tax districts continued to exist independently from the *pāygosh*es. These territories were subdivided into smaller units such as *ōstān* and *kūra*, one *ōstān* consisting of twelve *kūra*s.[25]

---

[21] Altheim and Stiehl (1954: 240–241).

[22] Braun (1915: VIII–IX).

[23] ŠKZ: 30–32.

[24] Wiesehöfer (1996: 198).

[25] MHDA 27. 12.

4.2   From Persian to Zoroastrian Law

The beginning Persian law starting its history as a customary law of the nomadic Persian tribes is unknown. This customary law may be similar to the custom of the Medes, if not identical with it, as the two tribal confederations parted ways only after entering Iran in the first millennium BCE. This ancient Iranian customary law again shows similarities with ancient Indian (Hindu) customs, which comes as no surprise since these Indo-Iranian people are common in origin, proven by similarities in their languages, religions, worldview and culture. We have only sporadic information on the ancient Persian traditional law, as no written sources have reached us if there were any. Some records are due to the time when Persia already established itself as a superpower and, therefore, some interest developed to know more about these people. It is again Herodotus who informs us about Persian customs, the accuracy of which could be doubted at some points.

The first turning point in the history of Persian law was the creation of a Persian state (there was no such a thing in the previous centuries), which became a hegemon in the Near East immediately. Persian law is, therefore, not to be confused with Persian imperial law if there was such a thing. Given the less centralised political structure of the empire and the autonomy granted for the various ethnic and religious groups living in Achaemenid Iran, it is reasonable to think that there was no uniformed imperial law binding for everyone. It is, of course, not to say that there were no royal edicts or commands pertaining to particular cases or issues, mainly administrative or political in nature. Surely there were such edicts, as scribes were responsible for their translation and dissemination and governors for their implementation. But these are quite different from an imperial family law or criminal law, for which there is not a single proof. Some Classical authors say that Darius I was engaged in legislation, the models of which was said to be the Laws of Hammurabi. Though some leading Iranists such as Olmstead and Ghishman accepted this claim, the majority still refuses to believe it.[26] Imperial legislation is a modern idea which should not be projected back to the Ancient Near East. In addition, it would have stood against imperial policy to grant legal autonomy to the conquered peoples enabling Jews, Egyptians, Babylonians, etc. to live in keeping with their own law. It is by far a more adequate question whether collections of local laws needed royal approval or not,[27] that is, was legal autonomy a freedom to do in matters of law whatever local people wanted or did, the Persian king kept his eye on what was going on.

Herodotus informs us that according to Persian customary law, it was the popular assembly consisting of armed men that made decisions about the most important issues, particularly about war and peace.[28] Members of the assembly discussed the matter and decided about it; Herodotus tells us, while being influenced by the consumption of alcoholic beverages. Next day, when they returned to their senses,

---

[26]Olmstead (1948: 119–134).

[27]Dandamaev and Lukonin (1989: 117). See also the articles in Watts (2001) dedicated to the study of this question.

[28]Herodotus I: 125.

they revised their previous decision and should they find it correct they upheld it, otherwise rejected.[29] This kind of primitive democracy was out of touch with reality when Persia became a hegemonic empire. Consequently, decision making process adjusted to the new political situation with a king in power whose standing resembled that of his Mesopotamian predecessors. As a result, the previous tribal structure gave way to a Mesopotamian understanding of kingdom and power that transformed Persian tribal confederation into a Near Eastern state, though in its Persian variant. This is how despotism, Mesopotamian in its origin and alien to primitive Persian tribal law, was introduced during the reign of Darius I and became dominant for long centuries to come (the same transformation happened in the early Islamic history when the tribal confederation of the Arabic tribes was changed to the ᶜAbbāsid caliphate the centre of which was Baghdad, a city in the heartland of Mesopotamian civilisation). The old structure was however not to abolish completely, therefore kings were obliged to rule in accordance with the council made up of the heads of the seven noble families, a less institutionalised form of government which remained in place for a thousand years or more.

The judiciary was secular and in the hands of the traditional elite and the royal judges (*dātābara*) who were appointed for lifetime to be removed only because of wrongdoing. Royal judges adjudicated cases presented to them, and interpreted traditional Persian law but remained subordinate to the king whose will qualified as law even if it contradicted traditional law.[30] Important cases were adjudicated by the Persian king himself even during military campaigns.[31] Persian kings paid special attention to the impartiality of the judges as *artha* (truth) is one of the most important concepts of Zoroastrianism. Herodotus underlines this with stories of doubtful accuracy. According to the most widespread story, a judge called *Sisamnes* was bribed and passed a false judgement. When the case was revealed to Cambyses, the king had the judge executed and made the judge's chair out of his skin; next he appointed the son of the executed judge in his place in order to remind him of the importance of his office.[32] The fourth-century CE historian, Ammianus Marcellinus, however refuted this story known also to the Romans and regarded the story as an invention or an extinct custom of old times.[33]

It is again Herodotus who tells us that the Persians did not sentence anybody to death for a crime first committed, they executed only those habitual criminals whose merits were less than their wrong. Modern scholarship believes, by contrast, that Herodotus here idealises Persian law as the cases known to us do not support this assumption.[34] Reality seems to prove the opposite: punishments were quite cruel, consisting of crucifixion, to smash the head with stones, to bury alive, to cut off limbs and, gouging the eyes. Torture was also applied during the procedure to extort

---

[29]Herodotus I: 133.

[30]Herodotus III: 31; The Book of Esther 1: 11–13.

[31]Herodotus V: 12.

[32]Herodotus V: 25; VII: 194.

[33]Ammianus Marcellinus XXIII: 81.

[34]Herodotus I: 137; Dandamaev and Lukonin (1989: 120).

confession from the suspect by whipping or with the help of scorpions.[35] Attempts against the king and his family were punished by death when the entire family of the perpetrator was also put to death, a consequence of the new political position of the Persian king. Marriages were not monogamous, at least not in the royal family where a large number of wives and concubines can be found. Fertility and the blessing by children were considered a great merit. This is the reason why Persian kings annually distributed gifts among the families where many children were born.[36]

The second turning point in the history of Persian law was the coming to power of the Sasanians and the Zoroastrian church. Persian law was secular in its nature until this period. When Zoroastrianism became the imperial ideology of the kingdom, law too was also Zoroastrianised, that is, more and more religious ideas entered the field of law. As a result, a previously secular customary law developed into a religious law, where priest and their dogmas gained prominence. This transformed both the institutions and the content of the law, as priests were sitting at courts, adjudicated criminal and sometimes also some private legal issues, laws of ritual purity became important, family law was adjusted to the priestly understanding of family and fertility, and criminal law was re-organised on Zoroastrian understanding of heaven, hell, and the fate of the soul. Law was not the Persian customary law any longer but a new, religious law of a religious community, based on some Persian traditions which fitted into this new legal framework. Law became therefore a normative expression of a religious community leaving behind its previous tribal and Achaemenid background. This is the reason why the third turning point, the fall of the Sasanians and the coming of Islam rooted it almost completely: Persian law was not the law of a nation any more but the law of the Zoroastrian community, a religious group constantly decreasing over time.

In this new understanding of law, a king only had limited role though he was, in theory at least, the supreme judge of the realm. It is important to note that there is no hint in the sources to legislation and no such a work has reached us, we know only some administrative orders of technical importance (the use of seals). Our most important source from this period is, therefore, not a Code but a law book, a compendium of hundreds of difficult cases and their laws. The Book of a Thousand Judgements as it is properly called (*Mādigān ī Hazār Dādestān: MHD+A*), is the work of a judge written most probably in the seventh century for educational purpose or academic interests but was surely not an official law book of a king.[37] Other sources at our disposal are priestly works concentrating on minor issues of ritual purity which contain no laws on secular matters save some criminal acts in correlation with purity laws. Works such as *Shāyast-nē-shāyast,*[38] *Nērangestān* and *Hērbedestān*[39]

---

[35] Herodotus III: 130; Dandamaev and Lukonin (1989: 120–121).

[36] Herodotus I: 136.

[37] The text was edited, translated into German and commented by Macuch (1981, 1993); translated into English by Perikhanian-Garsoian (1997).

[38] Text editions: Tavadia (1930), Kotwal (1969).

[39] Text editions and translation: Kotwal and Kreyenbroek (1992, 1995, 2003), Humbach and Elfenbein (1990).

are products of the late Sasanian period which reflect the legal worldview of the Zoroastrian clergy but explain little about contemporary legal life in general. This is the reason why the so called Martyr Acts about criminal procedures against Iranian Christians are such important sources for Zoroastrian criminal law.[40]

Along the third turning point in the history of Zoroastrian law, it was transformed from imperial law to the law of a religious minority, facing repressions and sometimes prosecutions. In this new historical context, criminal law lost its significance as Zoroastrians were denied of *ius gladii* by their Muslim overlords. Family law also underwent some changes while ritual laws remained intact. Former legal sophistication and institutions vanished together with their royal backing, the latter resulting in the intellectual monopoly of the Zoroastrian clergy. The priestly leader of the community, now called *dastūr,* was entrusted with maintaining law and order and to teach law on a basic level to the community at large. This is how *riwāyat*s, basic texts on ritual and law in the form of questions and answers were born in the ninth and tenth centuries, evolving later into a literary genre of its own right. Among them *Riwāyat-i Ēmēd-i Ashawahishtān* (REA), a compilation of the high priest *Ēmēd*, and the *Riwāyat* accompanying the *Dādestān ī Dēnīg* (PRDd) are of importance.[41]

4.3 Legal Theory of Zoroastrian Law

The idea that the rules are ultimately of divine origin is part of the Iranian worldview. The so called *daiwa*-inscription of Xerxes clearly proves this when he calls "to respect the law that was ordered by *Auramazdā*" (*dātā parīdiy tya Auramazdā niyashtāya*), as the "man who has respect for that law which *Auramazdā* has established, and worships *Auramazdā* and *Arta* reverent(ly), he becomes both happy while living and blessed (*artāwā bavatiy*) when dead".[42]

The laws of *Auramazdā*, whatever they might be, are not revealed to a prophet, to the sages or anybody else because revealed holy texts of Zoroastrianism contain no such rules. Contrary to the revelation of Moses and Muhammad, Zoroaster, the prophet of Zoroastrianism received not a single law in revelation, despite the fact that he was the addressee of ongoing revelations for long. Legal rules were however, exempt from Zoroaster's teachings which concentrated on ethical principles instead. This is why the Gāthās, verses which are believed to be composed by Zoroaster himself, stress religious and not legal understanding of his mission. Holy texts of Zoroastrianism compiled and later edited as Awesta have no direct reference to a revealed law, subject to no modification which makes Zoroastrian law different from Jewish and Islamic laws. Contrary to these religions, Zoroastrianism is not a strict monotheism since in addition to *Auramazdā,* other deities such as *Mithra* play also important role in it. Therefore, law could not be understood as the (legal) requirement

---

[40]Braun (1915), Hoffmann (1880).

[41]Text editions: Safa–Isfehani (1980), Williams (1990).

[42]Kent (1953: 151–152).

of a single deity to be followed by mankind but rather as an abstract cosmic order to be respected also by celestial beings. The essence of Zoroastrianism embodied in the three expressions of good thought, good speech and good action (*humad, huwarsht, hūkht*) are not legal rules but ethical principles on which laws, given by kings or others, should rest. One consequence of this is that law is less in the focus of Zoroastrian thinking than among Jews and Muslims and its function is replaced by rites and ritual purity.

The term *data* is a very important term denoting both divine "laws" and that of the kings entering in various Near Eastern languages as a Persian loan world. Darius makes references to it several times as his law corresponding to his will.[43] Thus, the will of the king has the force of law. After the fall of the Achaemenids, the term remained in use denoting not only law but also religion, presumably as a consequence of law being more and more tied to religion, that is, Zoroastrianism. This is how *dād*, the Middle Persian equivalent of the Old Persian *data* in the Middle Persian texts was used not only in the sense of 'law' but also of 'religion' in Sasanian times,[44] though there was a proper term for it which also entered the Arabic lexikon (*dīn*).

Dātā has a strong correlation to *arta*, another key concept of Indo-Iranian ethical and legal thinking to be found both in Zoroastrian and early Hindu texts (Rgveda), the proper meaning of which is subject to dispute in modern scholarship for long. Some scholars interpret it as a universal law and a cosmic order regulating not only human behaviour, while others interpret it narrowly as justice. Following the wider interpretation, justice is part of the cosmic order but fits into a larger cosmic framework where everything has its proper place, social justice being one among them.[45] A person living according to *arta* is called *artawān* (also personal name of so many Iranian kings) who is happy in this world and will be happy in the world to come just as the text of Xerxes quoted above has it. The opposite of *arta* is *drauga*, lie, which is the denial of *arta*. This is why Herodotus is right when saying that the most repulsive thing for Persians is lie, together with debt, which may bring one to lie.[46]

Against this background, it is understandable why Awesta is considered as the most important source of law since a sacred book containing rituals, hymns, blessings and some folklore is the best candidate for it. But this is only legal theory, not practice. Given the fact that neither the Awesta nor any other sacred texts contain revealed legal norms or law in general, the practical significance of the theory is reduced. As a result, claims of legal theory and legal practice do not correspond but are opposite to each other: though according to legal theory, Awesta is the most important source of law in everyday legal practice yet it has no relevance and this is the reason why there is no reference to it in judicial documents.

---

[43]DB I. 23: (Kent 1953: 117–119): "by the favor of Auramazdā these countries showed respect toward my law." DNa 21: (Kent 1953: 137): "my law—that held them firm ...."

[44]PRDd 7.2; Williams (1990: Part I: 47).

[45]Boyce (1975: 27). Schlerath (Enc. Ir. I. 694) and Gershevitch (1959: 6) interpret it merely as justice.

[46]Herodotus I: 138.

Chāshtag, usually translated as doctrine, came to fill in the gap. *Chāshtag* is the product of Sasanian jurisprudence based on custom, various interpretations of (religious and legal) texts and personal preferences of individual scholars. Out of these doctrines and the by joint efforts of some scholars, legal schools emerged which made late Sasanian law pluralistic as more schools operated parallel to each other, neither of which gaining prominence or monopoly. Various doctrines of the schools however, related only to detail and questions of technical importance, while fundamental pillars of the legal system seem to be understood uniformly. Unfortunately, we know very little about the history of these legal schools, since sporadic evidences do not allow us to determine the number of the schools and their chronology. Based on different assumptions and arguments, the third, fifth and sixth centuries were proposed to date the legal schools but conclusive proofs are missing.[47] The number of the schools is no less problematic as we have references to three and to four schools (Shāyast-nē-shāyast 1.3; 1.4.) but studying the latter means it is evident that the four schools schema is just a combination of two original schools which makes it probable that there were only two schools: that of Abarag and Mēdōmāh, each consisting of three generations.[48] Almost nothing is known about the scholars of the schools besides their names. Abarag and Mēdōmāh however, were well known commentators of the Awesta and that of the Wīdēwdād, Ērbedestān and Nērangestān,[49] that is, texts of purity laws which makes us believe that they were Zoroastrian dignitaries engaged in legal problems of ritual purity and related issues. As a result, Zoroastrian jurisprudence seems to be academic, concentrating on issues which were important for the clergy but not for the society at large, which made the legal schools ivory towers rather than real succour to everyday legal practice.

The third source of law called *hamdādestān ī wēhān* and interpreted as the consensus of the scholars may well be of more help, at least one may infer to this since some of the sentences in the MHD+A were based on it. To our misfortune, we know less about it than about the schools: we do not know whether *hamdādestān ī wēhān* was the consensus of all legal scholars or only that of the members of a given school; was it a complete consensus or only that of a given generation with no reference to the understanding of previous scholars, etc. Despite this, it seems clear that *hamdādestān ī wēhān* is not to be compared with *ijmāᶜ* in Islamic law in its epistemological value.[50]

The custom of the courts referred to as *kardag* was of importance in everyday legal practice. Perhaps it was not accepted as a former legal source, though we do not know as both positive and negative claims are missing from our sources. In judicial practice, however, as a material legal source, *kardag* was taken into consideration. What is more, there are cases which demonstrate that *kardag* was sometimes contra legem, that is, legal practice was at variance with legal doctrine and courts followed *kardag*

---

[47] Macuch (1993: 29) argues for a third century dating, Perikhanian and Garsoian (1997: 418) for the fifth century, while Jany (2006: 295–305) for the sixth century.

[48] Tavadia (1930: 28–29).

[49] Macuch (1993: 13).

[50] Jany (2005: 297–303).

instead of relying on doctrines, making Zoroastrian law thus flexible to adaptation to changing social reality. *Kardag* therefore not only filled in gaps in the legal system but also modified it, as courts did not follow some doctrines, the reasons of which we do not know. Perhaps some doctrines were outdated at the time when *kardag* established itself as a legal source, perhaps some doctrines were against local customs or the interest of some influential persons or groups who were powerful enough to bring about some modifications at courts. To be clear, these modifications were about minor points of technical importance and not about gradual changes. Despite this, the changes reflected an alternative view on society and law and contributed in the long run to gradual changes which were at variance with the original legal doctrines. As post-Sasanian sources reveal, it was the *kardag* understanding that was followed, meanwhile old doctrines fell into disuse and were forgotten. The compilers of the *riwāyat*s, seemingly unaware of old rival doctrines, do not discuss them but present *kardag* laws as the doctrine itself. Here are some cases to illustrate. According to traditional doctrine, a letter of divorce (*hisht-nāmag*) produced by a husband is invalid should it not specify the guardian over his former wife. By contrast, *kardag* did not follow this rule strictly and considered a document without specifying such a person also valid, giving husbands more freedom to divorce their wives yet at the same time entitling women to be without a guardian, a novelty in a strictly patriarchal society as Sasanian clearly was. Similarly, following the old doctrine the income of a wife (*windišn*) belonged ipso iure to her husband but *kardag* ruled in favour of her saying that a woman could dispose of her *windišn*, again a significant novelty in order to enhance women's rights. The same tendency could be observed in the law of inheritance where *kardag* was also in favour of women.[51]

4.4 Substantive Law

4.4.1 Family Law

In the Sasanian period, marriage was polygamous because of two reasons. One is that a man could marry more wives in one type of marriage, the other is that there were three types of marriages in which one could have, in theory, more than one wife. The typology of marriages is not only important because of the number of wives but also because of their different legal consequence in inheritance.

The most common form of marriage was called *pādikhshāy* marriage, a kind of prototype in comparison to which particularities of other marriages could be demonstrated. A *pādikhshāy* marriage came into being by a marriage contract unless the girl was abducted. Abduction is widespread among nomads (see, among others, the Hittite and the ancient Hindu law) and there are some traces of it also in the Persian/Zoroastrian law. Similarly to Hindu law, abduction was tolerated, though

---

[51] For more see Jany (2005).

certainly not encouraged, perhaps not as a genuine form of marriage but in order to bypass the long process of marrying for whatever reasons. We do not know whether abduction had to be legalised later with the help of some formalities or not. In the Sasanian period however, abduction may have been the exemption not the rule.

In a contract creating a *pādikhshāy* marriage, the legal position of the spouses and their pecuniary rights had to be regulated. A *pādikhshāy* marriage was a marriage *cum manu mariti*, it was therefore, a precondition for the husband to acquire *sālārīh* (manus) over his wife. Should it be otherwise, the marriage was null and void.[52] Property rights, dowry, divorce money and maintenance of children are the most common issues in a marriage contract. A *pādikhshāy* marriage could be concluded only with the permission of the guardian of the woman (*sālār*)[53] otherwise it was null and void or was regarded as a *khwasrayūn* marriage if some conditions were fulfilled. It was an important rule protecting the girl that she could not be forced into a marriage against her will.[54] If the marriage contract was concluded when she was only a minor[55] she had the right to nullify the marriage when coming of age.[56] In such a case, the contract had to be annulled and the girl was not to suffer any disadvantage because of her decision.[57] This is at least what the law says but we do not know contemporary social practice.

Family fathers enjoyed considerable competencies in managing the family. Family members under his *sālārīh* were required to follow his decisions called command (*framān*) without hesitation. Obeying such *framān*s was a legal obligation for those under his authority, that is, wives, children and slaves, if there were any in the family. Disobedience was a serious issue called *atarsagāyīh* (literally: not fearing) the definition of which was not to do the good thing that was commanded and do the bad thing that was not commanded.[58] When disobedience manifested and the husband wished to do so, he produced a document about *atarsagāyīh*,[59] but it could be challenged at a law court since a wife could prove that she was in fact obedient.[60] If she failed to convince the court, it produced a document certifying that she was disobedient.[61] Again, we do not know the chances of a wife against her husband at a court consisting of local elderly men. To produce such a document by the court, had in itself no consequences. A husband could disinherit his disobedient wife only while referring to a court document about *atarsagāyīh*, but in absence of such a will, the document itself had no legal consequences of its own. To disinherit a wife, her

---

[52]MHD 4. 15–5. 3.
[53]MHD 36. 2–5.
[54]MHD 36. 9–16.
[55]MHD 106. 7–9.
[56]MHD 89. 15–17.
[57]MHD 89. 17–90. 2.
[58]MHDA 4. 6–8.
[59]MHDA 7. 2–3.
[60]MHDA 6. 1.
[61]Perikhanian (1983: 648).

husband had to use proper formulas,[62] otherwise his will was void. If done everything properly not only the disobedient wife but also her children were disinherited.[63]

A *framān* of a husband included his right to give his wife into a temporary marriage with another man. This was, it seems, an irregular situation driven by the necessity to have children and heirs as a requirement of both Zoroastrianism and family interest. If a man, though married, was "in trouble" regarding marriage and children he could reach out to an already married man (a relative or a friend) to help him and provide a woman to bear him heir(s).[64] If the husband agreed he gave his wife to him in a temporary marriage for which the consent of the wife was no precondition, she could be given to this marriage against her will. Such marriages were agreed upon by the men involved who drafted a contract about it. It was not against the law to conclude such marriage for some remuneration.[65] A husband could, moreover, sell his wife also to slavery together with his children. A husband enjoyed also a privileged position in managing family wealth as he was the sole authority to decide about monetary matters. Though a wife could have her own income (*windishn*,) her husband was entitled to dispose of it without her consent with the only restriction that after divorce he was obliged to give her *windishn* back.[66]

A head of the family was obliged to maintenance toward family members under his authority. The obligation lasted lifelong toward his wife, until reaching maturity toward his son, and until her marriage towards his daughter.[67] If the head of the family did not meet this obligation because of his own fault and someone else brought up his children (presumably a close relative), he could demand compensation from the father.[68] Maintenance meant supply of food and garments.[69] If a husband donated valuable goods to his wife it did not reduce his duty of maintenance. A wife could dispose of her property freely, which was not to be reduced with the costs of her maintenance.[70] Authority was inherited in the family, therefore, when her husband died, the widow was put under the guardianship of her adult son. Consequently, he had the right to decide whether his mother could remarry or not.[71] If there was no adult son in the family a close male relative was entrusted with the guardianship of the family, who usually married the widow. When her son came of age however, his permission was necessary to continue this marriage.[72]

A *pādikhshāy* marriage could be dissolved by divorce, initiated only by the husband but accepted by his wife. If the wife was not asked or she did not consent

---

[62]MHDA 6. 5–14.
[63]MHDA 7. 3–8.
[64]MHD 110. 4–8.
[65]MHD 108. 6–8.
[66]MHDA 2. 17–3. 1.
[67]MHD 32. 12–14.
[68]MHD 33. 3–6.
[69]MHDA 7. 8–11.
[70]MHDA 7. 8–11.
[71]MHD 26. 3–5.
[72]MHD 26. 3–5.

to it, the divorce was void. To have legal effect, a document called *hisht-nāmag* was produced, regulating monetary matters and appointing a person to the guardianship of the woman no longer under the authority of her former husband.[73] Only children born of a *pādikhshāy* marriage inherited their parents and also a widow inherited her deceased husband. The share of the widow and the male children was equal while that of the unmarried daughters was half of it; married daughters received nothing from the bequest (because their share was already given to them as dowry, an idea widespread among traditional Asian legal systems).

Temporary marriage was only of help for a childless person when he was still alive. When, however, a man died childless, obviously no temporary marriage could produce him an heir and this is the reason why *chagar* marriage was introduced into Zoroastrian family law. To help such deceased persons was a legal duty for relatives, referred to as *stūr*, to enter into a *chagar* marriage because children born of this union were regarded as the children of the deceased and not of the parents. This institution was more complicated than levirate marriage because a *stūr* could not only be a brother, but anybody in the family, perhaps, also outside of it (a friend). If the *stūr* was a man, the identity of the *chagar* wife was unimportant, if the *stūr* was a woman, the *chagar* husband could be anyone in principle, but presumably a husband was sought for among the near relatives of the deceased. When a *stūr* was a female who entered into a *chagar* marriage, she could not live in a *pādikhshāy* marriage which had to be dissolved, at least in theory. *Chagar* husbands had no authority in their family because authority and inheritance were two sides of the same coin: should he have the right of guardianship, his children would inherit him and not the deceased person, thus making the *chagar* marriage lose its mission and rationale. This is, however, exactly what happened in the post-Sasanian times upon the requests of the *chagar* fathers whose interest was to have their own heirs. As a result, *chagar* marriage became a second rank marriage losing its original social and religious rationale.[74]

Khwasrayūn marriage was the third, though atypical, form of marriage of less social prestige. Similarly to the Indian (Hindu) understanding, it was one of the most important duties of a family father to arrange marriages for his daughters which resulted in child marriages (more on that in the chapter on Hindu law), as nobody wanted to be ashamed by unmarried girls living at home. Should a family father (or any other guardian) neglect his duty, it was the right of the daughter to marry someone she liked without the permission of her guardian or even against his will.[75] This is the reason why *khwasrayūn* is called "love-marriages", similarly to the Hindu *gandharva vivaha* based on the same lines of arguments. Such a marriage provided an escape for a girl from her shameful situation, yet at the same time it was a kind of sanction for a neglecting guardian who was unable to do anything to protect his fame and prestige. Despite this, such a marriage was of low esteem, as a husband was not

---

[73] MHD 87. 7–10.

[74] Carlsen (1984: 108–112).

[75] MHD 33. 1–3.

denoted as such but as *gādār*,[76] that is, a lover.[77] No surprise that authority remained with the guardian of the woman and the husband had no control over his wife, which made him also free of the duty of maintenance. If his wife had no property on her own right it was the duty of the guardian to provide maintenance for her.[78] A *gādār* obtained guardianship only when his wife had no guardian at all, which must be an exceptional constellation as women were permanently under the authority of a male. When the *gādār* was also her guardian he was also obliged to maintenance.[79]

Finally, to say same words about incest is in order. Incestuous marriages seem to be widespread in Ancient Iran referred to as *khwēdōdāh* or *khwēdōdād*. The term goes back to the Awesta[80] where its meaning is broader, reflecting to a cosmological idea according to which vital force is important against the struggle against Evil and had to be spread among close relatives. Zoroastrian cosmology emphasises this idea since the first couple, parents of mankind, Mashya and Mashyānē were brother and sister. When this cosmological myth was connected to the incestuous marriages to legalise them is unclear, therefore, its origin is subject to disputes. According to Herodotus, Cambyses fell in love with his elder sister and wanted to marry her but it was against Persian customs which caused royal judges a sense of discomfort. Not willing to allow an incestuous marriage yet not daring to contradict the king, they finally resolved the issue answering that though there is no law that legalizes incest there is definitely a law which grants Persian kings to do whatever they please. If it is not only a folkloristic story of doubtful accuracy then incest was a taboo in Achaemenid times and the story serves to underlie the notion that Cambyses was a godless tyrant, a common theme in contemporary Persian texts driven by political motivations at the Persian court (Herodotus, too, has many such stories). This is why some of the leading Iranists such as Cameron believe that incest is Elamite in origin since during the Eparti dynasty heir to the throne could be only a son born to the ruler by his marriage to his sister. Since Persian tribes settled just on the Elamite border in Southwest-Iran, it was easy to transplant this custom, at least in the royal family. Other scholars however reject this hypothesis and point to the fact that Darius II also married Parysatis, his sister, and, what is more, this custom was not limited to the royal house, at least this is what Diodorus tells us.[81] Without concluding proofs, the question remains open.

In Sasanian Persia, *khwēdōdāh* was enlarged to marriages with other relatives, therefore, it has a broader meaning than a marriage between brothers and sisters. Again we do not know the reasons behind. One can speculate that this tendency was connected to the coming to power of the Zoroastrian church, when the *magi* (an endogamous cast-like entity) enlarged their own custom to society at large. Sound as it sounds, it is hard however to prove. High priest *Kardēr*, a leading person at

---

[76]Macuch (1981: 92–95).

[77]MHD 73. 7.

[78]MHD 33. 1–3.

[79]MHDA 14. 1–4.

[80]Yasna 12.9, Wīdēwdād 8.13, Wisperad 3.3, Yasht 24.17, Gah 4.8.

[81]Herodotus III: 31; Dandamaev and Lukonin (1989: 119; 121).

the Persian court who was allowed to have a rock inscription of his own near to those of the kings (in fact, he was the only commoner granted this privilege) proudly refers to his *khwēdōdāh* relationships already in the third century. Late Sasanian religious texts (*Shāyast-nē-shāyast* 8: 18) go further claiming that *khwēdōdāh* has miraculous effects smashing and killing demons by the thousands while expiating sins and allowing for entering Paradise even for criminals of capital crimes (*margarzān*).

Dēnkard, some kind of a Zoroastrian encyclopaedia, classifies *khwēdōdāh* into three types depending on the degree of relationships between the parties: (1) *khwēdōdāh* between relatives; (2) *khwēdōdāh* between near family members; (3) *khwēdōdāh* in the nuclear family that is, between father and his daughter, mother and her son, and between siblings.[82] Another religious text (*Riwāyat* accompanying the *Dādestān ī Dēnīg*) has a more complex structure listing six different combinations.[83] Accordingly, the most valuable relationship is between mother and her son as the son 'comes out' of the mother's body. The second most valuable relationship is between father and his daughter, followed by the relationship with the sister, the relationship between brothers and sisters of the same father, the relationship between half brothers and sisters from different fathers, ending up with the relationship between a man and his illegitimate daughter. Despite its alleged positive effects and the priestly propaganda to promote it, Persian society was seemingly reluctant to follow the rules of *khwēdōdāh*. Prophet Zoroaster rejects the idea in a fictive conversation with chief deity Ohrmazd (Auramazdā) who argues in the favour of it.[84] The law book of *Jesubocht,* an important text among Iranian Christians (see the next chapter), while condemning *khwēdōdāh* also highlights that the *magi* find it difficult to follow their 'dirty customs' and should they do so, they are doing it often with a bad conscious.[85] Perhaps it was one among the reasons why Zoroastrians abandoned it around the eleventh century and *khwēdōdāh* has fallen into oblivion. When western scholarship pointed to this ancient custom based on both classical authors[86] and Zoroastrian religious texts,[87] Parsees attacked modern Western scholarship to lend bad name to their religion by falsely accusing them with such practices, a vehement though unfounded critique which also shows their complete rejection of *khwēdōdāh*.[88]

---

[82]Macuch (1991: 143).

[83]RivDd 8d1–6: Williams (1990: Part I. 53, Part II. 12).

[84]RivDd 8o1–2. Williams (1990: Part I. 61; Part II. 16–17).

[85]Sachau (1914: 35).

[86]Herodotuos, Ctesias, Strabon, Sextus Empiricus, Diogenes Laertios, Origenes, Agathias, Bardesanes.

[87]Awesta; Dēnkard and the Riwāyat accompanying the Dādestān ī Dēnīg.

[88]Macuch (1991: 141).

4.4.2 Criminal Law

In order to understand Zoroastrian criminal law, we should bear in mind that its aim is not to retaliate the wrong, to restore the damages, or to protect society with preventive measures, but to save the soul of a criminal from the consequences caused by his criminal act in the world to come. After death, souls will be judged by the divine judge Mithra who weighs humans by their thoughts, words and deeds. If good thoughts, words and deeds (*humad, huwarsht, hūkht*) constitute the majority, the soul would enter Paradise, otherwise it will go to hell. A crime is obviously a bad deed, which weighs in heavily at the final judgment. And this is exactly the point where Zoroastrian criminal law enters with the doctrine that bad deeds are to the detriment of an individual soul only if it is not atoned for and punished properly. Consequently, a crime atoned for and properly punished would not be considered as a bad deed at the divine court of Mithra. The aim of punishment or criminal law in general is, therefore, to free the human soul from the consequences of his/her bad deeds and let them enter Paradise if their good deeds and words make it possible. Since Zoroastrianism was already a ritualistic religion in Sasanian times, it is small wonder that criminals were regarded as ritually impure, which could be removed also with proper repentance and punishment with the exception of criminals called *margarzān* (worthy of death) because they would remain polluted for ever.[89]

Religious texts emphasise that *margarzān*s would go to Hell irrespective of their good and bad deeds if they do not repent their sins.[90] Thus, divine punishment is due to both the criminal act and the lack of repentance. Repentance had to be public and sincere.[91] Repentance was to be expressed towards the plaintiff if the crime was against a person (against life, bodily integrity, property, etc.), and towards a priest (*rad*)[92] if it was committed against "the soul" (that is, it was a breach of ritual norms).[93] Repentance was, of course, followed by the sentence of the *rad* with unlimited competencies, who could pronounce also capital punishment if he believed this was the only way to save the soul from divine punishment.[94] The execution of his punishment, capital or not, immediately relieved the soul of the consequences of his sins and the person became ritually pure.[95] As a result, all his good deeds (thoughts and words) could be considered at the final judgement in his favour. By contrast, *margarzān*s without repentance are denied this favour.[96] Zoroastrian apocalyptic, a popular literature for centuries of which *Ardā Wirāz Nāmag* is a classic, has much

---

[89] Shāyast-nē-shāyast 2: 108.

[90] Shāyast-nē-shāyast 8: 7.

[91] Shāyast-nē-shāyast 8: 8–9.

[92] Rad is a priest and a spiritual leader going back to the Awestan times (Kreyenbroek 1994: 1–3).

[93] Shāyast-nē-shāyast 8: 1.

[94] Shāyast-nē-shāyast. 8. 6.

[95] Shāyast-nē-shāyast 8. 5–6 has the scholarly debate on the issue.

[96] Shāyast-nē-shāyast 8: 5.

to say about the sufferings of the soul in Hell, bringing together sins and crimes and their divine punishments sometimes in a sadistic vision.[97]

Zoroastrian texts classify crimes differently. According to one typology, crimes are of two kinds: one is 'against the soul' (*wināh ī ruwānīg*), the other is a crime against a third person (*wināh ī hamēmālān*), a classification also known to Hindu law. According to another typology, criminal acts are of eight kinds known as *framān, āgrift, ōyrisht, ardush, khwar, bāzāy, yāt* and *tanāpuhl*. This is a very unique and sophisticated system which takes into consideration both the gravity of the crime in order to arrive at a proportional punishment and other relevant circumstances which have influence on the final outcome (was it a habitual crime or not, was it done negligently or deliberately, etc.). These wrongdoings and crimes were not retaliated since they were punished by compensation. Accordingly, four stērs had to be paid for a *framān*, thirty stērs for an *ardush*, sixty stērs for a *khwar*, ninety stērs for a *bāzāy*, one hundred and eighty stērs for a *yāt*, and three hundred stērs for a *tanāpuhl*. Compensation for āgrift and ōyrisht was not established but left to individual agreement with the limit that it should be less than a compensation for a *framān*.[98]

It is important to note that these are categories and not individual crimes. Crimes were put together in these categories for reasons unknown to us, but they seem to follow their own logic. Examples help to clarify. Seemingly *khwar* consisted of sexual crimes, that is, illegal unions with prohibited persons such as a prostitute, a non-Iranian or apostate woman, or with someone who had committed *tanāpuhl*.[99] Here the common denominator is sexual relation with prohibited persons, that is, not the act itself is illegal (e.g. rape) but the person involved. *Tanāpuhl* is another example. *Tanāpuhl* acts are, among others, taking fire three steps to a corpse,[100] take fire into a house that is impure, or light fire in such a place,[101] to move a corpse not seen by a dog,[102] not to pull out a corpse from water,[103] to have sex with a menstruating woman,[104] sitting in water or walking in the rain by a menstruating woman.[105] In sum, these are acts violating rules of ritual purity which deserve the same punishment. Contrary to these cases where the common denominator is clear, other categories are less obvious. Take *ardush* as an example, which contains minor bodily injury and the wrong of a student of religious studies neglecting to learn the

---

[97]Snakes were stinging and tongues were ever eating (punishment of liars); killing his child and eating his brains (punishment of corrupt judge); suspended upside down from a tree and was ever masturbating (punishment of an adulterous man): Vahman (1986: 216).

[98]Jany (2007: 362–373).

[99]Hērbedestān, 12. 29.

[100]Shāyast-nē-shāyast 2. 40.

[101]Shāyast-nē-shāyast 2. 50.

[102]Shāyast-nē-shāyast. 2. 69. The sagdīd ("to see by a dog") is part of the burial ceremony the aim of which is to become convinced about the definite setting in of death.

[103]Shāyast-nē-shāyast. 2. 80.

[104]Shāyast-nē-shāyast 3. 26.

[105]Shāyast-nē-shāyast. 3. 28.

texts out of laziness.[106] Needless to say, there is not a single common thing in these two acts except their penalty which might bring them together.

The system is complicated further with the important consideration of whether the act was a habitual offence or not. If it was a habitual offence, its punishment was stricter than the sanction for the first crime. As a result, a pyramid of sanctions came into being, beginning with the lesser punishment and ending with the stricter. Again, an example helps to understand the logic. In the case of *āgrift*, the sanction for the first act was only ten lashes or the sum of compensation calculated on this basis. Next, it was followed by 20, 30, 60, 100 and 120 lashes and the compensation calculated on this basis, reaching the 180 at the top of the system for the seventh time of the same crime. Should a person commit the same crime for the eighth time, it was n o bnger an *āgrift*, but was put under the next more serious type of crime, that is, *ōyrisht*. As a result, such a person was punished as he would commit an *ōyrisht* for the first time. In sum, the frequency of a crime committed made it to belong to a stricter category than it originally belonged to. The system was absolute consequent: frequency of acts could transform a crime only to the next category but never to two or more grades ahead. It was, by contrast, impossible for a more serious crime to belong to a lesser category.

From this list, perpetrators of the most grievous crimes called *margarzān* are missing for unknown reason. Following the logic just outlined, *margarzān*s are of two kinds: one is when a crime in itself constitutes the perpetrator a *margarzān*, the other is when an act of lesser gravity, that is, *tanāpuhl* was committed frequently or continuously and it is the frequency of the act that makes its actor a *margarzān*. Apostasy is an example: it was a *tanāpuhl* and only after a year was his actor regarded as *margarzān*. This systemic logic explains why apostates were put to jail for a year where they were visited frequently by priests 'to convince them about the truth and their mistake to abandon Zoroastrianism'.[107] It was, of course, inquisition which Zoroastrian texts try to hide in vain. When a person was unwilling to confess his/her return to Zoroastrianism after a year, he/she was regarded as *margarzān* and was put to death. The majority of crimes the perpetrators of which were *margarzān*, without delay constitute breach of important purity laws such as carrying a corpse in rain,[108] carrying a corpse alone,[109] throwing a corpse into water and leaving it there, to ate carrion by a pregnant woman.[110] In addition to these, a soldier fleeing from the battlefield[111] and an assassin attempt against a king[112] was also put to death immediately.

---

[106]Hērbedestān, 17. 1.

[107]Nērangestān, Fragard II, 23. 4. Ibn Isfandiyār: (1942: 22).

[108]Shāyast-nē-shāyast 2. 9.

[109]Shāyast-nē-shāyast 2. 63.

[110]Shāyast-nē-shāyast 2. 76, 81, 85, 89, 105.

[111]The Christian martyrs refer to this custom Braun (1915: 43).

[112]Nyberg (1964: 10).

4.4.3 Law of Procedure

4.4.3.1 Criminal Procedure

Criminal and private procedures were separated during the Sasanian period or perhaps also earlier but we have no sources to prove. A procedure started either ex officio or on the request of a claimant, depending on the act committed. If the act was a crime against the king or the Zoroastrian church, the trial started ex officio and was conducted sometimes with extreme brutality. Confession enjoyed prominent significance which gave way to tortures during the trial to force out avowal from the accused. Such trials lasted for long years and there were long intervals between the hearings, during which torture was continued or the accused was just locked up in a prison. If the crime committed was apostasy, he was not left alone but visited regularly to "teach him the truth of Zoroastrianism", a form of inquisition already referred to. Officials had to report to the ruler about each phase of the trial to keep him informed. In cases of importance or in trials against kingly officials it was the king himself who passed the judgment.[113]

Administration of justice was a royal prerogative but kings did not, of course, adjudicate all cases. Royal courts were already established in the Achaemenid period which was continued and also modified by the subsequent dynasties. The involvement of priests and the establishment of ecclesiastic courts was an innovation of the Sasanians. Ecclesiastic courts, headed by *mōbeds*, played an important role in criminal procedures because some of the criminal acts consisted of violation of purity laws in which Zoroastrian priests were professionals without rivals. In such trials, *mōbeds* collected evidence and checked their accuracy, conducted the hearings and passed the judgment at the end of the procedure.[114] Personal involvement of the king became with the passage of time only an ideal which was emphasised in Zoroastrian writings as an essence and guarantee of justice which was, however, hardly realised. In theory, the last instance in a process was the king himself. This idea was implemented with the custom that everyone seeking remedy against an unjust sentence could appeal to the king directly in the first week of each month. It was a risky business to do because should the claimant lose his case and should the king decide against him and in favour of the officials and the courts, such a person faced severe punishment. This is what texts of Zoroastrian royal ideology tell us, but we do not know actual legal practice as not a single record has reached us from such hearings. The fact that the custom of royal hearing was abolished in the fifth century leads us to believe that it was not an effective means of control.[115]

A criminal procedure started with investigation which was in the competency of the *frēzwān*. His task was to identify the person of the culprit, to hear the witnesses

---

[113] Wiessner (1967: 167–168).

[114] Braun (1915: 198).

[115] By king Yazdagerd I: Braun (1915: 179).

and to arrest the accused.[116] The investigation consisted of collecting evidence—whatever they might be, to hear the accused and the witnesses, and to hold a view if necessary. After investigation, the procedure entered its next phase where the accused was informed about the accusation. The trial was conducted orally and the accused was given the right to defend himself against the charges. Both the arguments of the accuser and that of the accused were recorded in a document called *pursishn-nāmag* (question book).[117] The *pursishn-nāmag,* however, was more than only a record of statements, it was by contrast a document containing all the relevant information of a trial seeing as it contained the accusation and also the sentence of the court.[118] These documents were kept in archives which are unfortunately lost to us completely. When the trial was only about petty crimes, no *pursishn-nāmag* had to be produced, only if the court so wished. By contrast, in a trial of a *margarzān* such documents were compulsory.[119]

The procedure was left to the discretion of the court with no time limits or any attempt to protect the accused. Hearings were held at courts but accused were interrogated also between court hearings, often accompanied with tortures. Here, physical violence amounted to bodily mutilation when the tongue of the accused was cut off, his teeth were knocked out, and his bones were broken when his statement made his interlocutors angry (e.g. repeated apostasy).[120] Accused were put to jail or into house arrest between hearings, provided they were still alive after interrogations combined with torture. It is important to note that sentence to prison was not a sanction in itself, it was only a detention to prevent him fleeing or was a mean to force a confession if tortures resulted in no avowal.[121] For this reason, accused were put in heavy chains, were interrogated and beaten repeatedly each day, were left without food and drink for a long time, while visiting them and supplying them with food, drink and garment was prohibited, or were whipped with thorny branches of a pomegranate tree. Apostates were locked up together with robbers and murderers.[122] An official called *zēndānbān* was responsible for the order of prisons being personally liable for any detainee fleeing from the jail.[123] Despite this, some contemporary texts refer to the practice of corrupting *zēndānbāns* helping the detainees at least by providing them food and drink. Sometimes detainees were released on bail. Modern as it sounds it was in fact a way to free overcrowded prisons and to guarantee the continuation of the trial. Detainees were released and put to house arrest in exchange of a sum of money or two personal guarantors, obviously, from his family.[124]

---

[116]Macuch (1981: 202–203).

[117]Macuch (1993: 727), Braun (1915: 203).

[118]MHDA 34. 8–9.

[119]MHDA 34. 6.

[120]Braun (1915: 2–3).

[121]Braun (1915: 208).

[122]Braun (1915: 94, 101, 120, 122, 145).

[123]MHDA 13. 10–12.

[124]Braun (1915: 145–146), Hoffmann (1880: 37–38).

When court hearings ended, the court announced the sentence. We do not know the rules of deliberation if there were any. A sentence to death contained both the accusation and the sentence which specified also the way of execution. Capital punishments were executed usually by the sword by a professional executioner.[125] Sometimes condemned persons were tortured for the last time before their head was cut off: first fingers, then hands and feet were cut off, followed by decapitation only at the end. If a single executioner was unable to do his job, persons kept in jail for murder were ordered to implement death penalties.[126]

In addition to beheading, other means of execution were also applied. One among them was crucifixion,[127] which was the punishment for robbers and witches.[128] Sometimes condemned persons were cut to half (at the waist) or smeared with naphta and burned alive. We know a case where the eyes of the condemned were gouged out with a red hot needle and he was left to die, or was half dug into the earth and shot with arrows, or vinegar and mustard were squeezed into his eyes, mouth and nose.[129] Elephants were used to execute Christian martyrs and for the execution of killers and robbers.[130] Armed revolts were also punished by using elephants, proven by the case of Sus, a city which was completely devastated together with its inhabitants by elephants on the order of king Shapur II after an unsuccessful revolt. Pregnant women were not to be executed until delivery because children were innocent and were not let to die with their mother.[131] Executions were implemented in public where royal soldiers guaranteed order and guarded the corpses, a difficult business sometimes as huge crowds gathered in such places. Their failure ended in complete chaos which led some Persian kings to regulate executions in detail. A crucified person was left on the cross for three days and his corpse was removed from it only afterwards. When a king wanted to be convinced personally about the death of a person the head of his corpse was cut off and shown to the ruler.[132]

4.4.3.2 Civil Procedure

Litigation in private matters was legally possible but Zoroastrian ethics was not in favour of it as persons fighting for their rights with every means were of low esteem in the eyes of society at large. Partners wanted to avoid meeting at courts, which is the reason of some stipulations in contracts. One such a stipulation was, should one partner start a lawsuit it would make the contract in itself void.[133] According

---

[125]Braun (1915: 34, 55, 81, 95, 99, 104, 105, 148, 169), Hoffmann (1880: 16).

[126]Braun (1915: 84, 153, 176).

[127]Braun (1915: 185; 187; 268).

[128]Ibn Isfandiyār: (1942: 26).

[129]Braun (1915: 4, 56, 92, 183, 185). Hoffmann (1880: 33).

[130]Braun (1915: 183), Ibn Isfandiyār (1942: 26).

[131]Nyberg (1964: 10).

[132]Braun (1915: 3, 272), Hoffmann (1880: 112).

[133]MHDA 33. 3–7, 11–14.

to another agreement, between the parties one party definitely renounced his right to initiate a lawsuit against compensation.[134] With the help of such contractual conditions, the parties assured each other that they will settle their disputes not at court but by using other means of negotiations and compromises.

Despite this, the judiciary was at the disposal of the parties with a rather complex structure. Local courts and judges were called *dādwar* which seem to be the first instance and a general court. The number of law courts was determined by districts (*rōstāg*) in a royal decree. Courts had their own buildings called *mānāgān*.[135] *Mōbed*s had their role also in private litigations both as an appellate court against sentences of the *dādwar*[136] and as a particular court that had exclusive competency in some important cases of family law, such as appointing a *stūr* and a *sālār*.[137] It was also the *mōbed*'s task to authenticate private documents. The competency of the *rad*'s court was on the same footing with that of the *mōbed* excluding the appointment of a *sālār* and a *stūr*.[138] At the top of the judicial hierarchy was the *mōbedān mōbed* therefore no further appeal was possible against his sentence.[139] He enjoyed this power upon delegation since it was the king who was the supreme judge, at least, in theory.

There were also some persons at court with particular competencies. One such an official was the *āmārgar* who represented the king (treasury) in a lawsuit if the object of litigation was something belonging to the royal treasury. In addition to this, the *āmārgar* was responsible for recording and collecting taxes, and levy a fine for those who caused damage to things owned by the royal treasury.[140] Another was a representative of a party who was, however, not a legal representative. The designation of such a person was *jādag-gōw,* which indicates precisely the role such an advocate had in a lawsuit, that is, speaking in a case (like the original meaning of *advocatus*). A particular advocate was the representative of the poor called *driyōshān jādag-gōw,* whose function is not yet clear. It certainly had some religious connotation since Zoroaster himself was called the protector of the poor.[141] It was also an honorific title for provincial *mōbed*s who had it on their seals,[142] a seemingly widespread usage in Sasanian Persia.[143]

Litigation began with calling the defendant to court, which was the task of the plaintiff, courts did not call defendants to court ex officio. Women and slaves were no plaintiffs on their own right, they participated in a lawsuit together with their guardian. The date of the hearing was set by the acting judge[144] when parties were

---

[134]MHDA 17. 4–7, 22. 1–7.

[135]MHD 78. 2–11.

[136]MHDA 26. 14–15; MHD 110. 13–15.

[137]MHDA 26. 12–16.

[138]MHDA 26. 17–27. 4.

[139]MHDA 27. 4–5.

[140]MHDA 27. 13–28.3.

[141]Perikhanian-Garsoian (1997: 354).

[142]MHD 93. 7–9.

[143]Macuch (1993: 600).

[144]MHDA 25. 16–17.

obliged to go to court. Hearings could take place only in the morning and the judge had to make his decision up to noon of the same day at the latest.[145] If one of the parties was absent it was to be recorded in the protocol.[146] Absence for three times resulted in the loss of the lawsuit.[147]

When both parties arrived to court, the lawsuit began with the identification of the persons involved with information about age (literally: the blackness and whiteness of the hair), gender, name and seals of the parties.[148] After identification the procedure continued with the hearings of the parties: first the plaintiff (*pēshēmār*) *and* next the defendant (*pasēmār*) was heard. The terms for the parties reflect to their order of pleas at court as *pēshēmār* has the meaning "who speaks first" and *pasēmār* "who speaks later".[149] According to a very rigid protocol at court, parties had to stand three steps away from the judge. Pleas of the parties were recorded in court minutes which had to be sealed by both parties.

The process then continued with giving evidence. Among means of evidence, testimony of witnesses was the most common, but documents, oaths and ordeals could also be used. It was not always clear who bear the burden of proof, therefore it was the judge who had to decide about it on a case to case basis. Judicial formulas used in the contracts were of help since the burden of proof varied according to such formulas. It was a moral obligation to give evidence once one was called to court as witness. Should a witness neglect this obligation, it was recorded by the proceeding judge.[150] The number of witnesses varied according t o cases, and there was no general rule pertaining to their number: sometimes only a single witness was sufficient to prove a statement,[151] while in others three witnesses were necessary (e.g. in an oral testament). If a claim was proven neither by testimonies nor by documents, oath and ordeals were administered in order to continue the procedure. Oaths and ordeals were outside the competencies of the proceeding judge who was responsible for a lawsuit but not for such religious institutions. Therefore, if oath or ordeal was necessary, the judge suspended the procedure until oaths or ordeals were properly performed. Oaths were taken outside the court at a particular place, under the supervision of an official (*war sālār*) who recorded the taking of the oath, sealed the minutes about it and send it to the court which could then continue the process.[152] If the plaintiff deliberately hindered the process the defendant could demand compensation for wasting time.[153]

After taking evidences, the court announced its sentence. Here again, underlying social understanding how to resolve disputes outside courts has a strong impact on procedural law because until this time the parties could come to an agreement.

---

[145] MHDA 13. 17–14. 1.

[146] MHD 73. 13–74. 5.

[147] MHD 10. 16–11. 2.

[148] MHDA 25. 15–26. 11.

[149] Macuch (1981: 160).

[150] MHDA 25. 16–26. 12.

[151] MHD 107. 9–12; 12–14.

[152] MHDA 27. 7–9.

[153] MHD 77. 15–78. 2.

Therefore, a plaintiff had the right to ask for the suspension of the procedure with the consent of the defendant before the sentence of the court was announced.[154] Parties could also come to a formal agreement ending the case definitely at court. Such an agreement was, however, no hindrance to start the process again for whatever reason.[155] In the absence of such mutual agreement the court announced its judgment which ended the process at the first instance. Judgments were committed to writing in all probability by the clercs to the court, and their copies were kept in the archive.[156] After the judgment was announced, the parties could decide whether they accepted it or appealed against it. Should they appeal, the court of first instance forwarded the documents of the case to the court of appeal.[157] The case was then reconsidered by the court of appeal. If the judgment violated the laws of procedure, it was considered "not good",[158] but if it violated substantial law, it was considered a "false sentence". If the parties first accepted the judgment they could not make up their mind later and appeal. An accepted judgment came into force immediately, but courts did not execute it ex officio only on the request of the party winning the case. This makes the rule comprehensible as to why the winning party could decline the execution of the judgment.[159]

4.5 Zoroastrian Law in Modern Times

The fall of the Sasanians had enormous impact on Zoroastrianism and its law. Iran was no longer an independent state, not to speak of a great power but only one territory among the many in the caliphate. Zoroastrianism was no longer a state religion, but a tolerated (beyond limits) religion, the adherents of which decreased with time as more and more formal adherents converted to Islam. With the loss of state's support, its refined institutions and the position in power, Zoroastrian law was transformed into a customary law of an ever smaller religious community with no chance to official recognition, as Muslim courts and bodies did not execute the sentences of Zoroastrian (and Jewish and Christian) courts.

As a result, communal life was completely reorganised. A new priestly office called *hudīnān pēshōbāy* ("chief of those of good faith") emerged, who then took over the intellectual and administrative control of the Zoroastrian community. The powerful mobedan mobed lost function and was replaced by the *dastūr,* while teaching priests (*ērbad*) continued to exist since their task was to teach the next generation about ritual and law, among others.

---

[154]MHD 90. 6–8.
[155]MHD 74. 9–12.
[156]MHD 93. 3–4.
[157]MHD 3. 6–8; 110: 13–15.
[158]MHDA 14. 5–6.
[159]MHD 3. 1–3; 3–5; 5–6.

   The ninth and tenth centuries bear witness to an intellectual renaissance of Zoroastrian thinking, manifested in important works such as the *Dēnkard* and the *Dādestān ī Dēnīg*, encyclopaedic works about Zoroastrian theology, rites, ethics, prayer and law sometimes coloured with folkloric stories. In addition to these, a new literary genre known as the *riwāyat* came into being, which focused on ethics and law containing rules on civil and criminal matters while neglecting theology, cosmology and other religious topics. The aim of these works differed however from that of the legal works of the Sasanian period. *Riwāyats* were composed to have a comprehensive book about basic laws regulating family law, inheritance, and some purity issues touching also upon some criminal matters, despite the fact that Zoroastrian community was deprived of *ius gladii*. *Riwāyats* were composed in a structure of questions and answers which—though a widespread literary form in Zoroastrian work—could be more than a literary device and contain questions put to Zoroastrian leaders in everyday life. Legal precision, refinement and hair-splitting arguments are missing, as are references to legal schools. *Riwāyat* were not works written by judges and scholars to their peers about hard and irregular cases to show mastery in law but were comprehensive texts for the community at large to teach the faithful the basic principles and laws of Zoroastrian legal understanding. In short, *riwāyats* were manuals to keep the community and the Zoroastrian teaching intact in a constantly changing and sometimes antagonistic environment. *Riwāyats* were of eminent importance to preserve Zoroastrian identity of the isolated communities in Iran and later also in India. This is the reason why such works were produced up until the eighteenth century.

   Social and legal conservativism coupled with religious dogmas preserved Zoroastrian law, intact with very few changes during the centuries. With the disappearance of legal schools, legal pluralism ended, as did legal debates, with the result that only one interpretation continued to exist. Lack of sources prevent us from determining which doctrine fell into oblivion and why. What is discernible, however, is that some *kardag* rules remained in practice even to the detriment of *chāshtag,* which modified Zoroastrian law mainly in family law. One such a change concerned *chagar* marriage in which the natural father was not the legal father of the children produced, which might result in him dying without an heir. Pursuing their interest, *chagar*-fathers wanted to obtain the right to adopt at least some of their children to have legal heirs, an idea to the detriment of the rationale of *chagar* marriage. The issue was already disputed in late Sasanian times when *chāshtag* was against adoption but *kardag* in favour of it. With the passage of time, the understanding of legal practice became dominant against legal dogmatics and this is the reason why *riwāyats* have *kardag* rules in the belief that it corresponds to legal doctrines. Another more important change during these centuries was that *khwēdōdāh* was abandoned for reasons unknown to us. Perhaps it was the Muslim environment with its very strict rules against incest that contributed to it but we have no sources to prove it. Dogmatic precision was also abandoned in criminal law, where former categories and their complicated structure gave way to a more simplistic understanding which maintained only two categories, that of *tanāpuhl* and *margarzān*. This is of course no wonder, since without the right to implement sentences, criminal law as a topic lost its significance. Despite this, Zoroastrian community leaders did the best they could to prevent mass conversions, with the help of criminal law too. This is the reason why apostasy, a grievous crime also in Sasanian times, was preserved as a *tanāpuhl* crime, the culprit of which became *margarzān* after a year. Consequently, such a person lost all his property, the items of which were free to be kept by anyone as a property of his own.[160] Similarly, inter-community marriages were also prohibited to prevent women from embracing Islam and losing her and her children to the Zoroastrian community. Zoroastrian men too were prohibited to marry a Muslim woman, an act that qualified as *tanāpuhl* crime. If the child born to such couple reached maturity and remained a Muslim, his progenitor became *margarzān*.[161] All this remained on paper of course, as no Zoroastrian community could execute its sentence on a former Zoroastrian, newly converted Muslim person enjoying the protection of the Muslim society and its institutions. Zoroastrian leaders were perfectly aware of the contradiction between theory and practice of which they made no secret.[162]

Some Zoroastrian communities decided to leave Iran and this is how they came to Gujarat after a long and tiresome journey. Indian Zoroastrians (Parsees) now living in a completely different social and physical environment had to adapt to the new reality where inherited legal traditions were at times hard to follow. Since it is not law but ritual, purity laws and basic theological doctrines that constitute the essence of Zoroastrianism and the identity of its followers, emphasis was not on law and jurisprudence but on rituals, prayers and other cultic activities. Zoroastrian law was of course not abandoned as basic laws were continuously followed, but jurisprudence was de facto non-existent. Even priests were unversed in legal matters since they were—together with their co-religionists—poor, whose livelihood was secured by ceremonies, prayers and rites and had no energy for any science. In addition to this, they did not have access to ancient texts, firstly because there were none in India, secondly because they lacked the necessary qualification to read, understand and comment such texts. But they were safe and could make their living in India while preserving their identity. Things changed with the coming of the British who relied on the service of the Parsees who were willing to learn English and the new skills of the modern age and cooperate with them in both public administration and business. As a result, the influence of the Parsees became more proportionate than their number would indicate, being a very small community indeed. Pursuing their interest they successfully lobbied for a particular status and a personal law similarly to that of the Hindus and Muslims according to which they enjoyed autonomy in respect of personal and family law matters. The two basic laws, the *Parsee Marriage and Divorce Act* and the *Parsee Intestate Succession Act* were passed in 1865, which were in line with inherited customs and traditional legal and social understanding being sometimes at variance with contemporary requirements. The Act preserved the patriarchal model and ensured privileges to the males while discriminated women. This is why growing criticism was focused on the Act and

---

[160]REA 25.

[161]REA 42.

[162]REA 25.

even influential Parsee leaders regarded the correction of the Act desirable, resulting in the second *Parsee Marriage and Divorce Act* in 1936 which remained somewhat controversial. In the same year, the *Parsee Public Trusts Registration Act* was passed, an important law making the financial support of the Parsee community possible and therefore contributing to the material maintenance of the community.[163] Despite these moderate successes, Parsee communities preserved their ancient attitude to isolate themselves and did not allow anyone to enter. This issue was hotly debated in a lawsuit in which the wife of the industrial magnate Ratan Tata, a French woman claimed that she is a Parsee by her marriage to a Zoroastrian man and therefore the Act also pertained to her. The court however rejected this argument and did not regard her as a member of the Parsee community. This exclusivist attitude combined with low number of children, very late marriages and a rather high number of persons living outside marriage have been the factors that contribute to the further decline in numbers of the Parsee community.[164] The figures are alarming: while according to the 1951 Indian census they numbered 111,000 adherents, they lost 10% of this figure in a decade numbering only around 100,000 in 1961.[165] This trend is on going, now they are estimated to have around 60,000 souls with a 12% of decrease every decade in India, which produces 20% population growth in every census. No wonder they are worried due to the demographics.[166]

References

Sources

Back M (1978) Die Sasanidischen Staatsinschriften. Brill, Leiden. I. Shābuhr Ka^{c}ba-i Zardosht-i felirata (ŠKZ)

Braun O (1915) Ausgewählte Akten Persischer Märtyrer. Bibliothek der Kirchenväter, Band 22. Kempten, München

Gershevitch I (1959) The Avestan Hymn to Mithra. Cambridge University Press, Cambridge

Herodotos (1989) A görög–perzsa háborúk (ford. Muraközy Gyula). Európa Könyvkiadó, Budapest

Hoffmann G (1880) Auszüge aus Syrischen Akten Persischer Märtyrer. Leipzig

Ibn Isfandiyār (1942) Tārīkh-i Tabaristān. (ed. ^{c}Abbās Eqbāl). Tehran

Kent R (1953) Old Persian: grammar, texts. Lexicon. American Oriental Society, New Haven

Kotwal FM (1969) The supplementary texts to the Šāyest-nē-šāyest. Kobenhavn

Kotwal FM, Kreyenbroek Ph (1992) *The* Hērbedestān and Nērangestān, vol. I. Hērbedestān. Studia Iranica, Cahier 10. Paris

Kotwal FM, Kreyenbroek Ph (1995) *The* Hērbedestān and Nērangestān, vol. II. Nērangestan, Fragard 1. Studia Iranica, Cahier 16. Paris

Kotwal FM, Kreyenbroek Ph (2003) The Hērbedestān and Nērangestān, vol. III. Nērangestān, Fragard 2. Studia Iranica, Cahier 30. Paris

---

[163] Sharafi (2014: 75–82; 165–192).

[164] Irani (1968: 275–276; 283–284).

[165] Irani (1968: 275).

[166] http://www.bbc.com/news/world-asia-india-35219331.

Macuch M (1981) Das Sasanidische Rechtsbuch Mātakdān I Hazār Dātistān (Teil II). Wiesbaden
Macuch M (1993) Rechtskasuistik und Gerichtspraxis zu Beginn des siebenten Jahrhunderts in Iran. Die Rechtssamllung des Farrohmard i Wahrāmān. Wiesbaden
Nyberg HS (1964) Kār Nāmag-i Ardakhšēr: a manual of Pahlavi, 1–18. Harrassowitz, Wiesbaden
Perikhanian A, Garsoian N (1997) The book of a thousand judgements. A Sasanian Law Book. Persian Heritage Series, No. 39. Mazda Publishers, Costa Mesa
Sachau E (1914) Corpus juris des persischen Erzbischofs Jesubocht. Erbrecht oder Canones des persischen Erzbischofs Simeon. Eherecht des Patriarchen Mār Abhā. Verlaf von Georg Reimer, Berlin
Safa-Isfehani N (1980) Rivāyat-i Hēmīt-i Ašawahistān. A study in Zoroastrian Law. Harvard Iranian Series vol 2. Harvard University Printing Office, Cambridge
Tavadia J (1930) Šāyast-nē-šāyast. A Pahlavi text on religious customs. Hamburg
Vahman F (1986) Arda Wirāz Nāmag. The Iranian Divina Comedia. Scandinavian Institute of Asian Studies Monograph Series. Curzon Press, Malmö
Williams AV (1990) The Pahlavi Rivāyat accompanying the Dādestān ī Dēnīg. Part I: transliteration, transcription and glossary. Part II: translation, commentary and Pahlavi Text. Copenhagen

Literature

Altheim F, Stiehl R (1954) Ein Asiatischer Staat. Feudalismus unter den Sasaniden und ihren Nachbarn. Limes Verlag, Wiesbaden
Boyce M (1975) A History of Zoroastrianism, vol. I. E. J. Brill, Leiden
Carlsen BH (1984) The Cakar marriage contract and the cakar children's status in Matiyan I Hazar Datistan and Rivayat I Emet I Asavahistan. In: Middle Iranian Studies. Peeters, Leuven, pp 103–114
Dandamaev M, Lukonin W (1989) The culture and social institutions of Ancient Iran. Cambridge University Press, Cambridge
Daryaee T (2009) Sasanian Persia. The rise and fall of an empire. I. B. Tauris, New York
Fried L (2004) The Priest and the great king. Temple-Palace relations in the Persian Empire. Biblical and Judaic Studies, vol 10. Eisenbrauns, Winana Lake
Frye RN (1963) The heritage of Persia. The World Publishing Company, Cleveland and New York
Gnoli Gн (1989) The idea of Iran. Roma
Irani F (1968) The personal law of the Paris of India. In: Anderson JND (ed) Family law in Asia and Africa. George Allen Ltd., London
Jany J (2005) The four sources of Law in Zoroastrian and Islamic Jurisprudence. Islamic law and society 12, vol 3. Brill, Leiden, pp 291–332
Jany J (2006) The Jurisprudence of the Sasanian sages. Journal Asiatique 294/2. Paris
Jany J (2007) Criminal justice in Sasanian Persia. Iranica Antiqua vol XLII, pp 347–386
Kreyenbroek Ph (1994) On the concept of spiritual authority in Zoroastrianism. Jerusalem Stud Arabic Islam 17:1–15
Macuch (1991) Inzest im Vorislamischen Iran. Archaeologische Mitteilungen aus Iran, Band 24. Dietrich Reimer Verlag, Berlin
Olmstead AT (1948) History of the Persian Empire. The University of Chicago Press, Chicago
Perikhanian A (1983) Iranian society and law. Camb Hist Iran 3(2):627–680
Sanjana D (1888) The alleged practices of Next-of-Kin marriage in Old Iran. London
Schippmann K (1980) Grundzüge der Parischen Geschichte. Wissenschaftliche Buchgesellschaft, Darmstadt
Schippmann K (1990) Grundzüge der Geschichte des Sasanidischen Reiches. Wissenschaftliche Buchgesellschaft, Darmstadt

Sharafi M (2014) Law and identity in colonial South Asia. Parsi Legal Culture 1722–1947. Cambridge University Press, Cambridge

Tafazzoli A (2000) Sasanian Society. Bibliotheca Persica Press, New York

Watts JW (2001) Persia and Torah. The theory of imperial authorization of the Pentateuch. Society of Biblical Literature, Atlanta

Wiessner G (1967) Zur Märtyrerüberlieferung aus der Christenverfolgung Schapurs II. Vandenhoeck and Ruprecht: Göttingen

Wiesehöfer J (1996) Ancient Persia from 550 BC to 650 AD. I. B. Tauris Publishers, New York, London

Chapter 5
The Law of the Church of the East

5.1 Emergence of a New Tradition

How exactly Christianity spread to the East is unknown to us. Concerning the first two centuries, we mainly have legends at our disposal and it is difficult to separate historical facts and hagiography. Here the journey of Apostle St Thomas to India comes to mind which is regarded as a legend despite the fact that Indian Christians have called themselves Thomas Christians for centuries.

We get closer to the truth if we assume that the most important role in the eastern spread of Christianity was primarily played by the Jewish communities living in the eastern part of the Mediterranean, particularly in Syria. Here Damascus, the ancient metropolis was just next door together with a city like Antioch, one of the most important cities in the Roman Empire (later home to an influential theological school). Christianity had set out from here and moved towards the East, where arriving at the northern part of Mesopotamia reached the Roman–Iranian (Parthians, Sasanians) border. Crossing the border, Christianity reached Persia relatively fast and from here missions reached out to Central-Asia and finally to China.

Before moving ahead, it is worth clarifying terminology. The Church of the East is also known as the Eastern Syrian Church (so that it may be distinguished from the Western Syrian or Jacobite Church), the Persian Church, and also as Nestorian Church, but this designation is misleading. This Church had emerged actually as a result of the early missionary activities, that is, its beginning precedes Nestorius by centuries. In addition, Nestorius himself did not found a church, neither this nor any other. By contrast, he participated in a theological dispute in which he was defeated, and then subsequently moved to the desert where he lived alone in the hopes that his interpretation would finally emerge victorious. As a modern researcher put it: Nestorius was not Nestorian.[1]

After having clarified terminology, let us see, why is it worth studying this legal tradition? Basically it has three reasons: (1) because this Church had the

---

[1] Baum and Winkler (2003: 4).

© Springer Nature Switzerland AG 2020
J. Jany, *Legal Traditions in Asia*, Ius Gentium: Comparative Perspectives on Law and Justice 80, https://doi.org/10.1007/978-3-030-43728-2_5

largest territorial extension in the East; (2) because it can be considered as the last major transmitter of Near Eastern legal culture before Islam; (3) because this is an extraordinarily rich and complex legal tradition transmitting the culture of late Antiquity through scholars and thinkers whose works embraced law, theology, philosophy and medicine. The law of the Church of the East is linked to the Mesopotamian legal tradition not only because it shares some of the legal *koine* of the Ancient Near-East and Jewish law but because it encapsulates the Mesopotamian approach to society and law, that is, a social environment which left its traces on all Near-Eastern legal tradition including Jewish and Islamic law, too.

The beginnings of the Church of the East are known from legends which claim apostolic origin to it. These legends are widely known in the Near-East and even medieval chronicles preserved them. Accordingly, the East was evangelised by Apostle Thomas and his followers, Addai, Mari and Aggai. Addai and his disciples evangelised Edessa, Mosul and the vicinity of Nisibis, that is, Northern Mesopotamia, while Aggai concentrated on Southern Mesopotamia and Persia.[2] Following this tradition, the Persian Church was founded by Mari, the first *catholicos* and founder of the patriarchate in Seleucia-Ctesiphon (the capital of the Parthian and Sasanian Empires), whose work was continued by Papa, his disciple (historically, however, Papa can be identified only in the fourth century). According to the Doctrina Addai, the ruler of Edessa, Abgar fell ill and wrote a letter to Jesus asking for healing. Jesus praised his faith and promised to send one of his disciples to him. It was Addai who went to Edessa and healed the king and preached the Gospel which was continued after his death by Aggai, his disciple.

Though the story is a legend, the protagonists are historical persons. There were several rulers named Abgar in Edessa, and presumably it was Abgar VIII (177–212) who took up Christianity, a theory that cannot be proven for certain. But it was Abgar V who actually lived in the first part of the first century and was thus a contemporary of Jesus. The person of Addai is also a well-known figure as the most successful Manichean preacher in the Near-East, and it is in fact strange how the Doctrina Addai—a strongly anti-Manichean polemical work—put him into the Abgar legend as a disciple of Jesus. Perhaps this is the reason why only such a later work as the Chronicle of Eusebius (fourth century) has it, while it is missing from the Chronicle of Edessa. Modern scholarship sees little merit in these stories, and regards them as a late effort to lend apostolic foundation to the Church of the East and thus enhance its prestige.[3]

Despite this, it is no wonder that the Abgar legend links the spread of Christianity to Edessa, since it already reached the Parthian Empire via Edessa and Nisibis in the second century. In the third century, Christians were to be found in Adiabene, Khuzestan, Pars and the area around the Persian Gulf. The first Christian communities grew out of the local Jewish communities which had been present in Mesopotamia for centuries where they enjoyed autonomy as a result of a tolerant religious policy of the Parthian Empire. As the western part of the Silk Road passed through

---

[2]Moffet (1998: 45–70).
[3]Baum and Winkler (2003: 12–14).

Mesopotamia and Syria, long-distance trade offered excellent chances to locals, Jewish merchants and legal scholars among them. Christianity reached Mesopotamia with the very help of these merchants coming from Jerusalem, Antioch, and Edessa and moving toward to the East up to the Persian Gulf. The spread of Christianity was greatly facilitated by the common cultural and religious background as well as by the Aramaic language, the *lingua franca* of the age. In addition to the Jewish–Christian missions, Christians were sent to the East also by deportations, a source of internal tensions later. This happened because the Sasanians continued the offensive policy of the Parthians with more success and defeated the Romans in the third century. As a result of these victories, the population of some conquered cities and territories such as Antioch, Cilicia, Syria and Cappadocia were deported to Persia where they were allowed to live as merchants and craftsmen. These mainly Greek Christians maintained their identity and thus remained separate from the Jewish-Christian community. This separation lasted up to the fifth century and during these centuries both communities preserved their own ecclesiastic organisation and language. Perhaps this is the reason why Persian texts used different terminology in the third century when referring to Christians. It is our misfortune that we no longer exactly what the name of the Nazarenes (n'cl'y) and the Christians (klstyd'n) indicate, where Middle Persian has the word *tarsagan* (those who are afraid of/fear God) to refer to Christians in general.[4] Parallel to its spread, Christianity also developed its ecclesiastic organisation. Seleucia-Ctesiphon slowly rose above other episcopal seats, though the priority of this city was challenged by bishops of other communities. The above-mentioned Papa, however, asserted his will with the assistance of western (Roman) bishops with the argument that the imperial capital had supremacy. This is how Papa had finally become the first head of the Persian Church.

Internal disagreement was the lesser evil, international politics contributed to more problem to come. When Rome adopted Christianity as its state religion, the situation of Christians in Persia changed drastically. Protected by Roman rulers but suspected by Persian kings, Iranian Christians were torn between the superpowers and it was international politics that shaped their destiny. Intolerance intensified, sometimes resulting in violence and prosecutions depending on both domestic and international political situation. The first mass prosecutions took place during the long reign of Shapur II (309–379) which gave rise to a new literary genre in Iran, martirology, commemorating and praising the life and death of Christian martyrs.[5] Relations between the Persian court and the Iranian Christians remained controversial in the next century, too. Sporadic acts of violence sometimes gave way to cooperation when Persian kings relied on the services of bishops in diplomatic missions sent to the Byzantine court which, on its turn, also sent bishops for negotiations. Perhaps the most successful of them, Bishop Marutha, convinced the Persian king Yazdagerd I (399–421 CE) to put an end to prosecutions and to allow Iranian Christians to rebuild their demolished churches. In addition to this, Yazdagerd I called a synod to the capital which unanimously agreed to the creed and canons of the Council of Nicaea and put

---

[4] Asmussen (1983: 929, 947).

[5] Baum-Winckler 2003: 7-11; Hoffmann 1880; Braun 1915

an end to the dual organisation of the Aramaic and the Greek Christian communities. The bishop of Seleucia-Ctesiphon was elected as head of the Persian Church by the synod which confirmed metropolitan centres at Khuzestan, Prat de Maishan (Basra), Kirkuk, Arbela and Nisibis. As a result, a centralised Persian Church came into being, which followed western theology. International politics again left its hallmark on the life of Iranian Christians when after a new peace treaty between Theodosius II and Wahrām V, a new synod was organised which declared the independence of the Persian Church (424 CE). Accordingly, issues of the Persian Church were ultimately decided upon by the bishop of Seleucia-Ctesiphon and no appeal could be made against his decisions to Antioch, that is, Church authorities in the Roman Empire could not interfere into the business of the Persian Church. With this, the leading role of the bishop of Seleucia-Ctesiphon now called *Catholicos* was strengthened and Christians could not be (falsely) accused any longer with being unloyal to their Iranian homeland.[6] From the fifth century onwards, Church organisation consisted of five metropolitans and 80 episcopal seats headed by the *Catholicos*. However, this organisation did not mean a very strong centralization, as every bishop controlled his own territory independently and supervised the property of monasteries and churches.[7]

Organisational autonomy did not lead to an intellectual isolation of the Church of the East, which followed the theological disputes of the West dominated by the Antiochian and Alexandrian theological schools. Nestorius became Patriarch of Constantinople under such circumstances. The views of Nestorius were significantly influenced by the Christological interpretation of Theodore of Mopsuestia, a leading theologian of Edessa, refuted by Cyril of Alexandria. Ultimately, the issue was decided in favour of Cyril and his theology by the third Ecumenical Synod of Ephesus (431 CE) which removed Nestorius from his office. This theology was reinforced in Chalcedon (451 CE) after the failure of the Monophysite synod of Ephesus (called the Robber Synod), which decided otherwise (449 CE). The final decision was a complete defeat for the theological schools of Antioch and Edessa, the latter being closed down by Emperor Zeno (489). The teachers of the school of Edessa, being driven away from their home, crossed the Iranian border just nearby and this is how the school of Nisibis came into being. This school was established by Narseh, a former Zoroastrian who converted to Christianity and followed the theology of Theodore of Mopsuestia. As it was the school of Nisibis that dominated intellectual life among Iranian Christians, it is no wonder that the synod of Ctesiphon voted for the Christology of Antioch on the basis of the writings of Theodore. It was not Narseh but Bar Sauma ('Son of Fasting'), a teacher at the school of Nisibis and a determined opponent to the Alexandrian theology who was the mastermind of this decision. In addition to accepting the 'Nestorian' teachings, celibacy was lifted and marriage was made compulsory even for the clergy. With this latter decision, the spread of monasticism criticised by Bar Sauma and other Church leaders was slowed down and the constant critique of Zoroastrian priests against Christianity was made impossible

---

[6]Baum and Winkler (2003: 14–21), Vine (1937: 47–49).
[7]Spuler (1961a: 123).

(Zoroastrianism considers marriage a duty for everyone including priest and regards celibacy as an aberration of the natural order set by creation). Though the methods of Bar Sauma were profoundly criticised (his name was written upside down in the Jacobite manuscripts which shows both the hate felt by the Jacobites towards him and the influence of Iranian culture as it is the name of Ahriman, the Devil that was written upside down in Zoroastrian documents), his teachings were accepted in his Church. As a result, the Church of the East turned away from the earlier Jewish–Christian tradition favouring ascetic, monastic Christianity and became a Church much more adjusting to the contemporary Iranian cultural environment. The cost of all this was that monks unable to accept the resolutions turned their back to their own Church and joined the Monophysites instead.[8]

After having found its own organisational structure and theological understanding, the Church of the East entered its new epoch of history, that of consolidation and expansion reaching out to some Arab tribes in the west and Central Asia in the east. Internal consolidation took place under the leadership of Mar Aba (540–552), a former Zoroastrian dignitary who converted to Christianity and studied in Nisibis, Jerusalem, Alexandria, Athens, and Constantinople. Upon his return, he was teaching at the school of Nisibis and after having been elected *catholicos* he founded his own school in the Persian capital. Mar Aba was among the most important leaders of the Church of the East, who not only strengthened its organisation but contributed to its spiritual renewal as well. To this end, he had prohibited incestuous marriages known from Persian customary law (*khwēdōdāh*) which was widespread also among the families belonging to the Iranian Christian elite. This was an attack against Zoroastrian understanding of morality, family and law, and this is the reason why Mar Aba was accused by the Zoroastrian priests and sentenced to exile and house arrest by the court (this was, in fact, a sentence in his favour since as a convert he could have been sentenced to death because conversion from Zoroastrianism to any other religion was a capital offence). When not in prison Church leaders were continued to be sent to the Byzantine court for diplomatic missions. King Hormizd (579–590) sent *Catholicos* Ishoyabh II to Maurice to negotiate before the Byzantine-Persian war (604–628) while Queen Boran wanting to put an end to the decades of war, sent not only the *Catholicos* but almost the entire Church leadership including all the metropolitans to Aleppo to the Byzantine emperor for negotiations. The resolutions had brought about success and peace, the Church was once again strengthened and its messengers reached as far a s China. Under Ishoyabh II new metropolitan seats were established in Herat (today in Afghanistan), in Samarkand (Uzbekistan), in India and in China too. Parallel to this however, the Sasanian Empire was defeated and rooted by the invading Arab-Muslim army (651 CE) and the Church had to come to terms with the new masters of the Near East.[9]

In the early decades of Islamic conquest, Muslims were still a minority in the occupied territories where the population continued to practice its former religion.

---

[8]Vanyó (1988: 681–697), Baum and Winkler (2003: 21–30), Vine (1937: 21–42), Spuler (1961a: 126–128), Asmussen (1983: 942–944). For the history of the Jacobite Church see Spuler (1961b).
[9]Baum and Winkler (2003: 28–42), Vine (1937: 70–72).

Conversion to Islam was a long and complex process lasting for several centuries, thus Zoroastrianism remained the dominant religion in Persia. Adherents of the Church of the East preserved their religion too, though some changes had taken place in their life. The poll tax they had to pay was now called *jizya*, which was a privilege granted by the Muslims for adherents of the "people of the book" (*ahl al-kitāb*), that is, believers of the tolerated religions. To this end, caliphs and provincial leaders concluded contracts (*dhimma*) with non-Muslim communities (Jews, Christians) specifying the sum of poll tax they had to pay and other restrictions they had to follow which enabled them to live peacefully in Muslim territories. The legitimacy of these contracts rested on the agreements concluded by Mohammed in his lifetime called *dhimma*. Details of these contracts were elaborated later by Muslim legal scholars. The subject matter of the *dhimma* was the paying of the *jizya* and the numerous restrictions *dhimmī*s had to accommodate to. Restrictions are of two kinds, one symbolic and the other real. Symbolic restrictions are about garments, greetings, building of houses, religious symbols, drinking wine while real restrictions are related to blood money (the blood money of a *dhimmī* is just a half of that of a Muslim), marriage law (a *dhimmī* could not marry a Muslim woman while a Muslim could marry a *dhimmī* woman), criminal law (theft sanctioned according to Islamic law). The paying of *jizya* and the observance of the rules specified in the *dhimma* guaranteed *dhimmī* communities their religious and legal autonomy, at least in private law, and also some welfare institutions (hospital, school).[10] This was the legal and political environment that determined the history of the Church of the East for long centuries.

Respecting internal autonomy was rather a principle and not the practice in many cases, as caliphs played a particularly active role in appointing the *Catholicos* thus continuing the practice of the former Persian kings. Internal divisions among Christians contributed to this trend as rival groups made every effort to acquire the backing of their own candidate from the caliph. As Christian intellectuals worked at the courts of the caliphs as physicians and secretaries, at times very close to the person of the caliph himself, they could take their chance to influence the Muslim leader in his choice. It is revealing that 12 of the 30 *Catholicoi* in office were directly appointed by the caliphs. The outstanding leader of the period of transition from Persian to Muslim rule was Ishoyabh III (580–658) whose excellent diplomatic qualities were greatly needed in such a difficult time. Ishoyabh was already a member of the Persian delegation sent by Queen Boran to Byzantium and Al-Tabarī, the prominent Muslim historiographer of the tenth century credited Ishoyabh the diplomatic success of the return of the Holy Cross, carried away previously by the Persian army as booty, to the Byzantine emperor.[11] His diplomatic experience was needed both in negotiations with Muslim authorities and in setting internal disputes because the leading role of Seleucia-Ctesiphon was still challenged by some who were seeking independence (such as Simeon, the Metropolitan of Rew-Ardakhshēr). During this period, monastic life harshly condemned previously by Bar Sauma and other Church leaders, flourished and monasteries mushroomed. Currently 150 archaeological sites

---

[10]Cahen 1991: 227--28; Kruse 1979: 82; Al-Misrī 1994: 607–609.

[11] For this rather complex issue see the recent works of Stoyanov (2011) and Payne (2015: 177–189).

of monasteries are known. In the changing environment it was these monasteries that were the strongholds of Eastern Christianity which ensured not only physical protection but emerged also as centres of learning, particularly the Mar Abraham monastery on top of the Izla Mountain near Nisibis (for more see Chapter 2).[12]

The spread of Islam did not stop the further expansion of Christianity towards the east starting from Merw, a very important oasis town in eastern Iran where Christianity set foot already in the fourth century. From here, Christianity advanced to central Asia and this is the reason why the metropolitan of Merw (Elias) converted the Turks to Christianity in 680. Already in the last decades of the Sasanian period, Christian monks arrived to the Chinese court, presumably from Sogdia on the same trade roads that Sogdian merchants used during their business travels to China. First, Chinese emperors guaranteed freedom for Christianity in the belief that it was a religion teaching harmony among people and thus it could be of benefit for the Chinese society. As a result of this policy, even a monastery was built in the capital. The welcoming of Christianity continued in the subsequent decades and was promoted by the translation of Christian texts into Chinese. Yet Christianity remained foreign to Chinese society, the believers of which were mostly Sogdian and Persian merchants. It is no wonder, therefore, that Christianity was called 'Persian religion' in China. In addition, imperial attitude toward Christianity also changed in the subsequent centuries and Christianity died out without traces in China by the eleventh century. The same goes for India where the missionaries of the Church of the East were first welcomed and Christians enjoyed some privileges (were allowed to sit on carpet, could mount an elephant), moreover, their merchants had their own guilds to protect their interests in Kerala.[13]

During the ᶜAbbāsid caliphate (750–1258), both domestic considerations and international politics determined the situation of the Church of the East, that is, the situation resembled that of the Sasanian period. Subjective attitude of some caliphs coloured the picture further. The situation deteriorated under the early ᶜAbbāsīs: Caliph al-Mansūr either supported or locked up the *Catholicos*; Caliph al-Mahdī (775–785) persecuted Christians resulting in the first wave of emigration towards Byzantine territories, to be continued under Caliph al-Ma'mūn (813–833) as well. History repeated itself: Christians were believed to be the fifth column of the enemy by the Muslim elite just as Sasanian kings and priests thought the same about them previously. The case of Caliph al-Mansur is a good example to illustrate the point. He was convinced that Christians were praying night and day for the victory of the Byzantine armies and he could be convinced about the opposite only when the statement of Isha, a Christian physician was confirmed by Byzantine prisoners. Accordingly, Isha argued that they did not pray for Byzantine victory because the Byzantines hated them more than Jews. Byzantine prisoners of war agreed to this independently, saying that Nestorians were more Arab than Byzantines. This confession, however, came too late because the caliph had many Christian churches demolished already. Reconstruction was left to *Catholicos* Timotheos I, who obtained

---

[12]Baum and Winkler (2003: 42–44).
[13]Baum and Winkler (2003: 46–57).

his office by corruption yet became one of the greatest Church leaders. He transferred his office to Baghdad, to the new capital where he had a new residence built on the right bank of River Tigris (*Dayr al-jathaliq*: the monastery of the *Catholicos*), though consecration was left at the church of Seleucia-Ctesiphon (Kokhe) where deceased *Catholicoi* were continued to be buried. During his long term in office for 43 years, he had to cooperate with five caliphs of whom Harun al-Rashid held him in greatest esteem and supported the reconstruction of churches. In addition to rebuilding churches, Timotheos paid attention to missions as his missionaries reached India, China and the Yemen. He founded a metropolitan seat in China and Tibet, and a bishopric in the Yemen. During his leadership, the Church of the East reached its heyday with millions of adherents, 27 metropolitans and 230 *dioceses*. Timotheos was not only a talented administrator but also a gifted scholar who collected manuscripts from all over the world (even from rival Byzantium) and produced works on law and philosophy, some of which have been lost by now. The ninth and tenth centuries witnessed rather cooperation than tensions when Persian Christians obtained rather high positions in the caliph's court. We can find a good number of Christians among the physicians of the caliph because medical science was on a high level among Christians who were outside court intrigues and caliphs could thus trust their lives to them. Christian intellectuals took up jobs in provincial administration too, since there was a great need for literate and educated people to run the administrative system smoothly. They could even be promoted to offices higher in rank, but if they wanted more (to become vizier) they had to convert to Islam which did in fact happen in some cases. Such advancement was seen by envy and hatred by both Christians and Muslims. Egyptian Christians accused the adherents of the Church of the East to contributing indirectly to their oppression because they took up positions in the administration of the caliphate and thus cooperated with their oppressors. Muslims also condemned the progress of Christians and did not understand why non-Muslims administered a Muslim state. To reduce tensions, caliphs lowered the number of Christians in office from time to time. In addition to their official positions, the wealth of Christians was another source of envy as diligent Christian craftsmen and merchants often lived better than Muslims did.[14]

Despite this, the number of Christians continuously decreased due to conversion to Islam and emigration, proven by the sum of *jizya*, the poll tax. In the tenth century, the sum of the poll tax paid was 130,000 dirhams, yet a century later it was only 16,000 dirhams. The Mongol invasion and destruction contributed to more losses of souls, despite the fact that the Mongol elite was favourable towards Christians. During the siege of Baghdad, for example, the Mongols spared the life of Christians and Shiites, which made the false impression that Christians were allied to the Mongols. It was, however, not political alliance but religious sympathy that was the reason behind, because some members of the Mongolian ruling family were Christians, for example Doquz Khatun, the wife of Hulagu and their children. The new masters of the Near-East, the Mongols did not follow Islamic law and its restrictions of religious minorities, thus making Christians regain their freedom. This situation, however,

---

[14] Vine (1937: 100–103), Baum and Winkler (2003: 59–62).

came to an end soon when Ghazan Khan, the ruler of the Iranian Mongols embraced Islam and revived the old restrictions. Yet, this is the period of the last intellectual blossoming since Abdisho bar Brika, the last polymath of the Church of the East lived at that time. Abdisho bar Brika is the author of a Church history, a two volume law book and a work on calendar. After his death (1318), no scholar of his stature was born and the attacks of Timur Lenk and his devastations ultimately reduced the Church of the East into the status of an insignificant minority who live in small communities o n he spot where it emerged, in Northern Mesopotamia.[15]

5.2   Intellectual Life: Sciences and Schools

Intellectual activity in the Church of the East concentrated, predictably, on theology, already from the third century onwards. The centre of learning was the city of Nisibis near the Roman–Persian border where a lesser known teacher called Ephrem began to teach. His disciples gathered around him and this is how the school of Nisibis came into being, which lacked any organisational and institutional framework in the beginning (similarly to the Jewish and Muslim schools).

When the invading Persian army conquered Nisibis, local Christians fled to Edessa, a safe haven on the other side of the border on Roman territory (363 CE). Here the school now called as the school of Edessa, continued to flourish and reach maturity in the fourth century. The influence of the school of Antioch increasingly asserted itself in Edessa in the early fifth century and therefore works of Theodore of Mopsuestia and his master, Diodorus of Tarsus were translated into Aramaic, paving the way to the school's "Nestorian" understanding. After the defeat at the Synod of Ephesus, the school of Edessa was increasingly losing its ground and Emperor Zeno ultimately had it closed down (489 CE), which made the members of the school once again to cross the border, now back to Persia. Here they re-established the school of Nisibis under the leadership of Narseh and Bar Sauma, the Bishop of Nisibis. The school was organised along the pattern of the school of Edessa and its first teachers and students were also recruited from among the refugees coming over to Persia. The organisational genius of Bar Sauma and the scholarly reputation of Narseh developed the school soon into the intellectual centre of the Church of the East where 800–1000 students registered in its heyday. After this time, all the leaders of the Church of the East studied at Nisibis. One of the reasons of its success was discipline. Curriculum was regulated, the three-year training included writing, reading, rhetoric, philosophy and Biblical exegesis. The statutes of the school were drawn up by Narseh (called 'the Harp of the Holy Spirit' because of his lovely poems), the first head of the school, and by one of his follower in office, Henana, an autonomous personality with the quality of a genius.[16]

---

[15]Spuler (1961a: 159–162), Baum and Winkler (2003: 69, 84–103), Vine (1937: 111).

[16]Baum and Winkler (2003: 26–28); for a detailed history of the school under Narseh and Henana see Vööbus (1965: 45–121, 234–276).

Accordingly, the school was headed by the *rabbaita*, elected annually. In controlling the school the *rabbaita* had to cooperate with the council of leaders (*rabban*) and other leading personalities outside the council. The decisions of the leadership had to be accepted without dispute and whoever challenged them was excluded from the community. *Rabbaitas* were under the control of the community in order to prevent misuse of power. This is the reason why leaders of the school could only make decisions in monetary matters in the presence of three witnesses and they were also not allowed to make decisions on punishments alone, only in concert with the council. Members of the school had to observe celibacy, the violation of which resulted in immediate exclusion from the community, similarly to theft, intrigue, libel or riot. In addition, school members were prohibited to have commercial or industrial activities, were not allowed to cross the Roman border under any circumstances, and could not lend money for usury. They lived in their own (single or plural) cells and were not allowed to live in the city, but had to join the community while taking their meals. This was an important point of public life, as several statutes stress the importance of communal eating and learning, and prohibit separation. It goes without saying that visiting the city taverns and public gardens, and participation in any urban entertainments were also prohibited. The statutes regulated hairdo (no one should have his head shaved or of long hair but tonsure was compulsory), and garments. It was prohibited to teach women or even to talk to them. As theology was believed supreme to any other science, students of the school of Nisibis were not allowed to live together with medical students because "books of the craft of the world should not be read with the books of the holiness in one light."[17] Teaching was free of charge but in order to allow for the students to cover their own and their families' expenses, the school had a break for the duration of the agricultural works (from August to October),[18] a model to be found also in the Jewish and Islamic centres of learnings.

This system established in the formative period continued for centuries with little change. The first significant reform of the school took place at the beginning of the Islamic period, during the leadership of Ishoyabh III, who changed the statutes of the school and added medicine, logic and music to the subjects taught. In addition, translation activity remained important for centuries. Greek and Persian texts were translated into Syriac to ease communication and maintain doctrinal unity. This is the reason why the bishop of Rew Ardakhshēr (Pars) translated a series of writings into Syriac in the early fifth century and sent them to the East and to India in order to safeguard missionaries there.[19] Modern scholars also benefit from this because a significant number of documents have reached us only in their Syriac translations since the original works (composed in Middle Persian) are now lost.

In addition to the theological school of Nisibis, other centres of learning also emerged. One among them was the Mar Mari monastic school, the most famous scholar of which was Abu Bishr Matta b. Yunus, who engaged in logic and Aristotelian philosophy. He was also known to his Muslim peers and highly esteemed

---

[17]Based on the statutes of Narseh and Henana, in Vööbus (1962: 73–101).

[18]Vööbus (1965: 109).

[19]Baum and Winkler (2003: 26–27, 44, 53).

by the famous Muslim traveller and scholar al-Bīrūnī. Abū Bishr Matta b. Yunus translated the Poetics of Aristotle and most probably all the subsequent Arabic, Syriac, Hebrew and Latin translations go back to this work. In the course of the seventh century a new intellectual centre, Beth Abe also emerged, where attention was primarily dedicated to issues of monastic life which gained growing significance in both preserving the tradition and scholarly life from the beginning of the Islamic period. *Catholicos* Giwargish (George) I, successor to Ishoyabh III in office, asked one of the monks living there to collect the biography and sayings of Egyptian monks which he did. To this core of hagiographical material, biographies of Mesopotamian monks were added later. Henanisho, successor to Griwargish produced homilies, letters, and a commentary to the Organon of Aristotle. *Catholicos* Timotheus I, a talented administrator was engaged also in scholarly activity. He produced 200 letters out of which 59 has reached us, in which he discussed various problems of theology and philosophy testifying to the influence of Aristotle (Poetics and Rhetorics). For a legal historian, however, it is his law book which is of primary importance, discussed in the next paragraph. He also wrote a refutation to the resolutions of the Synod of Chalchedon and a theological dispute with Caliph al-Mahdi. According to the framework story, the dispute took place in the caliph's court and lasted for two days. Since such disputes were organised frequently at the courts of the caliphs with the personal involvement of the Muslim ruler, it may reflect to such discussion and could be more than only a literary form necessary to the exposition of the subject matter. Such discussions and refutations show that Muslim intellectual life was more tolerant in the Middle Ages than it is today permitting, even encouraging, theological disputes with scholars of other creeds who were not persecuted because of their views but hold in esteem because of their prudent participation. Such discussions would be impossible however, without the profound knowledge of Arabic, since no Muslim was acquainted with Syriac, the language of the Church of the East. Therefore, we can witness a shift from Syriac to Arabic in this period. Works of polemics with Islam were already written in Arabic and Christians spoke Arabic in their daily life anyway. As a result, Syriac remained only the language of liturgy and learning for centuries. The polemical work against Mohammed and the Qur'ān of Rabban al-Nasranī ('the Christian'), secretary to the *Catholicos* already indicates this tendency, followed by ᶜAmmār al-Basrī in his apology for the Holy Trinity and by Kashkari Israel in his work against Mu'tazilite doctrines. Ishaq al-Kindī followed suit in both Christian apologetics and in critiques of Islam. Al-Kindī was a well prepared apologist who knew the Koran and Mohammed's life profoundly, causing his partner some unease in their (fictitious or real) dispute. Al-Kindī's criticism focused on the wars waged in the name of Islam which he compared to the Bedouin raids, Mohammed's polygamous marriage with fifteen wives, the contradictions in the Koran, and the pilgrimage to Mecca which ultimately rooted in a pagan Sun-cult. He compared the legal principles and institutions of Islam with Christian thoughts, and contrasted the idea of holy war with the Christian doctrine of love, the Paradise promised to the soldiers dying in war with the fate of the Christian martyrs. He came to the conclusion that Mohammed did not teach anything new that (Christian) children did not learn at school, but even this was falsified by successive generations of Muslims. Al-Kindī's work was known both among Muslims and in Europe: Al-Bīrūnī, a Muslim scholar of reputation made reference to it, and Peter of Toledo produced a Latin translation of the work (1141). Theodore Bar Konai was also engaged in Christian apologetics and in pointing at the weak points of other religions. In doing so, he criticised not only Islam but Zoroastrianism too. He was also the author of a work on ecclesiastic history, which has become a model to works of the same topic.[20]

Jundeshāpur, an ancient city funded by the Sasanians was also an important centre of Christian learning, where we can find schools of theology and medicine. The school of theology was referred to first at the end of the sixth century but the medical school may have been older. In this school, the tradition of the Greek, Syrian and Indian medicine were known, making it the centre of learning in this field. The significance of the Jundeshāpur medical school is proven by the fact that all important physicians studied there during the centuries. Jundeshāpur was as important in medicine as Nisibis was in theology. The school had a huge library which was later shifted to Baghdad.[21] This school produced dynasties of physicians, the most talented of which were the doctors of the caliphs. One such a family was the Bochtisho dynasty, the members of which were the caliph's physicians for generations. The founder of the dynasty, Giwargish, was invited to Baghdad by Caliph al-Mansur where, in addition to his activities in healing the ruling family, he translated Greek works on medicine. His son entered the service of Harun al-Rashid, while his grandson Gabriel lobbied to relax the restrictive rules pertaining to Christians making use of his close contact to the caliph as his doctor. Gabriel managed to obtain permission to bring the bones of Nestorius to Seleucia-Ctesiphon, in vain since his place of burial was forgotten by that time. Gabriel had contact with the polymath Hunayn ibn Ishaq, another outstanding scholar and founder of a dynasty of physicians. Hunayn, the descendant of an Arab tribe was no member of the school of Jundeshāpur but came from Baghdad. In his youth he travelled a lot and visited scholarly centres of fame, among others Constantinaple and Alexandria. Upon his return, he became the physician of Caliph Al-Mutawakkil, yet he is primarily known by his scientific works. Hunayn ibn Ishaq was a gifted translator who started to translate scholarly works at the age of 17 as he knew Arabic, Persian, Syriac and Greek. He translated altogether 260 works, and was author of another one hundred. He had made progress particularly in ophthalmology, an important field of medicine in the Near-East because diseases of the eye were widespread due to the physical environment. His talent in translation was inherited by his son and grandson too, thus the translation of the works of Aristotle, Galen, Euclid, and Ptolemy is the product of his dynasty. According to a letter of Hunayn, 129 of the altogether 400 works of Galen were translated into Arabic or Syriac of which he himself translated one hundred. In addition to his talent in languages, what made this remarkable work possible was his efforts to collect and preserve manuscripts to which he has made access during his travels.

---

[20]Baum and Winkler (2003: 45, 61–68).

[21]The Iranian government re-established the university on its antique antecedents in 1955. The university is still in operation in Ahwaz, running an English-language international periodical in microbiology (Jundeshapur Journal of Microbiology).

In addition to works on medicine, he produced a book on logic and history which recounts the events from Adam to his own age. His excellent knowledge of languages made it possible for him to write works on lexicography and linguistics too. His translation of the Septuagint made him famous among Muslim scholars, praised by its outstanding quality by the historiographer al-Mas⁶ūdī. Unfortunately, this work is now lost. Hunayn ibn Ishaq had written Christian apologetics, rejected to embrace Islam, and argued against the practice of such religious opportunism (obviously not everyone was as steadfast among his contemporaries as he was). In the course of his long and prolific scholarly activity, he made his mother tongue, the language of the Bedouins suitable for scientific discussions by developing new terminology and adding neologisms and foreign terms to it. No wonder, therefore, that Hunayn ibn Ishaq is called the "Erasmus of Islamic renaissance" where Islamic refers to a period of Islamic history and not to the religious affiliation of its participants.[22] In sum, scholars of the Church of the East preserved and transferred the philosophical and medical heritage of Antiquity to the post-Hellenistic and early medieval Near-East with the translation of its works to Syriac and to Arabic the significance of which in cultural history cannot be overestimated.

In addition to theology, philosophy and medical science historiography was also a field of learning, though less emphatic. The Church of the East followed the Persian custom to base the calendar on Alexander the Great, the starting point of which was 1 October 312 BCE, though some scholars started to count the years on the date of the death of Jesus in 30 CE. Christian scholars produced mainly local histories. One of them is the Chronicle of Arbela covering the period between 100 and 550 but its accuracy is subject to scholarly dispute. The Chronicle of Edessa is a local history of Edessa between 130 and 540. Perhaps the most significant historical source is the Chronicle of Seert named on the episcopal seat of Kurdistan, Seert, where its manuscript was found by Addia Scher, the scholar bishop in the early twentieth century. The text that is known to us is about ecclesiastic history and the Roman–Persian wars. Equal in importance is the world history of Elias bar Shinaya in Arabic and Syriac, an eleventh-century polymath, the only manuscript of which is to be found in the British Museum. This work relies on earlier Byzantine, Syriac and Arabic works.[23]

5.3 Jurisprudence and Legal Sources

There was no such thing as jurisprudence in its own right having its own methods, sources, principles and ways of thinking. By contrast, jurisprudence had to be situated in this web of science where various disciplines developed in constant interaction to each other. This is the reason why there were no legal scholars as such but polymath, who were masters in various fields, the most talented among them in theology,

[22]Spuler (1961a: 147–148), Baum and Winkler (2003: 65–67).
[23]Baum and Winkler (2003: 69–70).

medicine, philosophy and law. Law was not regarded as an autonomous field of study but as part of theology and morals (similar to the medieval European understanding) with the consequence that the majority of outstanding legal scholars were *Catholicoi* and theologians.

The law of the Church of the East evolved in a particular social and political environment, because, contrary to the European experience, it could not rely on a state and society in which Christian thinking was dominant. The law of the Church of the East developed in a less supportive environment during its entire existence. Relative autonomy was granted and persecution was not a constant but rather a hectic threat, depending on a variety of domestic and international factors. Despite this, Christian population remained something as a secondary citizen with limited rights and competencies but a lot of obligations to follow. To this, one can add the general problems of the entire region which affected, obviously, Christians as well (economic decline, Mongol invasion, etc.). Legal environment was also challenging because both Persian and Islamic laws were well-developed systems and should the law of the Church of the East not react properly to their challenges, Christians would turn away from their own legal system and would follow that of rival religious communities (Jewish communities faced the same problem). As a result, the law of the Church of the East was not merely a law on church organisations and institutions, but a legal system that had to regulate a variety of mundane affairs, including marriage, inheritance and commerce. Institutions were adapted to this situation, too. To prevent Christian merchants to go to Muslim courts to settle their disputes, bishops were granted the power to settle such conflicts as well (*episcopalis audientia*). This could be the reason why two important law books on Roman law were included in the law of the Church of the East (Sententiae Syriacae, Syrian-Roman Law Book). In addition to commercial activity, the protection of the community was another challenge law had to face. Mixed marriages and apostasy were the two main channels through which Christian community could lose its members. It is not surprising, therefore, that Church leaders made every effort to prevent their decrease in number to which law was a tool. This explains why topics of mixed marriages and its legal consequence in family law and inheritance have an important place in this legal system. These were elements that separated the Christian community from their fellows.

There were, however, a lot of common things, too, which brought the law of the Church of the East closer to the Persian, Jewish and Islamic law, that is, to its legal and social environment. As demonstrated in the previous chapters there are a lot of similarities among Near-Eastern legal systems, both in principles and institutions which I labelled legal *koiné*. These are elements of social life that are shared by all communities in the region irrespective of religion. To illustrate: though monogamy separates the Christian community from all other Near-Eastern societies which follow polygamy, customs related to marriage are rather similar (arranged marriages by the parents, negotiations about marriage already in childhood, contracts about propriety rights, rules for dressing, etc.). In short, the law of the Church of the East is a unique, yet at the same time very Near-Eastern, legal system that shares a variety of legal *koiné* with its neighbours but developed some particular institutions that make it distinctive from its rivals.

Sources of the law of the Church of the East fit into this general pattern. Sources are of three kinds: (1) late Roman legal texts in their eastern reception; (2) decisions of synods and law books with their summary (synodica); (3) compendia edited by scholars focusing on some legal problems (primarily in family law) or producing a comprehensive survey of the law. Two important texts belong to the first group. One is the Sententiae Syriacae containing Roman law from the time of the Dominate. Its legal material originates from the late third century to which supplements were added in the following decades. It contains paraphrases and laws in a simplified style. This legal collection was written in Greek and then translated into Syriac. The other text is the Syrian–Roman law book that came into being about a century later. It was composed also in Greek, but was later translated into Syriac, Arabic and Armenian, making its influence broader than that of the Sententiae Syriacae. This law book does not contain pure Roman law but its eastern reception, that is, Roman law modified by local legal practice. Its title, Leges Constantini, Theodosii et Leonis, can be, according to Walter Selb, only a later addition.[24] According to the modern editor and translator of the text, the author lacked the intellectual capacity to put the legal material to writing in a terminologically correct way, therefore the text was difficult to understand and confused in many places. At the same time it shows how Roman law was interpreted and put into practice in the eastern Mediterranean where the text was born. The law book may have been written in the late fifth century (476), but its name is misleading as there are only five references in the text of 130 articles which could be linked to either Constantin or Theodosius. The popularity of the text is due to its simplicity in both language and content which made the text intelligible and the law applicable in the social and economic environment of late Antique Syria, and to its Roman legal elements that could be used also after the Schism among Christian (the Church of the East, the separation of Monophysites) which would have been impossible with later legal texts such as those of Justinian. In fact, while the Syrian–Roman law book was translated into several languages and even used in the Middle Ages under Muslim rule, Justinian's codification had no traces whatsoever in the Near-East. For a modern researcher the merit of the law book lies rather in its unique comments added to the text of the law by its editor. In these notes he added the legal practice of his age as comments to the Roman legal rules allowing us not only to know the law in books, but also the law in action which makes it a rather unique legal source.[25]

The second group of sources contain legal materials of the synods, a genre known in every Eastern ecclesiastic law. Synodikon is the law of synods in chronological order, a collection of the law of the Church of the East composed in the eleventh century with 80 titles on 2000 manuscript pages. It contains, among others, the synodic canons of Ankyra (24), Neokaisarea (14), Nicea (14), Antioch (25) and the synodic decisions of the Church of the East which were recorded under the name of the presiding *catholicoi* (Dadisho, Yahballaha, Babai, Mar Aba, Ishoyahb, etc.). In addition to synodic law, the Synodikon contains some parts of the Syrian–Roman

---

[24]Selb (1993: 180–181).

[25]Bruns and Sachau (1880: 317–333).

law book, tractates dealing with laws of inheritance, and relevant letters of some *Catholicoi*. The entire work is still not edited and translated but some parts of it are.[26]

The first work dedicated only to legal issues is the small tractate of Mar Aba, a convert from Zoroastrianism who became the leader of the Church of the East after long journeys and studies during the reign of the Persian king Khusrau I (531–579). In this period, Zoroastrianism was again reinforced and understood as the ideological basis of the rigid late-Sasanian society and political structure. It was this environment in which Mar Aba's work on marriage law came into being, the aim of which was, obviously, to defend Christian morals against Zoroastrian understanding of family and sexual relations. As a former Zoroastrian believer, Mar Aba was well acquainted with Zoroastrian teachings on family in general, and its elements in particular that were unacceptable for Christians, such as polygamy and incest (*khwēdōdāh*). These practices however, seem to enter Persian Christianity, and this is the reason why Mar Aba wrote a tractate on family law to reject, refute and prohibit them. Mar Aba's work was targeted primarily against Persian customs, but he rejected Jewish customs based on the Old Testament both of which were contrary to Christian understanding of family relations. Consequently, he prohibited every form of incest elaborated in Persian law (marriages between father and daughter, mother and son, siblings, etc.), bigamy, and levirate. Anyone who married the wife of his father, his daughter-in-law and sister should be expelled from the Church. Mar Aba granted them a period from one month to one year to have time to settle their affairs. Should they not dissolve the prohibited marriages, they were excommunicated from the Church. This was seen as an attack on Zoroastrianism and this is the reason why Zoroastrian authorities demanded him to withdraw these laws and to prohibit him from exercising legal authority over Christians in civil cases. Mar Aba rejected these demands and he was, therefore, put on trial. Though not executed, he remained in prison for ten years. Just some days after his release from prison he died as a consequence of the tortures suffered there.[27]

Another short tractate on practical legal issues is that of Henanisho, who was elected *Catholicos* in 686 amidst internal and external difficulties. He had to balance between rival Muslim groups struggling for power and to defend himself against his own rival, Iohannes, Bishop of Nisibis who ultimately achieved his removal in 693. During this short and politically hectic period in office, Henanisho succeeded in compiling a law book primarily for practical purposes.[28] The brief text contains sentences, letters and laws related to a given case, mainly in family law because according to the author's introduction his intent was to protect widows and orphans with its help.[29]

An important collection is the law book of *Catholicos* Timotheos, compiled upon the request of bishops in 805. It was written in dialogue, a popular style in Persia

---

[26] Selb (1981: 58–63) has all the 80 titles.

[27] Sachau (1914: XXII–XXVII).

[28] Sachau (1908: VI–XII).

[29] Selb (1993: 182).

proven also by Zoroastrian law books. The text soon became an authority quoted for centuries both in daily routine and in producing new legal compilations. As the Syriac language was not spoken any longer after the tenth century, Ibn al-Taiyib translated it into Arabic in order to ensure its continuous use. The text contains 99 articles dealing mostly with marriage and law of inheritance.[30] In his preface, the author apologises for writing this treatise which makes the text rather curious. In his view there would be no room for law if people followed the religious ideals because in that case it is love and not egotism that would dominate social interaction thus litigation would not emerge. In an ideal society, no law is needed but Timotheos is aware that reality is different and Christians also litigate on mundane affairs hence their relations have to be settled by law. This antinomian attitude is to be found also in other Christian law books (see, for example, Ishobokht) and is shared by various Asian societies as well (e.g. Confucianism). The author goes on to say that he should have written this compilation previously but illness and other obstacles prevented him from doing so and this is the reason why he wrote it only at the end of his career at the age of 65.[31]

The fame of the text is certainly not due to its cohesion and structure. Unfortunately, the final editing of the text is missing and this is the reason why there are issues that emerge at least three times in various parts of the text (like the share of the widow from the heritage of her deceased husband). On the other hand, contradictions are missing too, and Timotheos gives the same answer for the same question every time. This structural imbalance may be due to the fact that dialogues reflect reality and these questions and answers might preserve the very questions Christians put forth to their leader. As these questions and answers were put together later, no one checked that the same problem was already dealt with in another question. No wonder, therefore, that it is casuistic that dominates the work from which academic interest is completely missing, particularly in the law of inheritance where any kind of system is missing. Timotheos just answered properly all the questions which emerged in a particular situation (what if the deceased had sons, daughters and widow but one of his parents is also alive (Art. 66); how to distribute the wife's bequest among her relatives (Art. 47, etc.)) but made no attempt to create a system. Without references we do not know the basis of the answers, however detailed and precise they are. Timotheos was seemingly more concentrated on the legal precision of his answers, while cared less to demonstrate their authenticity. This casuistry in the field of law of inheritance makes the law book similar to the Koranic legislation on inheritance which is also a compendium of questions and answers without any attempt to create a system (which was left to generations of Muslim legal scholars).

In addition to producing his own law book, Timotheos also translated a law book written in Middle Persian into Syriac, enabling modern research to study the text since the original was lost. We do not know the reason behind but it may be related to a constant power struggle between the *Catholicoi* in Seleucia-Ctesiphon and the

---

[30] Sachau (1908: XVII–XX).

[31] Introduction to Timotheos, in Sachau (1908: 55–56).

Church leaders in the province of Pars who were reluctant to acknowledge his supremacy and strove to become autonomous. Pars was controlled by metropolitans in Rew Ardakhshēr, not far from the ruins of Persepolis, who challenged the authority of the *Catholicoi* for centuries until the conquest of Islam. No wonder numerous letters were written by *Catholicoi* to stress the importance to preserve unity and the supremacy of Ctesiphon. Perhaps it is more than an accident that the *Catholicos* Timotheos translated the Middle Persian law book of Ishobokht, a metropolit in Rew Ardakhshēr and a senior contemporary of his.[32]

Ishobokht's law book resembles more the work of a legal expert than to that of a metropolit. Theological expositions that have an important place in law books are missing from this work. The author hardly makes any references to synodic canons, and topics of Church organizations, institutions and discipline, important for Timotheos, also have no place in the compilation. By contrast, the author focused on mundane affairs, first of all, on the favourite topic of all Christian law books, marriage and the law of inheritance followed by law merchant. Though the text makes no reference to the Syrian–Roman law book as his source, yet its influence could be proven without any shade of doubt testifying to the popularity of this late Roman law book. Another source of the law book was local custom to which the author refers several times, particularly to the customs of merchants. Ishobokht followed in the food steps of Mar Aba to produce a legal apologetic in defence of Christian understanding of sexual ethic and in refuting some Zoroastrian customs such as incest.[33]

It is worth mentioning that we can find legal apologetics only in Christian legal works which were written by either former Zoroastrian converts or Persian Christians, but not by others. In addition, legal apologetics go on vehemently even after the collapse of the Sasanian dynasty when Zoroastrianism was no longer a state religion. Ishobokht dedicated his attention to argue against the Persian customs at the beginning of the Abbasid period, that is, 150 years after the fall of the Sasanians. This shows that Zoroastrian (legal) customs were still alive at that period in Persia, but only there. Persian Christians however, faced the challenges of Zoroastrian ethics and this is the reason why Ishobokht wrote some parts of his texts very emotionally, for which there is no room in a legal work. Ishobokht not only refuted Zoroastrian customs but even cursed his prophet, unthinkable in Sasanian times. Now, under Muslim rule however, he was safe in doing so because Muslim authorities obviously cared less about what a Christian bishop was saying about the prophet of Zoroastrianism.

Ishobokht's law book has more to offer than some harsh words on Zoroaster. In the introduction of his work he was engaged shortly in what we call now legal theory, missing from other Christian legal works. According to him, norms are of three kinds. One is *namosa* (*nomos*), the ideal understanding of the New Testament, teaching man to what is good and to be followed and what is bad and to be rejected. This is Jesus's attitude with no emphasis on mundane affairs. By contrast, *dina* is law that focuses exclusively on mundane affairs, regulating social relations, propriety

---

[32] Sachau (1914: VIII–IX).
[33] Sachau (1914: X–XII).

rights, commerce and other issues important in everyday life. The third kind of norms, *terishuta*, is between the two understood as justice, correctness, honesty, that is, the moral content of deeds which may or may not be in harmony with *dina*. He illustrates his point with an example: if someone promises to give his daughter to a man, he has to marry her to this man because of the force of his promise, being a form of *terishuta*. According to *dina*, however, he could marry off her daughter to another man though will face some monetary sanctions because breaching his previous promise. In Ishobokht's understanding, *terisutha* has three forms: thought, word and action, testifying to the Persian environment in which this legal text came into being, since these are exactly the 'three words' of Zoroastrianism (*se gowishnih*) summarising Zoroastrian ethics: *humakth* (good thought), *hukht* (good speech), and *huwarsht* (good action).[34]

This shows that Ishobokht's attitude toward Zoroastrianism was complex. While he refuted its sexual ethics, he nevertheless incorporated key concepts of Zoroastrianism into his Christian understanding of law and morality, reflecting to the complex identity Persian Christian had in late Antiquity and the early Middle Ages. In addition to this, Ishobokht makes some observations in 'comparative law' saying that legal systems are different according to time and space since previous legal systems are different from that of his contemporaries. In shaping legal systems—Ishobokht goes on to say—religions have important, though not exclusive role: meanwhile Jews and Zoroastrians only have one law, Christians have many because Roman legal understanding differs from that of the Church of the East where regional differences are also to be found.[35]

Similarly to the law book of Timotheos, the work of Ishobokht also gained prominence and was referred to for centuries. Its Syriac version was well understood among Christians in the Near East and this is the reason why later compilers such as Abdisho bar Bahriz (eleventh century), Ibn al-Taiyib (eleventh century) and Abdisho bar Brika (thirteenth–fourteenth centuries) rely heavily on this work. It is more regrettable that the original Middle Persian text is lost and the Syriac version is also not complete (the final part of the last chapter is missing, other chapters are completely lost, known only from references in other works (about wells, bridges, canals, grape and palm tree plantations, the wages of labourers, procedural law and penal law)).[36]

Parallel to Ishobokht's work a small law book on marriage and inheritance was produced by Mar Simeon in Pars province, in Middle Persian. This tractate is also lost but a Syriac translation—made presumably in the East Arabian Church (Bahrain?)—is extant. Though by far not as comprehensive a work as that of Ishobokht's, the law book of Mar Simeon was also quoted by scholars of the next generations when discussing problems of family law.[37]

---

[34] Sachau (1914: XII–XIII).

[35] Introduction to Ishobokht, in Sachau (1914: 9–11).

[36] Sachau (1914: XIV–XVI).

[37] Sachau (1914: XVII–XXII).

Isho bar Nun, opponent and successor to *Catholicos* Timotheos in office also produced a law book. According to ecclesiastic chronicles, he hated his former schoolmate and rival whom he criticised in several of his writings. This biographic information is important because there is no trace of rivalry in Isho bar Nun's legal collection. He seems to accept the work of his predecessor and did not produce a rival text but completed it. This is the reason why the text rather deals with exceptional cases which were left out from the work of Timotheos. Even if the author intended it as a supplement, yet it became somewhat longer than the supplemented text was (130 articles). This is also due to new elements in this law book such as the protection of servants and debtors, and laws against magical practices (amulet, astrology, sooth-saying) seemingly widespread also among Christians.[38]

The law book of Isho bar Nun was the last great compendium of its kind. From the eleventh century, new legal compendia emerged which differed from their predecessors in their editing principles. Until this time, legal compendia rested on chronological order, putting (mostly synodic) law in chronological order following the dates of their producing but not their content. Now the demand emerged to systematise law according to topics and not to chronology, a new yet practical consideration making it easy to find laws pertaining to a particular field. Thus, the new collections followed the topical principle of editing and put both *canon*s, that is, laws on Church organisation and institutes and *nomos*, secular law, into a single work. This is how *nomo-canon* compendia came into being, a literary genre in law that was also widespread in Byzantium in the same historical period. The first such a collection is the work of Gabriel, a legal scholar from Basra in the eleventh century, who summarised both ecclesiastic and secular law in two volumes, arranged by topics, in Syriac. This was a text of great importance because authors of the most influential *nomo-canon*s, Ibn al-Taiyib and Abdisho bar Brika based their work on it. It is our misfortune that we know this text only by fragments. Gabriel's contemporary was Elias al-Jauhari, bishop of Damascus, who also compiled a thematic collection in Arabic, a text that is still awaiting publications.[39]

Perhaps it is Ibn al-Taiyib's compendium called *Fiqh al-nasraniyya* ("Jurisprudence of Christianity") that is the most influential among the legal works of the Church of the East. Ibn al-Taiyib was a secretary to *Catholicoi* John and Elia in the eleventh century. He was a polymath, a priest, a monk, a philosopher, a physician and a legal scholar who produced significant works in various fields. He wrote comments and critiques to Aristotle's Logics and Metaphysics, commentaries to Galenus' work on medicine, commentaries to the four Gospels, and defended the doctrine of the Holy Trinity against Muslim theologians in a separate tractate. In his legal work he combined the chronological and the topical approach, and produced a two volume work: in the first part he edited the laws in chronological order, and in the second volume according to topical arrangement. Family law remained the most important topic for him but he also dedicated his attention to property law and to the management of public services such as hospitals and prisons. As a prominent

---

[38] Sachau (1908: XXI–XXII).

[39] Selb (1993: 184), Selb (1981: 74–75).

intellectual, he considered education crucial for the well-being of the community, therefore founded a school where he had been teaching. Among all his works, it was his legal compendium that made him known in the entire Near-East, proven by the fact that it was the model for Copts when they produced their own law collections. The popularity of the text is also due to its language, Arabic, a vernacular of Christians under Muslim rule.[40]

Ibn al-Taiyib's *Fiqh al-nasraniyya* dominated the field for a long time making neither necessary nor possible to produce another work of this kind. It was only the last polymath of the Church of the East, Abdisho bar Brika (known also as Ebed Jesu) bishop of Nisibis under Mongol rule who compiled his own law book. Though historical circumstances discouraged scholarly activity, he was nevertheless engaged in it producing commentaries to the Old and New Testaments and works on Greek philosophy. In addition, he wrote tractates on natural sciences and composed poems. Abdisho bar Brika wrote two law books, one contains canons of synods arranged by topical order (*Collectio canonum Synodicorum*), the other contains ecclesiastic decisions (*Ordo iudiciorum ecclesiasticorum*), later translated to Latin. Both works are used in the Church of the East today.[41]

5.4 Substantive Law

Family law, particularly laws about marriage was of crucial importance for Christians living in Persia and the Caliphate as a religious minority. As Christian understanding of family and sexual ethics differs from that of Zoroastrianism and Islam, it was family law that was of help for Christians to preserve their identity. Though, the laws of the Church of the East shared a great deal of Near-Eastern legal *koiné* with other local legal systems, family law made it markedly different. In addition to reflecting moral understanding, family law also contributed to preserve the Christian community, intact with a variety of legal restrictions against mixed marriages and conversion. Law of inheritance, evidently an important tool to distribute material wealth among family members, was also a mean to protect the community with restrictions on converts. These considerations make marriage law the most important field of law among Persian Christians, to be followed by law of inheritance.

By contrast, laws on property, obligations and commerce were secondary in importance and thus left out of some law books. These fields of law are to be found only in law books that concentrate exclusively on material issues or are comprehensive enough to cover every field of law (*Fiqh al-nasraniyya*). It is important to note that law books that contain laws on property and obligations have nothing to say about Church organisation and canons about the domestic affairs of the Church. This is not by accident but reflects a clear vision on law, society and religion, defined best by Ishobokht (see above). Since compilers of law books were

---

[40]Baum and Winkler (2003: 72–73).

[41]Selb (1993: 185).

clerics and sometimes metropolitans and *Catholicoi*, these legal compilations reflect their understanding of normativity where law was not of high esteem. Disputes about material goods which are subjects of the law of property and obligations is a concern of a materialistic man concentrating on mundane affairs and not on eternal values and salvation which are the real message of the Church. It is this anthropology, therefore, that prevents Church leaders from concentrating on private law. It is this understanding that makes it clear why compilers who also put laws on property and obligations into their law books apologise to do so in their preface and explain with rationalistic arguments why it is necessary to deal with such issues too. An important point among them was that bishops were entitled to settle such disputes which they did with due care in order to prevent litigants to go to foreign, that is, Persian and Muslim, courts. The preservation of identity and cohesion was, therefore, an important consideration, also in matters of property and obligations.

Obviously laws on public administration are missing from the law books as there was never a Christian state in the Near-East. Their place was taken over by laws on Church organisations, regulating the competencies of bishops and metropolitans, rights and duties of priests and clerics. Criminal law is also missing from the law books since religious minorities (Christians, Jews) were deprived of the right to implement penal sanctions in both Sasanian Persia and the Caliphate. In absence of criminal law, the only sanction that remained at their disposal was excommunication, a final solution when violating basic rules. Only two cases are preserved in the law book of Isho bar Nun about criminal law: homicide and homicide by poisoning. Accordingly, their sanction is excommunication (Articles 125 and 129) since it was the most the Church could do while state authorities, evidently involved in such matters followed their own, and not that of the Church of the East, law to investigate such cases in Sasanian Persia and the Caliphate.

Laws of procedure are also missing from the law books, which is not as evident as the lack of criminal law since litigations did take place at courts. Here again, anthropology and principles of procedure could clarify the point. According to Ishobokht (V/VIII: 3.§; V/XI: 6.§; V/XIII: 7.§), efforts should be made to reach an agreement and compromise between the parties during the course of the proceedings while he condemns asserting one's right at court without taking into consideration the interest of others. He particularly warns the wealthier to be guided by mercifulness in their disputes with the poor and emphasises mediation as the most important task of the judge. A judge should produce a peaceful settlement of the dispute acceptable to the parties and be flexible enough while doing so and avoid applying the letter of the law strictly. Evidently, Ishobokht formulates here a general understanding, not only his personal view. This attitude has its origin partly in Christian ethics, and partly in the general understanding of procedures in the Near-East which highlights mediation and compromises to the detriment of asserting individual rights. This principle, an important piece of the Near-Eastern legal *koiné* can be found, as we have seen, both in Jewish and Persian law and is not missing from Islamic law either. Parties are entitled, even encouraged, to settle their disputes by compromises and judges make a final warning to do so just before making their sentence public which hinders any compromise. In short, a flexible way of procedure and the need for compromises might be a reason for the lack of procedural law. Another reason might be the lack of rights to implement court decisions which was another factor that enhanced mediation and compromise. Finally, we can suppose that local (and ecclesiastic?) customs were at play when regulating procedures and it is our misfortune that we know nothing about them as they are missing from the written sources.

As demonstrated in the previous sections, law books on marriage were polemic and apologetic when written by Persian authors and normative when produced by others. Influence of Iranian culture in general and Zoroastrian family law in particular challenged Christian sexual ethics and it was Persian Christians who had to face them. To protect the identity of Iranian Christians, law books sometimes levied harsh attacks on Zoroastrian law and this is the reason why I call these works legal apologetics, particularly the law books of Mar Aba and Ishobokht. Mar Aba's law book is actually a treatise against Zoroastrian sexual ethics and family law. In this work, substantive laws on Christian marriage are pushed to the background while we can read long arguments in favour of Christian interpretation (supported by Biblical quotations) and against Zoroastrian customs which are referred to as that of demons. Mar Aba, a former Zoroastrian convert was well versed not only in Zoroastrian family law but also in the myths and theological arguments that underpin Zoroastrian concept of family. The emotions of Mar Aba (he calls Zoroastrians the disciples and slaves of Satan)[42] show how important family law was for him to discipline Iranian Christian aristocrats who were more integrated into contemporary Iranian (Zoroastrian) aristocracy than the bishop wanted (this is the reason why we can also find Christian aristocrats among those who accused the bishop at the royal court which led to his sentence to prison).[43]

Ishobokht too, argues against Zoroastrians at the beginning of the Abbasid caliphate but has nothing to say about Muslim marriages which are also not in harmony with Christian ethics. Obviously, to criticise Zoroastrians was without risk but to argue against Islamic law was not. As a result, Ishobokht's law book is more normative than that of Mar Aba though does not lack apologetics. The first book on marriage law is about prohibitions, enlisting women of every kind who are prohibited to marry. Prohibitions rest either on family relations or on religious considerations. Women prohibited to marry are classified in fifteen categories according to line and grade including collaterals, ascending and descending relatives. To these categories non-Christian women are added, since only Christian women could be married. In his next chapter Ishobokht explains in lengths why exogamy is useful and rational while endogamy is not. It is his way of thinking that makes this chapter worth mentioning because he did not refer to the Bible, Christian ethics or already established legal norms, but to rational arguments. His argumentation is in line with that of modern sociology and anthropology, claiming that exogamy is better than endogamy because it creates very important social networks. According to the Persian bishop, exogamy creates a network by bringing outsiders into the family, the members of which are obliged to mutual help for the benefit of individuals and the family as a whole. It

---

[42]Mar Aba 2.§ in Sachau (1914: 267).

[43]For more on this topic see Payne (2015: 93–117).

is true, he goes on to say, that endogamy keeps property inside the family yet its aggregate benefit is less than that of the networks of relatives which can mobilise contributing members in a way that an endogamous family cannot. This is a very modern argumentation though, evidently, it was targeted against Zoroastrianism, whose prophet Ishobokht condemns at the end of this chapter (Book 2, Chapter 2).

The chapter against levirate marriage of Jewish law is shorter and less emotional. According to him, to marry the wife of a deceased brother is not a general command in Jewish law only an exceptional rule if a man dies childless. The bishops emphasises that Jews did not believe in resurrection and eternal life at the time when the Laws of Moses were revealed to them, therefore, their only chance to live on remained in their descendants. Christians, by contrast, do believe in eternal life and resurrection and do not need such legal practices any longer. Contrary to the Persian endogamy, levirate is not an evil but an unnecessary institution of family law. This view is identical with that of Mar Aba.[44]

After refuting non-Christian types of marriages, Ishobokht turns to another debated issue, divorce. The prohibition of divorce is one among the few points that makes Christian law and ethics different from all the Near-Eastern legal systems and contributes to establish a particular Christian identity. Divorce was prohibited as a general rule, permitted only in exceptional cases such as blasphemy, adultery and murder. Adultery was, however, a legal title only for a husband but never to a wife, a sign of male supremacy that is part of the Near-Eastern legal *koiné* shared by Christians too. Ishobokht argues otherwise of course, with an argument similar to that of a Roman lawyer, referring to the maxim that 'a mother is always sure' while a father is not. Therefore, a husband of an adulterous woman may never know for sure the father of the children raised in his family, and this is such a blow on the family system that it makes lawful to divorce an adulterous woman. By contrast, if a man commits adultery, the child thus born does not belong to his family and will not inherit in the paternal family, therefore, it cannot be a title to divorce. Seemingly, this line of argument did not convince all and there were Christians who believed that the imbalance between the sexes in adultery as a title to divorce was only due to the fact that males create laws and sit at courts and thus enforce privileges. Though Ishobokht did not share this view, the very fact that he mentions such a rival explanation testifies how widespread this understanding was in his time (Book 2, Chapter 12).

Ishobokht was surely not naïve. He warns against men who want to get rid of their wives for any reason and would, therefore, accuse them with adultery, the only lawful legal title to divorce. The bishop makes it clear that law should protect such innocent women from the false accusations of their husbands. To this end, evidence must be presented to prove the husband's unilateral accusation, usually by two or three witnesses. In the absence of such witnesses, adultery could not be proven. But here too, some licence is given to men with laws relaxing the strictness of evidence if the woman's lustful way of life was publicly known or she got pregnant while her husband was away for long. The possibility that pregnancy could be a consequence of rape too is neglected (similarly to Islamic law). If a man accused his wife with

---

[44]Ishobohkt, Book 2, Chapter 6.

adultery but was unable to prove his claim his wife was obliged to take an oath to prove her innocence. Her oath put an end to the trial and divorce was, of course, not granted. She was free from suspicion and the couple remained married (Book 2, Chapters 15 and 16). If a husband could prove his claim, divorce was only a possibility and no husband of an adulterous wife was obliged to neglect her. Here again, Ishobokht informs us also about local customs and not only about written laws when claiming that usually adulterous wives are not divorced but families try to solve the conflict by negotiations, compromises and compensation. It is understandable against this background why the bishop stresses that an adulterous wife of a cleric should be divorced and sent away, because she bring shame to the Church. Divorced partners may re-marry in the future if they so desire, but Ishobokht turns against this interpretation and prohibits divorced partners to re-marry (Book 2, Chapters 16 and 17).

Ishobokht has almost nothing to say about legal routine, how to conclude a marriage because after discussing the legal problems of divorce he turns his attention to exceptional and difficult cases. A modern reader has the impression that the author took it for granted that basic norms of family law were known by all and there was no need to repeat them in a law book. His task was, seemingly, to collect laws for exceptional cases, unknown by the public at large. Here are some examples. When discussing engagement he only deals with obstacles that prevent marriage without mentioning how engagement leads to marriage in a normal case. He has much to say about eloping girls (an Iranian custom that can be found also in Zoroastrian law) and concubinage (defined as a partnership without wedding) and cites also some laws on the marriage of slaves and the waiting period for an absent husband.

Ishobokht was very careful when discussing such non-typical problems and took both legal and social factors into consideration. If, for example, someone slept with a virgin girl, first the parties were asked whether they wanted to marry. If the parties wanted to marry and their relatives agreed to that in the belief that they were suited to each other (which probably meant social position) the case was solved with a wedding. By contrast, if the man was unwilling to marry the girl, he had to pay compensation the sum of which was determined by the girl's social position. Elopement was more complicated. If the girl was not yet engaged, the man could marry her if he so wished, but if she had been engaged then she had to marry the bridegroom. Law discouraged the custom of elopement, since if the girl was taken away with her consent she had to marry a third person and the culprit had to be punished (Book 3, Chapters 4 and 5). Obviously, we do not know how widespread elopement was in late Antiquity among Iranian Christians but the mere fact that it is a topic of a law book about family law leads us to believe that it was part of their social life. One may agree with Walter Selb who is of the view that elopement was a widespread custom, a daily routine that resulted in conflicts between extended families and villages leading the Church of the East to prevent it with legal means.[45]

The apologetics of Mar Aba and Ishobokht disappeared almost completely from the law books in the next centuries because Zoroastrianism lost its influence also

---

[45]Selb (1981: 153).

in Iran. Later works such as *Fiqh al-nasraniyya* have almost nothing to say about incest such an important a problem in previous law books. The second part of Ibn al-Taiyib's law book begins with a list of obstacles that hinder a lawful marriage. Family tie is one among them, but he does not devote more than a paragraph to it. He condemns incest, highlighting that such relations may produce bodily deformed children, a claim which is completely missing from earlier apologetics and may be due to Ibn al-Taiyib's medical practice.[46] For Ibn al-Taiyib, it was not Zoroastrianism with incest but Islam with conversions that caused headache. No wonder, therefore, that for him religious difference between the parties was a greater concern by far. Accordingly, a Christian man could marry a non-Christian woman because one may hope in her conversion, while a Christian woman could never marry a non-Christian man otherwise she and her children would be lost to the Christian community (Islamic law has the same argument). The sanction of such a union is excommunication: both the parents and the girl should excommunicated, unless the girl did not consent to the marriage.[47]

Ibn al-Taiyib's work is more normative than that of his predecessors, focusing less on apologetics and more on a systematic arrangement of the laws. Therefore he did not follow the structure of Ishobokht to concentrate only on hard cases but produces a comprehensive compilation of the law of the Church of the East. Presumably, Christian marriage customs differed little from the local customs, besides some important points of Christian ethics (e.g. prohibition of divorce). Christians in the Near-East, therefore, followed local legal *koiné* with these differences. For Christians too, marriage was a family matter and to decide about it was not left to the parties alone. Agreements, a result of long negotiations were bonds between families and not between individuals, this being a Near-Eastern (Asian) understanding of marriage regardless of religious affiliation. It was only the head of the family who was entitled to enter such negotiations and detailed rules were established to define who could represent him in cases of necessity (death, long journey). Only adult males were exempt from the authority of their fathers, as they were entitled to negotiate their own affairs. Marriage contracts regulated monetary matters and all related subjects. When agreement was reached, the next step was engagement, a ceremony in the local church with the help of priests (their absence making the engagement null and void) and the ring as a symbol. Engagement was more than a promise to marriage, it had some legal effects. For instance, an engaged girl had to wait for her bridegroom for three years if he went away to a distant place, but if he supplied her with maintenance she had to wait for seven years. The waiting period of a girl engaged in childhood for her bridegroom was ten years. Despite this, the engagement did not result necessary in marriage. Since family agreements were concluded already in childhood of the partners, they were entitled to reject it when reaching maturity. If they declined to marry they could not be forced to marriage but their family had to pay compensation for the other family. The sum of such a pecuniary compensation is set by the law (400 Drachmas and three series of garments) for the rich and by the priests (considering

---

[46] Ibn al-Taiyib Part II, Chapter 1: 1.

[47] Ibn al-Taiyib Part II, Chapter 1: 7–8.

all relevant factors) for the poor. A marriage may also fail because of illness setting in after engagement but before wedding. In case of illnesses for which there was no cure such as leprosy and epilepsy, the separation of the parties was necessary if the other party was not aware of the illness, otherwise one could wait for healing. If a party agreed to marriage with a profound knowledge of the illness of his/her partner, illness was not a legal cause later for separation.[48]

Concerning divorce, Ibn al-Taiyib follows Ishobokht's system and arguments but modifies them at some points. Perhaps the most important difference is that while Ishobokht argues, admittedly, on shaky grounds, for the husband's unilateral right to divorce his adulterous wife but denies her right to do the same, Ibn al-Taiyib— referring to Isho bar Nun—emphasised the right to divorce of both partners on the basis of equity. In addition, Ibn al-Taiyib raises the number of witnesses to prove adultery to four or six with an interesting argument. Accordingly, the number of witnesses in the previous law books (2 or 3) should be understood as witnesses of one party which makes the total number of witnesses to four or six.[49] Obviously, it is next to impossible to have six witnesses for such a case and it was perhaps the intent of Ibn al-Taiyib to make it impossible to prove adultery at courts and let family matters be settled by negotiations. If so, he did the same what Muslim legal scholars had done when raising the number of witnesses from two to four, making it very hard to prove the accusation of adultery and to avoid the implementation of its sanction (stoning).

Concerning the law of inheritance, casuistry remained the leading principle of edition in the *Fiqh al-nasraniyya* too, but Ibn al-Taiyib made some efforts to arrange some order in this ocean of legal cases. His sources were the works of Ishobokht, Timotheos and Isho bar Nun. Details of the law of inheritance were seemingly matter of disputes as Ibn al-Taiyib refers often to rival legal doctrines without specifying his own view. This part of the work is rather a compendium of the disagreements of the authorities. Despite uncertainties in detail, important institutions are clear. Accordingly, there was room for both intestate and testamentary succession. A man was entitled to make his last will regulating the shares of the family members in his bequest. In his testament a husband could disinherit his wife but a minimum share was due to her in order to prevent her to do illegal things and to guarantee a living for the widow. In the absence of a will, the husband's bequest was shared in equal parts by the widow and his male children, while the unmarried daughters' share was only a half. A married daughter inherited nothing because her share was—according to Ishobokht's argumentation—already given to her as a dowry. Here, not only law but also its justification is in accordance with Zoroastrian law of inheritance, resting on the same arguments. No wonder later authors have different laws when the influence of Zoroastrian law was in decline. According to Isho bar Nun, a widow inherits the half of the house where she has been living and is entitled to live there under her death. By contrast, Abdisho bar Bahriz would give a widow only one share, a widower two shares, a daughter four and the son eight shares out of the bequest. Here

---

[48] Ibn al-Taiyib Part II, Chapter 2: 3–9.

[49] Ibn al-Taiyib Part II, Chapter 3: 3–5.

Ibn al-Taiyib made no effort to harmonize contradictory laws as he was content with enumerating them in all their detail in a thematic order.[50] It is not surprising that this chapter is the longest (Part 2, Chapter 4).

Ibn al-Taiyib had something to say about law of procedures too, but not in a thematic order and without a glimpse to the entire procedure. By contrast, he only picks up some issues relevant to him and leaves others untouched. These are rather about prohibitions relating to a legal procedure. The most important among them was a prohibition to go to a pagan (Muslim) court which resulted in excommunication, a law that occurs more than once in the text, testifying how Islamic law challenged the identity of Christians living in a Muslim society. Another prohibition made it unlawful for women to enter courts, and could take part in a proceeding only through their representatives, this being another piece of Near-eastern legal *koiné*. The law according to which one cannot start a lawsuit until another proceeding of him came to its end is of Persian origin and originates, predictably, from the law book of Ishobokht.[51]

It is worth mentioning, in brief laws the aim of which was to protect Christian belief and communities. Isho bar Nun, for example, prohibited turning to magical practices, particularly in issues of love. Accordingly, a young man should be excommunicated if he turned to a magus to convince a girl unwilling to marry him. A woman who relied on the help of a magus to make her husband love her should be driven away from her family amidst the greatest humiliation. Persons suffering from various illness and disease who turn to magi and astrologists in the hope of recovery were also excommunicated and denied from taking the sacraments. This was the fate of those who had become victims of robbery and wanted to find their stolen goods with the help of magi and voyeurs, too. Only excommunication was the fate of those who wanted to cause damage or even death to others, through magical practices because Christians were denied the right to implement criminal sentences. Therefore, Isho bar Nun was unable to find a more serious sanction for such fellows but emphasised that their sin was double: one was to turn to magical practices and the other was their intention to cause harm or death.[52]

The law of the Church of the East protected the slaves, particularly Christian slaves. Any participation in slave trade was prohibited for Christians, the violation of which was punished by excommunication. With this law voted for human dignity against profit, since slave trade was among the most profitable businesses in the Near-East at the end of Antiquity and in the Middle Ages in which both Persians and Muslims were involved. A freed slave could not be claimed back, any such demand led to immediate excommunication. A slave who became disabled or was injured so that he/she was unable to work was guaranteed a living by a law according to which the slave owner had to care for him until the death of the slave, an obligation inherited by the heirs of the slave owner. A Christian slave can be sold only to a Christian slave

---

[50] Ibn al-Taiyib Part II, Chapter 4: 1–11.

[51] Ibn al-Taiyib Part II, Chapter 11: 7, 17, 20; Ishobokht: Book 6, 1: 7.§.

[52] Isho bar Nun: 34–40.§.

owner, the violation of which resulted in immediate excommunication.[53] A slave family was not to be split up and the married couple had to be kept together even if they were sold.[54] In short, though keeping slaves was not forbidden, law made every effort to humanise the institution of slavery.

Finally, it is worth pointing out that the law books paid attention to various public institutions like hospitals, prisons, and schools. Each city had to run a hospital where physicians had to be employed to cure the sick. A person educated in finances ('a person who understands incomes and expenditures') had to be delegated from the monastery to manage the financial issues of the hospital and if the income of the hospital did not cover the expenses (we do not learn from where the income originates), the inhabitants of the city have to cover the loss. The law book of Ibn al-Taiyib tries to limit the building of new churches because there were numerous churches in ruin, and the author encouraged the community rather to restore these old buildings. This text clearly indicates the decline of the Christian community: there was an increasing number of abandoned churches that were no longer restored.[55]

References

Sources

Al-Misrī A (1994) ᶜUmdat al-Sālik. Reliance of the Traveller. A Classic Manual of Islamic Sacred Law. In: Arabic with facing English Text (Trans: Keller NHM). Beltsville, Maryland, USA

Braun O (1915) Ausgewählte Akten Persischer Märtyrer. Bibliothek der Kirchenväter, Band 22. Kempten, München

Bruns KG, Sachau E (1880) Syrisch-Römisches Rechtsbuch aus dem fünften Jahrhundert. Brockhaus, Leipzig

Hoenerbach W, Spies O (1957) Ibn at-Taiyib: Fiqh al-Nasraniya. L. Durbecq, Louvain

Hoffmann G (1880) Auszüge aus Syrischen Akten Persischer Märtyrer. Leipzig

Sachau E (1908) Syrische Rechtsbücher. Zweiter Band. Richterliche Urteile des Patriarchen Chenanischo. Gesetzbuch des Patriarchen Timotheos. Gesetzbuch des Patriarchen Jesubarnun. Verlag von Georg Reimer, Berlin

Sachau E (1914) Syrische Rechtsbücher. Dritter Band. Corpus juris des Erzbischofs Jesubocht. Erbrecht oder Canones des persischen Erzbischofs Simeon. Eherecht des Patriarchen Mar Abha. Verlag von Georg Reimer, Berlin

Vööbus A (1962) The statutes of the school of Nisibis. ETSE, Stockholm

Literature

Asmussen JP (1983) Christians in Iran. Camb Hist of Iran 3(2):924–948

---

[53]Isho bar Nun: 64–66.§; 105.§.

[54]Timotheos 77.§.

[55]Ibn al-Taiyib: Part II, Book 7, 1–8.

Baum W, Winkler D (2003) The Church of the East. A concise history. Routledge, New York

Cahen C (1991) Dhimma. In: The Encyclopaedia of Islam, vol. II. E. J. Brill: Leiden

Jany J (2011) Criminal procedures against Iranian Christians in late Antiquity. In: Béli G, Duchonová D, Fundárková A, Kajtár I, Peres Z (eds) Institutions of legal history: with special regard to legal culture and history. Bratislava-Pécs, pp 205–213

Kruse K (1979) Islamische Völkerrechtslehre. Bochum

Moffet SH (1998) A history of Christianity in Asia, vols I–II. Orbis Books, Maryknoll, New York

Payne R (2015) A state of mixture. Christians, Zoroastrians, and Iranian political culture in late Antiquity. University of California Press, Oakland, California

Selb W (1981) Orientalisches Kirchenrecht. Band I. Die Geschichte des Kirchenrechts der Nestorianer. Verlag der Österreichischen Akademie der Wissenschaften, Wien

Selb W (1993) Antike Rechte im Mittelmeerraum. Böhlau Verlag, Wien

Spuler B (1961a) Die Nestorianische Kirche. In: Leipoldt J, Widengren G, Adam A, Spuler B, Dietrich EL, Fück JW, Arberry AJ, Strothmann R, von Gabain A (eds) Religionsgeschichte des Orient sin der Zeit der Weltreligionen. Handbuch der orientalistik I/8/2. Brill, Leiden, pp 120–169

Spuler B (1961b) Die Westsyrische (Monophysitische/Jakobitische) Kirche. In: Leipoldt J, Widengren G, Adam A, Spuler B, Dietrich EL, Fück JW, Arberry AJ, Strothmann R, von Gabain A (eds) Religionsgeschichte des Orient sin der Zeit der Weltreligionen. Handbuch der orientalistik I/8/2. Brill, Leiden, pp 170–216

Stoyanov Y (2011) Defenders and enemies of the true cross. The Sasanian conquest of Jerusalem in 614 and Byzantine ideology of anti-Persian warfare. Verlag der Österreichischen Akademie der Wissenschaften, Wien

Vanyó L (1988) Az Ókeresztény Egyház és irodalma. Szent István Társulat, Budapest

Vine A (1937) The Nestorian Churches. A concise history of Nestorian Christianity in Asia from the Persian Schism to the modern Assyrians. Independent Press, London

Vööbus A (1965) History of the school of Nisibis. University of Louvain, Louvain

Part II
The Islamic Legal Circle

Chapter 6
Pre-Islamic Arabia

6.1 Historical Overview

Historical events of Pre-Islamic Arabia are recorded in sources produced by neighbouring peoples such as the Assyrians, Babylonians, Jews, Romans and Persians. This is why our knowledge concerning this historical period is dependent on what they regarded as important enough to put into writing about the state of affairs in Arabia. Arabia in itself was not important enough for them to record events there on its own sake, they did so only when they came to contact with Arab tribes, mainly in wars. These struggles, however, affected only some Arab tribes but left others untouched.

No wonder, therefore, that the first Arab *sheykh* known by name was Gindibu ('locust') who participated in the anti-Assyrian coalition of Ahāb, King of Israel, adding one thousand camel riders to the joint army.[1] However, it was the Assyrians who emerged victorious from the battle of Qarqar (853 BCE) which had, of course, negative consequences for both the Arabs and Israel. During the reign of the Assyrian King Tukultu-apil-Ēsharra III (744–727 BCE), Arabs brought 'gifts' to the Assyrian king including gold, lead, iron, silver, and ivory, that is, commodities that Arabs could acquire exclusively through long-distance trade. Assyrian King Sharrukīn II reports in his inscription that he deported the defeated Arab tribes to Palestinian Samaria in 715 BCE. From this time on military conflicts with nomadic Arab tribes continued under the reign of Sīn-ahhē-eriba (704–681 BCE) and Ashshur-ah-iddina (680–669 BCE) who gained military victories in Arabia about which they reported in their inscriptions. Ashshur-bān-apli (668–627 BCE) personally led a punitive military campaign against Arab tribes breaking their agreement with the Assyrians. In the end, Arabs were defeated and their leaders executed. Despite such military successes, Assyrians could not conquer the territories of the Arabs who did not become Assyrian subjects.[2]

---

[1]Goitein (1955: 4).

[2]Klengel (1985: 95–99).

© Springer Nature Switzerland AG 2020
J. Jany, *Legal Traditions in Asia*, Ius Gentium: Comparative Perspectives on Law and Justice 80, https://doi.org/10.1007/978-3-030-43728-2_6

After the fall of the Assyrians, the new masters of the Near-East, the Babylonians, had nothing to report about their victories against Arabs, seemingly because there were none. It was Nabū-na'id (555–539 BCE), the last ruler of the New Babylonian Empire who spent a decade out of this seventeen-year reign among Arab tribes, reported about in his inscriptions in Harran, an astonishing move that calls for explanation. His contemporaries were as puzzled as modern scholars are. Some believe the Babylonian king was just fleeing from a deadly epidemic in his home town, while others think he was engaged in persuading Arab tribes to form an alliance against the Persians, a rising threat to Babylon from the east. Still, others think the Babylonian king was there only to prepare for a military campaign against the Arabs. The problem with these theories is that neither of them explains why Nabū-na'id remained there for ten years and also let a royal palace be built in the oasis of Tema. Whatever his motivations might be, he returned to Babylon only when forced to do so by his troops, but this came too late as the city was conquered by the Persians led by Kurush II (Cyrus) in 539 BCE.[3]

In the Persian period, Arabs played an important role in the conquests of the Achaemenians. Arab tribes agreed to Cambyses II to help the invading Persian army to conquer Egypt with water supply throughout their campaign across the desert.[4] Herodotus reports further that Arabs were never conquered and included into the administrative system of the Achaemenid Empire in exchange to their military help.[5] The Behistun inscription of King Darius I however, contradicts this while enlisting the land of the Arabs (Arabāya) also among his provinces.[6] If we assume, however, that Darius lists all the countries that belonged to him (Arabs included) and not only those which were subjugated, put into the administrative system of the realm and obliged to pay taxes (Arabs excluded), there is no contradiction between the sources.[7]

Meanwhile, northern Arab tribes were involved in the history of the Ancient Near East; we can witness a completely different development in the south. Here, four kingdoms emerged such as Saba', Maᶜīn, Qatabān and Hadramaut. At the beginning of their history, these kingdoms were headed by *mukarrib*s interpreted as priest-kings, though the exact meaning of the term is still disputed. As a result of the de-sacralisation of power, the rule of the *mukarrib*s was replaced later by kings (*malik*). The office of the king was inherited. South-Arabian kings ruled in concert with the powerful leaders (*qayl*) of the tribes whose opinion was not to be neglected in important decisions. In the south, a tribe was a territorial unity rather than only a group of relatives as it was among northern tribes. It was the kingdom of Saba' that was the strongest among the rival states, which as a result of continuous expansions, conquered its rivals and united the southern territories in the years around 300 BCE. Saba' was guaranteed a solid economic basis for its campaigns through long distance trade with luxury goods such as frankincense and myrrh. The monopolistic southern

[3] Klengel (1985: 101–103).
[4] Herodotus, III: 9.
[5] Herodotus, III: 88.
[6] DB I. 6.§.
[7] Dandamaev and Lukonin (1989: 98–99).

sea trade was extremely lucrative, which secured a high living standard to people living there. This economic prosperity and the luxury items found there had created a romantic illusion that led classical authors to call this area Arabia Felix. However, when Ptolemaic Egypt discovered the secret of the monsoon and established its authority over the Red Sea, the southern Arab sea trade declined.[8] Economic decline led to political chaos resulting in wars. In addition to this, the centre of international commerce was shifted to the north, making the emergence of new political centres such as Petra and Palmyra possible. Parallel to this, Ethiopia, a strong rival in Africa emerged, which after Negus ᶜĒzānā converted to Christianity became a close ally to the Byzantines.[9]

The Nabateans with UNESCO World Heritage Petra as their centre converted their economic strength to political influence when they supported the revolt of the Maccabees[10] and interfered with arms into power struggles in Palestine (e.g. Herod and Malichus).[11] Their success was a t he same time the cause of their fall too, as Romans began to look at them as local rivals. As a result, Petra was conquered (106 CE) and Emperor Trajan established Provincia Arabia on its remnants. After this time, the power of the Nabateans declined but from time to time they participated in the power struggles of Roman generals. The most important support was their backing to Septimius Severus, despite the fact that all neighbouring states supported Severus' opponent Pescennius Niger.[12]

The rise of Palmyra can be dated back to this period, too. This Hellenistic city reached the peak of its political power under Queen Zenobia in the third century when Roman power was in decline and Sasanian Persians dominated the Near-East. Persian King Shābuhr I (240–272) defeated the Romans twice in the middle of the third century. After Emperor Gordian died in the Persian wars, Roman army voted for Philippus, a brave soldier of Arab origin as their next ruler.[13] Philippus Arabs—as he became to be known—signed a peace treaty with the Persians but was murdered for that, as Roman elite regarded the agreement as a betrayal of Roman interests. The next Roman-Persian war brought however more humiliation to the Romans,[14] and only the Palmyran army—accommodated better to desert warfare than the Romans—could stop the advance of the Sasanians.[15] Encouraged by this success, Palmyrans wanted more and ambitioned also Asia Minor and Egypt, which made them a dangerous local rival for Rome. Emperor Aurelian, therefore, destroyed the city and captured its powerful and beautiful Queen, Zenobia.[16]

---

[8]Shahīd (1970: 7–13).

[9]Shahīd (1970: 13).

[10]1 Makk 5: 25–26.

[11]Bowersock (1994: 42).

[12]Bowersock (1994: 112–113).

[13]Roman chronicles preserved Philippus in bad memory; for an excellent anthology of sources see Dodgeon and Lieu (1991: 36–45).

[14]ShKZ 12/9/19-15/11/26.

[15]Bowersock (1994: 130–137).

[16]Dodgeon and Lieu (1991: 83–110).

The demise of Palmyra did not reduce the importance of Arab tribes in Roman (Byzantine) and Persian history nor in the wars of the great powers. Both Persia and Byzantium created buffer states along their borders to ward off nomadic incursions and to defend their borders against their enemy. These buffer 'states' (in fact: tribal confederations) were created with the help of local Arab tribes: Christian Ghassānids were allied to Byzantium while their local co-religionist rivals, the Lakhmids sided with the Persians.[17] These wars produced heroes such as the king of the Lakhmids (al-Mundhir) whose courage inspired Arab poets patronised by both the Lakhmids and the Ghassānids.[18] Despite this, neither the Romans nor the Persians trusted their allies and this is the reason why these buffer states were eliminated during the sixth century.[19] In addition to this, a *limes* was built from North Mesopotamia to the Red Sea (called *Limes Orientalis*), which ran just through the heart of the territory populated by Arab tribes cutting their home into half: those living inside the limes were called *rhomaioi*, while those living outside Saracens. Contracts (*foedus*) were signed with some Arab tribes to guard the borders, thus making them *foederati*. The military assistance of the *foederatis* was crucial in the wars against the Goths and the Vandals.[20]

Parallel to the demise of Palmyra, the Himyarite kingdom rose to prominence in the south under the leadership of Shammar Yuhar'ish, uniting southern territories. This kingdom which abandoned former polytheism and converted to Judaism was ruined by the invading Ethiopians led by general Abraha whose army came close to Mecca at the early decades of the sixth century. The memory of the elephants used by them and their devastation is preserved in the 105th Sura of the Qur'ān called The Elephant.[21] Muslim tradition has it that Muhammad was born in the same year (570), a claim already rejected by Theodor Nöldeke at the end of the nineteenth century.[22] The military success of the Ethiopians alarmed the Persians who invaded the rest of Southern Arabia and after defeating the Ethiopians kept the area under their control. With this, Arab-Iranian contacts were further intensified.[23] It seems plausible that the spread of horses in Arabia and their change to fight on horseback from their earlier method to sit on camels was due to their close contacts to the Persians proven by Iranian loan words about horse-keeping in Arabic.[24]

The demise of Palmyra opened the way to the rise of Mecca as a centre of long distance trade and pilgrimage. Long distance trade made various markets develop, one among them was a weekly market always held on the same day of the week in the open air. Another form of market was that of cities and small villages. Transit

---

[17]Lapidus (1998: 16).

[18]Shahīd (1970: 22).

[19]Lapidus (1998: 16). The chronicle of *Al-Tabarī* has the history of the Lakhmids, see Nöldeke (1879).

[20]Dostal (1997: 13–14).

[21]Dostal (1997: 10).

[22]For more on this subject see Conrad (1987).

[23]Nöldeke (1879: 86–88).

[24]Dostal (1997: 17).

places and caravan cities had their own markets (Palmyra), while the most populous were the annual markets held in the holy month, accompanied with games, poetry competitions and weddings.[25] Home to both the Ka^{c}ba and the Mount ^{c}Arafāt, cultic sites of pre-Islamic polytheism in Arabia, Mecca was an important place in Arabia already before the rise of Islam. Lying in the middle of a long trade route from the south to the north, Mecca soon evolved into a trading centre too. Independent from the Roman (Byzantine), Persian and Ethiopian powers, local Arab tradesmen could make good profit from their long distance trade for which Mecca was one among the few important centres.[26] Known as Makoraba on maps produced in the Ptolemaic Egypt it was not a place for permanent settlement for long. This only changed when members of the Quraysh tribe under the leadership of Qusayy b. Kilāb settled down there in the fifth century. Qusayy united the Quraysh tribe with the help of his priestly office and consolidated his power in Mecca. Unity did not last for long however and the Quraysh tribe became fragmented along rival commercial interests, a division that contributed to the later Umayya–^{c}Abbāsī rivalry as well.[27]

6.2 Political Institutions

This long pre-Islamic period when Arabs were not yet aware of the revelations of Allāh is called *jāhiliyya* by Muslims, that is, the age of ignorance. As Muslims see history through the lenses of religions[28] they have an ambivalent attitude to the history of pre-Islamic Arabia since this period was the age of polytheism and idolatry, yet at the same time it witnessed a flourishing tribal culture (e.g. poetry) which is part of their own cultural heritage.

Pre-Islamic Arabia is fragmented not only by religions (polytheism, Christianity, Judaism) but also according to way of life: while some, mainly northerner tribes, were nomads, others in the south settled down to establish cities and states. No wonder, therefore, that the political institutions of nomadic tribes were different from that of the sedentary population. Societies of pre-Islamic Arabia were divided also along professions: while nomads were engaged mainly in long distance trade, others opted for agriculture to guarantee their living. As elsewhere, in Arabia, nomads and the sedentary population had an ambivalent relationship; though they developed a mutual disrespect against each other, they cooperated in their daily life, which was channelled mainly in local markets where commodities were changed.

The basis of social structure in pre-Islamic Arabia was extended families which were grouped together in clans. Multiple clans formed a tribe which could create tribal confederations for a shorter or longer period to harmonise joint military activities. They were headed by a tribal leader called king (*malik*), who were sometimes

---

[25]Dostal (1997: 23); for more on local markets see Simon (1975: 138–154).

[26]Shahīd (1970: 24).

[27]Dostal (1997: 25–32).

[28]Weiss (1998: 148).

recognised also by emperors and thus were given additional honorary titles such as *dhū al-tāj* ("the one with the crown": the title given to the head of the Lakhmids by the Persian king).[29] Tribal confederations were created and controlled by the strongest tribes and clans. If their military enterprises were successful, the respect of the leaders grew and this is how a kind of 'military aristocracy' emerged.[30] Similarly to the Germanic tribes (Herzog), it was also customary among Arab tribes to elect a military leader called *ra'īs* for a single campaign.[31] The symbol of the military leaders was the sword called *sayf al-ri'āsa*, the sword of command which was hung above the entrance to their place of residence.[32]

A tribe was headed by the *sayyid*, whose authority depended on his own abilities. The office of the *sayyid* was usually linked to the clan of the greatest authority and prestige (*ahl al-bayt*) within the tribe as he could not rely on any coercive force while implementing his decisions. This is also the reason why he had to consult continuously with elders and other persons of influence. The prestige of *sayyid*s rested on the number of his warriors, his material wealth and his contacts to other tribes. There was competition among the clans for leadership since the leader was elected by the *majlis*, the meeting of the senior clan leaders. Leaders sometimes designated their sons as their successor in office in their last will, but this was a deviation from the original concept.[33]

In this system: *ᶜasabiyya*, group solidarity, is of utmost importance. This fundamental concept of both sedentary and nomadic tribes guaranteed cooperation in everyday life, mutual help in war (blood feud being some kind of an extension of it) and political cooperation in electing a new head to the tribe. This is an additional reason as to why greater clans have more chance to power than others and why aliens joining a clan/tribe have almost none: they lack a group of common descent supplying them with group solidarity necessary for any candidate to become a leader.[34] This is why proving descent was so important since enlisting all eminent ancestors into one's name enhanced the prestige of a person giving him an aura of authority. The coming of Islam brought about no change in this: the descendants of Mohamed wear a particular turban and enjoy additional prestige only because of their lineage even today. For the same reason, the Hashemite rulers of Jordan claim to be descendants of the Prophet to underline their legitimacy.

Group solidarity was necessary, not only to become a leader but also to be able to carry on with leadership. Lacking any formal institutions, *sayyid*s were dependent on their prestige within their group. Since *sayyid*s had to adjudicate all domestic conflicts and legal disputes, the decisions of persons lacking the necessary prestige were not accepted and implemented. In judging intra-group conflicts, leaders had to rely on established and widely known customs because decisions at variance with

---

[29] Al-Tabarī in Nöldeke (1879: 258–259).
[30] Noth (1994: 13).
[31] Athamina (1999: 10–11).
[32] Athamina (1999: 11).
[33] Athamina (1999: 13–15).
[34] Khaldún (1995: 137–143).

Arabic customs would not be accepted by anyone.[35] To introduce a novel concept or a law would amount to disregard the customs of the ancestors, an act of disrespect. This is also one of the reasons why Arabic customary law changed little during the centuries.

A *sayyid* was also the group's representative in contacts with others. It was he who signed agreements with other groups, freed the captives belonging to his clan, arranged the payment of blood money agreed upon with other groups and decided the request of foreigners wishing to join the group. Part of his office was t o bok after the poor. In order to guarantee the monetary means to his office, a *sayyid* was entitled to one fifth of the booty. *Sayyid*s controlled their clans in concert with the tribal meeting (*majlis*) in which leading role was due to the leaders of influential families and men of authority.[36] Decisions of the *majlis* were compulsory for everyone irrespective of functions or personal qualities.[37]

Inter-group conflicts were settled either by arms or with the help of a mediator. Mediators called *hakam* were persons of enormous prestige known in a wide geographic area. Such, usually elderly men, were trusted by both parties of the conflict who approached him to hammer out a compromise. Only mediators known for their honesty and impartiality were trusted, therefore it was their very interest not to be corrupt or partial otherwise no conflict would be brought to them. Mediators were not judges. As a result, they pronounced no judgments, but only made proposals for a compromise. To accept them was left up to the parties to decide, no *hakam* enforced his decision ex officio. Obviously, *hakam*s too followed Arabic custom in their decisions, but they did so in a flexible way in order to arrive at a compromise acceptable for all. Such decisions later became a kind of precedent on which similar cases could be judged. In this way Arabic customary law could be slightly modified, which gave the system the necessary flexibility. Mohamed, who was a *hakam* himself, introduced some new norms in this way.[38] If no agreement was available, the conflict was solved either with arms or with the help of religious institutions. Taking of an oath in a holy place or shrine in the presence of a priest called *kāhin* was one opportunity to end a dispute. If this failed for any reasons, parties turned to violence, particularly in cases of homicide when blood feud was the norm, a state of affairs that Islamic law tried to restrict.[39]

In South-Arabia, nomadic political institutions gave way to state institutions. If we interpret the term *mukarrib* correctly, early states were governed in some kind of a theocratic regime with a priest-king at its head. Land was owned by the state and a deity. A temple and its priests were not the owners but only the 'managers' of the landed property of the deity who communicated his wills through oracles. Territories conquered by the state were also put under the protection of the deity

---

[35]Lapidus (1988: 14).

[36]Watt (1986: 892).

[37]Dostal (1997: 40).

[38]Serjeant (1995: 34–35).

[39]Dostal (1997: 41).

to become inviolable.[40] This attitude toward property rights has found its way into Islamic law, where the property of God (*māl Allāh*) is a category of its own right. Kings had their own landed property separated from state-owned lands. Royal lands were either cultivated by agricultural labourers or donated to the elite clans by the king to guarantee their cooperation or redeem their loyalty. The cooperation of the nobility with the king was crucial for him because prominent persons of this landed aristocracy were members of a council that had an important role in governance and legislation. In Qatabān there was also a council in which leading bureaucrats were additional members. Decrees of these councils were first made public orally by heralds, then placed around the southern city gate to make it visible for anyone entering the city. The copies of these decisions were also kept in state archives. In the kingdom of Saba', kings could not control landed aristocracy which resulted in a continuous decline of royal power. Here a dual system of governance was established, headed by the king and his appointed heir which later led to a further disintegration with two capitals for each ruler. As a consequence of the increase of power by the aristocracy and the further decline of royal power, the king was elected by the nobles. Thus, the constitutional development of the southern is a move from a theocratic kingdom to a system of government with some feudal characteristics.[41] Kings lost almost all power when noble families elected no member from the royal clan but the first born son of a leading noble family as the next king, a custom reported about also by Strabo.[42]

Bureaucratic organisation was rudiment, yet important in managing state affairs. Leading role was entrusted to *kabīr*s ('great'), originally a priestly function, who headed the college of priests and was in charge of the royal palm groves and of supplying warriors. With the decline of this office, *qails* (speaker) elected by soldiers and landowners, rose to prominence. Important official in legal life was the *hāfī nafs*, who made royal decrees public and decided upon disputes related to water.[43]

6.3 Customs

To understand Arabian customary law, two important factors are of importance. One is group solidarity, a crucial term on which fundamental legal principles and rules are based. The other is the lack of individualistic approach, as everything was seen through the prism of the family and the clan. As a result, there is no word for 'person',

---

[40]Grohmann (1963: 125–126).

[41]Grohmann (1963: 126–130).

[42]Strabo, XVI. IV. 3. Accordingly, power was not inherited by the king's son but by the boy who was first born in the families of nobles after the king ascended to the throne. Hence guards were placed next to pregnant women and the first born baby was regarded as heir, therefore he was educated to fit his office.

[43]Grohmann (1963: 131).

only synonyms such as *qalb* (heart), *rūh* (spirit), *nafs* (soul), and *wajh* (face) are at disposal to refer to an individual person.[44]

I have already shown the significance of genealogy and clan affiliation. Descent was recorded on the father's side, yet patrilineal descent was perhaps not the only system in operation in the entire history of pre-Islamic Arabia as there are hints to matrilineal descent too. Some scholars believe that without a matrilineal system there would be no queens in pre-Islamic Arabia, though we know such rulers. Assyrian inscription already referred to Arab tribes and their queens in the first millennium BCE who were followed in the next centuries with outstanding authorities such as Mavia and Zenobia of Palmyra.[45] What is more, Montgomery Watt is of the view that there were tribes even in the age of Muhammad which recorded descent along matrilineal line. Matrilineal descent was replaced only later by patrilineal lineage and the authenticity of later Muslim scholars making attempts to prove patrilineal descent for everyone is historically doubtful.[46]

Walter Dostal agrees in seeing matrilineal descent important, though not exclusive in any period of pre-Islamic history. According to his view, both lines were important, at least among the northern tribes. To prove this, he refers to marriage customs according to which parties should prove their genealogy in both maternal and paternal lines in order to show to be of "pure blood", that is, a belonging to clans and families. Despite this, paternal line was dominant, proven by the role of males in family and clan matters, the authority of the father and the grandfather, and the loyalty to the custom of the fathers referred to also in poetry. This also explains the subordinated position of women.[47]

This and other matters are difficult to ascertain because pre-Islamic customs called *sunna* were not put into writing since *sunna* was, evidently, oral customary law. The same also goes for the southern kingdoms as well, though some laws were put into writing there. But what were committed to writing were only laws on details or some decisions about important matters but not the customary law as a whole, as it was known to everyone. To our misfortune, royal decrees have reached us only fragmentary, thus reducing our understanding further. Some of these decrees are about land disputes and distribution of landed property, which were in no possession of any clan. Perhaps such decisions were made by the king only as a mediator between clans and not as a sovereign ruler of a state. Other royal decrees are about some criminal matters and problems concerning irrigation. There are also decrees which summarise some laws of the customary law without mentioning the name of the king who proclaimed it.[48]

A unique set of laws are to be found on the city wall of Timnaᶜ, the capital of the ancient kingdom of Qatabān. The text is about homicide, to be judged by the king alone without mentioning blood feud as a mean to end such cases. Interestingly,

---

[44]Lapidus (1988: 18–19).

[45]Shahīd (1970: 21).

[46]Watt (1986: 890).

[47]Dostal (1997: 42–47).

[48]Korotayev (1996: 114–120).

the laws have nothing to say about penalties of homicide, seemingly left to the discretion of the ruler but emphasise that the decision of the king had to be accepted by everyone. Disobedient persons, by contrast, faced death penalty which might be an effort to underpin royal authority also in criminal matters in a tribal society unwilling to accept it. Other laws are about pledge, sale and purchase. Accordingly, a purchaser was granted a period of one month to terminate the contract if he wished so for any reasons. The seller had to take it back but the purchaser had to pay a rent for the object in his possession. If it was an animal which died during the first seven days, the purchaser was obliged to cover the loss. Concerning pledge, the law emphasises that a creditor could also rely on the labour of the debtor's servants and wife. Market regulations are also known from Qatabān (around 300 BCE), protecting local merchants against competition of others. Laws define market prices and should a (usually not local) merchant sell his goods on a lower price, he was obliged to pay a fee for the state. Foreign merchants were further restricted in their freedom since they could stay only in a definite quarter of the city and thus could not compete with local merchants on their place of residence and the local market. Further on, foreign merchants entering the city had to pay a fee at the city gate and were obliged to do their business personally. Concerning the sale of landed property, the laws prohibit any transaction of a land on which there was a grave. Landed properties were separated by sacred and untouchable stone landmarks to which annual sacrifices were presented. Any violation of this law was punished.[49] Here, obviously, the analogy of Mesopotamian *kudurru* comes to mind, testifying that Near-Eastern legal *koiné* extended over land ownership, too.

In addition to these laws, Strabo's report on Arabia Felix is another important source for South-Arabian customs. Accordingly, in the 'country of spices' as he calls this region, the law of inheritance was primarily based on brothers, not on descendants but the role of primogeniture seems to contradict his claim. There was no individual ownership as commodities belonged to the entire clan. More men, usually brothers, had one wife who visited their wife in a regulated way to prevent disputes, but first born males had the privilege to spend the night with her. If one of the husbands was visiting the wife, he left his stick at the entrance to inform others. As everyone had its own, particular stick, males could be identified easily. Adultery was punished by death provided the adulterer belonged to another clan. Strabo underlines his report with a rather folkloristic story about the difficulties of a young wife married to more enthusiastic husbands and her trick to slow them down.[50]

Since lacking written legal text produced among northern Arab tribes, we have to rely on the (sometimes folkloristic) reports of Herodotus concerning their legal life. Accordingly, a contract was confirmed by oath in the presence of witnesses and other assistants. To administer an oath, seven pieces of stone were put between the parties, next they cut their hands with a sharp knife and had the blood dripping on a piece of cloth cut off from their mantle. This blood was next smeared on the stones,

---

[49]Grohmann (1963: 131–139).
[50]Strabón, XVI. IV. 25.

meanwhile parties took their oath. All this was done in the presence of witnesses to guarantee publicity to the act.[51]

Laws of the Nabatean kingdom seem to be more developed, at least we can infer to this from a private archive found near the Dead Sea called the Babatha-archive. Babatha was a Jewish widow who fled to a cave during the campaign of Emperor Hadrian (132 CE) to save her life and her documents. The thirty-five documents taken along with her survived the catastrophe but she did not. These documents prove a landed property ownership of her father Simeon, a right to exercise guardianship over her son, and some claims of her second husband. The earliest documents referring to land ownership are dated to 93 CE, while the latest to 99 CE, that is, some years before the Roman attack against the Nabateans (106 CE). These documents testify to a legal system with fine institutions. There were land records about lands and their owners to which Simeon's land was no exception. The contract about the transfer of landed property regulated every detail, including irrigation, setting the exact time (days and hours) for the irrigation of the land. The breach of contract resulted in paying compensation to the other party and a fee to the Nabatean king. Interestingly, her documents related to guardianship date from the time after the Roman conquest and show Roman legal influence.[52] Roman law continued to play an ever increasing role in Syria in the next centuries, proven by, among others, the popularity of the Syrian–Roman law book (for more on this see the Chapter on the law of the Church of the East).

Among northern tribes it is family law that is known to us because Islamic family law was established on these customs and, therefore, Muslim authors refer to them. Some customs were adapted to Islamic law while others were rejected on ethical grounds. There are traces of monogamy and polygyny (one man having more wives) and—in the south—polyandry (one woman having more husbands) too. In addition, marriage of widows, marriage of cousins, and 'temporary marriage' (*mut^ca*) were also known.

Preconditions for a marriage (*nikāh*) to be lawful were genealogy proving descent, free status (*hurr*), and *kafā'a*, that is, a belonging to the same social status. One could marry a partner belonging to the same tribe, but inter-tribe marriages were more frequent.[53] Polyandry was not precisely regulated, save the number of husbands which could not be more than ten.[54] Polygyny, by contrast, was rather a symbol of wealth and social status. To maintain more wives and bring up all their children was a serious material burden which was beyond reach for many.[55] We do not know for sure whether marriages were consensual or not. There are some hints to the consent of the woman as a necessary condition of marriage but these are referred to only in some biographies telling us that a girl rejected her consent to a marriage arranged for her previously. Virgin girls were highly valued but lack of virginity was no obstacle to

---

[51]Herodotus, III: 8.

[52]Bowersock (1994: 76–79).

[53]Dostal (1997: 47).

[54]Fyzee (2002: 9).

[55]Dostal (1997: 48).

marriage. This is, perhaps, a hint to a sexual freedom of women referred to in poetry and a saying attributed to Muhammad. Pre-Islamic poetry has passionate love as one of its favourite topic, which was of course very popular. One can add to this a saying of the prophet of Islam, according to which he warned his followers not to rush home after prayer or a long journey but give time to their wives instead to put everything in order and make traces disappear.[56] To the horror of pious, Muslims prostitution was also tolerated. Prostitutes had their own flag over their tent interpreted as the symbolic expression of invitation. If a child was born to the prostitute, the father of the child was selected from among the men who repeatedly visited her tent on the basis of physiognomic similarities.[57]

A particular form of marriage was called *mut^c a*, concluded for a definite period of time between a man and an adult woman not living in marriage (divorced, widow), that is, virgin girls were prohibited to enter such a union. It is up to the parties to agree on the duration of their marriage contract after which their marriage is terminated. In addition to specifying the duration of the marriage, monetary issues should also be settled in the contract. Children produced in such a union were entitled to inherit their father. When the marriage came to its end the woman had to observe *iddah*, waiting period, before entering a new marriage. The attitude of Muslims toward *mut^c a* is ambivalent and subject to dispute for centuries. The Qur'ān refers to it once (4.24), and Muhammad is also reported to enter *mut^c a* marriage. By contrast, Caliph ^c Umar prohibited it, arguing that *mut^c a* is at variance with Islamic ethics and called it fornication. Sunnī Muslims follow the line set up by Caliph ^c Umar and prohibit this form of marriage, while Shi^c ī Muslims reject the prohibition of the Caliph making modern Iran a country where *mut^c a* is a lawful marriage.[58] Despite the prohibition of Caliph ^c Umar, Sunnis seemed to abandon *mut^c a* slowly, as according to the biography of Ibn Juray, an eighth-century Muslim scholar he concluded *mut^c a* marriages with 60–90 women during his life.[59]

Another particular type of marriage was called *nikāh al-istibdzā'*, a union between a wife of a man producing no children and another man whose person is not defined by law, leaving to the parties to agree upon. The precondition of the *nikāh a l-istibdzā'* was therefore a previous lawful marriage out of which no descendant was born. To change this and produce heirs, parties reached out to an adult male, most probably to a close relative of the husband, to enter *nikāh al-istibdzā'* and produce heirs to the first husband. Children thus born were the heirs of the first husband while their biological father had no claim for them,[60] otherwise this type of marriage would lose its purpose. In this and other features, *nikāh al-istibdzā'* resembles *chagar* marriage of Sasanian Persia (see Chap. 3 in part One).

---

[56]Serjeant (1993: 150); Dostal (1997: 51).

[57]Fyzee (2002: 8).

[58]Haerii (1996: 252–253). For more on *mut^c a* see Denffer (1978).

[59]Medieval Muslim sources vary in the number of marriages, one has 60, other 90, see Motzki (2002: 282–284).

[60]Dostal (1997: 46).

Regardless the type of marriage, monetary issues had to be settled. A bride's family was entitled to *mahr* ('purchasing price') while a bride was entitled to engagement gift (*saduqa*). The sum of the *saduqa* was not specified by law being dependent on the social rank of the parties. A bride was given a dowry, a wealth that remained in her family as her husband could not dispose of it by his own free will. It was not her husband but her brother who had the final say regarding female property, as the representative of her family. We do not know whether females were entitled to inherit or not. It is true that *Khadīja*, the first wife of Muhammad, a widow of a rich merchant of Mecca, *Abū Hāla b. al-Nabbāsh*, inherited significant wealth from her husband,[61] but we cannot infer from a single case to a general law about female's legal capacity to inherit.

Divorce was easy and frequent, lacking any formal act to be lawful. In pre-Islamic Arabia, women were entitled to divorce their husbands by declaration or symbolic acts. By replacing the entrance of the tent to another side (if it was placed to the west, to the east or vice versa, which is a symbol to deny wedlock) they communicated divorce to their husbands just coming home. Perhaps their right to unilateral divorce was a result of their capacity, albeit restricted, to propriety rights that enabled them to be relatively free from their husbands and thus not completely dependent on their maintenance.[62]

In criminal procedure it is *qasāma* that is worth mentioning. If a corpse was found near a village or in a territory belonging to a tribe and the killer was unknown, fifty male members of the community should take an oath confirming that they have nothing to do with the case and the murder is also unknown to them. Such an oath was called *qasāma* which made inhabitants free of criminal liability, though they had to pay compensation to the relatives of the victim.[63] This oath is again part of the Near-Eastern legal *koiné* going back to archaic times since it is known to the Laws of Hammurabi (Art. 23–24), the Laws of the Hittites (Art. 6), and the Old Testament (Deut. 21: 1–9).

References

Sources

Herodotos (1989) A görög–perzsa háború (ford. Muraközy Gyula). Európa Könyvkiadó, Budapest
Khaldún I (1995) Bevezetés a történelembe (ford. Simon Róbert). Osiris: Budapest
Nöldeke T (1879) Geschichte der Perser und Araber zur Zeit der Sasaniden. Aus der Arabischen Kronik des Tabari. Leiden
Strabón (1977) Geographika (ford. Földy József). Budapest

---

[61] Dostal (1997: 48–49).

[62] Dostal (1997: 50–51).

[63] Hallaq (1997: 6–7).

Literature

Athamina K (1999) The pre-Islamic roots of the early muslim caliphate. Der Islam, Band 76, Heft 1

Bowersock GW (1994) Roman Arabia. Harvard University Press, Cambridge, Mass, USA

Conrad LI (1987) Abraha and Muhammad: some observations apropos of chronology and literary topoi in the early Arabic historical tradition. Bulletin of the school of oriental and African studies. University of London 50(2):225–240

Dandamaev M, Lukonin W (1989) The culture and social institutions of ancient Iran. Cambridge, Cambridge University Press

Denffer D (1978) Mut^{c}a: Ehe oder Prostitution? Zeitschrift der Deutschen Morgänlandischen Gesellschaft 128

Dodgeon MH, Lieu SNC (1991) The Roman eastern frontier and the persian wars (AD 226–293). A documentary history. Routledge, London, New York

Dostal W (1997) Die Araber in vorislamischer Zeit. Der Islam, Band 74, Heft 1, 1–61

Fyzee A (2002) Outlines of Muhammadan law. Oxford India Paperbacks. Oxford University Press, Oxford

Goitein SD (1955) Jews and Arabs. New York

Grohmann A (1963) Arabien. Kulturgeschichte des Alten Orients, Dritter Abschnitt, vierter Unterabschnitt. München

Haerii S (1996) Mut^{c}a: regulating sexuality and gender relations in postrevolutionary Iran. In: Masud M, Messick B, Powers DS (eds) Islamic legal interpretation. Harvard University Press, Cambridge, Mass

Hallaq WB (1997) A history of Islamic legal theories. Cambridge University Press, Cambridge

Klengel H (1985) Nomádok az ókori Elő-Ázsiában. Budapest

Korotayev AV (1996) Pre-Islamic Yemen. Socio-political Organisation of the Sabean cultural area in the 2nd and 3rd centuries AD. Wiesbaden

Lapidus IM (1988) A History of Islamic Societies. Cambridge University Press: Cambridge

Lapidus IM (1998) A history of Islamic societies. Cambridge University Press, Cambridge

Motzki H (2002) The origins of Islamic jurisprudence. Meccan Fiqh before the classical schools. Brill, Leiden

Noth A (1994) Die Higra. Geschichte der Arabischen Welt (Hrsg.: Haarmann). CH Beck, München

Simon R (1975) A mekkai kereskedelem kialakulása és jellege. Budapest, Akadémiai Kiadó

Serjeant RB (1993) Zinā, some forms of marriage and allied topics in Western Arabia. In: Gingrich (ed) Studies in oriental culture and history. Frankfurt, New York

Serjeant RB (1995) Sunnah, Qur'ān, ^{c}Urf. Law and the Islamic world. In: Toll, Skovgaard, Petersen (eds) Law and the Islamic world past and present. Copenhagen

Shahīd I (1970) Pre-Islamic Arabia. The Cambridge history of Islam 1A:3–30. Cambridge

Weiss BG (1998) The spirit of Islamic law. The University of Georgia Press, Athens and London

Watt M (1986) Badw. The encyclopaedia of Islam I:892. Brill, Leiden

Chapter 7
Classical Islamic Law

7.1 The Caliphate and Public Law

At the peak of his success, Mohammed was—in political terms—the lord of Arabia, uniting various tribes fighting against each other for centuries. His political and military achievements were carried on by leaders of the next generations known as Caliphs, though such an institution did not exist at this time. These leaders were rather military commanders, hence their title: *amīr al-mu^cminīn* (commander of the faithful) which was incorporated later into the power of the Caliph. As a result, Arabia and its inhabitants entered world politics out of a provincial insignificance. At the death of Mohammed, little could be seen of this, as his sudden death produced a leadership crisis: he did not leave behind any kind of political testament which could have offered guidance. As the Muslim community (*umma*) was not a tribe or a clan anymore, its leader could not be a *sayyid*, leader of tribal political organisation either. On the other hand, commander of the Muslim army could not be called a Prophet either since according to his own teaching Muhammad was the last among the prophets. First they were called only military commanders (corresponding perfectly to the current situation), which was after a short period of time changed to deputy, Arabic *khalīfa*, and this is how the Caliph as a title was born. With such an ad hoc decision, the current leadership crisis was solved but it did not create a political and legal institution with elaborated competencies. This happened only after a century when Muslim thinkers, mostly experts in law, began to think about the legal position of the Caliph and his relationship vis-a-vis the *umma*. This was the time when the early political theories emerged, again as reflections to their own contemporary events. After defeating the Umayyas and seizing the power for themselves, the ^cAbbāsīs needed legitimisation for their own rule for which a more elaborated theory of the Caliphate was a perfect tool. This is how the first theories were formulated in order to establish the Caliphate as a legal and political institution.[1]

---

[1] More on this in Jany (2006: 17–32, 47–52).

© Springer Nature Switzerland AG 2020
J. Jany, *Legal Traditions in Asia*, Ius Gentium: Comparative Perspectives
on Law and Justice 80, https://doi.org/10.1007/978-3-030-43728-2_7

Before that period, there was neither need nor time to such intellectual undertaking because the first Caliphs were successful military leaders under whose leadership Muslim armies conquered large territories. The first Caliph, Abū Bakr conquered Yemen and took Syria from the Byzantines. His successor, ᶜUmar, the greatest conqueror of Islam, defeated and annihilated the power of the Persian Sasanians in Iran, occupied Iraq and Iran in the eastern front, Jerusalem and Damascus in the Syrian front and Egypt in the West. With Caliph ᶜUthmān, the commercial elite of Mecca, opposing Muhammad's mission for long, ascended to power. After his assassination, ᶜAlī the son-in-law of the Prophet became Caliph, but his rule was challenged by the adherents of the murdered Caliph. Even armed struggle (Siffin) was unable to settle the matter between the parties and subsequent negotiations failed both. Impatient followers of ᶜAlī, later known as *khāriji*tes, turned their back to him and created their own political and military organisation supported by their own understanding of Islam (to be rejected by the majority). Though they endeavoured to kill all their enemies only, ᶜAlī was assassinated and thus *khāriji*tes unwillingly opened the way for Muᶜāwiyya, leader of the traditional Meccan elite, later known as the Umayyas, to unrivalled leadership. These events marked the split of the entire *umma* into rival factions, later to be known as braches of Islam: adherents of ᶜAlī are the Shiᶜīs, a minority group right from the beginning, while followers of the majority are called Sunnīs, though it is a historical anachronism before the tenth century. *Khāriji*tes remained marginal and disappeared from the scene after splitting into insignificant rival groups. Their legacy is only their bad name since doctrinaire, impatient and violent figures, among them *jihādī*s, are called *khāriji*s even in modern Arabic parlance.

Umayyas, now in power, continued the successful military conquests: in the West, Muslim armies reached North Africa and the Iberian Peninsula, in the East the Indus valley and Central Asia. Outstanding ruler such as ᶜAbd al-Mālik also patronised culture and art thus the Dome of the Rock in Jerusalem and the great Mosque of Damascus were built during his rule. As Umayyas considered themselves rather Arab kings but not Muslim Caliphs, that is, they emphasised the national and secular character of their rule against a theocratic and universal concept of the Caliphate. Dissatisfied groups, therefore, started to protest against the rule of the Umayyas in religious terms and concepts, highlighting the importance of the Caliph as a religious leader. Making use of numerous unresolved political and economic problems of the late Umayya period, the opposition led by the ᶜAbbāsī family was able to win social support for their case and swept away the ruling dynasty (750) in an armed revolution.

With the coming to power of the ᶜAbbāsīs, the Caliphate reached maturity both in theory and practice. The first half of the long ᶜAbbāsī rule (751–1258) witnessed the flourishing of legal literature dealing with, among others, public law affairs, centred on the figure of the Caliph. It was this period, therefore, when legal and political theories about the competency and power of the Caliph were formulated, together with the personal requirements of the Caliph and his relationship to the Muslim community. As their claim to power was based on the Caliphate, that is, on a newly formulated theocratic concept, ᶜAbbāsī rulers had to live up to the expectations of their office, but they failed more often than not. With establishing a new capital for themselves in Baghdad, they cut up ties to Mediterranean-oriented Syria (headquarter of the Umayyas) and opened the door for Iranian cultural influence for centuries to come. Iranian influence dominated not only in state administration but also in law, art and science (medicine, astronomy, mathematics). ᶜAbbāsī Caliphs wanted to resolve theological and methodical controversies by force, siding with the rational mu'tazilite school against the more traditional understanding of law and theology. The following *mihna* (inquisition) lasted for decades but ended in a complete defeat for the Caliph marking also the end of the mu'tazilite influence. As a result, instead of rational arguments, it was the tradition of the prophet (*sunna*) that gained pre-eminence in Islamic thinking, thus making the adherents of this understanding Sunnīs. Theological retreat was followed by political and military defeats since the Caliphate began to disintegrate already in the tenth century: East-Iran was lost to local ruler dynasties (Saffarids, Sāmānids, Ghaznawids), Egypt to the Fatimid Caliphate, while Andalusia remained at the hands of the Umayyas right from the beginning of the ᶜAbbāsīd rule. The century long rule of the Shiᶜī Buyid dynasty made the Caliph a de facto prisoner of Baghdad, while the Sunnī Caliphate was administered by a Shiᶜī military aristocracy of Daylamite (NW Iran) origin (934–1062). Buyids were defeated at the end by the Seljuqs coming from the East, thus the Caliph in Baghdad only changed his overlord, though his titular rule remained acknowledged by the new conquerors, keen to have legitimacy. The final blow came, again from the East two centuries later: the invading Mongol army devastated almost the entire Caliphate, ransacked Baghdad and killed the last ᶜAbbāsī Caliph (1258). After a long interim period, it was the Ottoman Sultan who declared himself Caliph and united Middle-Eastern territories inhabited by Sunnīs into a single political unit. Needless to say, Ottoman rule was based on military hegemony and not on classical concepts about the Caliphate, therefore, Ottomans only used, some would even say, misused, the Caliphate to legitimate their own rule and conquests. It was the new Turkish republic, headed by reformist Kemal Atatürk which abolished the Caliphate when dethroning the Ottomans, a controversial move that provoked anti-Kemalist sentiments among Muslims worldwide.

As Islam was born in the context of pre-Islamic Arabia, so was its political institution, the Caliphate, though with significant modifications. As we have seen in the previous chapter, political institutions of tribal Arabia rested on family and clan relations being fundamental entities of reciprocity and solidarity. The coming of Islam altered this, at least, in theory, as a universalist religion with no preference for clan affiliations. With adopting Islam everyone could join the Muslim community (*umma*) irrespective of ethnicity, wealth and social status. Exactly this is what happened since we can find among the earliest generations of Muslims not only members of Muhammad's clan but also that of others from Mecca and Medina, the latter also outside of the Quraysh tribe of Mecca. Despite this, old tribal logic continued to influence institutions and decisions. It is no accident that all the Caliphs were from among the Quraysh tribe, thus excluding the Medinan elite from power, a fact that later became a prerequisite for power in political theories. According to classical theories, only a member of the Quraysh tribe could be Caliph, a claim at variance with the underlying principle Islam but a continuation of the former tribal logic.[2] Newly converts from the conquered territories also become part of the *umma* enjoying, in theory, the same privileges, but they were denied their rights and were considered only as clients, mawālī, instead, which was also an institution of the tribal society securing only limited rights to outsiders just joining the clan (this is the reason why mawālīs supported the ᶜAbbāsis, believed to be in their favour against the Umayyas). In theory, however, there was no place for tribal logic in an Islamic political institution designed for the entire *umma*. Authors of legal theory, therefore, highlighted the Islamic component of the newly created institution, while remnants of the tribal way of thinking could be discerned with careful reading only. As a result, the leader of Muslims was not called *sayyid* any longer, since *sayyid*s were tribal leaders while *amīr al-muᶜminīn* was also soon abandoned since this office encapsulated only military leadership out of the complex functions of Muhammad (prophet, arbiter, military commander, political leader). To highlight the religious component of their office, Caliphs were called also *imām,* as they led the prayers. The two terms were synonyms in the works of medieval legal scholars: when they referred to the office as a secular authority they used the term Caliph, while when referring to the same authority as a religious leader they used the term *imām.*[3]

It was an ex post facto endeavour of the medieval authors to establish the religious and legal position of the Caliph since jurists began to formulate their first theories the office already had a history going back to more than hundred years. In doing so, they looked on history as a model, a precedent which guided them to settle issues of debate. For example, when the question of how could a Caliph ascend to power emerged, the answer was either election or designation by the predecessor in office because in the course of events these two ways had realised (Abū Bakr was elected while he appointed his heir while in office). In short, legal theorists based their theories on already existing practices giving ex post facto sanctions to political routines challenged by many (the Medinese, the shiᶜīs, the khārijīs), referring to them as models. In so doing, the first four caliphs were given extra attention (since no one wanted to refer to Umayyas in the ᶜAbbāsid period) and this is how their legendary exalted position came into being (al-khulafā' al-rāshidūn: the orthodox or the rightly guided Caliphs). Finally, the doctrine evolved according to which only the rule of the first four Caliphs corresponded to the requirements of the imamate, at least according to the Sunnites.[4]

It is worth mentioning that legal theories focus exclusively on the Caliph, while other institutions are considered marginally. The reason behind this is that the *umma* came into being as a religious community in a tribal society with no territorial considerations. Therefore, early *umma* was not a state in need of administration, political organisation and territorial division but a religious community in need of a competent leader after Muhammad passed away. They have found it in the Caliph/imam, who happened to be also a military leader during the wars aimed at spreading Islam.

---

[2]Noth (1994: 32–35).
[3]Lambton (1981: 14–15).
[4]Lambton (1981: 17).

Territories won as a result of successful conquests and had to be administrated and this is how the Caliphate as a state came into being, but only at a secondary stage of development, the *umma* being a religious, and not a territorial community right until now. The Caliphate as a newly born state developed its new offices on military or foreign (mainly Persian and Byzantine) models to ensure daily operation and routine, but the Caliph remained the central figure of the system.

Scholars dealing with such issues came from among the jurists, though the Caliphate and "public law" (there is no such a term in Islamic law) were outside the scope of the *sharīᶜa*. Some philosophers (Ibn Sīnā, al-Fārābī, Ibn Rushd), it is true, dealt with questions of political theory too, but their approach was different: what they were writing about was a political utopia centred around the ideal city (bearing witness to the influence of Greek philosophy) and its ideal king which had almost nothing in common with the Caliphate as an existing institution.

The fact that political theories about the Caliph were developed by jurists could be explained by the special relationship that exists between the Caliph and Islamic law which did not escape the attention of legal scholars right from the beginning. According to Islamic legal theory, it is law that gains supremacy over the Caliph whose duty is to make sure that *sharīᶜa* prevails. The Caliph is, therefore, bound to law and could not change it as a law giver, since to be a law giver is the prerogative of Allāh only. The Caliph is, in short, subordinated to the law and could not transgress it without risking to loose legitimacy. Transgressing the law is not to follow its rules or enact laws contrary to the *sharīᶜa*. Muslims are not obliged to follow such laws and are relieved from their oath of loyalty (*bayᶜa*) to the Caliph, otherwise a lifelong obligation. Thus, loyalty is to the *sharīa* and not to the Caliph who is its symbolic embodiment, its servant but not its master.[5] Islamic law is, therefore, a limit on the power of the Caliph. On the other hand, should a Caliph not transgress the *sharīᶜa*, his power is almost absolute without any check or balance. In implementing Islamic law, Caliphs were free to choose ways and methods including legislation outside the scope of Islamic law, mainly in the fields of taxation, administration and the military. These qānūns, as this body of law came to be known from its Greek equivalent could be regarded as the Islamic variant of public law thought they are not part of the *sharīᶜa*.

Classical theories on the Caliphate concentrate on the person of the Caliph, his abilities and the mental and physical requirements for his office, the modes of creating a Caliph and his rights and obligations toward society. Appointment by the predecessor in office was an accepted way to create a Caliph, which was subject of no dispute. By contrast, election was a hotly debated issue that was never settled with consensus. Although, almost all scholars agreed that election was not a democratic issue which needed the participation of all (male) Muslims, they came to no agreement concerning the number of electors. Electors, known as *ahl al-hall wa'l-ᶜaqd* (men of unlocking and binding) were influential persons forming an electoral collegium with no fixed membership. On the one extreme there was the suggestion that only one elector is sufficient (based on the analogy of a judge who also adjudicates cases

---

[5]Lambton (1981: 18–19).

alone), on the other end the figure of 313 emerged only because this was the number of Muslims at the battle of Badr. Obviously, suggestions between these two ends are abundant and even outstanding authority such as al-Māwardī did not attempt to settle the issue in his classical work about the Caliphate. But he emphasises however that no candidate could be forced to the office by electors, therefore, acceptance of the candidate is a prerequisite, otherwise no election could create a Caliph. In his way of reasoning, al-Māwardī refers to the fact that there is a social contract between the Caliph and the Muslim society at large (this, six centuries before John Locke) and no one could be forced to sign a contact or, alternatively, a contract that came to existence by force is null and void. If the candidate accepted his election by his free will, the contract ($^c aqd$) came into being and a contractual obligation between the ruler and the ruled start to operate. This was ratified by a ceremonial act called $bay^c a$ with the help of which people swore allegiance to the Caliph provided he do not transgress Islamic law. Though important as it was, $bay^c a$ was significant only symbolically because the rejection of ratification did not annul the election and the 'social contract' born out of it.[6]

Caliphs were elected to perform complex duties, first among them was to protect and uphold the faith of Islam. According to al-Māwardī, nine duties are added to this gradual duty: to enforce law between disputing parties, that is, to adjudicate legal disputes following the laws of the $shari^c a$, to protect the realm of Islam, to punish wrongdoers, to defend the border with force in order to deter any attack, to spread Islam with every mean including violence, to collect taxes, to pay the revenue in time and correctly from the treasury for those entitled to it, to rely on wise men and seek their councel and advise before handling, to oversee matters personally.[7] Evidently, this list contains simultaneously real power (such as collecting taxes, defend the border, adjudicate cases) together with admonitions and wise councel from the Mirror for Princes and wisdom literature, widespread already in Sasanian Iran (to seek advice from the wise). Religious and scholarly duties are absent from this list, concentrating only on mundane affairs since the traditional elite, the $^c ulamā$ gained supremacy in Islamic sciences already at the tenth century when al-Māwardī put his theory in writing. In this period, the suggestion of Ibn al-Muqaffa' that the Caliph should decide alone in very important aspect of Islam with binding authority (making him something like a Muslim pope) was neglected, if not forgotten completely. The last admonition, to oversee everything personally is a remnant of the past, when $sayyid$s did in fact everything in person lacking any administration, court system or executive body.

By contrast, Caliphs experienced already during the first decades in power that it is impossible to oversee everything in person, therefore, they appointed persons they trusted to look after matters of the army or settle disputes among Muslims. This was the nucleus of an administrative system that developed during the centuries into a hierarchic, complicated and sometimes chaotic bureaucracy. Since Muhammad already delegated some tasks to his trustees (e.g. to collect taxes), the prophetic

---

[6]al-Māwardī (1996: 5–6), Lambton (1981: 14, 18).

[7]al-Māwardī (1996: 17).

practice served both as a model and a legitimation to create such a system. Therefore *ᶜāmil*s, known already from prophetic times were the first to act on delegated power in behalf of the community. The *ᶜāmil*s of this period collected *zakāt* and the taxes levied on non-Muslims yet at the same time they were also military commanders and provincial governors.[8] Military commanders and provincial governors however were referred to as *amīr* too, bearing witness to a confusion of terms and power during the first decades.[9] It lasted a while to clarify terms and power, though this development had already begun in the reign of the Umayyas, but it was not until before the tenth century when the system gained solid ground. As a result, the *amīr* was the political and administrative head of the province responsible for civilian and military administration. His political significance is indicated by the fact that the inhabitants of the province put their oath of loyalty (*bayᶜa*) to the Caliph into the hands of the *amīr*. His scope of authority included the maintenance of the army, conducting military actions just as well as leading prayers or building mosques. In the Umayyad period the *amīr* appointed the judges, and arranged for domestic security by the 'police chief' (*sāhib al-shurta*) appointed by him. Initially, the *amīr* also had the right to mint money out of which he covered the maintenance of the army. Later on, financial administration was separated from his authority to counter-balance his excessive power. The office of the *amīr* was expressly of confidence: when a new Caliph ascended to power *amīr*s usually lost their office and the appointment of new *amīr*s followed.[10]

Military administration was also of importance right from the beginning, therefore Caliph *ᶜUmar* already set up the first *dīwān* to register Muslim warriors and their revenue and settle issues of the treasury.[11] Based on this nucleus of central administration, the system was developed further by the Umayya Caliphs. As a next step, the *dīwān al-kharāj* was established in order to levy and collect land taxes. Soon the chancellery followed together with the *dīwān al-rasāᶜil* to manage the Caliph's correspondence with the help of scribes. The 'office of the seal' (*dīwān al-khātam*) was created to eliminate abuses, while the *dīwān al-jaysh* was responsible for military affairs including army supplies.[12]

The ᶜAbbāsī Caliphs were wise enough not to destroy the administrative system of their hated enemy in Iran but to develop it further. They not only created new units in the *dīwānī* system but put an official in charge of the whole system to oversee and control it. This is how the important office of the *wazīr* was born, who coordinated the work of the *dīwān*s with the help of the secretaries heading each unit. Documents were prepared by scribes and controlled by the *wazīr*, in extremely important cases the Caliph himself. A separate *dīwān* was set up to manage the income of the state treasury (*bayt al-māl*) which was split up into sub-units along the various sources of

---

[8] Duri (1986a: 435).
[9] Duri (1986b: 438).
[10] Duri (1986b: 438–439).
[11] Duri (1991: 323).
[12] Lapidus (1988: 72).

income.[13] The administrative unit to organise postal services (*dīwān al-barīd*) was
responsible not only for proper communication throughout the realm but also for
intelligence.[14] Though Caliphs did their best to control such a huge administrative
system (even with agents of the intelligence service), misuse of power and bribery
remained endemic problems for centuries.

In addition to systemic changes, the social background of the administrative system was also modified drastically during the ᶜAbbāsīd Caliphate. This was the time
of the Iranian influence since central administration (and the court, too) was built
upon the royal model of the Sasanians, which opened the way for experts of Iranian
origin into the capital. Iranian administrators filled not only provincial offices but
also central offices in Baghdad, the post of the wazīr included.[15] As the example
of the Barmakids and the Takhirids show, these influential families tried to make a
dynastic business from central administration and filled the system with members of
their own clan, making the Caliph sometimes captive of his own administration. As
harems were filled with noble Iranian women, many Caliphs were of Iranian descent,
too, on maternal line. Small wonder, then, that Iranian cultural influence was present
not only in administration but also in political theory, art and literature.

The collapse of the ᶜAbbāsīd Caliphate put no end to its administrative system.
States emerging on the ruins of the Caliphate or witnessing its cultural influence
continued to manage their affairs on this model. Governance in Egypt, Iran, India,
and the Ottoman Empire followed by and large the administrative system of the
Caliphate. Now *amīr*s were primarily military governors whose task was the protection of domestic and internal security with the help of the army maintained.[16]
Ottomans maintained the contours of the system creatively while creating the *dīwān-
i humāyūn* as the supreme central body of imperial governance. At the beginning,
sultans participated personally in the sessions of the *dīwān-i humāyūn*, but from
the early sixteenth century on they were represented by the grand vizier. A separate
building in the palace complex called *dīwānkhāne* was built for the *dīwān-i humāyūn*
which had sessions each day under the auspices of the grand vizier. Members of the
dīwān-i humāyūn came from among the leading officials of the administration. The
power of that body was merely consultative and with the growth of the authority of
the vizier, the *dīwān-i humāyūn* lost its significance. This traditional system of public
administration gradually yielded its place to a more modern governmental structure
because of continuous reforms[17] but a modern public administration system (based
on Western model) was created only in the twentieth century (Turkey, India, Iran).

---

[13]Duri (1991: 324–325).
[14]Lapidus (1988: 72).
[15]Duri (1991: 327).
[16]Duri (1986b: 439).
[17]Lewis (1991: 337–338).

7.2 Islamic Law in the Formative and the Classical Period

It is in order to clarify some terms of Islamic law. To begin with, the meaning of *sharī^ca* awaits some thoughts of importance. *Sharī^ca*, usually translated as Islamic law, has few in common with Western legal concepts where the term law has its origin. What is more, some scholars, either in the past or very recently (Fazlur Rahman, Wael B. Hallaq), believe that *sharī^ca* is not law, but ethics and should be looked at in this way and not as a set of legal precepts defined once and for all. The term law is, therefore, contested even among Muslims and our translation of the *sharī^ca* as Islamic law is justified only because we have no better term for it.

Even understood as law, *sharī^ca* differs from the Western concept of law drastically. The meaning of *sharī^ca* was originally a path leading to water, the importance of which is self-evident in Arabia. This was later re-interpreted symbolically, where water stood for God and hence *sharī^ca* became the way leading to God. Over the course of centuries, law became the corner stone of Islam (against the understanding of Sufis and philosophers), the way leading to God was re-interpreted again, now with the meaning of law that leads the norm-abiding believer to God. Law interpreted as the requirements of God (that makes it at the same time a tool for salvation) has nothing to do with laws defined by a mundane lawgiver of a territorial state (be it a king or a Parliament) for its inhabitants. This underlying principle of Islamic legal thinking makes *sharī^ca* closer to Jewish *halakha* than to anything else, both in theory and in practice.[18]

It also explains why the inner structure is so different from the Western (or other Asian) laws: public law is absent, while ritual law is at least the half of the entire legal corpus, to which private law (family, inheritance, law merchant) and a more rudimentary criminal law is added. As eating and dressing are relevant for both ethics and ritual these topics are included, while a legally important issue such as procedural law is absent from classical *sharī^ca* manuals. Such an inner structure explains why *sharī^ca* is composed of three legal areas: *^cibādāt*, that is, ritual laws, *mu'āmalāt*, private law, and *uqūbāt*, laws about punishments.[19]

Bearing all this in mind, it is small wonder that there is no mundane law giver in the terrain of the *sharī^ca* (Caliphs were, as explained in the previous paragraph, also no lawgivers) since the only law giver is Allāh. Norms defined by God could not be changed, modified, or be declared null and void just because circumstances (social, political, economic) have changed dramatically. This would make *sharī^ca* a very rigid law being at variance with contemporary realities, whatever they were in the past fourteen centuries. Without a mundane law giver and with no chance of change, Islamic law would be a frozen relic of the past, a consequence one wanted to avoid. Fortunately, as Islamic legal theory has it, God did not declare all his laws to mankind but invited Muslims to a joint effort to discover them in texts already known. This theory makes Islamic law flexible, the fundamental texts (Qur'ān and prophetic sunna) unavoidable and those studying them (legal scholars) the most

---

[18] Jany (2012).
[19] Schacht (1927: 321).

important intellectuals. It is important to stress that scholars do not produce new laws, therefore, they, too, are not lawgivers either. What they do is to study the texts and discover laws already there, as an English judge discovers the law in a precedent. It is not the legal scholar, therefore, who creates the law, he only informs the community about laws he happened to discover in these texts and thus recognised a hitherto unknown, though existent, norm.

Since human understanding is not infallible, scholars interpreted the same texts differently which led to different conclusions, though it is evident that only one interpretation could be identical with God's will. Lacking any proof, legal scholars were unable to select this out from among the other interpretations, which led to the acceptance of many doctrines. Laws thus formulated are, however, not to be confused with laws of the *sharīᶜa*, already known for certain. Therefore, legal science and all its achievements, that is, legal doctrines, is not called *sharīᶜa* but *fiqh*, understanding, to make this fundamental distinction clear. *Fiqh* law is uncertain as long as there is no clear proof that some of its doctrine is in fact divine law (consensus is the tool here), but nevertheless it is a living law and should be followed. The majority of norms is in fact *fiqh*-law, which led Joseph Schacht to claim that Islamic law is jurists' law and the result of legal science.[20]

But the consequences are numerous. One such a consequence is legal pluralism, an endemic and systemic feature of Islamic law giving room to legal schools to develop since all interpretations enjoy the same epistemic value. Another consequence is the exalted position of legal science as a discipline and legal scholars as professionals, since what they do is study texts revealed by God and discover the divine will in them. In studying law, they focus on God's will and show the way to salvation for Muslims. And the third consequence is that the history of Islamic law is not the history of legislation producing outstanding codices but that of great legal scholars and their schools. In short, the history of Islamic law is rather a history of Islamic jurisprudence.

The beginning of this history is obscure, as we do not know for certain things which would be essential to our understanding how Islamic law emerged from its tribal background. One such a question is the role of the Qur'ān in the early development of law. Joseph Schacht was sceptical about the role of the Qur'ān and the prophetic tradition in the early stage of development. In his view, both the Qur'ān and the prophetic traditions were latecomers, as Islamic law began to emerge only a century after the death of Muhammad, and references to the Qur'ān are merely secondary developments. Cases reflecting early legal practice being contrary to the words and intentions of the Qur'ān are cited to prove the claim.[21] Prophetic traditions, too, only came later in order to legalise already existing legal doctrines with the help of the alleged sayings and deeds of Muhammad. This is in harmony with Goldziher's view that the history of Islamic law started only a hundred years after Muhammad's death, and not in Arabia, but in Iraq.[22] Generations of scholars had the same view

---

[20]Schacht (1964: 71, 209).

[21]Schacht (1950: 224–227).

[22]Goldziher (1927: 102).

for long, doubts emerged only recently when some scholars challenged Schacht's arguments and claimed that the role of the Qurān was not a late development and Muslim community could actually rely on two sources, the Qur'ān and the customs of pre-Islamic Arabia.[23] The dispute is not resolved as both camps have followers of reputation making it one of the most interesting debate concerning Islamic legal history.

Despite this controversy, it is clear that Islamic law was non-existent at the time when Muhammad passed away, since it was inherited customary law that regulated everyday life for all and with revealed changes (Qur'ān, sunna) for Muslims. To have Islamic law as a distinct entity, further laws were needed to make Islamic law differ from the tribal customary law of pre-Islamic Arabia and to develop a distinct legal system. First Caliphs moved to this direction when they acted new laws to supplement existing norms, a practice at variance with classical theories that were formulated, seemingly, only later. A good example is Qur'ān 2.219 and 5.90, verses that prohibit the drinking of alcoholic beverages without specifying any sanction for not following the law. The first Caliph, Abū Bakr, supplemented the prohibition with a sanction of forty blows with a stick, which was later on increased to eighty by ^cUmar and ^cAlī, arguing that this was analogous to false accusation with adultery which is punished by eighty strokes.[24]

In addition to law making, administering justice was another important factor in shaping the early history of law. At the beginning, Caliphs participated personally in adjudicating cases brought before them in great number. In doing so, they based their decisions on existing customs, Qur'ānic law and their own personal judgment. It was family law and law of inheritance which required an active participation of the Caliphs because Qur'ānic law had brought about fundamental changes both in concept and detail making the new (Islamic) legal system gradually differ from the tribal customary law in these two fields. However, it soon became evident that a Caliph alone could not adjudicate all the cases and this gave rise to the judiciary. The establishing of the judiciary went parallel to the building of the new state administration making the first *dīwān* contemporary to the first *qādī* or judge. This was a turning point in the history of Islamic law because the tribal arbitrator was now replaced by a judge passing judgements and not hammering out compromises. The first judges were, however, not independent judges proceeding on laws of (at that time already non-existent) Islamic law, but subordinated officials to deal with military affairs. The first judges were sent to territories acquired by military conquests in order to settle conflicts within the Muslim army about monetary issues. These judges were subordinated to the governors who could place them from one office to the other if he so pleased. Islamic law as a well-developed legal system was non-existent in this period, so the competency of the first judges was also limited: they dealt with legal issues within the army but had no power to adjudicate other legal matters or to adjudicate cases of the residents of the conquered territories who continued, instead, to apply their own law at their own magistrates. With the passage of time, however,

---

[23]Hallaq (1997: 2–3).
[24]Hallaq (1997: 12).

Muslim judges became more independent from the governors and were not subordinated officials any longer. Parallel to this, judges turned their attention from conflicts in the military to Islamic law, which lend them a particular role in the history of Islamic law forming an elite attached more and more to the teaching of Islam.[25]

What role judges in fact had in shaping Islamic law in the first centuries is subject to debate. Schacht believed that judges (and other officials) had a crucial role in this development, creating laws in their praxis which were 'Islamised' only later, in the early eighth century.[26] Coulson agreed. According to this line of argument, judges relied not only on their own personal judgments but also on local customs which influenced their decisions. This however, gave rise to different legal practice in various geographic areas such as Iraq, Arabia and Egypt which ended up—in the absence of a unified Islamic law—in the first legal schools.[27] Recent scholarship however, challenges this interpretation. As Harald Motzki has shown, judges and governors played less important role in shaping the early legal material than it was believed previously. As a result, early Islamic law developed not on the basis of administrative and judicial practice but on scholarly doctrines formulated by early legal scholars. Thus, emerging laws were later on justified by prophetic traditions.[28]

Schacht's theory about the development of the early Islamic schools is no less controversial. According to this understanding, local customs and judgments based on them gave rise to various understandings of 'Islamic' law thus creating local variants. This is what Schacht called ancient schools of law, the legal corpus of which crystallized during the first decades. This is how the living traditions of the schools were born. Lacking any textual bases, the schools started to legitimise their own doctrines with authorities respected by all. As a result, first the idea of the tradition of the companions of the Prophet was emerging to be followed by the prophetic tradition with Muhammad as the last authority. This however has not altered the fundamental feature of the schools, that is, their geographic determination which made them Iraqi (Kufa and Basra) and Arabian (Mecca and Medina) schools. Members of these early schools were regarded as the elite of Muslim society who preserved their independence and studied law as private individuals led by their specific interest. There was, at the beginning, no formal structure, organisation or unified doctrine of the school. Early schools differed not only in points of detail but also in fundamental issues such as the sources of law or methods applied.[29] Outstanding persons obviously had greater influence than others in defining the methods and doctrines of the schools and this is how these ancient schools came to be associated with their own great scholars. This process transformed the local schools to personal schools and this is why the early school at Kufa became the Hanafite school (following their eponym Abū Ḥanīfa) or the legal school in Medina

---

[25]Coulson (1964: 29–33).

[26]Schacht (1950: 190–213).

[27]Coulson (1964: 30–31).

[28]Motzki (2002: 287–297).

[29]Schacht (1970: 550).

evolved into the Mālikite school, following the footsteps of its great scholar Mālik ibn Anas.

Though a leading theory for long, it is now seriously criticised by some scholars. Wael Hallaq claims that there were no regional schools and the whole theory rests on misunderstanding. Accordingly, the regional school is only the product of modern historiography and there were no regional schools which were later transformed to personal schools since the methods, the common teachings and the institutions are missing from the early schools. Lacking any common doctrine we cannot speak about a school as an entity. What we have instead are the doctrines of scholars on a personal but not on a geographical basis whose doctrine were developed further by their disciples or has fallen into oblivion if they had no followers, or were changed by his followers since strict adherence to a doctrine of the master was unknown at this time. These were individual doctrines also at variance with others in the same "school" not to speak about other schools. In short, Islamic legal schools were personal schools right from the beginning without a first period dominated by regional schools as Schacht believed.[30]

The first work on Islamic law is Mālik ibn Anas' *Muwatta'*, a comprehensive compendium of Islamic law. In this book, Mālik relied primarily on local customs and the Medinese tradition, as hardly any tradition outside Medina can be found in it. As a local of Medina he favours the tradition of this city seen as the city of the Prophet whose traditions are preserved in the local tradition which, therefore, must be given predominance in judging cases. It is not a work on jurisprudence, since theoretic issues are missing from it. By contrast, the work is a compendium of prophetic traditions (hadīth) and laws, based on the customs of Medina, to show the path on which every Muslim has to go (hence the title: *Muwatta'*: the "well-trodden path").[31] The material is arranged in books (*kitāb*), which are about a given field of law, subdivided into chapters (*abwab*) dealing with minor issues and detail that are linked to the topic of a book. Out of the five pillars of Islam (*arkān al-dīn*) four (prayer, alms, fasting, and pilgrimage) are dealt with to be followed by *jihād*. Basic laws of family law such as marriage, divorce and the law of inheritance feature before discussing various forms of business transactions. Penalties are, of course, not missing, together with traditions and laws on dressings, greetings and oaths. Because of its comprehensive nature, the *Muwatta'* is a thematic arrangement of prophetic traditions and local customs to which the author rarely added his own opinion. The work is casuistic, citing prophetic traditions and laws pertaining to a given problem without discussing theoretical issues, problems of methods and sources, important for Muslim legal scholars in the coming centuries. In short, the *Muwatta'* reflects the formative period of the history of Islamic law and is the first attempt at systematising the legal material. Traditions and laws are shown through the lenses of daily routine without giving weight to theoretic considerations.[32] Despite its shortcomings, it is a basic text still today among his followers, the Mālikite school (*madhhab*).

---

[30]Hallaq (2001a: 1–21).

[31]Dutton (1998: 30).

[32]Coulson (1964: 47).

Legal scholars of Iraq were less fortunate than their peers in Medina as they could not rely on Prophetic traditions preserved in local traditions since Muhammad made no entry to Iraq in his entire life. By contrast, Iraq was a territory inhabited by Semitic peoples and a tiny Iranian elite which accompanied the Sasanian dynasty there. With the capital of the former Persian Empire and a multi-religious society (Jews, Christians, Zoroastrians, Mandeans), the social landscape of Iraq differed enormously from tribal Arabia. As a result, there was neither a local (tribal) custom nor a prophetic tradition on which Iraqi scholars could base their own doctrines while formulating Islamic law. As a result, legal pluralism prevailed in some cultural centres where jurisprudence began to develop (Kūfa, Basra). As a next stage of development, doctrines of leading authorities evolved into a more central position while others were pushed into a background. This is how the doctrine of Abū Hanīfa, a contemporary of Mālik ibn Anas was elevated above the other doctrines and how Abu Hanīfa became the eponym of the school. Why however Abū Hanīfa was such a central figure remains obscure, as he left no book on Islamic law and we know his teaching only through the works of his disciples. Therefore the real founders of the Hanafi *madhhab* are, some scholars rightly argue, his disciples, notably al-Shaybānī and Abū Yūsuf.[33]

During the formative period not only different legal doctrines existed parallel to each other, but the problem of the legal sources of Islamic law remained also unsolved. To put a very long story brief, the question was this: if the Qur'ān has no law on a particular issue what are the sources on which one can base his judgment? Are prophetic traditions relevant sources for law and if they are, which are the authentic traditions to be followed and which are not? Could customary law of pre-Islamic Arabia be referred to as a source of law or not? Laws that antedate Islamic law but rest on revelation such as Jewish law could be referred to while shaping Islamic law or not? Human intelligence which rests on reason and not on revelation is also a source of Islamic law or should rather be rejected? These are theoretic issues which need clear answers but there were none in the formative period. Instead, each scholar followed his own understanding and this is the reason why some scholars relied heavily on reason while others preferred rather prophetic traditions.

Scholars who preferred rational arguments (*ra'y*) and based their doctrines on human intelligence when there was no law in the Qur'ān were called *ahl al-ray* (the people of reason). For them prophetic traditions were less important. By contrast, adherents of prophetic traditions built their own legal teaching on prophetic traditions and paid less attention to rational arguments or rejected them altogether, arguing that human intelligence is infallible and cannot, therefore, specify what divine will (=Islamic law) exactly is without a guidance. By contrast, prophetic tradition is a source of revelation in the understanding of the people of tradition (*ahl al-hadīth*) and, therefore, one should look after answers in the sayings and deeds of Muhammad instead of speculating without textual references. The adherents of this understanding regarded Muhammad's sayings and deed as paradigmatic, being a source of law, to be followed by Muslims because they rest also on revelation (though were not committed

[33]Wheeler (1996: 32–41), Hallaq (1997: 18–20).

to writing as the Qur'ān was). Since prophetic narratives called *hadīth* preserve these paradigmatic deeds and words, they are the most important source of law after the Qur'ān. With this, scholars belonging to this camp begun to re-interpret the term *sunna* which meant originally, as we have seen, pre-Islamic traditions or customs and restricted its meaning to the tradition of Muhammad. This is how the prophetic *sunna* was born.

The debate about tradition and rational thinking was not restricted to jurisprudence but was also important in theology and philosophy. Thinkers who favoured rational arguments were called Mu'tazilites, who based their own arguments on Greek philosophy which they wanted to adapt. Early ᶜAbbāsī Caliphs were among their supporters and followers who wanted to spread this understanding throughout the entire realm, also by force if necessary. This is how the Islamic inquisition, the *mihna* unfolded and lasted for some decades in the ninth century. The result was a complete failure since no theoretic problem could be solved by physical force. When adherents of the traditionalist camp were released from prison they were welcomed as heroes by the populace always supporting their case. From this very moment the majority of Muslims could be called properly Sunnī since they followed the traditionalist way of thinking, highlighting the importance of prophetic *sunna* to the detriment of rational arguments.

In jurisprudence this debate came to an end earlier, with the work of al-Shāfiᶜī (767–820) considered to be the founder of Islamic legal theory. His theory gave way to both rational and traditional arguments but gives weight to the latter. His *Risāla fi usūl al-fiqh* defines prophetic tradition as the second source of law after the Qur'ān thus pushing all forms of rational arguments into the background. Al-Shāfiᶜī however, distinguishes between various forms of Qur'ānic laws (*bayan*) which he arranged into categories. The first such a category contains obligations specified by the Qur'ān such as prayer, pilgrimage, giving of alms and fasting. Prohibited acts also belong to this category such as drinking wine, adultery, the consumption of blood and pork. The second category contains laws which are specified in the Qur'ān but details are missing which can be learned only through the Prophet's tradition. An example of this is the law about the number of prayers, or the due share of alms. Laws belonging to the third category are those which can be learned only from prophetic tradition but nothing could be found about them in the Qur'ān. Finally, the fourth category of laws contains rules which can be formulated by rational arguments only.[34] With his theory, al-Shāfiᶜī not only placed prophetic tradition on an exalted position within the system of the sources of law, but also lent divine legitimation to it as a particular form of divine communication (*bayan*). Compared to the detailed exposition of the Qur'ān and the *sunna* he hardly paid any attention to important concepts like *ijmāᶜ* (consensus), *qiyās* (analogy), and *ijtihād* (individual reasoning) showing that these were less important issues for him. Despite this, the well-known theory of the four sources of Islamic law (the Qur'ān, *sunna*, consensus and analogy) was first embodied in the work of al-Shāfiᶜī which is a fundamental pillar of Islamic jurisprudence ever since. With this theory, he put an end to the debate about the sources of Islamic

---

[34] al-Shāfiᶜī (1961: 68–71).

law and narrowed the sources drastically and defined their relative position. Since al-Shāfiᶜī's theory was accepted not only by his disciples but by the Sunnis at large, his theory was in fact a turning point in the history of Islamic law. This is the reason why he was regarded for centuries as the author of the theory of the four sources of law, a commonplace that was challenged only recently and with good reason. The compromise elaborated by al-Shāfiᶜī between the traditionalists and the rationalists fitted only to the ninth century but not to al-Shāfiᶜī's time. This might be the reason why his theory was unnoticed in his lifetime and was discovered only when the debate came to an end with the triumph of the traditionalist, who were however unable to get rid of rationalistic arguments completely. Al-Shāfiᶜī's theory fitted in this situation and this is the reason of its universal acceptance, otherwise a rare thing in Islamic jurisprudence, fragmented into schools. It was however, only his legal theory which became accepted by all school, but not his legal doctrines. Those who also followed his doctrines were the nucleus of a new school later to be known as the Shāfiᶜītes.[35]

Among the four legal schools of Islamic law, it is the Hanbalite that was a new-comer in the ninth century. Its history is connected to the *mihna* since its eponym, Ibn Hanbal was a leading figure of the traditionalist camp who was put in jail for long because of his traditionalist views and reluctance to accept Mu'tazilite doctrines. He was greeted as a hero by his disciples and the people of Baghdad among whom Ibn Hanbal enjoyed prestige and influence when he left the prison at the end of the *mihna*. He did not regard himself an authority in law, only a pious transmitter of prophetic traditions. He rejected the theory of al-Shāfiᶜī and the rationalistic meth-ods altogether. He forbade his disciples to follow doctrines of other jurisprudents as well, including his own, arguing that all legal scholars are human beings not free of sins and errors and are, therefore, not worthy of being followed. The only authority is Muhammad and this is the reason, Ibn Hanbal argues, why his traditions should be preserved and followed but not that of others. Should his disciples follow their master, the Hanbalite school definitely would not have come into being. But they rejected Ibn Hanbal's position in this and collected all his legal doctrines. This is how the fundamental text of the Hanbalite school, the *al-Jāmiᶜ li-ᶜulūm Ahmad ibn Hanbal* came into being with one of his famous students, Abū Bakr al-Khallāl as its editor. Though Abū Bakr al-Khallāl was heavily criticised by his fellows for dis-regarding their master's will, it is due to him that the school came into being from among the traditionalists of Baghdad. Abū Bakr al-Khallāl was not the only non-conformist among the Hanbalites: Ibn Taymiyya and his disciple, Ibn Jawziyya also scandalised contemporary society (thirteenth century) as did those extremist Han-balites who did not refrain from physical violence when they attacked shops, wine merchants, singing girls and broke musical instruments or attacked people hurrying to feasts in the open street of Baghdad.[36]

With the victory of the traditionalist in Islamic sciences and the unanimous accep-tance of theory of al-Shāfiᶜī in jurisprudence, the most important questions were solved. When Islamic law entered its classical period, after three hundred years of

---

[35]Hallaq (1993: 586–605).
[36]Melchert (1997: 137–155).

scientific turbulence, time has come to consolidate and systemise the doctrines of the schools and to put them on solid grounds. It is not to say, of course, that differences in doctrines among schools disappeared or were narrowed just because sources and methods were established universally. By contrast, schools continued to exist and to refine their own inherited doctrines on sources accepted by all. Parallel to this development the technical details of each school were elaborated and the geographical area of their influence established. As a result, the Hanafite school became prominent in the Middle East (the central territory of the Caliphate), Central Asia and in India, the Mālikite school in the Maghreb and Andalusia, the Shāfiᶜīte school in East Africa, Arabia and Southeast Asia. Hanbalites, by contrast, were unable to gain control over a definitive area but are present all around the Muslim world, predominantly in cities, with the exception of modern Saudi-Arabia where neo-hanbalism dominates exclusively.

With this, the personal schools gave way to the doctrinal schools since the space to intellectual manoeuver was narrowed down with established boundaries both in terms of doctrine and geography. Though great legal scholars were not absent for generations to come, their situation was different: time was not rape for completely new theories and methods any longer. What was to be done instead was to create a system, define details and preserve the doctrines of the schools. In short, classical schools were that of doctrines, not of persons. Great person of a school was only its eponym whose authority increased constantly with the passage of time. The methodology of the school, its principles and teachings were regarded formally as the teachings of the founder master irrespective of whether it was historically true or not. The aggregate of these teachings provided the internal structure and cohesion of the schools where the requirement of loyalty to the master was increasingly important. One consequence of this was that it was impossible to have legal opinions fundamentally different from that of the school, which restricted legal pluralism within the school. Since the preservation of the internal unity of the school was the most important underlying principle, creative thinking was pushed into the background. This is the reason why instead of the formulation of individual opinion (*ijtihād*), imitation (*taqlīd*), that is, adherence to the doctrine of the school gained prominence. As a result of this development, the meaning of the term *madhhab* had also changed: previously it referred to the individual doctrines of the scholars but from the ninth century onwards *madhhab* denoted the doctrines of a particular school. Properly speaking, therefore, we can speak about Hanafite, Mālikite, etc. *madhhab*s only from the early ninth century.[37]

The decline of creativity was a universal phenomenon shared by all schools. It was already noted by medieval Muslim scholars with their own expression, according to which: '*the gate of the ijtihād was closed*'. Modern academia took it for granted for generations, as did Muslims who believed it for centuries. Joseph Schacht argued that since the most important problems of jurisprudence were solved, few challenges remained that would keep jurisprudence on the same level than previously. Therefore, Islamic jurisprudence witnessed a decline already from the second part of the ᶜAbbāsid period when Islamic law became rigid and less able to keep pace with the

---

[37] Hallaq (2001a: 19–25).

changing social circumstances and with the new demands of commerce.[38] Ya'akov
Meron had similar views and called Islamic law after the twelfth century 'decadent
post-classical' law.[39] Currently, doubts have been raised whether the gate of *ijtihād*
was in fact closed (Hallaq 1984). Imitation is also seen in a different perspective:
accordingly, *taqlīd* was by far not a blind imitation but a framework of continuous
creative thinking in an age when the doctrines of the schools narrowed down such
possibilities (Jackson 1996). As a result of contemporary research, a handful of modern scholars do not share the pessimistic view about classical and early post-classical
Islamic law.

7.3 Sources of Islamic Law

As we have seen in the previous chapter, it was a matter of debate for long what the
sources of Islamic law were and what role human intelligence and prophetic tradition
has among them. After al-Shāficī's theory was acknowledged by all, the issue was
settled and only minor problems remained to deal with for the next generations.

Following al-Shāficī's theory and the consensus beyond it, it is the Qur'ān that has
eminence in the hierarchy of legal sources. The Qur'ān however is not a law book,
though it contains legally relevant verses as well. By contrast, Qur'ānic legislation is
rather meant to be ethical guideline for all Muslims to follow but certainly not laws
in the modern (Western) understanding. What is more, Qu'ānic laws are extreme
casuistic, since Muhammad did not create a new legal system but only changed
the existing tribal customary law wherever he found it necessary. These new laws
came into being as responses to various questions asked by his followers about some
mundane affairs such as marriage, divorce, inheritance and business activities. These
Qur'ānic verses testify at the same time to the social context in which they came
into being. To know about these circumstances is, therefore, essential to interpret
these verses properly. The new Qur'ānic laws only changed existing laws that were
at variance with the new religion while left the rest untouched. Emphasis was put on
morality and principles that shaped the laws and not on their legal content and technical elaboration. Details which are important for lawyers are missing, while ethical
and eschatological approach prevails. Proper behaviour and reward or punishments
are seen in eschatological prism and in the framework of Muslim's relationship to
God. It is clear from verses that deal with usury, drinking of vine and other wrongs of
utmost importance: sanctions are given only in religious terms, emphasising divine
punishments from which a lawyer however has no idea what to do next. What complicates matter is that verses of legal content could be found throughout the entire
Qur'ān with no connection to each other, standing completely isolated in different
textual contexts strengthening its casuistic feature and making contextual interpretation sometimes impossible. In addition to this, contradictory laws on the same issue

---

[38] Schacht (1970: 565–566).
[39] Meron (1969: 78–101).

could also be found in the Qur'ān (e.g. the drinking wine) and it was a great challenge to all Islamic sciences (law, theology) to harmonise them.

Since the majority of Muslim scholars interpreted Qur'ānic laws not as a modification of existent tribal customary law, but as the fundamental text of a new legal system that has to be created, Qur'ānic laws were, obviously, insufficient and more laws were needed. To this end, prophetic tradition was regarded as the second source in the hierarchy after the Qur'ān which rested, however also on revelation, properly speaking, on a personal revelation that guided the words and deeds of Muhammad. As Islamic legal theory has it, *sunna* differs from Qur'ānic laws in form but not in content: both contain God's revelation, the Qur'ān in a written form ready to recitations while prophetic traditions in Muhammad's words and deeds.[40] Prophetic behaviour is paradigmatic because it rests on two assumptions: one is his infallibility, the other is that norms that guided him are obligatory not only for him (as a Prophet) but for all Muslims (with some exceptions). If these assumptions are accepted then prophetic tradition must be considered as a source of divine law. Consequently, not only Muhammad's words and deeds are to be considered but also his absence from doing certain things.[41]

In al-Shāfiʿī's theory, the third source of law is consensus (*ijmāʿ*) but he interpreted it rather differently as the current understanding has it. In his theory, consensus was the consensus of the entire Muslim community which was based on a saying attributed to Muhammad according to which 'my community will never agree on an error'.[42] Consensus as a legal source was accepted by legal theorist but narrowed down to the consensus of the legal scholars arguing that only legal scholars study the sources and formulate their own doctrine based on their interpretation of the sources if neither Qur'āic law, nor prophetic tradition reveal the norm to be followed (*ijtihād*). These interpretations differ, of course, both in important issues and technical detail but no one is able to know for certain which doctrine is in accordance with the divine law and which is not. As a result, all interpretations and doctrines are accepted and to be followed by adherents of the legal schools. This is the reason why *fiqh* law, that is, law defined by legal scholars is not certain yet it is normative. Should however, all legal scholars arrive at the same conclusion concerning a particular case and its law, this consensus elevates the doctrines of scholars to certainty, that is, the former doctrines of less epistemic value is identified as a piece of divine law and treated accordingly. In creating consensus, every legal scholar had to participate actively, otherwise the consensus would be binding only for those who had participated in it. The meaning of consensus is taken very seriously since there is no consensus until everyone is convinced and the different doctrine of only one scholar could prevent consensus from emerging. Consensus (*ijmāʿ*) is a legal source only in this sense and is identic in its function with Jewish majority rule. In Jewish law, too, various doctrines of scholars and schools are tolerated until the majority of legal scholars agree on a definite interpretation of law and vote for them. When a law is defined

---

[40]Weiss (1998: 44–45).

[41]Weiss (1992: 167).

[42]al-Shāfiʿī (1961: 286).

by majority vote it becomes part of the *halakhah* and no one is allowed to neglect it and act otherwise. Islamic consensus has the same function and effect but is more "democratic" since it requires the consensus of all legal scholars. A t he same time, it is less operational because there emerged a lot of theoretic problems which were hard to resolve.

One such a problem was the legitimacy of consensus which had become one of the much disputed questions of medieval Muslim legal scholars. In addition to the issue of legitimacy, practical problems were also abundant. Just to cite some problems of the medieval legal scholars: who are the members of a given generation of scholars who should come to consensus? Is there a tacit consensus, that is, what is the legal effect if a legal scholar does not approve a particular law but raises no objection against it: could we assume that he tacitly supports the decision or not (because, for example, a legal scholar in central Asia has no information about things in the Muslim West). There was no agreement among legal theorists: some argued that silence could not be regarded as consent being given because there can be several reasons behind it (political pressure, the lack of information, etc.), while others regarded tacit consensus acceptable.[43]

Analogy (*qiyās*) features at the bottom of the hierarchy of legal sources and is, properly understood, not a source but a method of interpretation. Analogy, however, is a misnomer here, since *qiyās* reflects not only to analogy as a method of reasoning but also to other devices such as *argument a contrario, ad maiore a minus, reductio ad absurdum.*[44] Analogy or, properly speaking, rational arguments are, however, pushed into the background since one can rely on them only when neither Qur'ānic law nor prophetic tradition has a law on a particular issue and Muslim scholars were also unable to reach a consensus. Even so, the role and function of analogy continued to be subject of debate among Muslim scholars. Traditionalists were reluctant to accept analogy as a source or treated it at least with suspiciousness. Hanbalities in general and Ibn Hanbal in particular were very sceptical but accepted analogy at the end as an ultima ratio (this secured them their position within the orthodox Sunnī camp) while the Zāhirīte school rejected analogy altogether (resulting in their rejection among the Sunnī legal schools). By contrast, the majority of legal theorists who accepted analogy as a source and method devoted time and energy to define in detail how analogy operates and what are the crucial points of this method. Theorists identified four elements of an analogy called pillars (*arkān*) which are the basic case (*asl*), the new case (*far^c*), the *ratio legis* (*^{c}illa*) and the norm pertaining to the basic case (*hukm*). In modern Western terminology *^{c}illa* corresponds to the *ratio legis* or *ratio decidendi* indicating the common attribute which can be found both in the basic and the new case. *Hukm* is the legal norm pertaining to the basic case which is to be applied for the new case, too, if the *ratio legis* supports this.[45]

---

[43] Hallaq (1997: 78).

[44] Hallaq (1989).

[45] Weiss (1992: 556–592) has details on analogical reasoning and its methods.

7.4   Substantive Law

7.4.1   Family Law

Marriage for Muslims is a moral obligation, which is however a single contract between the parties without any formalities or religious ceremonies. The first step in the long road to marriage is the marriage proposal for which Islamic law provides detailed rules. Proposals are important because a proposal and its acceptance in the presence of witnesses actually creates a marriage. Therefore, Islamic law has a lot to say about who could be approached with a proposal to marriage and who cannot. No one can propose a marriage proposal to a woman to whom another person has already publicly made such a proposal, except if the first proponent consents to it. If the first proposal was not publicly accepted then there is no objection to further proposals.[46] In addition to this, prohibition of rivalry hindrances based on religious, social and economic considerations are abundant. Among these, the prohibited categories of women should be mentioned first.

Incest taboo is (contrary to Iranian law) very important in Islamic law, thus family relations are defined rather broadly resulting in the exclusion of a variety of women who could not be approached with a proposal (*mahram*). The result of such thinking is that women who are actually not relatives are nevertheless *mahram,* like a foster mother whose position is considered as that of a mother. Qur'ānic legislation also prohibits a marriage proposal to two sisters simultaneously (4.23.) which was later interpreted by Muslim scholars as a prohibition to also marry the paternal and the maternal aunt of the wife, an understanding that was supported also by prophetic tradition. Social standing was sometimes also an obstacle to a proposal. Though a marriage between slaves and free persons was not prohibited if the parties so wished (a slave can marry a female slave and a free woman if she and her guardian consent to it), but a free woman cannot marry her own slave because in that case she would acquire ownership over her husband. It was disputed however, whether a free man could marry his female slave or not.[47] The number of wives was also an obstacle to a proposal if a man already had four wives, the maximum number of wives stipulated in the Qur'ān. If someone already has four wives and wants to conclude another marriage, he has to divorce one of his wives. It became however a matter of scholarly dispute whether the number of wives and the laws following from this are also to be applied to slaves or not. Some believed that the same laws go for slaves, while others denied it and argued that they could marry only two women, based on an analogy that only a half of what is stipulated for free persons pertains to slaves (e.g. blows with a stick), and it should be applied also when determining the number of their wives.[48]

---

[46] al-Misrī (1994: 510–516), Ibn Rushd (1996: 1–2). Competing proposals were expressly prohibited by Muhammad, see Mālik (1989: 209).

[47] Ibn Rushd (1996: 47–51), al-Misrī (1994: 528).

[48] Ibn Rushd (1996: 47).

Difference in religion is also a hindrance, though there are different laws for the sexes. As a result, a Muslim man can marry a *kitābiyya* (a free woman belonging to the revealed [Christian, Jewish] religions) but a Muslim woman could not marry a non-Muslim man. Religious difference may complicate matters further if either of the non-Muslim partners converts to Islam, since their marriage was evidently not concluded with the observance of Islamic law. Islamic law developed complicated laws to solve the issue. Accordingly, if the man converts first and his wife is a *kitābiyya*, their marriage remains in force, but if she is not a *kitābiyya* and does not convert to Islam, they have to be separated. By contrast, if the wife converts first her marriage it remains sound only if the man converts to Islam during her *ᶜidda* period.[49]

Equality of partners *(kafā'a)* is also a precondition, though it was subject to debate for centuries with few points on which legal scholars could agree. One such a point is that equality mattered only from the man's side, that is, he had to be on the same social position as his wife was before her marriage, that is, *kafā'a* is an obstacle to marriage on the male line. By contrast, if a man wants to marry a woman of a lower rank than that of his, *kafā'a* is no obstacle since his wife would rise to a higher social position. It is evident from these laws that *kafā'a* is intended to protect women or, properly speaking, their social status which could not be deteriorated by a marriage. Descent, an important issue in pre-islamic Arabia, continues to play an important role in Islamic law, too, since without proving descent one cannot ascertain social status. Details, however, were and remained to be disputed since social status is by its very nature a social, and not a legal, issue, and it is hard if not impossible to define it with legal terms.[50]

If there are no obstacles to marriage and the proposal is accepted, negotiations follow between the families resulting in a marriage contract regulating monetary issues and the rights and obligations of the parties. Islamic law gives a relatively free hand here to the parties who could regulate their affairs on their own will, sometimes even contrary to Islamic law (for example, a marriage contract could rule out the possibility for a second marriage of the husband completely or could make it dependent on the consensus of the first wife, giving more power to her than provided by Islamic law). When the parties agree on all issues, they produce a marriage contract which should be presented to the couple for their approval. To present the contract loudly during the wedding is a constitutive element of the process, otherwise the marriage is null and void. The parties have to agree to the contract during the wedding and state clearly and unambiguously their agreement to it since according to Islamic legal understanding marriage is a consensual contract.[51]

Islamic law defines precisely the legal effects of a marriage. Accordingly, (1) sexual relations between the parties becomes legal and the children produced are

---

[49]Ibn Rushd (1996: 56–58).

[50]Ziadeh (1957: 509–517), al-Misrī (1994: 523–524).

[51]Ibn Rushd (1996: 3), al-Misrī (1994: 517), Mālik (1989: 209), Fyzee (2002: 91–92); Bakhtiar (1996: 396–400).

legitimate descendants of the parties; (2) the wife is entitled to *mahr* and to maintenance; (3) the husband gains authority over his wife; (4) the parties inherit each other in case of death of a party; (5) laws prohibiting marriage towards the relatives of the partner enter into force; (6) *ᶜidda* (waiting period) is compulsory for the wife in case of her divorce or becoming a widow; (7) the marriage contract enters into force and becomes enforceable; (8) parties keep their properties separated; (9) the wife continues to belong to her pre-marriage *madhhab* and there is no change in this respect.[52]

Islamic law—though ensures male dominance—also has laws to protect wives, both their persons and their belongings. An important law to protect wives and ensure harmony in a polygamous family is that husbands should treat their womenfolk equally, that is, a husband should share his time and energy proportionally among his wives and should provide the same material benefit for all his wives. In this all legal schools agreed. By contrast, obligation of a wife was subject to debate among the schools. Al-Shīrāzī, a prominent member of the Shāfiᶜite school denied that a wife has any obligation toward his husband except sexual relations and is not obliged to cook, wash and keeping the house. The Hanafite School on the other hand considered keeping the house and raising children the religious duty of women. If they do otherwise, it is a sin, though they cannot be forced to do their duty by the court.[53]

Monetary issues are important for Islamic family law in order to secure at least some independence for females. This is the reason why *mahr*, a sum to be paid for the wife is a precondition to a lawful marriage. The sum of the *mahr* is not specified by law and it is left to the parties to agree upon it based on the social and economic position of the families. This is the reason why *mahr* has no upper limit. But *mahr* also has no minimum either because it was specified differently by the schools and there was agreement among them.[54] What is more, the currency of the *mahr* was also not exactly specified since not only money but other objects, too, are among the goods that could be given to a wife.[55] In addition to *mahr,* the right to maintenance is the other prerogative wives enjoy in a Muslim marriage. Though all schools agreed on that principle, the reason behind it remained controversial. Some scholars believed that maintenance was the compensation for sexual rights which the husband enjoys over his wife, while others think that maintenance is due to the womenfolk because they are hindered in moving freely in the public space and to work independently from their family and could not, therefore, manage their own maintenance but are dependent on their families. Irrespective of the reasons, maintenance includes food, garments and securing a home which is the duty of the husband during marriage and the months of the *ᶜidda* period following a divorce. In exchange for *mahr* and maintenance, husbands have some prerogatives among which the right to enjoy their wives sexually is one of the most important. In addition to this, a husband could limit

---

[52]Fyzee (2002: 116–117).

[53]al-Misrī (1994: 948–949).

[54]The prophetic tradition is quoted by Mālik (1989: 210).

[55]Ibn Rushd (1996: 23–25), al-Misrī (1994: 533).

his wife's freedom of movement outside her home since a married woman cannot
leave her home without her husband's permission and cannot let anybody in the
house. She can leave the city where she resides only in the company of her husband
or another *mahram* male relative. It is also the right of the husband to control his
wife and warn her against any signs of disobedience, something which could result
in losing the right to maintenance. At first, husbands should warn their wives only
orally and advice to be obedient. If it proves to be insufficient and disobedience
continues, a husband could correct his wife physically, too, but in so doing he must
not cause bleeding, make a wound or break a bone. Should the conflict remain
between the parties they or, properly speaking, their family usually choose an arbiter
to reach agreement and restore harmony. Finally, the parties could divorce if neither
an arbiter nor any other means is sufficient to bring about peace.[56]

Divorce (*talāq*) is a male prerogative to terminate a marriage even without the
consent of the wife. If divorce is the wish of both parties, they could terminate
their marriage by consensus. A husband is entitled to declare *talāq* any time during
marriage, and in doing so he is not required to justify it nor is he obliged to refer
to some conditions on which his declaration rest. The agreement of the wife is not
necessary for a divorce to be lawful which could be pronounced even in her absence. A
husband may delegate the right to pronounce divorce to his wife, usually guaranteed
in the marriage contract and bound to some conditions. Such a condition is that a
husband is negligent to provide due maintenance to her or wants to marry a second
wife against the will of his first wife.[57] In the absence of such an authorization,
women could divorce their husbands on their own initiative, provided they pay back
everything their husband had spent on their maintenance during the marriage. The
name of such a divorce, *khulᶜ* (bail out) shows the most important point of this legal
institution.[58]

Law of inheritance is the most complicated field of Islamic law in which lawyers
have difficulty in finding their way. The science of distribution (*ᶜilm al-farā'id*),
as Muslim lawyers call this field, is extremely complicated because Qur'ānic laws
and the customs of pre-Islamic Arabia are brought together into one single system,
though their principles are different. What complicates matter is that there are almost
no general rules and principles, only laws pertaining to a particular situation, thus
creating an ocean of casuistry. In addition to these difficulties, one could add the
differences between the legal schools, itself a consequence of the uncertainties of the
sources and their interpretation. Shiᶜī law of inheritance in particular (otherwise not
very different from the Sunni schools in substantive law), differs considerably from
that of the Sunnī schools because it rests on an entirely different understanding.

Qur'ānic legislation brought about enormous changes in law of inheritance, providing new laws based on a completely different understanding from that of pre-
Islamic tribal customs. Arabic tribal society regarded the clan as the basic unit of
inheritance, with the result that (1) the closest agnate relatives were considered as

---

[56]al-Misrī (1994: 538–542).

[57]Ibn Rushd (1996: 84–87).

[58]Ibn Rushd (1996: 79), Fyzee (2002: 163–164).

heirs; (2) cognate relatives and females were excluded from the bequest; (3) the bequest was equally distributed among persons standing on the same grade. Qur'anic laws changed the fundamentals of this tribal system when stipulating that (1) married partners could inherit each other; (2) cognate relatives and females also have the capacity to inherit; (3) female relatives usually receive half of the share of males from the bequest. Sunnī schools consider these new rules not as a basis for a completely new system of inheritance on which further laws has to be established in the same spirit, but as a correction of existing tribal customary laws. Since Qur'āanic laws have, obviously, priority to tribal laws, therefore, Qur'ānic heirs also enjoy priority to other heirs. As a result, Sunnī legal schools created two types of heirs, the Qur'ānic heirs (ashāb al-far'āid), and the agnate relatives (al-ᶜasabāt), that is, the beneficiaries of the previous tribal system. In distributing the bequest, Qur'ānic heirs should be given their due shares first, with the rest going to the agnatic relatives if there remains anything to distribute. This system is complicated further with the laws on exclusion (al-hajb) that could be, in its turn, relative and absolute. Exclusion is a particular rule to exclude persons from the bequest, otherwise entitled to inherit, that is, it is an exception from the general rule that every living person has the capacity to inherit, including the foetus (provided it is born alive). Absolute exclusion is when someone is excluded from the bequest completely because of some conditions specified by law. One such a condition is homicide: whoever is responsible for the death of a person could not inherit his bequest. Religious difference is another cause for exclusion: a non-Muslim cannot inherit a Muslim as a Muslim cannot inherit a non-Muslim either (save the Shiᶜī laws). Slavery is the third condition, as no slave could inherit a free person. In contrast to absolute exclusion, a relative exclusion makes someone not incapable to inherit completely but transforms his/her legal title and status to a lesser degree. If there are other heirs whose title is stronger than that of others, heirs with a stronger title reduce the chances of their co-heirs who can inherit only the rest.[59]

In distributing the bequest, descendants enjoy priority since their claims should be met first. Descendants are followed by ascendants, collateral relatives standing only in the third place.[60] The principle of *ius representationis* is missing from Islamic law, according to which descendants of an heir who died before the testator could inherit up to the share of the heir who passed away.[61] Qur'ānic heirs are husbands, wives, fathers, mothers, daughters, daughters of sons, sisters, grandfathers, grandmothers, maternal siblings but their share is by far not equal. Even so, it may happen in some constellations that the sum of the shares that should be given to Qur'ānic heirs is more than the bequest (e.g. when ½ is due to the husband and 2/3 to the sisters altogether), since Sunnī legal scholars see Qur'ānic shares as obligatory for the beneficiaries to be given. To solve this anomaly, the principle and practice of

---

[59]al-Misrī (1994: 475–476), Bakhtiar (1996: 290–294, 311–312), Fyzee (2002: 394–396).

[60]Ibn Rushd (1996: 411).

[61]The modern states try to overcome this rule of the classical Islamic law considered unjust by legislation even in countries where the basis of law is Islamic law, like for instance in Pakistan (1961), see Fyzee (2002: 392–393).

al-ʿawl, correction (reduction) was born, according to which the share of each heir is reduced proportionally until the sum of their shares equals the bequest. Once Qur'ānic heirs received their due share, the rest is given to agnate relatives. If there was no Qur'ānic heir at all, the *al-ʿasabāt* could claim the entire bequest. The most important principle of the distribution of the bequest is that a relative on a closer degree would exclude a more distant one but the distribution is more complicated than that. In fact three factors should be considered: class, degree and the strength of blood relationship. Descending, ascending and collateral heirs form three classes, respectively, in this order of priority, allowing descendants to have priority over other classes. Degree means that the degree of relationship is a decisive factor to select the heirs, something which is taken extremely seriously which could rule out some descendants completely in the absence of *ius representationis*. Seen from a different perspective, it also means that no one could inherit a deceased person if a person is still alive by whom he/she is linked to the testator. For example, a grandson could not inherit the deceased if his father, that is, the son of the deceased, is still alive. The strength of blood relationship reflects the relative status of persons belonging to the same degree and class. For example, if there are two brothers (who are by definition members of the same class and belong to the same degree) among whom one is a brother through the line of both parents while the other is only a half-brother, priority goes to the former enjoying priority against the half-brother.[62]

Islamic law grants only a rather subordinate role to testamentary succession, since according to Muslim understanding, intestate succession enjoys priority over the last will of a person making arbitrary decisions about his belongings. This is the reason why Islamic law restricts the possibility to draft a testament by two restrictions. One is that a testator could dispose of only one third of his property in a last will, that is two third of his wealth remains untouched and should be distributed along the laws of intestate succession. The second restriction is that no testament could be produced for the benefit of the heirs of intestate succession. Now it is clear that the freedom to produce a last will is missing from Islamic law, which is remarkable since the same Islamic law does not restrict a person to dispose of his property *inter vivos*. As a result, one could dispose of his property without restrictions while alive, but is deprived of the same right when dying, in his last will. On the other hand, Islamic law guarantees a privileged position to the will of the testator, sometimes even to the detriment of Islamic law itself.[63] For example, Muslims and non-Muslims could inherit each other by their last will, something which is, as we have seen above, completely unthinkable in intestate succession.

---

[62]Fyzee (2002: 423–426).
[63]Fyzee (2002: 358–359).

7.4.2   Law of Property and Obligations

Law of property and obligation is a very important part of Islamic law which was
created during the Middle Ages for the benefit of the city-dweller merchants. This
is the reason why modern Islamist thinkers on the left, such as Sharī͑atī, criticise
this part of the law, heavily claiming that it privileges the bourgeois. By contrast,
conservatives allied to merchants defend this corpus of law with its underlying principle of the freedom of trade that comes close to a laissez faire understanding of
economic activity. Muslim scholars concentrated rather on the laws of obligations,
while propriety rights were elaborated less. Sale as a contract was understood as
a model also for other contractual obligations, thus purchase gaining an important
position among contracts. This is the reason why almost all *fiqh*-books begin with
sale in their section about the law o f property.

The first step to arrive at a sale (*bay͑*) i s t o make a n oral offer followed by either
its acceptance or decline. This is of course only in legal language, since in reality
an offer is followed by a long bargaining, most of all about the price. An offer and
its acceptance create a sale as a contract but it is important that the parties should
agree about essential elements of the contract such as the number, the quantity and
the quality of the commodities together with their price. Islamic law makes some
restrictions on the freedom of trade on ethical ground, the prohibition of usury (*ribā*)
as the most important among them. Though it is believed to be a law against usury
(or any interest according to another interpretation), it is more complicated than this.
There are two verses in the Qur'ān against *ribā* (2. 275, 278), it was however the
Muslim legal scholars who generated a general prohibition from the Qur'ānic texts.
In this interpretation, *ribā* means that the price of a commodity is not exactly known at
the moment of the conclusion of the transaction or the exchange of the commodities
is not immediate but the transfer of one or both of them is postponed to a later
date. In addition to *ribā*, the prohibition of uncertainty *(gharar)* is another restriction
on the freedom of contract on ethical grounds. Uncertainty may extend over: (1)
the commodities; (2) the price of the commodities; (3) the quality and quantity
of the commodities. Should there be uncertainty in these points of the contract,
the agreement is null and void on the bases of *gharar*. This is the reason why the
agreement of the parties should contain these elements.

Warranty for goods as a term was non-existent, though the idea itself was part
of everyday legal practice. Warranty included liability for any shortcomings in the
commodity itself and for any legal claim by a third party concerning the object of a
sale. If there was any fault (*͑ayb*) in the good, the customer had the right to return
it (*radd*) to the seller. The fault in the commodity however had to make the use of
the good impossible and should be missing from commodities of the same kind. In
absence to choose *radd*, a buyer could claim compensation. Should the buyer know
about the fault in the commodity yet agreed to the transaction, he was not entitled to
radd. He could assert his claim only if his consent was not given.[64]

---

[64]al-Misrī (1994: 392).

Contracts such as rent, deposit and other private legal institutions were modelled and elaborated on sale. The most characteristic Muslim legal institution remained however the pious endowment called *waqf*. Islamic law rejects the idea of a legal person, therefore, a *waqf* is closer to an Anglo-Saxon trust than to Continental foundation. Islamic law has two types of *waqf*, *waqf khayrī* and *waqf ahlī*. A *waqf khayrī* is a *waqf* for charitable purposes for the benefit of the entire society, such as maintenance of schools, hospitals, development of water supply, roads and bridges. By contrast, the primary objective of a *waqf ahlī* is to arrange for the material well-bing of family members, that is, of the founder's children and other descendants. The common feature in both forms of *waqf* is its religious content and purpose, since a *waqf* is a religious institution. The name *waqf* goes back to the verb to hold up, keep back, referring to the fact that all goods of *waqf*s are unalienable, being kept back from economic transactions. It is only the fruit of a *waqf* that could be used for the benefit of the beneficiaries of the *waqf*, but not its capital.

Any person, who is a mentally sane adult and of free status could establish a *waqf*. This creates an astonishingly wide circle of entitled persons, including women and non-Muslims, otherwise only with restricted legal competencies. When a non-Muslim establishes a *waqf* however, it should be compatible with Islamic purposes but not with others (a non-Muslim may establish a *waqf* to build a mosque but not for erecting a church). In creating a *waqf*, its founder has freedom to make his provision: could ascertain its wealth, objective, beneficiaries and basic rules. Islamic law guarantees considerable freedom for stipulators, while removing restrictions hindering to establish a *waqf* and defining only prohibitions that are self-evident (no *waqf* could be established for objectives prohibited by Islamic law).

Goods transferred for a *waqf* have to exist continuously and produce profits, that is, it cannot be created by commodities becoming extinct after a single use (such as food). It was land ownership that met the above criteria and this is also the reason why arable land was the most common good on which a *waqf* was created. Everyday management of a *waqf* was usually the task of the *mutawwalī*, appointed by the founder to administrate its business. A *mutawwalī* once appointed enjoyed considerable freedom in managing the *waqf* and could not be removed by the founder. Should a *mutawwalī* deliberately harm a *waqf* and act obviously against its interests, he could be removed from office, but not by the founder but by the court. A *mutawwalī* is obliged to act in person and not transfer his office to anyone else but could rely on professional help of deputies. A *mutawwalī* is not obliged to manage a *waqf* without remuneration and it is usually the founder who establishes the *mutawwalī*'s fee. In the absence of such a stipulation, a law court is entitled to supplement it and specify a salary for him, which could never exceed ten percent o f he income.[65]

One of the most difficult tasks of a *mutawwalī* is to distribute the profit among the beneficiaries. Profit however was not guaranteed, even missing in years of poor harvest. As the profit of the years of good harvest had to be distributed among the beneficiaries and could not be spared for less fortunate years, *waqf*s struggled against financial difficulties in many cases. In poor years when the income did not

---

[65]Fyzee (2002: 311–317), Makdisi (1981: 44–47).

meet the beneficiary's claims, it could be source of serious tensions. In managing the *waqf*'s business, the *mutawwalī*'s responsibility was restricted to intentional harm and utilisation diverging from the objective of the *waqf*. In order to prevent misuse, *mutawwalī*s were continuously monitored and controlled. In addition to the founder law, courts also supervised the management of the *waqf*s. A judge could monitor the activities of the *mutawwalī* who could take a loan only with his permission. It was also the task of the judge to supervise the distribution of the profit to the beneficiaries. As was the judge who removed a *mutawwalī* from office in case of deliberate mismanagement.[66]

*Waqf*s are designed for continuous operation, but they could be terminated in certain circumstances, for instance, when the founder apostatises or the objective for which the *waqf* was created becomes void. In such cases, the wealth of the *waqf* had to be utilised, according to majority opinion, to the benefit of the poor or should be returned to the heirs of the founder. Authorities, however, could not confiscate it. It is an important point because historical experience proves just the opposite. Confiscations, sometimes called euphemistically nationalisation were against Islamic law but driven by economic and rational arguments. Since lands of *waqf*s were kept out from the economic life the consequences were to be felt soon. Huge areas of arable lands were left uncultivated because of mismanagement or the lack of resources necessary for sowing, leading to hunger or starving. In such cases, secular authorities were left no option but to confiscate when they wanted to hinder catastrophic consequences. The problem was economic, but its cause was legal: laws on *waqf* separated instead of integrating the huge amount of wealth of *waqf*s into the economic system which became an obstacle against economic growth. *Mutawwalī*s were only administrators, not owners, being less interested in managing the *waqf*s properly. Monitoring was less effective and bureaucratic, left in the hands of judges responsible for implementing Islamic law and not for economic efficiency. In addition, huge areas of arable land were accumulated in the hands of *waqf*s which paralyzed the entire economy. In the Ottoman Empire, three fourths of arable land was in the (mis)management of *waqf*s. Egypt, too, was no less different, leading its great reformer, Muhammad ᶜAlī (1769–1848) to nationalise the *waqf*s in the early nineteenth century, a move that spared only houses and gardens. In Algeria, the French started reforms in the 1830s culminating in the Act of 1873, a law that brings all lands under French law and declares every diverging law and condition null and void. With this law, the French did not abolish *waqf* as an Islamic legal institution because they respected its role in Islam, they only restricted its operation, primarily in the law of inheritance.[67]

---

[66]Makdisi (1981: 54–57).

[67]Heffening (1993: 1099–1102).

7.4.3   Punishments

Criminal law as a branch of law in its Western conception does not exist in Islamic law. It is therefore more appropriate to speak about some specific criminal acts and their punishments. 'Criminal law' thus defined has three layers. One consists of the Qur'ānic legislation, defining some acts as crime against God and establishing sanctions to them (*hadd*, plural: *hudūd*). The other *(jināyāt)* consists of laws that had evolved in pre-Islamic Arabia, based on blood feud, the principle of *talio* and on compensation. The third layer has punishments *(taᶜzīr)* that can be meted out by secular authorities for wrongs specified by them.

These layers of law go back to different historical periods in their development and, what is more, represent completely different way o f łegal thinking, attitude and cultural background. It is, therefore, impossible to integrate them into a single system with common underlying principles. It is more appropriate to say that Islamic law has three different normative layers with their own logic than to define Islamic criminal law as a normative system of three subsystems. Obviously, it was customary law that developed first, to be followed by Qur'ānic legislation, and *taᶜzīr* being only a latecomer produced by medieval Muslim authorities running the Caliphate. These three criminal systems lived in parallel to each other for long centuries and even Muslim legal experts did not attempt to shape these rules into a uniform system.

The category of *hudūd* consists of crimes defined by the Qur'ān, such as adultery, false accusation with adultery, wine drinking, theft, highway robbery, and apostasy. These are crimes against God for which punishments are different but all are defined within Islam as a religion and not by custom or public authorities. On the other hand, crimes which do not figure in this list do not belong to *hudūd*, irrespective of their social relevance or brutality (like homicide). Punishment for these crimes is defined on a case to case basis, sometimes with an eye on social status.

In the case of adultery, the punishment of free but not virgin persons was stoning and one hundred lashes for virgins. As the punishment of slaves is half of the punishment of free persons, slaves could be punished by fifty lashes whether they were virgins or not, though there were also views according to which *hadd* could not at all be meted out in the case of virgin slaves. The execution of the punishment is the right of the *imām*, the head of the Muslim community (since the crime was committed against God), hence the plaintiff or his/her relatives are not entitled to do so. Punishment cannot be implemented on a pregnant woman until delivery or until a proper wet-nurse is found for the child or, in the lack of such a person until the baby can be weaned from its mother. Stoning has to be executed in an uninhabited place, outside the settlement. Stoning is prohibited in a mosque. In the case of lashes by whip, both the physical condition of the person and external circumstances (heat) are considered since the aim of this punishment is not the killing of the culprit. If the condemned suffers in an illness that does not allow for such a punishment, its execution has to be postponed until the culprit recovers. It is also prohibited to execute a judgment in particular heat or cold. The whip must not be new or worn as these circumstances strongly influence how the punishment can be endured.[68]

In the case of wine drinking the punishment may rest on either drinking an alcoholic beverage or drunkenness. Since the prohibition is against consumption, the quantity of the drink consumed does not play any role in the commitment of the act: the criminal act was realised even by drinking the smallest quantity. The sanction, however, was disputed because Muhammad did not specify the number of lashes: according to some schools the punishment was forty while according to others it was eighty lashes.[69]

The sanction for theft is to cut off the right hand below the elbow, irrespective of the culprit's gender, personal status and religion. The sanction of a recidivist thief had provoked heated disputes as the Qur'ān mentions exclusively the hand (5.38.) resulting in the impossibility to sanction a thief with third repetition. This was actually what Abū Hanīfa had taught. By contrast, according to Al-Shāfiʿī, the thief's left foot should be cut off if he committed this crime for the second time, and afterward his left hand, then his right foot, and the theft committed for the fifth time could only be left without *hadd* punishment.[70] This dispute reflects on the academic nature of Islamic legal scholarship, since it is very hard to find a thief with amputated hands and legs.

Highway robbery ('the cutting of the way') is composed of robbery and manslaughter, yet it is a *sui generis* crime. As it is part of *hudūd*, agreement between the parties is impossible and sanction must be followed because the crime violates the Law of God. The sanction of this crime however, remained disputed among the schools. According to *Mālik,* capital punishment is inevitable if someone was killed but if no harm was done to human life and only the road was blocked the *imām* can choose among crucifixion, other ways of execution and cutting off of limbs. Such a decision is based on his *ijtihād.* According to the Shafiʿites and the Hanafites however, if no one was killed no capital punishment is allowed.[71]

The punishment of apostasy is death but the opportunity to return to Islam should be granted to an apostate. To this end, three days are granted to her/him for considering it. If she/he does not return to Islam after this period of time the apostate should be executed. If the apostate is a woman she must not be executed according to the Hanafites, but should be condemned to jail until her conversion to Islam. Similar rules pertain to slaves as well.[72]

Crimes referred to as *jināyāt,* have their origin in pre-Islamic custom and not in the verses of the Qur'ān, albeit Islamic legal thinking modified it considerably. Blood feud was in its essence the responsibility of the community, that is, any member of the clan to which the killer belonged could be victim of blood feud by any member of the

---

[68]Ibn Rushd (1996: 527–528), al-Marghīnānī (1982: 178–182), al-Māwardī (1996: 243–244), al-Misrī (1994: 611).

[69]Ibn Rushd (1996: 535), al-Māwardī (1996: 248).

[70]Ibn Rushd (1996: 544).

[71]Ibn Rushd (1996: 548).

[72]al-Shaybānī (1966: 195, 205, 209).

clan to which the victim belonged. Now the coming of Islam restricted this collective responsibility and limited it to the killer himself based on a new understanding of criminal liability, individual responsibility. This individual approach was further restricted to deliberate homicide when it was proven beyond doubt. In addition to this, Islamic moral understanding preferred to reach agreement between the parties and to reject blood feud though, it was never declared illegal.[73]

Jināyāt consists mainly of crimes against life and physical integrity, that is, some kinds of manslaughter and assault. A person deliberately committing manslaughter can be punished if he is a sane adult and has acted out of his free will. The person of the victim plays an important role for the determination of revenge because *qisās* (revenge) becomes compulsory if the social position of the killer and his victim is identical. The definition of the social position rests on three criteria: (1) Muslim or of another religion; (2) free or slave; (3) male or female. *Qisās* is the right of the *walī al-dam* but in some cases it was disputed who these persons were. Generally, the *walī al-dam* is the heir of the victim but concerning detail, legal schools differ as to how to choose the exact person from among the many heirs. It is the *walī al-dam* who chooses between *qisās* and the acceptance of blood money. If he chooses *qisās*, the execution of the capital punishment is due to him in theory though, Muslim legal scholars criticised this, arguing that a victim's heir is nurturing hostile emotions toward the condemned person and would, therefore, overstep proportionality while executing the judgment which would be against Islamic criminal thinking. If a person entitled to *qisās* is unable to execute the sentence for any reasons (e.g. does not have sufficient physical strength), the Caliph would appoint someone else to act in his stead. Should the *walī al-dam* decline *qisās,* he could demand the payment of blood money *(diya)*. One can only demand blood money without recourse to *qisās* in case of (1) unintentional manslaughter, when the killer could not be subject of *qisās* because of (2) social status (e.g. a free Muslim kills a slave) or (3) personal consideration (e.g. is a minor or a mentally ill person). In these cases, blood money is the only option available for the *walī al-dam* who cannot opt for blood feud. The sum of the *diya* for Muslim men who are engaged in animal husbandry is one hundred camels[74] and the equivalent of this in gold and silver for those who are not engaged in animal husbandry. Blood money must be paid either in camels or in money, but there is no third alternative at the disposal of the parties. In case of deliberate manslaughter, blood money had to be paid immediately and could be demanded only from the killer but not from his relatives.[75] The sum of blood money for a woman is only half of the blood money to be paid for a Muslim man.[76]

Concerning assaults, the main concern for Muslim legal scholars was proportionality and similarity between the harm caused by the assault and its blood feud or punishment. Since legal scholars took this issue rather seriously, disagreement was abundant among them, mainly in cases where similarity was impossible to reach.

---

[73] Schacht (1964: 185).

[74] al-Māwardī (1996: 253), al-Misrī (1994: 589).

[75] Mālik (1989, 364–365), Ibn Rushd (1996: 495–497), al-Misrī (1994: 588–589).

[76] Ibn Rushd (1996: 500), al-Misrī (1994: 590), al-Māwardī (1996: 253).

Such an issue was—among others—whether *qisās* could be exercised if the injury could not be reproduced, for example in the case of a broken bone, since it is impossible to break the bone precisely at the point where it was broken for the victim. As a result, blood feud was kept at bay and was restricted to cases where similarity could be defined without any shade of doubt. Following this principle, only the right hand could be cut off for a right hand but not the left hand (the same applied to foot), and a lower tooth could not be knocked off for an upper tooth, and so on. Here, too, blood money was preferred to blood feud and this is the reason why blood money for assaults was elaborated in minute detail, based on the nature of injury. Injury of the head was considered as the most serious harm which was classified into ten sub-categories from the slightest injury to the skin up to an injury inside the skull. The blood money to be paid was adjusted to these injuries, usually set as a percentage of the sum total of blood money to be paid for death.[77] The blood money paid for a female victim of assault was the half of a male victim.[78]

The third layer of Islamic criminal law, *ta^czīr* is a punishment for a variety of crimes and harms which do not feature neither in *hudūd* nor *jināyāt*. Punishment for such deeds is within the competency of state authorities with unlimited power in establishing and executing punishments. It is impossible to enumerate all acts belonging to *ta^czīr* and this is the reason why Muslim legal scholars made no attempt to do so. Misdeeds concerned are acts against regulations of public administration and finance and unethical behaviour which have no legal sanction either in *hudūd* or *jināyāt*. False testimony is a good point to illustrate: Qur'ānic laws condemn only false testimony concerning adultery but not false testimony generally, while the whole issue is missing from *jināyāt*. In order to guarantee the smooth operation of the judiciary, false testimony had to be sanctioned which found its place in the framework of *ta^czīr*. Since Islamic religious law had nothing to say in this, the way was paved for secular authorities to regulate this segment of criminal law according to their own understanding. In doing so, they enjoyed very broad competencies. Muslim authors dealing with the issue emphasise primarily the separate standing of *ta^czīr* and the definition of the possible sanctions but remained silent about the criminal acts themselves. Contrary to the crimes belonging to *jināyāt*, forgiveness by a party is unthinkable in the framework of *ta^czīr* since state authorities acted on their own right and competencies. Special rules were developed for habitual offenders despite the fact that the term was unknown. Small wonder that more severe punishments were applied against habitual offenders coupled with additional humiliations when his deeds were announced publicly, his head was shaved (but the beard was not to be cut), his face was smeared, etc. Ultimately the condemned could be crucified alive within the framework of the *ta^czīr* but only for three days. During that time he was not to be deprived of food and drink. In case the condemned lost his life because of the punishment his blood money had to be paid, but it was a matter of dispute as who

---

[77]Mālik (1989: 361).

[78]Ibn Rushd (1996: 506–514), al-Māwardī (1996: 254–256), al-Misrī 1994: 592).

should pay it: according to one view it was the treasury's obligation while others believed that it was a burden on the ruler and his family.[79]

7.4.4 Laws of Procedure

Laws of procedure make legal proceeding very formal and rigid with twofold consequences. On the one hand, the formal character of the procedure guarantees that basic rules be observed and it is therefore impossible for judges to handle cases with absolute discretion (contrary to what Max Weber believed). On the other hand, the rigid rules were at variance with contemporary social reality, a fact already heavily criticised by some medieval Muslim legal scholars (Ibn Hanbal, al-Jawziyya). Islamic procedural law makes no distinction between civil and criminal procedure, the latter being modelled on the former because criminal procedure conserved its civil origin where the plaintiff, that is, the *walī al-dam* retained his important role during the trial.

At the beginning of the process, the judge examined the demand. Should he consider it unfounded, he rejected it without setting a date for the trial.[80] If the demand was not unfounded, the judge had to set a date for the hearing and it was his duty to arrange for the that defendant to appear at court, at least according to the Hanafite school. A hearing starts with the complicated issue how to seat the parties. After the very formal greeting procedure men had to kneel down and women had to sit down cross-legged. It was advised to judges to set a separate day to hear men and another for women though, to hear them simultaneously at the same hearing was not against the rules. A trial began with the declaration of the parties, but it was left up to them to decide which one would present his declaration first. If the parties could not agree on this issue, lots were drawn to decide or the judge sent them away until they reached an agreement.[81] After their declarations, the parties had to prove their claims. Oral testimony was preferred but written documents were also accepted.[82] The burden of proof rested as a rule on the plaintiff, but the distribution of this burden could change during the lawsuit.

In criminal procedure, all forms of torture were rejected due to the originally civil nature of the procedure and the scepticism Muslim legal scholars developed toward oral testimonies in general and forced confessions in particular. A forced confession was null and void, only its consequence remained subject to dispute. According to the Hanafites, a judge who ordered torture should be punished on the basis of lex talionis while other schools condemned such a judge to death. The reason is that the judge violated the principles of legal procedure, abused his authority and challenged the credibility of the administration of justice. In order to understand the logic behind

---

[79]al-Māwardī (1996: 258–259), Kamali (1993).

[80]Müller (1999: 143).

[81]Schneider (1990: 131–135).

[82]Müller (1999: 143).

the rejection of torture, we should bare in mind that in Islamic legal understanding it is not the task of the judge to explore the truth. By contrast, a judge has to control the procedure and decide the case on evidences what the parties presented during the trial and has neither the right nor the duty to go beyond that. A judge is the master of the procedure who controls the law suit, guarantees equal treatment to the parties and takes a neutral position on which his judgment rests at the end. In arriving to a final decision, a judge is exposed to the statements of the parties who bear exclusively the burden of proof. Should they fail to prove their claim, they will bear its consequences. As the proving of facts is not the task of the judge, a mistake in facts would not affect his sentence. The judgment has to be correct according to the facts presented in the lawsuit irrespective of whether those facts did reflect material truth or not. If a factual mistake is subsequently revealed, the judgment remained *res iudicata* since the burden of proof exclusively rests on the parties.[83]

The judge's work was assisted by various law clerks during the procedure. The door keeper led the parties in, kept them at distance from the judge if necessary, and acted accordingly when a break was introduced. In addition to this, he informed the judge about the identity and rank of the witnesses arriving so that the judge may greet them properly. However, the most important assistant of the judge was his secretary who was expected to know how to produce documents, to be familiar with the official language, to have good handwriting and to know how to draw up minutes. The judgement was recorded and deposited in the archive of the law court (*dīwān*). If the parties so requested, a copy was made of the judgment.

There is no court of appeal in Islamic procedural law, which has led Western scholarship to believe for long that a judgment at the first instance is at the same time the final judgment. The issue is more complicated than this. It is true that in the majority of the cases judgments are implemented without hesitation or any more former procedure. Despite this, Muslim legal scholars agree that a sentence which is obviously contrary to the rules of the Qur'an, the *sunna* and the *ijmāᶜ* must be revised. Some further causes for the revision of a judgment are (1) serious shortcomings and injustices during the trial: the judgment is based on a fact that was not proven or the person heard as a witness did not meet the requirements set for witnesses; (2) new facts emerged after the sentence was passed; (3) the court overstepped its competency and made a decision in a case to which it was not entitled; (4) the judgment violated the rights of a third person; (5) the judgment was not properly justified, that is, legal argumentation and proofs were missing; (6) the judgment is obviously unjust, that is, the judge was not neutral toward the parties, or the judgment was produced by corruption. In this case, the judge should be banned from his office and punished. In post-classical times when the doctrines of the schools became the most important factor of school identity, a judgment was to be revised also if the judge deviated from the doctrine of his school.[84]

The most frequent way of subsequent revision of a judgment was the revision made by the new judge after entering his office. A revision could be launched ex officio but

---

[83] Johansen (2002: 168–177).

[84] Johansen (1993: 34).

in the majority of cases the revision began upon the complaint of one of the parties. If the new judge has not found any legal mistakes, the former judgment remained in force, otherwise it was considered null and void. If the new judge realised that mistakes were made not only in individual cases, but the judge proceeded generally contrary to law (e.g. he did not have the proper qualifications), all his sentences were to be revised. Such a general revision was rare. Revisions in individual cases were also no daily routines and were implemented only when procedural rules were violated enormously or social considerations made it necessary (the case was scandalous, one of the parties was a person of influence and power, etc.). Finally, a proceeding judge could also revise his judgment if he realised that a mistake has been done during the procedure and could, therefore, withdraw his own judgment.[85]

7.4.5 The Law of War and Peace

The law of war and peace was not an important field of law in classical *fiqh* books which focus primarily on private law. The reason why this issue is discussed here in a separate chapter is not due to its importance in classical Islamic law but to it is its modern age relevance.

Before proceeding, to clarify basic terms and concepts is in order. One such a term is *siyar*, the plural of *sīra* denoting biography. These biographies narrate important events from the life of Mohammad and his followers with a particular mix of historical facts and legendary elements. These stories focus on Muhammad's struggle to spread his teaching among non-believers with words and swords. As a result, the meaning of *sīra* was enlarged to the struggle against infidels. Since the paradigmatic behaviour of Muhammad and in a lesser extent that of his companions became a source of law, in the next turn *siyar* evolved into a term to denote the law of war on Muhammad's example to struggle against unbelievers. In this understanding, the law of war encapsulates issues such as how to begin hostilities, the right and duties of combattants, laws related to booty and basic principles of peace treaties.[86] Given the history of Islam, it is small wonder that *siyar* was developed by the Hanafites, that is, legal scholars of the Caliphs in Baghdad, prominently by *al-Shaybānī* (eighth century) and *al-Sarakhsī* (eleventh century).

Now *jihād*, a term widely known but not properly understood, should be located into this framework. *Jihād* is a derivative of the root meaning making efforts and struggle for a definitive goal (*ijtihād* is another derivative from the same root), later to be understood as an effort to spread Islam with whatever means, war included. But *jihād* denotes not only war but all other means too. It is customary—mainly among Shiᶜīte theoreticians—to distinguish between two forms of *jihād:* the greater *jihād* and the lesser *jihād*. The former is understood as a struggle against bad habits and unethical behaviour in order to perfect one's character to meet the demands of

---

[85]Müller (1999: 144–159), Rebstock (1999: 11–23), Powers (1992: 323).
[86]Kruse (1979: 23–30), Khadduri (1966: 39).

Islamic ethics. Holy war against infidels to spread Islam is understood only as the lesser *jihād* clearly legging behind the first understanding. This distinction is known also to the Sunnis as it goes back to a prophetic tradition.[87]

There are some references to *jihād* in the Qur'an (2. 216; 4. 89; 9. 5; 9. 36; 60.1), but they do not reflect a coherent view and one can identify contradictions among them: while one verse is agitating vehemently for armed struggle other is very sceptical about it and about the enthusiasm of the early Muslims to do so to whom the verse is directed. After the death of Muhammad and following the early victories of the Muslim armies in the East (Iraq, Persia, Central Asia), the Maghreb (Egypt, the Vandal kingdom) and Europe (Hispania) references to *jihād* in the Qur'ān and the prophetic traditions concerning the struggle for Islam were re-interpreted in order to canalise it to the understanding necessary for both the ruling elite and the army: war. Hanafi legal scholars did their best and thus developed the law of war, doctrines which were less important for other schools. Dissenters who did not follow the line were outcasted from the Hanafi School such as Sufyān al-Thawrī who opposed the then current understanding of the Qur'ānic verses and denied the universal command for war. The laws of war clearly reflect the historical situation in which they were developed: authors took it for granted that it is the Muslim army which is the winner in the battlefield and laws were formulated accordingly. Soon, however, Muslim victories entered the pages of historiography and the victories of the Seljuqs, the Mongols and the Ottomans reshaped the Islamic world (the Crusader wars were just local history in a limited space and time). Despite this, the laws of war were not reinterpreted, only some minor changes were introduced in order to make the doctrines more realistic.

Though *jihād* could also be understood as the self-defence of the Muslim community, it is first of all an offensive aspiration which goes back partly to the great victories of the first centuries, and partly to the universalistic aspiration of Islam as a religion. As a result, *jihād* is a continuous and collective obligation (*fard kifāya*). The continuous nature of *jihād* is the reflection of the universalistic aspiration, according to which struggle cannot be stopped until the entire world embraces Islam. Consequently, there is no chance to conclude a peace treaty for an infinite period of time only to sign a temporal agreement, otherwise the continuous obligation would be jeopardised. The collective (community) obligation places the responsibility for war on the shoulder of the entire community but not on all its members. As a result, the community and its leaders is the subject of the obligation and not the individual, a core concept radically challenged by modern radical *jihādists* who interpret *jihād* as an obligation of each Muslim individual. According to the classical concept however, *jihād* could never be an individual obligation, making the majority of the Muslim community exempt from it. Some examples help to underline the difference. If *jihād* is a collective duty, not every Muslim male should participate in the war: when the sufficient number of warriors joined forces, others have no obligation to participate. If an enemy attacks the Muslim land, collective obligation has it that first inhabitants of the land affected by the attack should take up arms and Muslims at the other end

---

[87] al-Misrī (1994: 599).

of the land are exempt from the obligation when the inhabitants have sufficient force to expel the enemy. This collective duty however, may turn into individual obligation when the individuals concerned could not rely on others. This is for example the case in a besieged city where the inhabitants of the city have the obligation to defend it.[88]

The universalistic aspiration of Islam led not only to the continuous obligation of *jihād* but also to a particular worldview of medieval Muslim legal scholars. Accordingly, the world consists of either the world of Islam, inhabited by Muslims (*dār al-islām*) or the territory inhabited not by Muslims uniformly named as the territory of war (*dār al-harb*). To wage war on the latter territory in order to spread Islam is the obligation of the Muslim community led by the *imām* and this is the only lawful war. *Dār al-harb* is a uniform category irrespective of nationality, religion and international status of the people living there. Needless to say, there could be states on the territory of the *dār al-harb* with far greater military might than that of the Muslims but this typology does not rest on Realpolitik but on religious doctrines. To bring theory closer to contemporary political realities, some Shāfiᶜīte legal scholars introduced a third category, the territory of contracts (*dār al-sulh*; *dār al-ᶜahd*) whose inhabitants signed a temporary agreement (peace, truce) with Muslims (Hanafites vehemently opposed the existence of this category).[89]

According to Muslim legal scholars, the aim of warfare is dual: either (1) forcing conversion to Islam or (2) ensuring the payment of the poll tax (*jizya*) levied on non-Muslims. The two aims are alternatives, since if the first aim was realised and the people concerned had become Muslims, they could not be obliged to pay *jizya*.[90] On the other hand, not all non-Muslims have the privilege to retain their religion in exchange of paying tax, this way is open only for the "people of the book", that is, Jews and Christians who are part of the Abrahamic tradition.

To participate in *jihad,* one should be a person who is (1) a male; (2) adult; (3) sane; (4) physically fit and healthy, does not suffer from a chronic disease or epidemic; (5) of free status; (6) capable to finance his contribution to the warfare. These preconditions rest on the rules of the Qur'ān (9.91, 48.17.). In addition to the Qur'ānic conditions, legal scholars also required the consent of parents, a clear proof of very strong Middle Eastern patriarchalism. If a debtor went to war, the Shāfiᶜītes also demanded the creditor's consent. No consent of the parents and creditors were needed in defensive war when the attackers endangered Muslims.[91]

Before launching *jihad,* a call addressed to the non-Muslim community should be pronounced to urge them to embrace Islam to which reasonable time must be granted to them in order to think about it. Should they accept the call, no war is lawful since the aim of *jihād* was fulfilled without hostilities. By contrast, if non-Muslims reject the call, to attack them is lawful provided the conditions set by the laws of war are met. One such a condition is that it is only the Caliph who could decide about war and peace. The other condition is the declaration of war, a written

---

[88] al-Misrī (1994: 600–601).

[89] Khadduri (1966: 11–14).

[90] Ibn Rushd (1994: 455, 464–465), al-Misrī (1994: 602–603).

[91] Ibn Rushd (1994: 455), al-Misrī (1994: 601–602), Mālik (1989: 175).

document sent to the leader of the non-Muslim community, informing him about the beginning of hostilities.[92] Surprise attacks such as 9/11 are clearly against these classical doctrines.

The issue of lawful damages caused during the war was hotly debated, at least concerning some detail of minor importance. Muslim scholars made distinction between damages done to human life, physical integrity, freedom, and property. To kill a human being, otherwise intolerable, is a lawful act during war if the victim is an adult male enemy participating in the war. It is prohibited to kill women and children if they do not participate in the combat. These laws rest on prophetic tradition because Muhammad not only prohibited the killing of women but also war by scheming, intrigue and misleading the enemy. Beyond these issues, legal disputes are abundant. According to Mālik and Abū Hanīfa, it is also prohibited to kill blind, disabled, insane and old people. In addition, Mālik believed that food necessary to their survival should also be left behind. By contrast, al-Shāfiᶜī was less tolerant and taught that everyone can be killed from among the enemy, even monks and elderly people.[93] At the same time, Muslim scholars agreed that any form of mutilation of the enemy is prohibited, as one can fight against them only with weapons.[94]

Issues related to freedom were less disputed since Muslim legal scholars agreed that everyone (man, woman, child, old person) from among the enemy could be captured and enslaved irrespective of their social rank, with the exception of monks, at least, according to Abū Bakr's practice. The same applies to the 'people of the book', too, otherwise protected religious groups. The *imām* is the only authority to decide the fate of the captives in which no law restricts his competency. Though, al-Māwardī put into writing some good advice as to what to do with them, these remain what they were: advice to the Caliph without any legal effect. Accordingly, a dangerous enemy could be executed, but the rich could be freed against ransom. Captives with enormous physical strength could be sent to slavery, while those who seem to be sympathetic to Islam might be freed in the hope that they will embrace Islam voluntarily.[95] Captured women and children become *ipso iure* slaves with a consequence that the former marriage of a married woman is regarded as null and void.[96]

The issue of damages caused to properties is to be found in an ocean of casuistry without agreements among Muslim legal scholars. According to Mālik, destruction of buildings and trees was permitted, but animals should not be killed, nor palm trees set on fire. By contrast, Al-Awzāᶜī prohibited the destruction of buildings and the falling of trees. However, Al-Shāfiᶜī was of the view that the lawfulness of falling of trees depended on whether the enemy could use them for combat or not. Shāfiᶜītes also prohibited the killing of animals, unless the enemy used them in battle, or their destruction would weaken the enemy. Muslim armies must not leave anything on

---

[92]Ibn Rushd (1994: 461–462), al-Misrī (1994: 602–603).

[93]Ibn Rushd (1994: 458–460), al-Misrī (1994: 603).

[94]al-Shaybānī (1966: 95, 102), Ibn Rushd (1994: 460).

[95]al-Māwardī (1996: 146).

[96]Ibn Rushd (1994: 456–458), al-Misrī (1994: 604), al-Shaybānī (1966: 91).

enemy territory of which they would gain advantage but they must not destroy entire cities.[97]

It was necessary however, to maintain contact with some persons from among the enemy without facing all the disadvantages outlined above. To this end, security guarantee (*amān*) was given to private individuals from the territory of war (*harbī*). Such a person (*musta'min*) could move freely on the *dār al-Islām* and, what is more, was allowed to trade with everything he pleased except some commodities which were related to warfare such as weapons, objects made of metal and slaves. The reason behind that was despite hostilities and military operations, the complete break off of trade relations was against the interests of both parties, therefore, *amān* guaranteed security for merchants who were prohibited only to export objects of military significance. In addition to merchants, diplomats and emissaries of the enemy were also privileged by *amān* in order to make it possible to do their job properly. An emissary had to support his commission with written proof in order to qualify as *musta'min*.[98]

Islamic law of war and peace has a great deal to say about the distribution of war booty and other goods which Muslims gain as a result of their victory. Muslim legal scholars made distinction between *ghanīma* and *fay'*, legal categories to which a variety of goods belong. *Ghanīma* consists of war booty, which are gained directly as a result of violent action during the armed conflict such as prisoners of war, occupied land and movables taken by force. By contrast, *fay'* consists of goods which are the products of the victory of Muslims but are not linked directly to military activities such as goods left behind, sum of money paid for an accord of truce, the *jizya*, or land tax. The distinction between *ghanīma* and *fay'* is important because they are distributed along different rules, though issues of detail generated endless debates. According to Mālik, land cannot be distributed but should be given to a *waqf*, the income of which is to be used for the benefit of the entire community, whilst Al-Shāfi°ī believed that these lands should be distributed in the same way as the booty. Abū Hanīfa had a third view when saying that the right to decide is with the *imam*, who can have his choice: he either distributes the land or returns it to original owner who had to pay land tax (*kharāj*).[99]

As it is clear now, Islamic law on war and peace rests on the assumption that military victory is with the Muslims, something that went against historical realities from the second half of the °Abbāsid Caliphate onwards. By this time however, legal doctrines were defined and it was extremely difficult to modify them even when political realities were in favour of change. The most controversial issues were truce and peace treaty, documents that might testify to the victory of the non-Muslim enemy, a bitter experience and a hindrance to Islam's universalistic approach. At the end, legal schools acknowledged the temporary cessation of hostilities as lawful, provided it took place because of the interests of Muslims. However, the interest of Muslim remained ambiguous, a concept that could be interpreted rather broadly.

---

[97]Ibn Rushd (1994: 461), al-Misrī (1994: 603), al-Shaybānī (1966: 91).

[98]al-Shaybānī (1966: 158; 168–173), Ibn Rushd (1994: 457).

[99]al-Māwardī (1996: 152–153), Ibn Rushd 1994: 480).

According to Al-Awzā'ī, truce is lawful only if a more serious danger or damage can be averted by it, while Al-Shāfiʿī ruled that a truce can be concluded only if the enemy is superior in numbers. According to him truce can be concluded for a maximum of ten years because Muhammad also concluded it for that duration with the Quraysh tribe. When it expires, the truce is terminated but there is no obstacle in concluding another one.[100]

While truce meant the termination of mutual hostilities, a peace treaty (*muwādaʿa*) was a contract which did not necessarily presume warring conditions. When justifying the legality of the peace treaty, Muslim legal scholars referred to verse 8.61. in the Qur'ān which allows for the conclusion of peace. This *sura* is a key argument for those who argued for the legality of peace treaty which was difficult to harmonise with the concept of *jihād*. Here again, the ambiguous term necessity was introduced in order to disqualify contracts disadvantageous to Muslims. A peace treaty is lawful, therefore, if the enemy is superior in number or is in a more advantageous position by other considerations. Such a peace treaty is not for eternity but for a definite period of time. A contract should be terminated if the original necessity which mandated Muslims to sign the treaty was overcome (e.g. the enemy is no longer superior in number). In this case, the leader of the enemy should be informed about the termination and enough time should be guaranteed to him in order to inform his subjects about it (similarly to the declaration of war), during which it is prohibited to launch an attack. Obviously, citizens of the enemy who live lawfully in the abode of Islam should also be informed and allowed for a peaceful return to their homeland.[101]

7.5 Shiʿī Law

Shiʿī law is, similarly to Sunnī law, dominated by ritual and private law and there are only minor differences of technical importance that separate Shiʿī law from Sunnī law. In this understanding, Shiʿī law might be seen as the fifth legal school within Islamic jurisprudence, a view which was expressed in fact by some authorities. The problem is, however, more complicated if one looks at it from a religious perspective. In this prism, Shiʿī law is a legal expression of Shiʿīsm, that is, a particular reading of Islam which is at variance with Sunnism in a variety of religious doctrines. If one understands Shiʿī law as a kind of religious self-expression, Shiʿī law cannot be seen as just one school among the many legal schools within Islam. In addition, Shiʿīsm is also not a monolithic understanding of Islam but has three main variants (Zaydities, Ismaʿilites, Twelvers) in addition to other sub-variants. In short, Shiʿī law must be placed in this religious background and cannot be seen as only a legal variant of inter-Muslim legal controversies. The religious background is the more important when examining public law where imamate (*imāma*), one of the key concepts of

---

[100]Ibn Rushd (1994: 463), al-Misrī (1994: 605).
[101]al-Shaybānī (1966: 154–155); Kruse (1979: 85–124).

Shi^{c}ī Islam together with oneness of God (*tawhīd*), prophethood (*nubuwwa*), justice (*^{c}adl*), and resurrection (*ma^{c}ād*), determine law and legal theory.

Shi^{c}ītes do not accept Sunnī Caliphs as their leaders and also deny the principle of election because in their belief leadership was inherited within Mohammad's family in the line of ^{c}Alī ibn Abī Tālib. According to the Shi^{c}īte view of power, Mohammad appointed ^{c}Alī as his heir making all the Sunnī Caliphs' reign unlawful. Particularly the second and the third Caliphs are surrounded by hatred: ^{c}Umar is despised because the Shi^{c}ītes consider him the mastermind behind the political attacks against ^{c}Alī (the day of the assassination of ^{c}Umar is a festive day among the Shi^{c}ītes), while Caliph ^{c}Uthman is the subject of despise because the final text of the Qur'ān was completed during his time (from which passages referring to the lawful rule of ^{c}Alī were left out according to the Shi^{c}ītes). The unlawful reign of the Sunnī Caliphs turned to terror when ^{c}Alī's son, Husayn was massacred together with his family and followers upon the order of the Umayya Caliph Yazid (October 680: Kerbala). The assassination of Husayn shocked the entire Muslim community and not only the Shi^{c}ītes since the victim was Mohammad's grandson after all. Despite this, the military defeat marked the end of Shi^{c}ī aspirations to gain control over the entire *umma*, yet at the same time made Shi^{c}īsm to become a religion out of a purely political movement.[102]

This series of events determine the Shi^{c}ī worldview to this day, as they consider themselves victims of oppression and tyranny, persecuted by the majority, the Sunnis. As a result, martyrdom is a key element in Shi^{c}ī belief centred at Husayn's martyrdom commemorated in the bloody rituals of ^{c}Asūhrā. ^{c}Alī's prominent place in the Shi^{c}īte tradition is also visible in their creed (*shahāda*), as they supplement the Sunnī creed with reference to the prominent significance of ^{c}Alī (*^{c}Alī walī Allāh*). In addition to ^{c}Alī, all the *imām*s are extremely important in the Shi^{c}ī understanding of leadership since they differ considerably from the politico-religious and legal position of the Sunnī Caliphs. Shi^{c}ī *imām*s are infallible authorities whose opinion must be followed, which makes them more prominent intellectual and spiritual leaders than the Sunnite Caliphs. *Imām*s are without sin, are infallible who speak all the languages of the world and even understand the language of plants and animals, are capable of doing miracles, see the future in advance and are well-versed in theology, law, astrology and alchemy. Despite this, they are not prophets, thus Shi^{c}ītes also accept that Mohammad was the last in the line of prophets. Yet, *imām*s are elevated in jurisprudence to a level almost equal to that of Mohammad, since the *sunna* of the *imām*s is the most important legal source in addition to the Qur'ān and the prophetic *sunna*. The *imām*s' knowledge rests on three sources such as: (1) knowledge transfer from the earlier *imām*s, (2) knowledge obtained from books which are accessible only to the *imām*s, and (3) the acquisition of knowledge through angels.[103]

The issue is however more complicated than this, since it is exactly the religious-legal standing of the *imām* which caused Shi^{c}ī to split into three main branches. Zaydites, that is, Shi^{c}īs living in Jemen have only five *imām*s and reject all the *imams* coming after the fifth *imām*, Zayd. In their understanding *imams* are human beings

---

[102]Nasr (2007: 40–42).

[103]Kohlberg (1983: 1–9), Kohlberg (1988: 26).

just as anyone else without having any esoteric or superhuman ability. They are the leaders of the Shiʿī community but do not harbour competencies, which separate them from their fellows. In their religious, political and military leadership *imāms* of the Zaydites are closed to the Sunnī Caliphs. On the other end of the spectrum we can find the Seveners or Ismāʿīlites who invest divine qualities to their *imāms*. The Twelver Shiʿīs, by far the largest community (Iran) among the Shiʿīs developed a middle position, since they believe in the extraordinary abilities of their *imams* but do not attribute divine qualities to them. In what follows, Shiʿī law is presented as that of the Twelvers.

The failure of early political aspirations and the subsequent persecutions transformed Shiʿī ethos into an opposition movement that is unable to gain upper hand yet it is strong enough to oppose the tyranny of the majority. As a result, oppression by the majority (*zulm*) and the resistance leading to martyrdom are key concepts of Shiʿīsm even today, which mark their identity and world view (Kerbala-complex).[104] Another consequence of oppression is *taqiyya*, the right of Shiʿī believers to keep secret their religious conviction in emergency without being an apostate.[105] Curiously enough, *taqiyya* is open to the otherwise infallible *imāms* too, who can speak differently among Shiʿī believers and in the public. This controversy has its traces in Shiʿī jurisprudence, too, since it is hard, if not impossible to ascertain which is the only correct legal view from among the many doctrines attributed to an *imam,* since later generations are lacking the methods to prove which doctrines are just *taqiyya* and which contain the correct legal view. To solve this dilemma, Shiʿī legal scholars developed the notion that if controversial doctrines are attributed to an *imām* the legal view which is contrary to the Sunnī understanding should be understood as his own doctrine. The reason behind is not the revolutionary character of Shiʿīsm (otherwise a truism) but the assumption that doctrines identical with that of the Sunnis are or might be developed as a result of *taqiyya*, while contradictory doctrines are certainly free from the notion of *taqiyya*.[106] Despite this, only minor variances can be found between Sunni and Shiʿī positive law, mainly in family law.[107]

The leadership of the *imams* lasted however only for twelve generations because the minor son of the eleventh *imām*, Hasan al-Askarī disappeared and was never seen again. According to the Shiʿīte theology, the twelfth *imām* would re-emerge only when returning to the world at the last day as Messiah (*mahdi*). This is how—after a short transitory period—the great occultation of the *imāms* (*ghayba al-kubra*) started in Shiʿī history in the tenth century, creating a power vacuum which was filled in by the Shiʿī clergy who stepped into the footsteps of the *imams* as leaders, though without their abilities and competencies. As a result, Shiʿī political theory formulated the same point—though along completely different lines—as the Sunnis did in the eleventh century: the leadership of the *ʿulamā'*, the legal scholars. There are several hypothesises why Shiʿīs abandoned the autocratic leadership of the *imams* and opted

---

[104]Dabashi (2011: 83–90).

[105]For modern relevance see Sobhani (2001: 150–154).

[106]Kohlberg (1983: 11).

[107]Kohlberg (1983: 11).

for the less autocratic leadership of the *ᶜulamā'*. Perhaps the most convincing theory calls attention to the fact that this happened in the so called 'Shiᶜīte century', that is, during the dominance of the Shiᶜī Būyids who were a warrior dynasty of West-Iranian origin keeping not only their homeland but the entire Caliphate under control for more than a century (945–1055). The Būyids, however, were no descendants of *imām*s, thus with the 'disappearance' of the latter, the duality and rivalry in leadership also disappeared to the favour of the Būyids. The Shiᶜīte century was not only about political control but also about cultural and scientific progress: this was the time when Shiᶜī schools emerged together with works on law, theology and a genuine Shiᶜī hadīth-collection (*al-kutub al-arbaᶜa:* the four books), since Shiᶜīs do not follow the prophetic traditions of the Sunnis.[108]

What the leadership of the *ᶜulamā'* means exactly is subject to dispute among Shiᶜī clergy. While some believe that it is the mission of the *ᶜulamā'* to control society and the state with full political power and autocracy (Khomeinī and his followers), others deny such a mission and highlight the lack of the *ᶜulamā'*s competency in economics, state administration and other important elements of political control and think, therefore, that the Shiᶜī clergy should restrict its leading role to ethical guidance (Montazerī and his followers). Beyond this rather contemporary controversy, there is a deeper divide among Shiᶜī legal scholars, the dispute between the *usūlī*s and the *akhbarī*s. This intellectual controversy is not peculiar to the Shiᶜī legal scholars, since such a methodical dispute divided the Sunni *ᶜulamā'* too. At the centre of the debate was the role of rational arguments in Shiᶜī law with the question: can reason be considered as a legal source (like in Sunni jurisprudence analogy), or not? Scholars who believed that rational arguments have their proper place in Shiᶜī jurisprudence are called *usūlī*s, a reference to *usūl al-fiqh*, that is, Sunnī legal theory to which this thinking resembles, while those who cannot see any role for rationalistic arguments are referred to as *akhbarī*s, that is, a group of scholars relying exclusively on the traditions of the Prophet and the *imām*s (*akhbar*).

The most prominent *akhbarī* scholar is the Iranian Sharīf al-Astarabadī who lived in the seventeenth century, though *akhbarī* thinking might go back earlier. According to Sharīf al-Astarabadī, the only source of law is the *imām*'s tradition which is also a guidance to interpret the text of the Qur'ān since without the help of the *imams*, human intellect is unable to interpret the Qur'ān properly. Consensus should be understood only as the consensus of the *imams*, while analogy is the device of Satan. To understand this argument, one should understand al-Astarabadī's principle that the traditions of the *imām*s answer all questions and there are no problems to which they did not give guidance. This idea is also behind the requirement to interpret the Qur'ān according to the the *imām*s' interpretation (*tafsīr*), since the Qur'ān itself is difficult if not impossible for the human mind to understand. Astarabadī's main work, the *al-Fawāᶜid al-madaniyya* strongly criticises the work of al-Hillī, a famous medieval Shiᶜi scholar, accusing him of smuggling Sunnī elements into Shiᶜī jurisprudence. However, Astarabadī himself could not avoid criticisms coming from other members of the *akhbarī* school, prominent among them was al-Fayd al-Kāshānī who did

---

[108]Kohlberg (1983: 15–18), Kohlberg (1976a: 525–529, 533–534).

not agree with al-Astarabadī's theory, which actually identified Shiʿīte law with the tradition of the *imāms*. Despite al-Astarabadī's prominence, it is clear that the *akhbarī* school was not uniform either, as were all other Muslim schools, but was fragmented along principles and outstanding scholars. The dominance of the *akhbarī* school lasted to the end of the eighteenth century, when its refutation by the *usūlī* school, particularly under the extremely polemic al-Bihbihānī accomplished success. As a result, the *akhbarī* school disappeared without a trace and Shiʿī legal theory was determined in the past two centuries exclusively by the dominance of the *usūlī* school.[109]

The *usūlī* school emerged as a result of intense intellectual interactions with Sunnism, prominently with its Muʿtazilite understanding of theology, favouring rational arguments. The original understanding of Shiʿīsm was detrimental to rational arguments, highlighting the autocratic leadership and the infallible guidance of the *imāms*. With their withdrawing however, the Shiʿī community remained without its omnicompetent leader and the problem of how to find proper answers to legal and theological questions from the written sources of Islam. One way out of this dilemma was rational thinking, which was acknowledged by some early medieval Shiʿī scholars with the reservation however, that rational arguments could provide only some practical pieces of advice but not absolute truth (which is contained only in revelation and in the *imāms*' knowledge). One of the most prominent Shiʿī scholars of the Middle Ages, al-Tūsī (eleventh century) did not call this *ijtihad,* since he rejected this term because of its Sunnī connotation, yet at the same time he demanded precisely this. Two centuries later the influential scholar of the Middle Ages, ʿAllāma al-Hillī already accepted the concept of *ijtihād* in some fields of law (but rejected analogy), and elaborated the competencies of legal scholars engaged in this intellectual activity. Slowly the assumption was accepted that legal scholars were deputies and representatives (*nāʾib*) of the *imām*s in questions of law whose advice must be followed. This was however by no means a logical consequence of the occultation of the *imāms*, therefore it became widespread rather slowly. The theory of substitution was elaborated entirely only after the sixteenth century, when the Safawid dynasty ascended to power in Iran and declared Shiʿīsm its state religion (1501). In the subsequent centuries, scholars of the *usūlī* school divided the community into *mujtahid*s (legal scholars) and *muqallid*s (followers, imitators, actually lay people) who were prohibited to follow the opinion of a dead legal scholar. By the nineteenth century, the hierarchy of Shiʿīte scholars was established. Accordingly, scholars of the highest academic rank is referred to as the 'source of imitation' (*marjaʿ-i taqlīd*), a rank which is open only to very few and highly talented scholars. They are followed by more numerous *āyatullāh*s and *hojjatalislām*s with *mollah*s at the bottom. With this hierarchy, Shiʿīsm separated itself from Sunnism also in terms of scholarly structure.[110]

What made all this possible is the complete decline of the *akhbarī* school which denied the legal scholars' prominent role, whose human intellect is unworthy to

---

[109]Gleave (2001: 27–43), Kohlberg (1987: 134–137, 151–152).

[110]Newman (2000: 935–936), Vikor (2005: 132–135), Sadr (2003a: 51–52); Sadr (2003b: 48–53).

follow and imitate since only *imāms* must be followed and not legal scholars.[111] With the pre-eminence of the *usūlīs* however, this line of reasoning was pushed into the background and Shiʿīs witnessed the ever growing significance of their legal scholars who in addition to legal and moral guidance, also required political leadership in a completely Shiʿī country such as Iran. First, they led the opposition against Western-minded modernisation of the Pahlavi era arguing against its allegedly anti-Islamic character, then with the principle of the legal scholar's rule (*wēlāyat-e faqīh*) demanded autocratic political leadership.[112]

Autocratic leadership of the clergy has its basis in the belief that they are deputies of the *imāms* and it is next to impossible to challenge the authority of the *marjaʿ-i taqlīd*. His *fatwās* must be followed and also provide a basis for legislation in a theocratic system such as present day's Iran. In addition to political leadership, a *marjaʿ-i taqlīd* also provides guidance for the everyday life of Shiʿī believers with answering all their (legal) questions. Legal opinions of *marjaʿ-i taqlīd*s are usually published in books (*risālat-e amalīyya*) as well, which are important sources for daily legal routine of Shiʿīte law. Since the only criteria on which pre-eminence is based is scholarly reputation and talent, social mobility is also a feature of Shiʿī hierarchy, though it is not to deny that the majority of the Shiʿī clergy are descendants of clerical families.[113] The number of *marjaʿ-i taqlīd*s in a generation is not fixed for certain and the Shiʿīte community is almost never united under the authority of a single *marjaʿ-i taqlīd*. Even Khomeinī did not accomplish to be a single authority, since grand *āyatullāh*s opposing his theory on *wēlāyat-e faqīh* such as Kho'y and Shariʿatmādarī continued to be respected in matters of theology and law and criticised his theory as a novelty unfounded in *usūlī* political thinking.[114]

It is a truism among modern Shiʿī believers that they cannot follow the opinion of a dead legal scholar and have to choose a living *mujtahid* for guidance, thus forcing legal scholars to exercise *ijtihād* continuously. As a result, Shiʿīs proud themselves that contrary to the Sunnī experience, the gate of *ijtihād* was never closed in Shiʿī jurisprudence, a claim which should be treated with caution (see, for example, the *ahkbarī–usūlī* controversies). Despite historical uncertainties, modern urge for *ijtihād* is a continuous drive for renewal in Shiʿī jurisprudence that excludes the possibility of mere imitation of the past, making Shiʿī law more modern than some Sunnī traditional legal theory (e.g. wahhabism).

The pre-eminence of the *usūlī* legal thinking made the sources of Shiʿīte law very similar to the sources of Sunnī law, where only minor differences are to be found. One such a Shiʿī peculiarity is the interpretation of *sunna,* which incorporates in addition to the prophetic *sunna* also that of the *imāms*. Another point of difference concerns *ijmāʿ*, which could be a legal source only if *imāms* had participated in their

---

[111] Mallat (1993: 31).

[112] Keddie (1969: 47–53).

[113] Rostoványi (1998: 175–176).

[114] Nasr (2007: 126–127; 144–145).

formulation. The third difference is rather about terminology, as Shiᶜī legal theorists use the term ᶜaql (reason) instead of analogy (qiyas) to name rational arguments.[115]

Shiᶜītes have their own collections of hadīth as they do not trust Sunnī compilations. According to Shiᶜī tradition, already the disciples of the sixth imām Jaᶜfar al-Sādiq started to compile hadīths but the four most famous collections were produced during the time of the Būyids: (a) Al-kāfi fī ᶜilm al-dīn (Yaᶜqūb al-Kulainī's work) contains the largest number (sixteen thousand) of traditions; (b) Man lā yahduruhu l-faqīh (Shaykh Saduq's work) contains nine thousand hadīths; (c) Tahdīb al-ahkām: describes about thirteen and a half thousand traditions; (d) Al-istibsār fī mā ktulifa fīhi mina l-akbār (Shaykh Tūsī's work): contains about five and a half thousand traditions. Kāshānī, a scholar in the Safawid period added a commentary to them (Al-Wāfī), which was followed by similar works in the following century. Understandably, it was primarily the members of the akhbarī school who were interested in these compilations.[116]

Shiᶜīte positive law differs little from that of the Sunnis and this only in some hotly debated issues. Perhaps the most controversial legal problem is about temporary marriage (mutᶜa), a remnant of the pre-Islamic tribal custom of Arabia which has, curiously enough, its equivalent in Persian law. Temporary marriage is a marital bound set for a definite period of time between an hour and 99 years, otherwise sharing all other legal effects with non- temporary marriages (bride wealth, mahr, inheritance, etc.). First, Caliphs prohibited this custom because of its non-Islamic morality, a view which shared by the majority. As a result, Sunnis see temporary marriage unlawful and prohibit it, while Shiᶜīs do not share this view, arguing that Caliphs are not empowered to prohibit something which the Prophet of Islam did not. The second point of controversy is to be found in the law of inheritance, where Sunnis maintain pre-Islamic customs by ensuring the right to inherit for tribal relatives, that is, male members of the agnate family while Shiᶜīte law does not. In addition to this, Shiᶜīte law makes no distinction between agnate and cognate relatives, thus ensuring females a more favourable standing in matters of inheritance. A similar attitude is to be found in divorce law where Shiᶜī law limits the husband's unilateral right to declare divorce.[117]

Shiᶜīte concept of jihād also differs from its Sunnī counterpart Shiᶜī, legal theorists developed further the Sunnī concept of dār al-islām and dār al-harb adding a third category, land of faith (dār al-īmān) to it. Needless to say, dār al-īmān is the abode is Shiᶜī believers making dār al-islām the territory of Sunnism. Curiously enough, exactly this territory could be the abode of war as Shiᶜīs concept of jihād does not focus on combatting non-Muslims as a result of Islamic universalism but on Sunnism in order to make Shiᶜīsm victorious within the orbit of Islam. To turn against non-muslims might be just the next step.[118] Shiᶜī concept of jihād strongly emphasizes

---

[115]Löschner (1971: 134–145; 155–192).

[116]Löschner (1971: 92–94).

[117]Vikor (2005: 137–138), Kohlberg (1983: 11–12), Kohlberg (1988: 38).

[118]Kohlberg (1983: 10).

its religious background, ruling out any mundane motivation such as the acquisition of territory or other goals. This is why *jihād* can only be declared by the *imām*s.

This argument of the early Shiʿīsm lost its significance after the great occultation of the last *imam,* compelling Shiʿī theorists to develop the theory further. In addition, Shiʿī had to prepare for attacks from the Muslim majority against which they had to defend themselves in the absence of the *ā* too. As a result, Shiʿī legal theorists elaborated a dual concept of *jihād* during the Middle Ages. One was the holy war to spread Islam (= Shiʿīsm) against the Sunnites and other non-muslims, a *jihād* of purely religious motivation declared by the *imām* only. The other was the defensive *jihād* against any enemy attacking the Shiʿī community and threatening life, physical integrity and territory. This defensive war was also called *jihad,* though the motive to spread Islam is completely missing from it.[119]

Legal scholars began to develop their role in *jihād* too, in addition to law and theology, where they were deputies of the *imām*s, according to their own concept (see above). To enlarge this concept to *jihād* was by no means a great step, since *imām*s had their role in *jihād* and legal scholars as their deputies could find their place easily in the new theory. Already Abū Jaʿfar al-Tūsī, the greatest Shiʿī legal scholar of the early Middle Ages, declared that the defence of the borders (*ribāt*) is possible without the *imām*'s permission. Najm al-Dīn al-Hillī and Mutahhar al-Hillī, two outstanding thinkers of the late Middle Ages, developed the idea further when saying that it is possible to declare *jihād* by the *imām*'s representatives, though they did not specify exactly who they were. The next turn was due to the Russo-Iranian wars (1808–1813; 1826–1828), because the ruling Qajar dynasty could not declare *jihād* as purely secular authorities. To maximise mobilisation they asked for a *fatwā* underlining the religious motive of the war. Here the inherited concept of offensive (*daʿwatī*) and defensive (*difāʿī*) *jihād* was maintained, the latter being divided into four sub-categories (to defend the territory inhabited by Muslims; to defend the Muslim persons; to expel the enemy who had obtained authority over a group of Muslim persons or a given territory). Shiʿī legal scholars however, turned their back to the medieval tradition when declaring that a *jihād* in the absence of the *imām* is more praiseworthy than the war declared by him.[120]

The new concept of the *jihād* was elaborated in the Risāla-yi jihādiyya, a work containing *fatwā*s of the Shiʿī legal scholars and summarising the differences between the offensive and the defensive *jihād* in twelve points. Here are the most important differences: (1) offensive *jihād* is only possible with the *imām*'s permission, but no permission is needed to a defensive *jihād*, not even from the legal scholars; (2) persons who do not participate in an offensive *jihād* can participate in a defensive war (such as women); (3) offensive *jihād* can be launched only once in a year except in the holy months but there is no time limit for the defensive wars; (4) financing an offensive *jihād* must not lead to material burden to society, but the costs of a defensive war has no such limits; (5) contracts concluded during an offensive *jihād* must be respected, but in a defensive war, Muslims may cancel contracts unilaterally;

---

[119]Sachedina (1988: 110–112).

[120]Kohlberg (1976b: 82–84).

(6) before launching an offensive *jihad*, the enemy must be called to embrace Islam while in a defensive war there is no need to do that; (7) in an offensive *jihad*, cease-fire must be respected but not in a defensive war; (8) in a defensive war, all tactic is allowed while there are restrictions in an offensive war (felling trees, cutting off water supply, attack at night, etc.).[121] As a result of this development, the original concept of *jihād* to fight for purely religious motivation in the interest of Shi^cī Islam was gradually replaced with a war waged in the interest of a modern state (Iran) with or without the *imām*s' and their representatives' permission.

7.6 Islamic Law in the Modern Age

7.6.1 Ways to Re-interpret Islamic Law in the Twentieth Century

Classical Islamic law is the product of medieval culture representing the interests of the city dweller merchants having business worldwide. In the modern age, however, the world of Islam had no share in revolutionary developments which made the West what it is (discovery of the Americas, Enlightenment, industrial revolution, nation-states). In addition to this, the long decline of the Ottomans conserved socio-political structures that were detrimental to progress, creating an ever growing tension between demands and reality. Muslims were well aware of this and made efforts to find ways out. Unsurprisingly, however, Muslim thinkers had different conceptions in mind and believed in solutions which were at variance with each other more often than not. To analyse them would require a separate volume, here I have to restrict myself to some basic thoughts.

Both Muslim thinkers and scholars of modern social sciences developed terms to provide some order in an extremely confusing situation referring to various trends among Muslims which developed thoughts for solutions. Unfortunately, individual scholars have their own terms and classifications of Islamic movements not shared by others. Here are only some examples. Fundamentalism is perhaps the most widely used term though its meaning is far from being clear for purposes of scientific analyses. This term is further distorted by less accurate use in the media and elsewhere making some scholars to believe that the term is now absolutely useless for scientific purposes since its meaning is now only "bad guys" standing against the "good guys". The eminent French scholar, Olivier Roy on the other hand supplemented fundamentalism with neo-fundamentalism, because according to him it is not a coherent doctrine but rather a new kind of religiosity to which many trends and politically different views belong. A common element among neo-fundamentalists is their emphasis on the creative reinterpretation of Islamic texts (*ijtihād*), with the rejection of the medieval legal schools and their laws. Neo-fundamentalist groups are by no means

---

[121] Kohlberg (1976b: 84–86).

identical with adherents of Islamism, who are far more radical both in theory and practice (violence).[122]

Islamism (or political Islam) is another controversial term which also lacks a clear definition, though that of Mohammed Ayoub is perhaps the best. Accordingly, Islamism is the utilisation of the religion of Islam for the achievement of the political objectives of certain individuals or groups.[123] Consequently, he considers both Saudi Arabia and Iran states of political Islam while for others Saudi-Arabia is a Sunnite traditionalist society and Iran a Shiᶜīthe theocracy. Peter Mandaville agrees with Ayoub.[124]

Tariq Ramadan again has his own terms and understanding. Accordingly, there are six current trends in Islam, such as (1) scholastic traditionalism (followers of medieval legal doctrines); (2) Salafi traditionalism: they reject the medieval law books and follow only the basic texts (Qur'ān, *sunna*), Mohammad's companions and the Muslims of the first generation (Salafis); (3) Salafi reformism: a mixed group with Salafi theology but an openness to the modern world; this category includes very diverse thinkers such as the early social reformers Mohamed ᶜAbduh and Rashīd Ridā; Hasan al-Bannā, the founder of the Muslim Brotherhood, and Mawdūdī, his counterpart in India; (4) political Salafism: the most radical group ready to take up arms and violence; (5) liberal Islam: advocating co-existence with the West and modernising Muslim societies along western lines; (6) Sufism: a rather mystical way of thinking within Islam going back to a millennium of history.[125]

None of these categories of social and political science are adequate enough to analyse current trends in Islamic law. Therefore, it is more prudent to do so in a framework that is more relevant to legal analyses. Accordingly, there are three main trends with some varieties within each category. One trend is the westernisation-modernisation model, which believes in Western (legal) institutions and sees a guarantee for progress in them. As a result, adherents of this trend want to implement Western legal institutions in Muslim societies with a complete social, cultural and legal reform, to the detriment of Islam, if necessary. By contrast, the trend I call conservative-traditionalist sees it harmful to imitate the West and believes in Islam as the solution for all the social problems. The third trend rejects both modernisation on a Western model and the conservative traditionalism and sometimes offers radically new interpretation of Islam and its law for current problems.

Legal westernisation takes continental legal systems (French, German, Swiss) as its model for public, private, criminal and commercial, law. Needless to say, legal modernisation fits into a more general framework of social modernisation from above, some kind of a social engineering in political, economic, social and legal systems. The underlying principle is less Islam and more Western idea, since Muslims are backward vis-á-vis the West because they are lacking Western tools and institutions. When creating these institutions, Muslim societies will also be successful, the idea has

---

[122]Roy (2004: 232–254).

[123]Ayoub (2008: 2).

[124]Mandaville (2007: 151–168).

[125]Ramadan (1999: 239–245).

it, therefore, (legal) transplants are necessary. Ideological corner stones are secular political system, nation state with nationalism, a completely reduced Islam in public life and a modern, western-style legal system. As a result, constitutions and laws of some European countries were translated and promulgated without hesitation with only some minor corrections where the adoption of the western model would have been an obvious anachronism. History and geography determined the rest: in the Maghreb the French while in Turkey and Iran the German and the Swiss legal culture was taken as a model with some French influence. All this remained the program of a small, westernised elite with an ever more unwilling society to follow. The process was rapid and gradual, with a blind eye to problems created by the modernisation itself. As a result, social backing became eroded in the course of time, compelling these regimes to rely on more force but less democracy, a turn that was at variance with the very (legal) values they propagated (democracy, human rights, rule of law, secularism, sovereignty of the people, the separation of powers). Autocratic regimes such as Turkey of Kemal Atatürk and Iran of the Pahlavis are the best examples. Growing tensions led to a gradual abandonment of the western legal model the operation of which the elite was unable to guarantee. The break with the western model was either revolutionary (Iran) or gradual, but less revolutionary (Turkey in the past 20 years). The failure of the western legal modernisation started earlier, however, since a gap remained right from the start between the *law in books* representing western laws on paper and the *law in action* which was the inherited legal model to which society was acculturated. It was unrealistic to believe that bazari merchants would follow the Code Napoleon instead of their age old law merchant and business culture only because some politicians declared to do so. As a result, legal modernisation developed a parallel legal system: in addition to customary laws (local, tribal, professional) and Islamic law, it created a third western-minded system which was only for the elite and not for the society at large. This model did not reform but neglected Islamic law since western-minded legal modernisation cannot be accomplished with the reform of traditional Islamic law. It was only family law and law of inheritance which remained to some extent within the power of Islamic law but these too were reformed, sometimes gradually (monogamy in Tunesia) along western model (rights of women, divorce, head scarf).

Conservative-traditionalists see things completely different. According to their view, the solution for problems Muslim societies face is not less Islam and more western idea but exactly the opposite: more genuine traditions and no adaptation of foreign legal models. This way of thinking focuses on the importance of the medieval Islamic culture in which traditional Islamic law was born. The problem is, the argument has it, that Muslims neglected this model because of internal (unsuited leaders, corruption and the disintegration of moral values) and external forces (Mongols, Turks, Western countries). As a result, all foreign influence must be neglected and the primacy o f Islamic law of the medieval law books should be restored. Conservative-traditionalists do not necessarily deny the need for a state law (since secular authorities developed their own law during the Middle Ages) but believe that state law should be in accordance with Islamic law and in case of collision the former has to be adopted to the requirements of the *sharī͑ a*. Consequently this attitude rejects every (legal) innovation that emerged since the Middle Ages. Conservative-traditionalists' way of legal thinking is *taqlīd*, imitation, that is, adherence to the medieval doctrines and the rejection of *ijtihād,* the novel interpretation of texts.[126] This legal conservatism is wedded to a strong political and social conservatism which emphasises the leading role of the *ᶜulamā'*, the patriarchal family model and is hostile toward legal changes coming from both inside and outside the Muslim world. Curiously enough, this political conservatism advocates a liberal economic policy because Islamic private law is based exactly on that understanding. In order to understand this, we should bear in mind that the *sharīᶜa* is the law of the medieval merchant and Muslim legal scholars did their best to create law which is adequate to large scale business. Needless to say, in a medieval political environment there was neither state intervention to economic life (at least not in a way we understand it in the modern period), nor state capitalism. By contrast, commercial activity was free, even supported by Muslim regimes (in exchange for tax income) where freedom of property and business activity was a matter of course. This led to the astonishing result that the more conservative a legal scholar is in political terms, the more liberal in matters of economics, pursuing *laissez faire* economic policy (e.g. Ibn Taymiyya).[127] By contrast, Islamism, the opposing trend to conservatism is more inclined to advocate state interventions in economic life in the interest of social justice.[128]

With this, we now arrived at the third trend to interpret traditional Islamic law, Islamism (called also political Islam). This comprises of rather heterogeneous groups with different political agenda and attitude to violence. Adherents to this trend also wish to establish the primacy of Islamic law but at the same time they reject the world view of medieval legal scholars and do not follow the (legal) guidance of the traditional *ᶜulamā'*. According to their understanding, Muslims should not escape contemporary realities and lock themselves into the irrelevant world of the medieval lawyers but should find modern solutions for modern problems instead. Therefore, fundamental texts of Islam (Qur'ān, sunna) should be re-interpreted in order to make them fit to contemporary needs and to find guidance in them for modern problems, ethical and legal alike. This new creative interpretation leads them to turn against centuries-old doctrines and their advocates, the *ᶜulamā'* and to prefer *ijtihād* and reject *taqlīd.* Obviously, radically new interpretations could end up in completely different doctrines and this is exactly what makes this group so heterogeneous. For example, the Tunisian Islamist Rāshid al-Ghanūshī sees democratic and parliamentary political system to be in accordance with Islam[129] while global jihādists rejects this and divert fundamentally from the jihād-doctrine of the *ᶜulamā'*, who consider the violence of global jihādists anti-Islamic. In short, this third group has no uniform

---

[126]Taqlīd enscapsulates also the possibility of the creative interpretation of law though in a complicated way, see Hallaq (2001b: 86–120).

[127]Vogel (2000: 125).

[128]Qutb (2000: 132–138).

[129]al-Ghanūshī's party, the Ennahda won the first free Tunisian elections in 2011 but lost to its secular rivals in 2014.

world view, political objective, economic programme, social and legal vision. What is common, is their rejection of both legal westernisation and legal conservatism.

7.6.2 Legal Westernisation

Legal westernisation already started in the nineteenth century with a series of reform acts called *tanzīmāt* in the Ottoman Empire. These attempts were advocated by some Ottoman statesmen and diplomats who had Western education and succeeded in convincing the sultan about the need to reform.

The first step was the *Khatt-i Humāyūn*, issued in 1839 (also called the *Khatt-i Sherif* of Gülkhāne) which introduced some modifications in constitutional law and changed the system of taxation abolishing traditional taxes and levies and centralising the collection of taxes in order to save the budget from continuous deficit. This was followed next year by a new criminal code which however continued to be based on Islamic law. To encourage trade with European countries, a new code of commerce on the French model was introduced and a new law court was established to adjudicate legal disputes with European merchants. The second wave of reforms begun after the Crimean war with a new *Khatt-i Humāyūn*, published in 1856. Slavery was abolished and a new criminal code promulgated, now on the French model. A private law code was also produced but it remained to be based on traditional Islamic (Hanafi) law. In fact, the *Mejelle-yi Ahkām-i ᶜAdliyye*, as it was called, was a mixture of Islamic and European law since its content was a pure Hanafī law but its structure followed European pattern. The third period of reforms was launched as a result of riots in 1875. A constitution on a Prussian model was introduced, allowing for elections to create a legislative body but there was also a second chamber the members of which were appointed by the sultan. The Ottoman sultan remained a very strong power, however who set up the cabinet, appointed and dismissed ministers, signed new laws, appointed the members of the second chamber and continued to be Caliph. The constitution maintained an independent judicial system and implemented decentralisation in public administration.[130] Human rights and their guarantees were however, left out from the constitution. The sultan disliked even such a half-hearted constitution and dismissed the legislative body not to be reconvened again for thirty years. A constitutional reform in 1908 only introduced some passages to human rights issues but did not change the system any further. In addition to constitutional law, private procedural law was also reformed with a new code on French model and a new criminal law was also introduced based on the Italian *Codice Zanardelli* taking about 70 articles from it word by word.[131]

Egypt was another Muslim country where western-minded reforms were introduced. It was already Muhammad ᶜAlī, the Ottoman governor of Egypt who introduced profound reforms in the beginning of the nineteenth century. He modernised

---

[130]Davison (2000: 201–208).
[131]Bozkurt (1998: 284–287).

the army, built a maritime fleet, developed agriculture and heavy industries, encouraged exports. He also sent talented young people to France to study and translate the great French codices into Arabic. As a result, a new civil code on the French pattern was introduced in the 1870s, to be followed by a criminal law, procedural laws (private and criminal) and maritime trade law. Next, on the influence of the British a modern judicial system of European pattern was created while the traditional law courts and Islamic law were gradually marginalised.[132]

When *Mustafā Kemāl* took control of Turkey after the defeat of the Ottomans in WW I, he started to build a modern nation state immediately. A republic was created with a new constitution in 1921 with *Mustafā Kemāl* as its newly elected president. The capital was moved from traditional Istanbul to modern Ankara. The Caliphate was abolished together with the traditional judicial system, which gave way to create new law courts. The new constitution set up a single chamber legislature which elected the president of the republic. The government was appointed by the president but remained responsible to the legislature. In order to secularise public law all reference to Islam was removed from the constitution. In addition, Latin script and compulsory education was also introduced.[133] Western-minded legal reforms fitted into this policy: A new civil code with no reference to traditional Islamic law was created on the Swiss model (1926), to be followed by the translation of the *Codice Zanardelli* in the same year. Civil procedural law was promulgated on the Swiss model soon to be enlarged with the criminal procedural law of German influence.[134]

Persia under the Qājārs, followed suit slowly when western-minded reforms began already in the nineteenth century with wazīr ('prime minister') Amīr Kabīr (1848–1852) as its engine. Amīr Kabīr wanted to reduce the influence of corrupt Muslim intellectuals and mollahs and suggested a judicial reform. His attempt failed however, and he was first relieved from office, then assassinated. A new reform attempt with the same spirit was introduced by then Prime Minister Mirza Hoseyn Sepāhsālār which also failed. During the Constitutional Revolution (1905–1907), the Belgian constitution (1831) was seen as the best model for a new political system and, therefore, the text was translated to Persian. Freedom of religion and equality of citizens, cornerstones of European democracies however were unacceptable for the ^{c}*ulamā'*, backing the revolution. Both equality of citizens and freedom of religion would have meant equal rights for non-Muslims (Jews, Christians, Zoroastrians), a law at variance with traditional Islamic law. In addition to this, Shi^{c}ī Islam would also lose its eminent status as a state religion. Small wonder that the ^{c}*ulamā'* withdrew its backing and the constitutional revolution failed. Despite this, some progress has been made: a code on private procedural law was created which fit into a reformed judicial system: a new court of appeal was established (missing from traditional Islamic law) and the administration of justice was rewarded with a budget of its own, allowing for regular salaries for those working in the administration of justice. This was followed

---

[132]Hallaq (2009: 420–425).

[133]Karpat (1970: 533–535).

[134]Bozkurt (1998: 294).

by criminal procedural law on the French model (1912), and a decade later a new law of commerce was promulgated.[135]

Pahlavis pursued a vehemently western-minded policy in Iran for which Atatürk's modernisation was the model with minor variance. One such a difference was political system which continued Iranian monarchy because republicanism was alien to Iranian tradition and detrimental to the shāh's intentions. Reza Pahlavi wanted to build a nation state in which religious minorities were citizens with equal rights with their Muslim fellows. In addition to social, political and economic reforms based on Turkish experience, Reza shāh also introduced legal reforms on Swiss, Belgian and French models. In addition to traditional *sharīʿa* courts, a new western-minded judiciary was established, where legal experts with European training replaced traditional legal scholars. Next, a Faculty of Law was established at Teheran University to educate western-minded legal experts.[136]

A criminal law on the French model entered into force in 1926, to be followed by a code on private law as a result of a very long legal and political debate. Since Islamic law is focusing on private law, a non-Islamic private law threatened the authority of the ʿulamā' opposing such reforms for long. At the end, a mixed committee was established in which both modern lawyers and traditional legal scholars were members of in order to produce the country's first private law code, which they did. The *Qānūn-e Madani* as it was called, consists of three parts with 955 articles. The code is a mixture of Western and Islamic legal thinking, just as its Turkish counterpart was: its structure is a copy of the Code Napoleon, its content preserved a lot of traditional legal matter. The first wave of legal reforms came to an end with the creation of the criminal procedural law (1939), also a hotly disputed law. The next decades were spent on the continuous revision of these laws with the only exception of family law (1967), which limited the husband's rights and delegated disputes to civilian courts because its aim was to strengthen the rights of women in a strongly patriarchal society.[137]

The experience of Turkey and Iran cannot be generalised however when discussing legal westernization, because they were independent countries after all, something that was rather an exception when colonisation reached its peak at the end of the 19th and the beginning of the twentieth century. Legal westernisation was something very different in Muslim societies which were colonised by European powers, because legal reforms were not advocated by a western-minded though native elite, but by the colonising powers themselves for both practical considerations and as a 'civilising mission'.

Perhaps one of the best examples is Algeria, which got into French sphere of interest in 1830. As a result, French law was introduced, producing permanent legal difficulties for the Algerian society. It was clear enough that family law was not to be reformed along the western model and, therefore, it was left within the competency of

---

[135]Talesh (1986: 101–129).

[136]Hambly (1991: 224, 231).

[137]Talesh (1986: 101–129).

sharīᶜa law. Law of property was also alien to local laws and customs and was abandoned in the course of time. After gaining independence, Algerian elite was divided how to proceed with legal reforms. The western-minded elite regarded colonisation a bad experience, yet saw legal westernisation as an important tool to develop their country. By contrast, the conservative elite wanted to restore the primacy of the *sharīᶜa* after the long rule of non-Muslims, but failed to achieve their goal. Islamic law remained only a supplementary legal body vis-á-vis the law of the state, yet some concessions has been made to restore peace. For instance, the prohibition of usury was transplanted into a modern legal language and incorporated into the codes. Direct legal transplants from French law were avoided and thus the basis for the new Algerian private, criminal and procedural law was Egyptian law, which followed, on its turn, French law. Since Egyptian legal scholars already developed an Arabic legal vocabulary for western legal institutions, the adaptation of the Egyptian codes had the advantage to incorporate them to the Algerian legal language. Family law was another field of controversy between the westernising and the traditional elite. At the end, a code was produced (1984) which satisfied neither camps: according to the traditional elite, Islamic law only had a minor share in it, while the westernising elite saw too much Islam in it. These legal controversies reflect the deep division in Algerian society, which came to surface in 1992 in a bloody civil war that lasted for more than a decade.[138]

In sum, legal westernisation was a significant attempt to modernise traditional Muslim societies along western patterns with only formal results. Though legal codes were produced in all important fields of law, they remained in paper in the majority of the cases since Muslim societies continued to rely on their own laws and customs. The rootless western legal culture, the opposition of the traditional elite, the violence that accompanied the reforms and the meagre social prestige of the westernising elite made all the attempts subject to ever growing critique. As a result, legal westernisation was slowed down or come to a halt in the 1970s, a decade which witnessed also the first victory of political Islam, the Islamic revolution in Iran (1979).

7.6.3 Legal Traditionalism

Legal traditionalism is linked to Islamic universalism because of this way of legal thinking, it is the *umma* which has priority and not a territorial state. Legal traditionalism thus differs from legal westernisation not only in its perspective (looking backward to a glorious past instead of looking forward to a prosperous future) but also in its cohesion and loyalty: while legal westernisation is necessarily bond to a state, that is, a political community, legal traditionalism favours the community of all Muslims, that is, a religious community. This is the reason why legal traditionalism can be found all over the Muslim world, though with various intensity, but gains

---

[138] Aoued (1996: 194–198).

superiority in a state rather rarely (except Saudi-Arabia and Afghanistan under the Taliban).

Legal traditionalism simultaneously favours classical Islamic law as it stands in medieval law books and rejects everything foreign, be it a legal or any other idea. This, of course, not because of practical considerations but of principle: Islamic law is the essence of Islam which no foreign legal idea could absorb. A law based on revelation and the teachings of its prophet, elaborated by generations of respected legal scholars cannot be reformed, and certainly not along western models. Western law is that of non-Muslims promulgated by various states as a result of political law-making, while *sharīᶜa* is, at least, in part, a revealed law with no room for law making. In addition to this rather religious motivation of resistance, there is also a political aspect, since western law is that of the colonising powers, something that ought to be rejected irrespective of practical considerations.

For legal traditionalism, *sharīᶜa* as it stands in medieval law books is not a collection of age old doctrines that should be either reformed or pushed to the background in order to catch up with modernity and let fresh air in, but the essence of Islam which should be studied and followed. What is more, for legal traditionalists the crises of Muslim societies is not due to the enorm presence of Islam in all aspect of life (politics, business, family) but to its negligence. Islam is, in their understanding, not the cause of the problem, but the solution for every social wrong, law included. If Islamic law has all the answers including for current problems, the only thing one has to do is to study *sharīᶜa* in all its aspects (legal theory, argumentation, schools and their doctrines) and find the solutions suitable for every case, already present in the legal corpus. Thus, there is no need for reform or renewal, even *ijtihād* should be neglected, and it is *taqlīd*, the imitation of medieval doctrines that is important in this camp of legal understanding. This is by far not a new thinking in Islam (one would say in the Middle East), since common understanding has it that outstanding authorities belong to the past and contemporary scholars are only their imitators. The difference between *mutaqaddimun* and *muta'akhirun* goes back centuries, highlighting the eminence of previous scholars and the inferiority of the contemporaries. Small wonder, then, that legal traditionalists favour medieval legal texts, the treasury of classical Islamic law and reject to study contemporary legal scholars or to be engaged in innovative legal exegesis, that is, *ijtihād*. It is legal innovation that legal traditionalists see with extreme caution. In situations like this, there is a need for great scholars who could convince all his fellows that at least technical innovation is not as bad as they believe. This was the case when printing was taken to Istanbul by Ibrahim Müteferrika, a native Hungarian in the eighteenth century, but was rejected by the majority of Muslim scholars as an innovation not to be tolerated. The ground breaking argument by one of the most talented scholars was that printing could be useful for Islam and therefore be lawful, because in this way more Qur'ānic texts could be produced. Something very similar happened in Saudi Arabia in the first part of the twentieth century, when the problem arose weather radio is an innovation to be neglected or not. Here too, a Muslim legal scholar persuaded his fellows that the radio was not a satanic invention because one could listen to the text of the Qur'ān through it.[139]

Saudi Arabia is the only state with a traditional legal system since it is the *sharī͑a* which is the law of the country supplemented by royal legislation. As a result, it is the Qur'ān, prophetic traditions and the medieval law books which shape Saudi legal life. Works most often quoted are medieval scholarly writings of eminent Hanbalī scholars such as Ibn Taymiyya (more), *al-Mughnī* of Ibn Qudāma (thirteenth century) and the *Sharh muntahā al-irādāt* of Yūnus al-Bahūtī. Needless to say, the teaching of ͑Abd al-Wahhāb should be added to this, since Saudi law is Wahhābī law, that is, a variant of neo-hanbalism. Here the question arises: how can modern Saudi legal authorities be followers of ͑Abd al-Wahhāb, a scholar of no sympathy t o innovations, yet underlying the necessity of ijtihād and at the same time followers of the Hanbalī school, and true heir to ͑Abd al-Wahhāb, something that requires more *taqlīd* than *ijtihād*. The contemporary observer rightly claims that Wahhābīs teach the importance of *ijtihād* to a far greater extent than exercise it. In everyday legal practice, Saudi *͑ulamā'* apply the doctrines of the Hanbalite school and judges voluntarily follow the *fatwās* of legal scholars, that is, the intellectual influence of the traditional *͑ulamā'* does not differ from the medieval model. But this is only in a limited scope, since arbitration is more important than court judgments and therefore 90% of judicial decisions end in a compromise of the parties actually making judicial sentences unnecessary.[140]

Royal legislation is only secondary and subordinated to Islamic law, that is, it cannot be in variance with Islamic law and cannot establish laws for which Islamic law already has some. This is of course, nothing new, since medieval legal theories already empower state authorities to create law within their competencies (*qānūn*). Saudi law differs only in its name (*nizām*). The sphere of competencies however is not always clear and boundaries are flexible, something that can make the system complex. To illustrate: a violation of traffic rules has nothing to do with the competency of the *sharī͑a* courts, but if a violation of traffic rules results also in damage (personal, material), the same case can end up in a *sharī͑a* court as damages belong to classical Islamic law. In short, though royal legislation has free hand in regulating traffic, some of its consequences are adjudicated in a *sharī͑a* court. Royal legislation is operative right from the beginning (1932) and embraces, among others, punishments outside Islamic law (the classical *ta͑zīr*), establishing a judiciary for commerce (which goes back to the Ottoman and ultimately to the French pattern), traffic rules and a series of other issues that are indispensable to a modern state. Saudi *͑ulamā'* tolerates royal legislation within limits but refuses the idea of codification which transforms a judge to a servile implementer of a law code while he is responsible only to God for his decisions.[141] This is one of the main reasons why legal westernisation was impossible in Saudi-Arabia and why i t remains an example of legal traditionalism.

Without social support, legal conservatism of the *͑ulamā'* would hardly be more than one item among the many in a mental museum. It is social understanding that

---

[139] Vogel (2000: 286).

[140] Vogel (2000: 8–9, 11–13, 75–77, 117, 120).

[141] Vogel (2000: 175, 285, 336).

lends support for the legal values of the ^{c}*ulamā'*. Societies are (mainly in the Middle East) rather supportive and what is more, sometimes more conservative than legal scholars or at least some of them. This conservatism extends to family and family roles, gender issues, age hold habits and routines of everyday life and legal values. In addition, there are some social customs which are not only more conservative than the world view of the ^{c}*ulamā'*, but are against their understanding of Islam, or Islam in general. Here are two examples to illustrate this rather confusing situation.

Extreme conservatism of the Afghan Taliban movement is the first point. Though influenced by both the conservative interpretation of the Deobandi School and Saudi Wahhābism, the legal doctrines of the Taliban shocked even their masters, not to speak about the entire Muslim world. The destruction of the Buddha statues at Bamiyan is perhaps the best example to point at the issue at hand: these monuments were symbols of a tolerant local interpretation of Islam for a thousand years and no one ever came to the conclusion that these Buddhas are idols to be destructed. Yet, it is exactly what the Taliban believed and so they acted though conservative ^{c}*ulamā'* from all over the Muslim world protested (in vain) against such an act of barbarism. It is, of course true, that classical Islamic law is against idols and their worship, but it is by far more than ambiguous what exactly an idol is and what to do with it, more so if it belongs to another religion. It was one point among the many in the debates of medieval legal scholars preserved in centuries old law books which remained unnoticed by the Taliban. Their doctrinaire understanding of Islam however, resulted in the destruction of a world heritage site protected by the UN and Muslim legal scholars jointly but unsuccessfully. The same spirit of interpretation allows the Taliban to see the capital, Kabul, the city of sin, moral degradation and Western influence and to prohibit women from entering the schools, the work market and public life. To control moral values as they interpret it, the Taliban established a moral police following the Saudi model to implement their extreme conservative version of Islamic law.[142] In doing so, they not only followed one very conservative way of legal interpretation, but mixed their own primitive tribal customs into Islamic law, the two sometimes being in variance with each other. *Pashtunwali*, the tribal ethos of the Pashtun tribes to which the Taliban belong is more conservative than any school of Islamic legal interpretation and it is their own tribal customs that makes them prohibit women to walk loudly (to wear high heels and boots), to compel men to wear long beards, to prohibit all kinds of music and dance, to confiscate every cassette and disc, and to prohibit the flying of kites, a favourite pastime of the entire Afghan society (because it was seen by them as an idol).[143] In extending their own tribal customs the Taliban ruined their own country with a conservative legal understanding that was not even supported by the conservative legal scholars themselves.

The second point to illustrate social conservatism is honour killing, a practice demanding lives of hundreds of women in the Middle East every year. Exact numbers are missing, though estimates have it that in less developed countries such as Yemen and Pakistan about 400–600 women are killed, while less conservative countries such

---

[142]Marsden (1998: 64–65, 88–101).

[143]Rasanayagam (2009: 177, 198).

as Jordan and Egypt produce figures between twenty and fifty annually. These murders are committed exclusively by family members who kill one of their womenfolk in the belief that they ruined the honour of their family with their behaviour. This fits to the concept of a shame society developed by anthropologist Ruth Benedict, for which the most important value is honour, not human life. Honour (*sharaf*) o f the family may increase or decrease according to the behaviour of family members. One of the most important elements in the honour of the family is *ird*, female sexual morality which could be decreased or lost immediately, a turn that affects the honour of the entire family. To regain honour, the family has to kill its female member whose deed is seen as threatening the family's reputation. It is no retaliation since it is the family itself which kills its own member, something which is contrary to the logic of lex talionis. In addition, there is no crime committed and clearly proven at a law court, only rumours in a small village that destruct families and their reputations. There is no investigation whatsoever by anyone about the truth of the rumour, bad language is enough to act. Women killed committed no crimes, only disrespected some very strict local customs. Here are some examples to illustrate: (1) a thirteen-year old boy killed her elder sister because she phoned a male who was not a family member; (2) a twelve-year old girl was beaten to death by her father and brother because she was walking alone in the street; (3) a seventeen-year old boy killed his elder sister because she was talking to a man in the market standing before her in the queue; (4) a mother of three was killed by her brother (to the consternation of her husband) because he had heard her being immoral (the accusation was immediately refuted by autopsy); (5) a girl who was raped was killed by her own family because she became pregnant, a fact that ruins family honour if outside marriage. It is interesting to note that killers are agnate male family members (father, brother), while a husband cannot be found among them. It is because rumour ruins the honour of her family and not that of her husband's, who can divorce her if there is no other way out. A divorced woman sent back to her family is a great last as she could not be married off again, but incorporates the shame of the family. More often than not, these women are killed at the end of the day and so her families get rid of both the shame and a mouth to be fed. Unsurprisingly, honour killings are frequent in regions that are poor but densely populated where rumours spread fast. The reactions of Middle Eastern governments differ in detail but not in essence: though honour killings are not lawful, they are tolerated in one way or another (e.g. sentences are moderated). To reform the law is against society, backing honour killings. The case of Jordan is a good point to illustrate. The new law on honour killings initiated by the government wanting to restrict it was rejected by legislation, backed by the two-third of Jordanian society seeing the government's attempt against Islam, local customs and morals, and promoting Zionist and Western values.[144]

Needless to say, all this has nothing to do with Islamic law, even if some Muslim societies think it otherwise. Islamic law is against lynching and killing but prefers criminal procedure where guilt could be proven or not. A family and its members are not masters of life and death who can kill family members as they wish. Islamic

---

[144]Tellenbach (2003: 2–5; 13–14).

law protects human life and does not tolerate to kill innocent people without proper investigation and court procedure. Muslim societies are however, clearly more conservative as their law is and it is clan logic and familiarism which is for social conservatism and not Islamic law and its legal scholars.

7.6.4 Legal Understanding of Islamism

Islamism or political Islam is a comparatively new phenomenon within Islam, going back to a century when the last great Muslim empire, that of the Ottomans lost its global significance and vanished. Islamism shares the idea with conservatives that the solution for the problems Muslim societies are facing is not the adoption of foreign (legal) methods but genuine tradition, while disagrees with conservatives that the true Islamic solution is in the medieval law books to be found.

Islamists disrespect the medieval tradition (in which they are not well versed) and the ^{c}ulamā' representing it. By contrast, they are proud to be engaged in *ijtihād* and find new solutions for modern problems within the Islamic tradition itself. In this way, Islamic law (as they understand it) is the corner stone of Islamism which sees *sharī^{c}a* as a condition sine qua for a Muslim society. According to their view, the only criteria is the implementation of Islamic law without considering any other factor such as politics, economics, social conditions, etc. This is why in all countries where Islamism rules the first order of an Islamist government is to implement *sharī^{c}a* and nullify everything contrary to it (Sudan, Iran, some provinces in Nigeria) without hesitation.

Islamism however, is not a school about legal interpretation but first of all a political movement with diverse aims and methods from non-violent Salafism to radical jihādism. For them, legal interpretation is not a scientific activity but a method to underline their political message and to legitimise their actions. A good example is the radical re-interpretation of *jihād*, diverging considerably from classical law when claiming that *jihād* is not a community obligation but an individual obligation, thus making *jihād* a religious act for every Muslim (vehemently criticised by non-Islamists). They also want to end legal pluralism and declare their interpretation as the only normative force with no respect to the very history of Islamic law and its schools and legal pluralism. In addition to enforce their own legal interpretation, Islamists want to control the entire political order, too. This they realised in a Shi^{c}ī country, Iran.

Medieval shi^{c}ī theory of law underlines the importance of the deputies of the *imām*s later to be identified with the ^{c}ulamā' but this was not about a theocratic political order in a particular state where clerics rule supreme. By contrast, Shi^{c}ī theorists focus on the moral guidance Shi^{c}ī scholars could provide for both individuals and the general public without being engaged in everyday political routine and public administration. For Shi^{c}ī theorists, scholarship and teaching in holy places like Qum is more important than political activism. Against this background, the new Islamist political theory of Khomeinī was a departure from a long tradition which explains why it was vehemently criticised by some leading scholars. On the other hand, what made it possible for Khomeinī to formulate his own doctrine is first the decline of the akhbarī school and the monopoly of the usūlī school in legal theory and secondly, the Shiᶜī notion of perpetual ijtihād which makes taqlīd impossible and hinders to follow the opinion of a legal scholar who is not alive anymore.[145] Khomeinī formulated his theory on Islamic government already during his exile in Iraqi Nejef, where he met both enthusiastic followers and critics. His lectures were by no means about a well-developed theory proven by authorities of Shiᶜī tradition, but a new political understanding about the supreme role of Shiᶜī clerics in a newly fashioned political order. Key concepts in this political theory are the principle of *welāyat-e faqīh* (the legal scholar's rule), the supremacy of Islamic law and the denial of monarchy.

Monarchy is a non-Islamic form of government because it is a hereditary rule and a hereditary political system is against Islam, Khomeinī believed. To this, he added old notions of Muslim political theorists who dislike monarchies which they qualify as oppressive, such as the Pharaoh, the Byzantine emperor and the Sasanian king of Persia. Sasanian kings are further disliked because they fought long wars against the conquering Arab-Islam forces to defend their country and are regarded, therefore, as an enemy of Islam.[146] To counterbalance monarchy, the republic was born not because this is a political system deeply rooted in Islamic history but because there is no other candidate among modern political systems. Republicanism, however, is a western idea and this is the reason why it had to be Islamised. This is how the Islamic republic, as a concept and the new name of the country was born.

The principle of *welāyat-e faqīh* is the central concept in both Khomeinī's theory and the Iranian constitution. This is at variance with the traditional apolitical role of the Shiᶜī ᶜulamā' represented by, among others, Ayatollah Burujerdī, Khomeinī's mentor and teacher. With the help of radical reinterpretation of the fundamental sources (Qur'ān, prophetic tradition), Khomeinī was able to defend his new theory and lend political victory to it during the revolution.[147] A leading Iraqi Shiᶜī scholar, Muhammad Bāqir al-Sadr, executed by Iraqi authorities in 1980 contributed to its success as he drafted a constitution based on the principle of *welāyat-e faqīh*, which is identical to the Iranian constitution, both in its principle and in some points also in its wording.[148] Despite this, the concept of *welāyat-e faqīh* was rejected by some leading Shiᶜī legal scholars, while those who were in favour of it, such as scholars and clerics belonging to Khomeini's inner circle restricted the legal scholar's rule to moral, religious and legal guidance and rejected to lend him a constitutional position and a daily political decision-making.[149]

Yet Khomeinī was able to overcome all opposition, clerical and secular alike and lend victory to a constitution based on his political theory. The new constitution rests on the concept of *welāyat-e faqīh*, a key point of Khomeinism, securing the

---

[145] Sobhani (2001: 183), Al-Sadr (2003a: 53), see also 5.§.

[146] Khomeinī (1981: 31).

[147] Arjomand (1989: 120).

[148] Mallat (1993: 50–54, 69–78, 212).

[149] Schirazi (1997: 71), Keddie (2006: 260), Mottahedeh (2003: 32).

most eminent role to the leading legal scholar referred to as *rahbar* (leader) with very broad competencies. According to the constitution, the *rahbar* determines the political direction of the state and decides upon the most important issues of domestic and foreign policy, is the supreme commander of the army, decides on war and peace, appoints and dismisses members of the Guardian Council, the supreme judge, the head of the radio and television, the commanders-in-chief of the Revolutionary Guards, appoints the president of the republic after elections and initiates his dismissal from office and exercises clemency.[150] To all these competencies, he is not responsible to any constitutional body or the society at large and his office is not limited in time. Needless to say, such a political system is everything but a republic.

One cannot over emphasise the importance of the principle of *welāyat-e faqīh*, which is more than a political ideology and a constitutional principle: it is a theological dogma. Whoever doubts it, challenges the theological basis of the political system with serious consequences. It is not by accident that reformers of the Green movement demonstrating against the election frauds to their detriment (2009) also claimed that they do not challenge the principle of *welāyat-e faqīh* and the decision of the *rahbar*, a declaration which was contrary to their own political agenda, democratisation. The alternative however, is death penalty, with no respect to the person proven by the case of Hāshem Āqājerī, a professor of history and a veteran of the Iraqi war who challenged the principle of the *welāyat-e faqīh* and was therefore sentenced to death with the accusation of blasphemy in 2002, provoking massive protests in a number of universities in the country.[151]

The supremacy of the *sharīᶜa* (in its Shiᶜī understanding) is also a key concept, one with which Sunnis could also agree with. Accordingly, Islamic law is above all norms and there should be no laws which are at variance with it. This has double the effect of law, making is impossible in cases for which Islamic law already established a norm, and where no regulations are to be found, the new law promulgated by state authorities should also follow Islamic law both in spirit and wording. To oversee and control legislation a separate constitutional body called the Guardian Council (*Shūrā-ye Negahbān*) was established, composed of twelve members. Six members from among the traditional ᶜ*ulamā'* are appointed by the *rahbar*, while additional six members are elected by the legislature upon the supreme judge's recommendation.[152] Though equal in number, the Guardian Council is led by its ᶜ*ulamā'* members and is seen as a constitutional body strengthening the *rahbar*'s position. The Guardian Council is however, not an Islamic variant of a constitutional court since (1) it takes Islamic law and not only the constitution as the basis of its decisions which opens the way for a variety of non-constitutional interpretations; (2) there are no reasonings at the end of the decisions, whilst in a constitutional court's judgment reasoning is inevitable; (3) the Guardian Council disqualifies candidates from taking part in national elections on political reasons in order to prevent any harm to the system.[153]

---

[150]Constitution of Iran: 110.§.

[151]Amanat (2007: 120).

[152]Constitution of Iran: 91.§.

[153]Schirazi (1997: 105).

Sunnī Islamism shares the idea of the supremacy of Islamic law with Shiᶜī Islamism since it is the central concept in both versions of Islam. As a result, in every country where Islamists were able to gain control on regional or national level, Islamic law was implemented without hesitation since they believed it to be a cure for every social problem. Reality has not proven this belief. By contrast, wherever Islamic law was implemented without considering any other circumstances, it escalated conflicts rather than contributed to their solution. This was particularly the case in Sunnī countries with Shiᶜī and other religious minorities where Sunnī Islamic law was seen as a tool for oppression. Christians in Nigeria protested against implementing Islamic law in regions where mixed populations reside. The Shiᶜī minority in Pakistan obviously rejected Sunnī Islamic law as its legal system, the implementation of which resulted only in atrocities and hatred. Yet it is precisely what can be observed at the peripheries of the Islamic world: the unprecedented violence connected to the ruthless implementation of Islamic law which has been present for two decades in Nigeria (Boko Haram) Algeria (GIA), Somalia (al-Shabāb) and nowadays also to Iraq (IS) by Islamist forces which has few things in common with classical Islamic law in the name of which they act.

To conclude, the crises of Muslim societies, Islamic law included, is more evident now than it was a century ago. Though, legal westernisation achieved some success on the surface, it met social resistance which made it an ever growing authoritarian policy being incompatible with legal values to which these systems paid lip service. Legal traditionalism is completely out of touch with the modern and the post-modern world, with no intention to find legal solutions for contemporary legal problems. Islamism, by contrast, is proud to be engaged in finding new solutions in the name of Islamic law but all its efforts are connected to violence at the end of the day. All discourses among Muslims are, therefore, about Islamic law, its interpretation, relevance in the modern world and its contemporary crises. Some contemporary scholars like Saᶜīd al-Būtī deny the crises of Islamic law, but the majority of Muslim thinkers like Abdulkarim Soroush, Fazlur Rahman, Saᶜīd Ashmāwī, Muhammad Shahrūr recognise it and try to find ways for renewal and figure out solutions for contemporary issues.[154] The discourses of these intellectuals however, remain within academic boundaries and their influence is, therefore, limited among Muslims.

References

Sunni Law: Sources

Ibn Rushd (1994) Bidāyat al-Mujtahid. The Distinguished Jurist's Primer, vol I (trans: Nyazee I). Center for Muslim Contribution to Civilization. Garnet Publishing Ltd, Reading

---

[154]See the presentation of the views of these contemporary thinkers and their criticism in Hallaq (2009: 511–542).

Rushd I (1996) Bidāyat al-Mujtahid. The Distinguished Jurist's Primer, vol II (trans: Nyazee I). Center for Muslim Contribution to Civilization. Garnet Publishing Ltd, Reading

Mālik ibn Anas (1987) Muwatta'. Beirut. Al-Muwatta of Imam Malik ibn Anas. The First Formulation of Islamic Law (Trans: Bewley AA). London, 1989

al-Marghīnānī (1982) Hidāya. A Commentary on the Musulman Laws (Trans: Hamilton C) (Reprint edition), New Delhi

al-Māwardī (1996) Al-Ahkām al-Sultāniyya w'al-Wilāyāt al-Dīniyya. The Ordinances of Government. Great Books of Islamic Civilization. Garnet Publishing Ltd, Reading, UK

al-Misrī A (1994) ᶜUmdat al-Sālik. Reliance of the traveller. A classic manual of Islamic Sacred Law. In: Arabic with facing English Text (Ford: Keller NHM). Beltsville, Maryland, USA

Qutb S (2000) Social Justice in Islam (Trans: Hardie JB). Revised edition by Islamic Publication International, Oneonta, USA

al-Shāficī: Risāla (1940) Al-Shāficī's Risāla (1961) Treatise on the Foundations of Islamic Jurisprudence. Translated with an Introduction, Notes, and Appendices by MAJID KHADDURI. Baltimore

al-Shaybānī (1966) Siyar. The Islamic Law of Nations. Shaybānī's Siyar by Majid Khadduri, Baltimore

Sunni Law: Literature

Amanat A (2007) From ijtihād to wilāyat-i faqīh: the evolution of the shiite legal authority to political power. In: Amanat A, Griffel F (eds) Shariᶜa. Islamic Law in the contemporary context. Stanford University Press, Stanford

Aoued A (1996) Algeria: reconciling faith and modernity. In: Örücü E, Attwooll E, Coyle S (eds) Studies in legal systems: mixed and mixing, 193–209. Kluwer International, London

Arjomand SA (1989) Constitution-making in Islamic Iran: the impact of theocracy on the legal order of a nation state. In: Starr J, Collier F (eds) History and power in the study of law. New directions in Legal anthropology. Cornell University Press: Ithaca and London

Ayoub M (2008) The many faces of political Islam. Religion and politics in the Muslim world. The University of Michigan Press, Ann Arbor

Bakhtiar L (1996) Encyclopaedia of Islamic Law. A compendium of the major schools. Chicago

Boskurt G (1998) The reception of Western European Law in Turkey (From the Tanzimat to the Turkish Republic, 1839–1939). In: Der Islam, Band 75, Heft vol 2, pp 283–295

Coulson NJ (1964) A history of Islamic Law. Edinburgh

Davison R (2000) Tanzīmāt. In: The encyclopaedia of Islam. X. Brill, Leiden

Duri AA (1986a) ᶜĀmil. In: The encyclopaedia of Islam I. Brill, Leiden

DURI, A. A. (1986b) Amīr. In: The Encyclopaedia of Islam I. Brill, Leiden

DURI, A. A. (1991): Dīwān. In: The Encyclopaedia of Islam II. Brill, Leiden

Dutton Y (1998) The origins of Islamic Law. New Delhi, RoutledgeCurzon

Fyzee AAA (2002) Outlines of Muhammadan Law. Oxford University Press, Oxford India Paperbacks, 4th edn. Oxford

Goldziher I (1927) Fikh. In: The encyclopaedia of Islam, vol 2, pp 101–105. Brill, Leiden

Hallaq WB (1984) Was the gate of Ijtihad closed? Int J Middle East Stud 16:6–41

Hallaq WB (1989) Non-analogical arguments in Sunni Juridical Qiyas. Arabica 36:286–306

Hallaq WB (1993) Was al-Shafici the master architect of Islamic Law? Int J Middle East Stud 25(4):587–605

Hallaq WB (1997) A history of Islamic legal theories. Cambridge University Press, Cambridge

Hallaq WB (2001a) From regional to personal schools of law? Islamic Law Soc 8(1):1–26

Hallaq WB (2001b) Authority, continuity and change in Islamic Law. Cambridge University Press, Cambridge

Hallaq WB (2009) Sharīᶜa. Theory. Practice. Transformations. Cambridge University Press, Cambridge

Hambly G (1991) The Pahlavi autocracy. Rizā Shāh. In: The Cambridge history of Iran, vol 7, pp 213–293. Cambridge University Press, Cambridge

Heffening W (1993) Wakf. In: First encyclopaedia of Islam 1913–1936, vol 8. Reprint Edition. Leiden, New York

Jackson SA (1996) Taqlīd, legal scaffolding and the scope of legal injunctions in post-formative theory: Mutlaq and ᶜĀmm in the Jurisprudence of Shihāb al-Dīn Al-Qarāfī. Islamic Law Soc 3(2). E. J. Brill, Leiden

Jany J (2006) Klasszikus iszlám jog. Egy jogi kultúra természetrajza. Budapest, Gondolat

Jany J (2012) Judging in the Islamic, Jewish and Zoroastrian legal traditions. A comparison of theory and practice. Cultural Diversity and Law Series, Ashgate, GB

Johansen B (1993) Legal literature and the problem of change: the case of the land rent. In: Mallat C (ed) Islam and Public Law. Arab and Islamic Law Series, London, pp 29–47

Johansen B (2002) Signs as evidence: the doctrine of Ibn Taymiyya (1263–1328) and Ibn Qayyim al-Jawziyya (D. 1351) on Proof. Islamic Law and Soc 9(2):168–193

Kamali M (1993) Apellate review and Judicial Independence in Islamic Law. In: Mallat C (ed) Islam and Public Law, pp 49–84. London, Boston

Karpat K (1970) Modern Turkey. In: The Cambridge history of Islam 1/B. Cambridge University Press, Cambridge

Keddie NR (2006) Modern Iran. Roots and results of revolution. Yale University Press, New Haven, London

Khadduri M (1966) Translator's introduction to Shaybānī's Siyar. Johns Hopkins Press, Baltimore

Kruse H (1979) Islamische Völkerrechtslehre. Studienverlag N. Bochum, Brockmeyer

Lambton AKS (1981) State and Government in Medieval Islam, Oxford

Lapidus IM (1988) A history of Islamic Societies. Cambridge University Press, Cambridge

Lewis B (1991) Dīwān-i Humāyūn. The Encyclopaedia of Islam, vol II. Brill: Leiden

Makdisi G (1981) The rise of colleges. Edinburgh University Press, Edinburgh

Mallat C (1993) The renewal of Islamic Law. Muhammad Baqer as-Sadr, Najaf and the Shiᶜi International. Cambridge Middle East Library 29. Cambridge University Press, Cambridge

Mandaville P (2007) Global political Islam. Routledge, New York

Marsden P (1998) The Taliban. War, religion and the new order in Afghanistan. Oxford University Press, Karachi, Lahore, Islamabad

Melchert C (1997) The formation of the Sunni Schools of Law: 9th–10th centuries C. E, Leiden

Meron Y (1969) The development of legal thought in Hanafi texts. Studia Islamica 30:73–118

Mottahedeh RP (2003) Introduction. In: Al-Sadr MB (ed) Lessons in Islamic Jurisprudence (trans: with Introduction by Mottahedeh PR). Oneworld, Oxford

Motzki H (2002) The origins of Islamic Jurisprudence. Meccan Fiqh before the Classical Schools. Leiden, Brill

Müller C (1999) Gerichtspraxis im Stadtstaat Córdoba. Zum Recht der Gesellschaft in einer mālikitisch-islamischen Rechtstradition des 5./11. Jahrhunderts. Brill, Leiden, Boston, Köln

Noth A (1994) Die Higra. In: Geschichte der Arabischen Welt (hrsg. Haarmann), 11–57. München

Powers D (1992) On judicial review in Islamic Law. Law Soc Rev 26:314–341

Ramadan T (1999) To be a European Muslim. A study of Islamic sources in the European context. The Islamic Foundation, Markfield, Leicester

Rasanayagam A (2009) Afghanistan. A modern history. I. B. Tauris, London

Rebstock U (1999) A Qādī's errors. Islamic Law Soc 6(1):1–37

Rostoványi Z (1998) Az iszlám a 21. század küszöbén. Budapest

Roy O (2004) Globalized Islam. The search for a New Ummah. Columbia University Press, New York

Schacht J (1927) Sharīᶜa. In: E. J. Brill's first Encyclopaedia of Islam, vol 7, pp 320–324

Schacht J (1950) The origins of Muhammadan Jurisprudence. Oxford University Press, Oxford

Schacht J (1964) Introduction to Islamic law. Oxford University Press, Oxford

Schacht J (1970) Law and justice. In: The Cambridge history of Islam, vol 2B, pp 539–568
Schirazi A (1997) The Constitution of Iran. Politics and State in the Islamic Republic. I. B. Tauris, London, New York
Schneider I (1990) Das Bild des Richters in der »Adab al-QāĀī« Literatur. Islam und Abendland, Band 4. Peter Lang, Frankfurt, New York, Paris
Talesh NMA (1986) Modern law and Judiciary Reform in Iran—An Islamic Society. In: Chiba M (ed) Asian Indigenous Law. Routledge and Kegan Paul, London, pp 81–165
Tellenbach S (2003) Ehrenmorde an Frauen in der arabischen Welt. Anmerkungen zu Jordanien und anderen Ländern. Wuqūf- Beiträge zur Entiwicklung von Staat und Gesellschaft in Nordafrika. No. 13, Hamburg, pp 74–89. www.gair.de
Vogel FE (2000) Islamic law and legal system. Studies of Saudi Arabia. Brill, Leiden, Köln
Weiss BG (1992) The search for God's Law. Islamic Jurisprudence in the Writings of Sayf al-Dīn al-Āmidī. University of Utah Press, Salt Lake City
Weiss BG (1998) The spirit of Islamic Law. The University of Georgia Press, Athens and London
Wheeler BM (1996) Applying the Canon in Islam. The authorization and maintenance of interpretive reasoning in Hanafi Scholarship. State University of New York Press, New York
Ziadeh F (1957) Equality in the Muslim Law of marriage. Am J Comp Law 6(4):503–517

Shī°i Law: Sources

Baqir al-Sadr M (2003a) Principles of Islamic Jurisprudence. According to Shi'i Law (trans: Hussain AA). Islamic College for Advanced Studies Press, London
Baqir al-Sadr M (2003b) Lessons in Islamic Jurisprudence (trans: Mottahedeh RP) Oneworld, Oxford
Khomeini (1981) Islam and revolution (trans: Algar H). Mizan Press, Berkeley
Sobhani J (2001) Doctrines of Shi'i Islam. A compendium of Imami beliefs and practices (trans: Shah-Kazemi). I. B. Tauris, London

Shī°i Law: Literature

Dabashi H (2011) Shi'ism. A religion of protest. The Belknapp Press of Harvard University, Cambridge
Gleave R (2001) Akhbārī Shī°ī usūl al-fiqh and the juristic theory of Yūsuf al Bahrānī. In: Gleave R, Kermeli E (eds) Islamic Law. Theory and practice. I. B. Tauris: London, pp 24–48
Keddie NR (1969) The roots of the Ulama's power in modern Iran. Studia Islamica 29:31–53
Kohlberg E (1976a) From Imāmiyya to Ithnā-°ashariyya. Bull Sch Oriental Afr Stud 39:521–534. Reprinted in: Kohlberg E (1991) Belief and Law in Imāmī Shī°ism. Variorum, Aldershot
Kohlberg E (1976b) The development of the Imāmī Shī°ī Doctrine of Jihād. Zeitschrift der Deutschen Morgenländischen Gesellschaft 126:64–86. Reprinted in: Kohlberg E (1991) Belief and Law in Imāmī Shī°ism. Variorum, Aldershot
Kohlberg E (1983) The evolution of the Shī°a. Jerusalem Q 27:109–126. Reprinted in: Kohlberg E (1991) Belief and Law in Imāmī Shī°ism. Variorum, Aldershot, , pp 1–22
Kohlberg E (1987) Aspects of Akhbāri thought in the seventeenth and eighteenth centuries. In: Levtzion N, Voll O (ed) Eighteenth century renewal and reform in Islam. Syracuse University Press, Syracuse. Reprinted in: Kohlberg E (1991) Belief and law in Imāmī Shī°ism. Variorum, Aldershot

Kohlberg E (1988) Imam and community in the pre-Ghayba period. In: Arjomand SA (ed) Authority and political culture in Shi'ism. State University of New York Press, Albany, pp 25–53. Reprinted in: Kohlberg E (1991) Belief and Law in Imāmī Shī^cism. Variorum, Aldershot
Löschner H (1971) Die dogmatischen Grundlagen des šī'itischen Rechts. Carl Heymanns Verlag, Köln, Berlin
Mallat C (1993) The renewal of Islamic Law. Muhammad Baqer as-Sadr, Najaf and the Shi'i International. Cambridge University Press, Cambridge
Nasr V (2007) The Shia revival. How conflicts within Islam will shape the future. W. W. Norton, New York
Newman AJ (2000) Usūliyya. In: The encyclopaedia of Islam 2, vol X. Brill, Leiden
Rostoványi Z (1998) Az iszlám a 21. század küszöbén. Aula kiadó, Budapest
Sachedina AA (1988) The just ruler in Shi'ite Islam. The comprehensive authority of the jurist in Imamite Jurisprudence. Oxford University Press, Oxford
Vikor K (2005) Between God and the Sultan. A history of Islamic Law. Hurst and Company, London

Part III
Hindu Legal Circle

Chapter 8
Hindu Law

8.1 Principles of Hindu Law

Dharma, the term which is usually translated as law into English and other European languages has very few in common with the western understanding of law. In the Hindu conception, law is not an expression of political will but something eternal, deeply rooted in the cosmic order. Unsurprisingly, law is thus connected to religious ideas rather than to mundane affairs, though Hindu concept of law differs enormously from Middle Eastern religious concepts of law (Jewish, Islamic, Persian).

Such a complex concept evolved in history through centuries. The core of the idea is to be found already in the Vedas, holy books of Hinduism which came into being in the second millennium BCE. Here *rta* (truth, order) as an impersonal concept maintains both the macrocosm and the microcosm and guarantees the proper function of all beings, gods and humans included. Gods innumerable as they are, help to maintain the cosmic order and could be approached with sacrifices in order to plea for benefits. Small wonder that Vedic Hinduism is ritualistic. Vedic ritualism could be observed in highlighting animal sacrifices (white horse), sacrifices dedicated to Agni, lord of fire, and the numerous hymns and songs composed to worship the gods. Law is part of the cosmic order as a set of norms regulating human behaviour which should be in accordance with the cosmic order and the will of gods maintaining it. This is the reason why the Vedas are considered as the main source of law, though it is a truism that the Vedas—contrary to the Old Testament and the Qu'ān—contain no legal percept whatsoever. The Vedas as sources of all relevant religious knowledge should therefore also be the starting point of legal knowledge, despite its overwhelmingly ritualistic content. This way of thinking also explains the elevated position of priests, a privileged group with the monopoly of ritual knowledge necessary to maintain the world order and to help both the individual and the community to achieve prosperity and well-being. But all this is too abstract and contains no milestones to everyday life understandable to all with clear cut rights and duties. After all, one should know

© Springer Nature Switzerland AG 2020
J. Jany, *Legal Traditions in Asia*, Ius Gentium: Comparative Perspectives on Law and Justice 80, https://doi.org/10.1007/978-3-030-43728-2_8

what to do in order to maintain the cosmic order with his own deeds. Out of this necessity, the concept of *dharma* evolved to fill the normative gap.[1]

Dharma however is more than a set of rules, the aim of which is to maintain the cosmic order with its own means. It is true that *dharma* has laws for both individuals and *varna*s, defining rights and duties. What is more however, is that with the passage of time *dharma* became prominent and absorbed the concept of *rta*, which lost its importance and thus gave way to the supremacy of *dharma,* which evolved into the basic concept of Hindu moral and legal world view. The British began to translate *dharma* in the sense of law at the time when works dealing with *dharma* were translated into English out of practical considerations. This is how, for example, *Manu*'s *Dharmaśastra* became The Laws of Manu, being regarded as a kind of law collection which could be implemented also at the courts of law. Needless to say, *dharma* had never had such a narrow legal meaning in India, being closer to religion than to law. Law proper was referred to as either *vidhi*, a term of Sanskrit origin or *qānūn,* the latter bearing witness to the influence of Islamic law. The problem with the translation of terms is more than a technical misunderstanding, it is a conceptual failure since the dichotomy of law and religion is a modern Western idea entirely unknown to Hinduism. Consequently, *dharma* has the meaning of both religion and law, but also that of morality, making it impossible to translate into any modern western language. *Dharma* originates from the root *dhr* meaning 'holding, containing', thus referring to the function of *dharma* to preserve world order. If someone acts in accordance with *dharma*, such a deed will contribute to the maintenance of world order and the personal benefit of the actor. By contrast, a deed contrary to *dharma*, *adharma* has a destructive effect for both the cosmos and the individual.[2]

It is important to note however, that *dharma* and *adharma* could not be understood simply as good and bad, concepts difficult to place within Hindu moral thinking. At this point, a genuine example will help to clarify the matter. To kill a living being is neither bad nor good in the Hindu understanding of *dharma*: to kill a living being for its own sake is certainly *adharma*, but if a lion kills an animal for his own nutrition it is not *adharma* since it is the very nature of the lion to kill for staying alive. This understanding of *dharma* is closely related to the doctrine *karma* and the new incarnation after death as all acts have their consequences. All deeds, either in accordance with *dharma* or contrary to it, have influence on *karma* and the new incarnation of the individual. Good or bad *karma* thus, depends also on *dharma* and the way an individual was able to live in accordance with it. It is not an exaggeration to say, therefore, that *dharma* is the core concept of Hindu religious and legal thinking.

Hindu sages were, of course, aware that human behaviour is determined also by less noble intentions as envisaged by *dharma*. Power, material gain and sexual desire are among the main motivations of human deeds that should be taken into consideration. There is nothing wrong with these motifs, Hindus believe, since humans are created with flash and bones and both desires (*kāma*) and material well-being and political power (*artha*) have their place in human life. In addition to *dharma,*

---

[1] Menski (2003: 86–93).
[2] Rocher (2012: 40–42; 87).

both *artha* and *kama* are important for humans and this is the reason why *Manu* underlines (II. 224.) that a complete human life is composed of *dharma, artha* and *kama* and one should find their proper place in life. On the other hand, one should be aware of the relative importance of these concepts and their role vis-á-vis to each other. It is beyond doubt, that *dharma* has precedence over both *artha* and *kama* and *artha* is superior to *kama*. In keeping with their relative importance, humans are able to enjoy life in which religion, material prosperity and sexual desire can find their proper place. In order to elaborate skills and knowledge pertaining to these aspects of life, a particular scientific literature came into being: works on *dharma* are called *dharmasūtra* and *dharmaśāstra,* works about the discipline of *artha* are called *arthaśāstra* while works about the art of desire are called *kāmasūtra.*[3]

Now it is clear that *dharma* could not be translated simply as law. On the other hand, *dharma* as a broad concept encapsulates law and legal matter which are dealt with in works on *dharma.*[4] The complexity of the issue however, becomes evident when studying works on *artha,* that is, politics and public administration (Arthaśastra), which also contain legal norms that are, perhaps, closer to contemporary social reality and legal practice than works on *dharma,* reflecting a more idealistic legal understanding. This is a hotly debated issue among students of Hindu law: Ludo Rocher, for example, argued that texts on *dharma* reflect actual legal practice and not only a priestly ideal, while Werner Menski is of the view that these texts do not reflect contemporary legal practice only the legal understanding of the authors of those texts.[5]

To learn one's *dharma* is however a complicated issue, as there are few, if any, abstract and universal rules. By contrast, norms are determined in accordance with social status, age and individual position. One's own *dharma* is called *swadharma,* which is determined partly by one's individual destiny, partly by one's social rank. To these, the idea of life cycles (*aśrama*) is added as requirements vary in accordance with the age of an individual: young adults have entirely different obligations to what old people even have within the same social group. Social groups known as *varna*s (translated usually but improperly as caste) have their own *dharma,* not to be confused with that of other *varna*s. This is a very important point of Hindu (legal) thinking exemplified by the advice of *Krishna* given to *Arjuna* before the final battle in the *Bhagavadgītā.* Accordingly, one of the heroes of the Mahabharata, *Arjuna* is unwilling to fight in the battle and kill his enemies since they are his own relatives and he wants to spear their lives. *Krishna,* however, convinced him that he should fight and kill because he is a warrior and it is his *dharma* to fight regardless of who the enemy is. Finally, kings have their own *dharma* called *rājadharma* determining his competencies and outlining the portrait of an ideal king.[6]

Hindu tradition has four *varna*s, the origin of which go back to *Purusa,* the mythical ancestor. Accordingly, *Brahmin*s came into existence from his mouth, *Ksatriyas*

---

[3] Menski (2003: 97), Lingat (1973: 5).
[4] Derrett (1973: 2–3).
[5] Rocher (2012: 73; 106–109; 117), Menski (2003: 106).
[6] Lingat (1973: 3–5).

from his arms, *Vaiśyas* from his thighs and *Śūdras* from his feet. This organic view symbolises the hierarchical relation between the *varnas*, Brahmins being at the top of the system (since it were they who created it). Brahmins enjoy privileges because God Brahma had put secret knowledge *(brahman)* into their mouths in order to dedicate their lives exclusively to learning, worship and to the teaching of the Vedas. *Ksatriyas* are gifted with strength *(ksatra)* in order to defend society from the enemy, guarantee domestic safety and to govern the state. *Vaiśyas* have the vigour and ability of work *(viś)* ensuring their capacity to cultivation, industry and trade, that is, the material prosperity of society. By contrast, it is the obligation of the *Śūdras* to supply the three upper *varnas* with adequate personal and material services while they are excluded from Vedic cults, teaching, learning and the rites of initiation with the help of which a young man becomes a full member of the community and thus a twice born' *(dvija)*.[7] In addition to these particular duties, it is expected from all the *varnas* to refrain from killing living beings, to be credible, sincere, honest, peaceful and merciful.[8]

It is difficult to tell whether this *varna* system is only a priestly ideal or has some historic roots. Perhaps it has something in common with the social reality of the ancient Vedic period but with the passage of time social structure became more complicated. This is one of the reasons why it is improper to understand *varna* as caste. In fact, the number of castes *(jāti)* is higher than the four *varnas*, while *Śūdras* are hard to find in Indian society as they are not identical with the 'untouchables' *(cāndāla)* living on the periphery of society. Needless to say, such a contradiction did not escape the attention of Hindu sages, who made every attempt to harmonise theory with social reality. According to this new theory, castes emerged as a result of the mixture of *varnas*, thus constituting new categories. For example, a child produced by a *Brahmin* man and a *Ksatriya* woman does not belong to of either of his parents' *varna* but to a third, newly created category *(ambastha)*. Children produced by parents belonging to other, different *varnas* belong to various, newly created categories while children of the parents of these categories belong again to various new categories. This is how a very complicated system of the mixed *varnas* came into being, the aim of which was to develop an explanation to the multitude of castes harmonising with the theory of the *varna* system. This new theory was developed already in ancient India since the *Dharamaśāstra* of *Manu* already has it.[9] The theoretical and artificial nature of the concept of mixed castes is shown by the fact that attempts were made to embed the Greeks into this system, who were born accordingly, from the (otherwise illegal) relationship between *Śūdra* men and

---

[7]The expression refers to thesecond'birth' of a person with the help of his guru who taught him the necessary knowldge and was, therefore, regarded more important than the father who was only a biological progenitor.

[8]Kautilīya: Arthaśāstra: III.1. 13. The prohibition to refrain from animal sacrifice was an innovation because rituals in the Vedas rest on animal sacrifice, particularly (white) horse sacrifice. We still do not know for certain what exactly led to this change of doctrine, see Doniger and Smith (1991: xxx–xl).

[9]Manu X. 1–69.

Ksatriya women. This concept was later extended to other peoples with whom Hindus came into contact with, such as the Persians, Sakas and Chinese.[10]

In addition to the mixed *varna*s, the theory of the four stages of life complicates the matter further. Accordingly, there are four stages of life with different rules and obligations. The first stage of life is that of the student (*brahmachārin*), which begins with the rite of initiation, abling the young boy to enter among the *dvija* and participate in rituals. The age of initiation is the eighth year for *Brahman*s and the eleventh or twelfth year respectively for members of the other two *varna*s. During this period, the student learns important texts and basic principles of Hinduism under the guidance of his spiritual leader called *guru*. A *brahmachārin* not only learns what is expected from him, but has to follow his guru's spiritual guidance, serve his guru and do everything he is commanded. This stage of life is closed by a ritual bath to be followed by the next stage, that of the householder *(grhastha)*. During this period, a young man is obliged to marry, raise children and live in accordance with the rules of his own *varna*. This period lasts for decades and it has no general time limit when it comes to close. Generally speaking, it reaches its end when the man's hair begins to grey or his grandchild is born. Now his third stage of life begins during the time when he moves away from his family, spends a large part of his time on studies and meditation and consumes exclusively vegetal food. This period of retreat is continued during the fourth stage of life, which could be considered as the same stage with stricter rules. Now a man lives the life of an hermit who is already a dead person to his family and the society at large (this is an important point in the law of inheritance). Such a man has no place to dwell, has to wonder constantly, can eat only vegetables he finds, etc. Yet again the question arises whether the theory of the four *āśrama*s reflects only a brahmanistic ideal as in the case of the rules of *dharma* and the *varna* system or not. It is, of course, beyond doubt that young boys had to study and adult males had to work and wage war i f necessary already in Vedic times as it is the case in every society. Ascetics and hermits were also known in India from ancient times as the observations of the Greek *Megasthenes* and the Persian *al-Bīrūnī* perfectly support it. But this does not mean that the last two stages were obligatory. By contrast, the last stages were not obligatory by law[11] and, what is more, there were opinions according to which they should be neglected completely.

Now coming to law, proper legal literature (both in works on *dharma* and *artha*) made less attempt to define law yet classified the various fields of law into eighteen *mārga*s (road, path) or *vyavahāra-pada*s (bases of legal dispute). Once established, this framework became standard and all legal works classified the legal material accordingly. Though artificial at some points, the system was widely accepted not least because the number eighteen is a sacred number in Hindu understanding to be seen, among others, in the 18 Upanisads, the 18 books of the Mahabharata and the

---

[10]Gautama IV. 17. The origin of the *varna* system is subject to debate, particularly because the Vedas do not contain references to it. The Vedas only differentiate between the *ārya-varna* and the *dāsa-varna* the latter referring to the enemy of the Aryas. According to some theories *Śūdra*s may be the offspring of the *dāsa-varna*, but this concept is also challanged by some, see Lingat (1973: 29–44).

[11]Lingat (1973: 45–51).

18 Puranas. The 18 *vyavahāra-pada*s are the following: (1) non-repayment of debt; (2) deposit; (3) purchase and sale by non-owner; (4) partnership relations; (5) not giving over gift; (6) non-payment of wages; (7) violation of agreements; (8) waiver in case of sale and purchase; (9) dispute between owner and shepherd; (10) border disputes; (11) verbal attacks; (12) physical attacks; (13) theft; (14) violence; (15) sexual violence committed against women; (16) legal position of husband and wife; (17) inheritance and its partition; (18) gambling.[12] Obviously, this list of disputes is insufficient to cover all the cases, yet it remained the basis of legal thinking. If new demands emerged, they were thus adjusted to this system. Debt was in the core of the logic as a sort of an archetype because Hindu sages regarded the non-payment of debts or, generally speaking, obligations created by debt as the basis of all legal problems. In this particular logic, debt was interpreted rather broadly as it included the payment of wages, mutual obligations in sale and purchase. In addition to this pecuniary issues, family law and law of inheritance was also seen from the angle of debt since a pater familias was indebted to his ancestors to marry, to raise children and to support his wife and children.[13] In short, Hindu sages regarded debt as the basic institution what Muslim legal scholars identified in sale: both Hindu and Muslim legal scholars derived their entire system from a single legal institution, they only differ in their basis: Muslims developed their own system from sale while Hindus from debt.

8.2   Principles of Hindu Political Theory

Wisdom on *dharma* concentrates on religion and law but has something to say also about politics in general and the state in particular. Despite this, political theory belongs rather to the science of *artha* telling how to manage mundane affairs.

According to classical Hindu theory, a state consists of seven elements, such as the king, the ministers, the territory and population, the capital city, the treasury, the army and its allies. Hindus developed—together with other Asian cultures—an organic understanding of the state in which the state resembles a human body with the king as its head. Kautilīya, author of the Arthasastra, however, leaves no doubt that however important other organs might be, the head is still the most important part. A state is a monarchy where power is hereditary on the male line according to the laws of primogeniture, otherwise small units would be created which would fall prey easily to the enemy. Princes with empty hands should be given important offices in the state administration to control them. The heir appointed should be given a perfect education in order to prepare him for his job which could begin already during his father's lifetime, what some sages even considered as advantageous. A perfect ruler is called *chakravartin*, that is, a king who governs the entire world

---

[12]Davis (2010a: 77).
[13]Davis (2010a: 77–82).

morally and with good intentions. There are some texts which call such a ruler a god, but the interpretation of these texts remained subject to debate for decades.[14]

In short, it is the ruler who is at the heart of the political system in Hindu understanding while abstract concepts such as the state are missing. By contrast, *dharma* has its proper place in political thinking because according to Hindu political theory, a king has his own *dharma* called *rājadharma* which could be seen as a composition of rights and duties to be expected from a good ruler. A good king would, obviously, act and rule according to his *rājadharma* while a negligent king cares less about acts to be classified as *adharma*. Neither *dharma* nor *adharma* are, needless to say, forms of institutional controls on a king who enjoyed a rather free hand in governing. As a result, Indian kingdoms remained without effective balance of power which transformed Indian monarchies into more or less autocratic regimes. Only Brahmins in general and some of them as the kings' advisors in particular were those who had some influence on royal decisions since following Hindu political theory a king should act according to the advice of his sages, that is, leading Brahmins. This was however, a rather informal way of political influence as was the bargaining of other influential social groups. Here, Western-oriented political thinking about institutional balance of power should not mislead us: while an Indian king seemed to be, it is true, an autocratic ruler, in fact his power was balanced by powerful actors such as the Brahmins, the court circles, the provincial elites, the landlords, and no king was able to govern against the interest of these lobby groups.[15]

Hindu sages were not enthusiastic about the state, as they were less optimistic also about law. According to their understanding, a state—together with law—is necessary only because current conditions leave us no choice, since without a state societies would fall apart entirely. This is because mankind is now living in an age called *kali yuga*, the worst among the *yuga*s, the cycle of which started with the golden age. Conditions on Earth deteriorated ever since and in the present age, humans do not even follow their basic duties but have become each other's enemies and follow the 'law of the fish'.[16] According to the 'law of the fish' *(mātsya-nyāya),* big fishes devour small fishes, a worldview similar to *Hobbes'* theory about humans (*'homo homini lupus est'*) with the significant difference that this social disintegration emerged as a result of a long process of degeneration and was not an assumed initial situation. In such a world of chaos, a strong authority was needed in order to guarantee at least the basic functions of society and it is exactly what makes a state legitimate. Since people are unable to realise their own *dharma* in such conditions, gods have invested kings with power and authority in order to protect people and their goods against the assertion of the 'law of the fish.' This explains why a king should be a *ksatriya*, that is, a warrior with *ksathra*, strength and authority. Though, some medieval commentator do not insist on this doctrine any longer and accept the rule of a non-*ksatriya* king if

---

[14]Rocher (2012: 316–330; 335–339).

[15]Derrett (1969: 427–431), Rocher (2012: 351–357) also doubts the merit of the dominant view which sees an unlimited autocratic ruler in the Indian king.

[16]Kautilīya: Arthaśāstra: IV. 1. 13.

necessary, such a rule however, remained an exception in order to avoid more evil.[17] Texts on Hindu political theory discuss the qualification expected of rulers only vaguely without going into details such as impartiality towards the subjects, working to the benefit of the subjects, skills in religious and mundane disciplines).[18] If a king is negligent in working for the benefit of his people, it would be an *adharma* for him, but it is left to him to decide how to meet his obligations, as a peter familias or a guru also enjoys free hand to handle. Small wonder then that kings are compared to head of families and gurus, a paternalistic idea fitting well into Indian social conditions.[19]

Kings have two prerogatives, levying taxes and the right to punish. Taxes are seen as necessary monetary assets for the king enabling him to realise his duties. The right to punish (*danda*) was not regarded as a consequence and a part of a legitimate rule but has its own legitimacy of divine origin. This again is linked to the corrupted conditions of *kali yuga* when people could be forced to minimal cooperation and solidarity only with the help of punishments. The right to punish is, therefore, at the same time also an obligation for a monarch since by neglecting punishments a king would risk minimal social harmony, the maintenance of which he is responsible for. As a result, the king's right to punish is not only absolute but also obligatory: should he let someone go free who would deserve a punitive sanction, such a man's deed would affect negatively the *karma* of the monarch. The right to levy taxes and punish is related also to the king's duty to defend his land and its people from both external and internal enemies. Security of the kingdom include defensive as well as offensive wars and international treaties. Works on *artha* give detailed tactical and strategic pieces of advice to kings in issues of war and peace in a rather Machiavellian spirit. It is particularly the *Arthaśāstra* of *Kautilīya* (presumably *Candragupta*'s minister) that emphasizes such notion, but neither are works on *dharma* shy about such tactical advices. The *Mānava* and the *Nāradīya dharmaśāstra*s have four methods on how to defeat an enemy: with negotiations, bribe, division and military force.[20] Domestic security could also be guaranteed by force, that is, by punishments which led to the development of royal judiciary for both criminal and private litigation.

The problem of royal legislation was treated separately by Hindu sages from taxes and punishments. Royal legislation was not denied completely, but was held at bay within limits. Accordingly, no royal legislation could be at variance with the laws of *dharma*, laws for the *varna*s and the four stages of life. In short, while *dharma* is eternal, royal legislation is limited in space and time since the purpose of royal legislation is only to guarantee social order. Despite this, royal edicts were laws to be respected and challenging them was a challenge of royal power, at the same time sanctioned with severe punishments. While legislating, kings have to respect local customs, the interests of his subjects together with common sense and logic but edicts at variance with these expectations were not regarded as null and void. It was however, the moral duty of the new ruler to revise and modify the unjust

---

[17]Lingat (1973: 209–210).

[18]Gautama XI. 2–6.

[19]Lingat (1973: 207–212).

[20]Manu VII. 107; Nārada XVIII. 5.

edicts of his predecessor.[21] As kings were denied the right to legislate in issues belonging to *dharma* (as were Caliphs in the terrain of Islamic law), royal edicts rather concentrated on issues of public administration, taxes and criminal law (again a significant parallel with the Caliphate), that is, fields in which a king's power was unlimited. Unsurprisingly, these edicts are missing from works on *dharma*, that is, sources on Hindu law on which our knowledge on Hindu law basically rests. Since these royal edicts were lost due to numerous reasons (wars, negligence, weather conditions, etc.) during the centuries, they are known to us only in fragments.[22]

In order to rule properly and follow *dharma*, kings were expected to consult Brahmins before reaching decisions. To this end, an advisory body was set up, consisting of sages and priests because it was they who have the necessary intellectual and moral authority to guide the ruler. Hindu political theory regards the political authority of kings and the intellectual authority of Brahmins as complementary, the cooperation of which is capable to ensure moral order in the world.[23] It was primarily important to consult the sages in legal matters as Brahmins were experts in *dharma* and thus also in law. Kings were advised to consult Brahmins also in issues on political strategy and tactics, though these are by far not matters of *dharma* but that of *artha*. Kings had their personal advisers (*purohita*) appointed from among the Brahmins to consult in every matter, though these priests evidently had no veto against any decision of a king. *Purohita*s were personal spiritual leaders to the king, educated in various disciplines, including law, politics and astrology. Brahmins were awarded for their services for the community and the king with donations and kings were advised to be generous since such donations would help them to compensate their wrongs necessarily committed during a rule.[24] In addition to donations, Brahmins enjoyed further privileges such as exemption from taxes and punishments, since they could not be sentenced to corporeal punishment, fine and exile.[25] By contrast, criminal acts committed against *Brahmin*s were sanctioned with vigour because they were sacrileges since *Brahmin*s were sacred persons.[26] As a result, Brahmins enjoyed more privileges in criminal law than kings who belonged to the *varna* of warriors with less privileges. Medieval commentators, therefore, tried to reduce these privileges (perhaps also on the influence of Buddhism criticising the power of Brahmins) to the most scholarly sages and denied that all *Brahmin*s enjoy all the privileges *ipso iure*. Despite all their privileges, Brahmins were no institutional balances to kings and their royal authority who, in their turn, could not neglect Brahmins and their religious and social prestige completely.[27]

Works on *dharma* have no more to say than pointing at the importance to consult Brahmins and to follow their guidance. Small wonder, since *dharmasūtra*s and

---

[21]Nārada XVIII. 8–9.

[22]Lingat (1973: 230–232).

[23]Gautama VIII. 1.

[24]Manu VII. 82.

[25]Gautama VIII. 13.

[26]Manu VIII. 381.

[27]Lingat (1973: 220–222), see also Derrett: 1975a.

*dharmaśāstra*s were composed by Brahmins. By contrast, works on *artha* have more to offer on practical matters of politics and administration. *Kautilīya's Arthaśāstra* enables us to have a look on the fine organisation of an Indian state in late Antiquity. Accordingly, there were ministers (superintendents) on various matters of life, sometimes astonishingly modern. The superintendent for weaving was responsible for garments and armoury. To produce these, women with low social prestige (widows, crippled women, women who left their home, women redeeming their punishment by money, old slave women) were employed and then craftsmen made garments out of the fabric produced by them. It was the superintendent's task to control the process of production and to pay wages. The superintendent for agriculture was responsible for collecting products of agriculture and for sowing. The text specifies in detail the seeds of which plants should be planted at what time and in what order. Liquors also had a superintendent whose task was to control the production and sale of alcoholic drinks. There was a superintendent to protect animals (who fined everyone who killed protected animals) and another one to protect prostitutes (with criminal authority in wrongs committed against prostitutes). In addition, there were superintendents for marine shipping, for horses, for cows, and for elephants (elephants were used in the military and therefore emphasis was laid on their protection, feeding and training). There were superintendents for gold mining and sale, for the control of commerce and for the collection of revenues. Superintendents for chariots, horses and infantry and the commander-in-chief were responsible for military administration. Both external and internal security was guaranteed by spies and secret services. Provincial administration included the collection of revenues and the control of villages: there were officials who registered the number and size of villages, delineated the borders of villages and kept a record of local properties, and collected revenues (by five or ten villages). Cities had their own official ('mayor') to guarantee law and order. Attempts were made to prevent tragedies (not always successfully) by regulations of fire control and hygiene (for instance, anyone placing garbage in a public place was fined). In order to prevent chaos, strict building rules determined the cityscape.[28] In short, a fine administration with a strong army supported by a secret service was to assist Hindu rulers already in late Antiquity, a model of governance which was more effective in practice than that of the Mughals one and a half millennia later.[29]

Needless to say, the model of public administration by *Kautilīya* was subject to change during the centuries. The empire of *Aśoka*, for example, was divided to vice-royalties adjusted to the cardinal points, each headed by a viceroy. The famous king's religious commitment is reflected by the appointment of moral supervisors *(dharma mahāmātra)* sent by him all over his empire to assert *dharma*, even concerning members of the royal family. *Harita*'s empire was less developed in terms of administration, leaving more opportunity for highway men and other criminals threatening internal security. As a result, more rigorous and cruel punishments were introduced to stop them. When Muslims took control in various parts of the subcontinent, a dramatic change was introduced since Muslims paid less attention to local

---

[28] Kautilīya: Arthaśāstra: 110–185.
[29] Smith (1964: 100).

traditions and made efforts to introduce their own system of administration. Thus, public administration rested on the *dīwān* system, while the role of the army became increasingly prominent. Provincial governance was in the hands of *sīpāhsālār*s, military commanders who had unlimited authority on their territory. Outstanding rulers such as the Mughal *Akbar* made efforts to centralise the system and to control local authorities in order to secure the collection of revenues, which continued to remain the greatest endemic problem of public administration for centuries due to the resistance of local leaders. British India governed by the English East India Company faced the same problem despite reforms introduced to the system. When the British Crown had taken control over India (1857), public administration was remodelled in order to enhance efficiency.[30]

8.3 History and Sources of Hindu Law

Hinduism lacks a supreme God reminiscent to that of Judaism, Christianity and Islam. Therefore, *dharma* was not revealed by a God to a single prophet like the Laws of Moses or the legal verses of the Qur'ān. Despite this, the most important sources of *dharma* are the sacred books of Hinduism, the Vedas, which were also revealed to a chain of sages and holy men called *rsi*s whose names are unknown to us. It is however, not their names and life that are important, but their wisdom which is to be found in the Vedas. This is why Vedic literature is called *śruti* (revelation), to mark its difference from any other form of knowledge. As a result, Hindu sages agree that the fundamental source of *dharma* are the Vedas though, these texts do not contain legal verses, as the Qur'ān and the Tōra do. Next to the Vedas tradition and good custom are also sources of *dharma*, according to Gautama.[31] To these, Manu adds a fourth source, self-satisfaction ('what is pleasing to oneself').[32] Sources of *dharma* are put into a hierarchic order since the principal source is the scripture of the Vedas, followed by tradition and good custom. If neither of these sources has a clear answer to a particular legal problem, free discretion is the guide to decide. A source of lower rank could be consulted only if a source of higher rank is silent about the matter. If there are contradictory doctrines in the sources belonging to the same category in the hierarchy of legal sources, either of the doctrines could be followed,[33] a clear sign of legal pluralism.

The Vedas consists of three works containing liturgical texts, such as the Rgveda, the Sāmaveda and the Yajurveda to which a fourth text, the Atharvaveda was added. Like the Awesta of Zoroastrianism, the Vedas contain predominantly liturgical texts, hymns and recitations accompanying various sacrifices. We do not know for certain when the Vedas came into being, but a scholarly hypothesis with a solid ground puts

---

[30]Smith (1964: 128; 181; 344; 359).

[31]Gautama I. 1–2.

[32]Manu II. 6; 12.

[33]Gautama I. 4.

the oldest text, the Rgveda into the later part of the second millennium BCE. It is important to note however, that for Hindus the Vedas are not only texts that could be consulted, but a universal knowledge which is only fragmentarily known to mankind. Thus, when Hindu authors refer to the Vedas as a source of *dharma,* they do not have only a particular text in mind but understand this reference in a far broader context. As any other fundamental writing, the Vedas too had to be interpreted, which gave way to various schools with their own interpretation and understanding which were put into writing in texts called Brahmanas, discussing the relation between hymns and sacrifices. In the subsequent centuries, philosophical speculations in a rather enigmatic language were produced and collected in texts called Upanisads. Vedic literature is, therefore, about religion, ritual and philosophy but not about law. As a result, the Vedas had to be understood as rather theoretic foundations of law, but not as a legal source in its technical meaning, though outstanding authorities such P. V. Kane try to prove the opposite.[34] To clarify the matter, an example may be of help. In the dharmic literature discussing family law, it is prohibited to marry a girl who has no brother. In fact, there is no such a rule in any of the Vedas, yet it is clear that in Vedic society such a girl had no social reputation. The wisdom not to marry such a girl was already known in Vedic times but a legal rule to prohibit such a union was formulated only in the subsequent *dharma* literature since such a law was not to be found in the Vedas. The reason of this law is that a girl without a brother may be lost for the husband and his family as after the death of her parents she may return to her original family and take up the brother's position.[35]

Tradition is the second source of law that is, obviously, not based on revelation but only on the memory of the sages, the texts of which they passed on through generations (*smrti*). The corpus of this tradition was also put into writing, serving as a basis for disciplines such as phonetics, metrics, grammar, astronomy, etymology and ritual (*kalpa*)[36] the wisdom of which were collected in a literary genre called *sūtra. Dharmasūtra*s, that is, scholarly works on *dharma* were part of *kalpa* at the beginning, but as their subject matter developed and grew, they increasingly became independent from *kalpa* and the Vedic schools. This might be seen as the birth date of law and jurisprudence leading to a new literary genre, the *dharmaśāstra* which are composed in verse and are more detailed works than their predecessors.[37]

The third source of law is called the good custom *(sadāchāra)* of outstanding authorities, which differs on conceptual level from social custom. Needless to say, in a huge geographical area such as India there are numerous local customs in provincial and local level not to mention tribal customs. To these, one can add the custom of the various social groups and professions making customs an inevitable social fact of everyday legal life. On the conceptual level however, such diverse customs could not be a source of *dharma* and this why the custom of outstanding sages was seen as a source of law. The custom of outstanding sages is the way of life and what is

---

[34]Kane (1968: 6–9).

[35]Rocher (2012: 64).

[36]Kautilīya: Arthaśāstra III. 1.3.

[37]Lingat (1973: 73–74).

expected from an ideal Brahman, that is, sages who dedicated their life to teaching and learning, whose ethics were beyond doubt and in harmony with moral principles thought by them. The model of traditions elaborated in the *dharmaśāstra* literature was most probably that of the Brahmins, to which later the custom of the warrior *varna* was added. In fact, these texts deal with the legal issues of these two castes in the second stage of their life (that of the householder) while problems of other stages of life are almost completely missing, as are legal considerations about the *Śūdras*.[38]

There was a committee called *parisad* to decide whether a particular behaviour was in accordance with *sadāchāra* or not. The number of committee members i s given differently by our sources: according to Gautama and Manu the *parisad* consisted of ten scholars: one who knew the three Vedas, one who was a scholar of logics, one for the interpretation of texts, one educated in etymology, one expert in *dharma* and three others who represented the last three stages of life: a student, a householder and a hermit.[39] *Manu* however, is inconsistent since according to the same book a *parisad* could consist of three members only who come from among those who know the three Vedas.[40] Irrespective of the number and composition of its members, *parisad*s contributed enormously to the development of law, which led Robert Lingat to believe that the *smrti* literature is actually the compendium of the decisions of the *parisad*s. Hence *smrti* literature became the most important source of *dharma* and law.[41]

Hindu sages also had to solve the contradictions among the sources and to deal with their practical consequences. All authors agreed that in cases of contradictions, the Vedas should be followed as texts with the greatest authority, a claim which follows logically from the hierarchy of texts (legal sources). A more serious problem emerged if Vedic texts were at variance. Attempts were made to solve the contradictions in such cases by auxiliary rules. Such a technique was, for instance, to classify laws into general and particular rules, the latter to be applied only to exceptional cases. With this, some contradictions were argued away. Accordingly, a *brahmin* could never be killed, while another text has it that he could be killed out of self-defence. But this is not a real contradiction, the argument goes on to say that because self-defence is a particular situation with a particular law, that does not make the general law null and void. Another method of legal reasoning focuses on the time frame when laws at variance came into being: according to this method, laws were not contradictory but came into being in different times, one earlier while others only later. If contradictions were not to be solved with these techniques one was free to make a choice which law to follow, a clear evidence for legal pluralism. The same principles and techniques were applied to interpret other legal sources with the additional argument that if a doctrine is supported by the majority view, this has to be followed. If the majority cannot be ascertained for any reason, the doctrine supported by rational arguments should be followed. To build a hierarchy of texts on academic quality was also an

---

[38]Davies (2010a: 146–151).

[39]Gautama XXVIII. 49–51; Manu XII. 111.

[40]Manu XII. 112.

[41]Lingat (1973: 14–17).

attempt to avoid contradictions. This is the reason why *Manu* had become such a highly influential text the laws of which was to be followed when at variance with texts of the same genre. Finally, it was a very important principle of interpretation that in cases of contradictions the law which was identical with the local norms and customs (*sadāchāra*) should be followed, a clear proof of how important these customs for legal practice were.[42]

*Dharmasūtra*s follow the particularities of *sūtra* literature as a genre, that is, they contain short and concise sentences about the essence of the doctrines in order to summarise *dharma* for didactic purposes. Several *dharmasūtra*s have reached us, among which the most important are the *dharmasūtra* of *Gautama*, Baudhāyana, Āpastamba and Hārīta. Unfortunately, we do not know when these works came into being. According to academic consensus, the oldest *dharmasūtra* is Gautama's compendium. P. V Kane believed that it was composed in the sixth century BCE because there is no reference to Buddhism in the work while Robert Lingat dates Gautama's *dharmasūtra* two centuries later.[43] According to the most recent hypothesis of Patrick Olivelle, the entire genre did not emerge earlier than the fourth century BCE.[44] What complicates matter further, is the problem of writing, itself subject to debate for long, which was presumably unknown in India before the third century BCE. Consequently, not only the Vedas, but all works before that date were composed and preserved orally.[45]

The author of the *dharmasūtra* of Gautama belongs to a well-known *Brahmin* family of learning, the members of which can be found in various Vedic schools. His work is divided into twenty-eight chapters of various length, dealing with issues of ritual impurity and purification, the duties of the four stages of life and the *varna*s, the king's legal position, punishments, and particular laws about women. The *dharmasūtra*s of Baudhāyana and Āpastamba were produced in the same school which was according to tradition, founded by Baudhāyana who was followed by Āpastamba, a scholar later founding his own school. Baudhāyana's *dharmasūtra* does not significantly differ from *Gautama*'s work, but contains some topics which were not treated by Gautama, particularly in the field of marriage and law of inheritance. On the other hand, Baudhāyana's *dharmasūtra* is a less edited work discussing the same problem repeatedly in various chapters. By contrast, Āpastamba's work is far more focused and has a more developed logical structure, though its language is more archaic.[46] Its content is identical with other works of the same genre dealing with issues of purification, inheritance, punishments, the duties of kings and the *varna*s, and Vedic studies. At the same time, Āpastamba specifically prefers monogamy and does not call the three upper varnas *dvija*, a term broadly used in the

---

[42] Kane (1950: 26–30), Francavilla (2006: 216–222).

[43] Kane (1968: 35).

[44] Olivelle (2010: 37).

[45] Scharfe (2002: 12).

[46] Kane (1968: 41–42; 59).

subsequent centuries. This led Patrick Olivelle to believe that Āpastamba might be one of the earliest among the *dharmasūtras*.[47]

Around the second century BCE, the *dharmasūtras*, becoming increasingly schematic both in content and form were replaced by a new genre of its own, the *dharmaśāstra*. *Dharmaśāstras* differ from their predecessors in style, content and edition because they are written in verse and in a less archaic language closer to classical Sanskrit, are significantly longer and better edited discussing legal issues in greater detail, and are less linked to *kulpa* and to Vedic schools, an important step in the development of *dharma* literature.[48]

Among the *dharmaśāstras* that of *Manu*, Nārada and Yājñavalkya are particularly important. In the West, it is the Manu-smrti or Mānava dharmaśāstra (*Manu* in short) which became well known due to their early translation to English. It is not the work of an author called *Manu*, since *Manu* was a mythical figure (*mānava:* human being, man) whose name only assigned authority to the work composed by authors unknown to us. The Rgveda mentions Manu among the sages who lived in the distant past, while in the Manu-smrti he is a king who invented sacrifice to god. It is not only the author(s) of the work who are unknown to us, but also the date of its composition. According to scholarly consensus, the Manu-smrti could have been produced between the second century BCE and the second century CE. A more precise dating is made extremely difficult by many interpolations to the text. It is also subject to debate whether it is the work of a single author or was produced by more authors, perhaps of subsequent generations. According to a most recent hypothesis, Manu was written in the second century BCE as the work of a single author.[49] Manu's *dharmaśāstra* was also believed to be the oldest of its genre, constituting a transition between the *dharmasūtra* and the *dharmaśāstra*. This view, however, was based only on the assumption that since the works of both Nārada and Yājñavalkya are more refined, detailed and precise than Manu is, they are consequently also later works, a doubtful inference because works of higher standard were not necessarily produced later.

Yet, it is true that Manu reflects the transition from pure Vedaism towards Hinduism. While the text underlines the absolute authority of the Vedas, it also diverts from Vedic practice at significant points. Perhaps one of the best examples of this transition is the doctrine of non-violence *(ahimsā)* which completely contradicts the bloody sacrifices of the Vedas and the 'law of the fish'. This new principle of non-violence brought about significant changes in religious thinking and led to vegetarianism. Manu made every attempt to maintain various doctrines, an intellectual effort that might explain the numerous contradictions in the text. A classic example is the *niyoga* marriage: while Manu condemns this form of marriage morally and prohibits it in one of its books, in a different locus it discusses at length how to conclude such a marriage. Such contradictions might be the result of attempts to

---

[47]Olivelle (2010: 38–39), Note 23.

[48]Lingat (1973: 73), Kane (1968: 21).

[49]Olivelle (2010: 42).

harmonise various doctrines or of later interpolations to the text or the inclusion of the teachings of various schools in the same text.[50]

Manu is a rather extensive work containing 2694 *śloka*s (couplet) in twelve books. The first book is a kind of an introduction narrating how great sages visited Manu asking him to reveal the rules of *dharma* to them. The second book is about the sources of *dharma*, the stages of life and the importance of Vedic studies. The third and the fourth book are about the householder's stages of life and its rules, together with the rights and duties of the *varna*s. The fifth book is about ritual impurity and prohibited food. The shortest book of the work is the sixth discussing hermits. Thus far, there is nothing new comparing what is already known by the *sūtra* literature. The last six books however, add valuable new elements to inherited wisdom by enlarging the material. The seventh book, for example, discusses the king's legal position and his duties in a far greater detail, taking over many elements from the *artha* literature expounding political tactics and the art of warfare, too. This book is also the proper place to discuss punishments along the logic that it is the right of the ruler to punish his subjects. The eighth and ninth books contain something entirely new: legal issues in the narrower sense of the term. They include the eighteen *mārga*s (road, path) also called *vyavahāra-pada* (causes for legal proceeding), that is, the genuine classification of Hindu law into legal causes. The entire ninth book is filled with laws of the *mārga*, marriage and law of inheritance. The tenth book is about the *varna*s and the mixed castes that emerge from the mixing of *varna*s. Further on, laws to be applied in exceptional situations are also given here. The eleventh book discusses sins, while the last, twelfth book returns to the topic of the first book and sheds light on the religious, ethical and philosophical foundations of *dharma*. This is, of course, not the logic of a western legal work, but it does not make Manu a work of disarray and logical inconsistencies. Criticism on this ground can clearly be refuted. Manu follows its own logic built upon the theory of the stages of life. Now it becomes clear why the work begins with the studies of the Vedas and the relationship between students and masters to be followed by the stage of a householder. Since the second stage of life is about economic, social and political activity, regulated by law, it is exactly the second stage of life when legal issues and norms are discussed at length. By enlarging the material with wisdom from the *artha* literature, Manu was able to arrive at a more comprehensive understanding of a Hindu king and his rights and duties, including the right to punish. It was the innovation of Manu to incorporate issues of politics, state administration and judicial procedure into *dharma* literature, topics which otherwise belonged to *artha* literature.[51]

Next to the Manu-smrti, it was the Yājñavalkya-smrti that enjoyed authority among Hindus. *Yājñavalkya* too, is a mythic figure who had got acquainted with the *Yajurveda* through revelation. As a modern Indian author put it, Indians may acknowledge Manu as a source of wisdom but actually live according to the Yājñavalkya-smrti. Its time of composition is unknown, but it was written after the Manu-smrti: according to Jolly it could be composed in the fourth century CE while Kane dates it

---

[50]Doniger and Smith (1991: xxx–lviii).
[51]Olivelle (2010: 41).

a bit earlier, somewhere to the first two centuries CE. The popularity and influence of this *smrti* is shown by the fact that the British had also used it in their Indian legal practice because this is the best edited and most elaborated of all the *smrti*s, while its style is simple and hence understandable to a wide audience. Though its length is only one third of the Manu-smrti, it contains laws that cannot be found in Manu. The Yājñavalkya-smrti is free of contradictions and repetitions, despite the fact that the author based his work on different traditions and sources. The Yājñavalkya-smrti consists of three large books, the first dealing with religious customs *(āchāra)*, the second with legal disputes *(vyavahāra)*, and the third with punishments. This structure is a break with *Manu*'s divisions, also followed by medieval commentators. Concerning its contents, the Yājñavalkya-smrti is close to *Manu* discussing the same issues and laws with some important differences in detail: it has nothing to say against *niyoga* marriage, keeps quiet about the privileges of *Brahman*s and makes possible for widows and girls to inherit if there is no male offspring in the family.[52]

Among the *smrti*s it is the shortest, the Nārada-smrti, which focuses mostly on legal issues. This *dharmaśāstra* could have been composed between the third (Kane) and the sixth centuries (Jolly).[53] The work consists of two parts divided into chapters. The Nārada-smrti follows the logic of Manu when discussing the legal material in eighteen *mārga*s in its second part, while the much shorter first part is dedicated entirely to the issue of court procedure. The Nārada-smrti is close to Manu also in its content, since several wordings literally agree with the verses of Manu, yet the Nārada-smrti is not just an imitation of its predecessors because it has laws on some topics which were treated rather vaguely in the two other *smrti*s, particularly in the law of procedure. The Nārada-smrti is the most precise work among the *smrti*s.[54]

Though written in Antiquity, *dharmasūtra*s and *dharmaśāstra*s continued to play a crucial role for Hindus until modern times. This is the reason why the British, eager to adjudicate Indian communities according to their own laws, discovered these texts for themselves when they were looking for legal norms in order to provide guidance for the British judges trained in common law. Such legal norms, however, did not exist, so they translated and *applied the Manu-smrti*. One of its consequences was that the *Manu-smrti* had become the best known *dharmaśāstra* in Europe, a work subject to scholarly studies while the same text in India was a symbol of obstacles to social reform underlying the privileges of *Brahmins*, the oppression of women and the exclusion of the untouchables. No wonder that there is hardly any other text that had been burnt as many times in protest as the *Manu-smrti*.[55]

During the Middle Ages, *dharmasūtra*s and *dharmaśāstra*s were no longer produced, nor were they changed or enlarged because of their authority. As a result, a new literary genre, the commentary came into being, the authors of which interpreted the texts according to their own understanding. Consequently, the commentators argued against each other but never challenged the texts, the authority of which remained

---

[52]Lingat (1973: 97–100).

[53]Jolly (1875: xix), Kane (1968: 467–480).

[54]Dareste's opinion is quoted by Lingat (1973: 102).

[55]Doniger and Smith (1991: lix).

beyond doubt. Commentaries were produced either to interpret a particular *sūtra* or *śāstra* and its laws or to analyse legal issues in a thematic order comparing several *sutras* and *śāstras*. Great number of commentaries were written to Manu and Yājñavalkya smrtis, the oldest among them is that of Bhāruchi written to Manu. Bhāruchi's commentary was also a source to the most famous commentary on the Manu-smrti, the work of Medhātithi, a rather extensive writing also using other smrtis. The best known commentary to the Yājñavalkya smrti is the Mitāksara, wrongly regarded by the British as a legislative work and thus, translated into English in order to help the judges. In addition to commentaries digests, that is, extensive works on laws and their commentaries were also produced, the number of which is near to five thousand.[56] Two works are worth mentioning from this ocean of texts. One is Laksmīdhara's long text written in the twelfth century (containing 30,000 couplets making it ten times longer as the Manu-smrti), which is the best arranged text with internal logic of all the commentaries. The other digest came into being on the commission of Sir William Jones and was written by Jagannātha, an outstanding scholar of the late eighteenth century. This work was immediately translated to English and became soon an important source to the study of Hindu law in Europe.[57]

Finally, the Mahābhārata, the longest epic in world literature should also be mentioned among the sources of law. Though clearly not a legal work, the Mahābhārata is often considered as a *dharmaśāstra,* since its objective is to teach proper behaviour and not just to entertain.[58] Wisdom put into the mouth of one of its heroes, *Bhisma,* who embodies wisdom, justice and selflessness, also contain legally relevant elements. In addition to this, the work is an important source about the duties of kings.[59]

The history of Hindu law has been written almost entirely on these sources for long, a method that could be challenged on good reason. After all, *dharmasūtras*, *dharmaśāstras* and their commentaries are academic treatises about *dharma* and a Brahmanic ideal but not about everyday legal practice. Needless to say, no legal history could be produced in India or elsewhere only on books on jurisprudence while omitting sources which came into being in judicial practice. Studying only texts produced by Brahamanic scholarship is a one sided approach to legal history, but the authority of these texts has hindered any other approach so far, a method that seems to be challenged only very recently by a new scientific program focusing on legal practice.[60] Sources are abundant to the realisation of such a programme, as inscriptions (royal inscriptions, donations of land), temple archives, rulers' edicts, administrative and legal documents are available by the million.[61]

[56]Olivelle (2010: 54), Rocher (2012: 55).
[57]Kane (1968: 573–583), Lingat (1973: 107–122).
[58]Scharfe (2002: 17).
[59]Funk (1988: 194–195).
[60]Davies (2010a: 156–161).
[61]Michaels (2010: 61–68).

8.4 Substantive Law

8.4.1 Family Law

As we have seen in the previous chapters, the second stage of life is about mundane affairs, work, marriage and family life. Therefore, it is a moral duty for both men and women to get married and raise children. The pressure of this moral duty, combined with other social factors led to the widespread custom of child marriage, an issue to be discussed later. Marriage was defined along the analogy of plant production: the woman stands for the earth and the man for the seed sown. As the particular features of each plant are determined by the seed and not the earth into which it was put,[62] in marriage, too, the man's position is privileged by law as well as by social understanding. Land symbolising the woman is owned by the man, therefore in disputed cases what matters is 'ownership right': if a foreign seed is sown into the earth its fruit belongs to the owner of the land and not to the person who had sown it.[63] This is one of the reasons why Hindu law is mistrustful towards women and follows the principle of perpetual guardianship, that is, women always had to be under the authority of a male relative.[64]

Hindu marriage law is determined by the *varna* system. *Dharma* literature emphasizes that the members of each *varna* should look for a partner in marriage within their own *varna* but crossing over the boundaries of the *varna* is possible under certain conditions. The principle is that a male belonging to a higher *varna* may marry a woman belonging to a lower *varna* but a woman belonging to a higher *varna* cannot marry a man belonging to a lower one. According to this principle, a *Brahman* male can marry a woman belonging to the three *varna*s, a *Ksatriya* male can marry from two, and a *Vaiśya* from two *varna*s, but a *Śūdra* male can marry only from his own *varna*. Conversely, a *Brahman* woman can marry only within her own *varna*, a *Ksatriya* woman can marry a *Brahman* or a *Ksatriya*, and a *Vaiśya* woman can choose from among the members of all the three *varna*s.[65]

There are more forms of marriage in Hindu law, but their exact number differs by authors. While early *dharmasūtras* have six forms of marriage, the later *smrti*s enlarge this number to eight. These works classify the marriages into two main categories, marriages with higher and lower value. It is important to note that marriages of lower value are also lawful marriages, though some authors expressed their doubts (Nārada XII. 45.). The second aspect in this classification is the *varna*-system with the result that not all eight forms of marriage are lawful for members of every *varna*.

---

[62]Manu IX. 33–37; Nārada XII. 18–19.

[63]Manu IX. 51–53.

[64]Manu V. 147–148:'A girl, a young woman, or even an old woman should not do anything independently, even in (her own) house. In childhood a woman should be under her father's control, in youth under her husband's and when her husband is dead, under her sons'. Trs.: Doniger and Smith (1991:115).

[65]Nārada XII. 4–7.

The four marriages *(vivāha)* of higher value are the *brāhma,* the *prājāpatya,* the *ārsa* and the *daiva.* The *brāhma* marriage is of highest value (originally it may have meant the marriage of *Brahmans)* in which the father gives his daughter to his son-in-law as a gift, while in the case of the *prājāpatya,* it is the son-in-law who initiates the process. In an *ārsa vivāha,* the bridegroom gives garments and a couple of cattle to the future father-in-law, while the marriage is a *daiva* marriage if the bridegroom is a priest. The most accepted marriage among the last four marriages is the *gāndharva vivāha,* also called love marriage because it comes into existence by the joint will of the parties, without the consent of the parents. Marriage called *āsura vivāha* is lawful only for *Vaiśyas* and *Śūdras* since in this form of marriage material compensation should be given for the girl, a custom which higher *varnas* dislike. It is the reason why our sources condemn the sale of girls when a father sells his daughter like any other object of value. This is of low morality and is prohibited for members of the two higher *varnas.* Despite moral disapproval, this was the most frequent form of marriage, therefore it was also called *mānusa vivāha,* 'marriage (characteristic) of people'. The last two forms of marriage include physical violence: *rākṣasa* is an abduction of a woman while *paiśācha* differs from this only in that a man attacks the girl in her sleep or makes her a drink and abuses the situation. The abduction of women was reserved only for *Ksatriyas* and was obviously a survival of the customs of the warrior Indians. This might be true for *paiśāča* as well, but it became prohibited to *Ksatriyas* because of moral disapproval and remained lawful only among the *Śūdras.*[66]

Child marriage was (and continues to be) one of the main problems in Hindu law, something which is related to a basic principle of Hindu legal and social understanding. Accordingly, a father has to marry off his daughters and it amounts to child murder if he is negligent in this duty. In addition, such a father would lose guardianship over his family, receive no marriage gift and his daughter could marry a partner on her own wishes, without the consent of his father, humiliation everyone wants to avoid. As a result, fathers want to marry off their daughters as soon as possible, which led to child marriages. Works on dharma specify the seventh and the eight year as a minimum age limit, while others such as *Manu* also have an ideal age difference between the partners. Accordingly, a thirty year-old man had to marry a twelve year-old girl, and a twenty-four year-old man had to marry an eight year-old girl.[67] We do not know whether this council was followed, but the practice of the girls' early marriage was conspicuous for both the Ancient Greek travellers and *al-Bīrūnī* in the Middle Ages.

Polyandry is by no way a less disputed issue. There are references which suggest that polyandry was known in India, particularly the *Mahābhārata* refers to it since the heroes of the epic, the five *Pandava* brothers, have a common wife, *Draupadī.* Also verse IX. 182 in *Manu,* a text difficult to understand, is explained by some commentators as referring to polyandry. Some authors believe that this custom, foreign to the Aryas, has its origin in the native population. The probability of this hypothesis

---

[66]Nārada XII. 39–45; Jolly (1896: 49–54).

[67]Manu IX. 94.

is enhanced by the fact that polyandry survived as late as the nineteenth century in regions which the Aryas hardly reached, such as the South of India and the high mountains of the Himalayas. This custom was declared as contrary to the customs of the Aryas, and the *Brahman*s did all they could to eliminate it.[68]

Monogamy was also not free of contradictions. According to Hindu understanding, marriage is a unique bond between the partners for eternity, yet polygamy remained in practice for centuries. Men were obliged to remarry immediately after the death of their wife (but efforts were made to hinder it by all means for widows), and they had the right to conclude further marriages even during the lifetime of their wife, since the number of marriages was not limited. The first chief wife *(mahisī)* however, enjoyed privileges, the effects of which were realised even in the law of inheritance. A chief wife could not be a *Śūdra* in the case of higher *varna*s.[69] Despite this, *dharma* literature set obstacles to second and further marriages and protected the housewife: if she observed the prescribed ritual duties and gave birth to a male child, her husband could not marry for the second time, he could do so only if one of these two preconditions were missing.[70] *Manu* has different laws. Accordingly, a second wife could be taken to a barren wife after eight years, and to a wife bearing only female children after eleven years. A husband could immediately look for a new wife if his wife is quarrelsome.[71] According to *Nārada,* such a wife must be thrown away, otherwise her husband would also share her sins. If such a woman who did not deserve it is forsaken by her husband, the king will have to punish him severely.[72] Women can remarry only if their husband died, disappeared, went abroad, was impotent or was expelled from their caste. For the case of disappearance, a waiting period was specified, the length of which varied between two to eight years depending on which *varna* the parties belonged and whether the woman had a child or not.[73] The main reason for the expulsion of women was adultery punished by either exclusion from their caste or by death (she was devoured by dogs alive in a public place) according to Manu[74] but Nārada is far less severe with the punishments of cutting off the hair or doing the work of a slave for a year.[75]

Perhaps the most debated issue of Hindu family law is *satī*, a term for a widow who steps voluntarily into the fire where her husband's corpse is burning. It is important to note that it was never a legal obligation and remained only a voluntary act which remained disputed even among Hindus. Medieval commentators made efforts to circumvent it by stressing that such an act is suicide and does not lead the couple to heavenly bliss, a claim at variance with the original idea. In addition, to become a *satī* was prohibited if the wife was pregnant or had minor children. The overwhelming

---

[68] Jolly (1896: 47–48).
[69] Jolly (1896: 64).
[70] Āpastamba II. 5. 11–12.
[71] Manu IX. 81–83.
[72] Nārada XII. 94–95.
[73] Nārada XII. 97.
[74] Manu: VIII. 371.
[75] Nārada XII. 91.

majority of widows stayed alive of course and *sati* was only the exception not the rule. Widows avoiding to be a *sati* however, had to face legal restrictions for the rest of their life: they had to pray and do sacrifices daily, could eat only once a day, could only wear over worn garments, were forbidden to pronounce the name of other men, etc. If widows driven by their distress approached a man, they were regarded as adulteresses with the punishment of exclusion from the family and caste combined with full ritual impurity, thus becoming untouchables.[76] Re-marriage of widows was lawful only in a *niyoga* marriage which is an auxiliary bond if a husband passed away without an heir. In such a case, his widow receives authorisation (*niyoga*) from her husband's family (*gotra*) to marry with a family member in order to produce an heir for the deceased person. The reason of this custom is not economic but cultic: there must be a male heir to do the cult of the dead for the man passed away and *niyoga* was an institution to provide such a person. But it is less compatible with the ethics of Brahmanism and, therefore, some attempts were made to limit it by rules that could hardly be observed, such as the parties could not be motivated by corporal desire, the relationship could be maintained only up to the birth of the child or until the woman did not feel pregnant. If these rules were not observed, the child was excluded from inheritance and the parties committed adultery.[77] Despite restrictions, this custom existed as long as the end of the nineteenth century, particularly in the northern provinces of India.[78]

The law of inheritance is based, of course, on the typology of marriages which produced the heirs. This is the reason why there are only a few general rules and laws are fragmented into casuistry instead. One of these general rules is the privilege of boys, but their relative order remained disputed. Primogeniture was not a unanimously accepted rule, though the majority was in favour of it. Particularly the legal position of a son born of a *niyoga* marriage was disputed. Sons were followed by other descendants with the law that the closer *parentela* excludes the more distant one. Only the male line mattered originally but later on, after long debates, cognate relatives were given rights to inherit, though to a limited extent. The most debated issue remained the inheritance of widows. According to *Nārada,* a widow was entitled to a son's share. Some other authors, too, argued in favour of their inheritance, while others challenged such a view, stressing that widows were entitled only to maintenance if they continued to live among their husband's agnate relatives. In the absence of male offspring, the daughters of the deceases inherited and if there were no daughters either, members of the ascending line inherited. If there was not a single heir, the bequest went to the king save the *Brahman*s because their bequest was inherited by their master, pupil or the community of *Brahman*s. Female wealth was inherited by the deceased woman's children (it is of importance in a polygamous family), primarily by her yet unmarried daughters because wealth had to be spent on marrying them off. The system of the law of inheritance was elaborated for the first time by the medieval commentators which gave way to two schools, the Bengali

---

[76]Nārada XII. 51; Jolly (1896: 68–70).

[77]Manu IX. 59–64, 147; Nārada XII. 80–81.

[78]Jolly (1896: 71).

differing from the northern traditions in many respects. It is the northern tradition which corresponded more to the laws of the *smrtis*.[79]

8.4.2 Crimes and Punishments

Criminal acts and sins are inseparably intertwined with the concept of *dharma* and *adharma* in Hindu law. According to Hindu theory, crimes and sins cause impurity for both the offender and the victim, the extent of which was determined on the *varna*-system. As a result, the degree of impurity is based partly on the act committed and partly on the persons involved as offenders and victims. Acts committed against persons belonging to a higher *varna* led to more serious impurity than acts committed against person of a lower *varna* because the victim originally enjoyed a higher degree of purity. By contrast, acts committed by persons of a higher *varna* led to less impurity, a law at variance with the logic of the system, yet it was necessary to define the level of responsibility of the upper *varna*s on a lower level.[80]

The theoretical foundation of punishments and penance caused some headache to Hindu thinkers, since an illegal act is *adharma* at the same time the consequences of which are manifest in the karmic cycle and not necessarily in the current life of the offender, something which forced Hindu sages to think about the aim and sense of punishment. *Gautama*'s *dharmasūtra* preserves this dispute, arguing at the end for the necessity of punishments with reference to the Vedas,[81] a doctrine that remained dominant for long. Punishments were thus regarded as tools that would relieve the offender from the consequences of his deed and would restore his ritual purity, thus making it possible for him to re-integrate to society. As *Manu* puts it, offenders with proper punishment by the king will be purified and go to heaven just as those who do meritorious deeds.[82]

To administer punishments is the right and duty of the king as a part of his *rājadharma*. A king cannot mercy an offender since by doing so he would violate his own *dharma* and would also hinder the offender from the possibility of purification. Such a ruler would take upon himself the crime committed by that person.[83] This attitude had led Hindu sages to recognise the principle of proportionality between crime and punishment, to distinguish between crimes committed intentionally or negligently,[84] and to classify criminal acts by other aspects. At the same time, punishments played an important role in deterrence to guarantee social order, an indispensable precondition enabling people to do their duty. In short, in addition to

---

[79]Nārada Chapter XIII; Jolly (1896: 84–90).

[80]Glucklich (1988: 96–105)

[81]Gautama XIX. 1–12.

[82]Manu VIII. 318.

[83]Gautama XVIII. 32; Āpastamba I. 9. 25. 5.

[84]Āpastamba I. 10. 29. 2–5.

religious morality, practical considerations also played a role in evolving the rigour of penal law.[85]

According to the common classification of crimes in all the *smrtis*—which vary in their subcategories—there is a difference between grave *(mahāpātaka)* and minor crimes *(upapātaka)*. Grave crimes are to murder a priest, to consume alcoholic drinks, to pollute the guru's bed, to kill a friend, perjury, to steal gold and to violate the incest taboo. A person having or maintaining social contact with offenders of any of the above crimes would be similarly judged.[86] The minor crimes include forgetting the Vedas, to recite Vedic texts to unworthy persons, to kill sacred animals, to abandon the guru and the parents and to deny to take care of them, to collect usurious interests, perfidy, to deny the repayment of a loan, to abandon domestic rites, theft of things of less value, the consumption of prohibited food, to fell green trees.[87]

The pollution of the guru's bed became a paradigmatic category as the gravest sexual crime to which all other criminal acts were weighed. This is the reason why the violation of incest taboo, for example, was declared as a criminal act of identical gravity.[88] The pollution of the guru's bed was a horrific criminal act because it was the violation of the hierarchical order between a master and his entirely subordinated disciple and at the same time a mean to hinder sexual relationship between a young wife of an older guru and his young disciple. Against this background, it is no wonder that both Manu and Gautama have laws that sanction such an act with rigour. Accordingly, the penis of the man must be cut off and facing south, he has to run until he collapses dead or, alternatively, he has to lie down on a heated iron bed, or has to embrace a red-hot image of a woman. The incoherence of the texts could be shown here too, since there are loci with less severe punishments, such as a series of fasts and penance for the same crime.[89]

It is not the pollution of the guru's bed to which sanctions are defined alternatively. A person deliberately murdering a member of the priestly *varna*, for example either had to throw himself into the fire or fight in the first line in the battlefield in order to meet his death there, or had to save the life of a priest or had to wander in the country with a skull in his hand begging for twelve years. This kind of penance lasted for six years if the victim was a *Ksatriya,* three years if the victim was a *Vaiśya.* In addition, he also had to give one thousand, or one hundred cattle, respectively, as compensation.[90] Similarly, a thief was punished alternatively since he either had to throw himself into the fire or had to undertake heavy penance.[91] If a person refused to do the penance, he was expelled from his caste. Expulsion had rather serious consequences: his family and the entire society broke off any social contact with

---

[85]Davies (2010a: 137).

[86]Gautama XXI. 1–4.

[87]Manu XI. 60–68.

[88]Gautama XXIII. 12.

[89]Manu XI. 104–108; Gautama XXIII: 8–10.

[90]Gautama XXII. 1–18.

[91]Āpastamba I. 9. 25. 4–8.

him, his wife could re-marry, he was excluded to inherit, he was denied the ritual of the dead when he died, and after his death his destiny was a place in hell.[92]

The interrelation of crimes and sins required the clarification of competencies between secular and religious authorities. To determine penances was within the competency of the *Brahmin*s and the king had no right to interfere. If the act committed was only a sin but not a criminal act, penance terminated the case without any further legal sanction. This was the case when a person offended against ritual laws. In such a case,secular authorities only checked the implementation of the penance set by the priests. If however, the act was also a criminal act, legal sanction executed by the secular authorities was added to penance. Legal sanctions remained in the competency of the king, though he had to follow the *Brahmin*s' advice.[93]

Punishments included fines, forced labour, imprisonment, corporeal penalties and the capital punishment among which fines were applied most frequently. In case of corporeal penalties, mirror punishments reflecting and symbolising the act committed were favoured. This is the reason why the genital organ of adulterers were cut off and the tongue of false accusers were also cut off. The cutting off of hair, parading on a donkey, smearing the head with urine, and tattooing the sign of the crime on the forehead were among the humiliating punishments. Capital punishments were executed by burning alive, being torn apart by dogs, crushing by elephants, impalement, quartering and choking. Imprisonment was implemented in jails with terrible conditions which were set up along highways to have a deterring effect.[94]

8.4.3 Law of Procedure

There is no conceptual distinction between civil and criminal procedure in Hindu law, yet civil procedure was different from criminal procedure in legal practice. The king's authority was far more important in criminal procedure, while in civil cases various forms of dispute resolution were in operation, too. Legal issues we now label civil cases are called *vyavahāra-pada* in Hindu legal literature, including family law (marriage and inheritance) and contractual law (disputes related to loans, deposits, gifts, purchase and sale). A procedure could be launched on any issue of *vyavahāra-pada* if either of the parties violated the rules of the *smrti*s or the customs and thus caused damage to a third person. Causing damage or the violation of a law in itself was no legal title to launch a civil procedure by a party (though it could be a cause to a criminal procedure). Conflict resolution was entirely left to society, as neither the king nor his officials could launch a lawsuit in issues of *vyavahāra-pada*.[95]

There were different bodies to adjudicate civil disputes. One of them was called *kula*, a kind of family court of justice which decided on disputes among family

---

[92]Manu XI. 183–187.

[93]Lingat (1973: 232–234).

[94]Jolly (1896: 129–130).

[95]Manu VIII. 43.

members. The *śreni* was the law court for members of the same profession ('gilds') including craftsmen, peasants, creditors, dancers, etc. Perhaps these organs were not law courts but rather fori of arbitration to hammer out compromises. Parties could turn to the king against any decision but given the huge number of such cases, evidently no king proceeded in person in such appellate procedures. There were local law courts in every city to adjudicate local legal disputes. In addition, there were courts entitled to use the royal stamp and also royal courts proper. Itinerant law courts were in service for densely populated areas. In legal practice these bodies contributed enormously to local conflict resolution though in theory it was only the king with the authority of jurisdiction. *Dharma*-literature underlines the importance of this office: according to *Manu,* the administration of justice is equal in importance to the most important sacrifices. Due to the primacy of royal adjudication, *smrti*s deal exclusively with procedures at the royal court of justice, therefore laws for other bodies are unknown to us.[96]

A royal court of justice consisted of a chairman and three members. A chairman had to be a *Brahmin* whenever possible but could never be a *Śūdra.* If the king participated in person in the trial, his *purohita* (personal advisor) also had to accompany him. A king was advised to wear modest garment and to avoid royal pomp during a law suit. *Brahmins*, even if not invited to the procedure could be present at all the trials and express their opinion. *Smrti*s have some advices for kings how to arrive at a just decision. Accordingly, kings have to explore the material truth, to listen to witnesses and to investigate the circumstances of the case carefully. In addition, kings have to consider the opinion of his *Brahmin* advisors during the course of decision making. Should he disregard legal advice, he remains liable for an unjust decision in his person otherwise his legal advisors are equally responsible for a wrong sentence.[97] There was an appellate review of decisions of law courts by the king but such a procedure was not without risk since the party was fined if the king found no wrong in the judgment. Should he however, find the judgment unjust, he fined the judges.[98] A case decided by the king was *res iudicata.* As *Nārada* put it, the judgment was *dharma* for the litigants (XVIII. 19.), but only for them. Hindu law was, therefore, no precedent law as a judgment was only the solution of a single, specific case without any significance beyond it. This is the reason why medieval commentators did not refer to royal decisions at all when they analyse passages difficult to understand.[99]

According to *Nārada,* a civil procedure consists of four parts. A law suit begins when the parties arrive at court. This is followed by the exploration of the causes, which led to the legal dispute. The third part is about evidence, while the last part is decision making and pronouncing the sentence. A defendant had to be brought to court by the plaintiff, and a reluctant defendant could even be forced by the plaintiff to appear. If a defendant did not answer meaningfully to the claims of the plaintiff at the court of justice, he was punished and declared to have lost the trial together

---

[96]Nārada I. 8; Lingat (1973: 243–249).

[97]Manu VIII. 8–46.

[98]Manu IX. 234.; Nārada I. 58–59.

[99]Lingat (1973: 256).

with all its consequences. Immediate decision had to be made in issues considered most important (theft, land, gold, women, livestock, libel) but not in cases of less importance.[100]

The burden of proof did not necessarily rest on the plaintiff alone during the course of the trial but may vary. According to Hindu legal understanding, only positive statements could be proven but not negatives, therefore, it is always the person claiming something who has to produce evidence. If, for example, the plaintiff states that the defendant is indebted to him, it is a positive statement and, therefore it is the plaintiff who has to prove his claim and not the defendant that he did not owe him anything. By contrast, if the defendant claims that he had truly been in debt but had already paid the debt back, then it was a positive statement on his side and, therefore, it is he who has to prove. Means of evidence were witnesses and written documents. The minimum number of witnesses was three. Witnesses were either *krta* or *akrta*. A *krta* (lit. made, that is, appointed) witness was a person appointed to a legal action, for example, a witness for a contract was *krta*. By contrast, an *akrta* ('not made') witness was not a witness to a legal transaction but a person with important information relating to the subject of the trial. There were persons however who were excluded from giving evidence due to various considerations. Women, children and mentally ill persons were excluded due to their limited ability while friends and enemies due to their bias. Thieves, robbers, violent persons, gamblers, assassins were denied to be witnesses out of moral considerations. As a sign of respect pilgrims, priests, ascetics and old men were also excluded as persons who should be kept away from legal disputes, a clear sign of negative attitude to litigation. For eligible persons, however, it was a moral and legal duty to appear at court and give evidence. Witnesses refusing to give evidence were punished since they were treated equally with false witnesses. It was the duty of the proceeding judge to hear the witnesses one by one and to investigate their person and reliability. Witnesses were heard during the course of the procedure in the building of the court of justice, in front of a wide public and the parties. Legal texts emphasize the prohibition of secrecy and the need for publicity [101] provided by an audience consisting of the relatives of the parties and the inhabitants of the local village.

In addition to witnesses, written documents were also among evidences. Documents were either private or public. Public documents were accepted without hesitation since they were guaranteed by state authorities (such as, for example, a document on the donation of a piece of land by the king). Private documents however were scrutinized carefully and treated with caution because of frauds, the victim of which may have been the large number of illiterate persons. As it seems, royal documents were also among the objects of fraud, otherwise the death penalty for such a deed would be meaningless. Circumstantial evidence was also taken into consideration (if a weapon was seen in someone's hands it was a proof in a case of manslaughter; if a man was playing with the hair of another man's wife it was an evidence for adultery, etc.), but legal texts emphasize that no conviction should be based on them

---

[100] Nārada I. 39–41; 43–50; 54.

[101] Rocher (2012: 365–375).

alone. Circumstantial evidence were only supplementary proofs supporting claims that have already been confirmed by other means of evidence but are insufficient in themselves to arrive at a decision. Ordeal was also considered as a supplementary means of evidence to be applied in criminal procedure. The most frequent ordeals were fire, water and poison all sharing the basic idea that if a person is innocent, no harm would affect his/her body. Ordeal by fire was therefore a mean to cause harm for the body of a person by holding a red hot iron ball while walking and see if he/she is cured from the wounds or not. Ordeal by poison followed the same logic by drinking a definite amount of poison. Since ordeals were matters of life and death, Hindu legal texts defined which kind of ordeals should be used for which gender, age, occupation, caste and physical condition of a person. No wonder, in the case of old persons, women and children, only ordeals with less harm could be applied.[102]

8.5 Hindu Law in Modern India

British influence in the administration of Indian affairs started when the *dīwānī* right was transferred from the Mughal emperor in Delhi to the British East India Company. One among the problems very hard to solve was the administration of justice. It was, of course, impossible to follow only one legal system, given the religious (Hindus, Muslim, Parsees, Christians) and ethnic pluralism in the subcontinent which compelled Governor-General *Warren Hastings* to guarantee in his famous law reforms of 1772 (Judicial Plan), each religious community its own personal law in respect of family, inheritance and other fields of private law. In his reform of the judiciary, he eliminated the exclusive competency of the *qādīs* who were substituted by British judges. With this decision, *Warren Hastings* laid down the foundations of the later Anglo-Indian law.[103]

British judges, however, faced problems they were unable to solve alone as they were not versed in Hindu law. British judges were troubled not only by often contradictory doctrines but also by the logic of the entire system they were not used to. To cure the situation Hindu sages well versed in the *śāstra* literature (*pandita*) were appointed to assist the courts. The british, however, soon noticed that they were exposed to the *pandit*s who interpreted the texts as they wished without any control, a situation which gave way to mass corruption since it was always possible to find a text from among the contradictory doctrines that supported their view. To have a reliable text on Hindu law therefore became a necessity which resulted in the English translation of *Manu*'s *dharmaśāstra*, a text that was increasingly read by British judges as a law book (and not as a treatise on *dharma*). *Manu,* however, was only one text among the many, therefore the English asked Jagannātha, an eminent Hindu sage of the age to compile a law compendium for them which was translated into English by the eminent scholar Sir William Jones. Cultural differences soon manifested, since

---

[102]Nārada I. 4. 2; 5. 7, 15, 35–36, 55, 58, 92; VI–VIII; Rocher (2012: 378–381; 386–391, 421–433).
[103]Jain (1966: 92–94), Davies (2010b: 25), Baxi (1986: 224).

what the British wanted was a uniform law book for every day legal practice, whilst what Jagannātha did was a work on dharma. As the eminent scholar Duncan Derrett noted, Jagannātha would have ridiculed the British if he understood what they had wanted from him. Despite such misunderstandings, the British proceeded in both the intellectual understanding of Hindu law propelled by the discovery and translation of various Sanskrit texts and the judicial reforms to modernise the system. As a result, the appellate review was guaranteed, which made the sentences of the courts of law of the East India Company to be appealed at the supreme courts set up in the three big cities (Calcutta, Bombay, Madras) which could be reviewed, in their turn, ultimately at the *Privy Council*.[104]

The daily practice of the British judges, however, significantly transformed Indian law because they were thinking in terms of precedent law also in India. As a result, they began to refer not only to legal texts but also to former sentences, thus introducing a method alien to local legal understanding. In addition, they were authorised to fill legal gaps on the basis of *justice, equity and good conscience,* which actually meant the implementation of the British legal norms they were used to. This process made Hindu law become increasingly shaped by British judges, which resulted in an extraordinary conglomerate of law called the *Anglo-Hindu Law. Anglo-Hindu Law* is the mixture of British and local laws based on Hindu legal understanding but operating along precedents. The law reform, then, produced more confusion since this artificial legal system was unknown to both the local people and the British and was a terrain only for experts specialising in it, a law which was hardly in touch with Indian social reality. Werner Menski is right therefore to consider this law as the caricature of *śāstra* law missing unity of concept.[105] The same thing happened to Islamic law, properly speaking to its Hanafite variant, which was applied in India resulting in the *Anglo-Muhammedan Law,* a hybrid legal system based on both the fundaments of Islamic law and precedent law.

The low professional standard of local judiciaries, the contradictions of *Anglo-Hindu Law*, and the mutiny of 1857 encouraged the British to give up the policy of small steps thus far followed and to introduce significant legal reforms. As a first step, Hindu and Muslim legal experts were dismissed from the law courts, thus cutting off a living connection to Hindu/Muslim law what these experts embodied. Parallel to this and to the detriment of the *dharma*-literature, more influence was allowed for local customs, the collection of which had begun (see, for example, the well-known work of Rattigan about North-Indian legal customs). In addition, the British resorted to codification too, a method which is at variance with precedent law but reached them by *Bentham* and *Mill,* two representatives of utilitarian philosophy. With the codification of Indian law, the British attempted to arrive at a possible legal unity and to abolish legal institutions and traditions which the British considered displeasing or incompatible with the modern world. Attempts were already made by individual laws before codification, this is how *satī* was abolished relatively early (1829: Sati Regulation Act). In addition to this law, the British made efforts to improve the

---

[104] Derrett (1968: 229–249; 276–278).
[105] Menski (2003: 178).

situation of women. Hindu Widows' Remarriage Act (1865) guaranteed their right to re-marriage, a law at variance with the dharma-literature. The objective of the Age of Consent Act (1891) was to circumvent child marriages, while the Prohibition of Female Infanticide Act (1872) was passed to protect girls. These laws were welcomed by the educated Indians who were in favour of law reforms in general and women's rights in particular. But the process was slow and reforms were hard to implement: the age limit for the marriage of girls could be raised at first only to ten, then to twelve, and finally to eighteen years, but this only by independent India in 1978.[106]

The first result of codification was the Indian Criminal Code (1860), which was passed immediately after the suppression of the mutiny. This act was modelled on the French *Code Penal* and the criminal code of the State of Louisiana written by Livingstone. Though a western law code, it nevertheless opens the door to local particularities too. By combining European jurisprudence on criminal law and local legal understanding, this Code is considered as the most successful product of Lord Macaulay, the intellectual father of Indian codification. The transparent structure of the Code, its precise definitions and clear wording of its text had provoked the admiration of the well-known legal historian, Sir Henry Maine, then in governmental service in India. Critics pointed only at its rigour since Macaulay was blamed for the Draconian rigour of his law, resorting to corporeal punishment. This is the reason why the Code was changed several times by moderating its punishments, though it remained in force for a century. The criminal code was followed by an Act of Criminal Procedure (1882) introducing a uniform procedural law, which was soon replaced (1898) by a new code still in force in the 1960s. This new code is a very long law, consisting of 46 chapters and more than half a thousand articles regulating every aspect of criminal procedure. We can witness similar processes of codification in the field of private law too. With the contribution of Sir Henry Maine, the Indian Succession Act (1865) was produced, which introduced English law of inheritance in a simplified form in India. Since Hindus and Muslims could retain their legal autonomy in this field, the Code was addressed to Jews, Christians and the Europeans living in India. A less successful Code was the Indian Contract Act, which remained in force despite criticisms for decades with only some modifications.[107]

Codification did not come to a halt after independence, though its usefulness remained disputed. It is still on the agenda of the advocates of modernisation and legal reform who believe that Hindu law belongs to the past and has no relevance in a modern age. By contrast, authorities such as Derrett and Menski warn that traditional Hindu law is still part of India and a legislation neglecting traditional moral and legal understanding may produce results contrary to its objective. Hindu law is an integral part of Indian society to this day, if not always as official law but on the basis of social conventions *(unofficial law)*.

---

[106]Menski (2003: 291; 324; 336–339), Davies (2010b: 26).
[107]Jain (1966: 660–684).

References

Sources

Doniger W, Smith BK (1991) The laws of manu. Penguin Classics, Delhi, London (Mānava Dharmaśāstra)

Derrett JDM (1975a) Bhāruci's Commentary on the Manusmṛti. Franz Steiner Verlag, Wiesbaden (Bhāruchi: Manu-śāstra Vivarana)

Jolly J (1875) Nāradīya Dharmaśāstra or the Institutes of Nārada. Würzburg. (Nāradīya Dharmaśāstra)

Kangle RP (1972) The Kautilya Arthaśāstra, part I–II. Delhi. (Kautilya: Arthaśāstra)

Olivelle P (1999a) Dhamrasūtras. The law codes of ancient India. Oxford World Classics, Oxford University Press, Oxford, pp 3–74 (Āpastamba Dharmasūtra)

Olivelle P (1999b) Dhamrasūtras. The law codes of ancient India. Oxford World Classics, Oxford University Press, Oxford, pp 127–244 (Baudhāyana)

Olivelle P (1999c) Dhamrasūtras. The law codes of ancient India. Oxford World Classics, Oxford University Press, Oxford, pp 74–127 (Gautama Dharmasūtra)

Literature

Baxi U (1986) People's law in India, the Hindu society. In: Chiba M (ed) Asian Indigenous law. Routledge and Kegan Paul, London, New York

Davies DR (2010a) The spirit of Hindu law. Cambridge University Press, Cambridge

Davies DR (2010b) A historical overview of Hindu law. In: Lubin T, Davis DR, Krishnan JK (eds) Hinduism and law. An introduction. Cambridge University Press, Cambridge, pp 17–27

Derrett JDM (1968) Religion, law and the state in India. Oxford University Press, Calcutta, Delhi

Derrett JDM (1969) Rulers and the ruled in India. Recueils de la Société Jean Bodin pour i'histoire comparative des institutions. Editions de la Libraire Encyclopedique, Bruxelles, p 22

Derrett JDM (1973) Dharmasāstra and Juridical Literature. Otto Harrassowitz, Wiesbaden

Derrett JDM (1975b) Social and political thought and institutions. In: Basham AL (ed) A cultural history of India. Oxford University Press, Oxford

Francavilla D (2006) The Roots of Hindu Jurisprudence. Sources of Dharma and Interpretation in Mīmāmsā and Dharmaśāstra. Corpus Iuris Sanscriticum et fontes iuris Asiae Meridianae et Centralis, Torino

Funk D (1988) Traditional orthodox Hindu jurisprudence: justifying dharma and Danda. South Univ Law Rev 15:169–213

Glucklich A (1988) Religious jurisprudence in the Dharmaśāstra. MacMillan Publishing Company, New York

Jain M (1966) Outlines of Indian legal history. Tripathi Ltd., Bombay

Jolly J (1896) Recht und Sitte. Grundriss der Indo-Arischen Philologie und Altertumskunde II. Band. Heft. Verlag von Karl Trübner, Strassburg, p 8

Kane PV (1950) Hindu customs and modern law. University of Bombay, Bombay

Kane PV (1968) History of Dharmaśāstra, vol 1–5. Poona

Lingat R (1973) The classical law of India. Oxford India Paperbacks, Oxford University Press, Oxford

Lubin T, Davis DR, Krishnan JK (2010) Hinduism and law. An introduction. Cambridge University Press, Cambridge

Menski W (2003) Hindu law beyond tradition and modernity. Oxford University Press, Oxford

Michaels A (2010) The practice of classical Hindu law. In: Lubin T, Davis DR, Krishnan JK (eds) Hinduism and law. An introduction. Cambridge University Press, Cambridge, pp 58–77

Olivelle P (2010) Dharmaśāstra: a textual history. In: Lubin T, Davis DR, Krishnan JK (eds) Hinduism and law. An introduction. Cambridge University Press, Cambridge, pp 28–57

Rocher L (2012) Studies in Hindu law and Dharmaśāstra. In: Davis DR (eds) Introduction. Anthem Press, New York, London, Delhi

Scharfe H (2002) Education in ancient India. E. J. Brill, Leiden, Boston, Köln

Setalvad MC (1960) The common law in India. Stevens and Sons Limited, London

Smith V (1964) The Oxford history of India. Oxford University Press, Oxford

Chapter 9
Societies of Buddhist Law

9.1 Introduction: History and Concepts

This chapter focuses on Buddhist societies and their legal systems, a topic usually untouched in legal literature in general and works of comparative law in particular. Being some kind of a terra nullius, laws of Buddhist societies, mainly inhabitants of Southeast Asia, are left out from works on Asian laws which concentrate rather on Hindu, Chinese and Japanese laws, but ignore this area. I included this chapter not only for the sake of completeness, but also because the legal understanding of Buddhist societies is very unique and deserves investigation. As it is commonly known, Buddhism reached both China and Japan along the northern and the southern routes moving through Southeast Asia. Meanwhile, Buddhist thinking—though important—never became the fundamental of Chinese and Japanese understanding of law and social order, Southeast Asian societies were more open to its influence. Buddhism as a religion differs enormously from Judaism and Islam, religions evolving along legal disputes. As a result, the influence of Buddhism on mainland Southeast Asian societies is completely different from Islam's impact on the island, that is, on Indonesian and Malaysian society. Since Buddhism has not too much to say on law and politics in general and certainly hardly anything on detailed legal norms in particular, it is the Buddhist ethic and world view that influences Southeast Asian legal systems. With the absence of a universal Buddhist law to be applied in every Buddhist society, Buddhist societies were able to maintain their own laws and customs rooted in their past which go back sometimes to their tribal history and formal nomadic way of life. As a result, a mixed legal culture came into being composed of local customs and on Indian influence in the form of Buddhism. Evidently, not all of Southeast Asia is Buddhist since Vietnamese society is Confucian, whilst Indonesia and Malaysia are Muslims and the Philippines are mainly Christians. On the other hand, there are countries which do not belong to Southeast Asia in the geographic term but are nevertheless Buddhists, such as Sri Lanka and some Himalayan countries (Bhutan, Nepal, and Tibet).

© Springer Nature Switzerland AG 2020
J. Jany, *Legal Traditions in Asia*, Ius Gentium: Comparative Perspectives on Law and Justice 80, https://doi.org/10.1007/978-3-030-43728-2_9

Buddhist law and the laws of Buddhist societies are terms reflecting completely different legal concepts. Buddhist law means a kind of 'ecclesiastic law' regulating the life of monastic communities, including the rights and duties of monks, issues of managing property and some aspects of religious rites (*vinaya*), but certainly nothing more, leaving secular aspects of Buddhist societies (family, inheritance, property, contracts, etc.) entirely untouched. This is the reason why there is no Buddhist law to be followed universally, an important feature at variance with Jewish and Islamic legal understanding. It is this normative vacuum which enables Buddhist societies to maintain their own customs and to create new laws through legislation. Inherited customs and local laws are indeed important for Southeast Asian societies who are immigrants in the territories they now inhabit, coming either from the archipelago or the southern provinces of China. For instance, Burmese people are relatively newcomers, defeating and incorporating the Mons, a people with a high standard of culture and civilisation, absorbing Indian traditions. Burmese however, developed their own laws before settling in the area now called Myanmar, customs that were preserved even after they embraced Buddhism. Thai people too, coming from the southern provinces of China have the same legal history. As a result, inherited tribal laws and customs were preserved and Buddhist legal understanding only modified and enlarged them but surely did not root them out.

In addition to customary laws, law making by state organs enormously modifies the laws of Buddhist societies. At the beginning, law making by the state was hardly more than collecting inherited customs and putting them to writing in various degree of systematisation. As a next step, individual edicts promulgated by kings were added to this corpus of law which either filled the gap left by customs or regulated completely new areas of law untouched by tribal law (public administration, finances, etc.). Law making became more important in the modern period when customary laws were, obviously, insufficient to run a modern state. As a result, law making had an ambivalent effect on customary laws in societies where state power was strong (Burma, Thai and Khmer kingdoms): it preserved customary laws by collecting and tolerating them, yet it also restricted them by defining their limit of influence and the new laws created by the state.

Indian influence has to be put into this broader context throughout the history of Southeast Asia. In addition to Buddhism, this region is indebted to India also for legal thinking, jurisprudence, and a literary genre which provides a scholarly framework to express ideas and explain laws. Unsurprisingly, we find *dharmaśāstra*s in all Buddhist societies which differ from their Indian counterparts only in technical detail but are very similar in structure, terminology and form. This led historians of former generations (primarily Forchhammer) to see Southeast Asian laws only as local variants of Indian/Hindu law, but surely not a sui generis category in its own right. It was Robert Lingat who challenged this view and argued that Southeast Asian laws are more autonomous than believed previously. While similarities in forms (legal texts, terms, categories, systematisation, names, language) prove Indian/Hindu legal influence, laws are Southeast Asian (customary and state laws) in their essence. In short, genuine local Southeast Asian laws were put into an Indian/Hindu scholarly framework. Adding to this, some fundamental differences between Hindu and

Buddhist understanding of social interactions (e.g. the *varna* system) make it clear that what we have here is not a local variant of Indian law but an autonomous legal tradition.[1]

Indian influence reached Southeast Asia from the north through Burma, primarily by the adoption of Buddhism. The catalysts of this process were the Pyu (Tircul as they called themselves), people coming from Yunnan (today a province in Southwest China) who settled on the banks of the River Irrawaddy during the second century BCE. The Pyu were by far not the first inhabitants of this region. Archaeological excavations provide evidence (metal) for a previous civilisation in this region but in the absence of written records, little is known about it. Only with the coming of the Pyu entered the region in the period of written history. The Pyu created a flourishing civilisation based on long distance trade between India and China, a route on which Buddhism also entered the Pyu city states, the inhabitants of which embraced this religion in the fourth century. The Pyu then created a Buddhist civilisation described by Chinese sources as a peaceful and humane society where war was practically unknown, despite significant political fragmentation among their city states located in the northern region of the River Irrawaddy. Archaeological excavations in cities like Sri Ksetra and Beikthano unearthed canal systems necessary to a flourishing agriculture that existed for long centuries.[2] Pyu city states collapsed in the ninth century when they fell victim to the conquering Mranma (Burmese), coming from the north on horseback. As a result of their victory over the Pyu cities, the dwellers of which were not used to warfare, Burmese newcomers created a centralised state thus putting an end to the previous fragmented political landscape. Pyus not only lost their political independence but even their identity and merged into the Burmese society during the centuries. The Burmese, by contrast, ensured their hegemony with their newly established centre in Pagan, experiencing its heyday between the eleventh and the thirteenth centuries.[3]

History seemed to repeat itself in the southern delta of the Irrawaddy where the Mons, people coming from the region that is now Thailand settled around the sixth century. Similarly to the Pyu, the Mons did not create their own country but established Thaton and Pegu in its stead, smaller kingdoms which were built on marine trade and Buddhist civilisation. Mons were famous for their riches and culture, and their mastery in Buddhist disciplines left traces on Southeast Asian (legal) culture. After defeating the Pyu, conquering Burmese regarded the Mons as their new target and occupied Thaton under the command of the Pagan ruler Anawratha in 1057, a victory of importance in the history of Burma. As a result of this conquest, the central core of what is Burma today was beginning to take shape. In cultural terms however, the defeated became the masters of their conquerors: Anawratha was impressed by the flourishing Buddhist culture found here and thus introduced Theravada Buddhism in his own country, together with important social and political reforms inspired by the Mon cultural elite. Burmese legal culture,

---

[1] Huxley (2002a: 142), Forchhammer (1884: 106).

[2] Stargardt (1990: xxix; 6–40; 343–373).

[3] SarDesai: (2013: 31–32).

inspired by Buddhism, based on previous Pyu and Mon experience and shaped by Burmese political control (law making, Burmese language) is one element among the many that came into being as a result of this cross-fertilisation in the next centuries. The heyday of Pagan lasted for two centuries when it was rooted by the Mongols in the last decades of the thirteenth century. Mongol dominance did not last for long and their legacy was again a fragmented political landscape with small rival kingdoms like Ava, the Shan kingdoms, and Ravannadesa. The kingdom of Ava, heir to Pagan, was unable to defeat the Mons, now gaining independence again, and disintegrated into smaller units. North to the kingdom of Ava, the Shan people came together with the Mongols but gaining roots here created its own political structure, making use of the political vacuum found here. Unlike the Burmese, these newcomers established only smaller kingdoms that were united in a federation for some time. This is the reason why they fell victim to the Burmese Toungoo dynasty, which began its military conquests and centralisation in the early sixteenth century. Following the disintegration of Pagan, the Mons regained their independence and when the Mongols finally left the region, they again established their own kingdoms in the Irrawaddy delta. These small power centres were united during the reign of Razadarit (fourteenth–fifteenth centuries), a necessary move to repel the attacks of the kingdom of Ava successfully. As a result, the second heyday of the Mon culture, based on Buddhism and marine trade, began and flourished until they were defeated, once again, by attacks coming from the north.[4]

Parallel to Burmese history, the Khmer, a population that lived for long in Southeast Asia organised its state. It was the kingdom called Funan by Chinese sources that emerged first in the first century CE. Very little is known about Funan, which seems to be rather a conglomerate of smaller political entities than a centralised state. The reaches of Funan were ensured by long distance trade as far as India and China and, what is more, archaeological evidence also testifies contacts with the Romans. Merchants from Funan traded with luxury goods such as gold, ivory and spices. As a result of a complex relationship to India, Hinduism spread in Funan around the second and third centuries, and was mixed with local religious ideas. This is important because Hinduism maintained a more significant influence in this region than in other parts of Southeast Asia. The Khmer, living around the Mekong delta were vassals of Funan for long and could gain independence only in the seventh century when Funan begun to decline. This is how the kingdom of Chenla was born, again a conglomerate of small political units rather than a centralised state. To complicate matters, Chinese sources have two Chenlas, one was the 'Water Chenla' at the Mekong delta and the other the 'Land Chenla' in the mainland. As a result of political developments impossible to reconstruct from the meagre sources, Chenla gave way to the Khmer empire (802–1431), growing to one of the most significant states of Southeast Asia with its centre at Angkor. The territory of the Khmer empire corresponded with that of the former kingdom of Funan and extended over Southeast Asia with the exemption of what is now Vietnam. The Khmer expansion was stopped by Dai Viet in a victorious battle which happened to be a turning point in Kampuchean

---

[4]Tarling (1992:165–168), SarDesai (2013: 32–33).

history, replacing victories with a slow decline. The lack of conquests, the slow decay of the canal system necessary to rice production and the attacks of neighbouring countries eroded the power of Angkor which lost significance and power. Finally, Thai forces occupied Angkor in 1431 which was abandoned by the last Khmer king who sought refuge in the Mekong delta.[5]

In addition to the Mon–Burmese and the Khmer power, Ayutthaya was the third important political centre in Southeast Asia. Ayutthaya was established by the Thai who entered the region they now inhabit from Yunnan and Guangxi, that is, southwest China around the seventh century. Thai people came to contact with the Mons and the Khmer who already settled in Southeast Asia and had their own culture, impregnated with Indian cultural influence. This is how the Thai learnt about Indian civilisation and converted to Theravada Buddhism and their kings began to take up Sanskrit royal names. The Thai were able to build their own political centres though, at the beginning only in the shadow of Angkor. It was Lan Na that first emerged in Thai history, close to the border to Burma. Continuous struggle for power however, weakened this kingdom which fell prey to Burmese invaders at the end of the day. Sukhothai, another kingdom of the Thai was a more significant power centre than Lan Na in the north which incorporated significant Burmese territories during its heyday. After a century of victories and prosperity, Sukhotai started to decline in the fourteenth century which was interpreted in Ayutthaya, the third Thai political centre, as the best chance to invade its northern neighbour. Ayutthaya emerged as a significant power in the fourteenth century which chose Theravada Buddhism as its religion in order to distinguish itself from Hindu Angkor. The favourable location of the city (on a piece of land surrounded by three rivers) and its wealth soon made it a decisive political entity which gained the upper hand upon two other Thai political centres, though it did not destroy them.[6]

Ayutthaya was known as the Kingdom of Siam to European powers, particularly the Dutch and the French, who established commercial links with this Thai kingdom in the beginning of the seventeenth century. Long distance trade both to the west and the east (China and Japan) made Ayutthaya a very rich city which grew to be the largest city of the world by the 1700s with a population of one million, a number that was reached by Peking, Tokyo and London only by 1800.[7] At that time however, Ayutthaya was no longer a prosperous city because the invading Burmese completely destroyed the city and burned it down after a bitter siege in 1767. In addition to buildings and palaces, written records of history and law were also destroyed, among them an important compendium of Thai law and customs. This is the reason why—in the absence of written sources—we are unable to reconstruct early Thai legal history.

The Lao, people with a close relationship to the Thai in language, origin and culture entered the region they now inhabit together with the Thai and created their first state in the fourteenth century. It is the *Nithan Khun Borom,* a complex historical narrative which informs us about the origin of the Lao, their migrations and legendary heroes

---

[5]SarDesai (2013: 22–30), Taylor (1992: 157–168).

[6]Taylor (1992: 168–173).

[7]Modelski (2000: 63) has further data about the global changes in urbanisation.

and also about their laws and customs. No wonder therefore, that it is a valuable source for the history of Lao law and identity to this day. After settling in what is now Laos, the newcomers established the kingdom of Lan Xang, which was the contemporary of the Thai kingdoms of Lan Na, Sukhotai and Ayutthaya. During its long history (1354–1707), Lan Xang was attacked by the Burmese, the Viet and the neighbouring Thai states, though none of them could invade and destroy the kingdom of the Lao. Its collapse was rather due to domestic strife and struggle for power which destroyed the state that disintegrated into several smaller units with Vientiane as the most prominent of them. In the absence of a powerful state with the capacity to stop invading forces, small Lao states fell prey to the invading Thai and Viet armies with no chance of resistance. By the later part of the eighteenth century, the Thai dynasty extended its rule over the Lao kingdoms which lost their independence and were languished as vassal states. A good portion of Lao society was resettled to Thai territories as forced labourers, a harsh policy that led to a brief and unsuccessful revolt (1826–1829), which, in its turn, lent reason for further oppression. Man hunting and slavery was a practice which provided the Thai elite with a large number of slaves and good profit. Though, the legendary Thai King Chulalongkorn prohibited slavery in the later part of the nineteenth century, it continued into the 20th century, a good reason for the French to interfere. Lao constitutional monarchy was already born (1953) one year before the French protectorate collapsed as the result of the defeat of the French in Indo-China (1954). Following continuous domestic troubles and the growing Vietnamese interference, the country sunk into war which brought the Communist Pathet Lao to power with the support of the Vietnamese forces in 1975.[8]

Burma entered its modern history with Toungoo, at the beginning only a vassal state of the kingdom of Ava which became independent in the fifteenth century. Following this victory, Toungoo rulers enlarged their military capacity in order to defeat their former master and conquer neighbouring territories as well. As a result of their campaigns, a centralised Burmese state was born, the biggest ever in Southeast Asia. At first, southern Mon states and the northern Shan kingdoms fell victim to it. During the reign of King Bayinnaung in the mid-sixteenth century, Burmese forces occupied the territories of the Thai kingdoms of Lan Na and Ayutthaya, and the region of present-day Laos up to the Vietnamese border. Only far away countries such as Vietnam, Champa, and the Khmer kingdom could resist the Burmese forces. Though, King Bayinnaung made every effort to create an effective public administration to have his kingdom intact, it was only an oath of loyalty to the Burmese king which guaranteed the unity of the state. Formerly independent states, of course, took their chances to regain independence after the death of this victorious Burmese conqueror. As a result, the Burmese kingdom disintegrated and it was a hard task for his heirs to restore it. After decades of fighting, they were successful at the end, though Burmese lost important regions to Thailand (with the exemption of the former kingdom of Lan Na). The stability of the Burmese state was due to its effective public administration and its legal system which rested on inherited customs and law making. Burmese kings replaced former local lords and petit kings

---

[8]Church (2009: 66–79), SarDesai 177–179.

of hereditary power with provincial governors appointed by the government, a new structure which enhanced centralisation enormously. In addition to this, an efficient system of taxation was created which secured financial means to run the state. As a result, a peaceful and prosperous period followed which was ended only in the middle of the eighteenth century with the decline of the dynasty. The weakening of the central authority was again seen as a chance to create their own independent state by the Mon in the southern part of the country with its centre in Pegu. Their success, however, did not last long because a new militant dynasty of the Konbaung took power in the north and defeated the Mon for the last time ending all their hopes of independence. The Konbaung governed Burma with strong hand until the fall of the monarchy (1885) following the model of their predecessors. This is how a centralised Burma was created, a state which changed domestic peace to bloody wars with its neighbours, particularly China and Thailand to which Burmese lost the northern province of Lan Na (a Thai province ever since). To compensate the territorial losses in the east, Burmese military operations turned west, where for their misfortune, crossed British interest. The resulting three wars with the British was a catastrophe for the dynasty with economic recession, further losses of territories and the loss of their power at the end. With the fall of the dynasty, the British took over Burma which regained independence only in 1948.[9]

Burmese forces destroyed Ayutthaya completely, once a global leading commercial centre which remained in ruin until now. It was King Rama I who drove out Burmese forces and united fragmented Thai political centres into a centralised Thai state with its centre in Bangkok. As mentioned above, Thai forces were able to reclaim Lan Na from Burma in the nineteenth century and this is how modern Thailand began to take shape. Treatises with the British secured the border to Malaya and with the French to Kampuchea and Laos. It was King Chulalongkorn, a celebrated king of modern Thai history (1853–1910) who began to modernise and westernise his country with political reforms. As a result, Thailand was the only Southeast Asian country which was not occupied by the colonising powers and was given the right to use its genuine name of Prathet Thai (Thai-Land) instead of Siam known in the West. Progress was slow however, resulting in domestic strife for power. This is why a revolt broke out in 1932, headed by military leaders. Thailand was thus transformed from an absolute monarchy to a constitutional monarchy which however, did not lead to domestic peace but to rivalries among Thai elite groups and to military rules.[10]

Compared to Burmese and Thai history, modern Kampuchean past was not rich in success. After the fall of the Khmer Empire, both domestic fight and international pressure made Khmer history bitter. In addition to neighbouring Vietnamese and Thai claims of Khmer territories, European powers also entered Kampuchean history. As a result, Khmers sank to the level of a Thai protectorate while losing large territories to the Vietnamese, particularly in the south, in the Mekong delta. Finally, the region became a French protectorate in 1863, and remained as such for ninety years when

---

[9]SarDesai (2013: 68–70, 98–110).
[10]SarDesai (2013: 118–124; 160–164).

King Sihanouk succeeded in achieving the independence of Kampuchea following the defeat of the French in Southeast Asia.[11]

It is clear from the above rather short historical survey that Southeast Asian legal history cannot be written in the framework of modern states, rather new entities compared to Southeast Asian culture going back to centuries with an astonishing high rate of cross-fertilisation among peoples. For example, Buddhism and Mon culture did not only influence Burmese law, but also Thai legal understanding, which, in its turn, was not without effect among the Lao. The laws of the Khmers, though Hindus and not Buddhist for long, also share similarities with the laws of other Southeast Asian societies, together with the Malayas who are Muslims. It is only Vietnam, a country of Chinese influence, the legal system of which is out of this Southeast Asian cultural web based on Indian heritage. This is because Indian and Chinese influence manifested differently. Chinese influence in Vietnam was due to political subjugation and military defeat which generated an ambivalent reaction in Vietnam. On political and military level, resistance to the Chinese was the guiding principle followed for centuries. On a cultural level however, to absorb Chinese ideas about society, law and political order was never seriously challenged, resulting in a Confucian and not in a Buddhist, society. By contrast, Indian influence among Southeast Asian societies manifested only with peaceful means, without political or military pressure. It was long distance trade which brought Indian ideas to Southeast Asia about society and law, particularly through Buddhism. In the absence of a great power and its threatening military forces, Indian influence was manifest where local societies were willing to absorb foreign ideas but was absent where genuine ideas were stronger. This is the reason why local customs and animism remained intact and were only combined with new ideas which never claimed exclusivity with the intent to root them out. Indian cultural superiority thus, was not linked to political subjugation, and this is the reason why the ambivalent attitude to be observed in Vietnam is missing.

Another common experience in Southeast Asia is the fragmented political landscape with city states (Pyu, Mon) and small kingdoms engaged in rivalry (Thai, Khmer kingdoms). More centralised states emerged only through violence and a centralising effort of a ruling dynasty (Burma, Thailand) which declined or disappeared from the scene completely once the central power was not strong enough to resist centrifugal forces. This situation had a benevolent affect on customary law since in the absence of a power centre, local variants of law and custom could be maintained intact for centuries. This state of affairs has only changed in the modern age when emerging states, now driven by the will of modernisation, saw an obstacle to progress in customary law and wanted to reduce its influence. It was modernisation, going hand in hand with westernisation (based on military, political and economic superiority of the western powers) that was proven to be fatal for local customary law.

Agriculture was also a significant factor in preserving local laws for centuries. Southeast Asia remained rural for long centuries where village communities retained

---

[11] SarDesai (2013: 114–115, 176–177).

their importance in economic, social and legal life. As disputes were resolved on local level either in the extended family or within the village community, the legal basis for such conflict resolutions was customary law known by every member of the community. Since customary law contained legal topics important for rural communities (family law, inheritance, land law), there was no need to intervene in the legal corpus from outside, a factor that limited foreign influence either in the form of Buddhist ethics or in the form of state law as a product of political law making. Obviously, such general statements need to be qualified since Thailand is more urbanised than Laos, a country where rural communities dominate the landscape even today, but taken as a whole, agriculture is an important factor for preserving local customary law everywhere. What is more, according to a modern observer, agriculture also determined how Southeast Asian empires came into being. According to this theory, it was not the land itself which was important for agricultural product but the labour force. It is because Southeast Asian agriculture is based on rice production which needs relatively small parcel of land but enormous human labour force. It was the community which organised such works and provided human labour whenever it was short, an important factor in the development of Asian centralised states. This is also the reason why victorious Thais brought Lao people in chain to Thailand and forced them to agricultural labour while annexed almost no Lao territories.[12]

9.2   The Mon-Burmese Customary Law

9.2.1   Sources

Burmese law is perhaps the best documented in Southeast Asia because legal sources are numerous and relatively well known. Indian legal thinking was mediated through the Pyu and the Mon centuries before the arrival of the Burmese to their homeland. Previous scholarship attributed this exclusively to the Mon (Forchhammer) but recently, this idea is subject to challenge advocating also the contribution of the Pyu people.[13] This is, of course, not to downplay the importance of the Mons in Burmese legal history who did a great job in the Burmese King Anawratha's policy of cultural revival. Legal life was already well structured in the peak of Pagan's power (tenth to thirteenth centuries) with a complex judiciary ranging from a local court (village or urban) to that of the capital and a supreme court as a court of appeal (*Alaintryā*). Courts also authenticated documents on important transactions such as the transfer of land and slaves. Columns marking the border of a parcel of land (The Burmese equivalent of Mesopotamian *kudurru*) were also erected in the presence of judges, highlighting the importance of such an act. No wonder, that to remove a column was

---

[12]Chandler (2008: 22).
[13]Huxley (1996a: 109–114).

a criminal act. Contrary to this, sophisticated legal practice jurisprudence witnessed only its formative period. References to collection of laws called *dhammathat* are few and what has reached us are epigraphic texts only. We can assume, therefore, that *dhammathat* as a specific genre of legal literature came into being only at the end of the Pagan period or after it.[14]

Dhammathat is the Burmese variant of *dharmaśāstra*, a term of Sanskrit origin which did not reach the Burmese language directly from Sanskrit but was mediated by Pali and its variants (*dhammsattham*). Pali is an important middle Indian language in which the earliest Buddhist texts, the Pali Canon, were written, hence it is the liturgical language of Theravada Buddhism. *Dhammathat*s are the most important sources to reconstruct the history of Burmese law for centuries. *Dhammathat*s are however, more than law books and instructions for judges as they contain also ethics and rules on morals and social interactions that could be expected from anyone. This is the reason why the effort of the British to see *dhammathat*s as a legal manual was a failure together with the Sparks Code. The Sparks Code is a legal compendium by Major Sparks designed for the British judges as a guideline, modelled on Burmese *dhammathat*s (1860). In practice however, neither the courts of law nor Burmese society at large saw it as a text with authority and was thus, abandoned in practice soon and no such an attempt followed it.[15]

There is no shortage of Burmese legal text because a large number of *dhammathat*s have come down to us. The royal archives keep fifty-seven manuscripts, but a significant part of them is relatively late, from the eighteenth century. The very first *dhammathat* is the work of a Mon monk which was named according to its author (Dhammavilasa) and is known as *Dhammavilasa Dhammathat*. The text was written in Mon and Pali languages, but this document is lost, we only have a Burmese variant of it from 1637 which may not be identic with the original. The first legal collection that has come down to us is the *Wagaru Dhammathat*, which was translated from Pali to Mon upon the order of King Wagaru of Pegu in 1281 (marking the importance of Mon culture in law 250 years after their conquest). Wagaru's text was appreciated for long centuries, leading the Burmese King Bayinnaung to declare the *Wagaru Dhammathat* as the legal authority to be followed in his empire in 1580. Yet new *dhammathat*s were produced in the next decades, including the *Mingun Dhammathat Linga* (1650), a curious text putting the legal material into verse, to make it easier to memorise (an Indian memotechnique). The seventeenth century was the heyday of Burmese *dhammathat*s and the flourishing period of Burmese jurisprudence when numerous legal collections of high standard were produced. Despite this however, it took a century to produce the next very important collection of law, the still cited *Manugye Dhammathat* (1762). It is an encyclopaedic work containing Burmese customary law and moral maxims. In the nineteenth century the compilation of *dhammathat*s still continued but no significant works were produced. Parallel to

---

[14]Okudaira (1986: 23–27; 31).
[15]For more on the Sparks Code see Okudaira (1986: 44–45).

this, earlier manuscripts, written on palm leaves, began to disappear due to armed struggles, weather conditions and the lack of care.[16]

In addition to *dhammathat*s, compilations containing legal precedents called *hpytahon* are also important sources for the history of Burmese law. *Hpyathon* is a literary genre, a compilation of texts on what a particularly *hpyathon* is about. Therefore, there are *hpyathon*s, for example, containing wise sayings of mythical persons, or guidance to religious obligations. Legal *hpyathon*s (*dhammathat hpyathon*) contain legal maxims and precedents among which thirty four are known to us. The precedents are decisions of kings and the royal court of law based on laws of *dhammathat*s, making these precedents no sui generis sources of law only illustrations how to interpret and implement some laws of *dhammathat*s. Royal edicts were also produced in order to implement laws of *dhammathat*s, or to fill the legal gap in them. The authority of these texts rested on the legislative power of Burmese kings to issue edicts on particular issues without neglecting customary laws. Each Burmese king had its own corpus of edicts which had, in theory, no binding force for their successors in office. In practice however, Burmese kings kept up the edicts of their predecessors and this is how continuity was created, making royal edicts an important source of law. Royal edicts are abundant: the royal archives keep 5650 edicts which were issued between the sixteenth century and the fall of the dynasty (1885).[17]

Legal tales, constituting a literary genre in its own right makes Burmese legal life colourful and vivid. There are no individual collections for such tales which are to be found mostly in *dhammathat*s. Such tales are produced, of course, not to entertain but to explain an important or a complicated legal norm in a story for the sake of easier remembrance and to focus on the aim and reason of a legal norm. Actors of these tales are sometimes animals, sometimes humans, the deeds of whom reflect conflicts that a particular legal norm is about to solve. Legal tales are important sources for centuries in Burmese legal history as a peculiar literary phenomenon of law[18] with very few parallel in global legal history except Tibet.[19]

9.2.2 Legal Institutions

The present survey of Burmese legal institutions is based on two important *dhammathat*s, Wagaru and Manugye. *Wagaru dhammatat* is one of the oldest texts with authority for a long time, known from a palm-leaf manuscript of 1707.[20] The structure of the text shows strong Indian influence since it is based on the 18 legal

---

[16]An almost complete catalogue of the most important Burmese legal collections is in Okudaira (1986: 30–35).

[17]Okudaira (1986: 35–38) has a complete list of hpyathons.

[18]Huxley (1996a: 109).

[19]French (1995: 91–97).

[20]Wagaru: II: I.

disputes of Hindu law. Yet, it is a secular work with no intent to discuss topics of religious philosophy like their Indian counterparts. It is only the introduction which has some extra-legal topic telling us the well-known story of how Manu found the text at the very end of the universe and brought it back to mankind to make use of it. Wagaru is therefore a professional law book dealing with issues of private law (debt, marriage, divorce, inheritance, deposit, illegally causing damage), and some issues of penal law (theft, violence, giving false witness).

Manugye dhammathat is the law book with the greatest authority among the compilations written in the modern period. Great significance was attributed to this text, particularly by the British since its English translation was used at the Anglo-Burmese courts of law almost exclusively. The significance of Manugye however, was already established in Burma before the arrival of the British who translated this very text just because they learned how important it was in Burma, though only one manuscript was available written on palm leaves. Manugye was written at a time (1756) when after the defeat of the Mons, classical cultural heritage and the shaping of Burmese identity was important. This is also the reason why the text was not written in Pali but in the colloquial language of Burmese society, a fact that contributed significantly to its popularity. Yet, Burmese experts on law do not attribute such an almost exclusive significance to this text as the British had done but also consult other legal sources. In case of doubt, one can turn to other *dhammathat*s too, though one of the reasons to produce Manugye was to eliminate contradictions in earlier texts and to explain inherited laws. This makes Manugye some kind of an encyclopaedia of Burmese law explaining why the British translated this text to English. Yet *Manugye Dhammathat*, like other works of this genre is a collection of customary law and not a compendium of law asserted at a court of law. Customary laws are subject to change and some of them just fade from legal life, though they are nevertheless preserved in such a law book. What is more, customs could, in theory, be overwritten by royal edicts (which rarely happens) and a royal edict by the agreement of the parties. This is a widely known Burmese legal principle (*dhammathat ko yazathat chouk thi, yazathat ko gatigavut chouk thi*), making royal law a ius dispositivum for parties who favour compromises over customary and royal law.[21]

According to Burmese understanding, law is not of divine origin. This is clear in the myth explaining the origin of law, because it is only truth which is eternal and unchanging but not law. According to the introduction to Manugye, humans had to work for their daily portion of rice with hard labour. In order to do so, they distributed the harvest and also the arable land among themselves. To have more, however, someone stole the portion of others, and this is why people decided to elect a king to punish criminals. In exchange for doing this job, kings receive 10% of everybody's portion of rice. Thus Mahathamada, a very honest and wise man was elected king who appointed a judge called Manu to help him in making decisions. Manu was a wise man and told the king that this job would not be without mistakes. His prophecy soon proved correct because he made a wrong decision in a case which was not too complicated: two neighbours were disputing a vegetable which was

---

[21] Okudaira (1986: 59–67).

cultivated in one parcel but hung over to the neighbouring piece of land. Manu first ruled that it is the owner of the parcel on which the vegetable situated who has a legitimate claim, but this decision was disapproved both in heaven and on Earth. Following this, Manu has changed his mind and ruled that it is the owner of the plant who has a stronger claim, a new decision approved by heavenly authorities and society alike. His ultimate success notwithstanding. Manu realised that the job is not without the risk of failure and asked the king to relieve him from office which the king did. Being free from obligations, Manu again set out to a long journey to look for truth. During his journey he reached a cave where he ultimately rose to heaven. Here, at the end of the solar system he discovered a huge wall where a text of law was written with letters of a size of an elephant. Manu copied the entire text and once returned, gave it to King Mahathamada in order to live accordingly.[22]

This story tells us not only the origin of law but also the origin of political power, the essence of which is securing law and order and domestic peace. The legitimacy to tax rests also on this myth securing kings 10% of income, at least, in theory. In practice however, kings enjoyed more rights and competencies also in economic matters because according to Burmese understanding, kings are the owners of land and waters, mines and the bequests of persons passing away without an heir. Burmese kingdoms were absolute monarchies without any institutional control, moderated only by religious and moral expectations of Buddhism according to which a ruler must be a just king entitled *Dhammayaza* (king of the law). Court institutions were not organs to limit the power of Burmese kings but to advise the king and implement his decisions. *Hluttaw* (Supreme Council) was the most important among them with legislative, executive and judicial functions. *Hluttaw* was an archaic form of government which also participated in issuing royal edicts. *Hluttaw* was also a court of appeal as a supreme court in both criminal and private law cases. Members were ministers and military leaders appointed by the king who could be removed at any time. Confidant persons to the king constituted the *Byedaik*, another important court body to manage the personal matters of Burmese kings. The administration of justice was in the hands of various law courts (*Tayayon, Sheyon*) at lower level with the *Hluttaw* as the court of appeal in the capital city. Criminal cases were dealt with at these courts, though it was a royal prerogative, according to the myth of Manu. According to Burmese understanding of law, the king's right to punish was almost unlimited, though Buddhism restricted this power with its moral teaching. Early *dhammathats* have a wide range of punishments, including capital punishment, corporeal punishment (whipping), exile and material compensation. Burmese society however, preferred compromise and material compensation instead of corporeal punishments (even in cases of manslaughter), an attitude which was proven a fertile ground for Buddhist ethics which disapproved capital punishment. As a result, capital punishment was expressly prohibited. This is why *Manugye* praises a king who does not sentence anyone to death and who is worthy o f he appreciation of both the gods and the people. The reason behind this is that according to Buddhist understanding, a bad act cannot be balanced with another bad act and justice cannot be enhanced

---

[22]Manugye (1847: 4–23).

with a wrong act (*papathat*) but only with a right deed (*dhammathat*). Therefore, the gift to a kingdom abolishing capital punishment will be prosperity and bliss.[23] Penal law was, therefore, humanised enormously.

This is not to say, of course, that penal law was missing from *dhammathat*s. By contrast, these law books not only deal with various criminal acts but also with their social background, an important aspect since compensation depended on the social status of the victim and the culprit. Distinction was made between crimes committed intentionally and negligently, the perpetrators of the latter with restricted punishments or freed from it. Street fighting men were also left unpunished even if one of them died; in such a case, the other party was to pay compensation or had to pay the cost of the funeral. A woman was not even obliged to pay for the funeral if she fought a man and he died, but violence against women was punished by compensation in the majority of the cases. Rape had to be compensated with a high sum which could be raised further by the social standing of the victim. Non-violent illegal sexual act was 'punished' by forcing the couple to marry; if the man was already married he had to marry the woman as his second wife. Adultery was considered as a crime against the man's honour. This is the reason why a husband was entitled to immediate vengeance, though moral arguments in the same text usually dissuade him to do so. Slander is among those few criminal acts which could be punished by corporeal punishment if it was committed against a Buddhist monk or a nobleman. In harmony with Buddhist ethics, a violation of a promise was punished by corporeal punishment.[24]

Burmese law books distinguish twenty-five forms of theft, a rather artificial classification at some points. Needless to say, this is a very broad category including a variety of criminal deeds such as to pick up a thing deliberately, to rob commercial caravans, to counterfeit scales, to falsify the border of a plot of land, to falsify accounts, to mention only some of them. All forms of theft were punished with material compensation and punishment, the sum of which depended not on the act committed but on the loss the criminal act caused and the social status of the victim (except for a thief caught red-handed who could be killed on the spot). Stealing from the king was, of course, punished vigorously: the thief had to repay ten times the value of the thing stolen and in addition to this, he was also exiled. Law books define exactly the sum to be paid for various objects and animals, creating an ocean of casuistry where it is not worth immersing. To pick up some interesting cases however which shed light on contemporary economic conditions is in order. In case of stealing an elephant for example, one had to return it twice, a horse five times, a buffalo fifteen times, and a pig or a goat fifty times. A slave had to be returned five times, a law showing its value equal to that of a horse and less than an elephant.[25]

Though social stratification was important in criminal law, Burmese society was far from a Hindu caste system. There were slaves and frees, nobles and commoners, an evident distinction in every complex society. The elite consisted of the royal family, persons with very high appreciation such as ministers, guardians of historical

---

[23]Manugye Book V. 1.§; Okudaira (1986: 68–71).

[24]Manugye Book IV.: 9, 13–14.§; Okudaira (1986:106–112).

[25]Manugye Book IV: 1; 21.§.

records, scholars, leaders of the army, provincial leaders (governors, heads of cities and villages), commanders of the units of elephants. Brahmins who rose to important political positions and were advisors to kings also formed part of this political elite. People of free personal status were landlords, artisans and merchants living in cities. Slavery was widespread. One became a slave either by being captured as a prisoner of war, or as penalty (for not paying compensation). Children born to a slave woman were also slaves. Slaves were classified into various categories yet *dhammathat*s produced at different times have different categories. Classification was important because it had legal consequences, this might be the reason why later works seemingly overcomplicate the matter. Manugye, for example, has an individual category for slaves who were enslaved because they were unable to the pay the fine for slander, and another category for persons who were enslaved because they were unable to pay compensation for manslaughter. The idea behind is clear: those who were unable to pay compensation became a slave, and the law books introduced categories which implemented this principle with their own means. According to another categorization, there were permanent slaves who could not redeem their freedom (e.g. slaves o f pagodas) and others who could, such as prisoners of war and debt. Those who could redeem their freedom became free if they joined the Buddhist monastic order. Slaves were object to transactions and could be inherited within the family. Pagoda slaves were numerous primarily in the countryside since they worked there in agricultural works. Slaves worked for the interest of their masters who were regarded as wage labourers without getting wages. *Servi res sunt*, the well-known principle of Roman law was however alien to Burmese thinking where masters had no right to decide about the life of their slaves.[26]

Family law was based on Burmese customs free from Hindu or Buddhist religious ideas. Marriage was a consensual contract which was rather a matter between families and not individuals. Families rested on male dominance which was advocated, among others, with the argument that men are more suited to spirituality than women. Polygamy was allowed in theory but rarely put into practice because to marry an already married man destroyed the social reputation of the second wife. Burmese law has three kind of marriage: one was concluded by families (parents), one with the help of a mediator and the third rested on the consensus of the marrying couple. As it was common in all of Asia, marriages were family matters and marriages came usually into being by the will of the parents. The consent of the family is a precondition to a marriage except for unusual cases when the woman was more than twenty years old. Family consent was no precondition for marriages of widows and divorced women. When a girl eloped her family with a man and the couple lived together for at least five years or had a child, the woman had to return to her native village to meet her parents who could, however, not separate the couple. Since engagement and wedding were separated in time during this interim period, either party could change her/his mind. If the parents of the girl already received the gift of engagement, they have to pay it back twice if they or the girl change their minds and retreat from marriage. We can witness gender equality in family life where husband

---

[26]Manugye Book VI: 5.§; Book VII: 26.§; Okudaira (1986: 75–79; 123).

and wife jointly decide upon their assets from which women would receive an equal share in case of divorce. Another important point in gender equality is that boys and girls inherit equally.[27]

Women were classified into seven categories, four supportive and three disadvantageous for their husbands. Women who are like a mother, a sister, a friend and a slave are supportive because they would look after their husband, would help him and supply him with advice and would not argue. By contrast, disadvantageous women are like a boss, an enemy and a thief, who do not care for him, keep a lover, do not respect him and are quarrelsome. No matter how subjective and naïf this 'typology' may be, it is important because legal consequences are attached to it. Accordingly, women of the four favourable categories cannot be rejected, whereas others can. Rejection means in the terminology of the *dhammathat*s not divorce but the right of the husband to take another wife without the consent of the rejected first wife.[28]

It is the duty of the pater familias to provide garments, food and shelter to his family. If he happened to be far away from his family because of a longer journey (trade, studies) he had to guarantee the livelihood of his family by leaving behind material support for the duration of his absence. According to Manugye, the wife of such a man had to wait for her husband for eight years and can marry again only when that period is over and her husband did not return. But if a man departs with the intention of becoming a monk, then his wife can marry again after having waited for seven days. If either of the parties falls ill, it was a marital obligation to properly look after him/her. Neglecting this duty had different legal consequences for a wife and a husband. If a wife did not care for her ill partner but left him alone instead and married again, she was exiled from the country. By contrast, a husband could take a second wife of lower rank, though he had to care for his first wife until the end of his life, that is, illness was no legal cause to divorce but to a second marriage for a man. A man could also take a second wife if they have no children after ten years of marital cohabitation or have only girls, his wife has leprosy or epilepsy (if the husband was not aware of her illness when concluding the marriage). Divorce was also permitted with a relatively easy form and procedure. Couples could divorce by mutual consent, unilateral statement, referring to unacceptable behaviour and by running away. Mutual consent was the easiest form of divorce, based on the common understanding of the parties who distributed family wealth equally. Both parties were allowed to pronounce unilateral divorce but in such a case the party who wished to divorce his/her partner lost everything from the family wealth which enriched the other party with no intent to divorce. This does not hold true if either of the parties initiated divorce because of unacceptable behaviour like adultery or cruel treatment. Adultery of men however, was not a legal cause in itself to divorce, wives could divorce their husbands only if it was accompanied by other intolerable deeds such as cruel treatment. By contrast, adultery of wives was a legal cause to divorce for their husbands who also had the right to kill the parties on the spot, or to demand financial

---

[27]Manugye Book V: 24.§; Book VI: 15–22.§ Okudaira (1986: 79–83).
[28]Manugye Book V: 11. §; Wagaru: III: 38–40.

compensation from the adulterer. In addition to adultery, cruel treatment, including physical violence, was also a solid ground to unilateral divorce (and to launch a criminal procedure). A drunkard and a husband addicted to gambling (cockfights) could also be divorced if he did not stop his unacceptable behaviour after warnings. Finally, running away (abandonment) was the fourth way to divorce. Accordingly, if a husband did not want to live together with his wife and left their common house for three years or if the woman left the common shelter for a single year, the parties may divorce and can remarry. To conclude, divorce was a simple procedure in which the main issue was to settle propriety rights and to divide family wealth properly. This is the reason why consensus was favoured since in such a case family wealth was divided equally. Unilateral divorce was also legal but the party initiating it had to pay its material consequences, leaving the family home in a set of garments. This also goes for the guilty party who was divorced because of unacceptable behaviour like adultery or cruel treatment.[29]

Relative gender equality is also manifested in the law of inheritance. Accordingly, married couples inherit each other, receiving a child's share while girls and boys were entitled to the same share. Couples could not disinherit each other because last will was alien to Burmese customary law. By contrast, children could be disinherited, and this is the reason why some categories of children were so important. Children entitled to a share were offspring produced in a marriage, adopted children, children born to concubines, children born to slave women, and children produced in a previous marriage of the parties. Excluded from their share were children abandoned and adopted by others, a child born to a wife but not conceived by her husband, and the *svānuttā* ('dog child'), disobedient persons behaving towards their parents as their enemy. Mentally or physically ill children—excluded from their share by so many legal systems—were entitled to get an equal share.[30] Positive discrimination was due the youngest daughter to compensate her losses relative to her brothers and sisters because it was she who cared for the older parents living in the same family house, while others already left the family home and had their own. Moreover, her sisters were already supported by the family while getting married, thus receiving extra share in advantage. To compensate these losses, Burmese customary law awarded the youngest daughter with a larger share in the bequest.[31]

It is now clear that Burmese customary law is not a local variant of Indian/Hindu law as believed for long, but a remarkable legal culture in its own right. Casts are completely missing, together with legal institutions based on it in both private and criminal law as we cannot find the eight forms of marriage either. By contrast, women were treated rather equally and were less oppressed, endowed with rights alien to Hindu legal understanding. This is the reason why they could divorce their husbands unilaterally, received an equal share when inheriting their parents and their husbands, and could remarry after divorcing or as a widow, important

---

[29]Wagaru III: 33–46; Manugye Book V: 17§; Book VI: 20–21; 30.§; Book VII: 2.§. Okudaira (1986: 84–90).

[30]Manugye: Book X and Wagarau VI; see Okudaira (1986: 90–100).

[31]Wagaru VI: 75; Huxley (1996b: 107).

rights completely missing from Hindu India. Criminal law was rather humane where compensation was favoured and capital punishment abandoned—on the influence of Buddhism—going ahead before Western countries for centuries.

9.3   Thai–Lao Customs

Ancient Thai-Lao customs are hard to reconstruct because during the siege of Ayutthaya important sources were lost. This is the reason why *Nithan Kun Borom*, a chronicle narrating the origin of the Thai and Lao people is particularly interesting. This text is an important source to reconstruct Thai-Lao customs but should be treated with caution because it mixes legends with historical facts. The chronicle focuses on Kun Borom, the legendary king of the Thai-Lao people (hence the title, too) while it is subject to debate among historians whether we have an authentic historical person here or not. We do not know the time of his rule either which is believed to be around the late seventh or the early eighth century, at least by those who do not doubt his existence. To complicate matters, the extant text which has come down to us is a rather late document which came into being long centuries after the time it is about, during the reign of King Visun (1500–1520) who perhaps wanted scaffold for his shaky grounds for power with this chronicle, presenting former kings as his ancestors in order to legitimise his own rule. Since the chronicle also has Kun Borom's laws, an unparalleled piece of text which sheds light on early Thai-Lao legal history, the problem of authenticity is of paramount importance. The question we now face and cannot answer for certain is what these laws are about: do they reflect in fact ancient customary law as some believe, or reflect the laws of the epoch when they were put into writing, centuries after Kun Borom's legendary (?) rule?[32]

Kun Borom's laws (Kotmay Thammasat Kun Borom) are norms of a rural community with primitive institutions or with no institutions at all. The king was rather a Weberian charismatic ruler with personal authority but without effective state organs. This goes for the Lao for long centuries since Lao society remained rural until modern times, making their former (Luang Prabang) and later capital (Vientiane) rather an enormous village than a proper city. Small wonder that early Lao legal system also reflects the problems of rural communities stressing the importance of conflict resolutions instead of legal precision. Legal texts lack any kind of systematisation or discernible logic on which they are based. Early Lao customary law is, like the Burmese, secular without any hint to Buddhism which became important only later. If religious thinking was at some point important, it was animism, the original religion of the Thai-Lao people which had an impact on law, both private and criminal. Compensation for a wrong, for example, may be a religious rite offered to the spirits, regulated by customs, including plant and animal sacrifices. Such sacrifices (and the concept behind them) can still be found in Laos and Thailand. When Buddhism entered the scene, it did not abolish former ways

---

[32]Ngaosyvathn (1996: 73).

of rites and religious concepts but supplemented them, which led to a syncretism consisting of animist ideas and Buddhist ethics, also colouring legal thinking. A good example is the Khamphi Phra Thammasat, an important text which was found and published by the French under the title of *Code de Vientiane* in the late nineteenth century. This collection of laws is impregnated by Buddhist ethics, both in principles and structure since the legal material is arranged by *pañca-sīlāni* (refraining from the killing of living beings, lying, alcoholic beverages, theft and sexual sins), that is, the five fundamental Buddhist laws which should be observed by lay people as well. As a result, the Code de Vientiane has five books, each about adultery, murder, theft, lie, drunkenness. No legal material of such a Buddhist influence had ever been produced in Southeast Asia. It is more disappointing that no legal source has come down to us between the chronicle of Kun Borom and the Code de Vientiane.[33]

Despite the lack of sources, continuity of legal thinking is manifest proven by "survivals" which are present even today or are just now disappearing. It is animism, merged with Buddhism which continued to shape the legal landscape of rural communities. This *village Buddhism*, as it is properly called in academic literature, is perhaps the most powerful survival of a past which is rapidly disintegrating due to massive urbanisation and the complex effects of globalisation in Thailand, contrary to isolated rural Laos. According to this world view, the globe is also inhabited by spirits who are capable of interfering with people's lives, it is thus in the interest of both the individual and the community to have proper interaction with them. Spirits are everywhere because both living beings and inanimate objects have a kind of spiritual essence called *khwan* which could depart and have a life of its own. This happens frequently as a consequence of an accident, a personal trauma or tragedy. In such a situation, the departed *khwan* had to be brought back by a ritual called *riak khwan,* when a sacred thread is fastened on the person's wrist. Without this ritual the person's *khwan* would leave the body, depart the world and move to places where only souls and spirits live but not humans (forest) and that can be dangerous for the individuals and the entire community (village). To reclaim the *khwan* is thus of utmost importance, the burden of which rests on the person who caused the *khwan* to leave (caused, for example, an accident). This is the reason why the punishment for causing damage is called in legal literature payment for the *khwan* rite (*kha tham khwan*). It also explains why other kinds of compensation are non-existent or rare. In addition to *khwan,* there is also a second element of spiritual identity called *vinyan,* which leaves the body in the case of death and would again incarnate at a proper time in the natural course of events. If however, death is a consequence of an attack, injury or accident the soul cannot continue its natural course and transforms into a highly dangerous, harmful spirit. This is because unnatural death stopped the natural course of events and the spirit wants to escape his situation as soon as possible. To achieve this, such a soul has to find a proxy for itself who would take over his role. Such a spirit would, therefore, kill another human just on the spot where he was killed in order to be relieved and continue his path. This is a very dangerous situation for the entire community since anyone could be the victim of such a spirit,

---

[33] Ngaosyvathn (1996: 74; 76–78).

a situation that could be avoided again through proper rituals. If unexpected death was the result of the act of a third party (e.g. in an accident), it was he who had to arrange for the ritual but was not expected to do more. It is because animism and the doctrine of *karma* constitutes a strange mixture, according to which the third party has to free the community from the bad will of a harming spirit but is not liable for the death of the victim because it is determined by his/her *karma*. As a consequence, the third party has to pay for the ritual because he is obliged to arrange that the soul (*khwan*, *vinyan*) would not harm anyone, but is not obliged to do more, that is, pay compensation for the loss he caused. Archaic as it seems, this way of thinking is nevertheless alive, though modern cities hardly have space for such rites and the number of rural cultic places is continuously decreasing. Despite this however, such ways of conflict resolution are practiced even today, which might explain why legal disputes concerning damage and wrong are taken to law courts only in a limited number, though modern Thai legal system has every institution to promote this. Take accidents on motorway as an example contribute to understand the point. As we have seen, according to Thai understanding a forest is a dwelling place for spirits but not for humans, who should avoid entering a forest, or enter it with extreme caution and with the permission of the spirits living there. Needless to say, this was not the concern of modern construction workers who entered the forest careless and fell thousands of trees, actually the dwelling places of spirits. Offended by such brutal acts, spirits seek to revenge the wrong and this is why some construction workers died on spot while at work and also why victims of accidents die on the motorway. People who die in the forest are persons whose karmic circle in this life comes to an end there while others depart safe from the forest and leave the motorway without any harm, a good example how animism and Buddhism come together.[34] The observations of a modern anthropologist and the laws of Kun Borom are thus identical both in their concept and terminology.

In cases where spirits were not involved, compensation paid for the harmed person was unavoidable, particularly in family matters and conflicts about landed property, cases which have the lion's share in the laws of Kun Borom. Family was patriarchal limiting the rights of women enormously who were not allowed to depart the family house without the permission of their husbands. Noble women were always accompanied by a servant when entering the public space and royal concubines were always protected by a royal guard created for this purpose when they left the palace. Such women were not allowed to speak to anyone on the streets and no one could even look at them without risking a beating, laws which reflect a somewhat extreme jealousy and a will to avoid situations with a ground for suspicion of adultery. No wonder husbands entering their homes have the right to kill adulterers on the spot, an Asia-wide competency of angry husbands. Should however, the lover kill the entering husband in the quarrel, he was sentenced to death. Property was protected with the same vigour. A land owner was entitled to kill a thief who stole rice from the storehouse or from the land. Thieves of water were also sentenced to death, but only after the third warning. Since water is an essential element for rice cultivation not

---

[34]Engel and Engel (2010: 56–76).

only thieves but neglecting persons were also punished who did not contribute to the construction and maintenance of irrigation canals "out of laziness". Such persons received no share from the water. Damages caused by animals such as elephants, buffaloes, goats and pigs foraging on cultivated land were dealt with casuistic. The underlying principle in these laws seems to be that no land owner was entitled to kill the animals on the field but had warn the owner of the animals to care about his animals. If despite warnings animals do more harm on the field, the owner could kill them with the exception of valuable animals such as buffalos and elephants. This, of course, is not a relief for their masters to pay compensation for the losses the animals caused in the field. Compensation was due either in payment or in personal work (if animals destructed newly planted plants their owner had to plant them on the land of the harmed person).[35]

Lao customary law remained unchanged for centuries preserved by the life of rural communities isolated from civilisation (roads, electricity, medical care, school) up to the French colonisation and to the twentieth century. People living close to the jungle and fearing the spirits are relying on each other's assistance, a fact explaining the importance of great families and villages organising public labour. If such local communities are insufficient to a task (planting, harvest, house building), men from neighbouring villages are asked to help with the promise to return their assistance when asked for it. It is agricultural labour and its cycle which lent rhythm to life, specifies symbolism and social institutions, particularly marriage. Though Lao society is patriarchal, the separation of genders is by far not very rigid which makes marrying easier. Lao youngsters could choose their partner on their own since young people go together to work in the fields where they have plenty of opportunities to meet. Moreover, boys could visit girls in their homes in order to chat and get acquainted. These are social mechanisms of rural communities which make it easier to find a proper partner for marriage.[36] The same goes for ancient China where agricultural labour also determined the life of rural communities. Here, young people enjoyed considerable freedom in selecting their partner for marriage, accompanied with a freedom of sexual relation before marriage. It was only Confucianism which introduced rigid rules and transformed previous laws to its own understanding of social interactions in subsequent centuries.[37]

When the couple agreed to marry, a long procedure started since it was not their private matter only, but a public concern for their families and the entire village. This is the reason why a mediator is appointed to help the negotiations. After proposing a marriage, the bridegroom's social position was examined by the girl's family, including his wealth, character, profession and fame irrespective of whether he is from the same village or not. As a result of the inquiries, the parents could decline the offer and their daughter had to accept parental decision with the only alternative to elope with her lover (for which there are examples). In the majority of the cases however, parents agree and thus it is now up to the families to agree on every detail of

---

[35]Ngaoshyvathn (1996: 75–76).

[36]Ireson-Doolittle and Moreno-Black (2004: 43–45; 57).

[37]Maspero (1978: 109–110).

pecuniary issues and the wedding ceremony. Before wedding, an astrologer is asked to clarify the best date for the ceremony. Such a wedding ceremony is a huge burden for both families because of the number of guests invited and the rules which should be observed. To prepare the bride for the ceremony was, of course, the task of her family as it was they who arranged for the bed of the young couple. However, this was sometimes a complicated issue because of rules, the aim of which were to avoid every bad omen. If the parent of the girl was widowed someone else had to arrange for the bed to avoid doing harm for the young couple. The carpenter, too, should not be a widower or a divorced person but an elderly man living in a happy marriage for decades. Once everything is prepared, the bridegroom enters the house of the bride to ask for her hand, accompanied by the elders of his family who meet the elders of the other family there and exchange greetings. Next, the bride's sister greets the bridegroom and washes his feet before entering the inner part of the house where the girl's parents formally ask for the price of the bride. After mutual courtesies, the girl is led out at the end and the wedding ceremony properly begun, a curious mix of animist customs and Buddhist ritual. At the beginning, there are prayers in Pali language followed by evocation of spirits, asking for their benevolent assistance. After the prayers, the fists of the couple is bound together and eggs are offered as symbols of vitality and sexuality. This is then followed by speeches by elderly men from both sides, who bind a new ribbon around the fists of the young couple to strengthen their bond. Once the last speech comes to its end, the ceremony called *baci* is over. After wedding, the young couple starts a new life usually in the girl's parental home, at least in the first couple of years. This matrilocality protects women since they are living among their relatives who might also contribute to resolve possible marital conflicts. Matrilocality specifies also the law o f inheritance because it is the youngest daughter with her family who remains in the parental house to nurse the elderly parents. Should they die, the bequest goes to the youngest daughter who cared for them.[38] According to a contemporary witness, hardly anything has changed and recent wedding ceremonies follow the old pattern.[39]

In addition to marriages, there are some festivals which cement the community and help maintaining their identity and solidarity. These festivals include rites of animist tradition some of them taking a whole day. One such a ritual is to win over the support of the soul of the departed, a ceremony led by an elderly person well versed in the sacrifices and the texts accompanying them. Plants, fruits and animals are sacrificed in such a ceremony. Since the souls are satisfied with the fragrance of the sacrifices, happy villagers could consume the meat and fruits. This is a particular ceremony, the aim of which is to strengthen communal identity. This is the reason why every member of the community should take part on such a ceremony but every non-local is excluded from it and is prohibited to enter the village, in fact the only occasion for such a prohibition in an otherwise friendly society. When returning to the normal way of life, common work is also an important element enhancing solidarity. This is the reason why lazy persons who do not participate in communal works are

---

[38] Ireson-Doolittle and Moreno-Black (2004: 57–62).

[39] Swearer (2010: 58–62).

punished and expelled from the village. The reverse is also true: a new settler is welcome only if his work in the benefit of the community has proved adequate.[40]

The customary law of the Lao has remarkable similarities with that of Lan Na, a northern Thai kingdom near the border the inhabitants of which speak a language close to that of the Lao. Their common cultural and anthropological background explains why there are only minor variants in detail, while the laws of Kun Borom and the later legal texts of Lan Na are, taken as a whole, very similar.[41] Little was known about the laws of Lan Na, but new findings contribute significantly to our understanding of northern Thai legal history. A research group of Aroonrut Wichienkeo reported that they have found 132 manuscripts in the archives of Buddhist monasteries which they catalogued and microfilmed. The majority of these texts may not be too ancient (eighteenth to nineteenth centuries), yet they are important texts because some of them contain earlier material as well (1472). A significant part of the sources found (40) is *thammasat*, showing the popularity of this genre in Lan Na too (*thammasat* is the Thai equivalent of Burmese *dhammathat*). In addition to *thammasat*s, royal edicts are also preserved in great number because Thai kings did not repeal the edicts of their predecessors, only completed them since according to Thai world view, the wishes of the deceased should be implemented and the words of the elderly respected. The third group of sources are precedents, that is, final judgments of kings in some important and complicated cases.[42]

Based on these sources, we can specify four phases in the legal history of Lan Na. The first phase is the formative period between the foundation of the kingdom (1296) and its capital (Chiangmai) and the rule of Tilokaraj (1441–1487). This is a period when customary law reigned unchallenged and kings of the Mangrai dynasty adjudicated accordingly without compiling *thammasat*s whatsoever. The second phase lasted from the rule of Tilokaraj up to the Burmese conquest (1558) ending the rule of the Mangrai dynasty. This was an epoch when Lan Na became a Buddhist society and Buddhist thinking on society and law started to penetrate into customary laws supplementing it. Tilokarai, a stark promoter of Buddhism, constructed Buddhist temples, invited Buddhist monks to his land and reshaped the legal system according to Buddhist ethics. This is why *pañca-sīlāni* were incorporated into the legal system and why Buddhist monks and scholars were given a share in the management of the judiciary. On the other hand, laws unaffected by Buddhist ethics such as laws on agriculture remained within the domain of customary laws. During the Burmese occupation (1558–1774), that is, the third period in the legal history of Lan Na, the administration of justice was in the hand of Burmese officials who relied on Burmese *dhammasath*s. The fourth phase was not about the restoration of independence, since Lan Na became a region in modern Thailand where local and customary laws were replaced by new Thai laws made in Bangkok from where judges were also sent. Particularly the reforms of King Rama V had brought about important changes

---

[40] Ireson-Doolittle and Moreno-Black (2004: 42–44).

[41] The differences are summarised by Ngaosyvathn (1996: 78).

[42] Wichienkeo (1996: 21–34).

which significantly reduced the influence of customary law though it could never be eliminated.[43]

Mangrayathammasat, the laws of King Mangrai (1238–1317) is our most important source about northern Thai customary law, though it is difficult to read and understand some parts of the text. The preamble of the text has a historical narrative of how King Mangrai invaded Haripunchai, the rich city of the Mon merchants with tricks and intrigue. Accordingly, the king found Ai Fa guilty, one of his trusted servants in a serious crime and expelled him from his country. Ai Fa fled to Hariphunchai and complained about his bad fortune to the king Phraya Ba, who took him in good grace and assigned him some offices. Having seen his abilities, the king entrusted him more and more until the administration of the whole country was in his hands. Now Ai Fa wrote a letter to Mangrai and invited him to come with his army to which all gates were open. This is how the northern kingdom Lan Na started to expand its territories, followed by more victories subjugating local political centres. As a result, the kingdom of Lan Na was born in the northern part of what is now Thailand and Laos with its capital at Chiangmai. Once the new state was established, the king published also his laws for his realm.[44]

The structure of the laws is less consistent since the same topics keep on re-emerging throughout the entire text. They either repeat the topic or have something different to say about the same issue. For instance, the text begins with sexual crimes, a topic also emerging in the middle (47) and the end of the laws (77). Issues of marriage and marriage property rights are completely scattered in the text (11, 18, 22, 49, 53–58, 74), just like the matter of theft (7, 9, 16, 27, 33, 35, 67), or damages caused by animals (17, 60, 62). This is why Aroonrut may be right in believing that the current text is an edited version of three different codes which were put together later, a theory supported by variants and inconsistencies in the text.[45]

The text refers to the legal disputes of primitive rural communities rather than to complicated issues of an urban society. This is why it might be the customs of Lao society and not that of the more urbanised Thais, a theory supported by the absence of laws concerning political, administrative and economic institutions except corvée obligation. The text has nothing to say about the body politic, what we have instead is a somewhat naïve categorisation of officials into good and weak. Good officials (*gunadhamma*) help people in their need, are fair and do not abuse their authority but weak officials (*gunamara)* abuse their authority, confiscate the peasants' property, abuse women and judge arbitrarily. While the text is obviously a kind of sociography it has nothing to say about the punishment of weak officials and confines itself to the wisdom not to appoint weak officials for important offices.[46]

The laws concentrate on rural communities and their conflicts and is by far not a code with systematic regulations. Instead, it is picking up a lot of subjects without going through other aspects of the same issue. A reader has the impression that it is,

---

[43] Wichienkeeo (1996: 39–40).

[44] Laws of Mangrai 1.

[45] Wichienkeeo and Wijeyewardene (1986: 13).

[46] The Laws of Mangrai 76.

in part, a collection of difficult and atypical cases because laws on typical cases are taken for granted. Here are some examples: what to do when a wife has been waiting for her husband for ten years and remarries only after this rather long waiting period, but her first husband returns (80)?; what is the punishment of a deserted soldier (45), someone who destructs ritual tools (19)? What are the laws for the ritual pollution of paddy fields by excrement (48), for the collision of boats of different sizes on water (50), for unnatural sexual intercourse with animals (78, 79)? Obviously, not every law in the law book deals with such irregular cases since laws on damages, divorce, theft and rent are also to be found in the text, but the proportion of irregular cases is nevertheless conspicuous.

Criminal legal thinking is dominated by compensation, where capital punishment is only the exception not the rule. Theft is punished by compensation without exception. Manslaughter—intentional and negligent alike—and assault are also punished by compensation except when such a crime was committed in the family. The punishments of such crimes depended on the position of both the victim and the perpetrator in the hierarchy within the family. If a father/husband killed a child or his wife or an elder brother killed his younger brother, they had to pay compensation only. Should however, a person of lower rank kill someone with a higher social position (a wife kills her husband, a child a parent, a younger brother his elder brother, a slave a master, a disciple a master, etc.) such a person faced death (26). This is a rather unexpected law in the social context of Buddhist Southeast Asia, dominated by customary laws and Buddhist ethics from which such a way of thinking is alien. By contrast, such laws dominate Confucian China from the first penal codes until modern times. A soldier to abandon the army also faced death (45) but perpetrators of crimes such as setting one's house on fire; killing a monk; stealing from a monastery; sheltering enemies, criminals and deserters; inciting for homicide were not necessarily punished by death. It was up to the king's discretion to decide from among penalties (death, exile cutting off of hands and feet) in such cases (72). An entering husband was entitled to kill the lover of his adulterous wife, as in almost every Asian law. Should the husband forgive him, the lover was obliged to pay enormous compensation (4). If a wife of a slave's owner committed adultery with a slave, such a woman became a slave (4), a law again representing irregular cases.

Irregular cases also dominate family law, where typical cases are almost completely missing (the conclusion of marriage, position of the parties, etc.). One among these irregular laws is that an adulterous wife having her third lover could be sold by her father in order to purchase another wife from the money for her husband (18), or the husband could take another wife from this money (53). This is a very interesting and important law showing the strong ties between the two families and the responsibility of the woman's family for her behaviour during marriage. It was the father of the wife who was responsible for the immoral deeds of his daughter and it is he who should act and compensate her husband at the end of the day. A marriage concluded for a limited period of time (one, two, three years) also seems to be an irregular case. According to the text, such marriages were concluded with poor women applying for works in a household (74), the aim of which was, perhaps, to give some legal protection for them.

Divorce was of course a matter with no law limiting this right of the couple. The text concentrates therefore on monetary issues and propriety rights after divorce. Equality of the parties is the underlying principle on which laws on detail are based. As a rule, each party can take away his/her property while the wealth accumulated jointly during marriage was divided equally after divorce. This, however, is not to be followed if divorce was pronounced unilaterally because of a misdeed of any of the parties. If, for example, a husband beats his wife, she is entitled to divorce him and also to his share in the property jointly acquired during their married life. By contrast, if a husband divorces his wife because of her intolerable behaviour, she would lose her share in the joint property (53).

We cannot find any law concerning judicial procedure. Law courts existed without any shade of doubt since the laws refer to them repeatedly. As a rule, judgments were not to be modified (73) but it is by far not clear what this law means exactly: is it the law court which cannot modify its previous judgment, or is it a prohibition for appeals, or is it a prohibition to officials to alter a judgment of a law court? Despite this prohibition, there were cases however, when judgments were subject to review. When a judgment was obviously wrong or was produced with massive violation of the law (the judgment was passed by a woman, the procedure took place at night, the procedure was conducted in a private house, the judge was a relative of one of the parties), it had to be modified. Sentences such as these are very informative and useful for the reconstruction of Thai-Lao customary law because otherwise we have no data on laws of procedure. Since we can infer from negative sentences to positive rules, it is clear that law courts had separate buildings for trials where neither women nor relatives of the parties could be a judge, and procedures were to be held only during daytime.

The laws are infused with common sense and practical consideration also in monetary issues. A good example is to be found among the laws on damages. Accordingly, if two boats have an accident on water, the liability for damages go to the person whose boat was smaller and lighter (50), obviously, because it is easier to manoeuvre with smaller boats. This kind of logic was then extended to other analogical cases as well. Common sense is also manifests in psychological observations prudently collected in legal tales at the end of the law book. The tale of the tiger and the sage is illustrating the point (82). Accordingly, the tiger was killed by a snake, but a sage happened to walk there and saved the life of the tiger by neutralising the poison. Coming to his senses, the tiger wanted to eat the sage who told him that it was h e who saved his life and, therefore, he should be thankful instead. As they could not agree, they went to the jackal asking for justice. The jackal thought that the tiger belongs to animals and the forest and also protected the forest against the intrusion of humans whereas humans were only harmful to the forest, therefore he ruled in favour of the tiger. Next they turned to the spirit of the forest who also said that the tiger was right because humans felled the trees on which the spirits lived. Next, they went to the ox that was afraid of the tiger eating him if he did not give justice to the tiger, hence he also judged to the benefit of the tiger. Then they asked the monkey who remembered that his grandfather was eaten by a man, so he also judged against the sage. The vulture also voted for the tiger because it hoped to get something if the tiger killed the sage. Finally, they turned to the hare who went back with them to the spot and asked them to show everything as it had happened. Thus, the tiger lied down on the ground and once the cobra came again he bit the tiger. The tiger passed away and the hare prohibited the sage to save him again. The text teaches us that all these sentences are wrong besides the last one, because they are based on personal position and subjective considerations: the jackal's judgement was based on affection, the spirit's decision on hatred, the ox's on fear, the monkey's on vengeance, and the vulture's on greed. It was only the hare who brought justice.

The legal history of the southern Thai provinces differs from that of the north. Though Burmese occupation was a bitter experience here too, it did not last for long and after their departure, a new Thai state emerged with its centre in Bangkok. During the Burmese occupation, 90% of ancient documents, legal literature included, were lost but despite this, everyday legal life remained unchanged because customary laws guaranteed continuity. Though a new dynasty was in power in a new political centre, law courts nevertheless did their everyday routine on inherited wisdom. This is why the decision of King Rama I to revise the entire legal system and produce a new code was somewhat sudden. According to a wide spread story, the king ordered to revise the entire legal system because he was presented a case for final judgment in which a husband appealed against previous judgments according to which he lost his wealth when divorcing his wife, though it is was evident that the couple divorced because of her misdeeds and misbehaviour. The law courts were believed to have bad laws and the king ordered to seek for other, better textual variants. When it became clear that all variants have the same laws and the law courts were right in their judgment, the disappointed king voted for the revision of the entire legal corpus which preferred, obviously, injustice. Since it was impossible to believe that previous Thai kings pronounced wrong judgments based on evident injustice, it was clear the official argument goes on to say, that inherited Thai laws were distorted by corrupt officials and the Burmese who brought only disorder and corruption. The King thus, immediately appointed a committee of judges and Buddhist scholars to clear Thai law from injustice and passages at variance with Thai legal understanding. The committee worked hard and put a legal compilation on the table which was also sealed by the three ministers governing the three administrative regions of the country (North, South and the Centre) within eleven months. This the reason why this new code is called the Three Seals Code (Kotmāi Trā Sām Duang) to this day. A copy of the text was deposited at the Supreme Court, in the royal archives and in the private residence of the king. In producing the code, the committee compared all laws with the original text found in the Pali Canon and where contradiction was manifest they restored the original text in the code. The committee thus produced not a new code based on new principles and legal understanding, only cleaned the traditional legal system from imperfect laws whatever the reason of their presence might be. It is next to impossible to say how far the committee has gone in order to introduce new laws in the *Kotmāi Trā Sām Duang* because we have almost no source from the period before the Burmese conquest and have thus, no opportunity to compare the code with earlier material. Apparently there are passages which go back to the edicts of King Ramaraja of Ayutthaya produced in the fourteenth century. It is also true, however,

that laws concerning public administration reflect rather the social conditions of King
Rama I with a relatively modern state compared, at least, to Thai kingdoms of the
previous centuries. Laws on the central government and the administrative division
of the kingdom reveal this apparently.[47]

We should not be misled with the arguments of the code highlighting only to clean
inherited laws and to avoid to create new laws, because—strictly speaking- no king
is allowed to do this since according to a legal theory of Indian origin, *thammasat*s
are not the territory of kings. The kings' power is restricted to produce only edicts
in their own name (*rājasattham*) which are in effect only for a limited period: the
rule of the king who pronounced it. Though, Thai kings uphold the edicts of their
predecessors for ethical reason creating thus continuity for these laws too, yet their
place remained only secondary to the laws of *thammasat*s, just as laws of *qānūn* are
secondary to *sharīʿa* in Islamic law. Laws of *thammasat*s have been known since
Manu, while laws of royal edicts were only derivative and supplementary which
cannot contradict eternal law, only facilitate its implementation. By the revision of
the old laws and by putting them into a uniform structure however, a chance emerged
to also incorporate royal law into a *thammasat* without mentioning such an aim even
by King Rama himself who mandated to produce the code. The authority of the code,
on the other hand, was guaranteed by the king and this is the reason why the Kotmāi
Trā Sām Duang remained so important for so long.[48]

Indian political theory about kings and their power is a latecomer in Thai
legal history which has a completely different role model for rulers. Thai kings
were, according to the original concept—manifest also in customary laws—rather
benevolent fathers of the nation who were living close to the society they ruled and had
no political and administrative institutions at their disposal to govern. This patriarchal
king was always within reach for everyone seeking justice which was symbolised by
the bell hung at the entrance to the royal palace. By ringing this bell anyone could
ask the king to hear him and adjudicate his case after proper examination. This is by
far not the concept of an absolute monarch but rather that of a shepherd of his folk,
an organic theory widespread through Asia. Indian influence entered Thai society
in the subsequent centuries mediated presumably by Hindu Khmers, architects of a
Hindu empire. Here Indian/Hindu theory on law and government was the basis for a
more absolute monarchy centred in Angkor as its political and administrative capital.
Ayutthaya was perhaps influenced by the long experience of the Khmers, though the
extent of such an influence is subject to debate. This dispute notwithstanding it is
clear that Thai concept of law and political power was increasingly influenced by
the Indian tradition. As a result, Thai kings moved from the role of the benevolent
father to that of the master of servants who are absolute monarchs, lord of life and
death (*chao chivit*) and a figure resembling god (*devarāja*). This theory on the other
end of the extreme was then mitigated by Buddhism mediated by the Mon people
to Thai society. Buddhist understanding of law and power represents a third variant
entering Thai society within a relatively short period of time. Accordingly, a king is

---

[47]Hooker (1978: 25–26), Ishii (1986: 143), Vickery (1996: 146; 174–175).

[48]Engel (1975: 6–8), Hooker (1978: 28–30).

not an absolute monarch but the guardian of law and order. This is how the *devarāja* of Hindu origin was replaced by the Buddhist king as the servant of law who is bound to both Buddhist ethics and the law. A king subject to an eternal law is a theory reducing the power of an absolute monarch of divine origin which also limits the legislative power of such a king. *Thammasat*s containing laws free from royal will, limit the power of kings in two ways. First, by their very existence since these laws are out of the domain of political power thus stopping arbitrary legislation. Second, by setting ethical standards for rulers such as non-violence, prohibition of oppression, honesty, self-control, a control of negative emotions, benevolence, justice, moderation and the observance of the laws. In order to rule accordingly, a king has to investigate the cases personally, he can only have lawful income, has to defend and support the honest persons and has to work for the promotion of happiness for the entire society. If a king acts accordingly, he will be *chakravartin,* that is, a virtuous king who 'turns the wheel'.[49] Despite this theory, Thai kings enjoyed almost unlimited power proven by, among others, reports of foreign travellers. In the absence of institutions, no effective control and balance moderated the power of Thai kings who ruled with the help of their edicts. The decision of King Rama I to collect the laws and arrange them in a code should be understood within this context.[50]

The Three Seals Code consists of 41 chapters. The introductory chapters (preamble, Manu's legend as he recognises the law at the edge of the universe written on a tree, etc.) are followed by laws on public law highlighting the role of the king, his family and the palace, the power of ministers, the structure of public administration and the judiciary, and some issues of procedural law. Separate chapters are dedicated to laws on family (marriage and inheritance) and contracts. Criminal law concentrates on theft and crimes against public order. Chapters between 28 and 41 contain royal edicts in annual order without any attempt to systemise the material according to topics. Five chapters (32–36) contain edicts from Ayutthaya, while the rest are the decrees of King Rama I. Compared to the significance of the text in Thai legal history its logical arrangement and legal gaps (criminal law and the law of contracts are rather vague) cause some disappointment.[51]

The preamble of the Three Seals Code tells the myth of the origin of the law already known from the Mon–Burmese legal tradition. The text is enlarged with a story, the aim of which is to legitimate Thai laws and anchor them in Manu's eternal laws. Accordingly, when Manu handed over the laws to the king, it reached first the Mon people in the original (Pali) language and from them it entered Siam making in the Thai translation of the original text. Chapters on law proper begin with public law issues, first by enumerating the territorial and administrative divisions of the kingdom, contradicted enormously by the next chapter on military and provincial

---

[49] Turning the wheel is common in Buddhism as well as in Brahmanism and also in Jainism, while the origin and exact meaning of this symbolism remain obscure to this day: it may refer to royal power, or to the dharma as well: Gethin (2014: 70–71).

[50] Hooker (1978: 31), Engel (1975: 1–5). Engel believes in Khmer influence on political thinking in Ayutthaya while Vickery challanges this view: Vickery (1996: 140).

[51] Based on Lingat's classification, see: Hooker (1978: 26–27), Ishii (1986: 146–147).

administration. Contradictions could be resolved by suggesting that the first text reflects the Ayutthaya period, while the next chapter the contemporary period of King Rama I, but it remains a theory as no textual proof is available in the code. Officials had to swear loyalty to the king, which had to be repeated—accompanied by a court ceremony (drinking the water of fidelity)—every two years. An official neglecting this duty faced death. Court protocol was rigid and formal and whoever violated it was punished seriously. Communication, particularly addressing the king and his family was regulated with precision and vigour. For instance, if someone was whispering to his neighbour during a royal audience, he was obviously executed for not respecting the king. The same happened to a person who attempted to climb on the wall of the royal palace. Persons flying kites in the neighbourhood of the royal palace also faced harsh punishments, depending on their rank. Palace laws were merciless concerning the members of the royal family too, who could also be sentenced to death. Members of the royal family were executed by being beaten to death with bamboo sticks, as it was believed to be an execution most compatible to their dignity. Buddhist teaching on non-violence and forgiveness was completely neglected in specifying punishments which allowed for Draconian rigor, particularly in criminal acts against the public order and the monarchy. In contrast to the Mon-Burmese legal tradition, capital punishment was not abolished but was sometimes extended to innocent persons as well, following the Chinese model. Treason, for example, was punished by death, a sanction extended to the entire family of the convicted person, too, whose entire wealth was confiscated. Treason was interpreted rather broadly. An attempt to overthrow the king qualified as treason, together with an attempt against the king's life by arms, poison or bad omens, conspiracy with an enemy and its armed forces, the revelation of secrets to the enemy, and the efforts of the governors to become independent. It is worth mentioning that Thai girls marrying foreign men of another religion were also traitors because of the fear that their children would later be spies acting to overthrow the Thai kingdom and the Buddhist teaching. The strictness of criminal law, fear from the governors' treachery and from Thai girls marrying abroad show a somewhat paranoid system fearing both the domestic and the external enemy, thus revealing its vulnerability. Corruption must have been widespread and officials abused their power frequently, proven by the strictness of the code. Accordingly, non-implementation of orders, abuse of official authority, assistance given to rebels and spies, illegal use of a non-existent official rank, forgery of documents and seals, oppression of the population by illegal means are crimes punished by decapitation or by dismembering the body (cutting off of hand and feet), completed with confiscation and a humiliating parading. It was within the discretion of the king to decide upon the punishment. [52]

Chōn was a complex category of criminal law referring to a thief, a robber or a bandit, or, in its broader meaning: everybody who acted against domestic peace and order or against a person and his physical integrity and property. No wonder that the text classifies *chōn*s into sixteen subcategories. Here too, the paranoia of the political system manifests itself in the way *chōn* was interpreted. In order to achieve complete control over society, it was the task of the governors to enlist the population by residence and follow their movement constantly to hinder conspiracy or an act of *chōn*. In addition, authorities had to arrest any non-resident who happened to be seen on the streets or on a boat even without committing any wrongdoing. If authorities failed to do so, it was a *chōn* for them and they were punished accordingly. Worse, if a *chōn* person did some wrong repeatedly, authorities were punished more severely. Thai kingdom took this very seriously and extended responsibility also to family members of officials who resided nearby and exempted family members only who lived far away and were thus, obviously, not acquainted with the wrong committed far from their home. By contrast, family members and relatives living nearby were kept in jail until the culprit was arrested. If a *chōn* person caused death, he was executed regardless of his intention. This was the case when a highway robber killed a person he robbed or a thief killed the owner of the house during burglary even though it was not his intention to kill, just to steal. By contrast, anyone defending his property and life enjoyed immunity if he killed a *chōn* person by force and weapons, provided the *chōn* person resisted his counter attack. Should the *chōn* person avoid any resistance, the person defending himself was responsible for manslaughter because his act was not proportional. Self-help was interpreted, however, very broadly since a keeper of the house could defend his property not only against robbers but also against drunkards losing their way in late hours and trespassing someone else's parcel of land. In such cases, if such a person got hurt or died it was considered the moment his karmic cycle ended. Street fighters were only fined except when someone died in the fights because in such a case capital punishment was the rule. Non-intervening bystanders were also punished for not stopping violence. Persons setting a house on fire were also sentenced to death irrespective of whether someone died or not.[53]

In sum, Thai legal system was less impregnated with Buddhist ethics in the field of public and criminal law, first of all because of political reason. The extreme fear of treason and loss of political power led to the complete control of society with a constant monitoring of the moves of its members, the penalisation of Thai girls marrying foreigners, the arrest of innocent non-residents, the punishment of family members of negligent officials and the routing out of the complete family of persons called traitors for a variety of reasons. As a result, capital punishment was not abolished, like in Burma, but applied frequently for a variety of crimes in a regime which wanted to establish itself through vigour and force. This is rather the Chinese way of legal thinking. Small wonder, thus, that we will see similar laws in traditional Vietnam, a society under Chinese influence.

Procedural law has some curiosities to offer. One of them is that a free person could not launch a lawsuit in his own right but only with the help of a person higher in rank (*munnāi*) who took the case to the court of law on his behalf. The origin of this system goes back to the fourteenth century when the population was distributed into various groups and a *munnāi* was appointed to head each group. The aim of the system was to facilitate a rapid mobilisation of labour force upon the order of the king. Such corvée obligation lasted for six months in a year in the Ayutthaya

---

[53]Ishii (1986: 164–166).

period, reduced to four months in the modern period and to three months with the Code. With the help of the *munnāi* system, society was subject to state control not only in public works but also in their private affairs since their right to go to court was limited and transferred to the *munnāi*s, agents of the government. If someone started a legal action in his own right, his case was rejected and he was degraded to the position of the king's man (*phrai luang*), a lower rank from which it was difficult to escape (a way out was to became a Buddhist monk).[54]

Another curiosity is that a judge had a rather limited function in a procedure because a great deal of his tasks was transferred to officials. Judiciary was extremely complex where some courts of law were under the control of central administrative units. When a complaint was handed over, it was registered by an official who then forwarded it to the *lūk khun*, an expert who decided whether the procedure could be started or not. If he decided affirmatively, the defendant was called to answer the claims of the plaintiff. The defendant's claims were also transferred to the *lūk khun* who considered the case and chose the law to be applied. The judgment thus born was pronounced by the judge at the end of the procedure. The role of a judge was thus reduced to a minimum in a process where responsibility was taken over by *lūk khun*s, experts delegated to law courts in order to guarantee law not to be abused. The Thai king was the final authority in disputed cases because every party could appeal to him for legal remedy, but this was a risky business. Should a party lose the case against an official or a judge, he was fined in a civil case and whipped in a criminal case (combined with confiscation). By contrast, should a judge lose the case, he was whipped and fined because it was believed that a judge passed a wrong judgment because he was corrupt. Judgments were based either on documents or on oral testimonies of witnesses. Buddhist ethics however, disqualified a variety of persons from giving testimonies. Altogether thirty-three categories of people were prohibited to give evidence as witnesses, among others prostitutes, addicts of gambling, conjurers, shoemakers, fishermen, beggars, and those who are known not to live according to the basic rules of Buddhist ethics. Buddhist ethics not only disqualifies some people from giving evidence but also discourages proper legal procedure as a shameful thing. This is the reason why people of higher rank did not attend a law suit personally but were represented by their representative instead.[55]

In family law, women were classified into three categories because polygamy allowed for such a typology. A chief wife (*mia luang*) was taken to marriage by "holding the hand", a symbol referring to parental consent. A minor wife (*mia noi*) was subordinated to a chief wife while the situation of a slave wife (*thasa phalays*) was the least enviable. Parents could not force their daughter to marriage without her consent but parental consent was required as a rule for a marriage. Elopement of girls was, perhaps, a way out in the absence of parental consent, at least this is what we can infer from the law allowing a subsequent marriage later in such cases. A woman giving life to a baby was also considered a wife even when no parental consent was at hand. Long cohabitation in a house built by the "husband" also ended in a lawful

---

[54]Ishii (1986: 172–173).
[55]Ishii (1986: 166–170).

marriage without producing a child, though the time limit was not fixed exactly. These are laws with the wisdom to accept facts that could not be altered. This is why authority over women was also transferred in such cases from the parental family to the husband. Apart from such rather extraordinary cases however, a marriage was a bond between families which was bound amidst formalities. As a rule, a bridegroom had to show great respect toward the family of his bride, expressed by a plate with betel leaves and areca nuts handed over to them. If they took this present, it symbolised their consent to the marriage. A husband was called the wife's master (*chao mia*) because he could punish her and could even sell her to debt slavery. A husband can punish an adulterous wife by sending her back home and withholding all her wealth. By contrast, an adulterous man could not be punished this way by his wife, but elderly people intervened in such cases from both sides to restore family peace. A husband usually had to swear an oath to refrain from such acts in the future, a promise to be put into writing too. Should a husband continue his adulterous behaviour despite his promise not to do so, the parties could divorce, a right open for both the husband and the wife. In order to divorce his wife, a husband produced a document and handed it over to his wife. A divorcing wife had to produce such a document too, but witnesses were also necessary when handing it over to the husband. A marriage was dissolved without such documents in extraordinary cases when a husband went to a long (commercial) journey or to war. When a man took the way to a distant country (China), his wife had to wait for three years. If this time passed without receiving any sign from her husband, she could remarry. A wife of a man going to war had to wait for seven years, but someone turning into a Buddhist monk lost his wife soon.[56] These laws are almost identical with that of the Burmese, the Mon and the Lao and thus point to a common legal understanding of Southeast Asian peoples.

Finally, *lamoet,* a specific category of Thai law is worth mentioning, designating damage or tort. There are two kinds of *lamoet:* one causes damage in the property or physical integration of a person, while the second also damages public order. This typology is important because legal consequences are architected accordingly. The first form of *lamoet* is sanctioned only by compensation, while the second form is sanctioned by both compensation and corporeal punishment. One part of the compensation was to be paid to the victim and the rest to the royal treasury. The first firm of *lamoet* included various kinds of assault, manslaughter, slander and cursing. The Three Seals Code have long laws about the sum of compensation to be paid in various acts of *lamoet*. The sum for a *lamoet* rested on the age, gender and social rank of the victim which was then doubled, since it had to be divided between the kin and the royal treasury. Theft belongs, obviously, to *lamoet* but, as we have seen previously, theft was also classified as a *chon*, making theft a crime to be punished with more rigor. Those under authority were not regarded as persons proper. This is the reason why acts committed against them like sexual violence and adultery were classified under *lamoet* against property. Compensation to be paid to the parents and the husband makes this system very clear, more when the husband's right to kill the

---

[56]Ishii (1986: 175–178).

lover was eliminated by a royal decree some years before the composition of the Three Seals Code.[57]

The Three Seals Code was a milestone in Thai legal history giving the summary of traditional law. The decades after its composition saw stark colonising efforts by the Western powers which, in its turn, led to the demand for more political and legal reforms. First of all, the power of the king became disputed first among the royal family then in ever increasing circles. Meiji-reforms in Japan had a clear effect in Thailand to be felt since it was regarded as a model to be followed. Since legal reforms constituted an important part in the Meiji-program, this objective became increasingly important in Thailand too, where an additional argument was added in favour of the reforms. Accordingly, the occupation of Thailand could be avoided only if the legal system would properly be westernised and modernised according to the European pattern confirmed by the European powers. This was in fact an important aspect because during the reign of King Mongkut, unequal treaties were forced on the country guaranteeing legal immunity to foreigners which could be revised only if Thailand would erect a modern (= western) legal system (the same happened to Japan, too). King Chulalongkorn, son of Mongkut understood the pressure of times and voted for cautious reforms which he implemented during his reign. He rejected both speed and enthusiasm for reforms and rigid traditionalism standing in the way of everything new. Though he was against the idea of constitutional monarchy, he did introduce some reforms in public law and abolished old, inherited privileges. With his manoeuvring, he managed to incorporate some western-minded reforms without risking his power and social balance and was therefore able to preserve the independence of his country, a unique achievement in Southeast Asia in this century. Changes included governance, the position of the king, public administration and the judiciary. On the other hand, democratisation was by no means part of his agenda and Chulalongkorn remained an absolute monarch, though some members of the royal family and his foreign advisors and experts in law (primarily professors of law from Harvard) argued in favour of democratisation. Procrastination then ultimately led to the revolt of 1932 which produced the first constitution of the country replacing the absolute monarchy with a constitutional monarchy.[58]

Legal reforms also included private legal matters, one among them was the introduction of monogamy which generated a very long and intensive debate. The issue was raised after Chulalongkorn's death during the reign of his son who expressed his view in a long memorandum. Despite the king's clear position, the problem was not solved for decades and was left to the constitution to settle since at that time the majority already stood for monogamy (1935).[59] New codes on private and commercial law were modelled on French law with the active involvement of French legal experts showing how intensively Thai political elite turned to the French despite the influence of common law in the previous decades (1923). French domination however, lasted only for some years since a new private and commercial

---

[57]Ishii (1986: 183–187).

[58]Chulalongkorn's reforms are analysed in Engel (1975: 33–95), Harding and Leyland (2011: 7–12).

[59]Wichiencharoen and Netisastra (1968: 89–98).

code was introduced on the German model (1925) with novellae in 1928 and 1934. Thus Thai legal modernisation rested on three Western models (British, French, and German), and it was the German that were followed at the end of the day.[60]

9.4   Khmer Law

Khmer law is less known compared to the Mon-Burmese and the Thai-Lao legal traditions because sources are meagre. In addition, sources which have come down to us are important either for archaeologist or epigraphers but surely not for legal historians. Small wonder, that Khmer legal history is a less researched area but despite this, contours of Khmer legal understanding could be drawn.

It is important to note that Khmer law was not based on Buddhist ethics since Khmers were followers of Hinduism. The early history of Hinduism in Khmer society remains in darkness but according to an inherited wisdom, it goes back to earliest times, perhaps to the Funan period. Hinduism remained dominant also in the Angkor period, though Buddhism began to spread due to some Buddhist kings who favoured religious tolerance. Hinduism influenced both jurisprudence and political thinking in the form of Brahmanism both as a theory and practice. The *varna*-system, however, was not entirely adopted from India just because Khmer society was so different from the Indian. Caste-belonging was important in criminal law but hardly in any other area of law. Brahmins had significant influence in Angkor as advisors to Khmer kings and his chief officials accumulating valuable practice in public administration. Both Siva and Vishnu were venerated in the Khmer court but the former was more important in religious life because his cult was linked to the cult of ancestors, a common theme in entire Southeast Asia, and to fertility, important for human reproduction and agriculture. It was the duty of the king (*rājudharma*) to protect his subjects as an incarnation of Siva. Since economics of Angkor rested exclusively on agriculture or, properly speaking, rice production, it was the king's task to safeguard it (this is why canals and tanks were built). A Khmer ruler had thus a complex function of being a religious leader with a specific relationship to gods (pledge for rain, ancestor cult), and a victorious hero whose heroic deeds were sung by poets. Ancestor cult was a heavy burden on kings who made beautiful temples to erect, the well-known complex in Angkor being the most important among them (now protected as a UNESCO World Heritage Centre). In addition, Khmer kings were supreme judges and head of an ever expanding public administration. Despite such complex functions, Khmer kings were no despots but rather heads of an oligarchic political structure governing by concluding alliances, donations and building a clientele. Monarchic power did not extend to far away territories but concentrated on the capital and the centre of the kingdom whilst population in the periphery were sometimes not acquainted with the name of the ruler. Distant regions were governed rather by local landlords and vassals of the king whose power was rather formal. Political fragmentation was enhanced

---

[60] Kasemsup (1986: 292–293).

by geographic fragmentation since huge territories were dominated by jungle with
tigers and elephants, separating the villages from each other. Rural population did
not easily embark on longer journeys even in the early twentieth century until roads
and navigable canals were built.[61]

In such political geography, political efficiency depended on able rulers and a
centralised public administration which asserted central will against local interests
but was controlled by the ruler himself in order to stop bureaucracy to proliferate
beyond limits. Khmer kings divided their kingdoms into provinces (*visaya-pramān*)
and provinces into villages. Provincial and local leaders had to maintain internal
peace, collect revenues, organise public works and mark the borders of landed
property. Representatives of central government were unable to solve these complex
tasks and thus had to rely on the assistance of the local gentry and rural elders.
To settle conflicts of ownership on landed property was particularly difficult in an
entirely rural society. This explains why it was one among the tasks of governors
to settle such disputes.[62] In addition to governors, Khmer kings were also involved
in agricultural affairs sometimes. Contrary to some archaic kingdoms where land
ownership belonged to the king and not to private persons, the private ownership
of landed property was not restricted in Khmer society. The acquisition of lands
however, was not completely free since transactions needed the approval o fkings who
decided by their own discretion in such matters. Khmer kings could also expropriate
any land for communal interests such as construction of canals but had to properly
compensate the owner of the land.[63]

The court of Khmer kings were not only political but also cultural centres where
disciplines of Indian origin were widely known, among them jurisprudence, too.
Works on law and politics, that is, *dharmaśāstras* and *arthaśāstra*s were studied.
Manu's *dharmaśāstra* was definitely known, proven by the inscription of Yasovarman
(889–900), the fourth king of Angkor who quoted passages from this text. A royal
inscription from the eleventh century informs us that the king had maintained the
18 *mārga*s referring to the titles of claims (*mārgavyavahāra*) developed by Hindu
jurisprudence that could be taken to courts of law. Criminal law was also influenced
by Hindu jurisprudence where social rank was an important factor in specifying
punishments. Brahmins were free of capital and corporeal punishments which were
the punishments of commoners. The judiciary was complex and hierarchic with
local and central courts headed by the king as the supreme judge of the realm.
Law of procedures also followed the Hindu model, making Khmer law a faithful
follower of Hindu law in Southeast Asia. The somewhat extreme dependence on
Indian jurisprudence is also marked in legal terminology where legal terms of Indian
origin were maintained and no Khmer equivalents were developed. This is to be seen
in the name of the court of law (*sabha*), and in the chairman of the court (*sabhāpati*)
too. This is however, small wonder since the name of Angkor can also be traced back

---

[61]Chandler (2008: 53–56), Ishizawa (1986: 209–210).

[62]Ishizawa (1986: 210; 215).

[63]Ishizawa (1986: 229).

to the Sanskrit *nagara* (city).[64] The dominance of Hindu law obviously excluded influence of Buddhist ethics, to be felt in criminal law. As a result, humanisation of punishments was not on the agenda and capital punishment, usually beheading and choking in public was frequent. Interestingly, foreigners enjoyed some privileges which locals did not: if a Khmer killed a Chinese, he was executed, but if a Chinese killed a Khmer, he had only to pay a fine. Corporeal punishments included the cutting off of hands, feet, ears, and nose; the mutilation of lips; and the squeezing of the head often combined with whipping, branding the chest and the back, and tattooing the face, cruelties which sometimes ended in death. No distinction was made by gender when implementing punishments, therefore women were punished the same way as men.[65] In sum, humanism of Burmese law inspired by Buddhism is by far not reverberated in Khmer criminal law.

9.5   Buddhist Law in the Modern Period

Traditional legal thinking reigned supreme for centuries in every Southeast Asian society until western powers entered the region. Political, military and economic weakness of these countries soon manifested itself giving a stark impetus for ground breaking reforms, legal reforms included. This is why traditional ways of legal thinking (customary law, Buddhist ethics) were pushed to the background giving way to new, western-inspired ideas. Legal reforms included both form and content, that is, Indian genres of jurisprudence (*dharmasūtra, dharmaśastra*) were replaced with western forms (code) while traditional laws were also changed to western legal norms. These changes not only touched upon the surface but also basic tenets of social life, too, like family law where polygamy was abandoned and monogamy introduced. Customary law was thus on the retreat (though never disappearing completely) making western inspired legal reforms a unique experience in the history of Southeast Asian societies. However, the situation varied country by country.[66]

Thailand remained the only country which was able to defend its formal independence. However, its price was a voluntary policy of reforms, political and legal reforms being at the top of the list in order to have a legal system acceptable for European powers demanding immunity from local laws until such a modern legal system was introduced. In Burma, *dhammasats* and *rājasats* were taken over by British legislation, thus creating a mixed legal system which was administered by British judges with limited competency in Burmese law and language who turned, quite naturally, to their own laws and legal understanding. As a result, Burmese legal system became more British in which judicial precedents grew to importance. French policy was similar in the belief that no *dhammathat* was superior or even equal to

---

[64] Hooker (1978: 33–34); Ishizawa (1986: 210–211).

[65] Ishizawa (1986: 222–224).

[66] For more on the new countries' constitutional systems see Hassal and Saunders 2002, Chen 2014, Harding 2001: 217–218

the Code Napoleon. A new legislation on French legal understanding thus begun with various grade of success: taken as a whole, cities were more open to new laws while the countryside remained closed and less willing to any change. Since legal reforms were attached to colonisation and a reform policy from above, conducted by the elite sometimes against the will of its own society, its effects were contradictory. Though reforms contributed enormously to the policy to build a modern country, its relation to colonisation made these reforms a bow to foreign powers in the eyes of many. This is the reason why in Burma for example, efforts were made to get rid of the British heritage and judges symbolising colonial past were banned from the courts of law i n 1973 and replaced by others not familiar with British law. As a result of this anticolonial policy, Burma did not return to the Anglo-Saxon legal heritage considered to be an unfortunate intermezzo only lasting some decades. The career of French law in Southeast Asia was even less successful since it was introduced in entirely agricultural societies like Laos and Kampuchea where even genuine legal and political institutions had limited influence in villages near to the jungle. The formal introduction of the Code Napoleon in these societies affected them as little as its abandonment after the departure of the French. By contrast, cities were more receptive to legal innovations since international trade demanded, among others, modern institutions of commercial law, private international law, stock exchange and other devices necessary to participate in the global market. Rural communities were, obviously, not interested in these matters and continued to live according to their inherited customs regulating land disputes, issues of family law, inheritance, and communal work.[67] It is the reason why the constitution of Laos stresses the constitutional protection of the customary laws of the various ethnic groups, tribes and rural communities (Art. 8.).

Ethical foundation of law is also important in constitutional law regulating political matters. Here too, Buddhist ethics about an ideal king and its duties toward his subjects and the Western idea about political institutions and their relation to each other are at variance. To solve the conflict, each constitution developed its own way of compromise being supportive toward their inherited cultural heritage.[68] Surprisingly, ex-Hindu society of Kampuchea raised Buddhism to state religion in its new constitution (43.§) which however, guarantees freedom of religion and specifies a rather broad catalogue of human rights. This is because post-Pol Pot Kampuchea voted for a new constitutional monarchy based upon the western principle of separation of powers. Notwithstanding this constitutional liberal democracy, Buddhism is anchored in the constitution with a particular protection since Kampuchea is a Buddhist society after the Angkor period. This however, was no hindrance for the architects of the new constitution to emphasise the Angkor period as the glorious past of the country referring to it as a kind of legitimacy. All this ended in a constitutional monarchy mixing Hindu Angkor with post-Angkor Buddhism and post-Communist western democratic political ideas. This is why Kampuchea is the

[67]Huxley (2014: 181–182).
[68]For an analyses of Buddhism's role in politics see Swearer (2010: 109–128).

most Buddhist society by now in constitutional terms because no other constitution specified Buddhism as state religion.

Sri Lanka chose a different path once it became independent after 450 years of colonial rule in 1948. Sri Lanka, a Buddhist society for long, avoided raising Buddhism to state religion but guarantees freedom of religion in its stead (Art. 9. of the Constitution). This is because Sri Lanka is not entirely Buddhist, but is a society with significant Christian and Muslim minorities where Buddhism is the religion of the majority (69%). Without provoking social tensions no religion could be specified as state religion and there is also no such initiative enjoying social backing because every community is interested in preserving the status quo. This is not to say, of course, that there are no constitutional disputes concerning Art. 9. of the Constitution but these did not lead to constitutional revision. Each community has its own reason as to why conserve the existing situation. Non-Buddhist minorities wanting to preserve their freedom are obviously against any idea to change their constitutional protection. Buddhist, particularly Buddhist monks are also against the idea to have Buddhism as state religion because they fear that this would allow for the state to intervene in their affairs, a right what they want to hinder. Liberal minded Buddhist are too against such an idea because it is incompatible with the fundaments of a liberal democracy and the secular state.[69]

Interestingly, formally still socialist Laos follows the same line. After the global collapse of Communism, the Lao regime implemented significant liberalisation in the early 1990s. As a result, a constitution was born (there was no constitution between 1975 and 1991 because Party leaders considered it unimportant) which declares the freedom of religion within the framework of the chapter on human rights. The introduction to the constitution specifying the principles of the political system expressly encourages Buddhists and followers of other religions to practice all their activities which are useful for Lao society (Art.9.). The constitution thus guarantees, parallel to the protection of ethnic minorities and their customary laws, a constitutional protection also to religions among which Buddhism is the only referred to by name.

The military regime of Burma approached freedom of religion in a rather curious way in its constitution. The constitution specifies Buddhism as the majority religion without defining what this actually means. The constitution does not guarantee freedom of religion in general terms, it only protects Christianity, Islam, Hinduism and animism as historically relevant religions of Burma (Art. 362.). By contrast, abuse of religion for political aim is prohibited, a clause directed not against religious terrorism but against domestic opposition since social resistance against the military regime grew in the previous years in which Buddhist monks played significant role.

It is rather difficult to make any comprehensive claim in respect of Thailand, since by now it is the nineteenth constitution which is in force since the revolt of 1932. The constitution of 2007 prohibited Buddhist monks to be members of the legislative body (House of Representatives, Senate) or to participate in elections while the same did not apply to Muslim and Christian clerics (Art. 100.), a strange law at first glance

---

[69]Schonthal (2014: 158–164).

in a constitution which commands the state to support and protect Buddhism (Art. 79.). Time was too short to evolve an interpretation of this law by the constitutional court because a transitory constitution was born in 2014.[70] The constitutional ban on political activities for Buddhist monks could not be understood through a western lens regarding it a negative discrimination hindering monks to practice first generation human rights. Bhutan, another strongly Buddhist society with a similar constitutional dilemma could help us to understand the point. Buddhism has a long tradition in Bhutan where monks are numerous, particularly if we compare their number to the size of the country. This Himalayan country is one of the most secluded societies of the world where television was permitted only some years ago, a decision accompanied with arguments according to which it might undermine the Buddhist principles of the country. The permission was part of a modernisation program which touched upon every segment of public life, constitutional law included. As a result, a constitutional monarchy was born (2005) with its first elections in 2007, from which Buddhist monks were excluded according to arguments similar to Thai constitutional thinking. Monks are excluded from elections because politics and governance are mundane affairs and monks have already renounced their interest in this world turning their attention to mediation, the argument goes on to say. It is thus appropriate to exclude them from politics, at least, according to the official version which provoked protest and generated debate about the political role of monks. Opponents to this law agree however, that monks are excluded from politics with good reason since they should have the active right to vote only but nothing more. This is a novel thought in a country where Buddhist monks have particular role in history.[71]

To sum up, there are three constitutional models in Buddhist Southeast Asia. Kampuchean constitution raised Buddhism to state religion and thus elevated it to a unique position in the region. The majority of the constitutions guarantee freedom of religion with a specific emphasis on Buddhism (Laos, Sri Lanka,), while the third model praises Buddhist tradition but restricts political activities of Buddhist monks considerably (Thailand, Bhutan).

References

Sources

Hooker MB (1986) The law of southeast Asia: the pre-modern texts, vol 1. Butterworth, Singapore
Jardine J (1892) King Wagaru's Dhammasattham: text, translation, and notes. Rangoon. (Wagaru: Manu Dhammasattham)
Richardson D (1847) Damathat or the laws of Menoo, vol 14. American Baptist Mission Press, Maulmain. (Manugye Dhammathat)

---

[70]To the practice of the constitutional court see Harding and Leyland (2011: 178–179).
[71]Whitecross (2014: 362–365).

Wichienkeeo A, Wijeyewardene G (1986). The Laws of King Mangrai (Mangrayathammasart). The Wat Chang Kam Nan Manuscript from the Richard Davis Collection. The Australian National University, Canberra

Literature

Chandler D (2008) A history of Cambodia. Westview Press, Colorado

Chen AHY (2014) Constitutionalism in Asia in the early twenty-first century. Cambridge University Press, Cambridge

Church P (2009) A short history of south-east Asia. Wiley, Singapore

Engel D (1975) Law and Kingship in Thailand during the reign of King Chulalongkorn. Michigan papers on south and southeast Asia no 9. Ann Arbor, Michigan

Engel D, Engel S (2010) Tort, custom, and Karma: globalization and legal consciousness in Thailand. Stanford UP, Stanford

Forchhammer E (1884) The Jardine prize: an essay on the sources and development of Burmese law from the era of the first introduction of the Indian law to the time of the British occupation of Pegu—primary source edition. Rangoon

French R (1995) The golden yoke: the legal cosmology of Buddhist Tibet. Cornell University, New York

Gethin R (2014) Keeping the Buddha's rules: the view from the Sutra Pitaka. In: French R, Nathan A (eds) Buddhism and law: an introduction. Cambridge University Press, Cambridge, pp 63–77

Harding A (2001) Comparative law and legal transplantation in south east Asia. In: Nelken D, Feest J (eds) Adapting legal cultures. Oñati international series of law and society. Hart Publishing, Oxford, Portland

Harding A, Leyland P (2011) The constitutional system of Thailand. A contextual analysis. Hart Publishing, Oxford

Hassall G, Saunders Ch (2002) Asia-pacific constitutional systems. Cambridge University Press, Cambridge

Hooker MB (1978) A concise legal history of south-east Asia. Clarendon Press, Oxford

Huxley A (1996a) Thai law: Buddhist law. Orchid Press, Bangkok

Huxley A (1996b) Thai, Mon and Burmese Dhammathats: who influenced whom? In: Huxley A (ed) Thai law: Buddhist law. Orchid Press, Bangkok, pp 81–133

Huxley A (2002a) Buddhist law as a religious system? In: Huxley A (ed) Religion, law and tradition. Comparative studies in religious law. RoutledgeCurzon, London

Huxley A (2002b) Religion, law and tradition. Comparative studies in religious law. RoutledgeCurzon, London

Huxley A (2014) Pali Buddhist law in southeast Asia. In: French RR, Nathan MA (eds) Buddhism and law: an introduction. Cambridge University Press, Cambridge, pp 167–182

Ireson-Doolittle C, Moreno-Black G (2004) The Lao. Gender, power, and livelihood. Westview, Colorado

Ishii Y (1986) The Thai Thammasat. In: Hooker MB (ed) The law of southeast Asia. The pre-modern texts, vol 1. Butterworth, Singapore, pp 143–201

Kasemsup P (1986) Reception of law in Thailand, a Buddhist society. In: Chiba M (ed) Asian Indigenous Law. Routledge and Kegan Paul, London, New York

Maspero H (1978) Az ókori Kína. Gondolat Kiadó, Budapest

Modelski G (2000) World cities:-3000 to 2000. Faros, Washington

Ngaosyvathn M (1996) An introduction to the laws of Kun Borom. In: Huxley A (ed) Thai law: Buddhist law. Orchid Press, Bangkok, pp 73–81

Okudaira R (1986) The Burmese Dhammathat. In: Hooker MB (ed) The law of southeast Asia: The pre-modern texts. Butterworth, vol 1. Singapore, pp 23–138

SarDeasai DR (2013) Southeast Asia. Past and present. Westview Press, Colorado

Schonthal B (2014) The legal regulation of Buddhism in contemporary Sri Lanka. In: French R, Nathan A (eds) Buddhism and law. An introduction. Cambridge University Press, Cambridge, pp 150–167

Stargardt J (1990) The Ancient Pyu of Burma. Vol. One: Early Pyu Cities in a Man-Made Landscape. Pacsea, Cambridge

Swearer DK (2010) The Buddhist world of southeast Asia. State Uiversity of New York Press, New York

Tarling N (1992) The Cambridge history of Southeast Asia, Part 1, vol 1. Cambridge University Press, Cambridge

Taylor K (1992) The early Kingdoms. In: Tarling N (ed) The Cambridge history of Southeast Asia, vol 1. Cambridge University Press, Cambridge

Vickery M (1996) The constitution of Ayutthaya: the three seals code. In: Huxley A (ed) Thai law: Buddhist law. Orchid Press, Bangkok, pp 133–198

Whitecross R (2014) Buddhism and constitutions in Bhutan. In: French R, Nathan A (eds) Buddhism and law. An introduction. Cambridge University Press, Cambridge, pp 350–368

Wichiencharoen A, Netisastra L (1968) Some main features of modernization of ancient family law in Thailand. In: Buxbaum DC (ed) Family law and customary law in Asia: a contemporary legal perspective. Springer, The Hague

Wichienkeeo A (1996) LanNa customary law. In: Huxley A (ed) Thai law: Buddhist law. Orchid Press, Bangkok, pp 31–42

Part IV
The Chinese Legal Circle

Chapter 10
Chinese Law

10.1 Chinese Law to the Tang Period

With the study of the Chinese legal circle (China, Korea, Vietnam, Japan) we now
enter the world of state-centred legal systems. In contrast to Middle-Eastern and
Indian legal systems (Jewish, Islam, Hindu, Buddhist), law is in the Chinese legal
circle rather as the command of the state (ruler) which only allows for a very limited
influence to religion, if any. This state centred understanding of law resembling
Western style legal positivism in its heyday is however not against legal customs
and their role in legal life given it does not contradict state law by any means.
Since law is one of the main means of state control, it focuses on areas which
are important for the Chinese state, be it an empire or a small political unit in the
periods of disintegration: public administration and punishments. The system of
public administration remained intact for long centuries until the twentieth century
where changes had to be interpreted only within the inherited framework of public
law. It is true, of course that details of public administration have changed a lot
according to space and time but these changes never went as far as to create a
completely new system based on a new philosophy (sporadic experiments were put
to a halt rapidly and effectively). To guarantee law and order, public law was assisted
by a rudimentary criminal law which was rather a conglomerate of offences and
their punishments since Chinese political philosophy insists on serious punishments
as an effective tool of legal control. Since legal relationships of private individuals
had no relevance for any Chinese state, Chinese law had nothing to say about private
law which did not exist for millennia. This is the reason why private law matters
belonged to local customs with its plenty of local variants. The history of Chinese
law is, therefore, the history of public and criminal law working along identical
patterns and thus continuously repeating itself for millennia without any ground
breaking change.

The first period of Chinese legal history is the time of the Shang (Yin) dynasty
(from the thirteenth to tenth centuries BCE). Though preserved documents allow little
insight into society and law, the basic traits of a hierarchical society had probably

© Springer Nature Switzerland AG 2020   309
J. Jany, *Legal Traditions in Asia*, Ius Gentium: Comparative Perspectives
on Law and Justice 80, https://doi.org/10.1007/978-3-030-43728-2_10

already developed in this period. The most important archaeological remnants of this period are the so-called oracle bones the number of which is above two hundred thousand. In this archaic monarchy, a ruler (*wang*) not only headed the state as its political leader but had numerous religious functions as well. The foundations of public administration were already laid down at this period. Monarchs governed with the help of the chief minister (*king-si*) who headed a well-structured apparatus (an official forwarding royal orders, controller of major ceremonies, administrator of the royal treasury, chief scribe and the scribes subordinated to him). Kings' authority was unlimited in theory, but a prestigious council at the court must have had significant influence on the decisions in reality. In disputed issues, decisions were made with the help of prophecies. Agriculture was in the control of the state which regulated labour on the fields in fairly great detail: the time of sowing and harvesting was decided by the controllers of lands who also supervised the works. Since agriculture was a matter of life and death, Chinese monarchs were continuously informed about harvests proven by innumerable oracle texts coming down to us. Human sacrifice, a cruelty which was not unknown earlier became far more widespread in this age. Some of the victims were prisoners of war but even women and children were sacrificed. Needless to say, the territory of the Shang dynasty was not identical with the China of today, and was smaller than the China of Confucius. It was however, the time when the migration of the Han people begun when Chinese succeeded in acquiring more and more land to the detriment of their neighbours regarded as barbarians.[1]

The rule of the Shang was terminated by the Zhou at the end of the eleventh century, who arriving from the west occupied the capital city and incorporated the territory of the abolished state into their own. Despite this, no uniform Chinese state was created since they parcelled the occupied territory and allocated some areas to the ruler's relatives and supporters. Little is known about the early Zhou kings because sources pertaining to this period are interwoven with legends and it is very hard to identify historical facts among them. Chinese tradition considers the reign of the conquering *Wen* and his son *Wu* as the golden age, a tendency of ex post facto idealisation. Early Zhou period was a time of success and conquests, signs of decay emerged only around the eighth century BCE when the dynasty had to give up its western capital and move to the east. Based on this, Chinese chronicles distinguish two periods, the Western Zhou period (lasting up to 771 BCE) and the Eastern Zhou period (from 771 BCE up to their fall in 256 BCE), the latter with the sub-periods of the Spring and the Autumn (722–481), and the Warring States (451–221). This might be interesting for chronological considerations but certainly not for legal history since both periods witnessed the lack of a uniform state and the growing independence of smaller political units waging constant wars with each other.

In the Zhou period, rulers were called Son of Heaven (*Tianzi*) with a mandate from Heaven (*Shangdi*), a designation of unlimited power and a privilege to perform important sacrifices in person. Since the territory of the Zhou dynasty was larger than that of their predecessors, the structure of public administration was more refined and complex. Particularly the activities of the three ministers (*san lao*: 'three elders') were

---

[1]Maspero (1978: 49–52) and Schirokauer and Brown (2006: 10–12).

of importance since they were ministers of agriculture, military affairs and public works, supervised by the chief minister (*king-si*) acting in the name of the king. It was the director of multitude (*se-t'u*) who controlled rural life: this official coordinated agricultural works from sowing to harvest, but to issue market regulations, judging about minor offences and to coordinate the marriage of peasants were also issues among his competencies. The director of horses (*se-ma*) was actually the head of the army, while the director of public works (*se-kung*) looked after the building and maintenance of canals. In addition, there was a minister (*tai-cai*) managing the business of the palace and controlling the king's property (maintenance and governance of palaces). The chief official of religious matters (*cung-po*) controlled tasks related to cults. There was also a head for the administration of justice called the governor of sinners (*se-kou*). Zhou social system basically rested on land and the cult of ancestors, this is why the law of inheritance was so important ensuring the status to the chief wife and her first born son. Land ownership however, guaranteed not only material well-being and economic strength but also political power for the elite, the member of which began to establish their own rule. This is why the Zhou state disintegrated as a result of a slow but unstoppable development and how small political units came into being. These principalities formally acknowledged the supremacy of the king (no one dared to call himself *wang*) but ruled de facto autonomously. Zhou kings made every effort to assert their will by sending royal inspectors to supervise local issues from time to time but this policy was unable to hinder disintegration. All in all, the semi-independent states administered their own affairs with a relatively great freedom and their rulers passed on their authority within their families. During this period (called the Chinese feudalism), some states succeeded in acquiring hegemony (*ba*) over others, that is, made decisions in certain matters of other states, but this system functioned only for a short time and did not bring basic changes. This is why the small political units of the Warring States period made every effort to solve the conflict with both warfare and diplomacy, a tendency which highlighted the importance of the military and public administration to the detriment of civil society (this situation resembles very much the agony of the Sumerian city states before the Akkadian conquest). Small wonder, that we can witness an ever growing significance of law, because it was an effective tool to state control. In addition, old laws of the Zhou were outdated and had to be adjusted to new circumstances. Law was particularly important in Qin, where legism (*fayia*) was an important ideological factor. Though chaotic and bloody, this period was nevertheless important in Chinese legal history since it was the time when the doctrine of legism was born, advocating the superiority of law and state over society, a theory that contributed to the short-lived success of Qin and his ruler, Huang Di (for more see 3.§). It was also the period of the Eastern Zhou when Confucius lived who, seeing the anarchy of his age believed that the way out of the chaos was a return to the conditions of the idealised golden age, the Western Zhou period.[2] *Kang kao*, the Admonitions

---

[2]Li (2013: 132–134, 147–148), Salát (2003:18–20), Maspero (1978: 73–77), Schirokauer and Brown (2006: 19) and Creel (1980: 28).

of King Wu (twelfth century BCE), the very first document of Chinese law was also made in the Zhou period, stressing the social importance of filial obedience.[3]

Among warring states, it was Qin which was organised along the doctrines of legism. As a result, it was more centralised and militarized, though less developed in culture, art and ceremonies. This utilitarian way of thinking was introduced by Shang Yang, a legist thinker who persuaded the ruler to follow his line. Qin was thus divided to provinces on territorial basis while Qin society was divided into units of five families in order to control each other (e.g. they had to report crimes, see also *goningumi* in Japan). His land reforms provoked resistance and this is why Shang Yang was accused of treason by his adversaries after the death of the king and was executed on the main square of the capital city (Xianyang). Despite his personal fall, his policy had made Qin strong. Thus, Qin gained superiority over other competing states and its new ruler Ying Zheng was not satisfied with the title of *wang* any longer and took up the title of *huangdi* ('emperor') after his final victory. Since he was the first (*shi*) such an emperor, his regnal name Qin Shi Huang Di was now complete. He advocated merciless centralisation and in doing so followed earlier Qin policy, but in contrast to earlier traditions did not distribute land among his supporters. Qin Shi Huang Di introduced a uniform public administration by dividing the country into 36 provinces headed by military commanders and governors. In the interest of further centralisation he unified the monetary system, the writing systems and measures. It was he who started to construct the Great Wall as a defence against nomads but dismantled the walls of former enemy states in order to hinder resistance against his rule. In developing infrastructure, Qin Shi Huang Di built canals and linked them to rivers, and established a long imperial road network (6800 km). The emperor wanted to reduce the influence of the old feudal aristocracy, a goal that was behind his land reforms and his law obliging aristocratic families to move to the capital city where he could control them. The importance of the emperor was emphasized more than ever witnessed previously, creating something like a personal cult around his own personality. To symbolise his absolute power, Qin Shi Huang Di had a palace built for himself together with a mausoleum where the world-famous clay soldiers were found. The basis of his system was pragmatism disregarding any other consideration. This is why he is accused of having destroyed all written works considered as useless, together with Confucian scholars who were against such a policy. In short, he was a good disciple of legist thinkers who implemented all their measures carefully. While doing so, an outstanding legist thinker and states man, Li Si was his chief advisor who not only elaborated legist theory but also participated in its realisation. It is fair to claim, therefore, that the reign of Qin Shi Huang Di was not only Qin's victory but also the victory of the legist philosophy. As a result, the first totalitarian Chinese state emerged.[4]

Perhaps it is more than an accident that a collection of law written on bamboo slips (altogether 1100 pieces) was also produced in this period. These bamboo slips were found at a place called Shui HuDi creating an archaeological sensation since

---

[3] MacCormack (1996: 2).

[4] Head and Wang (2005: 67–72) and Li (2013: 236–241, 246).

this document is one of the most important sources of Chinese law containing laws of public administration and criminal law along the following structure: (1) laws on control; (2) questions and answers about Qin's laws; (3) miscellaneous laws from Qin; (4) the eighteen kinds of Qin's law; (5) samples to seals and to investigation.[5] Given the importance of the texts, numerous text editions and translations to various languages were produced in the previous decades.[6]

The victory of Qin was due to legism and the policy inspired by this philosophical school. As well was its demise. Reforms were introduced very rapidly and implemented with rigor and without hesitation in regions where social conditions were different from that of Qin. Small wonder that already during the reign of the third ruler of the Qin dynasty, an armed revolt unfolded, headed by Liu Bang, a talented commander of a peasant army who succeeded in destroying the Qin dynasty and its political power and established one of the most famous Chinese dynasties, the Han. According to their propaganda, the Han dynasty restored Confucianism and condemned legism which was believed to be the main reason of Qin's cruelty and the negligence of traditions. In practice, however, Hans continued to apply the methods of legism, particularly in law and public administration but were wise enough not to go too far and apply these methods to their extreme while emphasised the importance of traditions and Confucianism in order to have general support which they get.[7]

Han rulers learned the lessons of Zhou and Qin politics: while the Zhou ran a state which was too decentralised leading to its slow decay, Qin politics was an example of the other extreme of centralization, which quickly brought about its complete collapse. Han emperors, therefore, tried to reach the balance and create a system which was more centralised than the Zhou but less than the Qin state. As a result, the Han empire was governed from the centre but divided into local units giving role also to the local elite. These local centres were administrative units, the number of which was about thousand. This administrative system was also extended to landed properties which were donated by the ruler for local beneficiaries but did not include military administration which was a separate system. In order to hinder local elite from exceeding their power in these local centres, Han rulers regularly controlled them through inspectors who supervised their action, an effective means of control introduced by emperor Wu. Han administration was also huge in numbers since around 130,000 clerks were in their service, a figure exceeding the number of officials in the Roman Empire by far. Officials were recruited from among the families of officials (usually the first born son of an official) and the disciples of a 'university' founded in the capital which issued well trained clerks in the thousands who studied a standardised curriculum based on Confucian works and ethics.[8] Education lasted for one year and the talented graduates immediately got jobs in the offices. The institution had a few thousand students in the early Han period but their number was above

---

[5]Salát (2003: 133–233).

[6]For the English translation see Hulsewé (1985).

[7]Csikszentmihalyi (2006: 24–27).

[8]Li (2013: 206–261, 284–288).

thirty thousand in the late Han period.[9] Education was regarded as of outstanding importance which ended with examinations in which Han emperors participated in person. Questions were sometimes put forth by the emperors themselves (Wen, Wu), and it was the emperor who presided over the third, highest level of exams in the palace.[10]

Society was controlled by the legist method of rewards and punishments, the latter manifesting in criminal law. Peasants were obliged to pay poll tax, to enter the army and to do public labour. Some groups were resettled in the empire in order to hinder revolts and to enlarge arable land since it was their duty to cultivate these fields. All these resemble the centralising policy of Qin, yet Hans abolished the cruel laws of the Qin period, and did not spare symbolic gestures showing their commitment to Confucianism. Thus, books banned by the legists and their followers were not on index any longer. More importantly, Chinese law was Confucianised again. As a result, progressive doctrines of legism such as equality before law were changed to Confucian ethics according to which social rank and position was the most important factor in law, even in criminal law, where sanctions depended on the social rank of the culprit. It was not only law where Confucianism gained the upper hand, since the entire cultural life was shaped by Confucianism, the Han period being one of its heydays. After the death of Emperor Wu (141–87 BCE), the Han dynasty was becoming increasingly the prisoner of court intrigues and highly powerful military leaders. One among them was Wang Mang, who succeeded in grasping imperial power (9 BCE–23 CE) ending the rule of the Western Han dynasty. Wang Mang, well aware of the problems tried to introduce significant reforms in government and public administration but he failed to implement them. By contrast, his reforms generated dissatisfaction and a revolt ended his reign. With Emperor Guangwu (25–57), the rule of the Eastern Han dynasty began, which witnessed the ever growing political influence of the landlords who were opposed by courtiers (eunuchs, influential empresses and their relatives). In their struggle for power, both camps reduced the influence of the emperor who became an ever more insignificant figure in the empire which was on the best way to disintegration. Final collapse was brought about by the Yellow Turban Revolution in 220, but real power of the Hans ended earlier when they were unable to stop the rivalry of local warlords who waged war against each other. With no centralised state emerging from the ruins, China remained divided for centuries, the number of competing states varying by space and time (in the third century there were three kingdoms, in the fourth century there were sixteen kingdoms in the north only). It was only the Tang dynasty who led China out of this long period of political anarchy (618). Though chaotic, it was nevertheless an important period in the history Chinese (legal) thinking since both Buddhism and Daoism enjoyed widespread popularity during these centuries which left their traces also on law.[11]

---

[9]de Bary and Bloom (1999: 312).

[10]Dawson (2002: 31).

[11]Li (2013: 260–265) and Gernet (2001: 102–106; 130–131).

As seen above, 'imperial Confucianism' of the Han dynasty was not a complete denial of legism, though, it is true, law was increasingly built on Confucian ethics. In order to make sure their understanding of law, Hans promulgated a Code (Han Code), the original of which was lost, but could partially be reconstructed from quotations in other works. The Code was compiled by Hsiao Ho, a minister of Liu Bang on the basis of the Fa Ching, the earlier laws of Wei from around 200 BCE. The original text consisted of six chapters (banditism, robbery, arrest, prison, other criminal acts, adjudication), and Hsiao Ho added three more chapters to it (taxes, stables, household). This is how the Jiu Zhang Lü ('Statutes in Nine Chapters') was born. Later on, the text was enlarged with additional 51 chapters and this is how the Han Code of sixty chapters was produced. In harmony with Chinese understanding of law, the text primarily contained criminal law, specifying various criminal acts, sanctions (capital punishments such as beheading and cutting into two, execution of relatives, burning, mutilations, forced labour, castration, exile, fines, loss of office), and the laws of criminal procedure (arrest, prison, torture, evidence). In the 1980s a very large text of 1236 bamboo slips was found by the archaeologists in Zhangjiashan at a small grave which has about 500 slips of legal material with 27 articles reflecting the legal life of the early Han period. This text, too, is about criminal law (manslaughter, robbery, arrest, punishments), but there are also some market resolutions (market ordinances, prices, transport of grain). In addition, 228 bamboo slips were found in another grave (No. 247) in 1993 which contain the full description of 22 precedents.[12]

The history of the Tang dynasty (618–907) began with the revolt of General Li Yuan, who was commissioned to organise defence against the nomads but, in turn, concluded an alliance with the Turks and marched in the capital Changan and declared himself emperor as Gaozu (618–626). With the coming of the Tang, centralisation was again on the agenda in order to have a Chinese empire again after long centuries of disintegration. Tang emperors invested in administrative, military and economic reforms. Canals were constructed, waterways made navigable, and the capital city was rebuilt. The system of taxation was reshaped together with the legal systems and education. The empire was divided into ten provinces headed by officials but controlled by inspectors. The internal consolidation made the empire strong enough for large-scale conquests: the Chinese defeated the Eastern and Western Turks and extended their control over the big oases in the west, marched into North India and reduced the kingdom of Silla in Korea to a tax-paying vassal state. During their heyday (eighth century), Tang rulers developed their capital, Changan into a huge metropolis absorbing influences from Iran, Central Asia and India and prouded themselves to have the biggest city on Earth with a population of two million. Conquests, however, lent authority to military leaders who begun to assert their own political will already during the eighth century (see, for instance, An Lushan's revolt). As a consequence of a domestic struggle for power, territories won by conquests were lost (Silla, Vietnam) while provincial leaders and military commanders

---

[12]Head and Wang (2005: 86–92), Li (2013: 288–290), MacCormack (2004: 51–52), Fairbank and Goldman (2006: 62–63) and Csikszentmihalyi (2006: 29).

acquired ever growing independence. Finally, a revolt swept away the power of the Tang (907) giving way to another century of fragmentation.[13]

In reshaping public administration, Tang rulers followed earlier patterns but adjusted the structure to their own needs. The supreme council, responsible for the most important decisions was headed by the emperor assisted by leading officials. The secretariat edited official documents while the chancellery forwarded imperial orders and checked their implantation. Six ministerial bodies organised matters important for state administration (public administration, military, justice, economy, public works, matters of ceremony). The judiciary was headed by the *Dalisi* ('supreme court'), a court of law for complicated legal cases without the consent of which no capital punishment could be executed. Waterways, arsenals, library and the palace guard were also controlled by their separate offices. This enormous apparatus was supervised by the office of control (*yushitai*) investigating abuses, corruption and the complaints of commoners. Important offices were located in the capital city of Chang'an, on an area of 4.5 km^2 called the 'imperial city', surrounded by walls south of the palace.[14] Tang period witnessed the increasing importance of Buddhism and Daoism. In fact, Buddhism enjoyed its glory in China in the Tang period, never witnessed previously and later. Though Buddhism already entered China in the first century, it only began to impress Chinese society when the texts of the Buddhist Canon were translated into Chinese. Empress Wu was perhaps the greatest patron of Buddhism while the majority of the Tang emperors rather preferred Daoism. Despite its toleration, Tang emperors always kept an eye on Buddhism in order to hinder a limitless intellectual influence which could jeopardise the foundations of a Chinese state.[15]

Law reform was an important achievement of the Tang period, ensuring a distinguished position to it in Chinese legal history. In promulgating their Code, Tang emperors followed old patterns and compilations. One among them was the law book of Wei, produced upon the emperor's order in the third century, which was an abridged version of the Han Code with some minor structural modifications. This law-book called Xin Lü (Wei Lü) is lost by now but had serious impact on contemporary China as it was also the pattern for the Tai Shi Lü (Jin Lü), a Code promulgated in the western Ch'in kingdom. This work, compiled by 14 Confucian scholars, consisted of 20 chapters dealing with criminal law, taxes, market ordinances and some issues of public administration. The Tang Code was built on this unbroken chain of legal tradition in which no ground breaking novelties were introduced. In fact, the excellence of the Tang Code is not to be found in its new ideas but in its system and logic which make it the first true systematic work, a tribute to contemporary Chinese jurisprudence. What we call now the Tang Code is however, a collection of laws promulgated by different Tang emperors. The first law was already produced upon the order of Gaozu in 617 which reduces criminal acts sanctioned with capital punishment to four (manslaughter, robbery, treason, and desertion from the army).

---

[13] Fairbank and Goldman (2006: 76–79), Gernet (2001: 191, 205–207) and Head-Wang (2005: 116).

[14] Gernet (2001: 194–195).

[15] Fairbank and Goldman (2006: 79–81) and Schirokauer and Brown (2006: 112–113).

A new variant was produced in 653, and then again the law was issued in 737, the variant known today corresponds to the Code of 737. Given its extreme importance, the text was copied for centuries and this is how the Code was preserved for us completely.[16]

The 502 articles Code consists of 12 books divided into 30 chapters. The backbone of the Code is again criminal law but there are legal matters, organised into separate books, which were also worth mentioning, such as the family, the army, the royal bodyguard, the payment of customs, the process of adjudication and the power of officials. The Code specifies ten criminal deeds (such as instigation to rebel, treason, incest, denial of child's obedience), which threaten the structure of the Chinese family and the authority of the state. Though not all of them were punished by death, no clemency was granted in these cases. The structure of the Code is this: (1) General principles; (2) The imperial guard; (3) Laws about public administration; (4) Marriage and household; (5) State stables and granaries; (6) Illegal collection of taxes; (7) Violent acts and robbery; (8) Attacks and accusations; (9) Fraud and forgeries; (10) Mixed rules; (11) Arrest and escaping; (12) Sentence and jail. Interestingly, the Code is organised around the number five, an important number in Chinese cultural heritage. The commentary written to the Code notes that insistence on the number five is actually based on the analogy of the five elements and it was included in the law as its imitation. This is why the law already defines five different punishments, classifies family and blood relations into five grades, and specifies five groups of privileges (when ruling about punishments).[17] The first part of the Code is particularly interesting because it has a chapter on general matters of criminal law like accomplices and associates, the execution of punishments, circumstances which mitigate punishment (age: below 15 and above 70), privileges of the royal family, and amnesty.[18]

10.2 Chinese Law from the Tang to the Fall of the Qing Dynasty

The disintegration of Tang Chine was again followed by a political chaos which was ended by the military commander Zhao Kuangyin, founder of the Song dynasty (960–1276). The unification of the country was however a long process, completed only by his successor Taizong (976–997). Military success was reduced however, to domestic fighting while attempts abroad were proven to be failures: Vietnam regained its independence and pushed back the attacks of the Song; the emperor was forced to conclude a disadvantageous treaty with the Khitan Empire, an emerging power in the northeast to which the Chinese had to pay indemnity annually. Because of the lack of overwhelming military power, neither the strategy of force nor the strategy

---

[16] Head and Wang (2005: 110; 118).

[17] Head and Wang (2005: 120; 124–125).

[18] As to the relevant passages of the Code see Johnson (1979: 49–61, 88–104, 150–152, 197–235).

of diplomacy were able to guarantee the Songs to be as powerful as the Tangs were. Despite this, the Song dynasty remained in power for long centuries and only the Mongol invasion destroyed them in 1276.[19]

Song power was consolidated by Taizong (976–997), the second emperor who created a simpler but practical and more efficient administration, compared to its predecessors. The system was centralised, more than previously, giving considerable power to chief ministers, obviously not without political hazard. The supreme council, headed by the emperor in person continued to be the most powerful body deciding in every important matter, political or legal. Members of the Council (5–9) expressed their views about issues on the agenda and voted, though the final decision was, of course, the emperor's. Public administration was organised along three bigger units. One of them was the 'three offices' for monetary matters such as the budget, state monopolies and the revenues paid by society (industry and trade), the other unit dealt with issues related to the armed forces, while the secretariat controlled the administration of justice, the officials' exams and their promotions. The system of exams was created by the Tang but reached its peak under the Song. In the Tang period, a successful exam was not followed automatically by an appointment to an office because various methods of recruitment were also employed, such as recommendation, a risky business because a person recommending someone was responsible for all the mistakes of the recommended person. The system of exams was reshaped in the Song period and a three-tier system was introduced in order to broaden the social base of the officials. Needless to say, a school system was also created in the capital and in the provinces to open the gates for talented persons of any social background. As a result, an autonomous body was created with competent officials which did not tolerate courtiers (eunuchs, favourites, families of empresses) to interfere into the affairs of the state, an anomaly which troubled previous dynasties enormously. On the other hand, it was extremely hard to control such a huge apparatus giving considerable power to ministers heading it. Only internal rivalries and confrontations were able to counter-balance ambitious officials. Despite this shortcoming, Song bureaucracy contributed to the stability of the political system and evolved into a barrier to progress only later.[20]

The examination system was organised hierarchically and was constantly more demanding. The first level of exam was organised locally, followed by the second level in the capital city. The final, third level of exam had to be passed in the palace, in the presence of the emperor. Attempts were made to develop an objective and anonymous system of examinations, free of family influence and patronage because it was in the interest of the system to recruit the most talented persons for the job. For this purpose, the tests of the exams were numbered in order to make them truly anonymous. In addition, the texts of the exams were copied by scribes before they were distributed for correction so that no one could identify the author out of calligraphic characteristics. Examinations or, properly speaking, the entire system rested on neo-Confucianism (a Western academic term unknown in China) since according

---

[19]Fairbank and Goldman (2006: 113–114).
[20]Gernet (2001: 241–242) and Lee (2000: 77–78).

to an imperial decree the curriculum for the examinations consisted of the classical writings of the Confucian school. Neo-Confucianism was more than a return to the doctrines of Confucius since it was shaped along the disputes with Buddhism and Daoism which left their traces on it. As a result, neo-Confucianism became more systematic and doctrinaire than previously, though no systematic works were produced. The cost of ideological unity was its distance from reality, a serious blow to the system. Exams were not about the administrative capabilities of the candidate but about his knowledge of Confucianism, the philosophical texts, poems and the writing of essays. Small wonder, that critics and opponents to the examination system were numerous. Despite their remarks, the system was not abolished up to 1906.[21] Examinations were very hard, demanding very long time to prepare, sometimes, in fact, a life-long learning. Exams for higher offices were more demanding, though there was no guarantee for a job after a successful exam. The rank of *jinshi* (accomplished scholar) was due to very few who could erect a triumphal arch in front of their house and in whose honour a festive dinner was organised. But even such an academic career was no guarantee for a job because there were less proper offices then scholars.[22]

Legal system was also based on Tang patterns but modified where Songs saw a need for reform. A new code was promulgated already in the fourth regnal year of the first Song emperor (963). It was an almost word by word repetition of the Tang Code with some insignificant modifications, albeit social and economic conditions were rather different from that of the previous centuries. Perhaps the enormous prestige of the Tang Code hindered any change in the text. Law was brought near to social reality, not with the help of the Code but with imperial decrees supplementing the Code, a secondary law making which did not jeopardise the authority of the inherited Tang Code. With the passage of time, imperial decrees were abundant. This is the reason why these texts were collected and edited in a separate volume. Altogether twenty collections of decrees (*pien-ch'ih*) were produced in the Song period, a great number proving the claim of a contemporary thinker according to whom the collection of imperial decrees had actually replaced the Code. In addition to decrees, 'legal manuals' summarising all relevant norms to particular cases were also produced in order to assist proceeding officials (*t'iao-fa shih-lei*). Moreover, important precedents of the courts of law were also summarised in separate volumes (*tuan-li*, 'examples of decisions') to facilitate the work of the judiciary.[23]

Law was seen to be the tool of officials and the judiciary, but not something for commoners. This is the reason of the secrecy of the legal norms in the Song period. According to this way of thinking, it was not appropriate to inform society about law because in such a case they would seek for legal gaps in order to circumvent the law to persuade their own interests. Therefore law should be kept in secret, while society has to submit itself to Confucian law and ethics and be afraid of the consequences of their violation. Needless to say, laws were not made public when creating new laws.

---

[21]Nansen (1997: 544) and Schirokauer and Brown (2006: 139–140).

[22]Dawson (2002: 42–44).

[23]Miyazaki (1980: 56–58) and Head and Wang (2005: 144–146).

What is more: the possession of legal texts was a criminal act: anyone possessing, copying or printing (printing was already known in China at that time) a piece of text of a code or imperial decree was to be punished with whipping (100 blows with a bamboo). In short, law was of no use for civil society because it was designed exclusively to the officials and the judiciary. Despite this, industry and trade were developing, accompanied by extensive banking transactions, the number of China's inhabitants was doubled, academic life flourished, to which printing was a great technical assistance (130 volumes of the Confucian classics were printed between 932 and 953, followed by the classics of Buddhism).[24]

A completely new understanding of society and law was brought about by Wang Anshi and his reform movement in the eleventh century. Wang Anshi was a chief minister from the south who brought along a more liberal attitude from his place of birth which was characterised by a more free trade and economic development in that period (as well). Wang Anshi opposed the dominant state economics and saw in the obstacles bureaucratic rules which hinder economics to prosper. This, of course, was a view completely at variance with inherited Chinese understanding of state, law and economics. Small wonder that Wang Anshi was in office only for less than a decade (1068–1076) until he was forced to resign, and when he was appointed chief minister for the second time (1078) he was again victim of a conspiracy in 1085. Wang Anshi believed in economic prosperity which would enrich state and society alike. Among the important factors hindering economic development was a n unjust taxation system which did not allow peasants, craftsmen and merchants to prosper. With a new taxation system, Wang Anshi wanted to create a more economic friendly legal environment which would make both society and state grow. Songs were in need of more strength and economic development since attacks from the north threatened their position and more revenue from a prosperous society was in a dire need. Wang Anshi, therefore, introduced a series of new laws along these principles between 1069 and 1073. He reformed the taxation system, regulated the price of grain, introduced state loans with low interest rate, expanded the irrigation system and started some state enterprises. In order to enhance efficiency, he increased the salary of officials and reformed their curriculum, giving more room for practical training (law, economics) at the cost of philosophy. As a result, revenues significantly grew. He also reduced the punishment for the possession of laws and organised a new, cost-efficient army. Though focusing on efficiency and economic development, he also had an eye for those who were in need of public help. It was he, therefore, who established the first orphanages and poorhouses, public storehouses and hospitals in Chinese cities where the poor, coming from the countryside caused some problems. To these institutions, inalienable landed property was attached which ensured permanent income to finance their activities. This form of a 'foundation' had been spreading increasingly in the Song period because wealthy families also created such institutions in order to support

---

[24]Head and Wang (2005: 146–150) and Miyazaki (1980: 58).

their clans,[25] making this institution very similar to *waqf*s known from Islamic law (see Chapter Three 4.§ 2).

Wang Anshi's reign was just an interim period and his reforms could not stop the decline of the Songs in the long run. When conquering Mongols entered China, there was no military force to resist them. Mongol invasion already started with the attack of Temüjin (Genghis Khan) in the North of China, followed by the siege and occupation of Peking (1215). Temüjin's successors, Ögedei and Möngke continued the invasion. Möngke appointed his younger brother Kublai to govern China who was declared emperor in 1260, thus founding the Yüan dynasty. Mongols continued their victorious march further south where first the southern Songs fell victim, followed by Vietnam, Burma and Kampuchea. Mongols even sent marine expeditions against Japan. Though very impressive at first glance, these campaigns to distant regions were rather victories of symbolic value since the Mongol empire grew to a size which was too big to govern from one centre. Small wonder that these regions were lost to them soon and Mongols concentrated on governing China. This was a hard task since Mongols had no experience in running a state with a complicated public administration ('China could be occupied from horseback but could not be governed from there'). Not being familiar with Chinese institutions, Mongols first introduced their own and some Central Asian traditions which were, of course, out of touch with contemporary Chinese reality. When they started to govern from Khanbalik (Peking) in the last decades of the thirteenth century they had taken over some Chinese institutions but still remained mistrustful to the subjugated people. Mongols governed China on ethnic bases, creating a segregation between the ruling Mongols, the Hans (Chinese) and the people of 'coloured eyes' (Turkic peoples, Tibetans, Tanguts, etc.). Most important positions could be filled only by Mongols which were hereditary offices. Less significant positions were also open for those of coloured eyes (often Muslims were appointed to deputies), while only the lowest positions of public administration were left to the Chinese where they were supervised by a Mongol official. It was so humiliating in many cases that southerners denied to work there and left public administration. As a result, Chinese influence and expertise decreased significantly in public administration during the Mongol period. Seeing the decline, the examination of officials was reintroduced (1315), but it was only a parody of the previous system because Mongols were guaranteed their share with quotas while the most educated south Chinese deliberately turned their back to public administration. Social segregation was also the underlying principle of criminal law, where crimes were punished according to ethnicity: if a Chinese killed a Mongol he was punished by death and his family had to bear the cost of burial while if a Mongol killed a Chinese he was only fined. Ethnic segregation was dubbed with a system of taxation with the only aim of exploitation. Mongols wanted to profit from Chinese economic success and tax was a very easy way to have their share. This is the reason why extra taxes were levied on the prosperous southern regions without an eye on how counterproductive it was in the long run. Chinese merchants were made less competitive in their own

---

[25]Schirokauer and Brown (2006: 144–145), Gernet (2001: 243–245) and Miyazaki (1980: 59; 70–71).

country with privileges given to non-Chinese (mostly Iranian and Central Asian) merchants. Chinese society reacted with continuous revolts and a stark demographic decline (1220: 108 million inhabitants; 1381: 67 million inhabitants).[26]

Decline and negligence was also not spared to Chinese law, particularly in the first half of the Mongol period when Chinese law was replaced by Mongol customs. Decrees were already issued by Genghis Khan in 1212 and 1229 which significantly differed from Chinese understanding of law. The Chih-yüan hsin-ko ('The new rules of Yüan'), promulgated in 1291 was a work based on Mongol legal tradition but also contained traditional Chinese legal elements. In the subsequent decades, Chinese officials did their best to bring Chinese law back and produced drafts of new codes in the hope of approval. Finally, their efforts bore fruit in 1346, when a Code entitled Chih-cheng t'iao-ko was issued as the last important legislative act of the Yüan dynasty, which was the model of the Korean code of 1391. It is a large collection with 150 decrees, 1760 articles and more than one thousand precedents. In addition to this Code, two important works were also put into writing. One of them is Ching-shih ta-tien ('The Great Institutes of State Authority') which was edited upon the command of Emperor Wenzzong, an educated ruler who was regarded as a great patron of Chinese culture. The first part of the work has an overview of important laws which corresponds more or less to the Tang Code, while the second part has *novellae* which were introduced during the Mongol period. The other work is *called Hsing-fa chih* ('Treatise on Punishment and Law'), which is part of the official chronicle of the Yüan dynasty. It is also about important legal institutions and therefore is not different in its essence from the *Ching-shih ta-tien*. Mongol rule brought about some changes in substantive law. Among punishments, choking was abolished, exile was defined more precisely (southerners were exiled to the north and vice versa) while new sanctions were introduced, such as compulsory military service, the cutting off of hands and new fines (the payment of the cost of burial and medical treatment). At the same time new laws limited torture and reorganised the supervision of prisons.[27]

Resistance against the Mongols was ultimately successful when a talented commander, Zhu Yuanzhang joined forces with the Red Turbans. Zhu Yuanzhang became emperor in 1368 (Hongwu) and thus a new dynasty, that of the Ming, was established. Contrary to the Songs and the Mongols who favoured commerce, the new dynasty chose agriculture as its economic base. Soon after the consolidation of their power, Ming emperors started to reorganise agriculture, restored the irrigation system, settled labourers on abandoned and fallow lands, and registered landed property and their inhabitants. As a result, agriculture started to flourish securing revenues for the state. These acts have already shown what the Mings believed in: statism and centralisation. Ming rulers classified society into peasants, soldiers and artisans, a rigid and hereditary system denying any social mobility, perhaps a legacy of the Mongol period. Soldiers lived around the borders, artisans around the capital city

---

[26]Schirokauer and Brown (2006: 177), Head and Wang (2005:152–154) and Gernet (2001: 288–292).

[27]Head and Wang (2005: 156–157; 171–173).

while peasants everywhere in arable land. The affairs of these three strata were controlled by three ministerial units such as the ministries of economics, war and public works. Centralisation was already manifested in Hongwu's reign who put the central secretariat governing the administration of the court and the six ministries (of public administration, taxes, ceremonies, war, justice and public works) under his direct control. Parallel to this, he set up the 'high command of the five armies' to control the army. Centralisation was personal rather than institutional, which was driven by the extreme mistrust of Hongwu who saw enemies everywhere. The show trial against his erstwhile companion, Hu Weiyong was also conceived in this spirit of mistrust. Hu Weiyong was accused of rebellion, secretly being in touch with the Japanese and the Mongols to overthrow the emperor. In this infamous trial of Chinese legal history, fifteen thousand people were brought to court, all of them supporters of Hu Weiyong. Needless to say, the trial ended with the execution of Hu Weiyong. After the elimination of his rival, the emperor centralised further and set up a secret police to spy on the bureaucracy. These decisions had long lasting effects because Huangwu's mistrust shaped not only his own reign but also an entire system for centuries. Small wonder that the number of officials was very low (even in the seventeenth century there were only ten to fifteen thousand), while public administration was becoming increasingly oppressive as a result of the activities of the secret policy, yet at the same time isolated from social reality. This is the reason why landowners were asked more and more to help implementing decrees in the countryside. This opened the gate, obviously, for corruption to flourish, yet created a system which tolerated a flexible adaptation to local customs. In the spirit of mistrust and also because of the inefficiency of the system, families were grouped into units of ten with the task of maintaining order, collecting taxes, organising public work and reporting about misdeeds and crimes. The destruction of a well-functioning public administration opened the way to court intrigues, a political illness for long. Though Hongwu prohibited eunuchs to interfere into political affairs on the cost of a death penalty, in reality they had considerable power, particularly when they had acquired the right to control the secret police from the fourteenth century onwards. The routing of an efficient bureaucracy was also manifested in numbers and symbols. After paralysing the central administration, Hongwu had to deal with almost every case in person: he received 1600 documents in eight days, resulting in 200 documents per day on average, an impossible number to study carefully given all the cases presented to him. Hongwu had no time to talk and listen to his ministers, but when they succeeded in arranging an audience they could talk to him but only standing on knees (Tang ministers seated in the presence of the emperor while Song ministers had to stand).[28]

Hongwu's personal and political style, combined with centralisation and oppression also manifested itself in law. Since Hongwu accused the Mongols of not being strict enough in legislation, his aim was to eliminate the 'laxities' of the Mongols. This is how the Ming Code came into being, a law which was neglected as a model

---

[28] Fairbank and Goldman (2006: 130), Schirokauer and Brown (2006: 191–192) and Gernet (2001: 307–310; 318).

by the Japanese because of its brutality. *Da Ming lü* (Great Ming law) was promulgated in its final form in 1389 after twenty years of preparation and five variants. The emperor set up a committee to compile the Code which they did on the basis of the Tang Code. Similarly to Napoleon, the first Ming emperor participated personally in the codification and determined the final version of the text. His successors did not modify the Code they only added some minor additions to it. Though modelled on the Tang Code, the Ming Code arranged the law more systematically than its predecessor did and became a pattern to be followed in the next centuries. The structure of the Code follows the six ministries devoting six chapters to their affairs with the first, introductory chapter about general principles and terminology: I. General principles; II. Law of public administration: how to prepare orders and official documents; III: Private law: marriage and law of inheritance, land ownership, market ordinances, taxes and customs; IV: Ritual rules: state ceremonies and their rules; V. Military law: bodyguard, palace guard, military administration, border defence, postal services; VI: Criminal law: some crimes (manslaughter, robbery, corruption, slander, sexual crimes), criminal procedure and prisons; VII. Public works: irrigation system and construction works. A logical structure however, could not save the legal system from stark failures which were again due to the first emperor. Though Hongwu thought of law as an important tool, the regulations of which had to be followed, it was he who first violated the Code whenever law stood in the way of his interest. As a result, he made decisions in individual cases against the law (and, obviously, there was no institution which could correct a wrong judgment) and, what is more, issued decrees against the laws of the Code, creating a contradictory legal environment. Individual decisions were about brutal punishments, in fact more brutal than the Code has in cases of corruption and revolt by officials and soldiers, the trial of whom ended in mass massacres more than once (see also Hu Weiyong's case). It was, of course, not about law but about the emperor's paranoia, who was aware of how destructive his actions for the entire system were and prohibited his successor to follow his line in vain who continued to issue decrees being at variance with the Code.[29]

Ming China aggravated all the inherited illness of previous Chinese empires and was unable to solve them, sometimes even made them worse. Lawlessness by the emperor combined with brutal punishments, an oppressive but insufficient public administration and a political chaos created by courtiers (eunuchs who did not refrain from poisoning the emperor standing in their way) in the centre and landlords in the countryside made the government weak both domestically and internationally. Revolts broke out here and there and finally the Chinese were unable to resist conquering Manchus in the seventeenth century. This is how the rule of the Qing dynasty began and with this China came again under foreign control. The victory of the Manchus was due to their modern weaponry and the professional Chinese military leaders who were in their service. Chinese were in great number not only in the Manchu army but also in their public administration in the subsequent centuries, though the early period of the Manchu government was not about Chinese traditions. By contrast, Manchus wanted to follow Mongols in their attempt to segregate

---

[29]Head and Wang (2005: 180–189).

society and introduce an exploitative taxation policy. For instance, the hair style of the Manchus was made obligatory with a capital punishment for not obeying this law. Since this hairdo was the custom of the people of the steppe being at variance with Chinese customs several revolts broke out against it with preventive executions in retaliation. Peasants were divested of their lands and forced into communities where no one was allowed to leave only at the cost of death penalty. Despite rigor, running away became permanent. This policy however, led to economic decline and Manchu government realised after fifty years that it was high time to change it. As a result of a new policy, agriculture started to grow rapidly while tax burdens were also reduced. Parallel to this development, both industry and trade began to grow, making the eighteenth century the period of flourishing and wealth shown among others by demographic figures: in 80 years, China grew from 143 to 360 million. Economic strength contributed to a foreign policy which made the Qing empire the largest Chinese state ever, with a bigger size than that of the present People's Republic of China (because it included Taiwan, Outer Mongolia and some outer peripheral areas occupied by the Russians since). Qing China was thus, no longer a home to the Hans but a multinational state. This is why official documents were edited in four languages (Chinese, Manchu, Tibetan and Mongolian) and multilingual dictionaries were also produced. The territories inhabited by the Chinese were governed by their traditional methods of administration, yet the positive discrimination of Manchuria continued in governance. The government relied on the assistance of the tribal leaders where they thought necessary (e.g. the Mongols), while in the newly occupied Xinjiang province military administration was introduced. Centralisation, a key term in every Chinese state continued but Qing emperors rewarded the service of the officials with a very low salary which gave way to large scale corruption and a paralysed administration. The examination system was not changed despite harsh critiques, producing officials well versed in Confucian classics, philosophy, literature and arts but without any skill in law and economics. This is why proceeding district officials (*hsien*) relied on the assistance of secretaries who were private professionals payed by the official out of his own pocket. The secretaries were experts in tax and law with a considerable salary, one of the many anomalies of the system.[30]

Manchus continued Chinese traditions in law, manifested at that time in the Ming Code. Two years after the siege of Peking (1644), the new Qing Code, the Ta Ch'ing lü chi-chieh fu-li ('Great Qing Code with Commentaries and Decrees') was produced which followed the Ming Code both in its content and structure. The legal material was still divided into seven chapters, six of them corresponding to the six ministries while the seventh was about general rules. The majority of laws was a word-by-word repetition of the Ming Code to which no real changes were added during the next century. As a result, eighteenth century China had a Code the content of which was composed five hundred years earlier. Obviously, such a law had few things in common with contemporary social reality, forcing Qing emperors to rule with decrees (*li*). With the passage of time, the growing number of decrees were collected into

---

[30]Gernet (2001: 373–375), Head and Wang (2005: 215–216) and Schirokauer-Brown (2006: 235–238, 240–242, 250–254).

separate volumes and this is how Hsien-hsing tse-li ('Currently Valid Decrees') was produced in 1679, which was continuously enlarged in the subsequent years. Decrees and their collection were far more important than the Code itself, firstly because they were closer to social reality, and secondly because in case of contradiction, it was the law of the decree and not that of the Code which was to be followed, despite the fact that the hierarchy of legal sources dictates just the opposite. Finally, the texts of the Code and the earlier decrees were united in a single volume in 1740, and this is how the Ta Ch'ing lü-li was produced, which had to be revised every third year in order to incorporate new laws to it. In addition to these compilations, legal commentaries were also produced, written by private individuals and also upon governmental commission in order to explain less understandable laws to officials implementing the law. Commentaries were of two kinds. Short commentaries added to the text of the Code (corresponding to the glosses of Medieval Europe) comprise the first, while large commentaries were edited in separate volumes in the second. If neither the law nor the commentaries were helpful for the official in a particular case, he could solve it with the help of collected precedents or by way of analogy.[31]

10.3   Chinese Legal Thinking

Though Confucianism is believed to be *the* Chinese social and legal thinking, it is by far not the case. Since China is a very complex society for millennia it is obvious that no theory could grasp this complexity in itself. While one theory highlights elements which are important in its argument, others focus on factors that are meaningful for their understanding of law and society. For Confucianism, for example, tradition, ceremonies, ethical principles, education and a harmonious, ideal society were important with a minimal state and a very limited room for punishments. By contrast, legism neglected almost everything that Confucian thinkers thought important and highlighted law, punishment and the overwhelming importance of the state in creating not a harmonious, but a realistic and efficient social order. Both theories are Chinese not only because both were formulated in China by Chinese thinkers but, most importantly, because both reflect Chinese social reality: Confucians are for an ideal society based on patriarchal families while legists for a centralised state with its pragmatism and struggle for power. Since both traditionalism and statism are dominant features of China for millennia, no one can claim that one theory is more Chinese than the other. No wonder, thus, that after the formative period when these two opposing theories were formulated, they began to merge both in theory and political practice. As seen in the previous chapter, this tendency already started in the Han period when ideology rested on Confucianism but political and legal practice on legism, a combination which has been followed ever since. In addition to these two mainstream theories, Daoism and Buddhism also contributed to Chinese understanding of morality and law. Law is not important either for Daoism or for Buddhism

---

[31] Fairbank and Goldman (2006: 184) and Head and Wang (2005: 199–209).

and they also do not have too much to say about how to run a government efficiently. By contrast, both have strict moral principles with an eye on the transcendent world, which supplement the rather mundane theories of Confucianism and legism. Daoism and Buddhism, it is true, were on the side line of Chinese legal thinking, yet their contribution could not be neglected.

10.3.1 Confucianism

Confucius (Kong Qiu or Kong Fuzi, that is, Master Kong; Latinised by the Jesuits in the seventeenth century) came from a poor family and lived at the turn of the sixth and fifth centuries BCE. He was in the service of some rulers as minister but was not very successful in his office. He started to teach at the end of his life and attracted disciples sympathizing with his views. He was no man of letters and composed no written work or, at least, not a single work has reached us. By contrast, he was a great teacher whose doctrines were collected and put into writing by his disciples. His doctrines, therefore, could be reconstructed only from the writings of later Confucian scholars with the constant problem of authenticity. Lunyu (Annales), a work attributed to him is also no exception and is in fact the compilation of later generations. Confucius believed in traditions and their overwhelming importance in social life. This is the reason why he denied teaching anything new. By contrast, he insisted on not inventing new ideas but only to emphasise old doctrines. Thus, he commented and explained old texts dealing with rites, music and literature. In so doing, he did not organise his teaching into a coherent system which was the work only of later generations.[32]

Harmony and social justice, guaranteed by benevolent governance was in the focus of Confucius' thoughts. Modern commentators believe that it is due to the fact that he lived in the Zhou period when small political units were in constant warfare producing anarchy and chaos and what Confucius thought was an idealised golden age of the previous centuries when traditions and order contributed to the welfare of society. What he wanted was to restore this golden age with its idealised kings who ruled as outstanding individuals of merit and wisdom but not through law, force and punishments. Rulers were benevolent fathers and teachers whose personal example is a guide enough for society to refrain from wrongdoings and to follow him. Kings were at the top of a hierarchic social structure, a corner stone of Chinese social experience, an idea in fact without any novelty. Emphasizing inequality as an experience of our world is however, important for Confucians who believed that it is difference and not equality that corresponds to mundane conditions. Instead of equality (which is against experience and thus an irrational thought), harmony in inequality should be created in family, society and politics. People are different by their morals, abilities and opportunities which must be taken into consideration also in the division of labour. Confucians separated intellectual work from physical labour,

---

[32]Li (2013: 210–211), Nansen (1997: 535–536) and Maspero (1978: 361–367).

emphasising the importance and prestige of the former. Intellectual work is that of the scholars and officials whose task is to study, teach and govern. It is the obligation of the multitude of physical labour to supply intellectuals with the goods produced by them. This theory about the division of labour is not a value-neutral, pragmatic division for an efficient political economy but an elitist ideology guaranteeing stark privileges for intellectuals who enjoyed higher salaries, better garments and shelter. This hierarchical system should be followed both on macro and micro level since the governance of society must be modelled on a patriarchal family where the head of the family enjoys privileges to the detriment of wife and children.[33]

Privileges are however connected to obligations, creating a social web where persons of privileges also have more duties in the favour of others while people of limited competencies are expected less. Proper behaviour is to realise the position of the individual in this web of social relations and to act accordingly. A father should always act as a father, a scholar as a scholar, a peasant as a peasant, etc. What regulates this complex system of behaviour linked to rank, age and social position is called *li*. *Li* is a term of a complex meaning without any corresponding equivalent in other languages and even Confucian scholars refrained from defining *li* precisely. *Li* is something that could be learned by studying the works and deeds of old sages. Manners, morals, customs are only approximate translations and interpretations to explain *li* which resembles Roman *mos* and *exempla*. This understanding of *li* made Confucians look backwards to the postulated golden age where the model behaviour of outstanding individuals could be found, a theory which made Confucianism conservative, vehemently criticised by its opponents. This intellectual privilege attributed to sages of old ages also radiated to their work, the knowledge of which was a prerequisite to enter the class of scholars and officials. This is the reason why these works featured in the curriculum of the officials who were not able to pass rigid exams without a deep knowledge of old works even in the nineteenth century. With the help of *li,* everyone can find a guideline relevant to his/her own position, family, background and profession. If everyone would be aware of his/her rights and duties, disputes could be avoided, unlimited individual demands be restricted, and harmony restored in society. Just rule and proper governance is thus to maintain a social system based on *li*.[34]

Confucians attributed prominent role to five social relations (*wu-lun*) of which four are hierarchic such as the relations between (a) nobles and commoners; (b) persons of higher and lower social level; (c) older and younger; (d) close and distant relatives. The first three sets of relations are the most important, called the three bonds (*san–kang*) in the Han period. The first two relationships are quite complex and include several kinds of relationship such as ruler and subject, king and minister, father and son, husband and wife. The distance in the degree of relations is important because rights and obligations are based on it (for instance the duration of mourning

---

[33] T'ung-Tsu (1961: 226–230).

[34] Salát (2003: 30–31) and T'ung-Tsu (1961: 230–234, 238–240).

in the mourning system). The fifth relationship is that between friends, the only one which is not hierarchic.[35]

In addition to *li* and *wu-lun,* it is the virtue (*de*) of the king what is necessary to arrive at a just rule. Virtue was a concept already known before Confucius but he lent new understanding to it. In its original concept, *de* was linked to the heavenly mandate (*tianming*) of the ruler, a privilege which was due to his office but not to his person and personal qualities. The doctrine of heavenly mandate crystallised in the Zhou period. Accordingly, the authority of the king was legitimate until his actions were in harmony with the will of Heaven. If Heaven turned away from the king because of his misdeeds, his authority would become illegitimate and his power could be overthrown, by revolts, if necessary. Confucius made this impersonal concept of *de* a personal quality of the king arriving at one of his few innovations. In his way of reasoning, *de* is an exceptional morality of the king which is the basis for his actions to be followed by society at large. A king with his immaculate *de* needs no other tools to governance (law, punishments) because his example will be followed without coercive means. The opposite also holds true: a king without a proper *de* may issue whatever decrees he wants and they will not be followed because he himself is not worth of a proper personal example.[36]

What *li* and *de* actually are is subject to study. This is why Confucians regarded education a very important mean to social control and harmony. Teaching and study should, therefore, focus on classical works of ancient sages and their doctrines, supplemented by arts and ceremonies and this is how Confucian curriculum came into being. A well-educated man is a gentleman (*kün–ce*) who is altruistic to be implemented best in the family (contrary to the understanding of Mo-Ce, Confucian altruism is not universal) accompanied by proper ceremonies. This altruism requires self-control from the superiors who are in a privileged position, yet cannot abuse their authority but should act in the benefit of their inferiors. Ideal Confucianism is thus, not the ideology of autocracy since leaders are morally legitimate if only they do not transgress their power as tyrants but act along the virtues for the benefit of others. Good will and humanity (*ren*) are essential parts of Confucian thinking being a virtue particularly expected of leaders.[37]

Consequently, Confucians do not attribute particular role to law, though do not deny its function completely. They stress virtue and rites in governance, which are better tools than punishments and discipline because in applying these means, people will be restrained from wrong without however feeling shame.[38] Reality however, was far from Confucian ideals and this is the reason why Confucius himself did not deny the application of law and punishment entirely. He did stress however, the principle of proportionality, according to which crimes and their punishments should be proportional. This was the way later Confucian scholars wanted to go along. Xunzi, a Confucian scholar living in the third century BCE regarded punishments

---

[35]T'ung-Tsu (1961: 236).

[36]Lunyu XII.17: Salát (2003: 31).

[37]Li (2013: 213) and Maspero (1978: 369–371).

[38]Lunyu II:3.

more important than the founder master did. According to him, virtues, ceremonies and education were important, though not enough to control society. In addition to education, fear was also a necessary factor to prevent wrongs which could be achieved by laws (*fa*), punishments (*xing fa*), and fear from punishments. Thus with Xunzi, the legal theory of Confucianism became more realistic, though far from believing in the omnicompetence of law. Such an idea was first formulated only by Han Fei and Li Si, disciples of Xunzi who were among the first to unfold the doctrines of legism.[39]

10.3.2 Legism *(fajia)*

At first glance Legism seems an antithesis of Confucianism, denying everything Confucius and his disciples regarded important such as traditions, education, inequality before law, a virtuous king and a just government based on morality and altruism. Legism is not a theory about an ideal society but a political and legal sociology highlighting facts and analysing them in order to arrive at a strategy to create an efficient state which was their ultimate goal. Since they believed law to be the most efficient tool for governance, legist thinkers focused their activity on law, hence their name (*fajia*, from the word *fa*, law). This name is, however, a latecomer since at the beginning this trend had neither a name, nor a founding master, nor coherent doctrines. The designation was first used in the Han period, summarising similar views of various authors about law, state and society thus, creating a school that never existed as a coherent and monolithic entity.

As we have seen in the previous chapter, Confucianism emerged in the late Zhou period as a reaction to contemporary political reality about chaos, anarchy and a constant quest for power ruining old values and social cohesion. Legism, too, was the product of this period which developed a completely different strategy out of this chaos. Early legist thinkers saw no reason to turn to ancient sages and their doctrines to develop an efficient state but insisted on the idea to find contemporary medicine for contemporary problems. Since political anarchy was the problem for centuries, what they believed was a centralised and strong state that could subjugate all its competitors and guarantee a stable domestic order, by force, if necessary. Confucian idealism was subject to the parody of pragmatist legist thinkers who wanted to have a strong state and not a virtuous king. Legist thinkers not only specified a strategy completely different from that of their rivals but also analysed ways, methods, tactics and government policies in detail, an intellectual achievement which was new in this early period of Chinese history. We could now call total mobilisation in the interest of the state (law, economics, society) that they advocated. It is small wonder that it was Qin, based on legist principles, that emerged victorious from the struggle in the late Zhou period. And it is also no wonder that the very Qin state disintegrated soon because it implemented these doctrines with rigor and neglected everything else.

---

[39] Salát (2003: 35–40).

Legist thinkers wanted to create stability, law and order, an antithesis of their own experience of the late Zhou period, at every cost. Virtues and ceremonies were useless to achieve their aim, together with the five social relations and the privilege of intellectuals in a hierarchic social system. What was important was to punish wrongs and to reward proper behaviour. Wrongdoings were actions which were against the interest of the state, economy and society, based on objective criterions where social rank was no matter for consideration. Legist thinkers urged to do away social hierarchy in law and introduce equality before law, an astonishingly modern concept in the interest of the state which cannot tolerate wrongs just because they were committed by persons of higher rank. Since emphasis was on the observance of the law, social hierarchy was no matter for legists, a point for long debates with Confucian thinkers. Legist thinkers, to make sure, did not deny the existence of the five social relations, they only rejected to consider them in law. Kings had to be neutral because just rulers do not favour members of their families and ministers. If such a person deserves punishment because of the wrong committed, a just king has to punish him/her according to law, a claim entirely at variance with Confucian thinking which exempts leading officials from punishment because of their rank in hierarchy. A just ruler is thus, bound to law and it is law in the final analysis which rules and not the king who is not entitled to break it. This embryonic concept of the 'rule of law' was a theory entirely against Chinese tradition, which highlights the sovereignty of the king and not that of the law. To make their ideas acceptable, legist thinkers did not claim that kings are subordinated to laws, only recommended kings to respect their own laws and not to violate them, because permanent autocracy would lead to downfall (thus rewording the Confucian idea of the ruler's good example).[40]

Legist thinkers did not trust the virtues of outstanding kings in governance. Instead, they believed in institutions which are always on duty, irrespective of the personal qualities of kings. Kings are, according to the testimony of Chinese history, not outstanding personalities, legist thinkers argue, but mediocre figures in the need of institutional help. Law is a very important tool just because it is impersonal and objective, while ad hoc decisions of rulers are subjective and would lead to chaos. Subjective decisions jeopardise the entire system and this is the reason why family ties should not be considered in legal matters. In short, the proper function of the state and the legal system is more important than family system, social hierarchy and loyalty to the five social relations, a claim no Confucian scholar would agree with. To illustrate: if a family father would commit a crime, he should be protected and supported by his son because of loyalty to the family, filial duty and respect despite the fact that his son may not agree with his deeds. Contrary to this, Confucian argument legist would advise the son just the opposite, that is, to help institutions to investigate the case and to bring his father to justice because this is the only way which corresponds social interest.[41]

Objectivity was also expected from officials who were forbidden to decide cases on their own discretion. Judicial discretion was seen as a danger to objectivity and

[40] T'ung-Tsu (1961: 241–244).
[41] T'ung-Tsu (1961: 246–247).

equality before law leading to anomalies, therefore, officials were advised not to do so. Officials were only monitored by their efficiency, an important factor for legists who regarded the proper selection of officials and constant monitoring of the bureaucracy a crucial point in maintaining an efficient public administration. The demand for control and selection was one of the most important contributions of legist thinkers to Chinese legal history. By contrast, legists saw no merit in education, something they considered unnecessary. According to their understanding, people need not be educated but should be frightened from committing criminal acts. For legists it was entirely irrelevant why people follow the law: out of virtue, personal commitment or fear. What was important for them was law and order which could be established by fear of punishments and not by education on virtues. Confucian virtues such as good intention and altruism were of no relevance for legist theories which emphasised only the need for observing the law. Since legist scholars had a rather negative anthropology, they relied on preventive punishments, creating fear which would hinder people to commit crimes. In brief, a just ruler has to hinder crimes but not promote virtues. Moreover, virtuous people were considered dangerous because they endangered the omnipotence of the law by their moral authority. Thus, legism differs from Confucianism not only in its methodology but also in its anthropology.[42] Though sanctions were important for legism to create fear, legist thinkers were however aware that in addition to punishments, reward could also be an efficient mean, but it was secondary of importance for them. This is why some legists specified a figure of 9:1 as the ideal proportion of punishments and rewards.[43]

No matter how important law for legists is, it is only a mean to achieve their end, that is, the proper governance of a centralised state. Economics was, therefore, also important for them, basing their system on agriculture. Here, again, legists played a zero-sum game with protecting agriculture but disregarding other economic activities such as commerce and industry. The Chinese state has to determine the prices, hinder speculation and control the monetary system in order to develop agriculture. For the same reason, people had to work on the fields because this is what guarantees livelihood. Legists were pragmatists to the extreme claiming that only professions necessary for state and society are useful (agriculture, the military), while any other activity is harmful and therefore, prohibited. Following this utilitarian attitude, legists persecuted activities and professions which did not produce immediate material or political gains. As professionals of 'unnecessary' activities per se, teachers and philosophers stood in the focus of their attacks. It is, therefore, not an accident that legists are said to burn books, particularly Confucian classics and to bury Confucian scholars alive when they were in power in Qin, under the rule of Huang Di. It was more than the annihilation of the intellectual rivals, it was rather part of a general programme because Confucianism embodied everything the legist disregarded: education, moral virtues, tradition and the imitation of the glorious past. By burying them alive, legists could get rid of them for good and could start their

---

[42]T'ung-Tsu (1961: 261–263).
[43]Shang (1928: 258–259, 274; 287–288).

program: to find contemporary answers for contemporary problems, a revolutionary idea in traditional China.[44]

To find answers to political problems in general is an intellectual activity which could remain on paper without *shu* and *shi*, two important terms in addition to *fa*. *Shu* refers to means and tools with the help of which decisions could be implemented while *shi* is a political position, necessary to have power enough to act. For example, *shu* refers to commands, decrees and control mechanisms while *shi* is a position which makes such acts possible (who is not king or minister has no competency). Legist thinkers such as Shen Buhai and Shan Dao highlight the importance of both *shu* and *shi,* yet they regarded them only as tools to implement the law.[45]

The utilitarianism of legist thinkers is due to their profession and position since the majority of them were ministers troubled with everyday problems of governance. Shang Yang was the chief minister of Qin (fourth century BCE), who wrote a treatise on the importance of the army and agriculture. Li Si was also a chief minister of Qin (third century BCE), who played an outstanding role in unifying the country and creating a bureaucratic system. In addition, he is said to be the intellectual father of Huang Di (the introduction of strict legislation, the execution of Confucians and the burning of their books, the execution of Han Fei, his schoolmate and fellow legist thinker). With the fall of Qin however, he was also destroyed, together with his family to the third generation. Han Fei, the most important legist thinker however never had any office and dedicated all his intellectual energy to the elaboration of legist theory; his work, the Han Feizi has come down to us completely. Han Fei was a disciple of a Confucian scholar, Xunzi, who broke away from Confucian anthropology and regarded human nature rather bad. Han Fei evolved this concept further, claiming that humans are selfish and only strive to assert their own interests against the common good if necessary. If rich families kill their new-born girls, Han Fei argues because they are not useful in their economic activities, what can be expected in political matters which are, after all, only about interest? This is why no ruler must trust either his ministers or his own family members and is advised to keep his intentions secret and to govern with strict and good laws.[46]

As a legist thinker, law was of course of crucial importance for Han Fei who specified the features of a good law. Han Fei went further than his colleagues and not only insisted on brutal punishments and fear but also elaborated requirements which must be fulfilled by the lawgiver in order to arrive at a law which in fact is in the service of both society and law. According to this, astonishingly modern legal sociology good laws have five virtues. First, they could be implemented easily. Han Fei believed that a king may not expect too much from society, otherwise people would not follow the law but turn against it, which would destroy the political system. With this observance, Han Fei prophecised the fall of the Qin dynasty. Second, good laws are easy to understand for all. It is a bad law, Han Fei argues, if its text is difficult for everyone to understand and it is only a privilege for the educated few

---

[44] Shang (1928: 175–197).

[45] Chung-ying (1997: 528–529).

[46] Schirokauer-Brown (2006: 46–47).

or the professionals to understand the law properly. Third, law must be general and not particular. With this, we arrived at one of the chief principles of legism believing in equality before law and destroying a legal system which is based upon social hierarchy and privileges for families, professions and age. Fourth, law must be predictable, which is a complex requirement because what Han Fei had in mind was that every crime must be followed by a sanction and it should be predictable that a crime or a wrong would definitely be punished. This is of course rather a requirement for institutions and not for the text of the law. Fifth, law must create well-being or, at least, not impoverish society at large because people who live in poverty and have thus nothing to fear would break the law in order to secure their livelihood with crimes or would revolt against the political system (a prudent advise which was not followed in Qin, leading to the revolt which destroyed the dynasty).[47] Art, disciplines and education are useless, therefore, are not worth of any state support. By contrast, soldiers and peasants are indispensable and deserve any support for the wellbeing of state and society.[48]

A king should govern with the help of his ministers and is not obliged to act in person in every issue. By contrast, he is advised to keep his will secret and run the state with ministers who are responsible for him alone. A king operating in the background is an astonishing idea in ancient China and with this Han Fei gave a unique political meaning to the idea of *wu wei* (non-action), well known from Chinese philosophy. Seeing things from the perspective of the king, combined with a pragmatist political sociology made Han Fei the Chinese Machiavelli in Western eyes.[49] If Ha Fei was a Machiavellian figure, then Shang Yang could be seen as an ideologue of the totalitarian state and its raison d'être. According to him, civil society would limit the competency of the state, a misfortune in the interest of the state and its representatives (kings, ministers). Civil society should therefore be weak, otherwise it would not be obedient to state control. This is the reason why Shang Yang, believing in a strong state and a weak society advised to weaken society wherever possible.[50]

Legist doctrines were implemented with all their extremes only by Huang Di and his short lived dynasty while other ruling dynasties concentrated their ideologies around Confucianism, with some variants. Despite this, legism was not outlawed from China in practice when it remained disqualified as an academic school. Control and examinations of officials, the primacy of bureaucratic law, the legal system focused on criminal law and the deterring vigour of punishments were important elements of legism which no Chinese state ever wanted to change, though they were realised in the garb of a Confucian ideology. To put it briefly, Confucianism and legism began to merge in Chinese political practice, which provided emperors with both legitimacy and efficiency.

This merger in practice was also formulated in the academic world in a school (or trend) called *huang–lao* which made attempts to harmonise Confucianism and

---

[47] Salát (2003: 70–73).

[48] Han Feizi 49: de Bary and Bloom (1999: 203).

[49] Peerenboom (1993:153–154, 160).

[50] Shang (1928: 303).

legism on a worldview similarly to Daoism. Followers of *huang–lao* did not share the worldview and anthropology of Confucius what they thought to be too optimistic, yet at the same time rejected the focus of legism on state and law and its very negative anthropology. According to *huang–lao,* law is in fact an important tool to achieve social harmony to which more role should be given than Confucians do. *Huang–lao* thinkers however, also reject the pragmatist and utilitarian cruelty of legism in punishments, representing a mediating position between the two extremes. It was exactly the ideology that early Han dynasty was in need of and it is therefore, small wonder that the *huang–lao* school had its heyday just in the Han period. Later on however, it lost its influence, particularly during the reign of Emperor Wu Di when *huang–lao* scholars were replaced by Confucian scholars at the court.[51]

10.3.3 Socio-legal Factors of Chinese Legal Thinking

What Confucians and legists disputed about was, after all, how to manage a stable political system in which the position of law was subject to dispute between them. Despite numerous differences between these two intellectual trends, what they had in common was that both believed law to be a set of norms given by a lawgiver (king, emperor, state) while paid limited attention (if any) to customs. To see law only from one perspective, that of the ruler is a mistake, since Chinese legal life is more complex than one would expect from studying the various Codes with minimal changes throughout the centuries. Official law was about laws addressed to officials on how to run the state but not about how to manage conflicts.

This is why conflict resolution followed extra-legal mechanisms in which officials were replaced by family elders, that is, by heads of families or clans who wanted to solve the conflict by any means without applying law. In the majority of the cases, such mediating processes ended with a result acceptable for everyone. Should however, such a procedure fail, village elders, landlords and the head of 'gilds' were asked to solve the dispute which they did. Similarly to clan leaders, these authorities too did not apply the law strictly but followed local custom and basic tenets of Confucianism, known to everyone. Local conflict resolutions were not only about a case at hand but also about prevention, that is, to hinder conflicts from coming to the surface. If a conflict was not solved by whatever means, the case was transferred to the official who was in no hurry to investigate it since his main task was to run the state locally and not to solve the disputes of private individuals (pledges were not dealt with from spring to autumn).[52]

This of course does not mean that laws of private law are completely missing from the codes since almost every great dynastic code has a chapter about private law issues, most of all family law and some transactions. These laws were put into writing in order to regulate basic institution since it was also in the interest of the state

[51] Peerenboom (1993: 73–103, 242–256).
[52] MacCormack (1996: 24) and Fairbank and Goldman (2006: 185).

to control family matters (marriage, inheritance) and land ownership since taxation was based on landed properties. Small wonder thus, that matters which were of secondary importance from the point of view of an emperor were missing from the codes and left to local society to decide.

In addition to Confucianism and legism, the *yin–yang* school also influenced Chinese legal practice, though it has nothing to say about law and political system. It is the worldview of this school which specified the date of executions. Since spring and summer are said to be periods of life and energy when *yang* forces are dominant, no one could be executed in those months because as a result crops would be reduced. Therefore, convicts were executed in the autumn and winter months, during the time of death and decay when the *yin* energy is dominant, to which restrictions were added which were also not considered suitable for executions. If an official violated these taboos he was punished by one year of forced labour.[53]

Law was kept secret in traditional China which was the also practice in Japan. Though striking at first glance for a Western (and Jewish, Indian, Muslim) lawyer, it is not at all against the logic of Chinese law, which is rather a handbook for officials on how to manage state affairs. Civil society has of course no business with these issues and is therefore, in no need to be acquainted with it. One could raise the question of how to act in conformity with the law if it is hidden, but the answer is at hand: Confucian ethics, known to everyone. What is expected from society (not to steal, kill, etc) is well-known since Confucian ethics continued to be the guide for millennia. Laws related to private legal matters were subject to local customs never codified in any Code. In short, laws important for Chinese society were known from other sources (ethics, local customs) and the various Codes and decrees of the emperor were just about running a state, no business for commoners. This is why law was a secret knowledge of officials but not a common intellectual good. In addition, following a negative but realistic anthropology of legism, the political elite was afraid that if people knew the law they would invent legal tricks for circumventing the law in order to profit from it. Prohibition was enhanced with strict punishments in the Song period when it was a crime to have a copy of the law, an understanding which was changed to the opposite by Wang An Shi during his short lived reforms. Interestingly, who followed Wang An Shi in this policy was the emperor who violated the law whenever he wanted: Hongwu, the founder of the Ming dynasty who rewarded persons with a copy of their own because he wanted to promote the law this way.[54]

Confucian ideology and its tendency to look backward to find answers instead of inventing in the future made Chinese legal thinking very conservative. Consequently, previous Codes were held at a very high esteem and no one dared to change them, though they were useful less and less. In order to keep in line with reality but respect old laws at the same time, Chinese elite invented the policy not to change the Codes but to govern with ordinances of emperors, the number of which are, obviously, numerous. Codification proves this since the Han Code served as a model to the Tang Code which was taken over almost word by word by the Songs. The Song Code

---

[53]T'ung-Tsu (1961: 219).
[54]Creel (1980: 36–37) and Miyazaki (1980: 58–59).

was followed by the Ming and then the Manchu dynasty, creating a legal continuity for two millennia. Chinese Codes remained by and large unchanged which means that (1) the legal material of the codes was constant, dominated by criminal law and public administration; (2) the structure of the codes remained unchanged with the first chapter about general principles and concepts followed by issues organised around the structure of ministries; (3) the system of punishments was not changed both in its principles and praxis; punishments were just copied from one Code to the other, some technical modifications notwithstanding. Out of the Codes produced by the great dynasties, it was the Tang Code which allocated the greatest respect because of its technical superiority (structure, precision and terms). To follow outdated laws was therefore, a sign of respect, which was in harmony with Confucian world view and not an atavistic anachronism.[55]

Legal conservatism was further enhanced by a remarkable continuity in politics, society, and economics. Though Chinese history is about the coming and going of dynasties and the integration and disintegration of the central political system, basic tenets remained unchanged, that is: (1) the structure of the political system, headed by the emperor advised by his ministers, and managed by a corrupt yet operative public administration; (2) Confucianism remained without a rival when doctrines of legism were incorporated to legal practice and the school itself disappeared; (3) agriculture remained the economic base of Chinese states except for the Songs and there were no essential changes in the structure of ownership and administration which would have required completely new laws; (4) customary law retained its influence in private law matters because there was no state intervention to local economic activities (except for agriculture) which would create a need for legislation; (5) the patriarchal family model and related familiarism was constant for millennia; (6) the system of punishments was finely elaborated and there was no need to introduce changes in this tradition; (7) hierarchy continued to be the basic principles of political and social structure (king and subjects, free men and servants, elderly and young, husband and wife and the scholar (official) and commoner)

Though law was important for the Chinese states, lawyers were not. Lawyers were disdained as a result of Confucian ethics focusing on peaceful conflict resolutions and mediation while neglecting the importance of law in social conflicts. Since Confucian ethics prefers compromises and rejects unilateral enforcement of individual rights at all costs, lawyers—believed to be troublemakers profiting from litigations—were at a very low esteem whose profession was sometimes prohibited. To be a representative in a lawsuit was rejected as a profession and as late as the Manchu dynasty penalised 'pettifoggers" and other swindlers who persuaded people to litigate in order to enrich themselves.[56] It was precisely the arguments on which Deng Xin, the first known 'lawyer' of China was executed two and a half millennia earlier because the accusation argued that he persuaded the parties to go to court, deviated from the customs of the ancestors and mixed up good and bad. In the absence of lawyers and their profession, people did not turn to them for help in their cases but

---

[55]MacCormack (1996: 13; 33).
[56]MacCormack (1996: 11).

relied on inherited ways of conflict resolutions like mediation, compromises and the intervention of (family, clan, village) elders which reduced further the significance of official law in everyday legal practice.[57]

10.4 Substantive Law

10.4.1 Family Law

In the official law to be found in the Codes there are some laws concerning family law matters but they are not coherent, systemised and comprehensive regulations. By contrast, dynastic Codes pick up some issues believed to be important and relevant for some reasons but neglected others, thought to be irrelevant. As a result, if a reader would study only these Codes, he would not acquire a deep knowledge about Chinese family law issues which are to be found in Confucian ethics in general and in the local customs in particular. Codes do not regulate family law entirely but incorporate only some elements of i t which are relevant for their criminal law approach. For example, cases of violence inside the family, a crucial point to be treated by almost all Codes was such an issue, which was solved on the basis of Confucian world view highlighting patriarchal family structure and hierarchy.

Traditional Chinese family model was patriarchal (patrilineal and patrilocal) in which female relatives were of secondary importance, though not excluded completely. Such a great patriarchal family was called *tsu,* in which the degree of relation was symbolised in the mourning system: the closer a relative, the longer his/her mourning period. A maximum mourning period for the closest relative was three years. A shorter mourning period of one year, nine, five and three months were due to more distant relatives, respectively. Members of a *tsu* did not necessarily live together: usually three generations constituted a bigger family which was also a unit for accommodation and economic activity. After the death of the parents, brothers moved to their own house with their own families. Family property was undivided and intact at the beginning but as early as the Han period the partition of family wealth was already a widespread practice.[58]

Being a patriarchal family, Chinese families were headed by a family father whose authority rested on family structure, social hierarchy and religious considerations, supported by the entire legal system. Since the cult of ancestors was a very important factor in traditional Chinese understanding, a family father was at the same time a family priest, too, in relation to the ancestor cult. All family members were linked to the ancestors through the head of the family and this is the reason why all the wives, children and grandchildren were under his authority, including also married partners, concubines and slaves. The authority of the head of the family was irrespective of

---

[57]Zhang (2014: 434–435).
[58]T'ung-Tsu (1961: 15–19).

age, therefore, adult married sons with their own children were also subordinated to him. It was also the head of the family who alone decided on matters of family wealth (sale, mortgage, loan, etc.). Where paternal authority manifested strong was the right to punish, a privilege of family fathers. It is certainly not an accident that Chinese writing system has a symbol of a hand holding a stick for a reference to a father. To punish family members, in order to correct them and maintain peace and order was a topic also in wisdom literature with advice to go along with punishments prudently but without hesitation. Subordination to punishments called filial obedience (*xiao*) was, on the other hand, a requirement of family members from which there was no way to escape. This is the reason why there were officials in elevated position who were beaten by their old fathers already in the Han period. The wife of the family father was also not without authority, since the married couple could agree that concerning their children she has the same rights as her husband has and in case of her husband's death, she will have authority alone. It is subject to dispute whether Chinese family fathers were lords of life and death (*ius vitae necisque*) or not. To kill a child was a crime, though punished differently in various historical periods. We can observe as a tendency that more recent dynasties such as the Ming and the Qing were more tolerant and did not punish parents with rigor for killing their children if they could prove that the victim violated filial obedience. Parents could pledge for acquittal if they proved that filial disobedience was the only reason for killing their offspring. Disobedience is, however, an elastic term without any hope to define it precisely. This is the reason why it was interpreted so differently even in the same historical period on a case-to-case basis, opening the door for subjective considerations and corruption.[59]

If parents did not want to punish their disobedient child on their own, they could ask for help from the authorities. If requested, authorities backed parental authority with the rigor of the law and the prestige of their office. If a child was accused of not following parental orders, he or she could be sentenced to two years in prison. If children were accused of disobedience, their punishment was more severe. This is the reason why dynastic Codes specified at least some cases which were regarded definitely as disobedience such as to raise a hand on the parents, slander, to marry during the mourning period, to move out of the parental house. Only the murder of a parent was punished by capital punishment and if a child killed with deliberate intention, his cut-off head was put to public view in the marketplace. By contrast, if a family father asked for a capital punishment for his child, authorities did not investigate the case and the child was executed without any further procedure. There are abundant court records to prove this from a period as late as the Song dynasty. Parents could also ask for exile which authorities accepted with a similar automatism. If a child was exiled to a distinct region, his punishment usually ended on the request of his parents who in the absence of any other relatives asked for his help to look after them when they got old.[60]

---

[59]T'ung-Tsu (1961: 20–24).
[60]MacCormack (2006: 60–65) and T'ung-Tsu (1961: 25–29).

All this was the result of a long historical development. The idea of filial obedience (*xiao*) is older than Confucianism and was, perhaps, understood quite differently from the interpretation of Confucian ideology and the rigid laws of the dynastic Codes. At the beginning it was connected to the cult of ancestors since living family members had the moral and religious duty to care for their ancestors, a requirement which was extended to living elders, too, with an obligation to supply them with food if necessary. A complete obedience to parents might only be a latecomer when an ideology was created from a living ancient custom which was by far not as unbalanced as Confucianism, and particularly Song neo-Confucianism was. The opposite of filial obedience, filial disobedience, *buxiao* was also invented, an immoral act threatening social structure at its heart. Small wonder, that it was also a serious crime to be punished without hesitation. On the analogy of *buxiao*, resistance to the older brother, *buyou* was also created. We can observe a similar development in the rules of mourning which was not a rigid set of rules to be implemented at all costs at the beginning but a privilege for some people working in public administration. Accordingly, officials were allowed to leave their office for a short period of time to bury their parents and mourn them. This privilege was transformed to an obligation, meanwhile its period was raised to a very long time frame of 27 months, a novelty which provoked resistance among officials and their superiors alike. It was the Tang Code which specified the obligation to mourn deceased parents for three years. If this period was violated for a short time, that is, an official returned to his office a month earlier, he was sentenced to three years of forced labour. Parallel to this, some acts were prohibited during the mourning period (dance, drinking of alcohol, eating meat, wedding, playing music, not wearing mourning garment).[61]

Family fathers were entitled to dispose of the wealth of the family exclusively. If any other family member did so, the transaction was null and void and the person was sentenced to whipping, the number of which depended on the value of the good he or she deposed of without authority. Chinese law took this very seriously and made almost no exception, even during hardship. For example, if a family father was far away from home, his family members were not allowed to sell valuable goods such as land, animal and servant unless authorities issued a document proving the head of the family was far away from home in a foreign country because of war. In the absence of such a document, the transaction was null and void and thus the good returned to its original owner, that is, the family and the buyer lost the purchasing price, a preventive law to discourage Chinese society to conclude transactions with unauthorised persons. To leave parental house before due time was taken of similar seriousness, since no son was allowed to leave the family and have property on his own right whilst his father or grandfather was still alive. The wealth of the family could be divided only after the death of the head of the family and the proper observance of the mourning period. If a family failed to observe the mourning period and divided the wealth before this period came to an end, family members were either jailed (Tang and Song), or whipped (Ming, Qing).[62]

---

[61] MacCormack (2006: 65–79).

[62] T'ung-Tsu (1961: 29–31).

Traditional Chinese marriages were, as everywhere in Asia, arranged marriages between families to which partners of the prospective union had little say. No marriage was concluded without the approval of a family father who also decided about divorce, irrespective of the will of the couple. Here again, the cult of ancestors was a decisive factor, since it was the very aim of marriage to produce heirs (=sons) to the family who would continue the cult of ancestors, otherwise they would became wandering spirits. A childless marriage or a union without a son is unnecessary since it misses the aim of marriage and should, therefore, be terminated in order to have a next marriage in the hope of an heir. This is the reason why Mencius believed that a marriage without a son is a filial disobedience. Ancestors also played an important role in the wedding ceremony since the ancestors' temple was the place for rites. In addition, family fathers had to inform the spirit of ancestors about prospective marriages and the names of the parties and ask for their approval which was mediated with the help of divination. Only after receiving their approval could the family father continue with the wedding process by sending gifts and presents to the girl's family. Negotiations were usually the business of mediators on behalf of the heads of the families until an agreement was reached. Breaking such agreements was against Confucian ethics and law. According to dynastic codes, if the family father of the girl neglected the agreement, he was punished by sixty lashes with the stick and the marriage had to be concluded. By contrast, if it was the other party who neglected the agreement, engagement presents and gifts were lost to him but he was spared of whipping, a distinction which was abolished in the Ming period. Marriage created a new bond between the young wife and the family and ancestors of her husband. To enter into this bond, she had to pay a visit to her husband's parents and present a sacrifice to their ancestors the morning after the wedding ceremony. This was the last but very important step in a long wedding ceremony, elevating a girl to the position of a wife and more importantly, the daughter-in-law of her husband's father because this is how the wife was integrated into her husband's family.[63]

Marriages were exogamous with a list of prohibited degrees and persons, including also persons with an identical family name irrespective of blood relation. Persons with identical family names were prohibited because a common descent was assumed behind it. To disregard marital prohibitions was a crime which made such marriages null and void with a punishment of prison or whipping, varying according to dynastic Codes. The name taboo however, was not taken as seriously as other taboos were since there are recorded cases in which married couples bore the same family name yet they were not punished and their marriage was not declared void. Despite this, name taboo was removed from the law only in 1910. Further prohibitions of marriage were based on relations between generations and on the system of mourning. Consequently, a marriage between uncle and niece, and aunt and nephew was prohibited. It was also prohibited to marry a woman belonging to the family irrespective of grade. A widow could re-marry but only outside the family of her former husband, otherwise parties were strictly punished. Here too, legal practice differed from the law in books: marrying the widow of the deceased brother was not unusual, a Mongol custom which

---

[63]MacCormack (1996: 88–89) and T'ung-Tsu (1961: 9–102).

become widespread primarily in the countryside and among the poor. Given the publicity of Chinese marriages, such unions were not kept secret, yet they were tacitly accepted. If an official learned about them and wanted to dissolve such unions, he never punished the couple according to criminal law but asked for their dissolution.[64]

Chinese family was patrilocal, therefore the young couple moved to the husband's family estate for residence. The new wife's ties to her previous family lost significance, though was not lost completely, a new situation which was also embodied in the mourning period: she had to mourn her relatives for a shorter period and vice versa. A new wife enjoyed all the privileges a family member shares with relatives (economic position, social status, ancestor's cult, etc.) but was also responsible for all duties and penalties. Therefore, if a family member was sentenced to death with the routing of his complete family (e.g. for riot), she was also executed though, obviously, had nothing to do with the criminal act. Being a daughter-in-law specified a daughter's position to the new wife who had to serve her in-laws with filial obedience. Absence of filial obedience was a cause for divorce. Obedience was due to her husband and his family for the rest of her life, a subordinated position from which there was no way out. This was expressed symbolically by binding her feet, a custom emerging among aristocrats in the Song period. Accordingly, girls' front of the foot was bound in childhood so that it may not grow and keep the length of 8 c m regarded as ideal. As the foot continues to grow the foot is deformed and becomes unsuited for walking and particularly for work. Both the Manchus and the Communist attempted to abolish this custom but failed; it disappeared very recently.[65] A wife was treated like a child in some private law cases (propriety rights) and also by criminal law. If she accused her husband, it was regarded as if a young would act against an old, a clear violation of Confucian ethics, social hierarchy and law. Worse, if her accusation proved to be false she was punished by death. If a wife hit her husband, she was sentenced to several years in prison while her husband was entitled to harm her without causing serious injury. Should a husband harm her beyond the limit of law, he was punished for assault but his punishment was two grades milder than for an injury caused for a person outside the family. Ming and Qing laws further relaxed the husband's punishment in such cases. The husband had the right to kill her adulterous wife but only together with her lover and *in flagrante delicto*. The same husband committed a crime if he killed only one of the parties or did not act immediately.[66]

Parties could terminate their marriages by declaring divorce, a privilege of the husband. Chinese lawgivers seemingly wanted to restrict this right and hinder arbitrary decisions. This is the reason why there were seven causes for divorce, specified by law. These causes were actually some misbehaviour of wives but were drafted so broadly that the text allowed for subjective interpretations. These are: (a) disobedience towards the husband's parents; (b) barrenness; (c) adultery; (d) jealousy; (e) incurable disease; (f) too much talk; (g) theft. These were the bases for a declaration of divorce with the majority of subjective categories with no hope for restrictions

---

[64]T'ung-Tsu (1961: 91–99).

[65]Fairbank and Goldman (2006: 173–176) and T'ung-Tsu (1961: 102–105).

[66]T'ung-Tsu (1961: 102–110).

of divorces. This is why extra requirements were added and no divorce was allowed if (a) a wife had not a single close relative who could look after her; (b) she spent three years of mourning for her husband's parents; (c) the husband's family was poor before the marriage but later on became rich. In cases of adultery and incurable disease however, even these extra requirements did not exempt the wife from divorce. Infertility was an understandable cause in a system where to produce heirs for the ancestors and their spirits was the very aim of the marriage itself. Yet few marriages terminated because of infertility, since concubinage was a way out of the problem. This is also the reason why jealousy was a cause to divorce since it hindered concubinage. Adultery was a cause to divorce because there was the danger of aliens being born into the family whose sacrifices would not be accepted by the ancestors' spirits who disregard sacrifices from persons outside the family. Disobedience to the husband's parents was an entirely subjective category to be interpreted by anyone as he pleased. Here are some examples. A disciple of Confucius divorced his wife because she did not cook the food well enough for his parents and served it half raw. Another man divorced his wife because she shouted at a dog loudly and the voice disturbed his mother. In another story the wife was divorced because it took a long time for her to carry water from the river to his thirsty mother. Examples could be quoted endlessly. In addition to these seven causes, there were also objective causes called *i-chüeh* (dissolution of the marriage) which terminated the union irrespective of the husband's declaration. These are assaults against the relatives of the husband or the wife, manslaughter and sexual relations with prohibited relatives. Divorce was compulsory in these cases irrespective of the will of the parties. Should they resist to divorce they were sentenced to prison.[67]

If a marriage ended by death, widows were, similarly to India, expected not to re-marry. What is more, this expectation was enlarged even to girls with a dead bridegroom, though they were no widows in the eyes of the law. Interestingly, here Chinese law was more lenient than social expectations and customs since according to Chinese law, a widow was prohibited to re-marry only during the mourning period but not beyond it. For a short period of time (Tang), a widow could be forced to re-marry by her parents but later on it was abolished and declared to be a criminal act.[68]

10.4.2 Criminal Law

Chinese understanding of law focused on criminal law from its very first period of history. It is certainly not by chance that the first compilation of law called *xing shu* (book of punishments) engraved to a tripod bronze vase around 536 BCE is about punishments. According to the Chinese tradition, punishments (*xing*) were

---

[67]T'ung-Tsu (1961: 118–123).
[68]MacCormack (1996: 93; 96).

first drafted by Lü Hou in the Zhou period in the Lü Xing, a work of nine chapters but presumably it goes back to earlier tradition.[69]

Chinese criminal law is about crimes and punishments with minor changes in the various dynastic Codes. Despite the centrality of punishments, there are some principles on which the entire system is based. One such a principle is proportionality, that is, the punishment of a criminal act should be proportional to the harm caused and also to the punishments of other crimes. This was one of the most important principles of legism, though perhaps the idea itself is older than legism and goes back to earlier times when crimes were believed to be a violation of the cosmic order which could only be restored by a proportional punishment. To be sure there are no traces of such thinking in the dynastic Codes which elaborate further points for consideration instead, such as intent (e.g. negligent) social position (old and young, husband and wife, etc.) and tools used (poison, etc.) when committing a crime. The second principle was the consideration of social rank for specifying punishments, a differentiation based on the social status of both the culprit and the victim because it was important whether a slave killed a free man or vice versa, or the victim was a scholar, an official or a peasant. The third is related to this principle, the principle of privileges. Accordingly, privileged groups (royal family, scholars, officials and their families) were not punished the same way as ordinary people because they were exempt from punishments or their punishment was milder. The fourth principle follows the same logic but differentiates between family members according to age and gender.[70] These principles do not constitute a coherent system because the last three principles ruin the first, since the first principle punishes crimes according to its harm caused while the three remaining principles disregard this and introduce a new consideration, that of social rank, privilege and differentiation according to age and gender. Obviously, these principles are the result of the Confucianisation of criminal law which are at variance with proportionality and equality before law, modern yet ancient Chinese legal ideas advocated by legist thinkers.

The Han Code was primarily about specifying punishments. There were four variants of capital punishment, one among them, public execution, was a legacy of the Qin dynasty. In more serious cases, corpses were left for public view in the market place for further humiliation. Cutting into two, cooking alive and burning were punishments less frequently executed. For political crimes such as riot and revolt, not only persons involved were executed but their families were also routed to the third generation and only after a long process of torture (cutting off of nose, hands and feet). No doubt, the aim of such cruelties was to deter others from participating in such political movements, and this is also the reason why pieces of the body of the executed were sent to aristocrats as a warning. Among the variants of bodily mutilation, cutting off the nose and castration were preferred, while tattooing and branding the face were rarely executed. Forced labour and exile were also often applied punishments while fines were rarely charged in the Han period. The most frequent punishment was no doubt blows with a stick which was applied for a variety

---

[69]Creel (1980: 35–36) and Head and Wang (2005: 52–53).

[70]Drapkin (1989: 154–155) and Creel (1980: 43).

of minor crimes. The Code specified the exact size and length of the bamboo in order to avoid mismanagement and insisted that person should be beaten while standing. With these laws, the Han Code actually laid down the foundations of criminal law which was followed by successive Codes too. Only minor variants and changes were introduced when new forms of punishments were specified and some punishments abolished. The continuous tendency to make the Codes increasingly conform to Confucian ethics was the only 'novelty' for centuries and this is how social rank, status, *wu-lun* and gender were considered in specifying punishments.[71]

The Tang Code continued the tradition of the Han Code, though introduced some changes and precision of terms. The Code specified four kinds of punishments (capital punishment with decapitation and choking; blows with a light and a heavy stick, forced labour, life-long exile) and ten most conspicuous criminal acts (e.g. revolt, instigation of a territory to break away, treason, filial disobedience, incest, turning against the authorities) which were against the very fundaments of traditional Chinese society. Interestingly, not all of them were punished by death but none could be pardoned by the emperor either. In addition, those found guilty and sentenced to death were also executed on days on which otherwise no executions could be implemented. With its prestige and structure, the Tang Code not only established its prestige in Chinese legal history but also served as a model for subsequent dynastic Codes and this is how archaic criminal legal thinking continued to modern times.[72]

Familiarism already which took root in the Han period, continued to influence Chinese criminal law in the Tang period. Branded as a disaster ruining the entire legal system by legist thinkers but advocated by Confucian scholars, familiarism was a mean by which social considerations were introduced to criminal law. Accordingly, punishments were not adjusted to the criminal act but to the actor. As a result, the same crime was punished completely differently, according to the status of the actor who committed it. With this act-centred criminal law was transformed to actor-centred criminal law with the simultaneous loss of equality before law and proportionality, being the first principle of criminal law. In addition to these losses, familiarism also made criminal law very casuistic since it was impossible to draft a text in general. Instead, criminal acts had to be specified according to a matrix, based on social status. To illustrate: there was no general law on assault, just cases of assault with varying punishments for an old attacking a young or vice versa, a husband assaulting a wife and vice versa, etc. Since the aim of the system was to maintain and guarantee social hierarchy and privileges, it is no wonder that persons of higher rank were punished mildly when committing crimes against persons of lower rank while ordinary people were punished more severe if committing a crime against a privileged person. Legal practice too, favoured persons of higher rank because law was interpreted leniently in their favour while it was understood more rigidly in the case of commoners. Here are some examples to illustrate. According to Tang and Song laws, a murder of an innocent child with intention (who was not disobedient) was punished by two years in prison, later reduced to beating. The same criminal act was however, punished

---

[71] Head and Wang (2005: 99–101).

[72] Head and Wang (2005: 121–123; 184).

by death (choking) if the victim did not belong to the family. By contrast, hitting the parents resulted in immediate decapitation of the child even if no injury or death followed the attack. This was brought to its extreme when intention was not taken to consideration at all. A point for illustration is the case of a son who wanted to help his father in a street fight where his father was attacked by some people. In the fight he also unintentionally hit his father, but it was the son, and not the attacker of his father, who was sentenced to death because of hitting a parent. Since both hitting and killing a parent was a capital crime, no distinction was made in punishments. Therefore, the way of execution was specified differently: decapitation was replaced by cutting into pieces for murder. If the child died before the sentence was executed, he was not exempted from cutting into pieces: his corpse was cut into pieces and put into public view. Children were also executed when they did not hurt or killed their parents because they committed suicide. If there was a suspicion that a parent committed suicide because of one of his child's behaviour (drinking, gambling, stealing), such an offspring was sentenced to death for 'causing a parent's suicide'. This, again, was interpreted to its extreme: there was a case of a parent who wanted to correct his child with a blow but while doing so fell and hurt his head and died on the spot for his misfortune. It was his child who was declared responsible for this unfortunate fall and was executed for 'causing a parent's suicide'. Young persons attacked by elders were denied the right to self-defence. If they resisted the attack with a tool (stick, knife, etc.) they were sentenced to death immediately, even though they were victims not attackers. Only if young persons defended themselves with bare hands were they not executed without further investigation. In such a case, a judge had to send all related documents to the emperor and wait for his final decision. The draft of the new criminal code in 1907 attempted to abolish restrictions on self-defence but met the protests of the traditional elite and gave way to the old laws at the end. The new approach was also left out from the Act of 1914.[73]

Taking over of punishment (*dai xing*) was a further extremity of familiarism and filial obedience in criminal law. Accordingly, if a family member was sentenced to a punishment (usually capital punishment), a family member asked authorities to execute him instead of the person convicted. Such persons were family members of a lower rank (a younger brother, a child) who wanted to save their superiors. *Dai xing* was, to be sure, not an obligation specified by law but a moral standard which was met only by a few. This is the reason why such persons were not always executed at the end but pardoned by the emperor who regarded their voluntary act as a particular example of filial obedience.[74]

Particular attention was devoted to sexual crimes which were also understood in the light of the mourning system. Sexual relationship between relatives belonging to the first three grades was incest which was among the ten gravest criminal acts punished by death (choking). Sexual contact between relatives who did not belong to

---

[73]T'ung-Tsu (1961: 41–64), MacCormack (1996: 78–87) and MacCormack (2001: 174–175; 181).
[74]Zhang (2014: 205).

the system of mourning was punished by beating with a stick or exile but the sanction varied according to historical periods. Rapists however were sentenced to death.[75]

10.4.3 Law of Procedure

Similarly to criminal law, we can witness remarkably continuity in the law of procedure too, which has changed only to a limited extent. Basic principles remained constant for ages, only institutional background was modified according to the ever changing system of public administration. There was no procedural law for courts of law because it was the official who adjudicated the cases. Since public administration was not separated from the judiciary, officials proceeded in cases of both public administration and adjudication. This lack of separation of powers continued up to modern times in China. In this complexity of cases, matters important for administration and criminal law enjoyed priority, while private law cases were only of secondary importance. This is why no private legal matters were on the agenda between the spring and the autumn equinox up to the Song period, proving both disrespect for private legal cases and the importance of agriculture. Chinese procedural law was rational, though torture was not uncommon in criminal procedure. Despite this oath, ordeal and other irrational means of proof were not in practice. The official's task was to identify the material truth which was proven with the help of documents and witnesses.[76]

Cases were dealt with at the local level first, by the district (*hsien*) official, who started the procedure upon request of the parties presented in a written document. There were scribes attached to the offices who assisted illiterates in preparing a document, examined the case and advised parties whether or not it is worth launching the procedure. These scribes were private individuals and no employees of the local administration who acted upon permission, and if they made mistakes (rejected well-founded cases or accepted unfounded cases) their licence was withdrawn. Complaints were put into a complaints box which was opened each morning and this is how a case started. The office of the district administrator (*yamen*) consisted of six departments, of which the department of punishments (*hsiang-fang*) dealt with criminal cases. Departments were filled with administrative staff who were classified into a definitive hierarchy (head assistant, second assistant, assistant, and trainee). Assistants first selected the cases that were to be rejected and presented only the remaining cases to the official. The case started with the hearing of the parties and witnesses who were summoned usually for the morning hours. Pregnant women and persons above seventy were exempt from hearing because they were also exempt from the punishment for giving false evidence (a markedly negative anthropology of witnesses and parties). Family members gave testimonies in their stead. In criminal procedure, a person suspected was taken into custody and locked up in the district jail for the

---

[75]T'ung-Tsu (1961: 64–70).

[76]MacCormack (1996: 15–16).

duration of the procedure, or his clan was made responsible for his appearance at the trial. The first phase of the procedure was about finding and proving facts relevant for the case. In doing so, officials shared their job with assistant officials, the head of the judicial archives and an official of the 'police' who also participated in the first phase of the procedure in ancient times (up to the Songs). Confession was regarded the best proof and for this reason, officials could also torture the suspected person in order to force his testimony. Torture was also applied when other proofs (witnesses, etc.) were proving the case, yet the suspected person kept on denying his involvement. When facts were cleared and proved the procedure entered its next phase when the law suitable for the case had to be identified. The head of the court archives played an important role in it because he presented all the relevant norms found in the codes, imperial orders and available precedents that were related to the case. Studying them, the official identified the relevant legal norm and composed the sentence. A sentence comprised of the important facts of the case, the decision of the official and its explanation, and also the rights and duties of the parties in a private case. Private law cases usually ended at local level but criminal law cases continued at the second instance when suspected persons appealed against a judgment or the judgment of the first instance was about exile or death. In such cases, the documents had to be forwarded to the next instance. The procedure also continued if the condemned withdrew his confession. Only punishments of beating with blows less than 100 by the stick were immediately implemented on local level.[77]

The second instance of procedure was the province where legal professionals were numerous compared to the first instance. These 'courts of appeal' examined both problems of facts and the relevant law. If there was any doubt about facts, the first phase of the procedure, that is, giving testimony, was repeated. If no party challenged the facts, yet the relevant law for the case was not applied, the original judgment was corrected but the procedure was not repeated. This decision then had to be sent to the district office of control for approval. In the absence of approval, the procedure had to be started from the beginning. In criminal cases, the emperor had to be informed if a person was sentenced to exile or death. If neither the facts nor the applicable law was ambiguous, the emperor was only informed in writing. Should there be doubts concerning the facts or the law to be applied, the case was presented to the emperor who decided as the final instance. Emperors were advised by the *Hsing-piu*, a central body specialising in criminal cases. Emperors also pardoned convicted persons if they saw it fit.[78]

In 'cases of small significance' (*xishi*), that is, private law matters, officials employed mediators to solve the case. Mediators entered the scene when social mechanisms (conflict resolutions at clan, village, gild level) failed and the parties turned to the official for judgment. In such a case, a mediator (*xiangbao*) was appointed who proceeded on the basis of the official's preliminary opinion. This is because officials studied every case before they assigned them to the mediator and wrote their comments about the case on the document which was a guideline for both the mediator

---

[77]Miyazaki (1980: 59–62).
[78]Miyazaki (1980: 63–69).

and the parties who were also given a copy. If parties reached an agreement on this basis, the case ended here. Almost half of private law matters (40%) ended this way even at the time of the Qing dynasty because compromise was a solid element of Confucian ethics. By contrast, those insisting on litigation (particularly if repeatedly) were regarded as morally failed persons (*xiaoren*).[79]

10.5 Traditional Chinese Law in the Twentieth Century

Nineteenth century China witnessed a series of misfortunate events (Opium wars, defeat from the Japanese, Boxer revolt, unequal international treatises) proving the need for ground breaking political and legal reforms. Finally, after long debates, the ruling dynasty gave way to such reforms around the turn of the century. As a result, public administration was reorganised, new ministries were created, the traditional examination system of officials was abolished, the budget was made public, and a new criminal code was introduced.

Though these reforms were Western-minded, the inspiration came from the east, that is, Japan, a country which had won great appreciation in China after its victory against Russia (1905). Japanese success was interpreted as proof for the belief that a modernised Asian country could defeat a hegemonic and absolutistic state. Japanese modernisation (Meiji-reforms) was therefore an inspiration and a model for Chinese political and legal reforms. Japanese scholars were invited to help draft new Codes which were at this point only radical reforms of the inherited laws but not an entirely new legal system built upon new ideas. As a first step, public administration was separated from the judiciary, giving more freedom to the latter. As a matter of symbol, the Supreme Court was renamed to *daliyüan* (instead of the centuries-old *dalisi*). Civil and criminal law were separated, torture was abolished, and corporeal punishments were replaced by fines. The first faculty of law was opened in 1906. These reforms were inspired by Japanese and German legal influence (since Japanese legal reforms followed the German model in these years) but were confronted with the resistance of the traditional elite who wanted to hinder them. Though they were unable to stop legal reforms, they nevertheless succeeded to bring back old laws making legal reforms half hearted.[80] Common law however, was unable to take root in China in these days partly because it is less systematised than Civil law tradition, and partly because it is based on an individualism which was incompatible with Chinese society. Civil law tradition is said to continue the ancient Roman idea of the family which was more familiar to the Chinese legal understanding.[81]

The reforms did not last long because the dynasty lost its power to Sun Jat-Sen who was elected president of a new republic in 1911. Next year, both the last emperor and Sun abdicated and this is how Yuan Shikai, a general came to power. Yuan Shikai

---

[79] Huang (2010: 63–64; 76–78; 194).

[80] Ladany (1992: 44–46).

[81] Chen (2008: 28).

headed a short lived empire with himself as its emperor and after its collapse, Sun returned. Struggle for power created chaos in China for long years. Making use of the lack of Chinese central government, Japanese forces occupied Manjuria which made Guomindang of Chang Kay-Sek and the Chinese Communist to join forces against the invaders. With the Japanese capitulation at the end of WW II, this coalition came to its end and a new civil war unfolded whit the victory of the Communists.[82]

History thus, provided no solid ground for legal reforms to be continued. Despite this, Chinese republic did not stop short and introduced a new private law on the German and the Swiss model. Commercial and criminal law followed, since inherited drafts of these Codes were already at their disposal. It was Wang Chonghui, an internationally re-known scholar who was the motor of the new codification. A new constitution was also completed by Wu Jingxiong, a young scholar of outstanding talent, greatly appreciated also in the US (O. W. Holmes; R. Pound) within a few weeks in 1933. The 'six laws' created by the Guomindang government (among which the criminal code of 1928, and the civil code of 1929 were the most important) lasted only for two decades since they were declared null and void in 1949 after the Communist takeover. Despite this, the effect of making republican law was to be felt for long decades because western and notably, German, jurisprudence influenced Chinese law, particularly private law, in its terminology, concept and dogmatics. When a new private law was published in 1986, a leading American sociologist of law called it practically a German private law, a claim admitted by Chinese legal scholars.[83]

During the Nanjing period, old ideas such as privileges linked to social status, torture and analogy, being at variance with Western principles were eliminated, while *nullum crimen sine lege* was introduced into the criminal codes (1928, 1935) and the laws on criminal procedure (1928, 1935). Private law was also codified, an enormous innovation compared to the traditional legal system. Polygamy was prohibited in family law and the share of both daughters and sons was specified equal in the law of inheritance of the new private law code (1929). Economics was modernised with laws on insurance (1929), companies (1929) and bankruptcy (1935). The system of the judiciary was re-structured and legal education was prioritised. All these were, of course, tremendous changes for which social backing was inevitable. In order to win society for reforms, traditional law and local customs were left intact wherever possible, that is, where old laws were in no collision with new laws. As a result, a mixed legal system came into being with traditional and new laws.[84] This balance was further challenged with revolutionary changes in family law such as female equality, protection of widows and a new understanding of divorce. As law became more and more important also for social and economic activities, the number of legal experts increased. At the end of the period, there were about ten thousand legal

[82]For details of modern history see Gernet (2001: 471–482), Schirokauer and Brown (2006: 30–308; 319–320; 323–338) and Fairbank and Goldman (2006: 279–342).

[83]Ladany (1992: 48–51).

[84]Jordán (2008: 30–37) and Chen (2008: 35).

experts, a very low figure for such a huge country, yet a milestone in a society where the profession of legal experts was in no esteem for centuries.[85]

Mao's China was an enemy of both traditional and Western legal systems which were ruined. By contrast, law was a weapon in the struggle against 'counter-revolutionaries' and 'reactionary elements', while no legal system was established. Individual orders and Mao's speeches were guidelines for newly appointed judges who were not well versed in law. Law was a tool for implementing new economic policy. This is the reason why the law on land reform was already published in 1950 which confiscated the lands of landlords, temples and foundations, accompanied by heavy casualties the exact number of which is still unknown. Marriage law followed the path of the earlier reforms but went further in its struggle against familiarism and arranged marriages. Accordingly, arranged marriages had to be dissolved, otherwise the parties were treated as counter-revolutionaries facing punishment. This is why public opinion called it divorce and not marriage law. The law on trade unions entirely followed the Soviet pattern.[86] Martial law courts were also created which annihilated counter-revolutionaries' and 'enemies of the system' within the framework of criminal procedure.[87] The first socialist constitution of China was drafted in 1954, modelled on the Soviet constitution of 1936 with some changes (for instance, the Soviet Union was a federal state while China was unitary). Criminal law continued to be uncodified which contributed enormously to legal uncertainties concerning penalties to which re-education camp as a sanction was added. Grotesque as it is, these camps housed people who said something bad about the Soviet Union in the 50s and something good about the Soviet Union a few years later.[88] After Mao's death, China came back to its age old policy to codify important laws. This is why criminal law was already codified in 1979, to be followed by a constitution in 1982 (after two short lived versions of 1975 and 1978) and a private law code in 1986.[89] Codification and law making continues ever since but it is not the topic of a book about traditional law to enumerate the new laws which is a subject of volumes on modern Chinese law.

As this rather short overview demonstrates, Chinese legal system has been changed gradually in the last hundred years. Westernisation was followed by Sovietisation and a centralising Maoist policy which resembles at some points the rule of Huang Di. All these are discernible only on the surface, while traditional attitude has changed little and certainly less in the countryside. Chinese society remained suspected and mistrustful towards law which is seen as a tool to realise the will of the state and the political elite and not a mean to promote their own interests. Privileges and the system of personal relations (*guan xi*) which has been serving the interests of the political elite for millennia are among the causes of why society still neglects law to solve conflicts. Personal consultations and mutual compromises are still preferred.

---

[85] Huang (2001: 44; 197–198).

[86] Ladany (1992: 58–61).

[87] Jordán (2008: 54–58).

[88] Ladany (1992: 67–70; 112–115).

[89] Jordán (2008: 133–140) and Ladany (1992: 82–84; 92–93).

If they fail, people turn to archaic social mechanisms such as conflict resolution by mediators, village and clan elders. If such mechanisms do not bring forth any result, turn people to law seen as an ultima ratio. To put it briefly, without an insight into traditional values, ethics and legal understanding contemporary China is still not understandable for an observer who is narrow-minded enough to concentrate only on promulgated laws.

References

Sources

Csikszentmihalyi M (2006) Readings in Han Chinese thought. Hackett Publishing Inc., Indianapolis
de Bary WT, Bloom I (1999) Sources on Chinese tradition. Vol I: from earliest times to 1600. Columbia University Press, New York
Johnson W (1979) The Tang code. Princeton University Press, Princeton
Konficius (1961) Lunyu. In: Tőkei F (ed) Kínai filozófia: Ókor. I. Kötet, Budapest
Kroker E (1955) Rechtsgewohheiten in der Provinz Shantung. Monumenta Serica 14(1949–1955):125–302
Okamatsu S (1902) Provisional report on investigations of laws and customs in the Island of Formosa. Keba Herald Office
Salát G (2003) Büntetőjog az ókori Kínában. Budapest, Balassi Kiadó
Shang Y (1928) The book of Lord Shang: a classic of the Chinese school of law (trans: Duyvendak JJL). Arthur Probsthain, London (Reprinted: The law book exchange Ltd., New Jersey, 2003)

Literature

Bell DA, Chaidonk H (2003) Confucianism for the modern world. Cambridge University Press, Cambridge
Black EA, Bell GF (2011) Law and legal institutions of Asia. Traditions, adaptations and innovations. Cambridge University Press, Cambridge
Chen PM (1973) Law and justice. The legal system in China. Dunellen Publishing Company, New York
Chen J (2008) Chinese law: context and transformation. Martinus Nijhof Publishers, Leiden
Chung-ying C (1997) The origins of Chinese philosophy. In: Carr B, Mahalingam I (eds) Companion encyclopedia of Asian philosophy. Routledge, New York
Church P (2009) A short history of Southeast-Asia. Wiley, Singapore
Cohen JA, Edwards RR, Chen FC (1980) Essays on China's legal tradition. Princeton University Press, Princeton
Creel HG (1980) Legal institutions and procedures during the Chou dynasty. In: Cohen JA, Edwards RR, Chen FC (eds) Essays on China's legal tradition. Princeton University Press, Princeton
Dawson R (2002) A kínai civilizáció világa. Osiris, Budapest
Drapkin I (1989) Crime and punishment in the ancient world. Prentice Hall and IBD
Eikemeir D, Franke H (1981) State and law in East Asia. Festschrift Karl Bünger. O. Harrassowitz, Wiesbaden

Fairbank JK, Goldman M (2006) China. A new history. Belknap Press of Harvard University Press, Cambridge

Gernet J (2001) A kínai civilizáció története. Osiris Kiadó, Budapest

Gillespie J, Nicholson P (2005) Asian socialism and legal change. The dynamics of Vietnamese and Chinese reform. Asia Pacific Press, Canberra

Head JW, Wang Y (2005) Law codes in dynastic China. A synopsis of Chines legal history in the thirty centuries from Zhou to Qing. Carolina Academic Press, Durham

Hooker MB (2002) Law and the Chinese in Southeast Asia. Institute of Southeast Asian Studies, Singapore

Huang PCC (2001) Code, custom, and legal practice in China. The Qing and the republic compared. Stanford University Press, Stanford

Hulsewé AFP (1985) Remnants of Ch'in law: an annotated translation of the Ch'in legal and administrative rules of the 3rd century BC. Sinica Leidensia, no 17. Brill, Leiden

Jordán G (2008) „Az ég magas, a császár messze van". Igazságszolgáltatás, jog és politika Kínában. ELTE Eötvös Kiadó, Budapest

Kaku S (2013) Patriarchy in East Asia. A comparative sociology of gender. Brill, Leiden

Ladany L (1992) Law and legality in China. Hurst and Company, London

Lee THC (2000) Education in traditional China. A history. Handbuch der Orientalistik. Brill, Leiden

Li F (2013) Early China. A social and cultural history. Cambridge University Press, Cambridge

MacCormack G (1996) The spirit of traditional Chinese law. The University of Georgia Press, Athens

MacCormack G (2001) Cause, status and fault in the traditional Chinese law of homicide. In: Cairns JW, Robinson OF (eds) Critical studies in ancient law, comparative law and legal history. Hart Publishing, Oxford

Maccormack G (2004) The transmission of penal law (*lü*) from the Han to the T'ang: a contribution to the study of the early history of codification in China. Revue International des droits de l'Antiquité

Maccormack G (2006) Filial Piety (*Xiao*) and the family in pre-Tang law. Revue International des droits de l'Antiquité

Maspero H (1978) Az ókori Kína. Gondolat Kiadó, Budapest

Miyazaki I (1980) The administration of justice during the song dynasty. In: Cohen JA, Edwards R, Chen FC (eds) Essays on Cina's legal tradition. Princeton University Press, Princeton

Nansen H (1997) Confucius and confucianism. In: Carr B, Mahalingam I (eds) Companion encyclopedia of Asian philosophy. Routledge, New York

Peerenboom RP (1993) Law and morality in ancient China. The silk manuscript of Huang-Lao. State University of New York Press, New York

Salát G (2003) Büntetőjog az ókori Kínában. Sinológiai műhely 3. Balassi Kiadó, Budapest

SarDesai DR (2013) Southeast Asia. Past and present. Westview Press, Boulder

Schirokauer C, Brown M (2006) A brief history of Chinese civilization. Wadsworth, Boston

Tarling N (1992) The Cambridge history of Southeast Asia, vol 1. Cambridge University Press, Cambridge

Taylor K (1992) The early kingdoms. In: Tarling N (ed) The Cambridge history of Southeast Asia, vol 1. Cambridge University Press, Cambridge

T'ung-Tsu C (1961) Law and society in traditional China. Mouton and Co., Paris

von Senger H (1994) Einführung in das chinesische Recht. Verlag C. H. Beck, München

Zhang J (2014) The tradition and modern transition of Chinese law. Springer, Berlin

Chapter 11
Societies Exposed to Chinese Legal Influence

11.1 Vietnam

What determines Vietnamese (legal) history is its complex and contradictory relationship to China, its northern neighbor, giant with its rich cultural heritage and threatening army. Vietnam is the only Southeast Asian country with too much Chinese influence and less Buddhism. By contrast, Southeast Asian countries experienced less China and more Buddhism which is an important difference not only for religious history. Buddhism or, Indian cultural influence in general was not promoted by force but by merchants, travelling scholars and everyday social contact of persons with different social and geographic background. Chinese influence however, was due to military superiority which also mediated cultural patterns for Vietnamese people who were either subjugated military or revolting the northern enemy but unable to resist the cultural influx. This is what made Vietnamese relationship to China so complex and paradox: though enemy in political and military terms yet a model in almost every aspect of cultural life. The limited role of Buddhism compared to Confucianism is just one example. The system of public administration and the mandarin-exams, Confucian theory of state and law, social hierarchy, respect of authorities and the elders are principles which further demonstrate this unequal partnership. In addition, technical terms and the writing systems also come from China since educated people of course read Confucian classics (Latin alphabet was introduced only in the twentieth century). What is more, Buddhism, the very embodiment of Indian influence also reached the country from China. This is the reason why Vietnamese Buddhism is Mahayana and not Theravada which is dominant in Southeast Asian countries where Buddhism spread without Chinese mediation. To be sure, Chinese cultural influence reached Vietnamese elite but left rural population unimpressed, relying on their customs and religion based on ancestor's cult and animism. This is why Vietnamese society was sharply divided between a rural community and an educated elite, which

J. Jany, *Legal Traditions in Asia*, Ius Gentium: Comparative Perspectives on Law and Justice 80, https://doi.org/10.1007/978-3-030-43728-2_11

followed Chinese cultural pattern and rather spoke Chinese and not Vietnamese, the language of the common people.[1]

This however, is only about the north of the country, the core of which lies around the banks of the Red River (Hong), called Nam Viet. Because of evident geographical reason, the northern part of Vietnam was exposed far more to Chinese influence than the south. This is why people of the north follow Confucian values strictly, such as respect for authorities, hierarchy and elder, insist on doctrines of Confucianism and take rules seriously. By contrast, people in the south are more easy-going, are no doctrinaire followers of Confucianism, do not follow authorities blindly and have an eclectic religiosity of their own. This difference is due to several factors. One is, obviously, the distance to China and its cultural influence. The other might be climate with tropics in the south and a cooler and less humid climate in the north. To this, history could be added as a third factor since what is now South Vietnam was inhabited by the Khmers and the original inhabitants of the Kingdom of Champa who were influenced rather by Indian culture which also manifested in their ways of life. This cultural dividing line is to be observed up to our modern times since it corresponds more or less to the dividing line which demarked the two halves of the country when it was split during the rule of the late Le dynasty, and also to the line marking the demilitarised zone (1954–1975).[2]

Vietnamese legal history fits into this pattern of overwhelming Chinese influence. Chinese legal influence was, however, different from Indian because it was about both content and form. As we have seen previously, Indian legal influence in Buddhist Southeast Asia was about form (systematics, jurisprudence, terms, genres of legal literature) but left inherited substantive law (tribal, national) intact. This is why Thai, Mon, etc. traditional law survived for centuries and Indian inspired systematisation preserved rather than ruined it. By contrast, Chinese legal influence was not only about forms and terms of jurisprudence but also about substantive law. It was not only the language and the structure of Chinese dynastic codes which were adapted in Vietnam but also their legal material. Interestingly, with the passage of time genuine Vietnamese law disappeared more and more from the Codes. While medieval Le Code still contained some original Vietnamese legal material, later Gia Long Code was hardly more than the simple translation of its Chinese model. Needless to say, Vietnamese Codes also focused on criminal and administrative law and private law matters played only a marginal role, if any. Confucianism also determined Vietnamese attitude to law which was, in line with Confucian ethics, negative. This is still alive, shown by these figures: while in the US there is one lawyer for 400 persons, in Japan for 7000, and in Vietnam for 20,000.[3]

---

[1] SarDesai (2013: 34–35).
[2] Church (2009: 184–185).
[3] Nghia (2005: 86).

11.1.1 History and Sources of Law

Legal sources which had come down to us are meagre since the majority was destroyed for various reasons. One is constant warfare which is, unfortunately, an obvious reason. Climate is the second reason since extreme weather conditions such as heat and humidity contributed to their loss. Lack of printing is the third main factor because texts were only in manuscript form and thus not numerous. In addition, these manuscripts were not collected because private intellectuals only collected Confucian classics and not Vietnamese laws. Ming brutality further enhanced this tendency when they took away important Vietnamese documents, legal texts included. This is why there are no sources prior to the fifteenth century. The most celebrated text of Vietnamese legal history, the Le Code was not preserved entirely either: we only have two copies and none of them are complete. Since however, they complement each other, we can reconstruct the text entirely (the text is now in Paris at the École Francaise de Extréme Orient).[4]

A strange narrative of local folklore tells us the beginnings of Vietnamese history. Accordingly, Lac Long Quan, a Vietnamese prince married, the story tells us, a fairy princess who did not give birth to children but to eggs. The princess moved towards the northern hills with fifty of her offspring and the prince to the south to the banks of the Red (Hong) River with his fifty offspring when the couple separated for unknown reason. Tradition claims to know the exact date of it: this happened around 2800 BCE.[5] Academics believe that the story is about the dual origin of the Vietnamese people but this does not help us any further to reconstruct early history. Fourteenth century chronicles attribute the first Vietnamese kingdom to Van Lang, a northern kingdom of the Lac Viet people in the seventh century BCE. Van Lang was conquered four centuries later by the Au Viet people who came to northern Vietnam from China and founded their state, the Au Lac kingdom in the Red River delta (257–208 BCE). History did not leave too much time to celebrate the victory, because Chinese general Trieu Da occupied the kingdom who, after the collapse of the Chin dynasty, founded an independent state in the south (Guangdon, Guangxi provinces). Nan Yueh or Nam Viet as this state was known with its capital near modern Canton was thus, half Chinese and half Vietnamese with Au Lac at its southern border. With the growing power of the Han dynasty, however, Nam Viet rulers were forced to acknowledge the supremacy of the Chinese emperor and to harmonise local law with Chinese law. As a result, cutting off of the nose was dropped from Vietnamese punishments. Despite this, Chinese influence on everyday legal practice was minimal, if any, but continued to rest on local customs. Vietnamese society remained tribal with clans as its basis where genealogy followed matrilineal descent. Real power was in the hands of tribal leaders without the assistance of whom no Vietnamese king was able to govern. The dependency of Nam Viet under the Trieu dynasty (207–111 BCE) was only a formal declaration, since governance was in the hands of local clan chiefs who maintained order and collected taxes. Things changed drastically when

[4]Huy and Van Tai (1986: 443).
[5]SarDesai (2013: 33).

powerful Hans decided for real annexation in 111 BCE. This is how Nam Viet was fully integrated and organised into provinces, in keeping with the practice of Chinese public administration. This was the time when Chinese influence began to penetrate Vietnamese society more gradually and deeply, particularly among the ruling elite. Growing Chinese influence and oppression provoked the revolt of Trung Trac and Trung Nhi, sisters who failed to defeat the Chinese (40–43 CE). With the collapse of Vietnamese resistance, Chinese law was reinforced, though local custom (levirate, matriarchate) remained intact.[6]

Chinese dominance returned with the Tang dynasty and their public administration which was in the hands of Chinese officials, except for local government which was preserved for local elite. In addition, Chinese law was declared to be the official law of Vietnam where local law was maintained only as custom. Despite this, it was again only the ruling elite which came to the orbit of Chinese culture, while society at large was kept at bay and hindered getting access to Confucian classics. This policy had soon paid off because in the absence of strong Confucian belief among locals it was easy for Buddhism to gain ground. With the fall of the Tang dynasty, Chinese influence ended in Vietnam (939), which brought about struggle for power and chaos but not peace. It was the time when Thang Long (today known as Hanoi), a northern power centre was created, which remained the country's capital to this day. Undecided struggle for power destabilized the country and brought military leaders to power whose short lived reigns were unable to bring peace, law and order. By contrast, constant rivalries created unprecedented cruelties, particularly when destroying enemies and their allies was at stake (executing with a poisonous snake, throwing to tigers, choking by the ebb and flow of tide, cutting into pieces with a knife, etc.). The country was led out of the chaos by Ly Cong Uan, founder of the Ly dynasty (1010–1225) who was a poor orphan boy brought up in a Buddhist monastery. With the royal name of Ly Thai To, h e became one of the most celebrated rulers of Vietnamese history because he was able to stabilise the northern borders, to defeat resurgents and rebels, to end anarchy by establishing public administration and to ensure revenues through an effective yet just tax system. All this was accomplished in the spirit of Buddhism, not Confucianism. Ly Thai To's reign was important for Vietnamese Buddhism since the ruler remained an enthusiastic Buddhist who was serious in the observance of Buddhist ethics. According to his belief, former rulers failed because they did not consider the will of Heaven and did not govern for the welfare of society, two important principles which Ly defined as the essence of his rule. This is why he reduced taxes, remitted debts and stopped cruelties of the previous decades. His successors followed him in this policy, particularly in humanising criminal law in the spirit of Buddhist ethics and principles. This is the reason why punishments were moderated significantly, specifying beating as a general punishment also for violent crimes such as manslaughter. What is more, persons engaged in political revolt were not executed but forgiven, unprecedented and unthinkable as it was in contemporary Vietnam. The new criminal code of Ly Thai Tong (1028–1054) (*Hinh Thu*) was promulgated in this spirit and it is a great loss that it was lost and

---

[6]Huy and Van Tai (1986: 435–437, 1987: 5–7).

we know it only from references in other sources. It is easy to identify these laws since they specify more human punishments than the laws of Chinese origin which they replace. New Buddhist criminal legal thinking was at variance with Confucian rigour and this is the reason why Confucian scholars of later generations condemned the tolerant ethic of criminal law, particularly the generosity toward rebels. In political terms, Ly Thai Tong was a more significant king in Vietnamese history than his father had been because of his military successes. He was also a patron of Buddhism as all Ly rulers were who wanted to reconcile local cults with Buddhist ethics and worldview. Buddhism was at its peak in this period since both public and intellectual life was built around it. Ly rulers also promoted Buddhism in the countryside, where great amount of shrines were built. Despite such enthusiasm for Buddhism Ly, rulers called themselves Emperor of the South who ruled the Southern Kingdom upon the mandate of Heaven, a Vietnamese variant of Chinese political theory.[7]

Tolerant Ly policy combined with the decline of dynastic authority pawed the way for militant Tran dynasty (1225–1440) to power. With a new dynasty a new policy entered Vietnam with a centralisation never seen previously as the other extreme of Ly tolerance. Public administration was refined and controlled, officials were obliged to pass exams on the Chinese model and successful candidates were appointed to provinces in order to collect tax and implement orders of the central government. Against Ly policy relying on local elite and granting a relative free hand for local communities in exchange for loyalty Tran policy was just the opposite: to abolish local autonomies, push local elite to the background and send agents of central government to provinces in order to implement central will. Trained officials were just one tool in this system. Centralisation was however not only about aggregating power, it was also about public works which required central planning. Most importantly, the construction of dams regulating the Red River was a great achievement which protected land and people from floods.[8]

Endogamy was also a method to enhance centralisation and protect the ruling dynasty from rivalries. Accordingly, Tran males married their nieces and sometimes their half-sisters in order to keep Tran females within the clan and hinder no clan members to enter the Tran clan by marrying a female of the dynasty. Internal struggle for power was reduced by the practice, according to which the king abdicated when his successor reached maturity and handed him over the management of the routine cases while he himself continued to reign as 'upper emperor' (*thai thuong hoang de*) until his successor was trained in office and was able to govern alone. This was the time for the upper emperor to resign and retire, usually to a Buddhist monastery. This unusual way of selecting and training the next ruler proved successful since early Tran rulers cumulated military victories, expanding their rule further south and were also able to resist invading Mongol forces in the 1270s and 1280s. In addition to the military, public administration and dynastic custom law was also an important tool to govern. This is the reason why already Thai Tong, the first ruler of the Tran dynasty, promulgated Quoc Trieu Thong Che in 1230, a Code which was about the

---

[7]Taylor (1992: 137–148) and Huy and Van Tai (1986: 437–438, 1987: 8–11).
[8]Dutton et al. (2012: 42).

revision of previous criminal law. A century later, criminal law was again codified, resulting in Hinh Thu (1341) and Hoang Trieu Dai Dien. Though faithful Buddhists, Trans did not follow the tolerant criminal policy of the Ly dynasty. By contrast, new Tran criminal law was for the other extreme with brutal punishments which even provoked the criticism of Confucian scholars. Not a single word has reached us from these codes, yet some laws are known from references in other works. Accordingly, thieves were crushed by elephants and officials caught gambling were whipped to death. Such extremes notwithstanding, Chinese influence on Vietnamese law was on the rise. This is why the system of five punishments was introduced, and the judiciary was reorganized, headed by a body at the court which approved capital punishments (*Tham Hinh Vien*). Officials trained in Confucian classics and passing the exams contributed to further sinicization of everyday legal practice. Rising Ming dynasty however, went a step further when entering Vietnam and conquering it with a casus belli to restore legitimate Tran power which was challenged by a pretender. Victorious Mings wanted to govern the country as a Chinese province but failed because of Chinese intervention, abuses of corrupt officials accompanied with economic and political decline provoked resistance headed by Le Loi, a rich landlord. After heavy fighting, Chinese troops were driven out the country and Le Loi declared himself king. This is how the rule of the Le dynasty began.[9]

With a new dynasty, a new area began yet again. Aristocratic Buddhist society gave way to an ever more Confucian Vietnam ruled by a military aristocracy which relied on neo-Confucian doctrines. In addition to Buddhism, territorial integrity was also lost because—apart from the early period—Vietnam was no longer a united country but only two halves headed by local landlords. The power of the Le dynasty extended over the entire country only in the first century of their rule (1428–1527). The integrity of the country was secured by centralisation and the rooting of the local petty lords but this policy no longer bore fruit from the sixteenth century onward, when the country was de facto ruled by local dynasties. Le dynasty retained its authority de iure but they were only puppets in the hands of the Trinh clan in the north and the Nguyen in the south. The political situation resembled medieval Japan where the military aristocracy headed by the shogun governed the country while the emperor was a shadow figure captive in his own palace. It is thus, not by accident that the Trinh clan established a military system similar to the Shogunate which did not tolerate disobedient Le monarchs who were either killed or forced to abdicate. Nguyen clan in the south was no less militaristic with their campaigns against the Khmers around the Mekong Delta and the former Kingdom of Champa which were annexed and attached to their territory. Nguyens, too, acknowledged the supremacy of the Le dynasty but this was no hindrance to wage constant wars against the Trinh in the north. It is only Le Tanh Ton, himself an educated Confucian scholar who is worth mentioning from this turbulent period because he was strong enough to rule a united country (1460–1497). Based on his superiority in Chinese culture in general and Confucian classics in particular, he introduced a series of reforms modelled on contemporary China. This is why the six ministries came into being (finance,

---

[9]Taylor (1992: 148–150) and Huy and Van Tai (1986: 437–439, 1987: 12–17).

rites, administration of justice, personnel affairs, army, public works) and he also separated civilian and military administration. Public administration remained in the hands of trained officials well versed in Chinese classics and passing rigid (though often corrupt) examinations. The country was governed by these officials down to provincial level while village elders were left in power to control local society. As a result, rigid neo-Confucianism of the Song court became the leading ideology for long, up to the nineteenth century. It was also during the reign of Le Tanh Tong that the most important work of Vietnamese legal history, the Le Code (Quoc Trieu Hinh Luat: The Criminal Code of the National Dynasty, or, as it is better known: Hong Duc Code) was edited. This huge work contains both genuine legal tradition and Chinese law (200 paragraphs of legal material go directly back to the Tang Code), the authority of which was never challenged. This is the reason why it was still in use in later centuries when the country was politically fragmented.[10]

Unity was finally achieved by the Nguyens who founded a new dynasty (1802–1945), making use of the chaos and turmoil accompanying the fall of the Le dynasty. Unity, however, did not last long. This time it was challenged by the French, progressing north from the south and colonising the central and the southern provinces. But this was yet no trouble for the founder of the dynasty, Gia Long (1802–1819) who, whilst reorganising his rule, promulgated a new criminal code (1813), which formally replaced the Le Code. Since however, the new code was less comprehensive than its predecessor, the Le Code remained in use in practice for several decades concerning issues for which laws were missing from the new code. The Gia Long Code (officially: Hoang Viet Luat Le) is above all, a copy of the Chinese Qing Code which differs from its model only in a few issues of detail. This unprecedented servile copying was due to some reasons, both political and legal. First, Qing Code has a clear structure and an easily understandable text which made it a reasonable choice to copy. Second, Chinese influence was growing rapidly in the court where officials of Chinese descent backed the new ruler. Foreign policy was the third factor since Vietnamese political elite considered their northern neighbour not a dangerous power any longer but a country which could help them in their struggle against more powerful colonising western forces. In addition, codification was not the only area where the Vietnamese ruler followed the Chinese court, because Gia Long had a new capital built on the model of the Forbidden City in the middle of the country (Hué) to express the unity of the country symbolically. This decision however, rather created domestic tension since the northern power centre was abandoned which was a blow to the pride of northerners. Rigid neo-Confucian doctrines implemented with administrative force contributed to more problems. The situation escalated with the persecution of Christians and the deliberate rejection of Western doctrines and ideas which ultimately provoked French intervention. French missionaries were active in Vietnam already in the seventeenth century and a century later helped Gia Long to accede to the throne. As a result of their activities, around half a million Christians

---

[10]SarDesai (2013: 37–39), Taylor (1992: 151–152), Huy and Van Tai (1986: 439–440, 1987: 17–19) and Huy (1981: 239).

already lived in Vietnam in the nineteenth century and their persecution and indiscriminate massacre provoked consternation in France. French troops took Saigon at first and then, moving from south towards the north, occupied the entire country. Westernising modernisation left its trace on the country: in addition to roads and canals, the Hanoi–Saigon railway was built, Saigon grew rapidly to become the most modern city of Southeast Asia and schools and hospitals were erected all over the country. One of the most important decisions was to bring virgin land of the southern region to cultivation which multiplied the arable land of the country with a figure of 420%. As a result, Vietnam was one of the leading rice exporting countries by the 1920s. Western inspired legal reforms fit into this framework of modernisation. Needless to say, the model for the new laws was the French Codes which remained, however, on paper because Vietnamese rural population remained unimpressed by these laws.[11] By and large, Vietnam remained a Confucian country where disputes are solved by social mechanisms, such as mediation and the authority of respected persons (elder, village and clan leaders). Law continued to be seen as a tool of the state but not a mean by which individual rights could be enforced. Communist rule contributed to this understanding. Even today, legal conflicts are solved at the courts of law as an ultima ratio when other mechanisms of conflict resolutions have been exhausted.[12]

11.1.2 Legal Institutions

Traditional Vietnamese legal institutions could be studied best through the lens of the Le Code because it is well structured, it is the most comprehensive legal text that has reached us, which contains both genuine and adapted (Chinese) legal material. The Code consists of 722 articles of which 342 have no direct equivalent in the Tang and Ming Codes. That is, though genuine law and Buddhist legal understanding were on the decline, Chinese influence was balanced and not overwhelming in the fifteenth century.

The Code consists of six books; each book has two chapters, except the third book which consists of three chapters. The structure of the Le Code is the following: Book One, I: Concepts, principles (1–49); II: Armed bodies (palace guard, border guard: 50–96); Book Two, III: Public administration (97–240); IV: The army (241–283); Book Three, V: Marriage law (284–341); VI: Ownership (342–400); VII: Sexual crimes (401–410); Book Four, VIII: Theft and other violent criminal acts (411–464); IX: Assault and judicial procedure (465–514); Book Five, X: Fraud, misleading (515–552); XI: Minor criminal acts (553–644); Book Six: XII: Arrest (645–657); XIII: Criminal procedure (658–722).

The structure of the Code is thematic. We can witness repetitions however, and also thematic disorder when a topic comes to a halt at the end of a book and the

---

[11] Church (2009: 186–188) and Huy and Van Tai (1986: 441–442, 1987: 29–31).

[12] Hop (2011: 207–209).

matter is not continued in the next book but only in another (for instance, in the case of books II and IV, and IX and XIII). Concepts and principles are usually drafted in general terms, while laws are presented casuistically resulting in very long paragraphs sometimes when the subject matter is complicated and the editor wanted to go along comprehensively. Unsurprisingly, it is criminal law which dominates the code. When the subject matter is not criminal law but another field of law (marriage, ownership, etc.), it is again the criminal aspect which comes to the fore and thus, the Code discusses crimes against propriety rights or marriage and sexual relations. In addition to criminal law, public administration and laws related to armed bodies are highlighted, following, of course, the Chinese model in this respect, too.

The Code begins with the system of five punishments, taken over from Chinese law (Book One I: 1), which were further classified into sub-categories. Beating with a light stick (*suy*) was the mildest corporeal punishment which was either a sui generis punishment for minor crimes or an additional punishment accompanying others (e.g. exile). Subcategories of beating were specified according to the number of strikes (first category: 10 strikes, second: 20 strikes and so on), altogether five subcategories (50 strikes) belong here. Beating with a heavy stick (*truong*) was a sanction for men, which differed from beating with a light stick. not only in the weight of the stick but also in the number of strikes (first subcategory: 60 strikes, and so on up to 100 strikes). Forced labour consisted of three subcategories depending on the difficulty of the task but it was also specified by gender (men were sent to the army or to elephant stables while women were sentenced to work in a kitchen or in the paddy fields). Exile (*luu*) was also of three subcategories depending on the distance (nearby province, distant province, province along the border). Exile was usually accompanied with tattooing. Death penalty (*tuu*) was classified according to the mode of execution: choking was the most human form of execution because it preserved the integrity of the human body which was an important factor in Vietnamese understanding. Decapitation with placing the head on public display combined the horror of annulling the integrity of the human body with humiliation. The most horrible form of execution was cutting into pieces because it destroyed the integrity of the body entirely.[13]

The Code dwells upon the ten gravest crimes (*thap ac*) at some length. The most serious among them was high treason, that is, attempt at the king's life, to be followed by disobedience (destruction of imperial palaces, mausoleums, and temples dedicated to the spirits of royal ancestors) and treason. The forth category consists of acts violating the principle of gerontocracy, which means various forms of violence against older relatives. Interestingly, manslaughter comes only at the fifth place which was regarded similar to cursing with magic power. The sixth category included various acts against public order such as stealing from court mausoleums, criticising the ruler, stealing the royal seals. The seventh was the violation of filial obedience and the mourning system. Family life was destroyed by acts belonging to the eighth (violence against family members which were further classified according to the degree of relations) and to the tenth (incest) category while disloyalty (killing a proceeding officer, killing one's teacher) was placed between the two. Crimes belonging to these

---

[13]I:I: 9.

ten categories were treated differently and were exempt from general laws pertaining to others. For example, if a king decided for amnesty, it was not extended to persons convicted for one of these crimes. In addition, punishments for these crimes were not subject to mitigation, though otherwise it was not impossible. These crimes were adjudicated by the principle of absorption, expressly referred to by the Code, that is, a person who committed more crimes and one among them belonged to the ten categories, he/she was convicted only for the most grievous act, the punishment of which absorbed the punishments of the less severe crimes.[14]

The royal palace enjoyed particular protection in criminal law. Persons who went through the first gate were heavily beaten by the stick, but those who went towards the residential quarters were put to death. Persons shooting an arrow towards the palace, climbing up the wall of the palace,[15] or entering the palace with due reason but not leaving it when their task was completed or before the dark at the latest, were also sentenced to death.[16] It was prohibited to meet or talk to women living in the palace, and particularly to exchange messages with them.[17] There was curfew at night in the capital city the violation of which was punished by beating except if someone went for a doctor or a midwife.[18]

The borders of the country were no less protected. Crossing the border was prohibited and punished by death. Border guards unable to stop anyone from fleeing the country were also put to death. Persons marrying foreigners were exiled and the marriage was null and void. What is more, a native selling land near the border to foreigners or just talking to them was also executed. It was not only land around the border that was protected by criminal law since persons selling an elephant, a horse, a weapon, a servant or a secret to foreigners were also put to death. Persons selling salt were however, only exiled.[19] Despite such harsh laws, hospitality was not prohibited right from the outset. This is why everyone housing a guest had to inform authorities and also the neighbours about his guest and his time of departure. Hosts were also required to spy on their guests and learn everything possible about them (family relations, luggage, etc).[20] Here we have a political system paralysed by the fear of foreigners who were suspected of overthrowing the regime to the degree of paranoia. This is the reason why local people talking to them were executed. This way of thinking was not peculiar to Vietnam only: we can witness the same attitude with almost the same laws in Thailand and in its Three Seals Code.

Court protocol was also strictly regulated, the laws of which have found their way i n he Code. Court etiquette and protocol was very rigid and strict resulting in a ritualistic behaviour and communication for which words and phrases—designed for various situations—were specified and were to be rejected only at the risk of

---

[14]I:I: 16, 37.

[15]I:II: 51–52.

[16]I:II: 54.

[17]I:II: 61.

[18]I:II: 64, 67.

[19]I:II: 71, 74–77, 80.

[20]III:V: 293.

punishment.[21] Needless to say, it is criminal law again through the lens of which court etiquette was understood. A physician not properly serving a medicine was exiled together with the chief cook not properly serving the meal. Oral criticism of the ruler resulted in immediate beheading. Persons criticising the government in writing or circulating letters without proper signature were also put to death. Persons receiving such letters had to destroy them immediately, otherwise they faced punishments, too.[22] The illness of the king had to be respected. This is why persons participating in musical events while the monarch was ill were rewarded with 60 lashes. Humour was anyway exiled from the court: anyone telling a joke about the king or criticising his policy with nursery rhymes or songs would go to exile or forced labour.[23]

Corruption must have been widespread, otherwise the Code would not dedicate a separate chapter to it. Bribery was punished by fines but if the amount was large enough, a corrupt official could be put to death.[24] Corruption was detrimental to the economic interest of the entire political system if it affected public work and the military because similarly to other Southeast Asian countries, the mobilisation of labour forces for agriculture and the military was of crucial importance in Vietnam, too. It was thus, the task of officials to register the male population above 15 in order to guarantee their services. If an official 'forgot' to register adult males in the area of his competency, he was exiled and the persons involved were conscripted to the army and they had to pay for the missed public work to the treasury in addition. People wanted, seemingly, to escape corvée obligation for which they invented various legal means. One such a trick was to change their names and move to another district or province, or to register as an old person, or to enter a Buddhist monastery. Editors of the Le Code were aware of all this and created laws with strict punishments for such acts. Only persons above 50 could become a Buddhist monk or a Daoist priest.[25]

Officials were also charged with social services. They had to look after the ill, the disabled, widows, and the orphans if they had no family. Officials had to supply them with shelter, food, garments and medicines as well. Officials not properly caring for disabled persons lost their office or were beaten with the stick.[26] Daily management of infrastructure was also in the hands of officials who controlled dams and ditches, managed the building and repairing of dams for which time was precisely specified (the first two months of the year). It was also the task of officials to build bridges and ferries over rivers. If rural population was damaged because of improper works (e.g. the dam broke), the officials had to bear responsibility for it.[27]

Family law was also approached through criminal law yet basic institutions of marriages and divorce can be reconstructed. The long process of negotiations started with the bridegroom's present to the girl's family. If accepted, discussion between

---

[21] II:III: 126, 147.
[22] II:III: 110–111; 132–133.
[23] II:III: 144, 216; IV:VIII: 411.
[24] II:III: 138.
[25] III:V: 285–287; 299; 311.
[26] III:V: 294–295.
[27] II:III: 181–182; V:XI: 575.

the families begun. If everything settled properly, a wedding ceremony followed, for which the bridegroom was also responsible for. If however, there was sexual contact between the parties before marriage, the bridegroom had to pay compensation, the sum of which varied according to the girl's social status, meanwhile the girl was condemned to 50 lashes by the stick. Should the father not give his daughter to the bridegroom after having accepted the presents, he was condemned to 80 lashes by the stick. If such a father gave his daughter to someone else in marriage, he was sentenced to forced labour together with the second suitor if he was aware of the former engagement. If he was not informed about it, he escaped punishment but his marriage was nevertheless null and void and the first bridegroom could marry the girl if he still wanted. If he declined, the second marriage would stand but the father had to repay the presents twice.[28]

While cancelling the agreement, fathers could however refer to some cases which would free them from punishments, for example, if the bridegroom committed a crime, was seriously ill (leprosy) or squandered away his property by debauchery. If proven, agreements could be cancelled without punishment but this had to be reported to the authorities and the gift received should be returned. Bridegrooms, too, could refer to these causes when cancelling the agreement but, interestingly, when doing so they did not retain the wedding gift back.[29]

Officials could marry women within their competency, only at the risk of losing their office and beating (70 strikes). Their punishment was the same if they married a singer or an actress. Officials were sentenced to forced labour if they married a woman of a tribe living along the border. Levirate (once a Vietnamese custom) was strictly forbidden by the Le Code, punished with exile. All such forbidden marriages were, of course, null and void.[30] A marriage of a woman who married during the mourning period of her parents or her late husband was also null and void and she was sentenced to forced labour. Solidarity among family relatives was required not to marry when a family member was in jail. Le Code agreed and this is why such a union was declared null and void by law. If such a marriage was concluded upon the will of the family father, the marriage was not declared null but no wedding celebration was permitted. Circumventing laws on mourning (e.g. not reporting the death of a parent, a grandparent or a partner) was not a good idea either, since such a person was sentenced to forced labour.[31] Vietnamese law on re-marriage of widows differed from Southeast Asian or Chinese law and concept because she could be forced to a new marriage. Le Code has it in a particular way when claiming that whoever forces a widow to re-marriage is subject to punishment and the marriage is null and void unless if her parent and grandparents force her to a new marriage. With this particular drafting, the law specifies the right of parents and grandparents to force a widow to a new marriage, a unique right in Asian laws.

---

[28]III:V: 314–315.
[29]III:V: 322.
[30]III:V: 316, 323, 324, 334.
[31]III:V: 317.318; II:III: 130.

Though parents were entitled to force their widow daughter to marriage, they could not force her or the couple to separate. If they did (e.g. because her husband was impoverished) they were punished by 60 strikes by the stick and the wife was returned to her husband. If however, a husband behaved disrespectfully towards the wife's parents, they could apply for the dissolution of marriage from the authorities. A husband not visiting his wife for five months lost his rights over her except if he was away for public work. Such an abandoned wife could get married again but she had to report to authorities about the state of affairs of her marriage in order to avoid complications and hinder tricks. A woman, by contrast, who left her husband without due cause was sentenced to forced labour and if she concluded a new marriage, her new husband too, except he was not aware of her former marriage but his wife had to be returned to her first husband anyway.[32]

The Code has a short chapter (10 articles) on rape, adultery and incest. Adultery with the first wife was punished by exile or death, with the second wife the punishment was one degree less. The wife was exiled and lost her propriety rights while her lover had to pay compensation to the husband. Adultery during the mourning period or committed by a servant with his master's wife was punished by death. Seduction of a virgin also resulted in exile or death but the girl was obviously exempt from punishment. Punishment of rape was also exile or death in addition to the payment of compensation. If someone killed the assailant during the fight, he enjoyed impunity. Intercourse with a girl younger than twelve was considered rape even if she consented to it.[33]

Concerning criminal acts against life, there are no traces of Buddhist inspiration and the leniency of former laws. Le Code has a clear Chinese impact with strict punishments, yet the influence of Confucian social understanding is also limited. This is best illustrated in punishment for manslaughter for which everyone is sentenced to beheading irrespective of the social position, gender and age of both the victim and the condemned. As Confucian ethics has particular punishment according to such differences, the lack of such differences indicates that the editors of the Code followed either legism or their own, genuine tradition. At the same time, parties were not allowed to settle the issue of manslaughter by negotiations or compromises (as against Islamic law) because reaching an agreement was expressly prohibited at the risk of exile, an endeavour to monopolise criminal law by the Vietnamese state in a society where blood feud was not unusual. Blood feud was, in theory, prohibited, yet this only half-hearted: as a rule, the punishment of a revenging person was milder than that of the first murderer and if a person avenged the death of a close relative, such a person had not to fear practically any punishment. Magic and the use of charms for harmful purposes, wishing to cause death (with death as a result) and keeping poisonous animals (primarily snakes) were regarded manslaughter, too.[34]

---

[32]III:V: 308–309; 321, 333.

[33]III:VII: 401–410.

[34]IV:VII: 415–416, 419, 423–425.

Robbery was punished by decapitation. If in addition someone died while fighting with robbers, decapitation was followed by placing the head on public view, otherwise reserved for high treason only. Thieves were not executed for the first time but were only exiled save they stole anything from the king or from a temple built for the ancestor's cult of the royal family. If anyone entered someone else's property at night, he was sentenced to forced labour even if he did not steal anything. If such a person was killed at night by the owner, he enjoyed impunity.[35] Assaults are treated casuistically, creating endless variations based on rank, degree of relations, kinds of injuries and the intent of acts (injuries of foot, head, nose, hand; committed against officials or commoners; committed by servants or free persons, etc.). Punishment for such acts varied between compensation and exile, depending on circumstances. Against Chinese practice, violence within the family was not tolerated since a husband hitting his wife was punished, the sanction depending on the person of the victim: beating the first wife was punished more severely than beating the second wife. If beating resulted in death, the crime belonged to the ten most grievous crimes and sanctioned accordingly. The punishment of the wife raising her hand against her husband's family members was identical with the husband's punishment.[36]

Similarly to other Southeast Asian legal systems, the Le Code has a separate chapter on damages caused by animals endangering the crops. If an animal (cattle, horse, etc.) destroyed the crop, its master had to pay compensation provided he survived the 80 strokes by the stick as his punishment. If animals caused harm also to human life, their owner had to be sentenced for negligent manslaughter. These rules pertained also to masters of elephants.[37] These rules are practically identical with the agricultural laws of the Burmese, Thai and Lao communities.

11.2   Korea

It is not an easy task to place genuine Korean legal custom and its role to Korean legal history for some political and academic reasons. One is the controversy concerning Korean legal custom, the existence of which is subject to debate. According to a leading contemporary Korean legal historian, Korean custom as a concept actually never existed. It was only a romantic invention of Korean nationalists of the late nineteenth century when legal scholars were trying to emphasize Korean customs primarily to counter-balance Japanese occupation. Korean customary law cannot be identified in this form; it was only an academic 'invention' motivated by politics and manifested in the idealisation of the genuine Korean customs.[38] It was not only against Japanese occupation, it was also to the detriment of Chinese influence to reduce its significance and highlight Korean tradition. Another reason is the relative

---

[35] IV:VII: 411, 426, 430–431, 450.
[36] IV:VII: 482–483.
[37] V:XI: 580–583.
[38] Kim (2012: 2; 14).

negligence of Korean legal history as a discipline, even in Korea itself. As an average, no more than two or three books have been published in this topic in a decade in Korea, and non-Korean academic literature produces even less. The few works dealing with Korean law rather underline the Chinese influence in general and the Ming Code in particular, the importance of criminal law and the administration of justice, leaving little space to genuine legal thoughts.[39]

Despite this, there are some particular Korean customs which determine Korean law, particularly family law. These are also important proofs in the debate supporting the existence of genuine Korean legal customs. One is the matrilocal (uxorilocal) form of settlement according to which young couples after wedding settle in the house of the bride's family and not in that of the husband's relatives. Uxorilocal settlement is relatively rare on global level and it is also not designed as the final form of settlement in Korea because after some years, usually after the birth of the first child at the latest, the young couple moves to the husband's family house to find their residence. It is also a Korean custom to distribute the bequest equally among offspring irrespective of gender. This genuine understanding however, was pushed to the background when Confucian ideology and neo-Confucian orthodoxy, promoting patriarchal thinking, the ancestors' cult and gender inequality was favoured to the detriment of inherited wisdom in codifications.[40]

With this, we now have Confucianism and Japanese occupation as factors determining Korean law. The third such a factor was Buddhism which influenced Korean legal understanding for a limited period because it was neglected for being at variance with leading Confucian social thinking. The fourth element was Western influence which came to the peninsula from the east, that is, Japan. Since Meiji reforms in Japan were just about how to adapt western legal ideas and institutions, the same western, notably German, ideas arrived in Korea simultaneously, mediated by Japanese forces.

Korean law is however by far not only about adapting foreign ideas and influences. The very first legal document which has reached us was produced already during the Gojoseon dynasty, an important period for Korean national identity and pride. Unfortunately, we have no proof for the chronology of its existence: though local tradition puts its birth to the very early date of 2333 BCE, Chinese sources refer to it only in the seventh century BCE. What we have is a fragment of three passages (Pal-jo-geum beob) about criminal law (death penalty for manslaughter, slavery for theft and material compensation for assault). With the fall of the Gojoseon dynasty, Korea was politically fragmented with three kingdoms ruling over the peninsula (Silla, Baekje, Goguryeo), dominated by clan politics. Korea was united again by the Goryeo dynasty, the name of the country (Korea) still encapsulating the name of this dynasty. Goryeo rulers (918–1392) choose Buddhism as their religion and ideology, which entered Korea already during the previous centuries from China. Goryeo court relied on Buddhism both as an ideology providing legitimacy and as a religion with intellectuals who were in the dynasty's service. This is why Buddhist monks were sent to diplomatic missions. Goryeo kings were generous in exchange:

---

[39]Shaw (1980a: 302–303).
[40]Kim (2012: 25–27).

Buddhist monasteries were built all over the country and the capital endowed with land and slaves.[41]

With the coming of the Yi (Joseon) dynasty (1392–1910), we can witness a drastic change in intellectual life, since the new masters of the country made Confucianism their exclusive ideology to the detriment of Buddhism which lost its privileged position. With this Chinese understanding of society and law, it became dominant in Korea for long centuries to come. Heavenly mandate of kings was propagated together with a paternalist understanding of political power. In addition, a centralised bureaucracy was developed in order to have a professional support and social relations were grouped according to the five relations of Confucian teaching. The beneficiaries of the system were the royal family and the *yangban*, leading aristocracy heading civilian and military administration with privileges and landed property donated by the ruler. *Yangban* were relieved from paying taxes and accumulated wealth from their office and lands which explains why they backed the monarchy to the last and hindered every reform during the nineteenth century.[42] This landed aristocracy was interested in preserving the less efficient agricultural production and hindering trade and commerce, a policy which was backed by referring to Confucian ideology against profit. As a result, Korea remained an isolated society for long centuries.[43]

In this period, Buddhism was no longer a rival to Confucianism since this religion was rooted from Korea, the monasteries and its wealth were confiscated and their monks were sometimes persecuted. With the advent of the monopoly of Confucianism, Korean law was immediately codified on this new intellectual basis. This is why Taejo, the first king of the dynasty, promulgated the Six Codes (Gyeongje Yukcheon) in 1397, just five years after he ascended to the throne. This was followed by the Great Code (Gyeong-guk-dae-jeon) during the reign of Seongjong (1484) in the next century, which was a very important text for the coming centuries. The intellectual father of this Code, Cheong Dojeon, diverged at some points from Confucian teachings and political ideology. Korean tradition attributes him the view that it is the people which are the most important constituent part of a political system with the right to depose of a king if necessary. Some modern Korean authors see this view as a genuine precedent of constitutionalism and of the principle of rule of law, at the risk of exaggeration. The judiciary was also developed under the Joseon dynasty: though private law cases and petty crimes were left in the hands of the local elite, for more serious cases, an appellate system was created. Provincial governors were the first instances to appellate against local judgments, while the office of justice at the royal court was the appellate court against the governor's judgment as the ultimate instance. In addition to the judiciary, public administration was further developed with the task of registering (for instance, the capital city of Seoul kept the marriage

---

[41] Nathan (2014: 260), Kwon (2011: 152–153) and Kim (2013: 2–4).

[42] Chun (1980: 5–7; 10) and Shaw (1980b: 33).

[43] Choi (1980: 57).

and land registers) and controlling (covered agents of the *am-haeng-eo-sa* were trying to investigate corruption). All this was modelled on Chinese experience in public
administration in general and the Ming Code in particular.[44]

The Code was adjusted to the structure of ministries with six ministerial bodies,
hence its name (Six Codes). Consequently, the Code consisted of six books, known
as: Ijon (persons); Hojon (finances); Yejon (rites); Pyongjon (army); Hyongjon (punishments); Kongjon (public works). Similarly to the Chinese and Vietnamese Codes,
the Six Codes is predominantly a criminal law dealing with various issues through
the lenses of criminal law. Other fields of law are underrepresented and have no comprehensive and clear structure. For instance, laws on marriage can be found in the
book on rites, while the related registration is in the book on persons. The book on
financial issues (taxes) also has laws on private law matters (land ownership, debt).[45]

Similarly to China (and Japan), law was kept secret in Korea where society was
not expected to know and follow the law but to be obedient to officials and their
ordinances while law remained a guidance and a command for officials. Law was of
low esteem in every segment of Korean society but *yangban* were even advised not
to have any business with law (while being exempt from punishments): 'do read ten
thousand books but not law'.[46] Small wonder that no jurisprudence emerged in Korea
where the educated elite read Confucian classics, while law and its science (*yulhak*)
was regarded a practical skill not worth of study. Law was thought for officials by
the Ministry of Punishments in order to have reliable professionals to adjudicate
criminal cases. In the absence of jurisprudence as a discipline, obviously no works
on jurisprudence were written. Scholars who touched upon legal problems were
politicians and statesmen who put legal problems into the framework of problems
of running a state. This is why the celebrated author of Korean political thinking,
Cheong Dojeon also devoted some words to law. According to him, authority is
actually a service in the interest of society in order to develop welfare, security
and prosperity. Should a king deviate from this path, he is advised to abdicate and
hand over power to a most suitable candidate. Should he however, continue with
his unjust rule, people are entitled to overthrow him by force if necessary at the
end of the day. Choen Dojeon was not followed by everyone, Yi Ik (seventeenth
century), for example, rather followed Chinese legism, joined the views of Han Fei
and advocated rigorous punishments.[47] Chinese seasonal thinking also took root in
Korea, this is why there were no trials between the spring and the autumn equinox.
Legal proceedings were regarded secondary in importance compared to agricultural
work and, therefore, no time and energy were spent on them when time was ripe to
work in the fields. Exceptions were only made in serious criminal cases.[48] Despite
this general view, there were some people who were ready to help parties fill in

---

[44]Nathan (2014: 270–271), Kwon (2011: 152–153), Kim (2013: 2–4), Shaw (1980a: 303–306) and
Choi (2005: 66–72).

[45]Kim (2012: 22–23).

[46]Chun (1980: 9–11).

[47]Choi (2005: 88–104; 137–138).

[48]Choi (1980: 65–67).

documents and help their cases in the proceedings for due revenues. These persons, usually coming from the bottom of society were regarded as robbers, particularly by the *yangban* who despised them for provoking conflicts, creating disharmony, hindering court procedure by all sorts of tricks and being harmful parasites acting against Confucian morality.[49]

A special social and legal institute of the period was *hyangyak*, an institutional mechanism of rural conflict management. The basic idea was Chinese, which was elaborated by the Confucian thinker Zhu Xi and adapted in Korea during the Song dynasty. The aim of the system was to settle local conflicts at local level and to spread Confucian values among the masses. The adaption of the system in Korea was not without difficulties, since both the bureaucracy and local rivalries hindered it, yet it played an important role between its introduction (late fifteenth century) and its final demise (early twentieth century). The meaning of *hyangyak* is community contract, a somewhat euphemistic term for an accord the contents of which is not specified by the parties but settled beforehand, being strict Confucian morals. The *hyangyak* specified the expected behaviour of individuals and also the punishments for wrongdoers. The administration of justice was however not left to royal officials but to the local elite, the *yangban,* hence it was also a tool for the decentralisation of power. Despite controversies, the system operated according to the expectations since it contributed to spread Confucian values, spared time and energy for the officials who were relieved to deal with petty local issues while conflicts were settled fast and effectively locally. In addition to conflict resolution, the *hyangyak* system also contributed to enhance solidarity since it was expected to render mutual assistance for work, burial or illness when missing labour force was supplied by it.[50]

To relieve officials from litigations in order to focus on the issues of government and public administration was an idea with good arguments. Korean society was—as records of the past two centuries show—willing to litigate if their private interest was at stake (land, slave, ownership). By contrast, Korean society did everything possible to hinder criminal procedures since not only suspected persons but witnesses, too, were subject to tortures. As a result, parties wanted to reach compromises in criminal law matters, something which is against Confucian understanding and thus unlawful. What is more, blood feud was a moral duty in case of killing a close relative, therefore, to reach agreements in such cases was also against common moral understanding.[51] Despite this, Korean society did everything possible to enforce private interest and this is in harmony with the result of modern legal sociology proving that the rejection of law is no longer a common attitude in Korea where people are aware more and more with their rights and are ready to enforce them.[52]

Korean elite wanted to maintain the Code for long centuries, though it was applicable less and less due to changing circumstances. This is the reason why the Code was amended and changed frequently but no new Code emerged. The will to reform

---

[49]Choi (1980: 69–70).

[50]The history of the *hyangyak* is presented by Kim (2012: 41–51).

[51]Shaw (1980b: 42–44).

[52]Choi (2005: 298–303).

was missing and hindered by the elite which was the beneficiary of the status quo. In the second part of the nineteenth century, that is, the last decades of the ruling dynasty the resistance to reforms was anachronistic and this is why king Gojong send experts to Japan to study legal reforms and to bring home expertise on how to adapt Western law in an Asian country. Korean scholars thus studied Meiji-reforms, though some of them also went to the US to learn there. Reforms started slowly but gradually. Separation of powers was introduced first, followed by the reform of the judiciary. The first constitution of Korea (Daehanguk Gukje) was promulgated in 1899, but too late. The Japanese–Korean treaty of 1907 reduced the power of the ruling dynasty significantly which was dethroned completely in 1910 when Japan took over the governance of the country. This is how Japanese occupation, in the eyes of Korean society the darkest period of Korean history, started, transforming the model of political and legal modernisation to an enemy force. History is, however, complex and full of contradictions. Though an Asian power, Japan nevertheless introduced a series of Western inspired political and legal reforms in Korea just because the long decades of modernisation had an impact on Japan transforming its own political and legal system. This is why a law based on German, American and French pattern was introduced in Korea as well. This was, of course, controlled beyond limits and laws which were at variance with Japanese interest were not introduced. Since law in general and legal reforms in particular was a tool to govern the peninsula, important laws which hindered this were dismissed, such as freedom and first generation human rights. The independence of the judiciary was narrowed for the same reason. By contrast, the competence and power of the government was enlarged in order to introduce Japanese direct rule in Korea. Korean society rejected everything Japanese which hindered legal reforms, progressive or not. A case in point is the law on haircuts (1895) contradicting local custom and Confucian manner which provoked an armed revolt after the failure of the protest of Confucian scholars. The end of Japanese occupation brought no relief but war and the separation of Korea to North and South which made common legal reforms impossible. In the South, German thinkers such as Hans Kelsen and Gustav Radbruch continued to influence jurisprudence during the decades when Korea turned toward common law countries and their legal system to find a model while the North followed its own steps.[53]

References

Sources

Dutton G, Werner J, Whitmore J (2012) Sources of Vietnamese tradition. Columbia University Press, New York
Huy NN, Van Tai T (1987) The Le Code, vols I–III. Ohio University Press, Athens

---

[53] Kwon (2011: 152–156), Kim (2012: 101–192, 2013: 5–6) and Choi (1980: 88, 2005: 162).

Literature

Choi DK (1980) The development of law and legal institutions in Korea. In: Chun BD, Shaw W, Choi D (eds) Traditional Korean legal attitudes. Korea Research Monograph, University of California, Berkeley

Choi C (2005) Law and justice in Korea. South and North. Seoul National University Press, Seoul

Chun BD (1980) Legal attitudes of the late Yi dynasty. In: Chun BD, Shaw W, Choi D (eds) Traditional Korean legal attitudes. Korea Research Monograph. University of California, Berkeley

Church P (2009) A short history of Southeast-Asia. Wiley, Singapore

Hop DX (2011) Vietnam: the past 25 years, the present and the future. In: Black EA, Bell GF (eds) Law and legal Institutions of Asia. Traditions, adaptations and innovations. Cambridge University Press, Cambridge

Huy NN (1981) The penal code of Vietnam's Le dynasty. In: Eikemeir D, Franke H (eds) State and law in East Asia. Festschrift Karl Bünger. O. Harrassowitz, Wiesbaden

Huy NN, Van Tai Ta (1986) The Vietnamese texts. In: Hooker MB (ed) The law of Southeast Asia. Volume I: the pre-modern texts. Butterworth, Singapore, pp 435–494

Kim MS-H (2012) Law and custom in Korea. Comparative legal history. Cambridge University Press, Cambridge

Kim K (2013) Overview. In: Korea Legislation Research Institute (ed) Introduction to Korean law. Springer, Heidelberg

Kwon Y (2011) Korea: bridging the gap between Korean substance and Western form. In: Black EA, Bell GF (eds) Law and legal institutions of Asia. Traditions, adaptations and innovations. Cambridge University Press, Cambridge

Nathan M (2014) Buddhism and law in Korean history. In: French R, Nathan A (eds) Buddhism and law. An introduction. Cambridge University Press, Cambridge, pp 255–271

Nghia PD (2005) Confucianism and the conception of the law in Vietnam. In: Gillespie J, Nicholson P (eds) Asian socialism and legal change. The dynamics of Vietnamese and Chinese reform. Asia Pacific Press, Canberra

SarDesai DR (2013) Southeast Asia. Past and present. Westview Press, Boulder

Shaw W (1980a) Traditional Korean law and its relation to China. In: Cohen JA, Edwards RR, Chen FC (eds) Essays on China's legal tradition. Princeton University Press, Princeton

Shaw W (1980b) Social and intellectual aspects of traditional Korean law, 1392–1910. In: Chun BD, Shaw W, Choi D (eds) Traditional Korean legal attitudes. Korea Research Monograph. University of California, Berkeley

Taylor K (1992) The early kingdoms. In: Tarling N (ed) The Cambridge history of Southeast Asia, vol 1. Cambridge University Press, Cambridge

Chapter 12
Japanese Law

12.1 Japanese Law to the Tokugawa Period

The first inhabitants of the Japanese islands arrived to their new home from continental Asia about twenty thousand years ago. It is clear from the archaeological evidence that the modern Japanese people are not the direct descendants of these fishers and hunters. By contrast, the so called Yamato people who settled down in Japan during the third century CE have more in common with contemporary Japanese population. The Yamato people came to Japan from South China and Korea in successive waves and brought along the use of metals and a high standard of rice cultivation. Rice production remained the main factor of agriculture for centuries and this is why investments concentrated on agriculture. The first dams and canals were built during the first centuries which significantly increased productivity. This development is linked to the Yayoi people, a population with common anthropological features with the modern Japanese and, therefore, believed to be their direct ancestors. Yayoi people were the first on the island who created a more refined and complex social and political organisation, which is, perhaps, the result of public works such as building of dams and canals which requires planning, mobilisation and enforcement. Yayoi rulers had huge tombs built for themselves (*kofun*) in which the quantity of earth and stone piled up is equivalent to that of the Egyptian pyramids. Because of the ancestors' cult Japanese law still prohibits archaeological excavations in these monuments which hinders us to know anything definite about them. The building of these tombs continued for centuries and it was only the spread of Buddhism and the Taika reforms which prohibited it because people wanted to use resources for different aims and purposes.[1]

During this early period of Japanese history, there was no uniform Japanese state, instead Chinese chronicles tell us more than one hundred political entities shared the political and geographical landscape separated by natural borders. Chinese court referred to them with degrading terms, though some of them sent envoys

---

[1] Steenstrup (1996: 1–7).

© Springer Nature Switzerland AG 2020
J. Jany, *Legal Traditions in Asia*, Ius Gentium: Comparative Perspectives
on Law and Justice 80, https://doi.org/10.1007/978-3-030-43728-2_12

to the Chinese emperor. When, centuries later, this degrading practice was revealed, the Japanese protested and demanded their country be called the land of *wa* (harmony). Among these rival states the Kingdom of *Yamata* was the strongest. According to Chinese chronicles, contemporary Japanese society was polygamous but in contrast to China, every woman was a legitimate wife and not a concubine, therefore, 'Japanese women are not jealous'. This was, perhaps, also due to a Japanese custom according to which couples did not live together but separately, continuing their former lives and wives kept their former place of residence where a husband only visited them. We are left in darkness why this form of marriage evolved and continued for centuries in Japan. Perhaps it is related to a relative free position of women in contemporary Japanese society where women were entitled to have their share in public life, Chinese chronicler reports somewhat scandalised. What is more, there was Pi-mi-hu, a queen with a harsh rule and religious authority whose burial was accompanied with human sacrifices. Perhaps these are hints to matriarchate but convincing evidences are missing. In addition to the role of women, Chinese chroniclers also noted the brutal punishments in Japan where convicted persons were executed together with their families, hence the subsequent low rate of crimes. Not only thieves were missing but lawsuits, too, because people did not turn to law courts, a habit continuing to modern times. Rival states waged continuous wars for hegemony which resulted in the final victory of Keitai (d. 531), an eminent general who founded a new dynasty. If Keitai is, as it seems, in fact the ancestor of all subsequent Japanese emperors, Japan may pride itself to have the most ancient ruling dynasty on Earth.[2]

An important document of Japanese legal history from this early period is the so called constitution of *Shotoku Taishi* (Crown Prince). Needless to say, a Japanese document dated to 604 CE is no constitution in the proper sense of the term. Instead, it is a long list of advice and prudent councils for politicians. The 17 articles combine Buddhist ethics with Confucian social teaching and with some legist thoughts featuring here and there. Among the aim of the document was to strengthen central authority against centrifugal forces, that is, contemporary Japanese political reality, and to stress the influence and importance of religion in public affairs. The first two paragraphs of the document bring genuine Japanese principle of harmony and Buddhist ethics together. According to the first article, peace and harmony were the most important factors in society because it creates solidarity within the group. The second article warns that it was highly important to observe the teachings of Buddhism and have a positive anthropology: accordingly, people should be taught and advised in order to be law abiding persons. The third article underlines obedience to the ruler, and the fifth stresses that judicial procedure must be impartial and fast so that it may reach its goal. The remaining eight articles address officials with various appeals (they must not accept gifts, they should be tolerant towards people, they cannot spend their time by doing nothing and with private chats). The last two articles underline that the guiding principle of governance must be the welfare of the community and important issues should be decided collectively.[3]

---

[2]Steenstrup (1996: 8–15).
[3]For the see Drapkin (1989: 334–335).

According to Japanese tradition, the same Shotoku was the first scholar who wrote commentaries to various *sūtras* and had Buddhist and Confucian texts brought to Japan from China. Shotoku also established diplomatic relations with China and sent Japanese students to Chinese Buddhist monasteries to study. With this, Japan entered the Confucian world which did not leave Japanese law uninspired. As a result, Chinese law was studied and adapted, particularly criminal law with its punishments and torture. Shotoku's vision however, soon created social tension between the newly educated Confucian professionals and the traditional elite (Soga) who governed rather autocratically and hindered the new thinking. This is why the court, sensing tension in social and economic policy, introduced the so-called *Taika* reform in 645 in order to hinder popular uprising and to guarantee its own power at the cost of rearranging the power structure within the elite (this policy was repeated during the Meiji reforms in the nineteenth century). As a result, Soga ministers were liquidated, arable land was distributed among peasants, a uniform taxation system was introduced and various local taxes were eliminated. In addition, public administration was refined when the state was divided into provinces and governors were appointed to head them. To ease communication, a central postal service was organised. Governors heading the provinces also collected taxes for the central government. Smaller districts were managed by the local aristocracy. The model for these reforms was Tang China, a rising power which could threaten Japan, too, and it was wise to avert this by using similar methods in governance. Reformers kept on referring to the writings of Shotoku Taishi, claiming that what they were doing was the practical realisation of his principles, arguments encapsulating pieces of truth and striving for legitimacy. In contrast to China where social mobility opened positions for talented persons by learning and diligence, Japan remained an aristocratic society where learning alone was insufficient for a career when not backed by privileges of birth. Taika reforms did not change this and it was far from the aim of the reformers to do so. Reforms in public administration however, required a permanent venue for the bureaucracy and this is the reason why a capital was founded (Nara) for the first time in Japanese history, modelled of course on the Chinese capital Changan. Nara was however soon abandoned, because the influence of Buddhist monks was very strong here and the central government moved to a nearby but entirely insignificant place which was called the capital city (Kyoto) which soon became the venue of a lively cultural life and remained the capital city of Japan for the next one thousand years.[4]

In implementing Taika reforms, law had an important instrumental role. Along the Chinese pattern, written (promulgated) Japanese law was classified to four categories: (a) penal law (*lü*, Japanese *ritsu*); (b) law of public administration (*ling*; Japanese *ryo*); (c) royal edicts (*ke*; Japanese *kyaku*) to implement ritsu and ryo; (d) particular orders (*shih*; Japanese *shiki*) concerning individual cases. On this basis, a rapid and large-scale codification was introduced. The first laws on public administration were already issued at the time of Tenji Tenno (662–671), while the first code was promulgated by Mommu Tenno (697–707), an emperor called the Japanese Justinian, in 702. His *Taiho Code* contained laws of public administration and criminal law

---

[4]Faris (2009: 29); Meyer (2009: 47–48); Steenstrup (1996: 16–18, 30–32).

(*ritsu-ryo*). Unfortunately, the original text was lost but we can reconstruct it with the help of a later commentary. The Code has about thirty chapters, half of which is ordinances for the royal court including issues of ceremonies, the duties of officials serving in the various parts of the palace (in the empress's palace, in the heir's palace, etc.). The other half is about various topics such as the storage of grain, land, military administration, salaries, supervision of the markets and public works. Only two chapters were dedicated to religious matters (Buddhist monks, rites) and to penalties and only one chapter (8) to the family. An important body was the religious council (*jingi kwan*) symbolically emphasizing the importance of Shinto and the divine origin of the ruling family. In addition, a state council was also created dealing with finances, the administration of justice, matters of war, taxes, and the control of officials. The entire apparatus was housing in the palace. The system was far more complex than its predecessor, but issues of the palace and governance were not separated.[5]

Taiho Code was replaced by the *Yoro Code* which modified and supplemented it in 757. *Yoro Code* is also a *ritsu-ryo*, and one of the most important documents of Japanese legal history since it was in force up until 1869. The criminal law of the Yoro Code consists of 500 articles divided into 12 chapters. In addition to the definition of legal terms, various criminal acts (theft, robbery, perjury, cheating, falsification of scales, illegitimate organisation of an army), were specified together with their penalties and the outline of procedural law. An important topic was public administration, the laws of which were divided into thirty chapters consisting of one thousand articles. Issues to be dealt with at some length were land, taxation, education, officials (appointment, promotion, payment), bodyguards, forms of official correspondence, the palace guard, court protocol and etiquette, the army, ritual, burials. In all this, Chinese influence was overwhelming but despite this, local understanding of law found its way into the Code. Because of the influence of Buddhism, the rigor and cruelty of some punishments was moderated. In addition, the death penalty was abolished and was converted to life imprisonment (810) following the influence of popular belief according to which harmful spirits of executed persons remain on earth and torture the living beings.[6]

Ground breaking changes such as Taika reforms required communication, control and expertise. This is the reason why the court sent officials to the countryside to explain the essence of changes and the new requirements to local leaders. Parallel to this, supervisors were also sent throughout the country to check governors and their economic activities. In addition to supervisors, armed forces were also roaming the country to guarantee domestic security. When such armed men joined forces with professional soldiers fighting on horseback, in the subsequent centuries medieval samurai emerged. Legal reforms also required expertise and professionals well versed in law. This is why legal experts (*myoboka*) emerged, in order to facilitate codification and legal interpretation from the ninth century onwards. Similarly

---

[5]Brinkley and Kikuchi (1912: 177–179).
[6]Frank (1996: 212–213); Steenstrup (1996: 34–37).

to their medieval colleagues at European courts, *myoboka* contributed to strengthening central authority, domestic order and a kind of 'legal certainty' also at the times of internal chaos and fights. It was a unique period in the history of Japan, a culture in which otherwise law plays no vital role. During this period, however, law was in a higher esteem and it is not by accident that it was the time when Japanese jurisprudence emerged with scholarly works out of which two are still available for us. Though important as they were, *ritsu-ryo* codes left some vital points untouched, for example, succession to the throne, because the emperor was above the law and no code could regulate his business. As a result, struggle for power emerged which law was unable to stop. Court custom, however, was helpful in this issue since Japanese emperors began to appoint their successor before death or their retreat. In the absence of such declaration, it was customary for the eldest son of the chief wife to inherit the throne which reduced domestic rivalries.[7]

Taika reforms did not leave Japanese society untouched since new laws were introduced not only in public law but also in private matters such as family. Following the Chinese model, the mourning system was introduced but it was adjusted to the structure of Japanese society. In rural communities, a new system called *goningumi* was created which consisted of five families with no blood relations. *Guningumi* was an artificial grouping of families without considering whether or not they were relatives because the system operated to guarantee state interest: families of each *goningumi* had to control each other, report about wrongdoings (to avoid collective punishments) and collect taxes. Parallel to this, the old Japanese custom of servitude was abolished, mainly due to the influence of Buddhism. Purchase and sale of human beings was prohibited by law but the same law was tricked out in the form of contractual servitude which was only a contract and thus lawful. As a result, servitude continued for centuries and the selling of girls to brothels could be finally abolished only after World War II. Family law was also changing but not because of ground breaking Taika legal reforms but due to slow but unstoppable Chinese social influence. As a result, genuine Japanese understanding of marriage and anthropology gave way to Confucian worldview, which resulted in an increasingly patriarchal family structure where women lost their former status and their rights were reduced to a minimum, particularly during the samurai rule. Marriage was no longer the private affairs of the couple but an alliance between families, an understanding with far reaching consequences. First, the consent of the parents and grandparents was needed to a marriage which was followed by a contract and a religious ceremony. Second, the parties were obliged to divorce if a family member of either of the families—no matter how distant relative—committed a crime against a member of the other family irrespective of the fact that the couple had no share in it and want to continue with their marriage bond (this is the adaption of Chinese *i-chüeh*). Parallel to these consequences, patriarchal structure was developed further and the husband's rights were enlarged: he managed the property of his wife and was entitled to correct his wife physically but was not allowed to kill her. Unilateral divorce was also the husband's privilege but he had to justify it and had to write a letter of divorce. Chinese influence modified genuine

---

[7]Drapkin (1989: 351); Steenstrup (1996: 38–42).

Japanese law of inheritance, too, which interestingly resembled more the European than the Chinese model. The uncritical adaption of Confucian law of inheritance however, would have led to chaos soon and this is why codifiers adjusted the new laws to contemporary Japanese social reality. According to the Yoro Code, a chosen heir received the half of the bequest while the remaining half was shared by the other heirs. Since only people with rank could choose an heir and others could not, we can assume that this way of sharing was not the practice among commoners who might distribute the bequest proportionally among heirs. Widows received the same share as the chosen heir while his other sons received the half of it and her daughters only a quarter of it. Parallel to this, inheritance by last will was also introduced.[8]

This was a completely new understanding on Confucian moral standard which was at variance with former practice and law which guaranteed women an equal share with men and a propriety right on their own without restrictions. This might be a consequence of a rather licentious sexual morals of the previous period which made it possible for men to visit girls at night (even more than one), and for girls to host men in their homes. These relationships usually did not last for a long time but if a child was born, the man simply moved into the girl's house where the children were brought up. Licentiousness sometimes ended in village orgies which the government tried to stop by repeated prohibitions (like in 797).[9]

Confucian influence however, stopped short in criminal law where legist thinking was favoured with its harsh punishments which were, it is true, somewhat mitigated with the exception of the rule of the samurai when criminal law was a tool also for deterrence. Intention was not taken into consideration since result was the only factor for judgment (e.g. death irrespective whether or not the killer intended this or it was only the result of accident, etc.). Lack of accountability (such as mental illness, etc.) was also no obstacle to find someone guilty. Collective punishment was applied for criminals who committed grievous crimes, since their (innocent) family members were also executed, a criminal policy for long centuries (the first attempt to restrict it emerged only in the eighteenth century). Members of the royal family, noblemen and high ranking officials were exempted from punishments or their punishment was moderated. Despite rigour, capital punishment was rarely executed, if it was then by beheading or choking. The most frequent ways of punishment were whipping (with bamboo), hard labour (in state mines) and exile. *Ritsu* codes specify the punishments of crimes in a casuistic manner and also the mode of their execution (the number of blows, the quality of the bamboo whip, etc.). Crimes were not investigated ex officio but upon the request of a claimant. The report had to be put into writing (in a society where the majority was illiterate), in which the accusation had to be specified together with the name of the suspected person. If someone was unable to prove his accusation, he was punished exactly the same way as the accused would have punished if the accusation would have been proven (this law agrees literally with the

---

[8]Steenstrup (1996: 50–57).
[9]Faris (2009: 50–52).

laws of Hammurabi). The procedure did not take place in a court of law (as there were none) but in the presence of officials who could apply torture as well.[10]

Political changes led to legal changes, too, after the ninth century when *ritsu-ryo* codes were abandoned in practice but continued to be the subject of jurisprudence. *Ritsu-ryo* codes were replaced by both local customary laws and the custom of some professions (e.g. the samurai). Centrifugal forces and struggle for power contributed to the erosion of the central government which was unable to secure domestic order at times. This is the reason why samurai from the countryside were settled down in the capital, being soldiers of the ruling system (hence their name). Being aware of their power, these soldiers were ready to take over political control, too, first attempted by the Taira clan (1156–1181) which failed at the end. The *Minamoto* (1183–1203), and the *Hojo* clan (1203–1333) however, were more successful and governed autonomously from their own capital city (Kamakura), which was the de facto political centre. During this period—usually called, though improperly, the period of Japanese feudalism—significant modifications were introduced to Japanese law. The new legislation was linked to *Hojo Yasutoki* (1232), but the *Goseibai–Shikimoku* was certainly not a codification, only an amendment of already existing laws with 51 new casuistic articles. The text was written by a Buddhist scholar monk in a simple language easy to understand by everyone, which evoked the admiration of a poet, too.[11] The new laws however, diverted enormously from Buddhist ethics and reflected the world view of the new ruling elite, the samurai (*buke-ho* or *bushido*: the moral code of the samurai). With this, the legal system was actually doubled: one was the *kuge-ho*, the law of the bureaucracy which kept the old *ritsu-ryo* system alive, and the other was the *buke-ho*, the law of the samurai and the new military aristocracy.[12]

Following the militaristic world view of the samurai, the legal position of everyone outside their own circles deteriorated enormously. Women and children were the first among the victims of a new family law. Accordingly, parents could force their children to marry against their will (usually due to political reasons) and could also disinherit them. Disinheritance was a social catastrophe since it was not only the loss of a share in a bequest but also a loss of social status. The brutal treatment of women— being one of the basic pillars of the samurai ethos—was enhanced and the law did not mitigate but institutionalised it. A wife was regarded her husband's 'vassal' who owed absolute obedience to him and who could be unilaterally repudiated for the minutest mistake. Since the value of girls was very low for the military regime, they were increasingly squeezed out of the bequest. Militarism influenced criminal law, too, which was increasingly characterised by draconian harshness with the aim of prevention and deterrence and not a proper and proportional punishment. Death penalty was specified rather broadly, extending not only to grievous crimes but also to acts of minor significance. In more serious cases, innocent family members (women, children) and even neighbours were also executed. A death penalty was usually

---

[10]Steenstrup (1996: 59–63).

[11]Drapkin (1989: 354).

[12]Frank (1996: 216).

preceded by cruel tortures. The military elite was, unsurprisingly, exempt from these sanctions since samurai were punished usually only by the confiscation of their land.[13]

Medieval Japan was not as closed a society as it became during the Tokugawa period. This is why Spanish Jesuits, following the footsteps of Portuguese coming first to the shores of Japan succeeded to convert some members of the elite to Christianity. One of them donated a small fishing village to the Jesuits who settled down there. This is how Nagasaki, an important port and commercial centre had grown out of this insignificant village which remained the port of the Portuguese for a long time. Later on, when Will Adams, an English seaman convinced the Shogun that Japanese Christians would help conquering Spanish, the Shogun prohibited Christianity and this is how the anti-Christian policy of the Tokugawa period began.[14]

12.2   The Law of the Tokugawa Period

Warrior clans constantly struggled for power with no clear cut victory on either side. Things changed dramatically when Tokugawa Ieyasu defeated all his enemies in 1600 and emerged victoriously. The emperor appointed him Shogun, which was a *de iure* legalisation of a de facto situation. With a new central power there was a chance to unify the country again and the Shogun did everything possible to achieve this aim and, of course, to enhance his own power. This is the reason why Tokugawa Ieyasu had all his opponents executed. Despite all drastic measures, Tokugawa authority only extended over one third of the territory of Japan directly. The rest of the country was ruled indirectly, through the vassals of the Tokugawas among whom they distributed the confiscated lands of the annihilated enemy. Tokugawas made every effort to hinder political fragmentation and to secure domestic peace. Therefore, they prohibited the building of castles and organising rival armies, monopolised foreign trade and hermetically closed down Japan from any contact with external powers. As a result, they could accomplish domestic security but at the cost of isolating the country. As a result, there were no technical developments and no foreign model was available to modernise the country. The isolationist policy of the Tokugawas kept them in power for centuries, but when the rival elite realised the significant backwardness of Japan in the nineteenth century the Tokugawa system immediately collapsed.

Despite such shortcomings, Tokugawas wanted to reform their country and, of course, create laws which help them to hold onto power. As a result, two laws were issued in 1615, legalising the existing political system. The emperor retained his position *de iure*, but lost all his political and administrative power. More influential Shoguns even determined the order of accession to the throne. The loss of power was compensated by donations of land, though the emperor remained practically a captive in Kyoto. It is revealing that European travellers of the seventeenth and eighteenth

---

[13]Faris (2009: 158–160); Steenstrup (1996: 71–72, 84–90, 97–98).
[14]Drapkin (1989: 342–345).

centuries called the Shogun monarch and the emperor, responsible for religious and ritual acts, the 'pope'. The Shogun established his headquarters in Edo, where he was protected by a huge fortification and where he placed the central administration. Edo was the biggest city of the world in the seventeenth century, with inhabitants of more than a million. After the fall of the Tokugawas, the emperor moved to Edo from Kyoto which was the symbol of his loss of power; it was at this time that the city was renamed to Tokyo (eastern capital). In short, the emperor was only a source of legitimacy but was excluded from political life while the actual leader of the Tokugawa system was the Shogun. This was an inherited title received from the emperor to govern the country politically and administratively with the help of the military and the *bakofu*, the bureaucracy in the service of the Tokugawas. Two thirds of the country was however, not governed directly by the Tokugawas but with the help of the *daimyo*, a feudal aristocracy of 250 families with enormous landed property. Being their rivals, Tokugawas tried to control them with the help of the system called *sankin kotai* which was an existential threat for these rich families. Accordingly, noblemen had to maintain a residence in Edo adequate to their social rank where they had to spend six months in a year. They could only travel to their residence in the countryside afterwards, but had to leave their family members in Edo (practically as hostages under the control of the Tokugawas). Since this system was very costly (one could travel only in keeping with one's rank), a large part of the revenues was spent on maintaining this system as a cost of relative political stability. This de facto political fragmentation is the reason why there was no uniform Japanese law during these centuries because *daimyo*s were allowed to create laws for their territories independently of the central government. To hinder further fragmentation and turbulence, Japanese residents were forbidden to leave the country and foreigners were prohibited to entry (save the Dutch merchants) Japan. Christianity was declared illegal and converts were punished by death.[15]

Hierarchic social structure established during the previous period continued without changes during the Tokugawa period. Samurais remained the beneficiaries of the system with the monopoly of bearing arms and participating in governance. Peasants responsible for agricultural production (rice) were at the bottom, while craftsmen and merchants acquired a growing economic significance but without political rights were between the two. The system was actually the Japanese variant of the Chinese social hierarchy where soldiers enjoyed the place of scholars.[16]

This exploitive system was maintained by strict rules of public administration and extremely high rates of tax. In theory, the basis of tax was the yield of the fields, in practice however, sometimes the entire crop of rice had to be handed over to tax collectors and peasants mostly lived on barley. If not even barley was left, peasants ate grass or starved to death as it happened in the 1780s when peasants died of famine in the millions. The tax burden was distributed by village elders representing the better-off locals who paid, not surprisingly, less than the poor. Peasants lived continuously at the brink of starvation with no chance to bring up all their children.

---

[15]Beer and Maki (2002: 1113); Frank (1996: 225); Steenstrup (1996: 108–115).
[16]Frank (1996: 222).

Since the killing of little girls was prohibited by law, people gave their daughters to urban brothels. To enhance local control, the *goningumi* system of tax collection was maintained. Despite such controlled mechanisms, peasants tried to escape the land and look for livelihood elsewhere. Central government reacted promptly with a ban on leaving one's place of residence and peasants were required to have a passport to leave their own village. Despaired peasants however, took the risk and still moved to the cities in the hope of finding some livelihood there. This domestic migration was the driving force of urbanisation in general and the enormous growth of Edo in particular. Peasants worked and died in vain since the enormous revenue was not spent on economic or infrastructural investments but financed the rather expensive livelihood of the samurai, the *daimyo* and the maintenance of the political system. Laws were kept secret in order to enhance fear. Officials however were given legal manuals with important laws and precedents in order to help their daily routine work. By contrast, ordinances for particular cases were announced and their observance was strictly controlled. Law privileged the samurai with particular laws. Samurai families could only marry among themselves since a samurai man could only marry a woman of another samurai family. The consent of the seniors of both families was needed to a marriage. Endogamy was strictly prohibited, even more so among the samurai than among the commoners. For instance, a samurai could not marry the sister of his former wife and a samurai woman could not marry the younger brother of her former husband. The right to divorce was restricted among the samurai: a samurai husband was not entitled to declare divorce unilaterally because such a declaration could be a source of strife or armed conflict between families, a conflict which the system wanted to prevent. Therefore, both families participated in the solution of a dispute and persuaded the parties to continue with their marriage bond. When a samurai disappeared, his wife had to wait for his return for one year but when it was over she could divorce him.[17] Law of inheritance was also modified to the benefit of the samurai who were interested in finding an heir by all means, otherwise the land of a samurai who died heirless would return to his senior. Adoption was the way out to at least secure an heir in the absence of a son. Limitless adoption however. was detrimental to the interest of a senior who wanted to restrict such a right. This is the reason why law of inheritance became a battlefield of political struggles.

Among commoners, two ways of marriages prevailed. One was the old custom to live together without formalities until a child was born. The other was a more formal way based on the new laws inspired by Confucian ethics which introduced engagement and a wedding ceremony. In theory, a husband could divorce his wife unilaterally, in practice, however, husbands rarely did so because they had to pay back the dowry which was a heavy burden and they were unable to do so more often than not. The Asia-wide right of husbands to kill the lover of their wives was also declared in Japan with a later amendment that in such a case he has to kill his wife, too, otherwise he was responsible for manslaughter. The same applies if he did not kill them immediately but only later. Full parental control continued since children could be physically assaulted, disinherited and in serious cases even killed. Children were

---

[17]Steenstrup (1996: 116–121, 128–130).

obliged to obey their parents entirely, yet at the same time they were also obliged to report authorities if they conspired against the political system or their superior. What we have here is a Japanese combination of Confucian and legist thinking with the later gaining the upper hand in the interest of the stability of the political system. This was the only matter when the solidarity within the extended family (*ie*) was declared of secondary in importance. Extended families were otherwise units of decision making and actions due to two reasons. One is the old Japanese custom to decide unanimously where a head does not decide alone or the majority votes but the entire community reaches a consensus. This is why family fathers discussed the matters with their wives and adult sons. In addition, *guningumi* system, making everyone responsible for the deeds of any member further enhanced group solidarity which required sharing all information and decisions. Such an extended family consisted of a main household (*honke*) and subordinated households (*bunke*), which jointly constituted an economic unit. Disobedient persons were simply expelled and taken back only when the reason of their ostracism was not a crime. Expelled persons lost all their rights: they were prohibited to reside with their former family which could not supply them with food and were disowned also from the bequest. Family councils decided also upon marriages, making such unions arranged marriages in the majority of the cases. In addition to group solidarity, economic consideration contributed to this way of marry making. Peasants were poor people who could bring up two children but certainly not more. One of them was declared heir since law did not specify the person with certainty. This is why local custom prevailed declaring either the youngest or the eldest son heir. Sons with empty hands were supported by the custom called *mukotori-kon*. Accordingly, it was not the bride who joined her husband's family but the new husband joined his bride's family, where he was subsequently declared an heir if there was none. Everyone benefited from such arranged marriages between neighbours which also reduced the number of the killing of children.[18]

Criminal law followed the Chinese pattern, particularly Ming codification which was known in Japan for centuries. During the Tokugawa period however, Chinese influence was reduced in criminal law, firstly because of the isolationist policy of the ruling elite, secondly, because the new, Manchu legislation was believed to be too harsh and brutal and therefore, was not considered worth copying. By contrast, local elite was entitled to legislate in criminal matters in conformity with the fact that two third of the country was de facto governed by them anyway. This is how provincial criminal law came into being with the only restriction that they could not be at variance with the laws of the central government. If in harmony with central legislation, provincial leaders could not only legislate in criminal law matters but also execute judgments, capital punishment included. Local laws rarely diverted from the criminal law of the central government because there was a common basis for both: the moral principles uniform all over Japan, and the laws of the Ming period which served as a model. Contemporary Chinese legal thinking entered Japan only during the reign of Yoshimune, the eighth Shogun (1716–1745) who was interested in law

---

[18]Katsuta (1996: 254); Steenstrup (1996: 130–136).

most among Tokugawa Shoguns. After thirty years of systematization, he published the collection of laws entitled *Kujikata Osadamegaki*, which remained in force with slight modifications up to the end of the Tokugawa period. Though the Code preserved original Japanese legal ideas, the Chinese influence is beyond any shade of doubt. The Confucianisation of law was also manifested in public administration where civilian bureaucratic control was increasing in a state of warriors. In criminal law proper, Yoshimune abolished the cutting off of ears and nose, introduced fines for minor crimes, and invented a complaint box for cases in which people suffered injustice in the hope for a less corrupt judiciary. Everyone was allowed to drop his own complaint who believed that his case was not adjudicated properly and it was the Shogun alone who had a key to the box. Despite such progressive laws, *Osadamegaki* remained a secret text which was not made public but was produced in order to succour officials adjudicating the cases.[19]

Substantive criminal law continued with the harsh punishments of the previous centuries but collective responsibility was narrowed to political crimes, such as revolt. Blood feud was not ruled out but kept at bay: if a parent was killed, it was the moral obligation of the descendants to avenge. In order to do so, descendants applied for authorisation by the authorities who saw no reason to deny it because such a blood feud was regarded as a lawful punishment for manslaughter. Punishment of elders could be mitigated but it was not compulsory, in contrast to the *ritsu-ryo* codes. Punishment of serious crimes was death, the execution of which depended on the act committed. Killers of parents or masters were crucified, robbers and arsonists were cooked alive, a punishment which was later replaced by beheading. Decapitation was executed within the walls of a prison but the cut-off head of criminals was put on public display outside the jail, while their corpses were used for anatomical studies. Thieves were condemned to whipping (50–100 strikes). Criminals who were spared their lives were usually sentenced to hard labour in state mines. Imprisonment was also a punishment for everyone, but separate cells were for the samurai, for peasants and citizens. The samurai were not punished for minor crimes; should they however be sentenced to death, they were granted the clemency to commit suicide.[20]

12.3   The Meiji Reforms

Tokugawa policy of isolation kept the political system domestically intact but resulted in backwardness in terms of economics, technical innovation and international politics. Japan was left untouched by developments in Asia, not to speak about the rapid changes in the Western world (industrial revolution, capitalism, political ideologies, constitutionalism, nation state, etc.). Ultimately, when new ideas and ideologies entered Japanese politics, the Tokugawa system collapsed immediately. This is what happened beyond the stages. What happened in the surface was a confrontation with

---

[19]Henderson (1980: 270–281).
[20]Steenstrup (1996: 150–154).

the US when President Millard Fillmore—supported by a warship under the command of Captain Matthew Perry at Edo—forced Japanese government to sign an unequal treaty with the United States in 1854. This was followed by more unequal treaties with several European countries which was seen as treason by the opposition of the Tokugawas. Tension among the ruling elite enhanced when the young (19 years old) emperor *Meiji* (*Mutsuhito*) sided with the opposition, resulting in a peaceful transfer of power within the ruling elite without revolution or bloodshed.

The new governing elite slowly launched reforms and with compromises but were unstoppable. The first document of changes was the *Seitaisho*, a document on the system of governance, published in 1868. *Seitaisho* is by far not a constitution, only a document about governance which granted considerable power to the executive power and did not even recognise the separation of powers but considered legislation and the judiciary as tools of the executive. Governance was transferred to the State Council (*Dayokan*) which immediately launched a significant modernisation program: the privileges of the samurai were abolished, a new national administration was created together with the national army, a modern school system and the judiciary. Parallel to this, we can witness some Western cultural influence in Western like fashion and garments, food and art. But there was still no constitution and Meiji therefore, issued a constitution as his donation to his people on 11 February 1889. This act is full of symbolisms: it was the emperor who granted the constitution and thus it has no reference to the sovereignty of the people, an entirely new idea in contemporary Japan. What is more, the date is also relevant because according to Japanese tradition, it was the day when *Jimmu*, the first emperor ascended to the throne in 660 BCE, Meiji being his 123rd descendant. The constitution was elaborated by *Ito Hirobumi*, an erstwhile leading figure of the opposition to the Tokugawas. The model of the constitution was the Prussian constitution, drafted by—among others—Hermann Roesler who participated also in the elaboration of the Japanese civil code. Since the Prussian constitution was the least democratic among the European constitutions, it did not bring about significant changes in the political system except the constitution as an idea and a document itself. In short, the form was Western but the content remained more or less Japanese. Consequently the constitution erected the political system on the sovereignty of the emperor who incorporated legislative and executive power, was the commander-in-chief of the army, decided on war and peace and signed international treaties. His person remained sacred and inviolable while his power was not limited by the constitution only by self-constraint. Thus, the Meiji constitution was a constitution of an absolute monarchy without the principle of the separation of powers where neither legislation nor the executive and the judiciary were autonomous powers but only political tools of the emperor.[21] What is more, this constitution granted more power to the emperor than they enjoyed previously when their only political role was to legitimate de facto Tokugawa rule. Now the emperor was granted authority without political and constitutional responsibility, an entirely new political situation in Japan which hindered the balance of powers and

---

[21]Oda (2009: 15–16); Beer and Maki (2002: 17–21).

the 'checks and balances' from developing and liberated the military from civilian control which led to militarism and all its tragic consequences.[22]

It is unsurprising that the two-chamber legislature hardly had any authority according to this constitution. The government was not responsible for the legislature which only had the following rights: (1) to put questions forth to the government; (2) to receive petitions; (3) to turn to the emperor with applications; (4) to control financial affairs. Though these competencies have nothing to do with real power (save the control of finances), the composition of the legislature was designed to hinder opposition to the system or the policy of the emperor. This is why members of the upper chamber were appointed by the emperor from among his family members and the nobility and members of the lower chamber were elected from among the elite, too, because both active and passive rights to vote were based on extremely high census. The constitution has almost nothing to say about the executive power, yet from 1885 the cabinet system was introduced. It is also unsurprising that the constitution had limited space for human rights since this was quite alien to traditional Japanese legal thinking. Though the second chapter of the constitution specifies a rather broad scale of first generation human rights (nullum crimen sine lege, privacy of letters, freedom of religion, freedom of private property, freedom to assemble peacefully, freedom of thought and press), it limits them at the same time with the stipulation that they should be guaranteed also by law, an authorisation for later legislation to restrict human rights specified in the constitution. And this is exactly what happened, particularly during the reign of the military regime. In addition to rights, the constitution also specified duties such as the payment of taxes and military service.[23]

Despite such shortcomings, the political system moved toward further democratization. In the first decades of the twentieth century, the party system began to emerge with prime ministers who were party politicians. Parallel to this, the influence of the army was reduced and the general male suffrage was introduced during the reign of Emperor Taiso. But Taiso democracy soon collapsed due to the lack of democratic thinking (the school system, too, advocated obedience, not democratic values) and the emerging power of the military. When the government signed a disadvantageous treaty with the US to reduce Japanese forces on the sea in Washington in 1922, army leaders were ready to overthrow the government and launched a fourteen-year war with China which led to the occupation of Manchuria. This is how the failure of Taiso democracy led to the killing of civilian politicians and Japan to WWII.[24]

Meiji reforms, however, were not reduced to the constitution but encapsulated the entire legal system. The driving force beyond a large-scale legal reform was the stipulation of the unequal treatises which ensured immunity for Western citizens and companies from Japanese law until it would be 'civilised', a blow to Japanese pride and sovereignty. A civilised legal system was, obviously, a modern legal system on Western principles, something which Japanese elite wanted to create in order to free the country from these humiliating treatises. In the lack of any expert in Western law,

[22]Haley (1991: 79–80).

[23]Beer and Maki (2002: 25–29).

[24]Morton and Olenik (2005: 168–177).

Gustave Boissonade was invited from the University of Paris who drafted the first criminal code of Japan on continental legal principles (1882), which was translated from French to Japanese by a student who used to study in France earlier. Parallel to this, Nobushige Hozumi was sent to Britain to study common law but he returned with the conviction that the adaptation of the Anglo-Saxon law was impossible in Japan. This is why he went to Berlin to study German law which he found far more suited for his own country. Despite his arguments, there were enthusiastic advocates of Anglo-Saxon law, particularly at the University of Tokyo.[25]

Enthusiasm for Anglo-Saxon law remained however, a minority view and this is why Japan turned to German legal experience for help at the end of the nineteenth century. As a result, Japanese civil code was drafted following the German Civil Code (BGB), together with the code of commerce and the code on civil procedure while French influence was pushed into the background. Not only codes but also their commentaries were used in Japan in order to achieve a deeper understanding of the texts. This is why a belief spread, according to which 'what is not German law is not law at all'. German legal model however left fields untouched which were of utmost importance for the social fabric like family and inheritance. This is why in these fields genuine Japanese legal understanding prevailed. Discrimination against women who could not attend universities continued, had no right to vote, and whose adultery continued to be a crime (in contrast to adultery committed by men). The situation was not easy, neither in fields where transition from traditional to Western law was required. To start with, the translation of the very term of law created both linguistic and political difficulties since the traditional elite rejected the view that the population has right to anything and thus the French *droit civil* had an additional 25 years to wait until it was included in the final text of the code. German legal influence however, was reduced due to political reasons when Japan entered WW I but the gap between law in books and social reality remained wide, a fact which contributed to the birth of the Japanese sociology of law. After WW II, American legal influence was increased in public law, labour law and commercial law but the barrier in language and concepts remained. For example, human rights were translated as 'rights donated by Heaven' in order to be in harmony with Confucian teaching. Problems were also due to simple technical reasons: the original text was not properly understood and was mistranslated.[26]

12.4 Japanese Legal Thinking

After decades of legal modernization, Japan's legal system seems to be—at first glance—a Western (civil) legal system with a constitution and some basic laws (*roppo*: civil and civil procedural law; criminal and criminal procedural law; law of commerce) which new laws should be in harmony with. Despite recent social,

[25]Röhl (2005: 23–28).
[26]Katsuta (1996: 251–252, 259); Oda (2009: 18–19); Chiba (1986: 314).

economic, political and legal changes, Japan remained an Asian country and it would be a mistake to forget about it and classify Japan into a western legal system. Elements of traditional legal thinking continue to influence Japanese legal understanding to this day.

Contrary to most Far Eastern countries, in Japan law does not have its origin in tradition or in the political will of the ruler (state) but, ultimately, goes back to the will of gods mediated by the emperor. *Nori*, typically translated as law, is rather a declaration encapsulating the clan ancestor's will, a concept which was continuously expanded to reach its final meaning as the will of the Sun Goddess Amaterasu Omikami. Now it is easy to understand why subjective rights of persons are missing both from legal practice and as a concept. In addition to *nori*, there is another term for law, *ho*, a word of Chinese origin denoting written law kept secret and designed to help officials and to supply them with points of references in their work.[27]

The ancient religion of Japan is Shintō ('the path of gods'), a set of beliefs which brings animism, ancestors' cult and polytheism together in which the emperor was also the high priest. This brings politics and religion together. This is the reason why old Japanese word for governance (*matsurigoto*) actually means 'to whom one has to pray' and even today the same word means a Shintō shrine and the emperor's palace (*miya*). Chief god in Shintō is Sun Goddess Amaterasu Omikami whose late descendant, Jimmu Tennō (divine warrior), Japanese tradition tells us, founded the Japanese empire. His successors defeated the hostile tribes and united the country. Shintō ensured the legitimacy of the ruling dynasty with this myth and offered an ideology to unite the country and centralise government. Shintō has, however, neither ethics nor a metaphysical teaching nor canonical texts and dogmas which opened up the way for foreign influences (Buddhism, Confucianism) with stark commitment to fill the gap. By contrast, Shintō concentrates on rites dedicated to gods, trees, groves, rocks and other natural phenomena (the number of gods is not exactly known but their number is counted in millions). Buddhism entered this world in which some of its important messages such as equality of persons were abandoned since they opposed diametrically traditional Japanese social understanding. Parallel to this, Japanese Buddhism turned more mundane and avoided its original otherworldliness. At the later stage of this development, the two religions merged into a syncretism when Amaterasu Omikami was believed to be an incarnation of the Buddha while people prayed for the well-being of the Japanese state. At the same time, Buddhism brought religious tolerance to Japan which always ended whenever attempts were made to hinder the merger of Shintō and Buddhism. Religious tolerance came to a drastic halt during the reign of the Tokugawas when Buddhism was declared a religion of foreign origin and thus of low value and Christianity was banned and Christians persecuted. Confucianism, though Chinese in its origin, was not declared foreign and persecuted but followed in social and political relations. Confucianism reached the shores of Japan in its form of the Han dynasty, emphasising *li* and the five social relations (ruler–subject; father–son; husband–wife; elder brother–younger brother;

---

[27]Frank (1996: 211, 227).

friend–friend) which are part of a cosmic harmony. In order to hinder disharmony, conflicts have to be smoothened and solved while individual rights and the assertion of individual interests produce disharmony and, therefore, be abandoned. In short, the religious background of Japanese law is a particular combination of Shintō, Buddhism and Confucianism.[28] Plenty of examples can prove this. There are usually two altars in a Japanese house, one *Shintō* and another, a Buddhist. New born babies are presented in a Shintō shrine, as marriages are also concluded in the presence of a Shintō priest. At the same time, the dead are buried according to Buddhist tradition and their ashes are placed in a Buddhist temple. Japanese states made no mistake to profit from religions and transformed them to a tool for total control. Tokugawas created a hierarchy of shrines and linked every household to a local shrine. Whoever refused to join a shrine, was accused of having become *kirishitan* (Christian) which was sanctioned by death. During the Meiji reforms, Shintō purified from Buddhist elements was declared state religion, the priests of which were appointed by the state and its temples were maintained by the state, too. Thus, religion was significantly secularised which contributed—according to social scientists—to a relatively smooth implementation of modernisation along the Western pattern.[29] Simultaneously, state Shintō was one of the symbols and engines of ultra-nationalism of the inter-war period. This is why modern Japan deleted it from the constitution and replaced it with freedom of religion. Such declarations notwithstanding Shintō and ancestor's cult continue to influence Japanese politics and law also in modern times. The person of a *Tenno* is only one example. A term for both governance and ritual (*matsuri-goto*) is another. A historical example is the Japanese victory in the war against the Russians (1905) when not only the Emperor but also his victorious admiral, Tōgō rushed to the biggest Shintō shrine (Isé) to give sacrifice. Meiji constitution also based the rule of *Tenno*s on their ancestors' line which goes back, ultimately, to their divine ancestor Amaterasu whose cult is particularly important. Thus, the ancestors' cult simultaneously meant the cult of the ancestors of a given family at the domestic altars and the cult of the ruling dynasty's ancestors regarded as the ancestors of the entire Japanese nation.[30] Shintō rite was banned from public life by the modern constitution of Japan (Art. 20, paragraph 3) which declares the separation of state from church and guarantees freedom of religion. Yet Shintō was not entirely banned, since we can witness some Shintō rites on more solemn occasions (like the official inauguration of a new school) which the Supreme Court has ruled constitutional.[31]

The striving for harmony (*wa*) is not a religious but rather a social requirement which was already emphasised in the 'constitution' of Shōtoku at the very beginning of these particular texts. Though important also in Confucian thinking, *wa* is a genuine Japanese concept of social cohesion and solidarity expressed symbolically in the writing system in which characters denoting *wa* also reflect Japan and the Japanese people ('people of *wa*'). This harmony is, to be sure, not perfect but the existing order

---

[28]Katsuta (1996: 255–256); Rahn (1980: 479–482).

[29]Obayashi (1996: 109, 116–117).

[30]Hozumi (2009: 30–31, 73, 85, 99).

[31]Haley (2006: 189–190).

in the framework of which law contributes to the maintenance of the system. This explains why individual rights should not be asserted at law courts but be solved by other mechanisms of conflict resolution leading to an extremely low number of litigations. In addition to *wa*, a social relation called *oyabun–kobun* is the second most important social factor in Japanese legal understanding emerging during the rule of the warriors. Its starting point is *bushidō*, the warriors' code of behaviour which highlights the subjection of the vassal to his senior. This medieval attitude of warriors then gradually permeated the entire Japanese society. It was more than obedience to commands since such a relationship required a superior to be propitious towards his subordinate who in return, subjected himself to his will like a child and served him with dedicated fidelity. This understanding of social relationship continues to this day, since it is not only about a hierarchic order but also about care and goodwill toward subordinated persons (for instance, leaders at working places help their colleagues to find a partner for marriage). *Oyabun–kobun* is not to be confused with *giri* norm, which creates a system of dependency for a shorter or longer period of time. *Giri-norm* may be roughly translated as an obligation of gratitude and a moral duty to reciprocate a gift. Though such an act cannot be demanded, no one would risk losing face by violating *giri*-norm. *Giri*-norm is articulated according to social rank, since a *giri* is different for a person of lower status than for a superior. In brief: *giri* norm created a system of mutual obligations which was not law but was nevertheless observed. Since *giri*-norms kept together the fabric of traditional Japanese society, it was at the same time an obstacle for legal modernisation/westernisation since private law matters are either governed by *giri*-norms or by modern civil law shaping a system of balance between rights and obligations but the joint application of the two systems was impossible. In addition to *giri*-norm, *amae*-relationship also creates a system of obligations though not on reciprocity. *Amae* is very difficult to translate to any language; denoting a hunger for affection and the efforts of a little child to acquire attention from his parents. Social scientists deduct all 'typically Japanese' forms of behaviour from *amae*, such as smiling continuously, to be extraordinarily polite, to be excessively modest and to avoid open contradiction. Historically, *amae* emerged in the framework of the extended family which controlled all issues and excluded the possibility of turning to law. Though in our modern times extended families are only history, particularly in huge cities, their role was taken over by large communities such as work places, creating an astonishing continuity in behaviour.[32] All these factors explain why private law was non-existent for centuries and why it was a long process for civil law to take root in Japan where law was regarded a tool for governance focusing on administrative and criminal law. The low number of lawsuits in contemporary Japan is also a proof of this. But we should not be misled by these figures: they did not tell us that Japanese society is unwilling to pursue his own interest, it only shows that the majority turns to traditional ways of conflict resolutions and avoids the legal way.

This is also due to the Japanese social understanding which prefers interpersonal relations to be regulated by personal contacts and communication rather than by

---

[32]Frank (1996: 228); Rahn (1980: 482–487); Chiba (1986: 343–344).

abstract legal norms logically built up into a faceless system. Human relations are not free from emotions which should be taken into consideration, too, and efforts should be made to find solutions for specific problems since all cases are viewed as unique, requiring a particular solution irrespective of whether it corresponds to an abstract legal norm or not. Therefore, attempts are made to solve conflicts by personal negotiations. Should they fail, leaders of groups of any kind (family, clan, *goningumi*, working place, etc.) are asked to help. Next, if they are also unable to reach consensus, a third party is requested to mediate. In many cases, a simple excuse is more important than a victory in a lawsuit won after long litigation in which a party could be satisfied in the law court but not in society at large. In short, Japanese society prefers to settle issues without law which is an effort to restore social harmony. Law has a wider room in public administration and governance but here, too, extra-legal mechanisms are important, sometimes more important than law itself, proven by *gyōsei shidō*. It is hard to translate what exactly *gyōsei shidō* is. This term denotes governmental decisions which express requests, advice, warnings and encouragements, that is, forms of political communications which are, obviously, not to be enforced with the help of state institution such as the police, law courts, etc. But they are not intended to be enforced either and no one ever came to the idea to do so. With *gyōsei shidō*, Japanese governments express political and economic aims in the interest of the public good and thus, every citizen feels morally obliged to respect them and contribute to their success meanwhile a law, interpreted as a command of the government (state) evokes resistance and efforts to circumvent it. In short, extra-legal ways of governance are sometimes more efficient than law.[33]

The role of law in Japan is now subject to debate in legal sociology, searching for explanations of particularities of Japanese legal understanding. According to the most widespread theory of Takeyoshi Kawashima, Japanese society insists on mediation, makes efforts to restore harmony and avoids litigation due to historical experience and cultural factors. Japanese insist on the mechanisms of earlier centuries and on hierarchy, this explanation tells us despite formal modernization, the legal understanding of Western legal systems is still missing which explains why individual rights are rarely asserted at law courts. This theory was already subject to criticism during the 1970s when a new theory emerged which denied the importance of historical-cultural factors but highlighted the shortcomings of the Japanese legal system, claiming that it is the lack of legal experts and the long-lasting and costly litigation which keep parties away from law courts, who had to turn to ways of traditional conflict resolution which are less expensive but more efficient (Haley). A third opinion, however, highlights just the opposite, claiming that Japanese legal system is transparent and clear which enables parties to calculate costs and benefits since the outcome of a lawsuit could be predicted with high probability. When chances are meagre, parties favour negotiations and mediation to avoid a worse outcome in litigation which proves, this theory tells us, how transparent and well-functioning

---

[33]Rahn (1980: 491–494).

Japanese legal system is (Ramseyer).[34] These theories are not necessarily at variance since Japanese society experienced rapid changes during the past decades and a theory already drafted in the 1960s (when historical and cultural factors were more important) could be enlarged with later theories which appreciate legal reforms and their consequences.[35] Such theories notwithstanding informal consultations and compromises are still more promising to Japanese than formal legal procedures because their advantages are numerous. Firstly, there is the tactful treatment of disputes, an important factor because Japanese people are reluctant to make their disputes public. Secondly, mediation allows parties to have a significant part of the autonomy of decision in their hands. Thirdly, legal norms need not be applied rigidly since compromises require a more flexible interpretation, making a higher degree of justice possible which would otherwise be impossible. Fourthly, through mediation parties could work out solutions which would be impossible with the mere implementation of law. Fifthly, compromises are cheaper, simpler and faster. Sixthly, more, interrelated cases could be resolved in one procedure. Seventhly, compromises are easy to implement. Eighthly, there are no victors and losers since a compromise is always a win-win situation. Because of such advantages, mediation is not impossible even when parties already started a formal law suit. Courts could also act as a mediator and help parties to reach an agreement. Often courts of second instance transform their role to mediation for which the decision of the first instance court is considered as a basic text on which the dispute can be settled with a compromise.[36]

Mutual understanding between the parties is also important in criminal law. Japanese understanding of criminal law regards the restoration of social relationship between a culprit and a victim important. This is why repentance, apologies and forgiveness are stressed on both sides, which could be a solid base also for compensation. As a result, vengeance and harsh punishments are less important in criminal law. If a culprit apologised and had shown remorse for his act which was accepted by the other party, the court may significantly moderate the punishment, a policy which contributes enormously to the rather low rate of crimes in Japan.[37] By contrast, those who do not show repentance, do not cooperate or are recidivists, have to face a rather tough and very rigorous prison life which is subject to serious domestic and international criticism (Human Rights Watch).[38]

---

[34] Anderson and Ryan (2011: 142–143); Ramseyer and Nakazato (1989: 429–430).

[35] Tanaka (1985: 386–388).

[36] Obuchi (1987: 526–533).

[37] Haley (1991: 135–136).

[38] Haley (2006: 82–84).

References

Anderson K, Ryan T (2011) Japan: the importance and evolution of legal institutions at the turn of the century. In: Black EA, Bell GF (eds) Law and legal institutions of Asia. Traditions, adaptations and innovations. Cambridge University Press, Cambridge

Beer LW, Maki JM (2002) From imperial myth to democracy. University Press of Colorado, Colorado

Brinkley F, Kikuchi D (1912) A history of Japan. From the earliest times to the end of the Meiji Era. The Encyclopaedia Britannica Co., London, New York

Chiba M (1986) Three-level structure of law in contemporary Japan, the Shinto society. In: Chiba M (ed) Asian indigenous law. Routledge and Kegan Paul, London, New York

Drapkin I (1989) Crime and punishment in the ancient world. Lexington Books, D. C. Heath and Company, Lexington, Toronto

Faris WW (2009) Japan to 1600. A social and economic history. University of Hawaii Press, Honolulu

Frank R (1996) Traditional legal thought and present-day law. In: Kreiner J (ed) The impact of traditional thought on present-day Japan. Iudicium Verlag, München, pp 209–234

Henderson DF (1980) Chinese influences on eighteenth-century Tokugawa codes. In: Cohen JA, Edwards RR, Chen FC (1980) Essays on China's legal tradition. Princeton University Press, Princeton

Haley JO (1991) Authority without power: law and the Japanese paradox. Oxford University Press, Oxford

Haley JO (2006) The spirit of Japanese law. The University of Georgia Press, Georgia

Hozumi N (2009) Ancestor-worship and Japanese law. Routledge, New York. Az eredeti szöveg megjelenése, Hokuseido, 1940

Katsuta A (1996) Japan: a grey legal culture. In: Örücü E, Attwool E, Coyle S (eds) Studies in legal systems. Kluwer Law International, The Netherlands, pp 250–261

Kreiner J (1996) The impact of traditional thought on present-day Japan. Iudicium Verlag, München

Meyer MW (2009) Japan. A concise history. Rawman and Littlefield Publishers, Lanham, New York

Morton WS, Olenik JK (2005) Japan. Its history and culture, 4th edn. McGraw-Hill Inc., New York

Obayashi T (1996) Shintō and Buddhism in Japan. In: Kreiner J (1996) The impact of traditional thought on present-day Japan. Iudicium Verlag, München

Obuchi T (1987) Role of the court in the process of informal dispute resolution in Japan: traditional and modern aspects, with special emphasis on in-court compromise. Law Jpn 20:74–101. Reprinted in: Fujikura K (1996) Japanese law and legal theory. The international library of essays in law and legal theory: legal cultures 9. New York University Press, New York

Oda H (2009) Japanese law. Oxford University Press, Oxford

Rahn G (1980) Recht und Rechtsverständnis in Japan. Entstehung und Wandel rechtlicher Traditionen. München, Freiburg, pp 473–467

Ramseyer JM, Nakazato M (1989) The rational litigant: settlement amounts and verdict rates in Japan. J Leg Stud 18:263–290. Reprinted in: Fujikura K (1996) Japanese law and legal theory. The international library of essays in law and legal theory: legal cultures 9. New York University Press, New York

Röhl W (2005) History of law in Japan since 1868. Handbuch der Orientalistik. Brill, Leiden

Steenstrup C (1996) The history of law in Japan until 1868. Brill, Leiden

Tanaka H (1985) The role of law in Japanese society: comparisons with the west U.B.C. law review 19:375–388. Reprinted in: Fujikura K (1996) Japanese law and legal theory. The international library of essays in law and legal theory: legal cultures 9. New York University Press, New York

Part V
Customary Laws

Chapter 13
Exclusive Customary Laws

13.1 General Remarks on Customary Laws

13.1.1 The Approach of Legal Anthropology

Asian customary laws, due to various reasons, are out of the scope of jurisprudence and legal history in general and Asian legal history in particular. To study Asian (and any other) customary laws, needs field work while to study the history and structure of written legal systems only requires some written sources to read and interpret. Since contemporary legal history focuses on the modern period (Nineteenth–twentieth centuries) when legal reforms were implemented and related sources are abundant, customary laws, understood for a rather long period as an obstacle for reforms and progress, were abandoned, if not treated with hostility. Scholars in both jurisprudence and Oriental studies, that is, professionals who are engaged in researching Asian laws, are accustomed to interpreting written texts but not to dwell in the jungle for long months in order to explore the custom of tribes who do not produce written texts even in our contemporary world. This is the research method of anthropologists who turned their attention, however, to African people during the last decades and to modern urban problems most recently, but neglected Asian tribal societies. As a result, an academic terra nullius has emerged which is home to very few scholars. Small wonder that only few academic writings have been produced during the last decades while we can witness an academic boom in more popular topics such as Islamic and Chinese law. To this we can also add a political reason, since some governments of Asian countries regarded customary laws a hindrance and therefore, neglected to study them in the favour of modern legal history and legal modernisation.

No book on Asian legal systems would be complete, however, without a glance to customary laws and this is why I have dedicated a separate chapter to this topic. This is not only about being as comprehensive as possible, it is also about importance. Only India has a tribal population with a figure between 80 and 100 million people. To this we can add the tribal population of the Indonesian and Philippine Archipelagos, the tribes living in Southeast Asia and the Middle East (particularly

© Springer Nature Switzerland AG 2020
J. Jany, *Legal Traditions in Asia*, Ius Gentium: Comparative Perspectives
on Law and Justice 80, https://doi.org/10.1007/978-3-030-43728-2_13

in Saudi Arabia, Yemen, Iran, Jordan and Iraq) which constitutes a huge number of population altogether.

Concepts and methods of legal anthropology can be used for Asian customary laws, too. Together with other customary laws, Asian tribal customs exist for centuries, the beginnings of which remain hidden from us. They have no history in the proper sense of the world, they only exist and their existence is taken for granted. This archaic existence provides further legitimacy for them and contributes to a general law-abiding way of behaviour. Customary laws are oral laws since they are part of an oral culture which neglects to put anything in writing. To put laws into writing is considered a danger to the original 'democratic' character of the system which does not favour a minority to the detriment of the majority of the illiterates. If law would be put into writing, it would be a privilege of the few who could write, a small minority which would, in its turn, have power because the majority would be exposed to their knowledge of law and interpretation. By contrast, tribal societies insist on the original system of orality which guarantees everyone to take part, share and contribute to preserve the system through generations without favouring any person or a particular group. This is the reason why tribal societies wanted to hinder, to put their system of law into writing by the colonial administrators and not without success in the long run. Unsurprisingly, important laws are known to anyone while laws on technical detail are missing since there is no need for them: the majority of the conflicts are resolved with the help of negotiations and compromises but certainly not within the framework of institutional procedures to which technical detail would be an important part. In case of doubt, collective memory is decisive and what is important is what the entire community thinks about a particular law in a given situation. Such laws are, therefore, free from formalities and authorities: a marriage and a divorce is only a simple declaration of will without any further requirements to be valid.[1]

Customary laws are less institutionalised, it is the council of elders which is the only authority that may be called an institution but even such a council is not universal (it is missing among the hunters). But even such a council has no 'competency' as an institution, its authority rests rather on the social prestige of its members. Such a system is called gerontocracy, the power of (male) elders whose influence is based on their age and proximity of the ancestors whose cult we can witness almost everywhere. The lack of law courts is also a proof for the negligence of institutions. People want to solve their conflicts flexibly and through social interactions but certainly not by applying rigid laws. Formal legal procedures are therefore neglected since conflicts are seen as wounds to be healed and removed with ending the chain of conflicts while formal procedures create losers and winners but no win-win situations. Customary laws developed a great deal of techniques of conflict resolutions ranging from individual and community talks and agreements to final reconciliations backed by magic and the ostracism of a trouble maker. Customary laws are at the same time green, that is, ecological, protecting their environment inhabited not only by humans but also by animals, spirits and gods which require care and protection, otherwise the

---

[1]Rouland (1994: 170–172), Glenn (2000: 58–64).

community would be punished immediately (see, among others the khwan in Thai animism), a stance which contributed enormously to the protection and maintenance of their physical environment for long generations.[2]

Legal anthropology makes distinction between hunters, nomads and sedentary population, a typology which is also relevant to some extent to Asian societies. Hunters are usually, but not always, nomads, with no concept of private property but with very few conflicts since they inhabit a relatively huge area (looking for animals) with a low density of population. As a result, there is no need for law, institutional mechanisms of conflict resolutions and political authority. It is the nuclear family, and not the clan or a tribe, which is the basic unit of social organisation. Such a family rests on monogamy, since only very talented hunters could provide food for more women. Relatives from both parental and maternal lines belong to the family, making the system cognate. Endogamy is prohibited which is in fact the only restriction on sexual relations which are, as a rule, free, particularly, before wedding. The lack of sexual taboos and restrictions is related to egalitarianism which is, though far from being absolute, also an important factor among hunters.[3]

For sedentary and nomad societies, private property and the web of agnate relatives is more important than for hunters. This is related to what Gordon Childe called the Neolithic Revolution, that is, domestication and the ever growing significance of agriculture for which land ownership was of crucial importance. As a result, it was necessary to narrow and to precisely define who belong to the family, which gave way to the unilinear understanding of family relations. In contrast to the cognate system, unilinearism takes either the paternal or the paternal relatives into consideration but not both. Though there are traces of matrilinearism here and there, it was patrilinearism (relating to male dominance) which became widespread in Asia and elsewhere contributing to an ever deteriorating status of women. It is not by accident that the status of women in societies favouring matrilinearism is far better than in patrilinear societies (see, for example, the Malay customary laws).[4] In sedentary societies, ownership is also more important than for hunters who see property items rather as a burden (since they have to carry everything with themselves). Land ownership guaranteed its use and, therefore, livelihood. But land ownership could not be afforded by private persons because of its size and value which gave way to collective ownership, that of the extended family and clan which is another reason for the agnate system to become dominant. Land was however, not simply an object of ownership but also the residence of the spirits of ancestors and the scene of the community living on it. Lands of clans were either distributed among individual families or were jointly cultivated.[5] This is how early Mesopotamian laws prohibiting the purchase and sale of land became understandable. But this is also the reason why land boundaries were marked and protected precisely with landmark stones (such as

---

[2]Glenn (2000: 60, 69).

[3]For more on hunters see Wesel (1985: 71–92).

[4]See Wesel (1985: 189–234).

[5]Rouland (1994: 216–222).

the Mesopotamian *kudurru*) and brutal punishments for trespassing (Hittites). For nomads, it is cattle that play the role of land ownership.

All this led to a changing attitude to marriage and inheritance. Since exogamy brings a woman from outside, the loss of her working force had to be compensated. What is more, her fertility should also be paid for since it is she who gives birth and cares for the offspring of her new family, a crucial point in a system which highlights agnatic relatives and propriety rights. Now it is clear why marriages are believed to be family issues and not the business of the parties and why long negotiations about economic issues accompany marriages. It is also not by accident that what was paid for a marriage was often equal to her blood money which was to be paid for manslaughter.[6] Needless to say, law of inheritance was also of great importance for such societies while there is no trace of it among hunters. Heirs however, inherited not only the bequest but also the social status and responsibility of the deceased person. The extreme form of such a thinking led to levirate marriages or to the custom that a son inherited also his father's wives except his mother.

13.1.2 An Asia-Specific Typology of Customary Laws

Asian peoples living according to customary laws are, obviously, either hunters or nomads or sedentary thus the typology of legal anthropology also makes perfect sense among them. Yet, there are important considerations which are beyond the scope of this typology and call for further explanations. These have nothing to do with the way of life of the people applying these customary laws but are related to the role law plays in their broader social context. Customary law in China for example, with a strong legal system focusing on criminal and administrative law has a completely different place and role in Chinese society than tribal laws have in India under the umbrella of Hindu law without an exclusive focus on public administration. Tribal laws in areas dominated by Islamic law also differ according to space and time, thus Muslim Yemen and Muslim Indonesia should be treated separately. In addition to this, we should also take political organisations and their influence into consideration: tribal laws in a failed state (Afghanistan) have quite a different social role compared to customary laws of people living in a centralised state (China, Iran). These are very important points which justify an entirely new approach to Asian customary laws. This is why I introduce a distinction between exclusive, concurrent and complimentary customary laws.

Exclusive customary law is a system without rivals which makes such a customary law the only player in the field of normativity. This is the case when a society is living only according to its tribal customary law without considering other, rival legal systems such as a religious law or a state law. There are, obviously, very few examples of such white areas in our contemporary world but we can find some in Asian legal history. Mongol customary law, for example, was originally such a system

---

[6]Rouland (1994: 211–216).

with some local variants (the laws of the Kalmyk and the Buriats) but without the influence of any religion with a claim for superiority in the detriment of customary law (Islam, Hindu law, etc.) and of a state law. In the absence of any state, Mongol tribal law remained an exclusive customary law which turned, interestingly, to the basis of a new state law, that of the Mongol Empire, founded by Genghis Khan and his successors. This is why Mongol customary law remained intact after the fall of the empire and was also reluctant to change later when Mongol tribes converted to Buddhism, the influence of which remained marginal and beyond limits. Customary laws of the Indonesian archipelago are also cases in point without a rival state law. Islamic law, it is true, entered Indonesia, but relatively late and peacefully and thus with a limited influence on customary laws going back to a very long tradition with no intent to change their legal understanding in the favour of a newcomer (some Indonesian and Malay customary laws are matrilinear while Islamic law is strongly patriarchal, etc.). Something similar happened in the Philippines where people were hardly impressed by Christian legal understanding.

Concurrent system of customary law is a parallel legal system which shares its influence with a religious or a state law. Concurrent legal systems preserve their dominant position which is acknowledged formally or tacitly by the parallel legal system. Hindu law, for example, has customary law among its legal sources thus providing a theoretical backing to local and tribal customary laws. What is more, Hindu law is not against the notion to prefer customary law against the written legal sources in case of collision, a remarkable flexibility not shared by Islamic law. Islamic law, by contrast, excludes customary laws from its formal legal sources stressing the importance of the will of Allāh, manifesting in the Qur'ān and prophetic Sunna, against the normative understanding of tribesmen, being irrespective of revelation. This was, of course, only legal theory (theology) not every day legal practice which provided more room for customs. As we have seen previously, local customs were in fact taken into consideration either as a contract between the parties (the normative content of an agreement was identical with local custom) or as a normative background for judgments when law courts decided disputes according to local custom. In this way, similarly to India, local, tribal customs and customs of some professions (e.g. merchants) found their way to manifest even against theoretic objections. This goes also for societies in which Islamic law is very strong like the Middle-Eastern countries. But here, too, local, tribal customs are important, sometimes more influential than Islamic law itself, despite theoretical discouragement. The further a tribe lives from state bodies (law courts) and religious institutions (qāḍī), the more exclusive influence tribal customs have (Yemen, Afghanistan). Where Islamic law is less influential, the lack of its dominance is more obvious. Central Asia is a case in point where various Turkic people preserved their customs even when nominally embracing Islam and its law. In addition to religious laws, a new rival of tribal customary laws entered the scene with state law, by the twentieth century at the latest in every corner of Asia. State laws were less generous than religious laws were towards customary laws because many modern states regarded local custom a backward, atavistic hindrance and an obstacle in their efforts to modernise (Westernise) their legal system. This was signalised with a policy to eliminate customary laws entirely or at least, reduce their influence to a minimum, like in Indonesia. India, however, with its more relaxed position towards age old customary laws never went this way but guaranteed constitutional protection to them and left their limited sphere of influence intact. As a result, tribal customary laws continued to govern daily life such as marriage, family, burials, etc. In brief, concurrent system of customary laws emerges where legal pluralism is granted either in theory or in practice by a parallel legal system (religious/state law) which tolerates the operation of customary laws.

This is not to be confused with a complementary system of customary law where a customary law cooperates with a dominant legal system on a tacit agreement to fill legal gaps which the dominant legal system has no intent to fill. In contrast to concurrent legal system where parallel legal systems regulate the same area of law, in complementary systems customary laws supplement the dominant legal system. Here is an example to illustrate: both Islamic law and Malay customary laws regulate family law with remarkable precision but on a different understanding of social organisation and anthropology, creating thus a parallel but concurrent situation in which one of the legal systems would prevail. By contract, in China state law did not regulate private legal matters focusing on criminal and administrative law in its stead. Important issues such as family, inheritance and etc. remained, obviously, not without normative regulations but to the almost exclusive terrain of local customs. In such a model of co-existence, dominant (state) law and customary laws are complementary regulating different issues of legal life constituting together a whole body of legal life. Now it is the more regrettable that only state (written) law is studied in China while oral customary law is almost completely abandoned for academic research, making our knowledge on Chinese legal understanding one-sided.

13.2 Mongol Customs

Due to historical reasons, it is the Mongol customary law among the Turkic–Mongol customary laws which is the best documented. Since Mongol tribes created an unprecedented empire it was their custom which dominated the Eurasian steppe and also influenced the legal life of the subjugated territories from China to Iran. This is why Mongol customs were put into writing, in contrast to the customs of the Turkic people which were not.

The Yassas of Genghis Khan, a law collection produced during the formative period of the Mongol empire remained influential for centuries and were, therefore, copied and preserved for us. We are, regrettably, less fortunate with the customs of Turkic people which were either not put into writing at all or the documents have not reached us. This is also the reason why there are only few scholarly works dedicated to the study of Mongol and Turkic customary laws. One among the exceptions is a monograph on Mongol law by Valentin Riasanovsky, written in Russian in 1935 and published in the United States in 1965. Kazakh customs are discussed in a more recent work of Virginia Martin, though the book concentrates on the Russian imperial policy of the nineteenth century where the study of customary laws is only marginal.[7] We can witness the same pattern in the work of Martha Brill Olcott in which a brief presentation of Kazakh customs is only an introduction to the analysis of Russian politics.[8] There is even less about Turkmen and Kirgiz customs, though generally speaking they are similar to the Mongol and Kazakh customs. In such a situation, the 130 years old work of the eminent Hungarian Orientalist, Vámbéry Ármin should also be consulted in order to fill the gap and have access to valuable information which should be treated, however, with caution.

Mongol customary law is not only better documented but also differs from other Turkic customary laws in its structure and content. This is because traditional Mongol custom became a basis of the Mongol empire which elevated it from a local custom to imperial law for a short period, though never with the intention to destroy others (Islamic law, Chinese law, etc.). As a result, Mongol customary law was infused with ideas and laws about running a state and managing institutions, a novelty which is lacking in other tribal customary laws. The need and effort to create a state altered Mongol customary law significantly in the long run, yet contributed to its diffusion in remote countries such as Iran. The history of the Mongol empire, therefore, is also a point of reference for the chronology of the history of Mongol customary laws. The first period lasts to the emergence of the Mongol empire, a long yet undocumented period, the beginning of which is unknown. The second period is that of the imperial age, that is, the thirteenth and the fourteenth centuries when the laws of Genghis Khan were created or, properly speaking, put into writing. The third period lasted until the seventeenth century when—after the collapse of all Mongol dominated states such as China, Iran of the Ilkhanids, the Golden Horde—Mongol tribes were unable to create their own state but continued to live in three territorial units instead (Eastern Mongolia (Kalkha); Western Mongolia (Dzungaria); Inner Mongolia. It was also during this period when Mongols converted to Buddhism. During this period, various law collections have been produced in these areas which differ only in detail but rest on a common tradition. The fourth period began in the seventeenth century, when imperial China occupied more and more Mongol territories and introduced Chinese law to the detriment of local customs.

During the first period, Mongol customary law was without rivals to regulate Mongol society which was organised along clans, consisting of several families. Tribes were rather political units with no or only fictive family relations among its members. Tribes were also important in warfare because in the absence of any political organisation Mongols went to war by tribes. Khuriltai was the decision making body, comprising of the tribal elite which decided about war and peace and elected the khan. Khuriltai also preserved its importance during the reign of Genghis Khan and his successors when all important decisions concentrated in the hand of the Khan. Yet, even the most powerful Khans such as Genghis did not neglect this consultative body since its prestige and long history together with the respect to Mongol traditions left no room for deciding otherwise. Khuriltai was, needless to

---

[7] Martin (2001).
[8] Olcott (1987).

say, an aristocratic body resting on gerontocracy and the power of the customary law which was at the same time also a limit on the power of the Khan. It was family law which was and for long remained the most elaborated part of Mongol customary law. Mongol family rested on a patrilocal, patriarchal agnate model which granted considerable authority to the family father over his wife (wives) and children. Marriages were exogamous and polygamous if a man could afford to guarantee the livelihood of more women. In such a polygamous family a chief wife, who was usually the first wife enjoyed privileges. Families were considered rather the possession of men, who lost them to their enemies when falling captive. Violence was a part of family life also when girls were abducted for marriage, an archaic custom which was later moderated to ransom and thus to purchase and sale. This is the reason why later it was purchase and sale which became the dominant model of marry making (*kalim*). Poor men with no chance to purchase a girl entered the service of their future father-in-laws for long years (6–8 years) in order to work for their partners. Exchange of wives was also part of Mongol custom, though rarely applied. Accordingly, a family exchanged its sons and daughters as partners for the daughters and sons of their partner family. As a result, a son of a family married the daughter of the partner family and vice versa, a custom known in pre-Islamic Arabia, too. As it is clear now from what has been said so far, women were almost completely subordinated to their husbands who could even kill their wives, though had to pay compensation (the price of a slave). Women were more powerful at home when their husband were away or died because they took over control and managed their families. Divorce was also a simple act without formalities. It was only the husband who could divorce his partner but later wives were also endowed with the same right. A divorce on mutual consent was also a possibility for a couple with the intent to separate. The right to divorce was important not only in the light of personal status but also of propriety rights since legal consequences varied according to the person who initiated the divorce. If separation rested on mutual consent, the dowry had to be returned by the husband. If it was the husband who wanted to divorce, he lost the purchasing price but if it was the wife, the purchasing price had to be returned to the husband. Law of inheritance ranks sons in their descending order and provides a greater share to the first born son while provides the household and the wives of the deceased to the youngest son who could either marry them (save his own mother) or marry them to others. In contrast to family law, other private legal issues are hardly to find in early Mongol customary law: there was no law on ownership and obligations. Individual ownership of immovable was unknown, goods such as land were in the hands of the clan or a tribe and used for keeping livestock and hunting.[9]

The second historic period of Mongol customary law begins with the Yassa of Genghis Khan, a document which is subject to debate for decades for two reasons. First, the original document has not reached us, we have to compile it from references and quotations in various sources. Since the Yassa was an important legal text in the contemporary world, it was copied and referred to in works written during the Mongol period. The main sources are medieval Persian chronicles but Chinese, Armenian and

---

[9]Riasanovsky (1965: 199–201, 238–241).

Egyptian sources are also known. Outstanding are the Persian chronicles of Rāshid al-Dīn and Juwaynī, Iranian viziers in the service of the Mongols who had access to Mongolian sources, otherwise hidden from outsiders, and were well versed in Mongolian legal and political issues. Their references to the Yassas are of utmost importance, though we have to keep in mind that these are only references but not the original text, therefore, the authenticity of these texts as a scholarly problem emerges. Second, there is the problem whether the Yassa should be regarded as a kind of a code or not. Yassa (Mongol *jasagh*) is a word for law, order, decree, that is, edicts pronounced by khans, notably Genghis and his successors to regulate issues on an ad hoc basis. These individual decrees might have been put together later and this is how the great code, the Yassa of Genghis Khan was born, perhaps a construction of modern Western historiography which was taken for granted for long.[10] Eminent Russian scholars such as George Vernadsky and Valentin Riasanovsky, believed in the existence of such a code, though some of their colleagues (Popov, Vasiliev) raised doubts and argued (on Chinese sources) in the favour of individual edicts which never constituted a code.[11] David Ayalon was also for the code hypothesis with some caution pointing at the important fact that all sources backing such a theory, including the often quoted work of the Egyptian Maqrīzī go ultimately back to the chronicle of Juwaynī.[12] By contrast, David Morgan challenged this view, arguing that no source refers explicitly to such a code, not even the chronicle of Rāshid al-Dīn and the Secret History of the Mongols, two important texts with the best insight to Mongol domestic politics. This is not to say, of course, that there were no individual edicts but they were, Morgan argues, not put into a single code.[13]

The text as we now know it from Maqrīzī and Juwaynī consists of 26 paragraphs with additional ten paragraphs known from other sources the authenticity of which remains doubtful. The text refers to the formative period of the Mongol empire when military conquest, the establishment of a postal service and institutions of public administration was o n he way. Despite concentrating on public law and military issues, the text begins with adultery, to be punished by death. Here, Riasanovsky calls attention to how alien this law to original Mongol customary law is with a more lenient and flexible attitude to sexual relations before and after the Yassa. This is why he believes in a Chinese influence in this law.[14] Being an entirely new law, this might also be the reason why the text begins just with this issue. What comes next (3–6. §) are also wrongs with a death penalty but they have, seemingly, nothing to do with Chinese influence being traditional Mongol customs such as lying, spying, interfering in the disputes of others, urinating into the fire, taking a loan three times without paying it back, giving food to a captive without the permission of his master. Obviously, these are not edicts of Genghis Khan and his successors but age old customs which were in existence prior to the dominance of the Genghisids, thus making the Yassa a complex

---

[10]Jackson (2013).

[11]Riasanovsky (1965: 25–26).

[12]Ayalon (1971: 100–140).

[13]Morgan (1986: 165–176).

[14]Riasanovsky (1965: 146–147).

legal document containing both edicts and customary laws. This is why the Yassa is also a law collection of Mongol customary laws which becomes evident with the law of prohibiting any interference to the quarrel of others and the prohibition to urinate into the fire, a clear influence of shamanism. Despite this, the Yassa stressed the freedom of religion (11. §) and declared the importance of what we now call the secular state without favouring any religion. In order to achieve this goal, the laws prohibit the notion of ritual purity (which is favouritism and exclusion in ritual language) and declare everything ritually pure (16. §). Laws interfere with religious affairs only in the modes of slaughtering, prohibiting the Muslim way at the cost of a death penalty (8. §), a law which created tensions in Muslim dominated areas. We can find rules on the organisation of the army which is rather important for the students of military history. It is also important for legal history, however that every soldier was responsible for his own equipment and whoever was lenient in this obligation was severely punished after a careful check before every battle (18. §). Domestic communication was made easy and rapid with the postal service, an important novelty in the Mongol empire (25. §). Finally, the laws emphasise the privilege of khans to select women for themselves and their offspring from among women presented to them because it was an obligation to introduce pretty young girls to the khans (21. §).

According to the fragments missing from Maqrīzī, hunters who let an animal escape during communal hunting were punished (27. §). Animals and slaves were of great value which is the reason why they were also seriously protected by law. If a horse of someone was found in the possession of a person without legal claim, he had to give the horse back together with nine others as a punishment and compensation. Was he unable to do so and had no children, such a person was executed like a sheep (29. §). If, however, a runaway slave was found in the possession of someone other than his master, such a person was executed immediately without the chance of compensation (7. §). This law shows the rigor attached to the stealing of slaves because its legal consequence was stricter than the penalty for manslaughter from which there was the chance to escape by paying compensation, the exact sum being regulated by the Yassa itself in the form of blood money (28. §). The last three paragraphs are dedicated to inheritance law, where no novelty is to be found (the order of sons determined by the marriage of their mothers, the privilege of the eldest son and the youngest inheriting the household and wives of the deceased). It is now clear that the text could be regarded as a code only at the risk of exaggeration if it was put into writing at all. The prestige of the laws was guaranteed, obviously, not by its legal precision but by its political significance, being the laws of the world conquering khans. This is the reason why the Yassa closely shares the fate of the Mongol empire: as long as it dominated subjugated territories and societies, no one dared to neglect it. Ögödei Khan, for example, prohibited to change a word in it. After the decline and fall of the Mongols, however, the law of the empire also vanished and continued to exist only as it had been previously: the tribal customary law of the Mongols. Contrary to the fame of its intellectual father the laws of Genghis Khan had fallen into oblivion and new laws, resting on the same tradition but regulating detail differently replaced them during the third period.

After the fall of the Mongol empire, Mongol tribes created no state but continued to live according to their tribal constitution in three territorial areas of Mongolia as autonomous units with their own laws. Western Mongols produced an important collection of their customary laws in 1640, which remained an important document for a rather long time but escaped the attention of western scholarship. Its first edition and translation was produced in Russian (*Mongol Oyratin Ikh Tsaaz*) followed by a German translation. There are some textual variants with one text consisting of only 120 paragraphs while others are a bit longer with 130 and 150 laws, but presumably the authentic text is the shorter version.[15] Studying these laws, we can come to the conclusion that Mongolian tribes witnessed no ground breaking changes during the centuries. The basic unit remained the family which were organised into ever more populous units such as the *aoul*, the *aimak* and the *otok*, headed by leaders with various titles, ranks, privileges and income. This tribal aristocracy constituted the 'white bones' with *khan*s, *noyon*s, and *shulenga*s. By contrast, commoners were referred to as 'black bones' including shepherd–soldiers, merchants and servants. The *aoul* (camp) was home to extended families. Such families with relatives living nearby constituted an *aimak* with several *aimak*s an *otok*. A tribe consists of more *otok*s and the alliance of several tribes resulted in the Oirat tribal federation.

This structure was not only a hierarchical social organisation but also an internal network of solidarity. It included the natural daily cooperation, such as putting up or dismantling the yurt, guarding livestock, hunting, etc. A camp site of a family was fixed and it was prohibited to move from there within the *otok* because land was not in the ownership of individuals and families but in that of larger social units distributing land among their members. Solidarity was also emphasised by laws, stressing the duty of elders to care for the poor, the homeless and the wanderers. It was everybody's duty to give kumiss to the thirsty and night shelter to wanderers. Similarly, everyone was obliged to help young couples who wanted to marry. At the same time, it was rewarded if someone saved the life of a person or an animal from any kind of danger or saved a child from under a horse. There was no essential change in family law compared to the previous period: the family remained patriarchal and agnate resting on exogamous marriage. The age limit for marriage for girls was 15 years. Purchase and sale (ransom money) remained the most popular form of marriage. In addition to paying the *kalim*, dowry was also to be given to the girls, the sum of which depended on the social status of the parties. A wife could be obtained not only by purchase but also by force as a booty: if someone killed her husband in battle, he could take along the deceased's wife as a reward, a law which goes back to the old Mongol customary law.[16]

We can witness more gradual changes in criminal law where punishments were milder (compared to the Yassa), thus restoring the primordial state of affairs prior to the emergence of the Mongol empire. It is material compensation which dominates criminal thinking while the death penalty seems to be only an exception. This might

---

[15]Riasanovsky (1965: 47–48). The following description of the legal collection is based ont he text of the source as published by Rasianovsky (1965: 92–11).

[16]Riasanovsky (1965: 100–101).

also be due to the influence of Buddhism to which Mongol tribes recently converted. The opening law of the Yassa with the death penalty for adultery was abandoned and manslaughter was also punished only with material compensation the sum of which depended on the victim's social status (confiscation of property for noblemen). Capital punishment was reserved for acts which were against the safety of the entire community, such as deserting the army or not reporting the approach of the enemy in heavy arms. Mutilation and corporeal punishment were punishments of crimes for which neither the death penalty nor compensation was believed to be appropriate, such as when one of the wives killed the other one (her ears were cut off and she was married off), or when a daughter-in-law beat up her father-in-law (whipping). Among pecuniary punishments, fines paid in animals were more common, specifying the exact number of animals to hand over (sheep, horse or ox). Sometimes it was only a relative number, depending on the social standing of the parties, but sometimes the law collection specified the number of blows to be given in absolute terms irrespective of social status. Confiscation of the entire property was reduced to some serious cases such as when someone robbed an entire *aimak*, or if a father killed his son or a son killed his father or mother. It is now clear that Mongol customary law is far more moderate and tolerant than Chinese criminal law was. In contrast to Confucian understanding, Mongol customary law did not privilege parents and elders in general but treated the murder of parents and children on the same level and with remarkable flexibility.

Similarly to the Oyrats, northern Mongols (Khalkha) also produced a law collection of their own (Khalkha Jirum). This is not a law collection edited at a certain point of time in history but a compendium of various texts written during the seventeenth century supplementing the basic text of 1709, containing the customs of the Northern Mongols.[17] These laws were still in force in the early twentieth century, though the text itself was hardly known because according to Mongol understanding, commoners were prohibited to have copies of important texts such as law collections and the Secret History of the Mongols. This is why there is only one copy of the law collection at hand. Basics of northern Mongol customs are, obviously, identical with that of the Oyrats making Kalkha Jirum differ only in detail.

One such a difference is the role of Buddhism: while Oyrat law collection had little to say about Buddhism or religious affairs in general, Kalkha Jirum is full of references to Buddhism. This is because Khalkha was the headquarters of Bogdo Gegen, one among the three important authorities of Buddhism together with the Dalai Lama and the Panchen Lama. The law collection echoes Buddhist confessions all over the text. As a result, Buddhist ethics prevailed in northern Mongol laws. This is why the killing of some animals (dog, stallion, goat, frog, etc.) was generally prohibited and all kinds of killings were also prohibited on certain days of the month (8, 13, 15, 25, 30). Buddhist shrines and their superiors enjoyed privileges and particular protection by criminal law since stealing from temples was strictly punished. Certain shrines functioned as asylums. Buddhist monks were exempt from taxes and corvée obligations but not from penalties: wrongdoings against their social standing

---

[17]The text of the source is presented by Riasanovsky (1965: 111–126).

were properly punished (theft, drinking alcohol). At the same time, assaults against monks were punished more severely than attacks against commoners. In addition to the Kalkha Jirum. religious affairs were regulated by general laws on Buddhism, including the legal status of temples, the rights and duties of monks, and the punishments of crimes committed against them. One of such a code was produced in the seventeenth century (*Arvan Buyant Nomiin Tsaaz*), which was at the same time also a law against shamanism. This is why the code prohibited the veneration of statues and figures of shamanism and the very ancient Mongol practice to bury servants, animals and treasures of noblemen together with the dead. Instead, they had to be donated to a Buddhist monastery. It also prohibited statues and figures linked to Shamanism and also the killing of certain animals.[18]

The second difference is that law merchant is relatively more elaborated compared to the Oyrat law collection. Interestingly, these laws are about restrictions and prohibitions marking the limits of otherwise free commercial activities. Merchants should be registered in order to pursue their business. It was prohibited to engage in any commercial activity at night, to approach caravans coming to a settlement in the desert, to sell wine, to sell and hire camels and land to Russians and the Chinese. Registering merchants was in the interest of both the khan (taxes) and society at large (to reduce fraudulent activities). The prohibition of selling wine is Buddhist ethics in a legal language. The prohibition of selling and hiring land and camels is a protective law to hinder Russians and the Chinese to legally occupy Mongol territories, an attempt which failed in the long run since the Manchu dynasty occupied Mongolia by force. The prohibition to ride out to a caravan was in the interest of fair competition so that no one could obtain economic advantages by concluding separate bargains in advance with merchants ignorant of local prices (we can witness the same law in Arabia).

Buryat customary law has some particularities to offer in family law. The exchange of wives called *anda* was a practice for long when a son of a family married the daughter of another family and vice versa. More particular, was a law of divorce when a wife was fleeing from her home. First, it had to be investigated whether a misbehaviour of her husband led to her escape, or not. If her husband was not to blame, his wife was whipped and taken back home. This was to be done when the wife escaped two more times but not when she escaped her home for the fourth time. In this case she was neither whipped nor brought back to her husband but the couple separated and all properties returned to the respective families.[19]

13.3 Kazakh and Manchu Customary Laws

Kazakh customary law is by and large similar to Mongol customs due to their common cultural heritage, a common way of life and a similar geographic environment. Taken

---

[18]Wallace (2014: 322–323).
[19]Riasanovsky (1979: 196–198).

this similarity in what follows, I concentrate only on differences in order to avoid repetitions. Kazakh customary law preserved its original Turkic language but both Persian and Arabic loanwords found their way to it coming from the terminology of Islamic law.

Kazakhs refer to their customary law as the custom of their ancestors called *ata dasztüri* (from Turkic ata: father and Persian dastūr: rule), or *babalar zsoly* (the path of fathers). Guardians and experts of customary law are the elderly called *aksakāl* (of white beard), respected because of their age, life experience and skills in conflict resolutions. These persons were no legal professionals but old men acting in concert, whose decision rested on the prestige of gerontocracy. By contrast, judges called *bii*s were well versed in law who were also consulted by the *aksakāl*s in difficult cases. Judges also acted on their own right without consulting *aksakāl*s. In doing so, they investigated cases, controlled procedures, heard witnesses and passed sentences. One of the tasks of *bii*s was to keep order and this is the reason why they have a whip in their hands. Impartiality and fairness were expected of the judges. As a Kazakh proverb has it: a just *bii* has no relative. Though not all judges were able to live up this expectation, all three Kazakh tribal federations have their famous judges who are remembered to this day though they lived in the seventeenth century.[20]

Kazakh social and political structure is similar to that of the Mongols, moreover, the Kazakh elites (*ak suiuk*: those of white bones) regarded themselves the direct descendants of Genghis Khan. By contrast, commoners, similarly to the Mongols, were of the black bones (*kara suiuk*). Supreme military command was in the hands of khans who were elected by a council of elder, judges and the heads of clans. This council also decided about important questions such as the distribution of land for winter settlement and planning the actions (wandering, summer and winter camps) of the coming year. Lacking any formal institutions khans were dependent on their personal abilities, charisma and prestige. Khans were elected for lifetime. After their death, authority was inherited by their brothers because Kazakhs follow the principle of seniority. But this was only a tendency, not a rule since a better qualified candidate could always be elected. Social structure also closely resembles that of the Mongols: extended families were organised into clans, though the *aul,* consisting of several extended families was more important since Kazakhs were wandering and foraging their animals in the framework of an *aul*. A winter settlement of an *aul* consisted of about 30–40 yurts. An *aul* was headed by an elderly man, an *aksakāl,* who represented the *aul*, distributed the pastures and together with other *aksakāl*s elected *bii*s for settling disputes. *Bii*s, members of Kazakh tribal aristocracy for long were elected judges only in the seventeenth century when Kazakh legal life became more complicated as a result of Tauke Khan's decision to collect Kazakh customary law for the first time. This is how the *Jhety Jharga* came into being with Mongol, Russian and Islamic legal influences but reflecting contemporary Kazakh social reality. The text was committed to writing only in 1820, upon the initiative of the Russians and remained in force for a long time with minor changes. As legal material became more complicated, *bii*s were selected for judicial service i n the

---

[20]Raushangul (2013: 132, 138).

framework of a more formalised procedure. In the absence of any building, it was the tents of the *bii*s which gave home to legal procedures and judges received 10% of the fee for their services. Though judges did everything possible to keep conflict at bay and hinder the spread of violence, they were not always successful.[21]

Legal disputes focused on animals and land, wells and the winter and summer residences, on women and on various cases of manslaughter and assault. In contrast to Mongol customs, Kazakh customary law is less lenient and human, with more capital punishment for grave crimes such as revolt, high treason, manslaughter and adultery. Blood feud was common but in case of manslaughter, the loss could be compensated by blood money called *khūn* (a Persian word for blood also in use among Pashtuns). Compensation paid for crimes other than manslaughter, that is, various forms of injuries were called *ayb* (from the Arabic word for mistake, fault) the sum of which was less than that of a *khūn*. Blood money for women, the half paid for men. For killing a man, 100 horses had to be given on average, for a woman only 50. For calculating *ayb* a unit called *toguz* was introduced, consisting of nine animals. For example, if *ayb* was to be paid for an injury, it consisted, on average, of 3 *toguz* (27 horses). *Barymta*, stealing animals out of vengeance was an ancient practice among Kazakhs, committed usually out of grievance and passion (*khūn* not paid for, jealousy, etc.). Stealing livestock at night, that is, driving away the entire stock of animals was a heavy blow to the owners since the livelihood of Kazakh families was completely dependent on their animals.[22]

Internal solidarity was a moral and legal duty within the extended family, ranging from help in seasonal works (for instance, to dig a well) to succour in case of natural calamity. These were basic duties which could also be enforced with the help of the *bii*s if family members refused to help. Solidarity was particularly important when organising weddings which was an outstanding event for the entire clan. Age limit for girls was 14 years of age, though families agreed on marriages usually earlier. Purchasing price (*kalym*, a term identical with its Mongol equivalent) depended on the social status of the parties: among tribal aristocracy, animals had to be given in the thousands, but among commoners the number of animals (usually sheep) has not reached one hundred. Polygamy was lawful in theory but was abandoned in practice: since husbands had to provide each wife a separate yurt hardly anyone could afford to keep more than one wife. Economic reasons thus pointed towards monogamy. Divorce was free of formalities but following the logic of patriarchal families, the children remained in the former husband's *aul*. Kazakh law of inheritance was no exception from the model of the Mongol–Turkic peoples. Only sons inherited the bequest because daughters were already given their share as their dowry when they married. It was the youngest son who inherited his father's yurt and looked after his widowed mother.[23]

Quite similar to the Mongol–Kazakh customs is the Jurchen (Manchu) customary law. Similarly to the Mongols, they also followed the principle of ultimogeniture in

---

[21] Olcott (1987: 13–16).

[22] Vámbéry (1885: 370).

[23] Olcott (1987: 16, 22–23).

the law of inheritance with the youngest son as heir to his parents who cared for them in their yurt during their last years. Abduction of girls was a wide spread custom with its own ritual: the girl was impatiently waiting for her abduction by his bridegroom heading a group of armed men supporting him. Engagement and other formalities could only follow suit later. Robbery was also among their custom when garments, horses and household implements were taken away. The owner could get them back only in exchange of gifts and wine if he could find out within a short period of time who the robbers were. Girls were also abducted during such occasions, and parents were informed about it only later. Such robberies usually took place around the first full Moon of the New Year because this period was regarded the most suited time for marrying. Similarly to the Mongols, sexual morals were far more liberal among the Manchus than in China. A wife committing adultery was not punished at all costs, at the most, her social appreciation changed and that too only among the elite. Levirate was wide spread and daily routine. Blood feud was also common, though attempts were made to introduce compensation in its stead. Manchu customs were regarded as barbarism by the Chinese, particularly the abduction of girls, the levirate marriage and the partition of the bequest (which was a crime against the family according to Confucian understanding). Manchu customs became sinicised slowly in the Middle Ages but difference remained visible even during the rule of the Manchu dynasty in China from the seventeenth century to 1911.[24]

References

Ayalon D (1971) The Great Yāsa of Chingiz Khān. A Reexamination (Part A). Studia Islamica 33:97–140
Franke H (1981) Jurchen customary law and the Chinese law of the Chin Dynasty. In: Eikemeier D, Franke H (eds) State and law in East Asia. Otto Harrassowitz, Wiesbaden
Glenn P (2000) Legal traditions of the world. Sustainable diversity in law. Oxford, Oxford University Press
Jackson P (2013) Yasa-law-code. In: Encyclopedia Iranica. http://www.iranicaonline.org/articles/yasa-law-code
Martin V (2001) Law and custom in the steppe. The Kazakhs of the Middle Horde and Russian colonialism in the nineteenth century. Routledge, London, New York
Morgan DO (1986) The 'Great Yasa of Chingiz Khan' and the Mongol Law in the Ilkhanate. Bull Sch Orient Afr Stud 49(1):163–176
Olcott MW (1987) The Kazakhs. Hoover Institution Press, Stanford
Raushanngul M (2013) A kazak szokásjog irodalmi megjelenése. In: Keletkutatás. Kőrösi Csoma Társaság, Budapest, pp 131–140
Riasanovski VA (1965) Fundamental principles of Mongol Law. Indiana University Publications, Uralic and Altaic Studies 43. Indiana University, Bloomington
Riasanovski VA (1979) Customary laws of the Mongol Tribes (Mongols, Buriats, Kalmucks), Part I-III, 2nd edn. Hyperion Press, Westport, Connecticut. Springer, The Hague
Rouland N (1994) Legal anthropology. Stanford University Press, Stanford, California
Vámbéry Á (1885) A török faj. Budapest. Reprint: Lilium Arum: Dunaszerdahely

[24]Franke (1981: 226–230).

Vernadsky G (1938) The scope and contents of Chingis Khan's Yasa. Harvard J Asiatic Stud 3(3–4):337–360

Wallace VA (2014) Buddhist Laws in Mongolia. In: French R, Nathan A (eds) Buddhism and law. An introduction. Cambridge University Press, Cambridge, pp 305–319

Wesel U (1985) Frühformen des Rechts in vorstaatlichen Gesellschaften. Frankfurt, Suhrkamp

Chapter 14
Concurrent Customary Laws

14.1 The Pashtunwali

Pashtunwali is the ethos and ethics of Pashtun tribes living in Afghanistan and Pakistan on both sides of the Durand Line. Pashtun is one of the world's largest tribal society, comprising of almost 50 Million people. Pashtuns are Sunnī Muslims of the Hanafi school the law of which is sometimes at variance with their own tribal customary law and ethos. Despite this, Pastuns believe that what they do is in accordance with Islamic law, though sometimes it is not (for instance, the death penalty of stoning is executed by destroying a wall to the condemned person). What complicates matter is the emergence of the Taliban movement representing an extreme understanding of Islamic law who are without exception Pashtun. Thus classical Hanafi law, Taliban interpretation of Islamic law and Pashtun customs merge into a crucial matrix with visible cross-fertilisation (e.g. some Islam-interpretation of the Taliban are in fact Pashtun customary law).

14.1.1 Values of Pashtunwali

Pashtunwali is a common cultural heritage of the Pashtun tribes which cement them—in addition to their language—together despite their conflict and wars fought for women, gold and land (*zan, zar, zamin*).[1] This is, though a very widespread notion, only a Persian alliteration and poetic fantasy since according to the Pashtun themselves, they fight for *mar, khadza, msaka*, that is death, woman and land, gold missing from the list. Rightly so, because gold is entirely missing from this poor, rural community living in the bare mountains of Afghanistan. By contrast, death is in fact

---

[1]G. Morgenstierne: Afghan. Encyclopedia of Islam I, 216 b.

© Springer Nature Switzerland AG 2020
J. Jany, *Legal Traditions in Asia*, Ius Gentium: Comparative Perspectives
on Law and Justice 80, https://doi.org/10.1007/978-3-030-43728-2_14

a cause for conflicts, referring to blood feuds fought for long decades. It is not by accident that *mar* stands first in the list.[2]

Pashtunwali is, it is important to note, not the customary laws of the Pashtun tribes but their ethos, moral guideline and a code of honour for a Pashtu male in order to keep his reputation and not to bring shame on his person and family. Milestones are bravery and fighting spirit, respect for the elders, pride, magnanimity and hospitality, revenge for wrongs and participation in public life and communal decision making. Those who live up to these expectations are the ideal Pashtun men called *ghairatman*. Customary law (*narkh*) is however, only a part of *Pashtunwali*, containing obligatory norms which could be enforced if necessary while extra-legal parts of Pashtunwali could not. *Pashtunwali* is about honour which should be protected and enhanced and shame to be avoided at every cost. The dichotomy of honour and shame is projected on family life, on fighting moral, on crimes and conflict resolution, including property disputes such as land. Disputes on property rights are not regarded claims on material objects but as a challenge on someone's honour and reputation.

Pashtunwali bears witness to the nomadic way of life of the Pashtun tribes who became sedentary only at a later period of their history. Though a significant number of the tribes are not engaged in nomadic animal husbandry any more, urban civilisation and its legal values had no influence on their legal understanding which led to tension with other peoples of Afghanistan (Persian, Hazaras, Uzbeks) and with classical Islamic law proper which is the product of the urban civilisation of the Middle East in the Middle Ages. Lack of private property is one among the examples: while classical Islamic law has the city dweller merchant with his private property and willingness to engage in business as its model, Pashtun customary law favours communal ownership and hinders private property to emerge and develop. Communal ownership of land, for example, is such a nomadic heritage which is at variance with Islamic law not only in letters but also in spirit, anthropogy and economics. Communal lands are distributed among the extended families of villages based on their number, origin and military strength. Sometimes land is distributed by drawing lots annually, a technique which hinders any investment in agriculture since no investor has any guarantee to have the land and his investments the next year, too. Such community ownership is typical to this day in Afghanistan, where the acquisition of land is impossible for persons living outside the villages. Similarly to Mongol and Baluchi (Iranian speaking tribes living in Iran, Afghanistan and Pakistan) customary laws, Pashtunwali favours group interest to the detriment of individual interest which hinders individual ownership of land and a modern agriculture and economy to emerge.[3]

Nomadic background not only determines propriety rights but also social organisation which rests on the clan system. Tribes (*tāyifa*) consist of several sub-tribes made up by clans (*zai*, or *khel*) to be fragmented further to *kahol*s, consisting of several extended families, the ancestors of which are said to have lived seven or eight generations earlier. Out of these categories it is the *kahol* which stands out in

---

[2]Steul (1981: 218–219).
[3]Rzehak (2011: 6).

importance because internal solidarity is manifest at this level of social hierarchy. Mutual assistance in agricultural labour and constructing a house, marriages and internal legal disputes are settled within a *kahol*. This is the reason why genealogy is so important for Pashtuns who could enumerate all their ancestors in a *kahol* down to eight generations or, in an ideal case, to Qaīs ꜥAbd al-Rashīd, the nominal ancestor of the Pashtuns.[4] Such a nomadic family is, obviously, patrilocal and patriarchal where one is looking always for common ancestors. It is thus, small wonder that Pashtun men meeting for the first time immediately enumerate their genealogy in the hope to find common ancestors. Should they find common links, their cool or distanced relation immediately turns towards mutual assistance.[5]

Ghairatman is a complex term with some sub-categories together denoting the ideal of a Pashtun man. One such a sub-category is *nang* (or *nanga*) meaning bravery and heroism which is the greatest praise one can say about a Pashtun man if used as an adjective (*nangialai*). Bravery refers to the promoting of self-interest without hesitation but also to the protection of the weak, thus encapsulating both an active/aggressive and a passive/defensive aspect. To defend personal and family honour is *nanga*, by which one can be a respected (*nangialai*) person and a respected member of a tribe. The defensive aspect is of importance because to protect the weak and particularly the womenfolk is a duty and a minimum of bravery with its own term (*namūs*). *Namūs* is closely linked to the sexual honour of women but its meaning is broader, to be translated as honour, reputation, esteem and chasteness. Women to be protected include the mother, the wife (wives), sisters and female children because the protection of married sisters is their husband's task. To arrange food and shelter is also part of *namūs,* yet the lion's share goes to the control of sexual morals and behaviour. Since immoral sexual behaviour of women destroys the social standing of their male relatives, efforts are made to control every step of women and to keep them separated from the world outside in order to hinder comments, critiques or glazes. Extreme separation of gender and dressing women in burqa have, therefore, less to do with Islam and more with Pashtun understanding of honour and shame. Pashtun society is, therefore, another example of what anthropologist Ruth Benedict called shame society (in relation to Japan) in which ultimate driving force behind every individual and social action is shame and the fear to lose honour. Should a woman escape the attention of all her domestic watchdogs and have a lover, a husband returning home has a moral duty to kill them both on the spot. The right of husbands to kill their wives and her lover on the spot is no novelty since a variety of Asian legal systems endove a husband with such a power. Pashtunwali, however, goes further when transforming this duty into an obligation because a husband can regain his honour only by killing them, an action which would lead to a series of blood feuds more often than not. The only way out to avoid bloodshed is to take no notice, that is, a husband could pretend not to be aware of the affairs because one cannot revenge an unknown shame. In addition to guard and protect women, levirate marriage is also a part of *namūs* because to care for the wife and children of

---

[4]Steul (1981: 28–34).
[5]Rzehak (2011: 8–9).

the deceased brother belongs to internal solidarity no one can escape from. Levirate marriage also has the advantage of keeping family and joint property together, a basic concern in Pashtun society. This is also the reason why marriages between nephews and nieces are preferred. A person neglecting duties from *namūs* is called *benamūs*, a person without *namūs*, an enormous shame for a Pashtun male. If someone is called *benamūs* without reason it is an insult which is rarely left without consequences.[6]

Another survival of the nomadic past is bravery and the quest for glory in warfare called *tura* (sword). A warrior who stands out in fighting is brave (*turialai*) while a coward, unheroic person deserves eternal shame. Pashtun heroism was a constant hindrance for foreign invaders to occupy Afghanistan in the last three centuries (Safavid Persia, Anglo–Afghan wars, Soviet and American invasion) with modern weapons and preponderance. This is not just the heroism of the individual but also a duty toward one's family and clan in order not to lose honour individually and collectively. Pashtunwali is a "mortal code" which praises honour at the cost of human life. It is worth quoting here the account of a British army officer from the late nineteenth century. Accordingly, after a battle, Pashtun women were collecting the dead in the battlefield and while doing so an elderly woman lifted the head of each corpse. She had found seven corpses and kissed six of them but slapped the seventh on his face. When the officer asked the reason of this strange behaviour, he was told that the woman had lost all of her seven sons, six of whom got their wound in the front. The seventh son was however wounded from behind, a shame which could be awarded only with a slap. Women were present in the battlefield not only after the combat but during the fight also, supplementing men with food and water and any help which was useful in the given situation. Here *Pashtunwali* comes to the rescue of women, because they could not be attacked despite their presence and active support for the enemy. It is arrogance and cowardice to attack them as an enemy of unequal strength and ability which is against the martial ethos of Pashtunwali. For similar reasons, it is prohibited to attack children, Sufis, *hajjis* (persons who were pilgrims to Mecca with particular social appreciation) and mullahs. To attack women also has material disadvantage because the families of both her father and her husband could seek blood feud and demand blood money.[7] Here it is important to note that *turialai* and the *nangialai* are not synonyms. *Tura* is an aggressive motive to assert self-interest, even with physical violence, if necessary, but such a person is not necessarily *nangialai* if he fights only for his own interests but does not defend others. By contrast, a *nangialai* person is also a *turialai* since no one can defend the weak without courage and bravery.[8]

Pashtun tribes fight not only against external enemies but also internal wars for *badal*, a term denoting exchange and reciprocity. Accordingly, every act, be good or bad, moral or immoral, deserves reciprocity. A positive act (help, donation) should be reciprocated by the very positive act itself, so a negative act too (attack, violating honour, murder). Thus, *badal* is a term with a broader meaning than just revenge

---

[6]Steul (1981: 137–142), Rzehak (2011: 9–10).

[7]Rzehak (2011: 11).

[8]Steul (1981: 151–152).

or blood feud as it is often understood. *Pashtunwali* requires reciprocity, creating rather complex social relations. Greetings formulae of politeness are good points to demonstrate. Pashtun persons spend long minutes asking about the well-being of their partner in conversation with those they just meet on the street. It would be however, a sign of arrogance to answer these questions since one has to ask the same questions in its stead. Answering these questions first is not a proper behaviour being an act against modesty. This is why Pashtun people are engaged in a rather long verbal rite of politeness at every meeting, a custom which we can witness also in neighbouring Iran (ta'arof). Central element in every kind of exchange is proportionality hindering to go beyond limits in either side: neither more nor few could be given back, be it the exchange of words in greetings, the exchange of food or goods and also the exchange of wrongs, the later leading to talio. To go beyond limits is arrogance and violence called *salem* even when honour is at stake since proportionality should be a guiding principle during blood feud, too. A *salem* is an aggressive assailant who extends beyond the limits of *badal* and causes unnecessary conflicts and emotions. Such a person is *turialai* because he defended himself, but he is not a *ghairatman* because he violated the code of proper behaviour. Such a person would be condemned by his own relatives, too, who would use opportunities to get rid of them if they evolve into a burden for the whole family. There was a case when such a trouble-maker was killed during the exchange of blood feuds. His family however, stopped the chain of blood feuds being content to be relieved from him. Exact proportionality however is not always to identify. Take, for example, the case when someone's wife was abducted by armed violence. It is not an act of *badal* to abduct the wife of the abductor in exchange because an illegal act cannot be avenged by another illegal act. This is why in such a case the abductor should be killed, even though the original crime was not manslaughter.[9]

Pashtunwali prefers collective instead of individual responsibility in cases of blood feud because it is the community (family, clan, etc.) and not the individual who was the object of a wrong or an insult. By insulting any member of the group, the entire group was shamed. This goes the other way around, too, that is, vengeance and blood feud could not only target the individual who was responsible for the act but also the entire group to which he belonged since the group is responsible for the acts of its members. This understanding opens the door wide open for blood feuds for generations since potential victims are numerous and cases do not end with the punishment of an individual. What constitutes a solidarity group depends on situations. A family or a clan is a natural unit for solidarity but sometimes the entire village could be a group for vengeance. If, for example, there is a dispute between villages concerning land, forest, etc. which escalates to fighting with bloodshed, victims had to be revenged by the entire village and not only by their relatives. Thus, *badal* calls for everyone to participate, an obligation no one could escape from only at the cost of being *daus*, that is, a person who has lost his honour. A *daus* person denies solidarity with his solidarity group which would also end his belonging to the group. This could be a social pressure that forces people to opt for death instead

---

[9]Rzehak (2011: 14–15), Steul (1981: 151–155).

of being *daus*. A case in a recent conflict helps to clarify the point. A man was
in conflict with another man and in order to escape he fled his home and did not
dare go onto the street. To his misfortune however, his group was involved in blood
feud for a different matter and he had to join his group for fighting to avoid being
daus. Thus, he left his home and entered the streets where he was immediately shot
to death by his adversary. It is impossible to predict how long the chain of blood
feud would last since there are no rules for this. In the majority of the cases, blood
feuds last for generations and are always terminated with negotiations between the
parties. Conflicts are solved with an agreement on blood money (*khunbahā*) to be
paid. Conflict on injuries are also solved with blood money which had to be paid,
however not for the proper injury but for the loss of honour caused by the harm itself
because suffering an injury is regarded as a weakness and thus a loss of honour. Such
a weakness and defeat is a shame (*sharm*) for which offenders have to pay *sharm*
money. By doing so, they acknowledge that the attack was unlawful and thus they
restore the honour of the injured person. *Sharm* money has no fixed ratio but depends
on the social status of the injured. In addition to *sharm* money, medical costs called
tipakai should also be paid.[10]

Martial ethos is only one side of the coin. On the other side there are hospitality,
friendship and generosity called *sakhāwat*. Hospitality (*melmepalana*) is one of the
values of *Pashtunwali* which also determines architecture: houses are constructed in
a form which enables families to host guests: guests are accommodated in a separate
part of the house the use of which does not hinder hosts in their daily life. Hospitality
is offered not only to friends but t o anyone pledging for it. A request for hospitality
could not be refused under any circumstances and hosts have to do everything for the
comfort of their guests. Should a foreigner turn up in a Pashtun village, locals would
compete for the honour to host him, which is, seemingly, just another field for combat
in a competition for prestige and power. It is, more often than not, the most prestigious
family which hosts such a non-resident person, the head of which could enhance his
being *nangialai* and *turialai* by hospitality. The worldview behind it is that the world
is dangerous and one can defend himself only with the help of relatives which is, of
course, missing for travellers during their journey. Hosts provide, therefore, shelter
and protection for travellers which is a substitute for the succour of one's relatives.
Hosts however provide not only accommodation but also food and drink. What is
more, hosts are obliged to arrange for entertainment, too: guest should not be left
alone and to be bored. This might also be a burden for guests who cannot move freely
and leave the house without the permission of their host. Needless to say, guests are
strictly forbidden to commit anything to the detriment of their hosts, even to refuse
the food offered to them which would be a gross insult. Hosts do more than expected
and take heavy burden on them to finance dishes for their guests which they could
not afford and would never prepare for themselves, a practice which led guests to
wrong conclusions concerning the financial situation of their hosts. Hosts have to
defend their guests against any insult, injury and assault. This is sometimes a good
possibility to solve domestic conflicts since persons fleeing from their pursuer and

---

[10]Steul (1981: 157–158), Rzehak (2011: 14–15).

finding shelter in one of the houses in the village are regarded as a guest who had to be protected. In such cases, hosts acts as mediators between the parties. Women fleeing from their bridegroom who are selected for them by their families but are not willing to marry can also find asylum in a house as a guest and enjoy protection, usually in a house of the man she wants to marry. This however, ruins her reputation and social esteem for her lifetime and is, therefore, rarely made use of.[11] Similarly to hospitality, a traveller could ask also for armed protection and assistance against robbers and attacks of any kind when travelling through the territory of a Pashtun tribe which cannot be denied.[12]

14.1.2 Institutions

Similarly to every tribal society, Pashtun tribes also have their formal institutions, based on gerontocracy and the principle of equality of Pashtun men. Equality of Pashtun men, an important part of Pashtunwali requires consensus for important decisions and disqualifies a vote by the majority. As a result, it takes a long time to arrive at a decision backed by consensus. Every decision making body consisting of men is called *jirga*, a world of Mongol origin meaning circle, be it a clan, a tribe or a village council. It is a moral duty to participate in the sessions of the *jirga*s, yet at the same time it is also a privilege for Pashtun men to do so, which they do with pride. Sessions last for long and do not end with a consensus for the first time. In such cases, decision is delayed and new sessions are called for. Rival factions and their leaders usually take advantage of this and have private talks to reach a compromise which they can represent during the next session of the *jirga* in the hope of having the final decision. Such discussions are, of course, free of any formalities and fit perfectly into the understanding of a tribal society and its striving for mediation and compromises.[13]

The outcome of such decisions might be binding or not. A not binding decision is an advice relying on the consultative function of the *jirga*. A binding decision, by contrast, is obligatory to be followed by all with a serious sanction for ignoring it. In such a case, a person disregarding a binding decision would be expelled from the community, both the clan and the village and his house would be demolished.[14] A particular *jirga* is called *Loya Jirga*, comprised of tribal leaders to solve inter-tribal conflicts and debates and to consider important issues such as war and peace, natural disaster, etc. *Loya Jirga* was institutionalised by the Afghan monarchy during the past two centuries to elect kings, or, more recently, to vote for the Constitution of Afghanistan (1977, 1985, 2003) and to elect its president (Hamid Karzai, 2002).

---

[11] Steul (1981: 164–168), Rzehak (2011: 15–16).

[12] Rzehak (2011: 15–16).

[13] Steul (1981: 120–124).

[14] Rzehak (2011: 12–14).

*Jirga*s are not only political institutions but also bodies with judicial competencies in order to keep legal disputes within the boundaries of tribal societies and to hinder bringing conflicts either to law courts proceeding on state law or to Muslim courts proceeding on Islamic law. A survey in the 1980s shows that 80% of local conflicts were kept within tribal institutions, and only 20% were allowed to go elsewhere, a huge figure showing the importance of *jirga*s. Tribal and local conflict resolution is particularly important when a wrongdoing was against the interest of an entire community and not only against a private individual or a family, such as to demolish a forest or to avoid communal obligations. Sanction for such misdeeds could be fines (to be paid in animals) or exile in more serious or recurrent cases.[15]

A particular form conflict resolution is called *nanawāti*, a rite of forgiveness which is applied if one of the parties is unwilling to blood feud because of weakness or any other consideration. The central point of this rite is the confession of the wrongdoer and his pledge for forgiveness by the offended person or clan. To ask for forgiveness, wrongdoer had to go to the house of the victim to ask for admission which cannot be denied because of the moral duty of hospitality. For the sake of security, such a man is usually accompanied by several members of his tribe (men and women) and even a mullah (symbolising a symbiosis between tribal and Islamic law). Previously repentant persons used to put a bunch of grass into their mouth in order to show their humble position and subservience. By encountering a repentant person, housekeepers have no choice but to forgive, otherwise they would act against hospitality which would bring shame on them and their family. Shame is however, also the share of the repentant person because he chose public humiliation in order to save his life: he should be forgiven but on the cost of losing his honour as a man living in accordance with Pashtunwali. The bunch of grass put into his mouth symbolises this notion transforming him, symbolically, into a goat or cow, preys of predatory animals to be killed at the discretion of their enemies. No wonder that anthropologists were unable to report about at least one case of *nanawāti* while claiming that even local elders could not remember a person taking part in such a humiliation. A special form of *nanawāti* is *wazer* for the case of manslaughter when the murderer, asking for repentance and forgiveness, digs a grave for himself and lies into it voluntarily in order to show himself as a person who can be killed. Such an extreme form of apology cannot be refused.[16]

Apology is, of course, only the first step to avoid blood feud because it just opens the door for further negotiations to arrive at the agreement about the blood money to be paid (*khūn*: blood, see also Kazakh customary law). The basic unit of *khūn* is the money to be paid for a bride, the basis on which blood money is calculated. Consequently, the blood money for killing a man is 2 *khūn*s, half *khūn* for losing an eye or foot, etc. It is also possible to pay the *khūn* by combining various means, for example, 2 *khūn*s could be paid by giving a girl (one *khūn*) and animals in the value of another *khūn*.[17]

---

[15]Rzehak (2011: 17–19).

[16]Steul (1981: 161–164).

[17]Rzehak (2011: 17–19).

In addition to *jirga*s, political leadership is due to persons called *khan* or *malek*, respectively, with almost identical power. *Khan* is a Mongol word meaning a leader, a prince, or a ruler while *malek* is Arabic in origin also denoting a ruler. There is no difference between a *khan* and a *malek* in their legal status, only in their wealth as the *khan* is richer than a *malek*. Usually heads of villages and clans are called *khan/malek*, a position which is inherited in a family. They are, however, not single person leaders of their respective communities but rather their representatives, heading negotiations with other villages and clans and with the agents of the government. *Khan*s and *malek*s are not entitled to decide in matters reserved for *jirga*s, bodies for important decisions. Should a *khan* or a *malek* overstep his competencies, he would lose his social prestige immediately and also be killed for a serious misuse of power. A prudent *khan/malek* would, by contrast, enlarge his social network by integrating as many clients as he could and achieve his goal by 'ensuring gifts.'[18]

In the everyday life of this rural society, the supervisor of the long network of canals called *mir-āb* renders a very important service. Since without irrigation almost no agriculture is possible in the area inhabited by Pashtun tribes, it is necessary to gain water from distant rivers and oases with the help of canals. Such canals provide fresh water for more villages and clans and it is vital to share both the water and the work and costs to maintain these canals between the communities which profit from them. The use of the canals is regulated precisely, specified to days and hours, otherwise distant communities would end up waterless because of the excessive use of other communities with a more fortunate location. To control this and to ensure the smooth operation of the entire system is the job of the *mir-āb* whose job is very important to guarantee water for every community and to hinder disputes arising from using water against the law and the agreement of the communities.[19]

In addition to formal institutions, the informal influence of outstanding personalities, usually elderly men is also of importance since gerontocracy is a notion which heavily permeates Pashtun society. Here is a story about the last Afghan King, Zāhīr sāh to prove this. Accordingly, the king stopped his car because he saw an elderly man waiting at the road and he let him cross. This might be, of course, propaganda, but the very fact that such a story is used for political purposes shows the overall attitude of Pashtun society. Elderly men called *those of white beard* (*spin gir*; see Mongol *aksakal*) enjoy public respect because of their wisdom, experience and mastery in conflict resolution and customary law (*narkhai*). These people are also spokespersons in the discussions in the *jirga*s because young men are advised not to argue with the elderly.[20]

Pashtunwali is, as it is clear now, the ethical codex of a tribal society with nomadic background praising martial values. This ceased to be a local issue when the Taliban, Pashtun fighters without exception, took over Afghanistan and introduced their own understanding of law, Islam and governance. To their rigidly, conservative and patriarchal understanding of Islam influenced by both the Deobandi school in India

---

[18] Steul (1981: 68–88).

[19] Steul (1981: 88–92).

[20] Steul (1981: 98–100).

and Saudi Wahhābism, the Taliban infused their own tribal ethos and worldview which they wanted to enforce in a non-Pashtun, non-Sunnī (Hazaras) and non-tribal society, living in cities such as Herat, Kabul and Mazār-i Sharīf. The rest is known from history: death of millions of Afghans, the exodus of the middle class and an increasing radicalisation leading to 9/11.

14.2 Adat Law in Southeast Asia

14.2.1 Adat Law in Indonesia

Adat is a term of classical Islamic law for customary law. In theory, *adat* is no formal legal source for Islamic law since social customs could not be accepted as a basis from which divine will could be discerned. By contrast, *adat* was a material source for the same Islamic law since no one could deny its influence on Islamic law during the formative and classical period. In addition to the customs of pre-Islamic, Arabia customary laws of distant regions where Islam only entered hundreds of years later were also important for the local understanding and interpretation. Such local customary laws are called *adat* in Malaysia and Indonesia, *ᶜurf* ('whatever is known') in North Africa and *dastūr* (rule, order and custom) in East Africa. Difference is manifested not only in terms but also in contents. To illustrate with one example: Islamic law is strongly patriarchal because it was dictated by both Arabian custom and social structure. When, however, Islam entered distant regions such as Sumatra where matrilocality and matriarchy was dominant, these basic principles of Islam came to conflict with local social structure and it was hard to give up either of them. Insisting only on the law in books would have meant to ignore social structure and customary laws, hardly in the interest of the new religion which had to adapt to the new situation and, therefore, to take local customary law into consideration. The same happened on the other end of the Muslim world, in Africa where tribal laws were tacitly acknowledged (see the Yoruba tribe in Nigeria) in issues of family law and inheritance.

 Adat law was subject to concern not only for Medieval Muslim legal scholars but also for their modern counterparts, particularly to the Dutch, colonisers of Indonesia, who did not approach the problem from a theoretic perspective but from a practical point of view. In order to keep peace among the locals, Dutch government did not interfere into local issues if it was not against their interests. In addition to the government, Dutch jurisprudence also began to show interest in local customary laws and this is how the *Adat*-law school came into being, founded by Cornelius Vellenhoven, a leading scholar for decades in this school. Unsurprisingly, the *Adat*-law school focused on the study of the institutions of the indigenous population and their positive law. Dutch Scholars thus collected enormous material with the help of field works in the first half of the twentieth century. An additional merit of this school was its emphasis on genuine concepts and terms correctly arguing that every society could be understood only with the help of its own social and legal understanding and, therefore, the uncritical use of Western terminology would lead to misleading results. *Adat*-law school was not only against the use of Western legal terms but also against legal Westernisation and struggled for the independence of local customary laws which had to be left untouched in its view. Since both Van Vellenhoven and Ter Har, his successor, enjoyed great academic prestige due to their experiences and field works for decades, their view was also shared by Dutch decision makers. As a result, no uniform codification extending over the Indonesian archipelago was produced on the basis of Dutch law. While protecting and encouraging local customary laws, Dutch administration hindered Islamic law to play an important law. Yet local customs were abundant, Dutch administration struggled for a more or less transparent system with an inner logic and cohesion. This is why they divided the area into 19 zones (*Rechtskring*) on the basis of the content of the various *adat*-law systems. The new system allowed for the continuous application of *adat* law, particularly in issues of private law in areas both under direct Dutch governance (*inlandse rechtspraak*) and where limited self-government was guaranteed for the locals (*inheemse rechspraak*). Obstacles to implement local customary laws were specified rather broadly when they were at variance with the principles of European law (French colonisers called it the 'civilizational clause'). Locals were also free to apply Dutch law if they preferred it against their own laws. This was initiated voluntarily by the local community or individuals since it was also possible to implement Dutch law only for particular cases and issues. Dutch law was called for in issues on propriety rights while family law and law of inheritance remained untouched in the sphere of local customs. In sum, the policy of the Dutch was clear and unambiguous: to maintain legal pluralism and to implement a law that suited the overwhelming majority of the local population.[21]

The opinion of van Vellenhoven had a significant impact on shaping this policy. He argued that though the legal tradition of the Indonesian archipelago was highly fragmented with many local variants, some common values could be identified, such as the primacy of community interest, an extraordinary relationship to the land, the prominent role of families and a kind of religious approach to customs. He considered these basic cultural attitudes important and believed that the influence of a foreign law would be harmful for the genuine legal understanding which should be, therefore, protected from external influences. Curiously enough, it was the new independent Indonesia which doubted the wisdom of such a view. Independent Indonesia, now under the leadership of nationalists with a strong willingness to rapid modernisation wanted to create a nation-state with a uniform legal system which was hindered, among others, by local *adat*-laws since every island, clan and village had its own customary law. In addition, local customary laws are very conservative, being highly suspective towards modernisation or changes in general while insisting on their own values protecting local interests. In short, local customary laws were against modernisation and should, therefore, reduced extremely, legal modernisers believed. This view was shared by Indonesian policy makers and academics alike. Legal protection of customary laws was thus reduced to a minimum, particularly in cases when local

---

[21] Hooker (1978: 11–20).

interest and customs were at variance with the intent to create an efficient economy. Landed property is a good example. According to customary laws, landed property could be owned only by members of the local community (clan villages), excluding any other person from the capital city and the neighbouring village. This paralysed Indonesian economy in general and the market of real estates in particular since Indonesian nationals were forbidden to acquire landed property in their own country. This and other similar issues made local customary laws an easy target for legal modernisers who were at the same time also extremely critical towards van Vellenhoven and his school, protecting local laws and cultures from external influences and thus, nationalists argued, hindering to create a modern Indonesia.[22] Despite harsh criticisms, no Indonesian government eliminated *adat*-law entirely, guaranteeing its influence in private law, primarily in family law and ownership because they understood that in the eyes of the locals *adat* is not only law but an expression of justice (*keadilan*) as well.[23] This moderated policy did not spare continuous criticism to Vellenhoven and his school charged with romanticisms that hinders the development of the Indonesian legal system.[24] Consequently, the significance of *adat*-law was declined by the 1970s and was left to the margins of scholarly and political interests. When however, re-traditionalism emerged globally (Islamism being the best example) twenty years later, *adat*-law also became important in Indonesia again but not as a disputed category of jurisprudence but as a living law sometimes also reducing the sphere of state law.[25]

Dutch colonial administration classified *adat*-laws according to family relations and territory, a model also adopted by modern Indonesia. By combining these aspects, a complicated system came into being with five variants. One of them (1) is the *adat*-law of the *non-localised clans:* this is the customary law of the exogamous, patriarchal clans that live under the authority of one clan; in a village several such clans may live, or, if they leave the village they still remain under the authority of the clan leader; (2) *localised clans* are settled in a village, the population of which, in the majority of the cases is identical with the clan, making the head of such a clan also the head of the village; such small communities usually evolve on smaller islands; (3) the *regional community of mixed clans* is a more populous community including several clans which constitute a regional community, the leadership of which is in the hands of the council of clan leaders; since such *adat*-system can be found primarily in the vicinity of Minangkabau (Sumatra), it is called *Minangkabau-adat*. Communities (*nagari*) within the system are acknowledged as individual entities if they have at least one official building, a mosque, a bath and a venue necessary to cock fight. One of the most important tasks of such *nagaris* is to decide upon land in communal ownership. (4) in the case of the *patrilocal clans,* more clans live in a village but one clan is dominant with privileges such as land ownership and leadership, rights that are denied from other clans living in the same village. Subordinated clans may

---

[22]A very characteristic opinion of the time is that of Alisjbbana (1968: 3–16).

[23]Hooker (1978: 20–29).

[24]For the most recent summary of criticism see Bourchier (2008: 94–99).

[25]Benda-Beckmann (2009: 188).

be obliged to grant wives to others (*hula hula*) while this is not reciprocal, it creates village customs asymmetric to the detriment of subordinated clans. Finally, (5) *desa* refers to villages organised exclusively on territorial basis with no regard to family ties; on the island of Bali ancestors' cult is due to married men who have landed property in a local villages (thus new settlers are excluded); a similar *desa* system can be found on the island of Java and in Aceh as well.[26]

Despite extensive fragmentation, various *adat*-laws have some common features which they share without exception. One is orality since every customary law is part of an oral culture, the history of which goes back to generations with no definitive date of birth but with a living memory. Customary laws are also oral because people resist recording their own laws in order to hinder anyone from gaining authority over them. This is not only the case in Indonesia but all over the globe, making only some pieces of Indonesian *adat*-law to put into writing (Sumatra, Java). A second common feature of Indonesian *adat*-laws is their less exact wording and the possibility of their broad interpretation. It is partly due to orality since human memory is failable and detail could be lost in a long way of tradition through generations, and partly due to a flexible understanding of law which regards law not a code of rules that should be followed at all costs but a guideline which should serve the interest of both the individuals and the community. There are, however, some areas where strict rules had to be applied in and observed, land ownership being one among the few such issues. The third characteristic of the *adat* system is the lack of an individual approach to law. Communal interests prevail, and individuals should find their function and role in the community of which they are a member of until they are outcasted for serious misdeeds. But sanctions in general are rare because the fear of shame is a social force enough to hinder wrongdoings. Instead of insisting on a legal code designed for the individual local people, focus on conflict resolution pragmatically in the benefit of the community and its members.[27]

To illustrate both similarities and differences, it is worth studying the *adat* law of Aceh and Minangkabau. According to the *adat*-law of Aceh, legal capacity was no subject of any restriction whatsoever irrespective of status and gender. Therefore, slaves were endowed with legal capacity (until slavery was finally abolished), though to a limited extent, and the legal capacity of free women was also not restricted since keeping women under guardianship was alien to the social understanding in Aceh. By contrast, free movement was restricted for both sexes since villagers could leave their dwelling place only upon permission if they were able to prove that they want to leave their place of residence for good reason (cultivation of a distant land, constant disputes with the neighbours, etc.). Women were allowed to move mainly for marriage (marrying the chief of another village). In order to move from one village to another the permission of both village leaders was necessary, particularly if new settlers wanted to obtain land ownership in their new village. Village chiefs (*köcik*) granted their permission upon the advice of village elders (*uroeng tuha*) and—in

---

[26]For more see Hooker (1978: 36–41).

[27]Hooker (1978: 52–54).

big villages—the representative of Islam (*töngkü*). In addition to granting such permissions, it was the task of village leaders to ensure public peace, to decide issues related to land, to proceed in family matters (marriage, looking after orphans), and to supervise some sorts of religious activities (such as giving an oath). In addition, village leaders also acted as arbiters and mediators in order to solve conflicts peacefully and locally. Local people favour such mechanism of conflict resolution because it is easy, fast and efficient since no party has to travel for days in order to launch a formal procedure and the compromises hammered out by local leaders are welcome in the majority of the cases. Formal administration of law, however, is not in the competency of village leaders but in that of the tribal chief. Very few cases end up here because the majority of the cases are settled by the village leaders. In addition, some professionals have their own means and seniors to settle disputes, such as fishermen. The procedure in the jurisdiction of the tribal chief has no particular rules, hence ordeals and oaths were routine to which torture was added sometimes. In order to assert at least the basic requirements of Islamic law, the presence of the *kali* (the local variant of *qāḍī*) was required in the procedure, though the only qualification to be expected was his capacity to read and write. Judgments of tribal chiefs were final and, therefore, executed, capital punishment including (choking, beheading). Fishing boats or fields of unwilling debtors were taken away by the tribal chief in order to force them to meet their obligations.[28]

Family law—built on both matri-and patrilinearity—was further complicated by the presence of Islamic law, strengthening the latter but never subdoing the former. Descent had to be proved, therefore, on both paternal and maternal line. Women were not deprived of their propriety rights and were able to own and manage their own wealth before and after marriage. Spouses are joint owners of goods acquired during marriage and no husband has privileges in this regard. After marriage, wives do not move to their husbands but continue to live in their paternal house where their husbands regularly visit them or move to this house provided they are of the same village. Children grow up in the maternal house therefore, if someone marries outside his own village, his children are lost to his community. In short, women are quite independent of their husbands in housing and maintenance which strengthens their social position, a significant factor in a Muslim society. In addition, the fact that women live with their own families where men are outsiders, strengthens them further since wives could always rely on the help of their relatives should a conflict with their husbands arise. *Adat*-law is very consequent in this and thus prohibits women from moving to their husband even voluntarily. Islamic law, by contrast, dominates marriage procedure, prohibitions (women who cannot be married) and other important aspect of marriage law, though with local variations. One of them is called *pulang balée* ('substituting marriage'), the basic idea of which is that if a man paid for a wife to a family, her father has to substitute her if she died because the price was already paid. Usually, a younger sister is married in such a case to the bride. Divorce is permitted, though very rare and governed by Islamic law. In Aceh, divorce is not a social catastrophe for women because they continue to live with their

---

[28]Vellenhoven (1980: 60–75).

own family and are independent of their husband economically, too. Children also remain in the care of their mother while their father lives separately after divorce.[29]

In Minangkabau *adat*-law matrilineality is more prominent since here social organisation is based entirely on family relations. Minangkabau consists of 22 clans (*kampung*), the members of which live dispersed in the countryside and do not constitute a village. Clans consist of families and families are usually composed of several households because some members of large families move away and establish their own house and residence. Despite this, the original family home (*rumah gadang*, big house) plays an important role in the life of the entire family. A household only means a mother and her children without a husband because children belong to the mother's family and the husband is not part of the consanguinity but lives as a stranger in the house. This is the logical consequence of matrilinearity and a strict understanding of exogamy which prohibits men from marrying women of their *kampong*. As a result, family fathers have no paternal authority and do not manage the wealth of the family and their wives because the wealth belongs to the family of their wife. Only properties acquired during marriage is subject to joint ownership between the parties which should be divided equally when the couple divorces. The sphere of influence of Islamic law is thus restricted to formalities, similarly to Aceh.[30]

Family issues are decided within the family. Final judgment is due to the head of the family (*mamak rumah*), usually the oldest male (the brother of the mother) who has to consider the opinion of the adult female members of the family and also that of men married into the family (husbands). Interestingly, a clan (*kampong*) lacks competencies to decide any issue, therefore, it is the *suku*, an alliance of clans that is endowed with the right to make decisions. A village is usually composed of 2–4 *suku*s and is also a decision making authority with a separate building in the main square for this purpose. Communal issues are decided here (land) but problems in which more villages are involved are solved by the *luhak*, the community of villages. This served as a model also for the Dutch who wanted to reduce fragmentation and merged villages into such administrative *nagari*s. One of the most important issues to decide in a village was land ownership to be granted to non-residents who were obliged to pay extra for such a permission. Such a decision is also about the right to cultivation, the use of water, and the right to settle in the village. Distinction between the original inhabitants and the newcomers however, remained for generations since newcomers were excluded from the public life of the village and could not participate in communal decision-making. Only heads of families who have been residents of the village ever since its foundation can participate in the council of elders. The use of land and water (*hak ulayat*) could be granted for a definitive period of time but not for an unlimited period because selling of lands is an unimaginable idea in this part of the globe. Land owned by an extended family cannot be neglected, sold or partitioned. Since land ownership and residence in a particular village go hand in hand, no individual is allowed to have a parcel of land outside his/her own village. This is the reason why males marrying to another village have no ownership in their

---

[29] Vellenhoven (1980: 84–89).

[30] Vellenhoven (1980: 123–125, 134–135).

new place of residence but continue to have land in their village of origin. Needless
to say, such archaic concepts cannot be maintained under new circumstances and we
can witness purchase of lands in the last decades, though with a clause of buying
back the land.[31]

14.2.2 Malay Adat Law

Malay *adat* law (*adat Melayu*) is—similarly to the Indonesian—a very complex system of customary laws because it contains various *adat* systems which go back to
different historical backgrounds to be complicated further with the advent of Islamic
law. There is no uniform Malay system of *adat*-law but variants by regions. The
beginnings of the Malay customary law is lost in history but its origin can be found
in the island of Sumatra (near to Minangkabau) since the ancestors of the Malays
moved from here to present-day Malaysia. They were not Muslims and adopted their
new religion only after having settled in their new home. As a result, they brought
their original customary laws to present-day Malaysia which was shaped by the
clan structure and matrilineality. What complicates matter is that Malays travelled
in various groups and waves and there were some who arrived first in Palembang,
dominated by local Hindu law where their clan structure disintegrated and a new
social structure, based on patriarchy, evolved under the influence of Hindu law. As a
result, two entirely different systems of *adat*-law developed differing in their fundamentals, social structure and legal thinking. One is called *adat perpateh* which was
the matrilineal system of those coming from the neighbourhood of Minangkabau, the
other is called *adat temenggong* which was the patriarchal customary law, modified
by both Hindu and Islamic law. *Adat perpateh* survived in its original form in the
states of Negri Sembilan and Malacca while other Malay states follow the tradition
of the *adat temenggong*[32] (Malaysia consists of 13 states and 3 federal territories).
    Malay folklore tells this story differently. According to their own myth preserved
in the *terombo*, a song about the origin of Malays two half-brothers were the lords
in the neighbourhood of Minangkabau: Parapatih was the lord of the hilly area,
and Tamanggungan was the lord of the seaside. Both were law makers and created
their own system of customs, but the *terombo* has no answer for why Parapatih had
chosen matrilineality and Tamanggungan patrilineality.[33] The *perpateh* tradition has
preserved the clan structure in which the basic unit is the family which are organised
to tribes. These tribes, however, constitute further provinces (*luak*) and the state is
made up by provinces, a structure which is made up by both territorial principle and
family relations. Gerontocracy is a leading principle in governance, this is why tribes
are headed by the tribal leader, the *lembaga*. Provinces are headed by the *undang*,
and the state by the ruler. It is important to underline that leaders are elected in Malay

---

[31]Vellenhoven (1980: 126–129, 138–139).

[32]Inche (1968: 107).

[33]Minattur (1968: 18–19).

tradition, a practice that has found its way also to the modern Malay constitution, though election is only a formality in many cases.[34]

The Malay *adat*, just as the other customary laws, is an oral tradition and part of a broad cultural heritage, coloured by sayings and short poems which are easier to memorise but not necessarily easier to understand. One of the sayings teaches that one should break the grains of rice in a mortar and cook the rice in a pot, not a passage from a cook book but a wisdom of *adat*-law, pointing at the advantage of doing everything in the proper place, and with proper tools. To translate it to legal language, complaints should be submitted to the proper court of law, punishments should be proportionate, and owners have to proceed with proper care. Needless to say, such an interpretation hardly derives from the text of the saying therefore, not only sayings and words are passed to next generations but also their proper meaning and interpretation.[35]

Malay *adat*-law preserved its influence mostly in family law in both the *adat perpateh* and the *adat temenggong* traditions. Minimum age for marriage is only specified in Sarawak, where it is 20 year for males and 17 years for females. Marriage is, as everywhere in Asia, not a private affair but a family business. This is why a young man, intending to marry has to inform his family about his plans first. Next, his family has to informally find out what kind of a reception a proposal for marriage would meet in the bride's family. A formal proposal is only made if it is believed to be positive. Negotiations about propriety issues follow. When everything is settled, the day of the wedding is specified. Symbols help to communicate easily and politely. This is why the bridegroom and his family send a ring to the bride or her family symbolising an offer to marriage. If the rings are returned, the offer is rejected. If they are accepted, both families begin to organise a party to celebrate the acceptance of the rings. This is followed by another meeting of relatives who formulate their opinion about the planned wedding. When relatives also support the marriage, a marriage gift is given to the bride's parents (*tekol*: usually money, gold or diamond). Parties have a month to organise the engagement (*pertunangan*), after receiving the *tekol*. During this time, both parties could withdraw from the agreement but men would lose the *tekol* and brides should return the gift what they received. After engagement, parties have a complete year to organise the wedding. Should they fail to do so, men would lose the *tekol* and brides should return the gift, depending on which party decided otherwise. Wedding ceremony is however, not the final step since Malay customary law developed *sarak belega*, a curious form of temporary divorce. Due to the influence of animism, parties could separate for a month if within a week after wedding they experience signs believed to be unfavourable (bad dream, seeing or hearing prohibited birds or snakes). Such a person may live separately for a month but should join his or her partner. Should a party fail to do so it is interpreted as divorce and the party has to pay a fine.[36]

---

[34] Inche (1968: 107–108).

[35] Minattur (1968: 22–23).

[36] Sandin (1968: 40–43), Inche (1968: 112–113).

One of the most important ceremonies in Malay family law is called *bersand-ing*, a custom of Hindu origin. The *bersanding* has its own procedure led by the *mak andam* (the hostess of the celebration). A symbolic sum has to be paid on this occasion, too, because the *mak andam* covers the bride with a parapet and removes it and lets the bridegroom go to the bride only if she is satisfied with the payment. Next, both the bridegroom and the bride are seated on the wedding throne made for them. This is a central element in Malay customary law in the absence of which there is no proper Malay wedding, despite the fact that the marriage contract has already entered into force. If there is a marriage contract but there is no *bersand-ing*, this marriage is called *nikah gantong*, suspended marriage because the parties cannot live together and cannot even see each other until the *bersanding* is properly celebrated. After *bersanding,* parties take a ritual bath as well. In some states it is customary to dress the bride in old Chinese garments, a custom that evolved from a historical precedent. A Malaccan king once married a Chinese princess who was obviously dressed in Chinese garments which was immediately emulated in higher circles and this is how the Chinese dress became a tradition. The end of the long formal process is the wedding itself where a buffalo is usually sacrificed to supply food for the guests. Traditionally, there are numerous guests from both sides among them also the leaders of tribes because it symbolises their tacit approval for the marriage. While indigenous ceremonies and other formalities are coloured by Hindu and Chinese traditions, Malay customary law proper was heavily influenced by Islamic law once Malays embraced Islam. Institutions of Islamic law were, however, not adapted as new elements but rather corresponded to already existing Malay customs. This is how *mahr*, an important propriety right in Islamic law was said to be identical with *maskahwin*, a traditional Malay marriage property donation. *Maskahwin* was originally a sum given to the bride's parents by the bridegroom but nowadays it is the bride who receives it, the sum of which varies according to regions and the social status of the parties.[37]

After the wedding, the new couple moves to the wife's tribal territory where a house awaits them to move in. This is because the wife's parents already cleared a house for them and placed it to their disposal while they move to another house with their unmarried children. In a family plot, therefore, there are as many houses as many daughters already married. The youngest daughter remains in the family house which she inherits in exchange to looking after her elderly mother (similarly to the Mongol–Turkic law of inheritance where the youngest son inherits the family house). Though very favourable to the young couple, this system also has serious shortcomings. Some elderly people may live poor and in miserable housing conditions because they had given all their houses to their daughters and to their husbands. In addition, this system does not encourage husbands to enrich their families and contribute to their well-being because they already receive their houses at the beginning of their married life and do not belong to their wives' clan anyway. This is why women are working very hard on the fields while their husbands are economically less interested to take over the lion's share of the work. No longer being a part of the clan system

---

[37]Inche (1968: 112–118).

when their wives die, husbands have to leave their houses, land and children since they are considered to have no reason to remain. This is why husbands leave after the 100th day following their wife's death, accompanied by a farewell ceremony, and leave their children behind, who would be brought up by their mother's clan.[38]

In addition to matrilocality, matrilinearity also influences obstacles to marriage and persons prohibited to wed. This is why a marriage is prohibited between nephews and nieces on both the paternal and the maternal lines and to marry a second wife during the first wife's lifetime from her clan or even to have a love affair with such a woman. Malay customary law takes this rather seriously, and breach of these laws is punished by death. At the same time, to marry a sister of a deceased wife is not only not prohibited but rather encouraged because this is the best way to look after her children (*ganti-tikar*). Matrilnearity also discourages polygamy which is, in theory, not forbidden but we can witness it very rarely since it is also a matter of wealth. This is why there is practically no polygamy in the countryside and polygamy is not a frequent phenomenon in the cities either. In Negri Sembilan, for example, the number of wives was linked to political position: only the ruler could have four wives, the *undang* three, the *lembaga* two, and everybody else only one. Monogamy was not only strengthened by economic considerations but also by the interest of the families since children remaining in the woman's tribe should be properly cared for. This is why a second wife could only be married with the consent of the first wife.[39]

Malay customs also modified Islamic law on divorce which is a very easy process, at least from the husband's point of view. Malay society, however, wanted to restrict the number of divorces and made everything possible to make divorce difficult and thus to hinder them, particularly separations hastily pronounced. Accordingly, if a man wants to divorce his wife, he has to organise a social event called *bersuarang* to which both his and his wife's relatives are invited. Here he has to narrate his grievances and explain why he wants to divorce. After listening to him carefully, elderly men from both sides join in and try to restore harmony and peace in order to avoid divorce. Divorce could be pronounced only if the parties were not satisfied with the result of this mediation. Divorce also terminates joint propriety rights which should be settled parallel to the pronouncement of divorce. Here the law is simple and clear: both parties receive their original properties while properties acquired jointly are divided equally among the parties. According to Malay custom, a divorcing man also gives a gift to his wife which is either a symbolic or a substantial contribution to the expenses of taking care of the children who remain in the custody of their mother and her tribe and after divorce their father has no obligation to their maintenance whatsoever. Malay customary law further restricts the influence of Islamic law in family law when backing women's right to divorce unilaterally. Such a right is usually guaranteed for women in their marriage contracts where their right to divorce their husbands is specified when they are mistreated, neglected, treated badly or are not properly maintained. What is more, in some areas such as Sarawak, a wife may divorce her husband if her husband could not be blamed for any wrong. This is

---

[38] Haji (1968: 187, 195).

[39] Inche (1968: 118–119), Haji (1968: 200).

hardly compatible with the strict patriarchism of Islamic law and the fine to be paid by the wife for such occasion does not make it closer to the *sharīᶜa*. A wife intending to separate has fifteen days for consideration and if she insists on divorce this right has to be granted to her and she has to return to her husband only if she is unable to pay the fine. Malay customary law diverges from Islamic law even more significantly in case of *zinā*, adultery. Contrary to Islamic law, Malay customs are rather tolerant toward adultery and regard it a private issue of the parties concerned. This is why only a fine should be paid in the majority of the cases and an exile for a year is a rather rare punishment. Most frequently, parties have to marry or are persuaded to marry, provided, they are not already married. Fine should be paid only if one of the parties rejects this.[40]

Customary Malay law of inheritance was also shaped by matriarchate, focusing on the female line among relatives. This is why a widow inherits her husband completely in the absence of children. If there are children, girls would inherit an equal share among themselves while sons inherit only their father's personal objects but not his land because they are supposed to acquire land either by transforming virgin land into arable land or by marriage. Tribalism is a leading principle in the law of inheritance too, this is why Malay *adat* makes everything possible to hinder the transfer of tribal property to foreigners. This is why basic principles of inheritance law are the following: (1) property is owned by the tribe and not by individuals; (2) acquired property becomes tribal by way of inheritance; (3) tribal property is inherited along the female line; (4) tribal property remains in the hands of the female members of the tribe.[41] Sons are discriminated negatively but this is no real hindrance for them since they have to be looked after by the female members of their family until they get married. This is the task of their mother but after her death, the sisters would take over this role. Maintenance includes accommodation, housing and other costs (which may also include debts deriving from fines or gambling). After marriage, it is the wife and her clan who is troubled with problems of livelihood while the man only 'hangs his hat' as the Malay proverb has it.[42] Since the entire system is based upon the female line, girls are extremely important for families. If there are no girls, they would be adopted from outside the clan and the tribe (similarly to sons in patriarchal systems). Such adopted girls are sometimes not Malays but Chinese. Adoption has to be made public because the entire clan has to learn about it. Ceremonies (*berkedim*) and hospitality accompanying adoptions are organised to guarantee publicity, where a buffalo is again sacrificed for catering services.[43]

There is no criminal law in the Malay *adat*-law but there are punishments for some wrongs. Punishments are, in general, not strict and inhuman since the restoration of harmony and peace is more important than to punish wrongdoers at all costs. Here the difference in principles between *adat perpateh* and *adat temenggong* is clear. *Adat perpateh* is definitely against talio since accordingly a wrong cannot be restored

---

[40]Inche (1968: 119–125).

[41]For more on the law of inheritance see Inche (1968: 132–145).

[42]Haji (1968: 191).

[43]Haji (1968: 190).

with another wrong. In this tradition there is, therefore, no room for mutilations and revenge even in the case of death. By contrast, *adat temenggong* rests on the principle of talio.[44]

Capital punishment is the exception, not the rule. The breach of basic rules of family law such as disregarding prohibitions to marriage (incest) may lead to the death penalty but other crimes are treated rather with material compensation or other mechanisms of reconciliation. In case of injury, blood money had to be paid while for manslaughter a person from the perpetrator's clan had to be handed over to the victim's clan. But as a sign of appeasement, the children of the murderer had to be invited to an expiatory festivity. Judges are expected to have extreme care and wisdom while investigating cases and are often compared to a swift wizard which reaches its target flexibly and with a technique suitable for the particular situation. The wisdom of this symbolism is that a judge should not follow rules rigidly but has to consider cases individually and flexibly in order to reach a proper conclusion.[45] Mythical beliefs sometimes influence criminal law as, for instance, among the animist Dayaks living in Sarawak. Dayaks are cultivators of paddy rice, that is, a kind of rice which can also be grown on hillsides and not requiring flooding but demanding a lot of human and animal labour. Since all their attention is paid to this work, stealing while others are on the field is considered a grave crime since it is against group solidarity. In such a case, a thief should not only be punished but a pig should also be sacrificed to the gods, otherwise they would destroy mankind by starvation and deluge.[46]

14.3 Customary Laws in India

Customary laws enjoy a privileged status in India both in their number and legal protection. Around 9% of the Indian populace live in tribal society which makes a figure of more than 100 million people who live according to tribal customary laws, a number which is significant in itself. Facing such a reality Indian (Hindu) legal thinking did not attempt to neglect or overrule local customs. By contrast, traditional Hindu legal theory considers customs (*sadāchāra*) legal sources and incorporates them into its religious-legal framework of the sources of law. In modern times, the same privileged position is reaffirmed when Indian constitutional law guarantees legal protection to local customary laws.

The situation is, of course, more complicated than this. In theory, only good customs can be followed and supported, pointed at by the prefix *sad* (good), reflecting to religious authorities with outstanding morals and qualifications. This provided a theoretical basis on which local customs could be acknowledged because local customs (province, village, tribe) were said to be the inherited good customs already in classical Hindu texts. In addition to local customs, castes and professionals (fishermen,

---

[44]Haji (1968: 196).

[45]Minattur (1968: 34–36).

[46]Sandin (1968: 40).

merchants, peasants, money lenders, etc.) have their own customs. These customs were taken into consideration at the courts of law because sentences were pronounced on such a basis. Moreover, wisdom literature recommends the ruler to judge local cases on local customs in order to make individual judgments acceptable and restore harmony in the provinces. Problems arose only when local customs contradicted the sacred texts, most of all the Vedas and the collision had to be solved. At first glance, the answer seems easy since one would expect that nothing could contradict sacred texts such as the Vedas which has priority over local customs. Though an argument easy to grasp, there was, interestingly, no consensus concerning it. Some authorities argued that in certain cases customary laws may enjoy priority because sacred texts have laws corresponding to social conditions of their own historical period and when social reality has significantly changed, the old rules should not be followed otherwise it would only provoke consternation and resistance. What is more, with a reference to a verse of Manu (I. 108), transcendental origin was attributed to customary law in order to raise its epistemological position significantly.[47] And when it was declared that among the contradicting *dharma* texts one should apply the laws which correspond to customs (*sadāchāra*), customary laws had acquired full recognition and had de facto gained the upper hand over written legal sources.[48]

Tribal customary laws in India are concurrent since they do not complement state law as in China but operate parallel to state law and religious legal understandings (Hindu, Christian) with the intent to dominate legal life. Though religious ethics modified tribal customary laws in some points (for instance, Christian tribes abandoned polygamy in keeping with the Christian teaching) they have nevertheless primacy in their respective societies. The concurrency of tribal and state laws results in parallel systems with a claim from both sides to regulate issues according to their own laws. Here is a legal case to demonstrate. Criminal procedure was launched against a man because of fraud. Since he was found guilty, he was fined. After having paid the fine, he returned to his own community where a procedure was again launched against him and he was fined again because he had brought shame with his unethical behaviour on his community and for this reason the court (*jāti panchāyati*) punished him.[49]

Indian policy was always tolerant and flexible toward tribes and their local cultures, a policy which was also adopted by the British, who did not interfere into local business and did not want to bring them to the aegis of their own laws. By contrast, they rather strove to get acquainted with the local laws in order to make the British public administration and the judiciary rely on them if necessary. Efforts were thus made to learn more about them. Pioneering works on local customs were produced already in the nineteenth century combining the methods of jurisprudence and anthropology. Outstanding among them is *Customary Law As at Present Ascertained* by Sir W. H. Rattigan who was commissioned to this work by the Chief Court. This magnum opus discussed the customs of Punjab systematically where laws are

---

[47] Kane (1950: 21–40).

[48] Francavilla (2006: 221).

[49] Ishwaran (1968: 234).

arranged by topic on almost one thousand pages. It was only a fragment of the material available at that time because it contains only customs of private law (family law, land ownership and the use of land) in Punjab. Unfortunately, works on similar niveau were not produced about legal customs of other regions. This underlines the importance of Rattigan's work which has been in great esteem in India ever since having 16 editions up to 2007, followed by two reprints (2012; 2013).[50]

Contemporary Indian policy is also supportive and tolerant and guarantees constitutional protection to local customary laws with the exception of laws designated as 'barbarism', and other worst practices unacceptable to the dominant legal understanding (the British and modern India), such as treatment of women as property objects, choking sick children, child marriage, slavery, alcoholism, and addiction to gambling.[51] Despite the lack of direct interference from outside, local customs change continuously and sometimes gradually. Conversion to Christianity in the last century brought about significant changes in family law (monogamy) and recent global changes are to be felt too. Traditional villages are abandoned, mostly by the young who move to the cities in order to find a job because they do not want to continue the life of their ancestors any longer. Since tribal laws are, of course, not applied in cities, with the disintegration of traditional societies their laws also disappear, together with tribal solidarity. This is a high price that young people are willing to pay in the hopes of coming closer to the new global world. Parallel to this tendency, state institutions such as elementary schools, courts of law, medical care also contribute to the disintegration of archaic society while improve, of course, local living conditions. All this evoke mixed feelings among tribal populace since not denying the benevolence of state institutions, the overwhelming majority prefers the inherited archaic laws being an important part of their culture which they are unwilling to replace with modern institutions.[52]

Concerning its policy to tribal societies, modern India faced a dilemma hard to solve. One way to follow was the 'museum' approach according to which tribal societies should be preserved intact as far as possible for the present and the future as some kind of a reservatum where societies of the remote past are maintained as a curiosity inherited from history. By contrast, the so called 'civilisation mission', also on the agenda of the colonising powers for long considers tribes barbarians who need to be civilised, that is, taught, by force, if necessary, about the basics of civilisation. Such a mission is the burden of the civilised world as it is its moral duty to help these undeveloped barbarians, the argument has it. Consequently, modern institutions and techniques have to be introduced among tribal societies, too, in order to raise their standard of living. Modern India tries to find a middle path between these two extremes with a slow progress of modernisation and a constitutional guarantee on autonomy. The result of this policy is different according to place and tribes: while tribes living in the inner part are more willing to cooperate, inhabitants of enclaves in the North-Eastern mountainous areas rely more emphatically on their

---

[50]Rattigan (1880).

[51]Baruah (1990: 37–38).

[52]Hina (2012: 132–133).

own customs. Debated issue is ownership of land and forests since tribes insist on their rights to land and forests, a claim neglected more often than not. As a result, local populace was driven away from its own land and forest and was re-employed as non-paid labourers. Scandals on these abuses were ineffective to stop this process which accompanied Indian history in the twentieth century. Constitutional protection, declared in the Indian constitution for scheduled tribes (education, healthcare, the protection of tribal forests) also proved to be less efficient, though the system of monitoring was also established. The Constitution set up a commissioner directly responsible to the President (Art. 338), to monitor constitutional legal protection. After long debates, it was replaced by a national committee by the constitutional amendment of 2003.[53]

Such a committee is certainly important in a land where more than 600 tribes live and constitute a populace, the number of which equals with that of the entire population of the Philippines according to the most recent census of 2011. With such a figure, India is home to the biggest tribal population after Africa.[54] The distribution of tribes is rather uneven within the country because they are populous in some regions while less visible in others. Tribes live mostly in the North-Eastern part of the country, in Mizoram, Arunachal Pradesh and Nagaland, a forested hilly area between the borders to Bangladesh and Burma, but we can also find them in Odisha, Gujarat and Rajasthan. The proportion of tribes is highest in Mizoram (95%) but Arunachal Pradesh with a lower figure is also home to 30 registered tribes and tribal laws.[55]

Tribes are far from being homogenous since they differ in ethnic, religious, linguistic and cultural terms. This is why tribal laws are also very different: though the majority is patriarchal and patrilocal there are some tribes who live in matriarchate like the Khasis in Meghalaya (whose centre, Mawlynnong was elected the cleanest settlement in India and Asia), and the more populous Garo at the North-eastern border. In addition to settled tribes, there are some nomadic tribes with their own customary laws. These tribes are engaged in what cultural anthropology calls *service nomadism*,[56] that is, communities are moving from place to place in order to sell their entertainment services to locals such as music, acrobatic performances, etc. Such groups constitute separate castes with their own system of customary law and a body for jurisdiction (*panchayat*) with a somewhat formalised procedure. In addition to life style, religion too, is an important factor which influence tribal laws. There are tribes who continued with their own, inherited animist tradition while others opted for one of the world religions such as Buddhism, Christianity and Hinduism. Conversions to new religions however, never put an end to ancient animism which continued to live on in one way or another. This is how local syncretistic religious variants came into being. The only thing that is in fact common in all tribal customary

---

[53]Narwani (2004: 78–89).

[54]Narwani (2004: 11).

[55]Bhagabati (1990: 22).

[56]Hayden (2000: 10).

laws is familiarism and tribalism, specifying social system, family and criminal legal tradition. In what follows there are some examples.

The Garo are one of the most significant tribes in the North-eastern mountainous area whose legal life is organised around three key words. One is *Asimalja*, a word which originates from the name of two mythical figures, Asi and her husband, Malja, denoting what we would call religious ethics. *Dakmalja* is rather a code of honour which contains only prohibitions. The third word is *nima* which can be interpreted as a kind of etiquette where, too, prohibitions dominate (women always have to go after men except in dangerous places because animals in the jungle attack those who go at the end of the line; if someone reaches some water he/she has to call attention by shouts in order to provide time enough to dress up if someone is taking a bath there; the portion of rice for men is due to them from the top of the pot and never from the bottom). The violation of either of these rules would provoke the vengeance of the otherwise benevolent spirits which can be avoided only by punishments. To administer legal consequences is the task of the village leader who specifies the sanction together with the elders as a consultative body to help him. Inside families, it is the pater familias who specifies punishments, moreover, they execute them in person. Since Garo live in matrilinear system, the head of the family is usually the brother of the mother. Clans (*māchong*) are made up by persons who have common ancestry along the maternal line. Clans are subdivided to extended families based also on the maternal line. *Māchong*s are exclusively exogamous and a marriage inside the clan is impossible. Law of inheritance is obviously built on the maternal line, too. Accordingly, family property would be inherited by a daughter of the mother, usually by the youngest, but family members may opt for another daughter if they want to for whatever reasons. Such an heiress daughter (*nokkrom*) lives in the maternal house with her husband while others move to their homes with their husbands who are chosen from among the paternal *māchong* or from other clans. *Nokkrom* daughters inherit the family land which is cultivated under their husband's control, who have, obviously, no right to dispose of the land. It is for this reason that *nokkrom* daughters may face difficulties to marry because only few would accept restrictions such as living with their parents-in-law, cultivate land which is not their own when they could also marry non-heiress women with a freedom to choose residence and a separate life from the parents. Men do not lose contact with their former family because they continue to have rights and obligations towards their female relatives (mother, sisters, nieces). This creates a dual obligation for men who have their tasks also in their new families where they enjoy no privileges. This is what makes sense for the Garo saying, according to which '*my stomach is for my mother and sisters, while my basket is for my wife and children*', that is, a man eats as much as he likes at home of his relatives in the female line but not in his wife's house because there he has to care for his wife and children without privileges.[57]

Garo marriage is monogamous, though in theory a second marriage was possible with the permission of the woman's *māchong*. With their conversion to Christianity this possibility was eliminated. Influence of Hindu law is completely missing

---

[57]Roy and Rizvi (1990: 53–55, 59).

from Garo family law (prohibition of re-marriage for widows, child marriages), but celibacy is rejected too. Widows could re-marry, and in the event of the wife's death, it is her family who has to provide a second wife for the husband. Interestingly but not surprisingly, in such a matrilinear system marriage proposals are made by women not by men, by sending a gift (food) through a mediator. The refusal of the food symbolises the rejection of the proposal. Abduction of a young man, an ancient tradition is still alive among Garo groups that have not converted to Christianity. This custom is the precise opposite to the abduction of women in patriarchal societies which is, more often than not, rather a rite than a violent act since it takes places with the consent of the parties and their relatives. Accordingly, a young man rejects the marriage proposal and 'hides' from the suitors who continue to look after him until they find him and bring him back. This is rather a rural festival and game in which the entire villages takes part. Commerades disclose his hiding place and help the suitors to find him. This is then followed by the proper marriage ceremony. Such abduction is to be distinguished from the escape of the young who simply flee home and live together. Garo people see no wrong in that and such cohabitations are acknowledged as marriages after some time if law was otherwise followed (e.g. exogamy). Exogamy is a crucial point in Garo family law, the breach of which was punished previously by death penalty nowadays by exile.[58] Adultery is considered less seriously and left to the parties to regulate because Garo people do not see it as a violation of the religious and moral order but as an offence against persons. Accordingly, the adulterous wife offends her male partner's wife while her lover offends her husband. This is why they have to pay compensation to the offended parties.[59]

Contrary to Garo matriarchate, the Mizo tribe of Mizoram developed a strict patriarchal system. Families are patrilocal with a privileged position of the youngest son who has to look after the elderly parent and to marry off his sisters. Marriages are strictly exogamous since according to their belief, incest between close relatives would lead to the immediate destruction of the crops, endangering the livelihood of both the family and the entire village. Marriage is proposed by a man to a woman. Before such a proposal, the parties may meet relatively freely and get acquainted but only in the girl's house and not in a public place. At the beginning, parents also take part in the conversation but later they discretely pull back in order to let the young alone who have to follow a strict etiquette (the young man has to pay great respect towards the girl's parents, all kinds of physical contact are prohibited, no alcoholic drinks can be consumed, etc.). Previously, polygamy was not illegal in theory but conversion to Christianity changed this completely. It brought about little changes since in practice no one was able to afford a second wife except sometimes for a village chief who had concubines. If negotiations between the parties and their families came to no result but the couple wanted to live together, girls were eloped (*tiandun*) and the young couple settled elsewhere by a distant relative. This is by no means illegal and if the couple continue with cohabitation, such a union is also considered a marriage without any restrictions. This is a consequence of a relatively

---

[58]Roy and Rizvi (1990: 55–65).
[59]Majumdar (1990: 52).

high number of such elopements. Time for wedding is June and October because the summer between these months is dedicated to agricultural labour with no time for time consuming ceremonies such as a wedding. In addition, the souls of the dead are said to return to their families during that period which makes the summer period less attractive to weddings. The belief in returning spirits is not the only proof for a syncretistic belief composed of an inherited animist tradition and Christianity. The other is the right to divorce which is guaranteed by Mizo tribal law to both spouses. Accordingly, there are eleven forms and causes for divorce, related to illness, mental condition (madness, impotence, frigidity, lasting separation, etc.) and the content of the marriage contact. Children are free to decide about their future life since they can stay in the custody of their mother or father according to their own choice.[60]

In the midway between Garo matriarchate and Mizo patriarchate is the customary law of the Ao tribe in Nagaland which rests on patriarchate but guarantees considerable power to women. An Ao pater familias manages the business of the entire family and is its chief priest in families which did not convert to Christianity. In doing so however, he has to rely on the advice of women who have traditionally significant influence since their consent is needed for the men's decisions. Marriage law is based on monogamy where polygamy and child marriage is prohibited. This is why girls usually get married between 16 and 20 years and boys marry between 18 and 25. Weddings are usually held in the spring months. Ao marriages were traditionally arranged marriages with a marriage fee to be paid for the bride but nowadays this custom had been abandoned. Ao youngsters are relatively free in their love affairs, can meet both in private and public spaces without supervision and formalities. The old prerequisite however is still in force, according to which a formal condition of marriage is an independent house built by the bridegroom. This is important not only for beginning an independent life together, a crucial point in a society based on neo-locality, but also for proving the young man's ability to support and maintain his family, for his independent income and his maturity for marriage. Widows can re-marry but their freedom to choose their partner is strongly restricted because they have to find their new spouse from among their former husband's brothers. Similarly, a widower has to choose his next wife from among his former wife's sisters. Divorce is not forbidden but is rare among the Aos and is the result of adultery in most of the cases. By law, children remain in the custody of their father but spouses can agree otherwise.[61]

Tribes who speak Tibeto-Burman languages have their own systems of customary law. One of them, the Reang tribe, maintained its archaic system of bride service, a particular method for paying for the bride. Accordingly, men have to work for a period agreed upon with their prospective father-in-law for their future wives. It is usually three to four years among the Reang. When the labour period comes to its end the young man can marry the woman he was working for and move with his new family wherever he pleases. He can also choose to stay with the advantage to receive

---

[60]Roy and Rizvi (1990: 76–86).
[61]Roy and Rizvi (1990: 65–70).

financial allotment from his wife's family.[62] Another tribe speaking a Tibeto-Burman language is the Nyishi, the most populous tribe in Arunachal Pradesh consisting of three big clans with a common ancestor, *Aabhu Thayni*, a hero in their folklore and myth who was engaged in cosmic struggles against evil spirits. This fits into their own cosmological myth, according to which supernatural forces have created the universe in several phases (Sun, Moon, stars, water, wind, to be followed by plants and animals) and tribal customary laws came into being during the last phase of this period in order to protect humanity. These legal customs are preserved in their folklore together with songs, tales and dances. The custodian of tribal customary law is the village council, the *nyelee*, which is competent in every legal issue. There are various councils for different legal issues. One of them has the power to adjudicate cases related to foreigners, and there is a separate council to decide upon conflicts between villages. There is also a *nyelee* for conflicts between clans, village dwellers and families. Domestic conflicts of families however, are rarely subject to councils because according to Nyishi understanding, family issues must not be taken to formal institutions but should be settled at home. Procedures are held in public and women are also not excluded from them, an exception in Asian legal systems. Ordeals and oaths are considered evidence which explains the presence of local priests in the procedures. Experts of customary law (*nyegam aabhu*) join the procedure only when their advice is needed in a complicated case. Tribal councils adjudicate in both private and criminal cases and rule pecuniary compensation in the overwhelming majority of the cases.[63]

References

Alisjabbana ST (1968) Customary law and modernization in Indonesia. In: Buxbaum (ed) Family law and customary law in Asia: a contemporary legal perspective. Springer, The Hague

Baruah TKM (1990) The customary laws and their applicability in the context of Indian Penal Code. In: Dutta PC, Duarah DK (eds) Customary laws of Arunachal Pradesh. A profile. Directorate of Research: Government of Arunachal Pradesh, Itanagar

Benda-Beckmann F, Benda-Beckmann K (2009) The social life of living law in Indonesia. In: Hertogh M (ed) Living law: reconsidering Eugen Ehrlich. Onati International Series in Law and Society. Hart Publishing, Oxford, Portland

Bhagabati AC (1990) Formalisation of tribal customary law in North-East India: some observations. In: Dutta PC, Duarah DK (eds) Customary laws of Arunachal Pradesh. A profile. Directorate of Research: Government of Arunachal Pradesh, Itanagar

Bourchier D (2008) Positivism and romanticism in Indonesia legal thought. In: Lindsey T (eds) Indonesia. Law and society. The Federation Press, Sydney

Francavilla D (2006) The Roots of Hindu Jurisprudence. Sources of Dharma and Interpretation in Mīmāmsā and Dharmaśāstra. Corpus Iuris Sanscriticum et fontes iuris Asiae Meridianae et Centralis: Torino

Haji M (1968) Malay customary law and the family. In: Buxbaum (ed) Family law and customary law in Asia: a contemporary legal perspective. Springer, The Hague

---

[62]Roy and Rizvi (1990: 95–97).

[63]Hina (2012: 136–139).

Hayden RM (2000) Disputes and arguments amongst Nomads. A caste Council in India. Oxford University Press, Oxford

Hina NN (2012) Customary laws of Nyishi Tribe of Arunachal Pradesh. Authors Press, New Delhi

Hooker MB (1978) Adat law in modern Indonesia. Oxford University Press, London, New York, Jakarta

Inche A (1968) Islam and customary law in the Malaysian legal context. In: Buxbaum (ed) Family law and customary law in Asia: a contemporary legal perspective. Springer, The Hague

Ishwaran K (1968) Customary law in Village India. In: Buxbaum (ed) Family law and customary law in Asia: a contemporary legal perspective. Springer, The Hague

Kane PV (1950) Hindu customs and modern law. University of Bombay, Bombay

Mazumdar DN (1990) Some problems of studying customary laws: a case study of Garo customary laws. In: Dutta PC, Duarah DK (eds) Customary laws of Arunachal Pradesh. A profile. Directorate of Research: Government of Arunachal Pradesh, Itanagar

Minattur J (1968) The nature of Malay customary law. In: Buxbaum (ed) Family law and customary law in Asia: a contemporary legal perspective. Springer, The Hague

Narwani DS (2004) Tribal law in India. Rawat Publications, Jaipur, India

Rattigan WH (1880) Customary Law as at Present Ascertained. Universal Law Publishing

Roy, S, Rizvi SHM (1990) Tribal customary laws of North-East India. B. R. Publishing Corporation, Delhi

Rzehak L (2011) Doing Pashto. Pashtunwali as the ideal of honourable behaviour and tribal life among the Pashtun. In: Afghanistan analysts network, Mar 2011. AAN Thematic Report 01/2011. www.aan-afghanistan.org

Sandin B (1968) Some Iban (Sea-Dayak) customary law in Sarawak. In: Buxbaum (ed) Family law and customary Law in Asia: a contemporary legal perspective. Springer, The Hague

Steul W (1981) Paschtunwali. Ein Ehrenkodex und seine rechtliche Relevanz. Franz Steiner Verlag: Wiesbaden

Vellenhoven von C (1980) Van Vellehoven on Indonesian Adat Law. In: Hollemann J (ed) Selections from Het Adatrecht an Nederlandsch-Indie (vol I, 1918; vol II, 1931). Springer, Dordrecht

Chapter 15
Complementary Customary Law

It is only the Chinese customary law which is complementary, particularly in the field of private law which is left for local customs by the Chinese state concentrating on public and criminal law. Unfortunately, while great Codes of Chinese legal history are studied and commented on, Chinese customary law is a field left for almost complete oblivion. Chinese customary laws attracted no scholarly interest in the last centuries. What we have are only some surveys and reports produced on the commissions of governments.

The first report was made on the island of Formosa (Taiwan) in 1900 for the Japanese government occupying it. Japanese leaders wanted to get acquainted with local customs of private law (family, ownership) in order to set up an efficient local administration which had to rule according to local customs to prevent unrest. This is why Santaro Okamatsu, a professor of law at the University of Kyoto produced a report commissioned by the governor of the island, a document which survived the withdrawal of the Japanese forces and is still available (though not easily). This report deals exclusively with private law issues, particularly land law (ownership, rent, loan, tax, etc.) and marriage law, to be compared to Japanese customs.[1]

The other collection of customary law was produced in China upon governmental initiative aiming at some legal reforms. This collection is a rather long text with 3432 individual legal customs arranged by provinces on 1800 pages. The text is lacking a logical system and an inner structure of academic standard, commentaries to individual or provincial customs. What we have instead is a rapid recording of data, calling for further academic studies which was never accomplished because the project was slowly abandoned. Unfortunately, its author died in 1926 and the text was only published four years later in Nanking on the commission of the Ministry of Justice. Political changes contributed to further negligence. As a result, the collection

---

[1]Okamatsu (1902: 20–155).

© Springer Nature Switzerland AG 2020

J. Jany, *Legal Traditions in Asia*, Ius Gentium: Comparative Perspectives on Law and Justice 80, https://doi.org/10.1007/978-3-030-43728-2_15

fell into oblivion. Though Edurad Kroker translated some parts of it to German which was published in the series Monumenta Serica in 1955, no further study followed it.[2]

These reports are, of course, extremely casuistic since they only enlist local customs but do not attempt to create a system. Some customs are hard to understand since they refer to particular cases which are hidden from the reader. In some places, customs follow social rank and material well-being. This is why the collection calls to attention customs dominant among the wealthy and among the poor. Sometimes there are explanations which contextualise some customs making them more understandable. Governmental efforts to legal reforms are clearly visible in some cases when the editor adds his comments arguing for some actions to be taken in order to abolish or alter some customs which are, in his view, ripe for changes.

The text has a detailed description of the so-called six rites accompanying marriages, reflecting to its six phases. During the first phase, gifts are given to the chosen girl (*na tsai*) in order to find out parental intentions. If the initiative is rewarded favourably, the full name and the exact date of birth (*wen ming*) of the girl is asked for to calculate whether the partners are suited to each other and what future the marriage will await (*na chi*). When astrologers see no reason to concern, engagement is the next step when all the property issues are settled (*na cheng*). The fifth phase is the determination of the exact date of the wedding (*ch'ing ch'i*). The last phase is the ceremonial greeting of the bride in the bridegroom's house (*ch'in ying*). The entire process is supervised by a person called *chu hun* who is usually the head of the family: he negotiates issues of property law and ultimately decides about the wedding while the couple itself has little to say in the entire process. Nowadays, *chu hun*s continue to have an important role in wedding ceremonies as masters of ceremonies but not as the person for the most important decisions anymore, though it varies by regions (villages are more conservatives than cities). Professional mediators are also available to *chu hun*s who know all the families of the regions and can help finding eligible partners and initiating the first contact as well. When doing their job well, their name is also specified in the marriage contract. Such a long and complicated procedure is only due to the first marriage but not for the second or subsequent marriages or concubinage, a tolerated institution to trick out the criminal act of bigamy. When someone takes a concubine, she has to kneel before the chief wife to greet her and serve her a tea. In some provinces, the chief wife then gives a new name to the concubine and the man organises a party to inform his relatives about the changes in his family life. If someone marries his concubine, the procedure is simpler because the woman had been admitted to the family already and acts symbolising this need not be repeated. In such a case, the concubine has to prostrate herself in front of the symbol of the husband's ancestors and his parents in the presence of his relatives and friends who are invited to the ceremony and has to serve them a tea. Next, the man has to announce that he has elevated his concubine to the rank of his wife. The aim

[2]Kroker (1955: 228–302).

of the entire procedure is obviously to ensure publicity.[3] The concubine has a great chance to become a wife if she had borne a male child.[4]

Marriage is a great burden upon families, particularly when there are more sons who have to marry properly, according to their social and financial status. This may cause difficulties even for well-to-do families while poor families may go bankrupt. This is the reason why some mechanisms were developed in order to decrease financial burden. These mechanisms vary from region to region and are specific to some customary laws while are missing from others. A specific custom, particularly widespread among the rural poor is to bring up the girl selected to become the wife of one of the sons in the family from her early childhood (*t'ung yang hsi*). This is, of course, no child marriage because there is no engagement and wedding. The girl is simply brought up there and the marriage would ensue only after the children were grown up. The reason of this custom is that the family of the bridegroom has not to pay the significant sum of money at the time of marriage which poor families could not afford. When, however, the wedding ceremony is approaching, the girl is sent home to her parents for some days to be taken back to the husband's house along festive formalities on an auspicious day set by divinations.[5]

The exact opposite to this custom is when a boy is brought up in the house of his future wife. This comes up less frequently, only when there is not a single son in a family, only daughters. In such a case, a boy is brought up and when he is of age, he would marry one of the girls and would take her family name or attach it to his own name. The exchange of wives solves the problem of poverty along a different logic: in such a case, the girls and the boys are married off in exchange between the families thus avoiding the payment of marriage gifts. According to this model, the son of family A marries the daughter of family B while the son of family B marries the daughter of family A. Another device to help poor families is to organise a web of families who cooperate in financing marriages. In order to do so, poor families establish a society with contracts at the time when their sons are still children. Such a society exists for decades and if a son of a family marries the other, families contribute to the costs according to the rules of the contract and the society. This mutual assistance of families by societies is widespread in several Chinese provinces. Finally, a special form of divorce should be mentioned in relation to poverty: if the husband moved far away in order to escape from poverty and unemployment and does not give any sign of being alive for 3 years, the wife's parents may ask regional authorities with the consent of the husband's parents to declare the termination of the marriage in order to enable the widow to remarry.[6]

A somewhat bizarre custom is the posthumous marriage of young men who had died young, between engagement and wedding. If his family so pleases, it contacts a mediator who may know a girl who had also died after engagement and would be buried next to the deceased young man. The reason of this custom may be high

---

[3]Chiu (1968: 45–48).

[4]Kroker (1955: 283–284).

[5]Chiu (1968: 49), Kroker (1955: 281).

[6]Kroker (1955: 282–288, 298–299).

mortality rate and an early date for engagement. Though there is no specified age limit for marriage in Chinese customary law, it was around 14 years of age for a man and it was a shame not to be engaged or married around 16 years of age, particularly among the better-off families. Posthumous marriages lifted such a shame from the deceased persons. Interestingly, age limit was higher for women, around 20 years of age because according to customary understanding, a wife has to be 8–9 years older than the man.[7]

Taiwanese customs follow the Chinese pattern but we can also witness local variants. The extended family is no longer a social reality, though its importance is beyond any shade of doubt. If a male member of a family married, he continued to live on a large family estate but moved with his family to a separate unit called *pan*. These units are numbered according to the sons' age (the first *pan* belongs to the eldest son, the second *pan* to the next one, etc.). Thus extended families do not live together any longer but their members live at least on the family estate disintegrating into small units where social cohesion could be maintained among its members. Taiwanese customs highlight the importance of bride money more emphatically than proper Chinese customs. This is why a Taiwanese marriage is considered null and void if the purchasing price was not paid. It goes to the extreme that someone could purchase a wife for himself and next sell her to another man for a good sum of money. There are examples for such transactions.[8] In concluding a marriage, go-betweens play an important role in Taiwan, too. First, they have to go to a soothsayer in order to find out important facts about the bride and to have a look into the future of the prospective marriage. If no reason for concern emerges, go-betweens also handle the material aspect of the union hammering out an agreement between the parties after negotiations. When everything is settled neither party can change his mind, and is obliged to sign the contract and specify the date of the wedding. On this day men hired by the bridegroom take the bride to his house on their shoulders, usually in an ornamented armchair. When she arrives, the bridegroom takes over the keys of her furniture and gently kicks her ankles indicating that she would be under his authority. The wedding ceremony closes with the young couple's sacrifice to the ancestors. Taiwanese custom diverge from that of mainland China in relation to adoption: while it is impossible to adopt someone in China, due to the teaching of Confucianism, Taiwanese people do not take it too seriously and made such a contract legal. As a result, adoption is a tolerated institution and, what is more, there are also examples for adoption against material compensation.[9]

Law of procedure did everything possible to hinder formal legal actions in a court of law and pursue parties to reach an agreement and arrive at a compromise. In addition to law, traditional ethics also forced the parties to avoid formal procedure. The various restrictions and hindrances can be understood only when bearing in mind this underlying principle. Issues of private law could be brought to court only on a few days of the month, no more than eight or nine days. Documents had to

---

[7] Kroker (1955: 281–285).

[8] Okamatsu (1902: III–V).

[9] Okamatsu (1902: VI–XI).

be drafted in a very formal language which was impossible to produce without the help of professionals who worked for their own pocket. If neither legal nor cultural (writing in a formal language), nor economic (cost of expensive experts) obstacles prevented the parties from continuing the procedure then they were summoned to the official for hearing. Here the parties have to present their evidence and witnesses are also heard. When the procedure came to its end, the official pronounced his decision but up to this point the parties were entitled to stop their case and reach an agreement. The official also persuades the parties to compromises throughout the entire process. An alternative and more favourable mechanism of conflict resolution is mediation which usually took place in tea houses where parties could drink the 'tea of mediation' (*chijiangcha*).[10]

Among evidence, oaths already played an important part in ancient China which were also taken when concluding alliances and contracts. Oaths were accompanied by bloody sacrifice when the left ear of the animal was put into a jug and its blood was put into another jug and sprayed on the altar thus evoking the gods and the ancestors' spirits. Next the parties drank from the remaining blood and swore on respecting the contract. Every oath also had a formula to curse the party violating the contract. After giving oath, a copy of the contract was dug on the spot together with the cadaver of the sacrificed animal and a second copy was deposed in the archive. Oaths were also used for deciding legal disputes when no convincing evidence was available. In such a case, the parties gave their oath supporting their own claim in front of the figure of a god in which they asked for a curse on them and on their family, should they gave their oath falsely (for instance, that they should die within 3 months). In addition to proving innocence in a trial (particularly in the case of theft), oaths were used to settle legal disputes between neighbours concerning the border of their parcels. Here again animal sacrifice accompanies the rite: the throat of a cock is cut with a very sharp knife symbolising a similar fate of a person giving a false oath. Usually a young white cock is sacrificed because it is the symbol of life and vitality and is cheaper than other animals. This rite takes place in the temple of the Earth god where the parties are accompanied with an expert in such sacrifices. The parties had to stand about 3 m away from this person to either side. Here the parties give their oath with identical words supporting their own legal claim. The parties also take the risk of dying, should they swear falsely and wish the same for their opponents if their oath is false. After such pronouncements, the master of the ceremony suddenly cuts the throat of the cock and throws it to the dust. The mortally wounded bird is wriggling and rolling on the ground and comes closer to one of the parties. The person to whom the cock comes closest to is the one giving a false oath for which he had to pay. The belief that dying animals are able to find the party giving a false oath is a broadly held view among non-Han peoples too, who occasionally use dogs for the same purpose.[11]

Non-legal remedies are also applied in conflicts, particularly in criminal cases where self-help is understood very broadly. In Taiwan, for example, thieves were not

---

[10] Katz (2009: 47, 50–51).

[11] Katz (2009: 61–78).

reported to authorities but were hung by their garment and beaten up or their Achilles sinew was cut. Persons accused of rape were simply caught and dug into the earth up to their neck and were left there to die, while persons wrongly accused of magic and witchcraft were simply lynched by the crowd before authorities had any chance to investigate their case. Though modern Taiwanese legal system follows the western pattern, traditional attitude to law and conflict resolution is still visible. There is a case from 2007 in which mediators sentenced a man committing adultery to kneel for four hours in the local marketplace, a decision also echoed in a local newspaper. Coming under public pressure, the chairman of the mediating body justified the decision saying that though it went against Taiwanese law, it was nevertheless the solution to which all parties agreed and the dispute could be closed.[12]

References

Chiu VY (1968) Some notes on Chinese customary marriage. In: Buxbaum DC (ed) Family law and customary law in Asia: a contemporary legal perspective. Springer, The Hague
Katz P (2009) Divine justice: religion and the development of Chinese legal culture. Routledge, London
Kroker E (1955) Rechtsgewohnheiten in der Provinz Shantung. Monumenta Serica 14 (1949–55), pp 125–302
Okamatsu S (1902) Provisional report on investigations of laws and customs in the island of Formosa. Keba Herald Office

---

[12] Katz (2009: 49).

Part VI
Concluding Remarks

Chapter 16
Conclusions

Having studied all significant legal traditions of Asia, time has come to arrive at some systemic conclusions. To begin with, legal circles have their own sphere of influence which developed over the course of long centuries of history and did not change to these days.

16.1 The Dynamics of Legal Circles

As I have demonstrated every legal circle developed around a dominant legal culture to which satellite legal cultures were attached. Factors which specified the sphere of influence of the dominant legal cultures are various including cultural and religious expansion (missionary activities), armed conquests and commercial relations. Once a legal circle reached the limits of its sphere of influence no force was able to alter it however strong it was. As a result, contemporary legal circles do not differ from that of the previous centuries. Take for example Japan, Korea and Vietnam, satellite legal cultures in the Chinese legal circle which were home to Buddhist and Christian missionary activities for long. Despite this, Buddhist understanding of law had no impact in Japan and Christian legal thinking was also unable to dethrone Confucian legal thinking neither in Korea nor in Vietnam, though people converted to Christianity in both countries in significant numbers. By contrast, Islam and Islamic law were able to attract Central Asian peoples because no Chinese government wanted to enlarge its influence on this territory which was thus left for Muslims. As a result, Central Asia became heavily influenced by Islamic law already in the Middle Ages and continues to belong to this legal circle today. In sum, legal circles are remarkably constant entities which were developed long centuries ago and colonisation was also unable to change this situation (more on this subject will follow).

Obviously, it was the dominant legal culture which evolved first and expanded only later in its subsequent period of development. There is no "Axial Age" for this because various legal cultures came into being and expanded in different historical periods. In China, for example, moral and social foundations of law were already specified in

© Springer Nature Switzerland AG 2020
J. Jany, *Legal Traditions in Asia*, Ius Gentium: Comparative Perspectives on Law and Justice 80, https://doi.org/10.1007/978-3-030-43728-2_16

ancient times when the first Codes were also produced. The same goes for India where *dharma*-literature already flourished centuries before our common era. By contract, Islamic law is rather a product of the Middle Ages when other legal cultures reached their zenith or were slowly in decline, lacking creative energy and vitality previously witnessed. Islamic law was a latecomer in Asia which spread to territories where it came into being (Near and Middle-East) or was abandoned by other dominant legal cultures (Central Asia, some parts of the Southeast Asian archipelago). There were tribal customary laws in both Central Asia and the archipelago which were unable to resist Islamic law armed with literacy, jurisprudence and formal institutions but were vital enough to preserve their own identity, even altering Islamic law at some points. As a result, parallel systems came into being with their own institutions and legal understanding.

When a dominant legal culture reached maturity it began to spread and evolve into a dominant legal culture within a legal circle. This was a long development all over Asia but was due to various reasons. In the Chinese legal circle, the dominance of Chinese law was the result of Chinese political and military power in regions which were important for the Chinese imperial thinking. This is why we can witness in Korea and Vietnam a completely Confucian legal tradition but not in Central Asia where Chinese strategists opted for defence and deterrence (Great Wall). Japan is the only exception since Japan was never attacked by Chinese armed forces yet it was Chinese cultural dominance (writing system, art, Buddhism, law) which introduced Confucian legal thinking to Japan which was unable however, to root out traditional Japanese understanding of law. In the Indian legal circle it was also cultural dominance which contributed to the spread of Indian (Hindu) legal culture, mainly in Southeast Asia with no army backing such a process. Islamic law combined force with economic activities and was able to gain foothold in Central Asia and the archipelago of Southeast Asia which were free of both Chinese and Indian legal influence.

Though different in their history, legal circles show remarkable similarities in their inner structure and dynamics. Once the dominant legal culture established itself as the main force within the circle, it was able to transfer its understanding, technique and institutions to all the satellite legal cultures. The adoption of the understanding and institutions of an alien legal system is due to various factors in which force is only one and by far not the dominant. The adoption is usually voluntary and is the result of cultural dominance or practical considerations. Japan is a good example which was open enough for Chinese cultural influence, law included, throughout its history though, it is true, on different grade of enthusiasm. It was, however an unbalanced relationship since Japanese students went to China to study but no Chinese student went to Japan with the same intention. Another example for cultural dominance are the Southeast Asian peoples who embraced Indian cultural (legal) dominance and adopted its institutions meanwhile Hindu law remained free of any Southeast Asian influence. In addition to cultural dominance, practical considerations also play important role in taking over some legal techniques, institutions and ideas when adoptive societies realise the advantage of taking over some legal element from a rival legal system. Advantages might be political (it is wise to have similar institutions then a giant neighbour), economic (when legal understanding rests on the same footing, at least in private law, it will enhance commercial activities), or legal, when the adoption of some external legal ideas fits into domestic legal policy and enriches the adoptive legal system with some new and wise legal ideas. The range of the adoption of legal elements may vary between two extremes from the adoption of the entire legal system with its fundamental principles, institutions and academic activities to its opposite end with the adoption of only some useful legal institutions without touching the system as an entity. There are three different models for legal adoptions within each legal circle.

(1) The first model unfolds the strongest ties between the adoptive and the parent society and law. In this framework in addition to legal institutions, fundaments of law are also involved, such as social understanding, religious thinking concerning law and society and the theory of law and state. The stronger the influence of the dominant legal culture is, the more it can be felt in a satellite legal system. Korea and Vietnam are textbook examples for this where Confucianisation of society, state and law have a long tradition without being ever challenged. Japan, too, fits into this model though less characteristically since Japanese society always kept its own tradition alive, despite enormous Chinese influence. Where genuine Japanese understanding of society and law was identical with Chinese thinking, the two parallel lines of thinking reinforced each other (e.g. law as a state command, hierarchic society, etc.). This logic is also true in its reverse: the stronger an adoptive society is, the more it resists the influence on the basic principles of its own law. Take Islamic law as an example, which gained supremacy also in its basics, in regions where Islam as a religion became dominant. Despite this, local society resisted Islamic legal influence in issues in which the adoption of Islamic law would result in a short and complete collapse of social order. This is why matriarchate remained alive in Southeast Asia and the law of inheritance of the Turkic peoples on the steppe remained intact. Hindu law shares a similar fate because no Southeast Asian society introduced the *varna*-system, despite being heavily influence by Hindu law and jurisprudence. By contrast, every Southeast Asian society resisted this and continued to live in the framework of their inherited, tribal society free of the *varna*-system, a position which was strengthened later with joining Buddhism.

(2) According to the second model, adoptive societies take over only the formal elements of jurisprudence but not the fundamentals of law. Societies working along this pattern do not necessarily borrow normative contents but rather the academic discipline of law and its genres and methods. (a) Language is one among the leading indicators proving the exalted position of the dominant legal culture. Islamic law is a clear example since it is a religious law with a demand of universalism, highlighting the importance of its language of origin, Arabic. The mastery of a dominant language within a legal circle is essential for all non-native speakers to participate in academic activities including having access to earlier works and expressing their own ideas. Islamic law is in the hands of scholars of Iranian, Syriac and Central Asian of origin while Arabs are underrepresented

(this is why it is a great mistake to confuse Muslim authors with Arab authors) among Muslim scholars in jurisprudence. Despite this, every single scholar spent long years studying Arabic in order to join their fellows in jurisprudence. Indian legal circle has a less chauvinistic attitude to the language of jurisprudence even when Sanskrit and Pali remained essential for centuries. Interestingly, though fundamental texts were produced in Sanskrit (Vedas, etc.) it is the Pali language which was more important for legal scholars for the simple reason that Indian legal influence was brought to Southeast Asia through Buddhism, the sacred language of which is Pali. By contrast, in societies which understand law as a state command (Chinese legal circle), such a cultural imperialism made no sense and, therefore, is missing, since it is useless to have law in Chinese in Vietnam. To put it in a more abstract language: legal circles and cultures which rest on Personalitätsprinzip (religious laws) conserve the universalistic aspiration of the language of the (previously) dominant (legal) culture (Arabic) while legal systems resting on territoriality give free way to national languages and do not exalt their own language to the disadvantage of satellite legal systems (Chinese). (b) In addition to language, the adoption of the genres of scholarly discourse is another indicator for the influence of the dominant legal culture. In Islamic law they are the monographic works, the *fatwā*s and the permanent oral disputes among scholars. Nothing has changed in this even in our modern times as Muslim scholars continue to write monographs and issue *fatwā*s in Arabic. In the Indian legal tradition, legal genres are the *śāstra*, the *sūtra* and the commentary literature. In China the legal genre as such was the Codex for millennia to be emulated by successive generations and satellite legal cultures. Buddhist Southeast Asia while resisting the *varna*-system and a lot of laws deriving from such a social structure, nevertheless adopted genres of Indian (Hindu) law. They produced works on jurisprudence according to the Indian model in Pali and changed to their national language only later in which they produced the same genres of works (*dhammatat, thammasat*). In Chinese legal circle it is the Code which has outstanding importance and significance in both the legal system and jurisprudence. A Code in China is more than only a compendium of legal norms to be followed strictly. A Code is part of the culture, the written memory of past generations and a work of respected scholars and glorious dynasties which have to be respected even centuries after their demise. This is why Codes are constantly modified to the needs of contemporary reality but not declared null and void, and if a new Code is produced, it rests on the previous work regarded to be a model and a prestigious predecessor. (c) Legal teaching is the third indicator pointing at the influence of dominant legal cultures. In the Muslim world (legal) teaching follows a medieval pattern of education in institutions (madrasa) established in the same historic period from Morocco to Malaysia. By contrast, there was no separate legal training because it was a part of a broader education aimed at producing eminent officials for the state in China and, unsurprisingly, we can find the same structure throughout the whole Chinese legal circle from Korea to Japan.

(3)   The adoption of laws is only the third model which creates only weak ties between the dominant and the satellite legal cultures. Though this might be the most visible part of adoption, it is still the lesser important because both the fundaments of law and jurisprudence remain untouched. This is the world of "legal transplants" (Alan Watson) where legal institutions are adopted from one legal system to another though such legal transplants remain, as a rule, within a legal circle and do not cross boundaries. Through studying the dynamics of Asian legal transplants we can witness entire and occasional adoptions of legal institutions which are either creative or emulative. Occasional adoption is a simple thing at both ends of the story: accordingly, there is an efficient and prudent legal institution in one of the legal systems (though, mainly, in the dominant legal system) which is attractive to the adoptive legal system for practical reasons, be it economic or legal. There is no cultural, religious or social influence or dominance, and political pressure is also lacking. A good example is medieval Jewish law which adopted some legal institutions from Islamic law in order to enhance trade and create a favourable legal environment to merchants who could do their business more easily with their Muslim counterparts. With the adoption of some institutions of the law of contracts, Jewish law was enriched without being forced to change its fundaments such as social structure, theory and theology of law, jurisprudence and basic institutions of private law (marriage, inheritance, ownership). By contrast, a complete adoption is a deeper encroachment into the adoptive legal system which adopts not only some institutions in a field of law but entire normative bodies. A good example is the adoption of Chinese criminal codes in Japan regulating criminal law on external model which was modified only in extreme cases (when the original penalties were considered too brutal by the Japanese and were changed to less inhumane penalties). Both complete and occasional adoptions could be creative or emulative. Adoption is creative when adoptive society examines critically and carefully its model and transplants only legal institutions which fit into its own legal system and understanding and reject others which do not. Japanese criminal code is again a good example because Chinese laws not compatible with contemporary Japanese laws and worldview were left out. Islamic law was also adopted creatively in a process during which incompatible elements were simply abandoned, such as laws of a strongly patriarchal society in tribal laws based on matriarchate. Hindu law was also received with caution and Southeast Asian societies rejected the *varna*-system, being completely at variance with their own social structure. By contrast, adoption is emulative when entire laws are adopted without being scrutinised carefully and regardless of the adoptive society and its legal system. Though such an adoption is, obviously, less prudent, it has rarely to do with the state of mind of the local elite but rather to do with the political autonomy in which such an elite is manoeuvring. Here are some examples to clarify the point. Southeast Asian Buddhist societies opted for creative adoption because room was left to them to do so since Indian cultural influence was mediated by merchants and intellectuals but not by heavy arms. Japan, too, was independent enough for centuries to select from among Chinese laws in order to implement

only laws which fitted into their own legal system. When however, Western (American) powers entered the political landscape and forced Japan to sign all the disadvantageous contracts, local elite had no choice but to opt for a complete and emulative adoption which took Western legal thinking both in principles and laws to its model. The absence of creative adoption and the careful study of laws was, therefore, not the result of the lack of intellectual force but was due to the lack of power to do so. In such a political environment, minor victories were also celebrated as creative adoption with good reason. A classic example is the new constitution of Japan after WWII in which Japanese diplomats were able to convince the Americans not to abolish the institution of the Japanese emperor if they want to hinder more catastrophes to come. Interestingly and more importantly: there is no example for such a complete and emulative adoption among Asian legal systems which were able to maintain at least some of their autonomy during the long centuries of history. Such a change was brought about only by the Western powers and their 'civilisation mission' to change all legal systems according to their own understanding of law, morality, society and state.

In sum, there is a linear connection between the strength of political and cultural influence on the one hand and the extent of adoption on the other. At the end of the spectrum there are the indicators of deep and irresistible influence touching upon the fundaments of law combined with complete and emulative adoption. At the opposite end we can witness occasional adoption with no influence on fundamentals of law and society. The sphere between these two ends are filled with indicators pointing at middle way influence such as creative adoption of law and the scholarly genres, forms and methods of jurisprudence and legal training. Diagram (Fig. 16.1) may help to visualise this complex relationship.

Adoption within a legal circle is asymmetric no matter what was adopted: only laws or fundamentals of law, too. As one may expect, the asymmetrical relation starts in the dominant legal culture which offers legal thinking and institutions to emulate or to adapt to the satellite legal system which, by its turn, has nothing to share with the dominant legal system. Consequences are mainly negative and to be felt at both ends. The adaptive legal system loses at first its independence which is reduced to autonomy or dependence, according to space and time. Here the local legal tradition is enriched at the beginning with external ideas, institutions and methods but later the same dependence reduces the openness to other legal systems which might be useful, too, but are outlawed by the dominant legal system and its political representatives. As a result, satellite legal systems became inflexible and closed to the outside world with no willingness to change (Japan, Korea). At the same time, autonomous and genuine ways of development are also missing because everything is expected to come from the dominant legal circle. Dominant legal systems are not better off either. Though they profit from being expansive and dominant in a relatively wide sphere of influence at the beginning, they lose creative energy later on and begin to stagnate. It is the point where asymmetry comes to their disadvantage because no impetus enters from the satellite legal systems which await new, creative energy

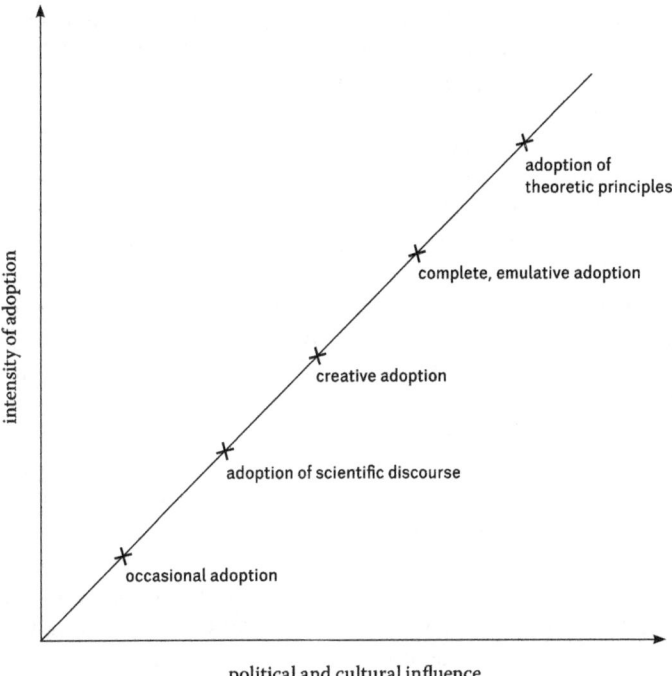

Fig. 16.1   Intensity of legal adaption

from the dominant systems though in vain. As a result, both systems paralyse each other because satellite systems are denied to look for changes outside their own legal circle and cannot thus contribute to the renewal of the dominant legal system which becomes more and more inflexible and inward looking. As a next step, dominant legal systems only repeat themselves and their unsolved problems and loose more and more ground in their own society and became isolated in the outside world. Changes here are dramatic and complete and always due to external powers to which dominant Asian legal cultures were unable to resist. It is important to stress that such a breakthrough was the consequence of Western colonisation and legal influence (others would say legal colonisation) since Asian systems had less impact on each other. The status quo between the spheres of influence among Asian legal systems and circles were constant throughout the entire legal history of Asia and no Asian legal circle was able to or willing to influence other legal circles to the extent of shaking their foundations and base them on different underlying principles. This happened only on Western impact when Japanese law had to be 'civilised', Chinese law was 'modernised' on western and later on Soviet model, Hindu law was almost completely abandoned in the favour of common law tradition and Muslim countries were also changed along secular French, German, and Swiss legal models.

Prior to Western colonization, Asian legal circles remained constant and stable without any cross-fertilisation among them. This is because the status quo lasted for a remarkably long historic period and each legal circle was closed and inward looking without any intent to learn or adopt anything from another Asian legal circle. This isolation was the policy of the dominant legal systems while satellite legal systems were more flexible, though this only beyond limits. Hindu and Chinese laws, for example adopted nothing from each other, despite their connection through various channels (trade, Buddhist missionaries). Dominant legal systems were, therefore, dominant not only in their relation to satellite legal systems in their own circle but also vis-á-vis their peers in other legal circles. In short, dominant legal systems were proud of their sovereignty and protected their unique status also from the influence of other dominant legal systems not only in their basic principles and genres of jurisprudence but also in substantive law. By contrast, satellite legal systems were more open to foreign influence, that is, to new ideas coming from outside their own legal circle which were however, sporadic and weak and provoked the wrath of the dominant legal system and its institutions. Buddhist influence on Japanese law is a case in point. Though Buddhism was welcome in Japan at the beginning (Shotoku) it was rooted from the country later. The same happened to Christianity during the rule of the Tokugawas. The message was clear: no foreign influence was to be tolerated which touched upon the basic principles of law since both Buddhism and Christianity provided ethical and legal understandings which were at variance with Confucian and traditional Japanese thoughts. Christian (Western) legal thinking flourished in Japan only when it returned as an irresistible force backed by gunpowder empires.

Ancient Near-Eastern legal systems do not fit into the model which is only operational for contemporary Asian legal circles because it lacks a clearly dominant legal system. Instead of one dominant legal system, there are at least two dominant systems: the Sumerian and the Assyro-Babylonian (with strong ties to each other) influencing neighbouring legal systems in Nuzi, among the Hittites, and elsewhere. Early Jewish law is also part of this tradition, similarities between agricultural laws prove close ties. Jewish law, however, began to separate from this cuneiform legal tradition and walked along its own path due to political and religious reasons. Thus, despite common roots in the formative period, Jewish law departed step by step from the Ancient Near Eastern tradition and developed its own independent legal culture against Mesopotamian legal tradition. In this sense, Jewish law is a revolutionary and as such, a unique legal culture which developed *against* and not along a dominant legal system (Assyrian, Babylonian, and Persian) within its own legal circle. Thanks to their common roots, Jewish law shares legal elements with other Mesopotamian legal systems which are part of the Near-Eastern legal *koine* on normative level but nothing in principles and jurisprudence. Post-hellenist new comers such as imperial Persian (and Zoroastrian) and Christian laws were in no contact with a once dominant legal system since Hammurabi's stele was already two thousand years old at this time. Both legal systems built their own legal understanding on religious beliefs and practices and were connected to Ancient Near Eastern laws only through legal *koine* which were widespread in the entire region. Despite the lack of a clearly dominant legal system, Mesopotamian legal circle was also inward looking and closed to foreign influences from a different legal circle. This is why there are no traces of Egyptian legal influence (despite extensive political, economic and cultural contacts)

and Greco-Roman law also took no roots. Though imperial Roman law was translated, it is true, to local languages, the Syriac-Roman law book had almost no impact
on local societies and vanished completely with the fall of the Roman Empire.

16.2 Functions of Law

Functions of law differ in Asian societies and there is no Asian understanding of
law and its functions. But there are clear tendencies, also visible in geographic areas
which separate contemporary Asian legal circles into three different models.

Jewish and Islamic law, both heirs to ancient Near Eastern legal systems represent
religious laws because each legal system is that of a religious community and not
that of a state. Christian (Eastern) law shares the same understanding. This is because
there was no state which acted as a lawgiver and followers of these religions were also
not necessarily citizens of a same state. Jewish law developed for long centuries when
there no longer existed a Jewish state but Jews lived in the periphery of various global
empires (Assyrian, Babylonian, Persian, Seleucid, Roman, the Caliphate). This also
goes for the Eastern Christian communities which never founded a Christian empire
in Mesopotamia but lived as secondary citizens in Persia and the Caliphate. At the
beginning of its development, Islamic law too was not the law of the Caliphate but that
of the *umma*, the Muslim community the members of which shared the same religion
but not necessarily the same tribe, clan or "citizenship". Since social cohesion and
identity linked members to a particular religion, it is small wonder that the legal
system of such societies also developed as a religious law and not as a state law.
By contrast, in the other end of the spectrum there are societies which are purely
political and not religious communities. It is the state which organises societal life,
law included, therefore, law is understood as a command of the omnicompetent state
(Chinese legal circle). Between these two extremes there are the Indian (Hindu) and
Persian (Zoroastrian) legal systems which are religious and state laws at the same
time, combining the logic of both, representing a transition between the Near-Eastern
and the Far-Eastern logic which also fits perfectly to their geographic location, too.
In this model, both religious and state institutions were developed which demanded
their own share in political, economic and legal life of these societies. Though both
religious and state institutions struggled for monopoly, both failed at the end because
rival forces were too strong to root them completely. As a result of rivalries for
centuries, religious and state institutions came to a compromise and changed rivalry
to cooperation. As a result, they created legal systems which were religious and
state law at the same time, representing the interests of both. Religions not only
ensured legality and legitimacy for state law and its institutions in exchange for
some privileges but demanded more role in legal life, jurisprudence and legal practice
including. This is exemplified best on theoretic level in the Hindu *varna*-system which
mandates the warrior cast with governance and politics (to run the state) but places
*Brāhmana*s above warriors who had to govern according to the prudent advices of
the first *varna* who are guardians of law (*dharma*), too. A similar ideology was also

born in Persia known as twin-theory (religion and state are twins born from the same womb). Though Zoroastrianism is no longer the state religion of Persia, it is not by chance that it is contemporary Shiᶜīte Iran which attempts to harmonise state law and religious (Islamic law) in a dual legal system which consists of laws enacted by political bodies but controlled by religious authorities. This duality also reached Buddhist South-East Asia where religion specified ethical principles, jurisprudence and some laws (the prohibition of capital punishment) but left enough space for emerging nation states to create their own legal system based on their own cultural heritage and legal history (Thailand, Myanmar, Cambodia). Going just one step further east to Vietnam, all these disappear and what we can witness instead is a state law, codified by political bodies and resting on Confucian principles. The sphere of influence of this model is thus demarked in Iran in the west and Vietnam in the east.

16.3   Legal Pluralism and Politics

Strongly related to the functions of law is the issue of legal pluralism which we can witness all over Asia except, of course, in societies of exclusive customary laws. Though effective in entire Asia, legal pluralism is due to various reasons in different legal systems.

In societies where religious law was dominant, emerging state law automatically created legal pluralism already during the Middle Ages when specifying administrative laws (public administration, tax, the army, etc.). As a result, a dual legal system came into being with an inward looking religious law with less willingness to change according to changing circumstances and a state law which was ready to fill all the gaps which were left by its rival. We can witness this state of affairs in all Muslim countries, though local variants are important. What makes the difference is what role state law specifies for the religious law in modern times. According to a secular model (Atatürk's Turkey, Iran of the Pahlavis) religious law only has a marginal role and that is only in family law. According to its extreme on the other end of the spectrum, religious law has the upper hand and all state laws had to be checked through its lenses (Iran of the Islamic Republic and Saud-Arabia). Between these two extremes there are numerous variants attempting to reach a stable modus vivendi (Egypt, Jordan, Morocco, etc.).

In some Muslim societies the situation is however more complicated because tribal laws also demand their share under the aegis of legal pluralism. Tribal customary laws were never accepted by Muslim legal theorists as a formal source of law but they are nevertheless a very important part of these complex legal systems to this day, representing the third layer of laws. In daily routine, tribal laws are in some cases more important than state law and Islamic law are: 80–90% of private cases end up in compromises, based on local customs and people, thus to avoid both Islamic and state law. What is more, tribal customary law could also overrule state law and Islamic law: honour killing is a case in point which is deeply rooted in local customs but is not backed by Islamic law and state law has a long struggle against it in vain. In addition to Muslim countries, India shares the same experience with this triad of legal systems. Since India is also home to various local and caste customs, these should be added to Hindu understanding of law and state law. Here, too, local customs are more important than any other laws with the difference that Hindu legal theory did not deny legitimacy to customary laws and state law even make efforts to safeguard them. Concurrent customary laws are, therefore, not only concurrent to religious and state laws but also take the lead in some areas of law.

In societies however, where state law was dominant right from the beginning, there was no room left for religious laws. As a result, legal pluralism in such systems is kept beyond limits, which also reduces confusions emerging from the triad of parallel legal systems. It is only complementary customary law which is tolerated to exist and, what is more, even encouraged to develop in order to fill normative gaps which are left consciously by state law in areas which were considered secondary in importance, such as law of inheritance, ownership and mechanisms of local conflict resolution.

There are also strong ties between legal pluralism on the one hand and the political system on the other. Less legal pluralism goes hand in hand with a centralised state since in such a system there are no rival institutions (society, religion, economy) which should be taken into consideration either in political or in legal matters. In such a system, parallel legal understandings have little or no room to assert their own laws without the approval of the central government. This is, needless to say, the Chinese legal circle with a dominant state and a subordinated society which could rely on its own local customs only with state approval and only in fields of law which are not important enough for the central government to regulate (local land law). When such an equilibrium is disturbed by an ideology which pushes political will to its extreme to the detriment of society and economy (legism, Maoism), consequences are catastrophic. Such tragic episodes of Chinese history clearly show that (legal) pluralism is a necessary component also in a political system controlled by a centralised state. This is exactly the lesson contemporary Chinese leaders were willing to learn. Maoist totalitarianism paralysed both society and economy with its failed attempt to annul any pluralism including family law and ownership of any kind. New laws produced in this spirit only led to chaos, famine, labour camps and death of millions of people. With the immediate end of this system by the time of Mao's death, new Chinese leaders restored the status quo ante between state and society. With this, they invented nothing new just re-introduced a very old structure which we can witness in China for millennia. Accordingly, the centralised state allowed Chinese society for a limited (legal) pluralism in some areas of law in exchange for not interfering to politics at all. When Chinese society became enthusiastic about new laws and a kind of freedom not experienced previously and wanted more, limits to such demands were shown promptly and brutally (Tiananmen square). Thus far, it is an old story. But there is also something new which immediately led to the Chinese economic miracle of the past two decades. Post-Mao Chinese leaders abandoned the age old policy of not interfering into economics and its law but took the lead and introduced new laws in a variety of fields of law which were completely abandoned by Chinese rulers for millennia. With this new policy of statism in economy, China emerged as one of the most important players globally which created a new relationship between society and the centralised state (entrepreneurship).

In less centralised systems legal pluralism has more room, yet the political system is less transparent and faces centrifugal forces represented by parallel tribal and religious legal and political institutions. Where it is only the tribal law of subordinated tribes which constitutes parallel institutions, the political system is stable and faces no challenges. This is the state of affairs in India where political leaders are not tribal leaders at the same time and tribes do not struggle for power in the central government but are contempt with the political freedom and legal pluralism they are granted by the central government. Such tribes living in the remote forests in the eastern part of the country are no rivals for the central government in Delhi and do not challenge the system unless they are left alone and are allowed to control their own life and are no victims of serious injustice by the police, local government or private companies looking for extra profit to the detriment of local society (oil, annihilation of rain forests, etc.). Put differently: a less centralised and more tolerant political system guarantees legal pluralism and political freedom for local society and its élite and limits the enthusiasm of the central government to modernise and westernise everything, even against the will of the local population. This was however, more theory than practice in the previous decades when modernising efforts, the abuse of power by the police and the companies led to scandals and sufferings of the locals. But the wisdom of such an understanding began to unfold recently to which constitutional protection is a good reference.

By contrast, in political systems where tribal laws are not subordinated like in India but are powerful actors, (legal) pluralism has a completely different role and function. Tribal societies may struggle for political power in the central government to control the state and its institutions or against a central government intending to interfere in their business which they no longer tolerate. When tribes or tribal confederations of equal strength struggle for power, it can lead to long and bloody yet undecided civil wars. Yemen in the last three decades and Libya after Gaddafi are text book examples. When however, one clan is remarkably stronger than others and could acquire power easily, this ends up in stability and a more or less peaceful coexistence. Post-Soviet Central Asian republics in general and Kazakhstan in particular are cases in point where the strongest clan with its powerful leader (Nazarbayev) guarantees stability and some kind of a prosperity for the whole country and not only for the leading clan. Here again, there is nothing new in the system since Genghis Khan's Mongol empire rested on the same foundations. To put it simply, in such a system state law and its institutions and tribal law and its institutions are not rivals but partners to run a state.

Where the rival of state law is not tribal law but religious law, the situation is more complicated. Religious and state institutions are not partners in constructing a stable system but rivals from ancient Egypt to modern Muslim societies more often than not. Identity, legality and legitimacy, cohesion and solidarity, sovereignty and power are at stake in a struggle where both religion and state demand supremacy. In western countries, the struggle ended with the secular state and the division of powers but in

Asian countries no such a compromise is visible. The continuous conflict between state and religious institutions may have led to a balance of powers between the two (as in the Middle Ages in the Caliphate), or to a chaotic situation where rival institutions paralyse each other (the modern experience of Muslim countries). The old Indian political wisdom could easily be applied to this situation: accordingly, where elephants are fighting, the first victim is the grass. Here, too, the victim is above all civil society which is not prepared and ill equipped to defend itself. Modern Iraq is a case in point where Kurds were attacked by both Saddam Hussein's army and the armed forces of ISIS. Where the competition of institutions is not kept at bay and controlled effectively as in Iran and Saud-Arabia, hostilities emerge sooner or later with devastating consequences. Post-Soviet Afghanistan, Pakistan after Zia ul-Haqq are tragic examples of states which lost more and more control to religious institutions and its allies and became de facto failed states. This problem has its roots in the universalist demand of Islam and its global membership (*umma*) which is at variance with a more particular yet also absolutist demand of modern Muslim nation states. This was an issue which Muslim jurists were able to solve until political bodies (Caliphate, Sultanate) were based on Islamic principles and laws. This situation changed dramatically however, with Western colonisation which ruined the inherited system and created a new, western-minded system in its stead. Since modern Muslim nation states are or, at least, are said to be resting on Western understanding of law and politics (constitutionalism, human rights, etc.), religious institutions were also pushed into the background to be in line with western demands of separation of powers and the secular state. This move however, destroyed the equilibrium lasting for long centuries and gave the state the upper hand. No wonder the influence of religious influence on politics were kept on to a minimum, archaic economic privileges were eliminated (*waqf*) and cultural influence was strongly limited (*madrasa*). Since such changes also met social resistance, the new order also required coercive force, thus creating a democracy-paradox (not in Huntingtons's understanding) when democratic Westernising elite introduced Western principles (democracy including) and institutions with increasingly antidemocratic policy. What we can witness recently is the failure of such policy and the revival of religious institutions and their wrath on state organs and laws.

The situation is more complicated when to this dichotomy a third factor, tribal law and tribalism is added which also have their own share in authority and power. Until recently, it was above all the legal aspect which was easy to grasp (arbitration instead of formal process in the judiciary, honour killings against Islamic and state law, etc.) while the political aspect was less important. With the coming of re-traditionalisation and re-Islamisation, this situation changed drastically and the political aspect became more important than the legal: the Taliban constitutes not a law school but a religious movement and a tribal confederation (Pashtun) at the same time; what we can witness in Yemen for decades and in Libya after Ghaddafi is a de facto tribal war between tribes and tribal confederations. What complicates matter in such societies is that tribal and religious frontlines rarely meet. Yemeni tribes, for example, may be rivals or enemies for pure political reasons but if they share the same religion (e.g. Yemeni shiᶜīs) they could find themselves on the same side in the end. This problem also arises the other way around: should a tribe fight for the same political goal if members are followers of different religions? Affiliation in minority religious communities like the Christians, the Shiᶜītes, and the Druzes in Lebanon might create an alliance on religious grounds, meanwhile they are rivals in tribal politics. In short, the problem is solidarity and identity and no one can answer for sure and once for all whether solidarity would go with the religious or the tribal affiliation or, seldom, with a loyalty to the state which is sometimes only an artificial creation of local and global diplomacy (Jordan, Iraq, Kuwait, etc.). Thus decisions are made on a case-to-case basis, which make such alliances fragile and their policy hard to predict, ending in a very unstable political and legal situation. A further complication arises when anarchic religious movements enter the scene which do not want to gain local power (Taliban) or back state authorities in order to share power and economic gains (Saudi and Iranian religious elite) but aim to ruin local powers and nation states in the utopian hope to create an all-inclusive political space for the entire Muslim *umma* resting on the glorified history of the Caliphate. Since it is absurd to struggle for and against state authority, at the same time tribes which align themselves to such policies and religious movements are unprepared to be in the spotlight of global rivalries which has devastating consequences for both such tribes (Taliban) and the state they are living in (Somalia, Yemen) which tend to disintegrate into failed states more often than not. In such a situation, state institutions and laws are non-existent and the struggle for power continues between tribal and religious institutions bringing such societies back to archaic times.

Here again the transition between Middle-Eastern rivalries and Chinese statism is to be found in a region between Iran and the Southeast Asian countries. Iran is, contrary to its neighbours (Iraq, Afghanistan) a stable state with a remarkable history and a long tradition of autocracy which did not tolerate rivalries or open hostilities between institutions and identities (tribal, religious and citizenship). It is the Twelver Shiᶜīa which has the same function as state religion in modern Iran that had Zoroastrianism in ancient Persia and less evidently for the Pahlavi kings until 1979. Iranian Islamism and the revolution created no chaos (except for the first years) but led only to a change of paradigm and strategy: the rapid, Western-minded modernisation from above was replaced by a similarly violent and rapid Islam-minded modernisation which gave no chance to rivalries between institutions and identities. Tribalism was never a decisive factor in Iranian politics anyway and the rivalry between state and religious institutions was brought to a rapid end with the victory of the latter. With the declaration of the primacy of religious law, state authorities were reduced to second rank in importance yet the constitution created a disputed but operational constitutional order which prevented the country from falling into chaos, unlike her neighbours. Similarly, there is no chaos either in India or in the Southeast Asian countries. Tribalism was never a decisive factor in Indian politics, despite the huge number of tribes living in the country. Religious sectarianism, though an important factor for growing concern recently, does not paralyse the country and is no cause for civil war in a state which was designated as secular in its constitution. Buddhist Southeast Asian countries are also secular, despite post-Communist Kampuchea's efforts to declare Buddhism a state religion where neither sectarian nor tribal conflicts paralyse the country and state institutions.

That said, now the various responses to colonisation and legal westernisation is easy to understand. Colonisation was a complex external force (military, economic, political, legal, ideologic) which brought about gradual changes in all Asian legal circles disrupting their status quo and internal cohesion. Needless to say, the responses to colonisation varied from country to country and there was no uniform policy within a legal circle which modified the relationship of legal systems within a legal circle. Take Japan as an example, which westernised its legal system already in the Meiji period and thus distanced itself from the Chinese influence. What is more, Japan took the lead and introduced a more western-minded legal system in occupied Korea which experienced no Japanese influence previously but was a satellite legal system in the Chinese orbit for long centuries. With the advent of legal Westernisation, Japan left behind its isolation and became an advocate of this policy in the Chinese legal circle. This however, did not modify the basic principles of Chinese legal circle in which the state continued to be the sole actor and legal changes also focused above all on state institutions (political system, public administration, legal system). But this was not an easy task to accomplish either, since Japan's efforts to Westernisation succeeded only after the devastating consequences of militarism destroying earlier achievements (Taisho-democracy) after WW II, China changed ideologies and political systems four times within some decades (the fall of the last dynasty and the bourgeois period, Maoism and post-Mao Communist rule) and now democratic South Korea also has its long history of autocracy. Such challenges notwithstanding Chinese legal circle continued statism as its leading principle leaving no room for religious or tribal institutions. The importance of this truism is easy to grasp when comparing this situation with that of the Islamic legal circle of the Middle East where tribal and religious institutions take the lead which—in contrast to state institutions— cannot be modernised or westernised. A legal system which rests, according to its legal theology, on divine revelation, cannot be modernised just because advocates of westernisation or some global organisations (e.g. AI) criticise its laws and practice (cutting off hands, etc.). Obviously, there is room for different interpretations of archaic texts in order to bring about some changes but its efficiency could not be compared to that of the law making of political bodies (parliament, government). As a result, no serious attempt was made to gradually change archaic Islamic law but efforts concentrated only on state institutions and political bodies and processes. Since however, religious law always had its share in power and competency, conflicts between state law and religious law soon emerged which paralysed further reforms. To overcome resistance, westernisers applied force which contributed to more social resistance based on religious ideology which again hindered further reforms and even the function of state institutions. This vicious circle is a huge obstacle for political modernisation and legal westernisation which reinforces re-Islamisation and political Islam campaigning against corrupt and inefficient state institutions in the favour of their own religious bodies and laws. In the early decades of the twentieth century this rivalry was closed down with the hegemony of state institutions and the marginalisation of religious laws and bodies (Kemalism) while the last decades are witness to the resurrection of religious laws.

Irrespective of social and political structures, legal westernisation touched upon the same areas of law all over Asia: constitutional law and the political system, private and commercial law, criminal law, and laws of procedure. Legislation had been in progress in these fields of law in Turkey, Iran, India, China, South Korea, Japan, Indonesia, and the Southeast Asian countries. Parallel to westernising legislation, traditional laws were reduced to a minimum and its sphere of influence was only kept in family laws (marriage, divorce, inheritance). Prudent regimes stopped at this point and did not go further, in order to secure social backing for reforms in other areas of law. Where governments did not respect this red line, they had to withdraw their proposal or lost power to their opponents (Iran, Afghanistan) because a complete reorganisation of society on foreign model was unacceptable throughout entire Asia. Remarkably, this only holds true not in countries where legal systems were reformed on the Western (common law, civil law tradition) model but also where the Socialist model had been followed. Needless to say, Japanese liberal democracy has nothing in common with the regimes of Pol Pot, Mao Zedung and other communist governments. Despite this, legal change followed the same pattern everywhere because it touched upon constitutional law, and, as a result, constitutions were produced all over the continent which was a great novelty since the very idea of constitutionalism was alien to Asian countries and is a Western legal way of thinking. In short, the idea of constitutionalism as a western model was introduced both in communist and non-communist countries but the content of the constitutions varied according to their underlining ideologies. This also goes for other areas of law reformed under the impact of western influence such as private law, criminal law and laws of procedures.

16.4   Importance of Law

Asian societies are said to be critical towards law which regard it as useless and harmful, something which is not worth studying and also raises moral concern. Such a view is, broadly speaking, an over-simplification though the essence of it holds true.

Though for different reasons, Chinese legists, Muslim and Jewish scholars regard law the most important field of study and there is no science, mathematics, geography, chemistry, physics, historiography, grammar, philosophy and theology included which is on equal footing with law. It would be however, a mistake to believe that law in itself was a very important thing in China, among the Jews and Muslims. By contrast, for Chinese legists, Jewish and Muslim scholars, law was only an instrument to achieve ends or arrive at goals which are more important than law is. Law is only a helpful and powerful mean but not the thing itself. This all-important goal for both Jewish and Muslim scholars is the will of God, which could be discerned while studying His laws since God is the ultimate Lawmaker. Law is the path (*shariʿa*, *halakha*) which helps believers find their way to God. This is why law has to be studied above all other sciences and legal commands had to be followed since breaking the law is at the same time the negligence of God's will. Despite this, Jewish and Muslim scholars did everything possible to avoid participation in everyday legal practice, above all, in judging because they were afraid of the supernatural consequences of wrong judgements and did not want to waste their time with mundane problems of commoners instead of being engaged in jurisprudence. Since the ultimate judgement is due to God, judges are responsible in person for their wrong judgements in the presence of God, a personal liability scholars wanted to escape from because it is easier to hide from the Caliph than from God. For Chinese legists it was the state and its interests what for Jewish and Muslim scholars the will of God was: the all-important end. For legism law was indispensable, a tool the importance of which they over-emphasised in all of their writings and decisions, yet it remained an instrument also in their hands. What they wanted was the total control of state, society and economics for which law was believed to be the best tool containing commands and punishments, two things legists celebrated in their works as the most efficient method of governance. Legists were not interested in any other aspect of law, such as philosophy, religion and ethics. What they concentrated on was the practical aspect of law and its contribution to build and maintain a totalitarian state, their ultimate goal.

Other Asian societies, cultures and ideologies considered the importance of law even less. Confucianism was strongly against it, believing in inherited customs, education, the proper performance of rites and the central role of families. For Confucians, the golden age of mythical times was the model to be followed where there was no law because people lived according to a moral standard which required no laws and punishments. Confucians remained distanced when they allowed room for laws and punishments as a result of a compromise with legism at later times. No serious Confucian scholar ever studied law at the detriment of the classics, an attitude prevailing in the entire Chinese legal circle. The Korean saying has it simply but revealing: 'read ten thousand books but not law'. We can find a similar way of thinking in Hinduism which also regards law as the tool of the most corrupted age, the kali-yuga in which egoism and violence prevail and 'big fishes eat small fishes.' Buddhism further neglects law while rejecting it completely since Buddhist teaching has nothing to say about law, punishments and running a state. The only set of norms which resemble law is vinaya, the regulations of Buddhist orders explaining the rights and duties of monks.

The education system and the relative importance of the various disciplines is also a good indicator of the role of law in a society. Looking at Asian societies through this prism, we arrive at the same result as above. It is Jewish society which adorns the study of law to the detriment of any other disciplines. Meanwhile, thousands of works has been produced in law and jurisprudence, we cannot find works on the same intellectual level in other sciences. Following an archaic Talmudic tradition, disciples of yeshivas do not study theology, philosophy or medicine but are engaged in the most hair-splitting analysis of law, coupled with techniques of textual interpretation and argumentation and the teachings of outstanding Rabbis (responsum). A Muslim madrasa does not differ from this in its essence and message, since education there concentrates on law, prophetic traditions and Qur'ān-exegesis and neglects any other discipline. This thousand year old curriculum is one of the most important factors as to why Muslim societies were behind Western countries in sciences, technical revolution and the social sciences in the last centuries.

Though with less enthusiasm, law was also studied in Hindu India, because law was part of *dharma* the study of which qualified as the most rewarding intellectual activity. This is why law collections were incorporated into works on *dharma* composed by priests and scholars (four chapters out of twelve in the Laws of Manu contain laws on private and public (the king) law issues). This is why *dharmasūtras* and *dharmaśāstras* are important sources for both Indian legal history and religious philosophy. The same fact explains why there was no individual legal training in India but legal education was an important part in the education of priests who were believed to be the guardians of law and order and were advisors to kings in legal matters. The ethical dimension of law bonded it to *dharma* but its practical aspect secured a place for it in works about more mundane affairs such as politics and economics. This is the reason why we can find legal material also in works on *artha*. Commentaries written to prestigious works on *dharma* further developed jurisprudence in the Middle Ages but not as an independent academic discipline but as a part of inherited ethical, religious and political wisdom.

A Chinese official had no formal training in law, though he was responsible for legal procedures. By contrast, he had to be qualified in disciplines which had little or no relevance to his job, such Confucian classics, calligraphy, rites and literature on a high level. This is why Chinese scribes were not well versed in detail of law and had to hire legal experts in procedures about complicated cases. There was no jurisprudence as an academic discipline in China, too, where law was studied only in works of outstanding legist thinkers such as Shang Yang and Han Fei but they remained isolated in the lack of followers and disciples for the next two millennia.

Similarly to his Chinese colleague, a Mesopotamian scribe (official) was lacking any formal education in law but it would be absurd to expect formal legal training in the Ancient Near-East four thousand years ago. Yet scribes were trained in almost all sciences and skills Ancient Mesopotamia is famous for and law was only a small part of. More importantly, scribes were trained in how to produce official documents of different kinds since Mesopotamian procedural routine was bound to strict formalism and scribes were required to master all these forms in order to get their job and earn their livelihood. But not a single work on jurisprudence was produced (at least, it was not unearthed yet) while a great deal of works were composed in medicine, astronomy, literature and religion. Persian (Zoroastrian) and Christian traditions also followed the middle path and did not neglect or adorn law to the extreme. Christians collected laws, above all canons of synods and edited and re-arranged the material either in logical or in chronological order to which some commentaries were added. Persian tradition collected rather precedents and court judgments—mainly for non-routine cases—without any discernible logic and order. Such collections were copied for centuries without any comments, critiques or changes which is a sign of both respect and neglect. These texts were respected to a certain extent, otherwise they would not have been copied for such a long time. On the other hand, there was only tiny progress because of the lack of jurisprudence and the relative unimportance of law. There was no legal training in either tradition because what was important for Christians was the orthodoxy of the doctrine and for Zoroastrians the orthopraxy of the rites. Law fitted into this framework only to reinforce doctrines and rituals and to fight heretics (Christian legal apologetics). This is why there was no separate legal training among Christians and Zoroastrians but legal education was only a part of a more comprehensive education of priests. Following the almost complete negligence of law in Buddhism, it is hardly surprising that there was no legal education and jurisprudence in Buddhist societies for centuries.

In sum, in Islamic and Jewish law, jurisprudence is an academic field to be studied by scholars of reputation which is regarded as the most important discipline. This is why both Islamic and Jewish laws are jurists' law where outstanding scholars take the lead and jurisprudence has pre-eminence over law making. By contrast, Chinese legal circle only has outstanding Codes but no outstanding legal scholars and, therefore, not works on jurisprudence but law collections embodying prestige and wisdom are copied for centuries. This is why there is legal education among the Jews and Muslims but it is lacking in the Chinese legal circle. India is, again, representing a middle path where the study of law is more important than in China but is not pushed to its extreme like in the Islamic and Jewish cultures thus leaving room also for a variety of other disciplines, too (mathematics, astronomy, philosophy).

Litigation is also a good indicator reflecting the importance of law in a society. In fact, there is no society in Asia which praises litigation and court procedures. By contrast, all Asian societies emphasise the positive aspect of compromises and the various methods of informal conflict resolutions. This old wisdom led many to think that Asian peoples are reluctant to assert their rights and do not stand for their share but are contempt with less. This is by far not the case because what they reject is a formal court procedure and the involvement of third parties in their own business (officials, legal experts, witnesses), but prefer less formal methods to resolve their conflicts. In short, the rejection of litigation does not mean that Asian peoples do not represent their material interests. The rejection of institutions related to law is not indifference but a permanent and inherited negative attitude. To be involved in a court procedure is a shame one has to avoid. This is why family affairs are not disclosed at courts because to let others have a look onto one's family life is a shame that hinders any conflict to come to court. This is why family affairs are solved by the head of the family and the clan but never by a judge sitting at a court. This way of thinking is pushed to the extreme when third persons who are not parties in the dispute but had to go to court (e.g. a witness) are also ashamed because of their involvement. Elderly persons are reluctant to appear at court and there are documented cases when some of them even died because they were summoned to court (stress because of shame and related heart attack or stroke). This understanding is the direct opposite of Western legal thinking, emphasising the right of individuals to litigation guaranteed by constitutions. It was, therefore, also a cultural change when Asian laws were Westernised, a process which provoked, understandably, resistance and also hatred sometimes. Small wonder that the Western attitude to litigation was slowly adopted even in countries where legal Westernisation had been accomplished successfully, such as Japan and South Korea where the number of litigations increased during the previous decades only to a very limited extent. Formal litigation is also unpopular because it is costly, long and is in remote towns, while traditional institutions such as the head of a family, a clan and a village is nearby, cheap and ends cases promptly with an authority (traditions, customs, ancestor's spirit, local religion) that is lacking by any formal legal institution.

There is thus no wrong in asserting one's own rights and interests. This should be done however with any eye to the interests of others, a very important aspect of behaviour and legal representation. There is no room for a completely individualistic approach to rights and interests all over Asia, a basic understanding uniting the entire continent regardless of culture, history and religion. Persons who would assert their own right with no willingness to compromise would meet social resistance which would make them de facto losers of the case even when they won the lawsuit in the courtroom. This is because conflicts and litigations are considered wounds on the body of society which should be healed. A formal litigation evidently produces losers and winners but this would not heal the wounds, on the contrary, it would deepen it because of the frustration of the losing party. Therefore, instead of court judgments, compromises have to be hammered out which create a win-win situation for all and would resolve conflicts which last for generations (blood feud, land ownership dispute). The restauration of social harmony is more important than the right of an individual to the detriment of others. Japanese *wa* is a good example to show the importance of this understanding. But legal minded experts such as Jewish and Muslim judges also highlight compromises and do everything possible during court procedures to call the parties' attention to their possibility to hammer out compromises with the help of the court and advise them not to wait for the court's judgment.

In addition to the rejection of formal litigation, another common feature of Asian legal systems is the importance of families and their protection. This is, of course, not completely homogenous since there are variants based on local customs, religion and social structure: Chinese familiarism based on Confucian tradition is not to be found in India while honour killings are missing from Buddhist societies. But these are rather examples of extremisms developed in a certain region by over-emphasising some aspects of family life which are, obviously, missing from other legal cultures. The importance of families is however, not a common feature of Asian laws but of Asian societies since it was not law that created it but, to the contrary, Asian legal systems only put principles and an anthropology into legal language that existed previously and independently.

What is in fact a common feature of all Asian legal systems is their understanding of rights and duties, neglecting the former and emphasising the latter. Law was never seen as a set of opportunities for individuals or communities but as a long list of duties reinforced by the punishments of authorities. Authorities vary according to time and place. In China, such an authority is the head of the family and the emperor, believed to be some kind of a collective pater familias. For Jews and Muslims the same authority is God, the supreme Lawmaker whose laws had to be studied and followed and never neglected. These are only variants in ideologies and authorities while their underlying (legal) understanding is identic. Duties also dominate Hindu legal understanding, though less emphatically because there is no hegemonic authority: Indian history is not the history of an empire but that of small states and Hinduism also lacks an all-powerful God punishing all sins and wrongs. By contrast, the doctrine of *karma* reduced the power of hegemonic supernatural powers in religion and law and with its automatism (good or bad *karma* for prospective lives) moral and legal duties became rather standards but not laws which are enforced here and now with the authority of political powers. Buddhism followed the same line and, what is more, with the doctrine of non-violence created the basis for a more human legal system (abolition of capital punishment) which however, continued to be centred on duties but not rights.

Glossary

Ancient Near-East

ālum town, city council, the leading political decision-making body of Assyria in the Old Assyrian period which issued decrees, was a court of justice and controlled diplomacy

awat ālim decrees issued by the *ālum* in the Old Assyrian period

awēlum a free commoner in the Babylonian period but its exact meaning has been subject to disputes for decades

bābtum city gate, the venue of legal procedure

bēl pāhāti provincial governor in the Middle Assyrian period who was responsible for ensuring supplies, guarantee safe routes of transport and to maintain communication with the capital

Codex Eshnunna law collection from the city of Eshnunna produced presumably during the reign of king Dadusha in the nineteenth–eighteenth centuries; it is an important link between the Sumerian and the Babylonian legal system

ditilla documents judicial notes and documents produced in the period of the Third Dynasty of Ur

e-dubba the 'house of tablets', school for scribes in the Sumerian period

en, ensi a ruler and priestly figure during the period of the city states in Sumerian history; the difference between en, ensi and *lugal*, also denoting a king is unknown to us; in the Akkadian period *ensi* was only a governor in the service of the Akkadian king

ibila a male heir offering sacrifice for the benefit of his ancestor and continuing his name and family in the Sumerian period

iginudu a free agricultural worker in the Sumerian period

ishiul contract signed by the Hittite ruler with his officials which stipulates their competency and responsibilities to which a personal oath of loyalty is added; this document served as a model for contracts concluded with client kings

© Springer Nature Switzerland AG 2020

J. Jany, *Legal Traditions in Asia*, Ius Gentium: Comparative Perspectives on Law and Justice 80, https://doi.org/10.1007/978-3-030-43728-2

hazannu governor of Hattusha, the Hittite capital guaranteeing the security of the
city; for this purpose the city gate was sealed each night and reopened next
morning

kittu expression of legality in the Babylonian period; together with *mēsharu* it was
part of a cosmic which gods also had to respect

kudurru border stone marking the border between parcels of land from the Akkadian
period the removal of which was a criminal offence

labarna title of the Hittite king

limmum Old Assyrian official elected by drawing from among the nobles of Ashshur
for a period of one year which was named after him; an office with no competency
but enormous social prestige with which royal authority was incompatible

Lipit-Ishtar's law book the law collection of Lipit-Ishtar (1934–1924), ruler of Isin,
the text of which has come down to us only in fragments; the complete text may
have contained about forty laws

lugal **(great man)** ruler, presumably a military leader at the beginning of the
Sumerian period

lugulabi well-to-do persons with social prestige and political influence in the
Sumerian period

MAL (Middle Assyrian Laws) the scholarly name of the most important source of
Assyrian law the original title of which is unknown (if there was one); it is a
private collection of law the author and chronology of which is not known to
us; the collection consists of several tablet but it is only the first tablet, mostly
about family law, which has been preserved in good condition, other tablets are
too fragmentary

mēsharu justice, a basic principle which should be considered both in law-making
and the administration of law in the Babylonian period; together with *kittu* it was
part of a cosmic order which gods also had to respect

mēsharu-edictum Babylonian custom according to which a new ruler cancelled the
debt of Babylonian citizens and restored the freedom of persons working in debt
slavery

mushkēnum a term subject to debate for long among Assyriologists; perhaps a
person living in the royal palace or a royal employee in the Babylonian period

nudunnū gifts given to the widow by her husband *inter vivos* in order to ensure her
livelihood because a widow did not inherit her husband in the Sumerian period

pankush a council consisting of the leading figures of the aristocracy and the army
in the Hittite empire which had no say in the election of the king but was entitled
by the laws of Telipinu to sentence to death a ruler who acceded to the throne
illegally

rab ekalli high-ranking official managing the royal palace (building, maintenance,
personnel) in the Middle Assyrian period

qēpu a court official controlling the governors in the Middle Assyrian period

sakallu rabiu General-in-chief, the second most important office next to the king
in the Middle Assyrian period who was responsible for military, administrative
and judicial functions

shar kibrātim arba'im (**lord of the four cardinal points**) title of the Akkadian ruler

sharru king (from the Akkadian period)

sheriktum a woman's dowry in the Babylonian period

shub-lugal owners of small plots of land in the Sumerian period

sukkalmah viceroy, marquis, governor of the border region during the reign of the Third Dynasty of Ur; the title was adopted in neighbouring Elam with the meaning of a ruler

terhātum a sum paid by the husband to his wife's family from the Babylonian period

ugulá the 'aristocracy' of city states in the Sumerian period

unkin a city council in the Sumerain period which lost significance already in the early phase of Sumerain history; the epic of Gilgamesh refers to it in some passages

UruKaGina's (Uru'inimgina) reform tablet new laws introduced in the city state of Lagash by its ruler UraKaGina to protect the poor, widows and orphans at the end of the period of the warring Sumerian city states

Ur-nammu's law book a law book attributed wrongly to Ur-nammu, founder of the Third Dynasty of Ur but issued more probably by his successor Shulgi; it is the oldest law book which has come down to us, though only in fragments

Jewish Law

cedūqīm the Sadducees, an aristocratic and highly influential group of priests and rich merchants who presumably derive their name from high priest *Cādoq* who rejected most of the doctrines of the Pharisees, denied the resurrection of the body, the immortality of the soul and the existence of angels

dayyān judge

gā'ōn head of the academies, elected from amog the prestigious scholars

genizah a room or a separated space of the synagogue where manuscripts were stored

get a document on divorce, drafted in a very formal language

gezerah order about prohibitions, usually issued by legal scholars

halakah (**literally: walking**) Jewish law, reflecting to a normative tradition containing in addition to private and criminal law also laws on kings, judicial procedure and the judiciary, agriculture and religious issues, such as cult, purity, and festivals

Halakōt Gedolōt ('**Great Laws**') a law collection modelled on the structure of the *Talmūd* but reducing its content enormously in order to give a comprehensive survey which was easier to put into practice; the work was very popular in the *gā'ōn*ic period and was composed by an author unknown to us, presumably in the ninth century to defend oral law challenged by the increasingly popular Karaite movement

Hillel a legal scholar and founder of the school named after him who lived in the first century and debated about hundreds of legal problems with his opponent *Shamm'ay*

issura' religious laws the interpretation of which is stricter than the laws of the more mundane *mamona'*

ketubbah agreement between spouses (from the word meaning 'to write') securing financial support for a wife in case of divorce

Maimonides **(1135–1204)** a polymath from Hispania who was a physician, a philosopher and a legal scholar, the author of innumerable *responsa* and the *Mishneh Torāh,* a work intended to be a code

mamona' laws about mundane affairs such propriety rights and obligations; contrary to issura' the interpretation of mamona' was more flexible and being a ius dispositivum parties were allowed to agree differently in their contracts

midrāsh interpretation, also including the interpretation of Biblical and Talmūdic laws; among techniques of interpretation, Jewish scholars favoured analogy, arguments *a fortiori*, contextual and historic interpretation and the distinction between general and particular laws; some techniques are also known as Hillel's seven rules but to attribute these norms to Hillel is a rather historic anachronism

minhāg legal custom with the help of which gaps in law were filled in and disputes between scholars were resolved while accepting the doctrine of a scholar which corresponded to everyday legal practice

Mishnah a law collection from the turn of the second century consisting of the oral law tradition of the Pharisees (*Torāh shebe^{c}al-peh*) arranged in six orders *(sedarīm),* such as (1) *Zerāīm* (seeds): laws on agriculture; (2) *Mō^{c}ēd* (festivals): laws on religious festivals; (3) *Nashīm* (women): laws on family law; (4) *Nezikīn* (damages): laws on private law and law of procedure; (5) *Qodashīm* (sacred things): temple laws; (6) *Tohorōt* (purities): laws on purification

mohar a sum to be paid to the girl's father at engagement, usually in cash; after mohar was handed over, the girl qualified for third persons as a woman living in marriage

nāśī some Jewish leaders (e.g. *Simon Bar Kokba'*) were designated *nāśī* in order to avoid being referred to as king in the second Temple period; rabbinic tradition narrowly interpreted the title as a legal scholar and the head of the judiciary presiding over the great *Sanhedrīn (bēt dīn ha-gadōl)*

P^{e}rūshīm Pharisees, an influential group of middle class persons appearing after the Hasmonean revolt who emphasised resurrection, ritual purity and their own oral law (*Torāh shebe^{c}al-peh*) which their adversaries, the Sadducees were unwilling to accept

Rashi (Rabbi Solomon ben Isaac) a legal scholar from France, author of the most famous commentary to the *Talmūd* which is jointly published with the basic text in the editions of the *Talmūd,* as if they constituted a single work; his disciples, the Tosafists continued his tradition of commentary after his death (1105)

rēsh galūta' exilarch, leader and political representative of the Babylonian Jews in the Parthian and the Sasanian periods

responsum answer given to a quiery about a legal problem by a private individual, issued by a rabbi who was addressed in writing

Sanhedrīn a court of law; the great *Sanhedrīn (bēt dīn ha-gadōl)* of 71 members in Jerusalem was the supreme judicial body during the Second Temple period

Shamm'ay a legal scholar from the first century, a disputant of *Hillel* and the founder of the school named after him

Shulḥān Arūk the law collection of *Joseph Qaro* published in Venice (1565), a work intended for the general reader and written in a clear language and a comprehensive style which are the causes of its uninterrupted popularity to this day; in producing his book, the author studied the works of Maimonides and other medieval scholars and followed the majority opinion in disputed cases

takkanah an ordinance prescribing positive actions

Talmūd (**teaching**) a storehouse of Jewish law and wisdom containing various interpretations of law, disputes of legal scholars and their deeds, anecdotes and legends, mathematical and astronomical observances; the work follows the structure of the Mishnah but is more than a simple commentary to it; the *Jerusalemi* or *Palestinian Talmūd* (PT) may have been compiled during the fourth or the fifth century in Tiberias while the *Babylonian Talmūd* (BT) came into being in the subsequent centuries after long centuries of editing in Mesopotamia; because of its encyclopaedic and more detail-oriented approach the BT is a more popular work than PT is, the use of which is further complicated by repetitions and contradictions

tanna recitor of law during teaching

Torāh shebeᶜal-peh oral law, the legal tradition of the Pharisees which was received accordingly by Moses also during the revelation at Mount Shinai and reached the Pharisees and the rabbinic sages through authorities such as *Joshua,* the elders, the prophets and the 'Pairs'; oral law was understood as a supplement to the written law which could not contradict it; despite its name, oral law was also committed to writing, its first collection being the *Mishnah*

Torāh shebeketab written law given by God to Moses during the revelation at Mount Shinai, containing 613 Biblical laws

Tosefta' a commentary and a supplement to the *Mishnah,* following its structure

yeshīva a legal academy, a venue of teaching and adjudication

Persian Law

Abarag Persian legal scholar from the Sasanian period, the third member and the most significant representative of the legal school named after him

arta justice, cosmic order

atarsagāyīh (**'not fearing'**) defiance of a person with authority in the family (father, husband); it was a criminal act which may lead to the exclusion from the bequest

chagar **marriage** a marriage; the aim of which was to produce a male heir to a man
who had passed away without a legal heir; persons obliged to enter a *chagar*
marriage were called *stūr*

chāshtag doctrine, opinion of legal scholars

dastūr priest, head of the Zoroastrian community after the Sasanian period

dāta (dād) law, religion

dāta-bara royal judge in the Old Persian period which continued to exist also in the
Sasanian period (*dādwar)*

dibīray registers containing documents produced in various fields of administration;
there was a separate register for legal matters, *(dād dibīray),* land ownership
which was the basis of taxation *(shahr āmār dibīray),* for the treasury *(ganz āmār
dibīray),* for fires *(ātash āmār dibīray)* and for the pious foundations *(ruwānagān
dibīray)*

ērbed teaching priest who was responsible for teaching of young priests

frasaka an official responsible for legal cases in the Old Persian period

ganzabara head of the treasury in the Old Persian period

gaushaka ('ears of the king'): secret agents directly responsible for the monarch
who controlled the satraps and the military governors

hāmārakara controller of the public treasury in the Old Persian period

hamdādestān ī wēhān consensus of the legal scholars, the third source of Zoroastrian law

hazārapati 'commander of the thousands': a military leader who was originally
the commander of the bodyguard of Darius consisting of one thousand men;
during the subsequent decades the *hazārapati* evolved into the head of the central
administration controlling diplomatic diplomatic negotiations with envoys and
controlling the chancellery

kardag legal custom, a juridical practice differing from the doctrines

khshachapāvan satrap, provincial governor in the Old Persian period who collected
taxes and was the head of the administration and the judiciary in a province

khwasrayūn **marriage** love marriage, that is, a marriage of a woman who selected
her spouse on her own without the approval of her guardian (father, brother)
because the latter failed to marry her for long years

khwēdōdāh marriage between close relatives

Mādigān ī Hazār Dādestān (**A Book of a Thousand Judgments**) a private compilation of precedents produced at the end of the Sasanian period, containing
complicated and irregular cases

margarzān ('worthy of death'): crimes punished by capital punishment

Mēdōmāh Persian legal scholar in the Sasanian period, the third member and an
important authority in the legal school named after him

mōbed (**magus**) Zoroastrian priest for rituals and the administration of justice;
*mōbed*s were part of the Zoroastrian church headed by the chief *mōbed*, the
mōbedān mōbed, who was the legal advisor to the monarch

pādikhshāy **marriage** a marriage with *sālārīh*

rad priest with a central role in the administration of justice

Riwāyat-i Ēmēd-i Ashawahishtān A law collection of high priest *Ēmēd* containing questions and answers on family law composed in the tenth century

sālārīh authority of the head of the family, *manus*

Shāyast-nē-shāyast a casuistic compilation of religious laws about irregular cases composed towards the end of the Sasanian period for a priestly audience

stūr a person obliged to produce a male heir to a man who passed away without such an heir, usually a near male or female relative who entered a *chagar* marriage

tanāpuhl legal term for various criminal deeds which were sanctioned strictly but without capital punishment

wuzurg-framādār commander-in-chief in the Sasanian period

The Law of the Church of the East

Abdisho bar Brika the last polymath of the Church of the East, living in the Mongol period (d. 1318); both of his law collections, the *Collectio canonum Synodicorum* and the *Ordo iudiciorum ecclesiasticorum* are used to this day in the Church of the East

Bochtisho dynasty an influential Iranian dynasty of physicians from the school of Jundeshapur; Giwargish, the founder of the dynasty was invited to Baghdad by Caliph al-Mansur where he translated Greek works of medicine; his son entered the service of Caliph Harun al-Rashid as his physician while his grandson Gabriel, also a court physician lobbied successfully to ease the restrictive laws on Christians and obtained permission to bury Nestorius to Seleuceia-Ctesiphon

Catholicos head of the Church of the East with his headquarters in Seleuceia-Ctesiphon in the Persian period and Baghdad in the ᶜAbbassid period

Episcopalis audientia the bishop's authority to proceed in legal cases and to settle disputes through mediation

Fiqh al-nasraniyya Ibn al-Taiyib's two-volume nomo-canon collection written in Arabic which due to its popularity served as a model for the Coptic Church

Ibn al-Taiyib priest, physician, philosopher, legal scholar, and secretary of the Catholicos of Baghdad, an author of scholarly treatises, among which the best known is the *Fiqh al-Nasraniyya*

Isho bar Nun opponent and successor of Timotheus in the office of the Catholicos who nevertheless continued his predecessor's law collection and added new material to it

Ishobokht Persian bishop in the ᶜAbbassid period producing a comprehensive law book in a systemic way about family law and the laws of obligation; being one of the best in its genre the work was translated to Syriac

Jundeshapur School important scholarly centre and rival to the school in Nisibis concentrating on theology and law, equipped with a library; a great deal of famous physicians were educated here for centuries, among them the Bochtisho dynasty who transferred the school to Baghdad where they were invited by the Caliph in the last decades of the eighth century

Hunayn ibn Ishaq Christian polymath, also called the 'Erasmus of the Islamic renaissance' who also visited Byzantium and Alexandria to study there in his youth; he was fluent in Arabic, Persian, Syriac and Greek already at the age of 17; though a physician of Caliph al-Mutawakkil and an expert in ophthalmology he is famous for his academic works: altogether he translated 260 works, and was the author of another one hundred; in addition to medicine, he also produced books on logics, historiography, lexicography, linguistics and Christian apologetics; his translation of the Septuagint, praised for its excellency is unfortunately lost; his talent in languages was inherited by his son and grandson this is why the translation of the works of Aristotle, Galen, Euclid and Ptolemy is associated with his dynasty;

Mar Aba a Zoroastrian convert to Christianity and Catholicos who excommunicated in his law book believers diverting from Christian marriage laws and following Persian customs, including incestuous marriage; he was imprisoned by Persian authorities (spent 10 years out of his 13 years in office) but did not give in

Mar Simeon Persian bishop, author of a brief law collection on the law of inheritance

Narseh a scholar and a Zoroastrian convert to Christianity, the founder of the School in Nisibis

Timotheus scholar and outstanding Catholicos who reorganised the Church and continued the missionary work towards the East in the early ᶜAbbassid period; though Ishobokht's work was translated upon his order from Persian to Syriac, he began to compile his own law collection

School of Nisibis a theological and medical school in the city of Nisibis

rabbaita the leader of the School in Nisibis, elected annually

rabban council of the former leaders in the School of Nisibis who governed jointly with the head of the school

Sententiae Syriacae a work containing Roman law, composed in the late third century in Greek and later translated into Syriac; the work paraphrases Roman law in a simplistic language for a broader audience

Syriac–Roman law book a law book produced in the fifth century in Greek and later translated into Syriac, Arabic and Armenian showing its influence in the Near-East before the Muslim conquest; the law book has a Roman law modified by local legal practice; the work is also known as *Leges Constantini, Theodosii et Leonis* but it is misleading because there are only five articles out of the 130 which are related to these rulers

Synodika one of the most important legal sources of the Church of the East containing synodic laws in chronological order with 80 titles on 2000 manuscript pages produced in the eleventh century; the work contains the canons of the synods of Ankyra (24), Neokaisareia (14), Nicea (20) and of Antiocheia (25), some parts of the Syriac–Roman law book, various tractates on inheritance law, and also relevant letters of *Catholicoi*; the complete edition and translation of the work is still missing but the individual works included in the compilation are already made public

Islamic Law

Abū Hanīfa a legal scholar in Iraq in the eighth century, the eponymos of the Hanafite School who left no written work behind

Abū Yūsuf disciple of Abū Hanīfa, an outstanding authority among the early Hanafites and one of the de facto founders of the school

ahl al-bayt the clan with the greatest authority in a tribe

ahl al-hadīth supporters of the Prophetic tradition who rejected rational thinking in matters of law and insisted on filling legal gaps according to the tradition of the prophet seen as paradigmatic

ahl al-ra'y supporters of the rational thinking who insisted to fill legal gaps based on rational arguments where revelation was silent

ᶜasabiyya group solidarity (family, clan, and tribe)

Babatha archive documents of the Jewish widow Babatha who fled to a cave near the Dead Sea together with all his documents including a variety of contract and other official notes during Hadrian's campaign and the revolt of Bar Kokba'; the documents are important sources for the Nabatean law and the Roman influence on it

fiqh (**understanding**) discipline pertaining to the *sharīᶜa*, jurisprudence

Gülkhāne-i Khatt-i Sherif (Khatt-i Humāyūn) a reform act promulgated by the Ottoman Sultan in 1839 changing some constitutional and tax laws, followed by a new criminal law act (still based on Islamic law) next year and new commercial laws in order to enhance trade with European merchants

hakam a mediator hammering out compromises in disputes between communities (family, clan, tribe), an important institution in traditional conflict resolution mechanism

hudd criminal deeds specified in the Qur'an (fornication, false accusation with fornication, drinking wine, theft, highway robbery, apostasy) which are acts against divine law and are punished as specified in the Qur'an

harām prohibited acts

Ibn Hanbal a scholar of prophetic tradition living in Baghdad at the turn of the eighth and ninth centuries who is the eponym of a law school that evolved after his death from among his disciples

ᶜibādāt ritual

ᶜidda a waiting period for women lasting for three months in case of divorce

ijmāᶜ consensus (of legal scholars), the third source of Islamic law

ijtihād intellectual effort, a mental process during which a legal scholar identifies a law on the basis of the sources of law studied by him; only scholars meeting the highest professional standard were entitled to practice *ijtihād*

jāhiliya the age of ignorance, an Arabic term referring to the pre-Islamic period and paganism

kafā'a social equilibrium of the parties, one of the requirements of marriage in pre-islamic Arabia for the male partner; accordingly, a man had to reach the social rank of his wife otherwise the marriage would decrease her rank which was not tolerated; by contrast, a man could marry a woman of a lower rank because the marriage was an increase in social rank for her

jināyāt criminal acts of various assaults and which are outside the scope of *hadd*

Khatt-i Humāyūn the second Ottoman reform legislation issued as a consequence of the war in the Crimea prohibiting slavery, introducing new private and criminal acts (on the French pattern)

madhhab legal school, doctrine

malik king

Mālik ibn Anas eighth-century scholar of Medina, the eponym of the Malikite School and author of the *Muwatta'*

mu'āmalāt 'private law'

mahr a sum (or its equivalent in gold, animal or other goods) to be paid for the bride when marring her

mahram prohibited persons, close relatives who could not be married

majlis council of armed men, an important political body in clans and tribes to decide about war and peace and other issues of importance; the name of the legislature in modern Iran

Mejelle–yi Ahkām–iᶜAdliyye the Ottoman 'civil code' issued in the late nineteenth century

mujtahid legal scholar entitled to *ijtihād*

mutᶜa a marriage for a definitive period of time specified by the parties, a legacy of the *jāhiliya* which was prohibited by Caliph ᶜUmar; his act of outlawing *mutᶜa* is followed by Sunnis but rejected by Shiᶜis who regards it a lawful marriage still today

Muwatta' the first significant work in the history of Islamic law composed by Mālik ibn Anas; the work is not a code but a thematic systematisation of the Prophetic traditions and local customs accepted by *Mālik* about prayer, alms, fasting, pilgrimage, *jihād*, oath, inheritance, marriage and divorce, purchase, sale and loan, last will and punishments

nikāh marriage

nikāh al-istibdzā' the marriage of the wife of a husband who had no children and a third person (usually a relative of the man) in order to produce heirs for him; this custom of the *jāhiliya* was prohibited by Islamic law

qādī judge

qānūn laws issued by political authorities (e.g. the Caliph) in fields outside the scope of Islamic law

qasāma a particular oath by fifty members of a clan, tribe or village confessing that they are not the killers and have no information about the killer of a murdered person found in their territory; this is Near-Eastern legacy to be found in addition to in pre-Islamic Arabia also in *Hammurabi*'s law book (Art. 23–24), the laws of the Hittites (Art. 6), and the Old Testament (Deut. 21: 1–9)

qisās blood feud

qiyās analogy, the fourth source of Islamic law

rahbar the leader of almost unlimited power in the present Iranian constitution since he specifies the line in both domestic and foreign policy, he is the supreme head of the army, appoints the president of the republic after elections and initiates his dismissal, decides on war and peace, appoints the supreme judge, the chairman of radio and television, the commanders-in-chief of the Revolutionary Guard and of the army

ribā usury, interest; it is prohibited in two verses of the Qur'an (2. 275, 278), but the laws on *ribā* were specified by subsequent generations of legal scholars who are debating some laws on detail still today

Risāla fī usūl al-fiqh the work of *al-Shāfiʿī* in which he defined the sources of Islamic law, the first book on Islamic legal theory

al-Shāfiʿī the first scholar to produce works on Islamic legal theory and the eponym of a school living at the turn of the eighth and ninth centuries

sharaf honour, social appreciation which may grow or decrease according to the behaviour of family members, mostly women whose sexual honour (*ird*) has a direct relevance to *sharaf*

sharīʿa Islamic law

al-Shaybānī an authority among early Hanafis and the author of the first book on the law of war

Shūrā-ye Negahbān Guardian Council, a body of legal experts examining laws passed by the legislature in order to find out their compatibility with Islamic law and the constitution; six of the twelve members are appointed by the *rahbar* and six are elected by the legislature; it is not a constitutional court because it also has functions incompatible with such a court (e.g. the political supervision of elections)

saduqa the engagement gift given to the bride, the sum of which depends on the social rank of the parties

sayyid head of a clan or tribe; it was i n his power to settle internal disputes, to represent the clan and to pay blood money to another clan; he was also the military leader receiving one fifth of the booty

sunna Prophetic tradition

talāq divorce, the unilateral declaration of the husband

taqlīd imitation, following the doctrine of a legal school instead of working on an individual opinion

taʿzīr deterrence, punishments outside *hudūd* and *jināyāt*, specified by political authorities with discretionary power

uqūbāt punishments

ʿulamā' scholars, the traditional Muslim intellectual elite

wājib compulsory action

walī al–dam a close relative entitled to exercise blood feud

waqf 'pious foundation', reminiscent to Anglo-Saxon trust with two types: while a *waqf khayrī* is created for charity purposes and for the benefit of the society at large (schools hospitals, roads, bridges etc.) a *waqf ahlī* is to arrange for the material well-being of family members

welāyat-e faqīh the rule of the legal scholar, the basic principle of the Iranian constitution according to which the most eminent legal scholar of Islamic law is entitled to lead the country as *rahbar* (leader) with powers specified in the constitution;

this is the theoretic foundation of theocracy which is not only a political ideology but also a dogma, and whoever challenges it may face capital punishment

Hindu Law

Anglo–Hindu Law an amalgam of inherited Hindu law and precedent-centred common law in India backing British rule and the administration of justice in the nineteenth century

artha mundane affairs, also a field of study on politics and economics; works on *artha* have also chapters on law

āśrama life cycle

Bhāruchi the best commentary on *Manu*

brahmachārin disciple

Brāhmana priest, the upper *varna* with privileges and the duty to teach, study and keep intact the wisdom of the *Varna*s

danda stick, power to punish (the prerogative of kings)

dharma a from the root *dh,* meaning to preserve, indicating *dharma*'s function to preserve the universe; proper deeds help to maintain order while its adversary, *adharma* refers to deeds of destructive and devastating consequences; human behaviour should be in accordance with *dharma* and therefore the study of law is an important part of Hindu religious philosophy about *dharma*

dharmaśāstra a literary genre in the *dharma* literature, the works of which were composed in verse, written in a less archaic language, that is, classical Sanskrit, are significantly longer than previous *dharmasūtra*s and have only loose contact to Vedic literature which came into being around the second century BCE; important works are the *dharmaśāstra*s o f *Manu, Nārada* and *Yājñavalkya*

dvija twice born

grhastha the second period in the life cycles, that of a householder when a man is obliged to marry, raise children and work

Jagannātha scholar of the eighteenth century who compiled a work on *dharma* upon the commission of the British in order to help British judges sent to India to adjudicate local cases; this is why the work was immediately translated into English

jāti castes which correspond to social reality; according to Hindu theory, *jāti*s emerged when persons of different *varna*s produced children who did not belong to either of the *varna*s of their parents but constituted a new category, e.g. a child born of a *Brāhmana* man and a *Ksatriya* woman does not belong to the *varna* of either of the parents but has its own category *(ambastha);* next generations complicate the matter further with producing more new categories in increasing number; this theory developed in order to harmonise *varna*-theory with social reality

kāma desire, sexuality

Kautilya perhaps a minister of *Chandragupta,* and the author of an *Arthaśāstra* which is a classic of Indian political literature

Kshatriya those who possess strength, warriors, the second *varna* with the duty to defend and the privilege to govern

kula family court, designed to resolve disputes of family members

Manu a *dharmaśāstra* in twelve books and 2694 *śloka*s (couplets) which was named after the mythic figure of *Manu* and composed between the second century BCE and the second century CE

mātsya-nyāya the 'law of the fish', the state of affairs in the present world, the *kāli-yuga* when big fishes eat small fishes; it is the mission of the king and the laws to reduce the law of the fish and maintain law and order in its stead

Medhātithi a well-known commentary on the *Manu-smrti*

Nārada-smrti one among the important *dharmaśāstra* produced between the third and the sixth centuries CE; the work arranged the legal material in two parts, the chapters of the first part deal exclusively with laws of procedure, while the longer chapters of the second part are about the eighteen *mārga*s (subjects of legal disputes)

niyoga **marriage** the marriage of a widow of a man died heirless and authorised (*niyoga*) by his family with one of the close relatives of her former husband in order to produce heirs for the deceased and thus to keep the cult of the dead intact; *niyoga* was subject to debate among Hindu scholars and schools

pandita experts of *dharma* and law, appointed to the British courts of law as advisors

parisad committee consisting of 3–10 scholars to decide about customs (*sadāchāra*)

purohita a *Brāhmana* and the king's personal advisor well-versed in various disciplines including law, politics and astrology

rājadharma the *dharma* of the king

rta cosmic order

sadāchāra good customs of authorities with a high level moral standard, the third source of Hindu law

satī a widow who steps voluntarily into the fire of her husband's pyre in order to burn alive together with the corpse of her former husband

śreni a court of 'guilds' to adjudicate disputes of its members; there were such courts of law for artisans, peasants, money lenders, dancers, etc.

Śūdra the last *varna* who had to serve the three *varna*s but were excluded from rituals and teaching and were thus not 'twice born' *(dvija)*

sūtra a literary genre produced in every discipline; wisdom about *dharma* and law were included in *dharmasūtra*s

svadharma the *dharma* of the individual determined by social rank, age and life cycle

Vaiśya those with the ability *(viś)* to work, the third *varna* engaged in economic activities such as trade, industry and agriculture

Varna caste, the four *varna*s are believed to come to being from *Purusa*, the mythic ancestor: *Brāhmana*s from his mouth, *Ksatriya*s from his arms, *Vaiśya*s from his thighs, and the *Śūdra*s from his feet

vyavahāra-pada bases of legal dispute, the indigenous classification of legal material in Hindu law including marriage and inheritance, loan, deposit, gift, purchase and sale and other transactions of the law of contracts

Yājñavalkya-smrti a *dharmaśāstra* of the highest standard yet with a simple style and thus easy to understand; the author(s) of the work are unknown since *Yājñavalkya* was not its author but a mythic figure; the text which is significantly shorter than that of Manu (one third of Manu) arranged the legal material in three books: the first deals with customs *(āchāra)*, the second with legal disputes *(vyavahāra)*, and the third with punishments; this is a complete break with the previous classification (followed also by Manu) which created precedence since medieval commentators also followed this system; *Yājñavalkya-smrti* was close to Indian social reality and was thus also applied by the British

Buddhist Law

Alaintriyā the supreme court of law in Burma at the heyday of Pagan

baci ceremony wedding ritual in the Lao customary law

Code de Vientiane: (*Khamphi Phra Thammasat*) Lao law collection found by the French and published under the title *Code de Vientiane* in the late nineteenth century; Buddhist ethics manifest in the law collections heavily since the material is arranged according to the *pañca-sīlāni* (adultery, murder, theft, lies, drunkenness), a basic term of Buddhist thinking; in fact, *Code de Vientiane* is the most Buddhist law collection in Southeast Asia

chakravartin 'turning the wheel': the ideal king in Hinduism and Buddhism

chōn thai legal term denoting various criminal acts against persons and properties; originally it had the meaning of a thief and a robber but later its meaning was widened to incorporate more crimes against public order

dhammathat the Burmese variant of *dharmaśāstra*

Dhammavilasa dharmaśāstra the very first Burmese *dhammathat* which was the work of a Mon monk (Dhammavilasa) composed in Mon and Pali languages but has not come down to us

Hlutaw Burmese political institution with executive and judicial competency, the members of which were appointed and dismissed by the king on his own discretion; *Hlutaw* was an advisory board with the power of a supreme court which also contributed to producing royal decrees

Hpyathon a literary genre and a treasury of Burmese judicial decisions serving as precedents to subsequent judgments which were collected and published as collected works (*dhammathat hpyathon*) out of which thirty-four are known

Khamphi Phra Thammasat the original Lao name of the Code de Vientiane

Kotmay Thammasat Kun Borom the laws of Kun Borom preserved in the Chronicle of Tithan Kun Borom

***Kotmay Trā Sām Duang* (Three Seals Code)** Thai law collection compiled upon the order of King Rama I.; with its 41 parts containing public, penal and private law it is the most important collection of Thai customary law

khwan Thai–Lao concept of a soul or a spiritual essence to be found in everyone and everything (even in objects)

lamoet Thai legal term of damage and tort of two kinds: one is a criminal act against an individual (assault, manslaughter, slander cursing, etc.) and his/her property, punished by monetary compensation and the other is a more serious criminal act against public order, punished by both fines and corporeal punishments

lūk khun Brāhmana legal experts sitting at traditional Thai courts of law who controlled the operation of courts to hinder the abuse of law, scrutinised the complaints and decided upon the law to be applied for individual cases

Manugye Dhammathat an encyclopaedic compendium of Burmese customary laws coupled with moral maxims and ethical standards (1762)

mia luang a chief wife in Thai customary law who was wedded by 'holding the hand', that is, with parental consent

Mingun Dhammathat Linga a compendium of Burmese customary law composed in verse in order to make the text easier to memorise (1650)

munnāi Thai head of social groups who were entitled to go to law courts on the behalf of individuals in their groups because commoners were denied to launch a lawsuit; this system was developed in the fourteenth century when Thai population was ordered into social groups each headed by a *munnāi* in order to guarantee the fast mobilisation of labour force upon the ordinance of the king; such corvée obligation lasted for six months

Nithan Kun Borom a Lao–Thai chronicle telling the story of the migration of the Lao–Thai populace under the reign of Kun Borom who is believed to be the ancestor of the Thai and the Lao people but whose historical authenticity is subject to debate; the text is however, a late compilation from the reign of King Visoun (1500–1520) who wanted to legitimise his rule with this reference to the royal ancestors

pañca-sīlāni five interdictions of Buddhism which are to be also followed by lay believers, not only monks: refraining from killing of living beings, from lies, from consuming alcoholic beverages, from theft and from sexual misdeeds

rājasattham Thai royal edict

riak khwan Thai–Lao rite in order to regain the *khwan* of a person which departed from his/her body and would otherwise join spirits that could be dangerous for the person and the entire community

Sparks Code a Burmese law code compiled by Major Sparks along the pattern of the *dhammathat*s which was intented to be a manual for law courts (1860) but was rejected by both the law courts and the Burmese society in general and disappeared soon from daily usage

svānuttā 'dog child', a disobedient child who was excluded from the bequest in the Burmese customary law

thammasat the Thai term for *dharmaśāstra*

vinyan Thai–Lao concept of the soul which leaves the body at death and would incarnate again in due time

vinaya teaching, discipline, laws regulating the life of Buddhist monks going back to the Buddha

Wagaru dhammathat The first Burmese *dhammathat* that has come down to us, translated from Pali to Mon upon the order or King Wagaru of Pegu in 1281; the text enjoyed enormous prestige during the centuries, King Bayinnaung specified *Wagaru Dhammathat* as the greatest legal authority in his empire in 1580

Chinese Law

Chih-cheng t'iao-ko the last important law collection of the Yuan dynasty promulgated in 1346 which contains 150 decrees, 1760 articles and more than one thousand precedents, and was the model of the Korean code published in 1391

Da Ming lü Great Ming law, modelled on the Tang Code and compiled by a committee of experts; the emperor participated in person in the work of the committee and it was he who decided about the final draft of the text (1391)

Dalisi the 'Supreme Court' of the Tang period the approval of which was obligatory to execute a capital punishment

de the moral of the king of very high standard, a key term for Confucians who believe that people would follow the good example of the king and would do no wrong when seeing the outstanding morals of their ruler

fa law, laws issued by the emperor

fajia legism, a political ideology emphasising the importance of law in governance

guan-xi a system of social contacts and a web of individuals which enables to assert interests even against the law if necessary

Han Fei important legist thinker in the third century BCE whose work, the *Han Feizi* is the best compendium of legist thinking

Huangdi emperor, the title of the ruler from the Qin period

huang-lao a philosophical school in the early Han period which harmonised the doctrines of legism and Confucianism and added some Daoist thoughts to it

i-chüeh a compulsory dissolution of marriage which was pronounced even against the wishes of the parties in some cases specified by law such as assaults, manslaughter and incest

Jiu Zhang Lü 'Statutes in nine chapters': the law compiled by **Hsiao H,** a minister of Emperor *Gaozu* based on Qin laws and precedence around 200 BCE; when later further 51 chapters were added to it, the Han code of 60 chapters was born

Kong Qiu Kong fuzi, Master Kong, whose name was Latinised as Confucius by Jesuits in the seventeenth century; he insisted that he taught no new ideas only repeated ancient wisdom which fell into oblivion already in his time, and this is why he produced no written work, even *Lunyu* (Analects), his most cited work is the compilation of later generations

li an amalgam of morals, customs and proper behaviour which can be learnt only by studying the works and deeds of outstanding sages

Li Si legist thinker and the chief minister of Qin in the third century BCE, the mastermind of the laws of Chin Shi *Huangdi* (unifying the country, legislation of strict laws and punitive actions, execution of Confucians and the burning of their works)

Le Code the most important Vietnamese Code produced under the reign of Le Tanh Tong (1460–1497) which mixes traditional Vietnamese custom with Chinese laws and Confucian ethics

Shang Yang legist thinker and the chief minister of Qin in the fourth century BCE who emphasised the importance of the army and of agriculture

Shuihudi texts administrative and criminal laws from the Qin period on 1100 bamboo slips found by archaeologist in the vicinity of Shuihudi

Ta Ch'ing lü chi-chieh fu-li (Great Qing code with commentary and orders): the Qing law book based on the Ming code both in content and structure

tianming mandate of Heaven, a political concept crystallised in the Zhou period according to which the emperor's policy should be in harmony with the will of the Heaven, otherwise his rule becomes illegal and could thus be overthrown by revolts

tianzi Son of Heavens, the designation of kings in the Zhou period

tsu relatives of the paternal line whose degree of relation is symbolised in the system of mourning consisting of 3 years, one year, 9 months, 5 months and 3 months, respectively

tuan-li a collection of precedents from the Song period

wang king of the archaic monarchies

wu-lun the five social relations

xing punishment

Xing shu books of punishments: a text on a tripod bronze vase about various punishments from 536 BCE

Xunzi Confucian scholar in the third century BCE who made concession to legist thinking and incorporated some of their views into his own; against inherited Confucian wisdom he insisted on the importance of law (*fa*), punishments (*xing fa*), and fear from punishments in order to maintain law and order because virtue and education are insufficient

Japanese Law

bakofu bureaucracy in the service of the Tokugawas

bushidō warriors' code, based on the subjugation of the vassal to his senior

daimyo feudal aristocracy of about 250 families under the control of the Tokugawas

Dayokan Great State Council, an important political body and the motor of modernisation in the Meiji period which abolished the feudal system and the privileges of the samurai, established a new public administration, the national army, a modern education system and the judiciary

giri–norm obligation of gratitude, a moral duty to be thankful for a gift or donation

goningumi a unit of five families which was responsible for paying taxes and control each other

gyōsei shidō announcements of governments which are not laws, yet Japanese society respect them

ie extended family

Ito Hirobumi a leading figure of the opposition of the Tokugawas who drafted the first Japanese constitution on the Prussian model in the Meiji period

Jimmu Tennō Divine Warrior who is believed to be the founder of the Japanese Empire

Kokkai National assembly, the legislative body in present-day Japan

mukotori-kon a social custom to produce a son for a family which has none; accordingly, the husband of one of the daughters is declared a heir for the father of his wife

Mommu Tenno (697–707) Japanese emperor known as Japanese Justinian who promulgated the first code in 702 (*Taiho code*) about laws of public administration and criminal acts (*ritsu-ryo*); the original text is lost but can be reconstructed on a later commentary

Nihonkoku Kempo the constitution of modern Japan which entered into force on 3 May 1947

nori 'law', the will of gods, the clan ancestor and Sun goddess Amaterasu Omikami

oyabun–kobun relationship between parent and child, a model for social behaviour and a moral standard for warriors according to which a superior has to be kind toward his subordinate while a subordinate owes him respect, loyalty and obedience

ritsu-ryo criminal laws and the laws on public administration specified on Chinese model at the time of the Taika reform

roppo the 'six codes' in modern Japan: the constitution, private law and private procedure law, criminal law and criminal procedure law and the law of commerce; all laws promulgated subsequently should harmonise with these six codes

Sangiin the upper house of the legislature consisting of 252 members

Shugiin the lower house of the legislature consisting of 480 members

Shotoku Taishi a prince and author of a text misleadingly called a constitution which is in fact a 17 articles compendium of Buddhist ethics, Confucian social teaching and political wisdom from 604 CE

Saiko Saibansho the Supreme Court of 14 members

sankin kotai a system of control in the Tokugawa period according to which daimyo families had to spend six months in their residence in Edo and could travel to their homes in the countryside only for the rest of the year but had to leave their families behind

Seitaisho the first document of the Meiji reforms which is not a constitution, only a document about a new political system which invested the executive with unlimited power and did not recognise the legislature and the judiciary as separate powers but as organs of the executive

wa social harmony, also referring to Japan and the Japanese people

Yoro code a law code about criminal law and public administration promulgated in 757; the code is one of the most important laws in the history of Japan which remained in force for 1100 years (1869); the text has 500 articles divided into 12 chapters about criminal law and 1000 articles divided into 30 chapters about public administration

Customary Laws

adat perpateh Malay customary law based on the matrilineal system originating from the region of Menangkabau and followed in the states of Negri Sembilan and Malacca to this day

adat temenggong Malay customary law based on the patriarchal system with influences from Hindu and Islamic law

anda exchange of wives in Buriat customary law, according to which a son of one family marries the daughter of the other family and vice versa

aksakāl (**men of white beard**) elderly Kazakh experts of customary law deciding on legal matters in council

ata dastüri custom of the ancestors among the Kazakhs, also called *babalar zsoly* (the path of the fathers)

aul a group of extended families migrating together with their livestock among the Mongols and the Kazakhs, headed by an *aksakāl*; the winter camp of an *aul* consists of 30–40 yurts

badal exchange, reciprocity, a key term among the Pashtuns according to which every deed requires reciprocation, be it good or bad; it is more than the ideology of blood feud since positive actions (assistance, donation) had to be reciprocated, too

barymta stealing of livestock out of vengeance among the Kazakhs

bii judges and professional experts of law among the Kazakhs who give advice also to the *aksakāl*s if they requested; all the three Kazakh tribal confederations had their famous judges whose name are still remembered even though they lived in the seventeenth century

bersanding a Malay wedding ceremony of Hindu origin without which a Malay marriage is null and void; accordingly, both the bridegroom and the bride have to sit on a wedding throne made particularly for this purpose during a particular phase of the festivities

ghairatman the ideal Pashtun male who meets all the requirements of the *Pashtun-wali*, their code of honour

jāti panchāyati caste judiciary of five members

Jirga circle, a word of Mongol origin referring to a Pashtun decision-making body be it a tribal assembly or a village council where proceedings last for long because decisions are made unanimously

kahol a basic unit among the Pashtuns consisting of several extended families whose ancestors lived seven or eight generations earlier; this is a group of solidarity and mutual help in economic activities (cultivation of land and building houses) and in family affairs (marriages)

Kalkha Jirum the compendium of the customary laws of the northern Mongols compiled in 1709, which is known only from a single source because the text was kept secret from commoners who according to Mongol customs could not have access to law

khun blood, blood money to be paid for assaults, injuries and murder among the Pashtuns and the Kazakhs, the basic unit of which was the bride money to be paid for a bride

Khuriltai Mongol tribal political body which elected the Khan and decided on issues of war and peace

mir-āb water inspector in Pashtun villages who supervises the use of a long network of canals

Mongol Oyratin Ikh Tsaaz the collection of customary laws of the Western Mongols promulgated in 1640 which has come down to us in some textual variants of different length containing 121, 130 and 150 articles, respectively

namūs a Pashtun concept of fame, honour and shame connected to the sexual honour of women who are controlled by a male (mother, wife (wives), unmarried sisters and daughters); this is why Pashtun women are dressed in burqa and are kept in houses far from the eyes of strangers; to arrange shelter and food for women is however also part of *namūs*

Pashtunwali code of honour among the Pashtuns highlighting bravery, militancy, respect for elders, pride, hospitality, revenge, participation in decision makings

Yassa (**Mongol jasagh**) law, decree and ordinance among which the most famous is the Yassa of Genghis Khan, a text which was lost and is known only in fragments in the chronicles of medieval Muslim authors